The City-State of Boston

THE CITY-STATE OF BOSTON

The Rise and Fall of an Atlantic Power, 1630–1865

MARK PETERSON

PRINCETON UNIVERSITY PRESS
Princeton & Oxford

Published by Princeton University Press
41 William Street, Princeton, New Jersey 08540
6 Oxford Street, Woodstock, Oxfordshire OX20 1TR

press.princeton.edu

Library of Congress Control Number: 2018940567
ISBN: 9780691179995

Portions of chapter 2 were originally published in
Early Modern Things: Objects and their Histories, 1500–1800
ed. Paula Findlen (New York: Routledge, 2013), 252–273.

An earlier version of chapter 4 was previously published within
Soundings in Atlantic History: Latent Structures and Intellectual Currents, 1500–1830
ed. Bernard Bailyn and Patricia L. Denault
(Cambridge, MA: Harvard University Press, 2009), 329–370.

Portions of chapter 4 were originally published in the
Massachusetts Historical Review 4 (2002): 1–22.

Portions of the conclusion were originally published in
"How (and why) to Read Francis Parkman," *Common Place* 3, no. 1 (October 2002).

British Library Cataloging-in-Publication Data is available

Editorial: Brigitta van Rheinberg, Eric Crahan, and Pamela Weidman
Production Editorial: Karen Carter
Text Design: Chris Ferrante
Jacket/Cover Design: Faceout Studio, Spencer Fuller
Jacket/Cover Credit: "A view of the Town of Boston in New England and
British ships of war landing their troops," 1768. Colored reproduction
of engraving by Paul Revere. Vector images © Shutterstock
Production: Jacquie Poirier
Publicity: Katie Lewis and James Schneider

This book has been composed in Miller

Printed on acid-free paper. ∞

Printed in the United States of America

1 3 5 7 9 10 8 6 4 2

For Mary, Rowan, and Thomas, and for Bud

Contents

Acknowledgments

This book has been a long time in the making. In fact, I began working on it years before I knew that's what I was doing. Serendipitous circumstances led me, as an undergraduate history and science concentrator at Harvard, to write a senior thesis on America's earliest institution for treating children with intellectual disabilities. Although I did not know this when I started my research, the origins of this institution lay ("of course," I might now say to my former self) in Boston. In one way or another, I have been reading, researching, thinking, and writing about the history of Boston in New England ever since. But twenty years passed before I had an inkling of the kind of book I wanted to write. Once I did, it took fifteen more years to complete it. I have had a tremendous amount of help along the way, and here I hope to express my gratitude, if not to everyone, then at least to those from whom I have learned the most and received indispensable assistance.

For the three family members to whom this book is dedicated, it has been the joy of my life to share with them the homework couch in our den of nerds, kept warm by a border terrier named Cricket. There, much of this book has been written and rewritten, argued over and edited. I doubt that my children, Rowan and Thomas, can remember a time when I wasn't working on the Boston book, and I thank them for tolerating its presence as a cranky and demanding extra family member. Mary Woolsey has been an extraordinary intellectual partner and editor. Her influence is evident on every page, and her love and moral support have sustained me throughout this project.

This book is also dedicated to Bud Bailyn, from whom I learned what it means to be a historian. I stumbled into his graduate seminar by accident, not intending to be a student of colonial North America and never having read any of his work. But I was immediately captivated by the scope of his vision, the spatial, temporal, and conceptual reach of his understanding of the subject, and the immense fun he was having in exploring it. How could I resist? I am grateful for his supportive friendship over the many years since then, including a typically thorough and critical reading of a much-windier draft of the entire manuscript of this book. The example of his teaching and scholarship has been a guiding light for me.

This book began to take shape during a research year in 1997–98 supported by Harvard's Charles Warren Center, where Professor Bailyn brought together a group of scholars working in various aspects of Atlantic history, just as he was launching his remarkable International Seminar on the History of the Atlantic World. Conversations with Warren Center Fellows Steve Behrendt, Rose Beiler, Eliga Gould, David Hancock, and Wim Klooster helped me think about Boston's connections across a wide range of places, peoples, and subjects. A similar year of research spent at the American Antiquarian Society in 2003–4, funded by a Frederick Burkhardt Fellowship from the American Council of Learned Societies, allowed me to dig deep in archival sources as well as expand the temporal scope of the project, thanks to the extraordinary collections of the society. The opportunity to work closely with Karen Ordahl Kupperman during that year was a great source of intellectual inspiration, and I also appreciated the insights and collegiality of Leon Jackson, Michael Jarvis, Molly McCarthy, and Meredith McGill. In addition, a Stephen Botein Fellowship from the American Antiquarian Society in summer 1999 allowed me to begin exploring the riches of the library of the Mather family of Boston.

The universities where I have had the privilege of teaching while working on this book have been generously supportive as well. The University of Iowa provided a Faculty Scholar Award in 2002, offering research and writing time to launch the project, along with Old Gold Summer Fellowship research funding. Colleagues at Iowa including the late Ken Cmiel and Glenn Penny were important interlocutors. The opportunity to develop a material culture working group with Rudi Colloredo-Mansfeld and cohost an eclectic conference titled Fleeting Objects supported by Iowa's Obermann Center were highlights of my time at Iowa—a chance to explore what Emerson called "the evanescence and lubricity of all objects."

The history department at the University of California, Berkeley, that great Pacific citadel of learning, has been in every way an ideal place to develop and complete this project. *The City-State of Boston* is a Berkeley book. The formal support of two semesters' leave from teaching, the history department's generous research funding, and a fellowship from the Townshend Center for the Humanities were all helpful. But I gained the most from Berkeley's intellectual community—the conversations over lunches, coffees, drinks, and bike rides that have shaped and rounded out my days here. My fellow members of the Gang of Five, Carla Hesse, Tom Laqueur, Ethan Shagan, and Jonathan Sheehan, as extraordinary a group of early modern historians as you'll find anywhere, read every page and many a draft over the past decade. Their advice and criticism have made this a much stronger and wiser book, and their friendship has buoyed my confidence.

Among the many brilliant historians I have gotten to know and work with in Berkeley, special thanks for many hours of companionship and enlightening conversation go to Beth Berry, Tom Brady, Margaret Chowning, John Connelly, Brian DeLay, Robin Einhorn, Susanna Elm, John Gillis, Mark Healey, David Hollinger, Abhishek Kaicker, Kerwin Klein, Margaretta Lovell, Massimo Mazzotti, Rebecca McLennan, Tom and Barbara Metcalf, Robert Middlekauff, Carlos Noreña, Caitlin Rosenthal, Daniel Sargent, Elena Schneider, Yuri Slezkine, Nick Tackett, Elisa Tamarkin, Jan de Vries, and Peter Zinoman. Among the equally brilliant graduate students with whom it has been my good fortune to work at Berkeley, and from whom I learned far more than I have taught, I have been inspired by Elliott Cramer, Alejandra Dubcovsky, Mattie Enger, Edward Evenson, Hannah Farber, Anthony Gregory, Charlotte Hull, Bobby Lee, Kerima Lewis, Derek O'Leary, Franklin Sammons, Hannah Waits, Russ Weber, and Ali Weiss. The Bay Area Seminar in Early American History, which I had the pleasure of co-organizing with Dee Andrews and the late and much-missed Caroline Cox, has also been a source of intellectual stimulation and conviviality. And I want to offer particular thanks to Caroline Winterer of Stanford University's history department and humanities center for being a happy coconspirator in organizing conferences and reading each other's work in progress, to my lasting benefit.

With a book this long in the making, I have had many opportunities to share bits and pieces of its progress at conferences, workshops, and invited talks far and wide, where I have received valuable feedback from many fine scholars and generous hosts. These include the Alternative States workshop at Duke University; American Antiquarian Society; American Culture and Politics Speaker Series at Oregon State University; American History Seminar and Early Modern Social History Seminar at the University of Cambridge; American Studies Institute at Heidelberg University; Atlantic History Seminar at Northwestern University; Britain's American Revolution and Object Relations in Early America conferences at the Huntington Library; British Group in Early American History's annual conferences at the University of East Anglia, University of Portsmouth, and University of St. Andrews; Center for the City in History at the University of Sheffield; Commemoration and the City symposium at the Savannah College of Art and Design; Cultural Studies Seminar at the University of California at Santa Cruz; Draper Chair Lecture at the University of Connecticut; Early American History Seminar at Columbia University; Early American History Seminar at the Newberry Library; Eighteenth-Century Studies Workshop on the City at Yale University; Early Modern Things workshop as well as the Enlightenment and Revolution Seminar at Stanford University; England's Age of Revolution conference at the University of Chicago; European Early American Studies Association Biennial Conferences at the University of Paris 7–Denis Diderot and Maria Curie-Sklodowska University at Lublin; Georgia Workshop in Early American History and Culture; Going Dutch: Holland in America conference at the University of Denver; Global City, Past and Present workshop at the University of St. Andrews; International Center for Jefferson Studies workshops at the University of Turin and University of Uppsala; John Winthrop's Worlds conference at Millersville University of Pennsylvania; Martin Weiner Lecture at Brandeis University; McNeil Center for Early American Studies at the University of Pennsylvania; Omohundro Institute of Early American History and Culture annual conferences at the University of Glasgow and Universite Laval, Quebec, as well as the Omohundro Institute–Early Modern Studies Institute annual workshops at the Huntington Library; Rensselaerswyck Seminar in New York City; Rocky Mountain Seminar in Early American History at the University of Utah; University of Southern California–Huntington Library Early Modern Studies Institute; Shaping the Stuart World conference at the University of Aberdeen; Seminar on Atlantic History at the University of Southern Maine; and Warwick University/Institute of Historical Research Seminar on Britain and America in the Seventeenth Century in Venice, Italy.

At all these events and many others, I have enjoyed the hospitality and benefited from the intellectual energy of many hosts, friends, and fellow scholars. At the risk of forgetting some, I nonetheless want to offer special thanks to Frank Bremer, Trevor Burnard, Christopher Clark, Frank Cogliano, Nina Dayton, Max Edling, Hannah Farber, Paula Findlen, Gary Gerstle, Ed Gray, Emma Hart, Eric Hinderaker, Steve Hindle, Jane Kamensky, Wim Klooster, Allan MacInnes, Peter Mancall, Paul Mapp, Simon Middleton, Stephen Mihm, Ben Mutschler, Simon Newman, Peter Onuf, Andrew O'Shaughnessy, Sarah Pearsall, Steve Pincus, Andrew Preston, Dan Richter, Jessica Roney, Benjamin Schmidt, Eric Slauter, Phil Stern, Jan Stievermann, Peter Thompson, Michael Winship, Phil Withington, and the late Alfred Young.

All historians are dependent on their archives, but historians of Boston and New England are fortunate to work in a field where, for many generations, dedicated scholars have preserved the records of the region's past and made them widely available to the public. This book's endnotes tell a fuller story of its many debts, although special thanks go to the expert librarians and archivists at the American Antiquarian Society, Boston Athenaeum, Boston Public Library, British Library, Massachusetts Historical Society, Massachusetts State Archives, New England Historic Genealogical Society, and Countway Medical Library, Houghton Library, and Widener Library at Harvard University.

Working with Princeton University Press has been a joy, and special thanks go to my agent, Geri Thoma, for arranging such a suitable match. Every writer should be so lucky as to have Brigitta van Rheinberg as an editor. Her enthusiasm for the project and careful review of the manuscript has made this a much better book. Amanda Peery, James Schneider, and Karen Carter have offered valuable assistance in bringing the book to publication, and thanks are also due to Steven Moore for his expert index making. The two external readers for the press, Jane Kamensky and Peter Mancall, deserve extra credit for their careful critiques and advice for a final round of revisions. Hannah Farber and Russ Weber provided diligent assistance in finding images and acquiring permissions; without Russ's help in particular, there would just be a lot of blank spaces where the pictures should be.

Thanks to all these, and many more, for making this book possible.

The City-State of Boston

FIGURE I.1. Royal charter of the Massachusetts Bay Company, 1629.

Introduction

In 1629, Boston's puritan founders acquired a charter from King Charles I. Unlike most royal charters, the governing document for the Massachusetts Bay Company—the joint-stock corporation that would govern the new colony—failed to specify a location for the quarterly meetings of its directors. The Crown must have assumed that like most English chartered corporations, its governing board would meet in London. But John Winthrop and company had no such intentions. Loophole in hand, the colonists brought their charter with them the next year on their three-thousand-mile journey to New England. There, far from royal oversight, they built their colony as they pleased. They erected a commonwealth remarkable for its autonomy, including an independent religious order free from the Church of England's scrutiny, and a self-governing republic centered in Boston, where the people chose their representatives and governors in annual elections.

Sixty years later, on April 18, 1689, Boston's leaders in church and state, supported by crowds from the surrounding countryside, many of them soldiers experienced in colonial wars, confronted the king's troops stationed at Fort Hill and a Royal Navy warship in the harbor. They disarmed the royal governor, Sir Edmund Andros, marched him to the town house at the head of King Street, the center of government in the heart of the city, and placed him under arrest.

Andros had been appointed by Charles's son, King James II, in an attempt to destroy Boston's autonomy and fold it into an authoritarian mega-colony, the Dominion of New England, stretching from New Jersey to Maine. The king assigned Andros, a veteran military officer, the task of stripping New Englanders of their rights, properties, and liberties. But the colonists' bold rebellion succeeded, in part because of the simultaneous overthrow of James II in England's Glorious Revolution. Boston's autonomy persisted.

Eighty years later, on March 5, 1770, crowds again gathered on King Street in Boston to stand up to British soldiers, who were

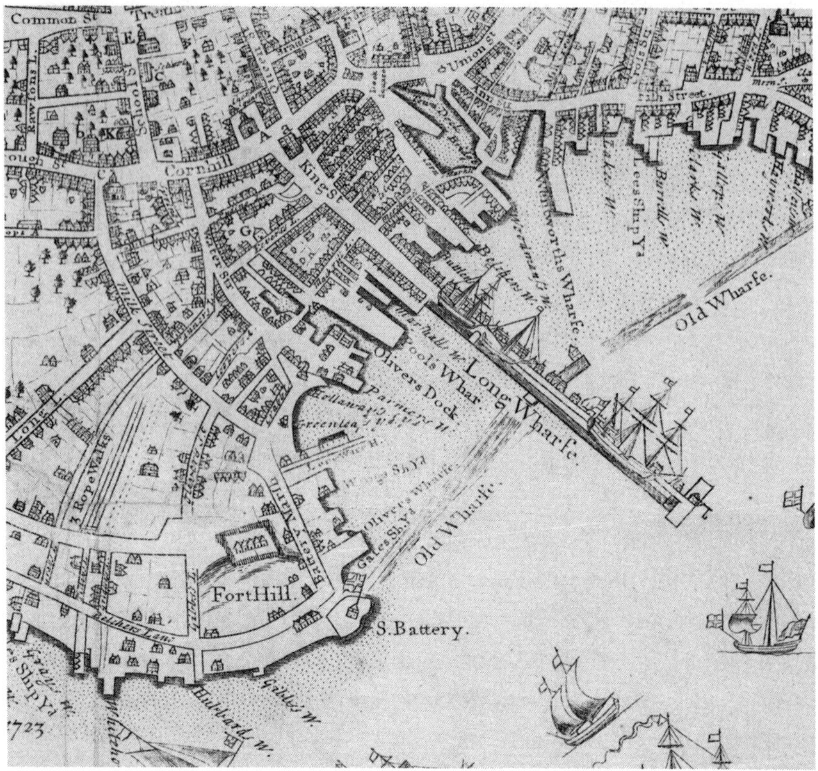

Map I.1. *The Town of Boston in New England*, by John Bonner, 1722. Detail. The crowd of soldiers seized Andros at Fort Hill, marched him up Battery March and along the wharves toward King Street and the town house, marked "a" on Bonner's map.

occupying their city to enforce Parliament's hated Townshend Acts. Five Bostonians paid with their lives that night. (See plate 1.)

The bloodshed of this "massacre" presaged more violence to come. Five years later the New England countryside, again encouraged to resist by Boston's leaders in church and state, erupted to repel the expeditionary force sent out from Boston on April 18, 1775, to seize arms and rebels believed to be in the nearby towns of Lexington and Concord. (See plate 2.)

By sundown the following day, militia volunteers numbering in the tens of thousands surrounded New England's metropolis, laying siege to the city for the next eleven months. King George's soldiers finally boarded Royal Navy transports to evacuate the city on March 17, 1776. Boston's autonomy was again preserved.

Another eighty years on, King Street, now renamed State Street after independence, was once more occupied by soldiers from beyond the commonwealth. The US government had dispatched the Marine Corps to ensure the successful rendition of Anthony Burns, an enslaved African American who escaped from his Virginia master and fled to Boston, where it was illegal to buy and sell human beings or hold them in bondage. Local laws against slavery were futile, however, in the face of national power. The Fugitive Slave Act of 1850 demanded the active cooperation of every US citizen, on pain of severe punishment, in the arrest of any person claimed by a slave owner to be a fugitive. Despite the encouragement of some (though not all) of the divided city's leaders in church and state to resist the tyranny of distant powers, Boston succumbed. From the foot of the Old State House down to Long Wharf, State Street was lined with marines armed with bayonets to control the crowds that thronged the streets after several days of rioting between opposing factions. Burns, surrounded by armed local ruffians, led by mounted marine cavalrymen, and trailed by horse-drawn artillery, was marched down to a US Revenue Service cutter waiting in the harbor to carry him back to slavery. (See plate 3.)

In the midst of this humiliation, Theodore Parker, a radical Boston clergyman, leader of the Transcendentalist movement and committed abolitionist, despaired over what had been lost: "There is no Boston to-day. There was a Boston once. Now, there is a north suburb to the city of Alexandria; that is what Boston is. And you and I, fellow-subjects of the State of Virginia."[1]

The first three of these episodes from Boston's vaunted history—the puritan founding in 1630, the rebellion against Andros in 1689, and the beginning of the Revolutionary War in 1775—ring like notes in a major chord from the familiar song that Boston sings about its past. This is a national song, as patriotic as "Yankee Doodle," in which Boston's colonial and revolutionary histories are understood as precursors to and central elements in the making of the United States. Boston's commemorative industry today is deeply committed to presenting the city's history in a national context. From the

Freedom Trail, developed in the 1950s to market Boston's history to tourists as the "birthplace of the American Revolution," to the Boston National Historical Park, organized by the National Park Service in the 1970s to show "how one city could be the Cradle of Liberty, site of the first major battle of [the] American Revolution, and home to many who espoused that freedom can be extended to all," this is the story it tells.[2] The same can be said for countless textbooks that place Boston's early history in the context of the United States' national founding, as do many scholarly monographs, popular histories, and biographies of Boston's leading events and figures. From Winthrop encouraging his fellow migrants aboard the *Arbella* with visions of a "city upon a hill," forward to the revolution with brewer-patriot Samuel Adams organizing resistance, the Boston Massacre and the Tea Party, Paul Revere's Ride, the "Shot Heard Round the World," the Battle of Bunker Hill, John Hancock's enormous signature on the Declaration of Independence, and Abigail Adams reminding John to "Remember the Ladies," then onward to the American Renaissance, abolitionist movement, and Robert Gould Shaw and the Massachusetts 54th Colored Regiment in the Civil War, Boston's popular history can seem like a long series of "just-so" stories and tableaux vivants, with the people and events that shaped its past perpetually available as usable exemplars for contemporary values and purposes.

As long ago as 1835, Nathaniel Hawthorne, in his story "The Gray Champion," lined up precisely these episodes in order to project a future consistent with Boston's independent past: "Should domestic tyranny oppress us, or the invader's step pollute our soil, . . . New England's sons will vindicate their ancestry."[3] But the last of these four episodes, the rendition of Anthony Burns, strikes a sour note, spoiling the tune we've grown accustomed to hearing. In 1854, New York's Walt Whitman, never overly fond of New England's pieties, wrote a darkly satirical "Boston Ballad" about the city's defeat by the national slavocracy. In it, the skeleton of King George III is exhumed and brought to Boston to watch the "Federal foot and dragoons" with their "cutlasses" and "government cannon" march Burns back to bondage in Virginia. The king gets his revenge for Boston's past rebellions in the sad irony that New England's sons failed to vindicate their ancestry against domestic tyranny and the invader's step—their hands restrained by the bargain that Boston had made with the slaveholders' union.[4] The consolidation of the United States, not the tyranny of British monarchs, was the death of Boston—the Boston that Theodore Parker lamented, the Boston that is the subject of this book.

From Boston's viewpoint, the narrow vote on February 3, 1788, by which Massachusetts ratified the US Constitution, turned out to be a fateful mistake. The nature of the union that Massachusetts joined in 1788, especially as it evolved under the leadership of southerners, from Thomas Jefferson and James Madison to Andrew Jackson and James K. Polk, was not what Bostonians had bargained for. The subsequent course taken by US politics and territorial expansion dramatically undermined the autonomy that Boston and New England had long enjoyed. During the colonial period, Boston's economy was closely tied to Jamaica and Barbados, but the islands' planter elites had no political authority over New England. Under the US Constitution, however, the seventeenth-century bargain with slavery came back to haunt the city, as its government now lay increasingly under the thumb of the slaveholders of the American South. Inclusion in the United States compromised Boston's autonomy, remade its political economy, and diminished its hegemony over New England, ultimately dismembering the city-state built in the seventeenth century and subverting its capacity to define, let alone uphold, a vision of the common good for all. By 1854, Parker was right to think that in its humiliation at the hands of federal dragoons, the Boston of old was no more. In the wake of the Union's surprising victory in the Civil War, even the memory of Boston's former autonomy and its resistance to the dominant course of earlier US history vanished within a reconstructed national narrative.

In this book, I argue that Boston in New England developed as a polity consisting of a city and its hinterland that together formed its identity, and pursued its aspirations as one among many such competing entities in the early modern Atlantic world. Until it was swallowed up by the United States in the nineteenth century, it can best be understood as the city-state of Boston, a self-conscious attempt to build an autonomous self-governing republic modeled on biblical and classical republican ideals in a New World environment. This is not a common way to understand Boston and its history, but I did not invent it; it has been lurking in the archives, unsought and overlooked, for centuries.

In the 1790s, Spanish colonial officials in Cuba registered the nationality, the *nación* of origin, of each slave-trading ship entering the port of Havana. The column on the register listing each ship's nation had entries for Spanish, English, Dutch, Danish, French, and American ships, and then a separate national category: "Bostonesa." Merchants from Boston had been trading in Havana for more than 150 years by this time, so perhaps it's not surprising that Spanish officials considered Boston to be an autonomous trading nation, requiring a separate category from the newly independent United States.[5] But Havana was not alone in viewing Boston as the metropolis of a distinct nation. In the 1660s, England's King Charles II sent commissioners to New England to investigate the loyalty of his colonies: Massachusetts, Plymouth, Connecticut, and New Haven. In their subsequent report, the commissioners referred to all the colonists from the region collectively as "the Bostoners."[6] King Charles himself would soon, in a formal decree to the Massachusetts General Court, address this body as "the governor and magistrates of our town of Boston in New England."[7] Several years later, when the French explorer Louis Jolliet drew a map of North America to depict his wide-ranging discoveries, he labeled the entirety of the English colonial settlement north of the Chesapeake with a single word: "Baston."[8] Later, during the eighteenth century's imperial wars between Britain and France, French troops commonly referred to all English colonial soldiers as "*les Bostonnais*." Their nineteenth-century descendants in Canada's maritime provinces came to refer to the New England region, where many of them would migrate, as "the Boston States." And during the American Revolutionary War, with France now an ally, French officers continued to refer to "*l'Etat de Boston*" in their correspondence.[9]

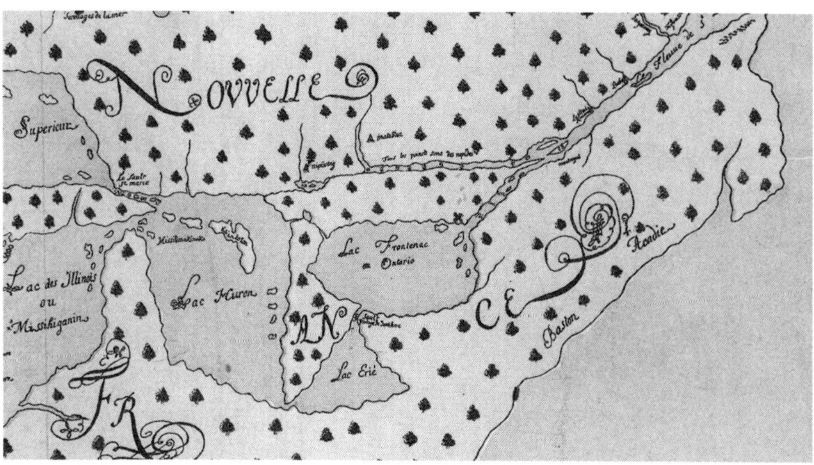

Map I.2. *Nouvelle decouverte de plusieurs nations dans la Nouvelle France en l'année 1673 et 1674*, by Louis Jolliet. Detail. Note "Baston" just to the right of the large "CE" of "NOUVELLE FR-AN-CE."

Today, these designations seem like misnomers. American schoolchildren learn that towns and cities are subordinate to states, which collectively comprise the country of the United States. Boston is not a nation or state; it is a city in Massachusetts—one of the states in the American nation. But King Charles and his commissioners, Jolliet, France's soldiers, and Havana's customs officials were not mistaken. Rather, they lived in an age when many a formal polity was built around a dominant city and its hinterland, and when our familiar hierarchies of sovereignty were not so clear-cut. And they were all witnesses to the emergence of one such powerful entity in the northeastern corner of North America. This was Boston in New England, known and regarded from Havana to Whitehall, from the fortresses of Quebec to the slave-trading factories of West Africa.

The persistent identification of Boston with New England, and widespread perception throughout the early modern world that Boston in New England was a *nación* or state in its own right, provide the rationale for my title. *The City-State of Boston* offers a new way of understanding early American history by tracing the long-term fate of the efforts that Bostoners made to transplant a viable and venerable form of European polity to American shores, believing that this was the best way to support the social and moral vision fostered by their religious convictions.

Modern American places have seldom been described as city-states—a term we commonly associate with the ancient Mediterranean, medieval Italy, smaller principalities of the Holy Roman Empire and Hanseatic League, and the rare modern holdover such as Singapore or Monaco. The residents of early Boston did not use this term to describe themselves. Then again, neither did the people of ancient Athens or Sparta, Renaissance Venice or Florence, or anyone else until well into the nineteenth century. Coined first in Denmark ("*bystad*") and Germany (the ungainly "*stadt-staat*"), the term "city-state" only entered the English language definitively in 1893, when W. Warde Fowler's *The City-State of the Greeks and Romans* gave the term its durable modern form.[10] Before the nineteenth century, small self-governing polities comprised of a city and its hinterland, relatively autonomous but not necessarily independent, were common sociopolitical forms.[11] There was little need for a special term of art to describe them until large consolidating nation-states began to devour them right and left. Thinking of the world that Boston made as a city-state allows us to think more flexibly about evolving forms of power over the three centuries from the earliest European colonies in North America to the consolidation of an American nation-state. It also offers an opportunity to assess the value, both the virtues and defects, of a once-common form of polity that has largely disappeared over the past two centuries. As secession and devolution movements arise in countries like Spain and Great Britain, two classic examples of consolidating nation-states from the early modern period, and as public confidence in the governing institutions of large countries like the United States or multinational entities like the European Union declines, the city-state model might be needed again as the nation-state falters.[12]

To bring this hidden history of the city-state of Boston to light requires unearthing and foregrounding many unfamiliar people and events from Boston's and New England's past, the importance of which has been obscured by the proclivities of America's national narrative. As a result, many familiar people and events from the just-so version of Boston's history will not appear in this book, or will make their appearances in unfamiliar guises. This is not to deny that there is a great deal of historical truth, meticulous scholarship, and narrative power behind the way that Boston's history has usually been told. The problem is that there is too much power, too profound a desire among authors and readers alike for narratives that sustain American national identities. The overly familiar narratives effectively drown out other stories that the rich archive of Boston's past affords.

The modern fame of John Winthrop's "A Modell of Christian Charity" illustrates this problem. Winthrop, the first governor of Massachusetts, wrote a discourse on "Christian Charity" as a principle that would unite the colonists and promote their survival. By the late twentieth century, it had become an unshakable belief, repeated everywhere from history textbooks to op-ed columns, that Winthrop delivered this address in a shipboard sermon to his fellow migrants, prophesying an exemplary future for the city they would found and the nation it would become: "We shall be as a city upon a hill."[13] President Ronald Reagan endorsed this image in 1984, adding the word "shining" to Winthrop's phrase and assuming that the "shining city upon a hill" was the United States.[14] Reagan's rendition was derived from Perry Miller, the twentieth century's most influential historian of puritan New England, who suggested that Governor Winthrop was "preternaturally sensing what the promise of America might come to signify."[15] Yet these interpretations badly distort the meaning and influence of the governor's words. Winthrop was warning against the danger of failure, not predicting a glorious future. Cities on hills are exposed places, their misdeeds visible to all, and if the colony were to fail, "wee shall be made a story and a by-word through the world."[16] The modern nationalist reading also misleadingly implies that Winthrop's words had a strong influence on his contemporaries and successors. In reality, we have no evidence that Winthrop's discourse was spoken aboard the *Arbella* or to any other audience.[17] The idea that "Christian Charity" was a foundational text in American history began only in the nineteenth century, when a Winthrop descendant discovered a manuscript copy. The manuscript was published for the first time in 1838, more than two hundred years after its composition.[18] Until then, it was essentially unknown. The prophetic interpretation of Winthrop's city upon a hill is a modern invention of American historians, journalists, and politicians in search of a usable past.[19] The demands on the past made by the modern American nation transformed Winthrop's obscure fragment of colonial planning into a dominant metaphor for the American nation-state's historical destiny.

Metaphors are not easy to dislodge. But stronger ones can displace them, and the foundational literature of Boston contains a powerful image on which the origin of the city-state of Boston rests. In spring 1630, in the city of Southampton on the English Channel, the Massachusetts migrants waited for the winds and tides that would launch their fleet across the Atlantic. Their spirits were buoyed by the preaching of John Cotton, vicar of St. Botolph's Church in old Boston, Lincolnshire, spiritual mentor to the colonists, and soon to be minister of the new Boston's First Church.[20] Cotton tried to assuage the colonists' fears about embarking on a dangerous journey to an uncertain future. He posed their doubts as a rhetorical question:

> *Quest.* But how shall I know whether God hath appointed me such a place, if I be well where I am, what may warrant my removeall?
>
> *Answ.* . . . [W]e may remove . . . to plant a Colony, that is, a company that agree together to remove out of their owne Country, and settle a Citty or Common-wealth elsewhere. Of such a Colony wee reade in *Acts* 16. 12, which God blessed and prospered exceedingly, and made it a glorious Church.[21]

Among the most gifted puritan writers and preachers of his generation, Cotton was not commonly at a loss for the proper word.[22] But the flurry of terms that he uses here—plantation, colony, company, city, commonwealth, and church—suggests that his vision for this venture was no simple thing to define. Nevertheless, a clue into the nature of Cotton's vision lies in his biblical reference: "Of such a Colony wee reade in *Acts* 16. 12."

Cotton's audience would have immediately understood its meaning. English Puritans strove "to live ancient lives," to place the drama of their existence on a continuous spectrum of time that stretched back to antiquity and to find inspiration in ancient texts for their dreams of a better world.[23] In this light, Acts 16:12 is central to the founding of Massachusetts, cited not only in Cotton's sermon, but in other documents justifying the puritan migration.[24] In the King James Bible, Acts 16:12 reads, "And from thence to Philippi, which is the chief city of that part of Macedonia, and a colony."

Why did Cotton comfort the anxious colonists by referring to the Macedonian city of Philippi? The answer lies in the layers of meaning buried in this cryptic passage, which reveal the founders' vision for the kind of city and colony they hoped to plant in America, rooted in the biblical story of the spread of Christianity and in classical models of ideal city-republics.

In 356 BCE, King Philip II of Macedon, father of Alexander the Great, built a fortified city on the Aegean coast to exploit nearby gold mines, granted it a charter for self-government under an assembly, populated it with Macedonian colonists, and named it Philippi. Two centuries later, in 168 BCE, the Roman Republic conquered Macedonia and reconstructed the main road to its eastern domains, the Via Egnatia, to pass through Philippi on the way to Byzantium and the Bosporus Straits, the traditional boundary between Europe and Asia. It was at Philippi, another century later, that the Roman Republic entered its twilight. Mark Antony and Octavius pursued Julius Caesar's assassins, Brutus and Cassius, along the Via Egnatia and defeated their armies in the Battle of Philippi in 42 BCE. Octavius (as Caesar Augustus) made Philippi into a Roman colony, repopulated by his former legionnaires, its land divided among them and administered by Roman law as a "miniature Rome."[25]

But this history mattered to Cotton and Boston's founders because Philippi became, after nearly another century, the first place in Europe to hear the Christian gospel. In 49 CE, the apostle Paul established the first Christian church in Europe at Philippi. As Acts 16 relates, Paul, Silas, and Timothy had been preaching throughout the cities of Anatolia (now central Turkey). During his mission in Anatolia, Paul had a vision in the night: "There stood a man of Macedonia, and prayed him, saying, 'Come over into Macedonia, and help us.' And after he had seen the vision, immediately we endeavoured to go into Macedonia, . . . to Philippi, which is the chief city of that part of Macedonia, and a colony."

Paul's plantation of a church in Philippi was the culmination of a series of colonizing projects that prepared the way for the gospel to reach Europe. The author of Acts self-consciously placed Paul's plantation of a Christian church and commonwealth at Philippi within the Greek and Roman colonizing tradition, but also as a challenge to that tradition. When Paul and Silas caused trouble in Philippi with their preaching, the locals complained that they "teach customs, which are not lawful for us to receive, neither to observe, being Romans." Paul's novel religion violated the emperor cult and worship of pagan gods that flourished among elite Romans.[26] Moreover, the early Christian churches practiced communal property sharing, renouncing private wealth in favor of the common weal. Caesar Augustus had reorganized Philippi, erased the traces of Greek and Roman republican traditions of egalitarian self-rule, and placed power in the hands of a military elite.[27] The customs of the Christian plantation challenged the imperial model. Philippi was the place where the Roman Republic had met its end, and Philippi would become the place where a Christian commonwealth in Europe began.

It is worth dwelling on the meaning of Philippi because it is fundamental to understanding the vision that framed the founding of Boston. Look no further for evidence than the Great Seal, created in 1629 when Charles I granted the Massachusetts charter. The words spoken by the figure in the Great Seal, "COME OVER AND HELP US," are taken from Acts 16:9, where the "man of Macedonia" spoke to Paul in his vision: "Come over into Macedonia, and help us."

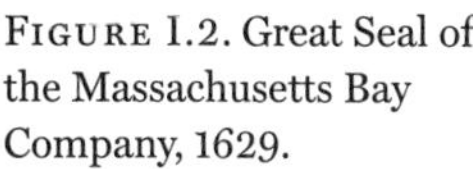
FIGURE I.2. Great Seal of the Massachusetts Bay Company, 1629.

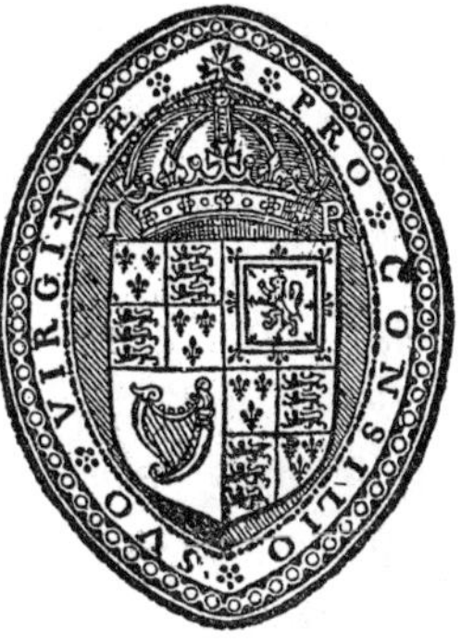

FIGURE I.3. Great Seal of the Virginia Company of London, 1606.

The Massachusetts seal was highly unusual. Its image of a Native American uttering a biblical quotation differed dramatically from the seals of other chartered colonies. The Great Seal of the Virginia Company of London (1606), with its regal expression of power and authority, adding "Virginiae" to the other realms (Britaniae, Franciae, and Hiberniae) over which King James ruled, presents a marked contrast.

More than simply a sign of the colony's missionary zeal, the Great Seal's reference to Philippi anticipates Cotton's use of this image in *Gods Promise to His Plantations*. As Philippi was the site of the first Christian church planted on a new continent, superseding the corrupt imperial remnant of the formerly virtuous Greek and Roman republics, so Boston in New England would bring the first reformed Christian commonwealth to a new continent, escaping the imperial decay and religious persecution that threatened England's government and church.[28]

Philippi's importance to Boston's founders highlights two aspects of their vision for the new plantation, and therefore two critical themes of this book: first, that it would strive to be an autonomous body, committed to republican self-government in both church and state; and second, that within the corporate body of voluntary members, the principle of mutual charity maintained by Paul and the early churches would be crucial to its success.[29] Neither of these principles was a necessary aspect of English colonizing ventures or

English Puritans' aspirations. Rather, they emerged from two significant influences on Boston's founders. One was the widespread interest in utopian, ideal, or reformed cities and commonwealths—"the best state of a publique weal"—that flourished in early modern England and Europe, and achieved a heightened intensity in the decade before the migrants' departure for Massachusetts.[30] Second and equally influential were the examples of many prior colonization attempts—most of them abject failures.

Boston in New England was not, strictly speaking, a utopian enterprise, nor can its particular features be traced to any specific one of these model colonial precursors. But these models are important because they help us recognize that the idea of Boston emerged in the late 1620s during a period of intense curiosity, debate, and disagreement about what an ideal society could possibly be like, tempered by careful observation of other colonial experiments. Thomas More inaugurated the discussion with his fictional satire *Utopia* (1516), which depicted an ideal republic on a remote New World island. Its 1551 translation from Latin into English, and subsequent editions in 1556, 1597, and 1624, made More's text accessible to a wide audience. But less familiar strands of thought, such as an early modern fascination with the ancient city of Jerusalem, also played a part in generating conversation about ideal cities and commonwealths.

In 1595, an English Puritan minister named Thomas Tymme translated and published *A Briefe Description of Hierusalem and the Suburbs Therof, as It Florished in the Time of Christ*. The book included a "beawtifull mappe" on which the famous sites of scripture could be easily located, giving the reader a view of "that faire and most auncient Citie . . . by God him self bewtified aboue all other Citties . . . the cheefe, most noble and famous Cittie of the world."[31] For the poor or illiterate, similar lessons could be learned from a busker in southwest England named Will Gosling, who built an intricate model of Jerusalem on a wheelbarrow that he pushed from town to town. For a few pennies, Gosling would pull away the cloth and allow customers to study the earthly Zion in miniature.[32] In 1621, Robert Burton's *Anatomy of Melancholy* described a "Utopia of mine owne," located on "one of those floting islands in the Mare del Sur" or else in the "inner parts of America"—a monarchical utopia, unlike the egalitarian commonwealths described in other works.[33] Further instances of this profusion of model cities included Johann Valentin Andreae's *Christianopolis* (1619), Tommaso Campanella's *Civitas Solis* (1623), and Francis Bacon's *The New Atlantis* (1624). All of these, like Burton, mimicked More's *Utopia* in being set on remote islands in the oceans surrounding the New World, whence travelers return to report on the inhabitants of strange commonwealths.[34] In the decade before the Massachusetts Bay Company received its charter, the discussion of ideal societies intensified with this remarkable series of new publications, growing discontent among Puritans over the policies of Charles I, and movement toward colonial projects spawned by this discontent.[35]

Juxtaposed with these utopian visions were recent efforts to create actual cities and colonies on new models. Some were the product of unusual circumstances, such as the great fire in 1613 that destroyed much of Dorchester, in southwestern England. Dorchester's destruction allowed its puritan leaders, especially the minister John White, later one of the founders of the Massachusetts Bay Company, to remake their city as "a reformed, godly community, . . . a new Jerusalem." White and his fellow Puritans directed their efforts toward charity, from the creation of new hospitals and schools to new methods for raising money for the poor. Earlier efforts by Protestant reformers in European cities, such as John Calvin's Geneva and Huldrych Zwingli's Zurich, served as models for the Puritans in Dorchester.[36]

Radical dissenters, whose strident critiques of the half-reformed Church of England were met with persecution that pushed them into exile, conducted other experiments. English separatists established churches in urban centers of the Netherlands, where free from English ecclesiastical authorities, they experimented in remaking church polity, taking the apostolic churches as their models. Among the clergymen who took part in these Dutch experiments were leading figures in early New England, such as William Ames, Hugh Peter, and John Davenport. The exiles argued fiercely with one another and their Dutch hosts about how to implement scripture, questioning everything from the legitimacy of a pastor's wife wearing silken finery to the theology of the Dutch Arminians. These experiences, like the utopian writings, offered conflict and disagreement, not a single model of a perfect church polity.[37]

In 1597, Francis Johnson, minister of an exile church in Amsterdam, took part in an Anglo-Dutch attempt to settle a colony of puritan separatists on the Magdalen Islands off the coast of Newfoundland.[38] Johnson's failed colony was one of many such experiments, most of them disastrous, and these forerunners also shaped Boston. American mythology imagines Winthrop and his fellow colonists, along with Jamestown and the Plymouth "Pilgrims," as the nation's beginnings, but we should remember how *late* Massachusetts came in the long series of English efforts to plant colonies in America. Many of these, like Johnson's Newfoundland venture, are now obscure or forgotten. But for Boston's founders, they created a litany of failure, illustrating how rapidly even the most hopeful and well-funded project might descend into bleak dystopia. Martin Frobisher's three voyages in the 1570s to Baffin Island, north of Labrador and west of Greenland, where he collected thousands of tons of ore that proved to be worthless; Humfrey Gilbert's Newfoundland venture in the 1580s, from which Gilbert never returned; Walter Ralegh's "lost" Roanoke Colony and disappointing Guiana venture; Charles Leigh's similar failures in Newfoundland and Guiana; the Sagadohoc Colony in 1607 in Maine, led by George Popham and Raleigh Gilbert, which lasted a year and gathered only a cargo of sarsaparilla before disbanding; George Calvert's failed attempt in the 1620s to create a Catholic refuge at "Avalon" in the "wofull country" of Newfoundland—all yielded nothing but wasted money, vanished settlers, and dashed hopes.[39]

Even the plantations at Jamestown and Plymouth that did manage to gain a toehold were not inspiring models. In 1610, three years after Jamestown's founding, all but sixty of its first five hundred colonists were dead. Some of the survivors staved off hunger by digging up the graves of their fellow colonists to eat the corpses. Over the next decade, Virginia's organizers coerced four thousand more of England's poor to cross the Atlantic. Three thousand of them had already died of disease and starvation by 1622, when an Indian attack killed a quarter of the remainder in a single day.[40] Plymouth's disasters were quieter than Virginia's, but the "starving time" that killed half the original colonists in 1620–21 was well known. Their English investors abandoned the colony, leaving the "pilgrims" to buy out their debts and fend for themselves.[41]

These dreadful examples, no less than the utopian dreams of godly commonwealths, were in the minds of Winthrop and his fellow organizers as they weighed the decision to migrate in their "General Observations for the Plantation of New England":

> Ob[jection] 4. But we may perishe by the waye or when we come there, either hanginge, hunger, or the sworde etc., and how uncomfortable it would be to see our wives, children, and freindes come to suche misery by our occasion?
>
> Ob[jection] 7. We see those plantations, which have been formerly made, succeeded ill.[42]

Such conversations among potential migrants to the New World mimicked the fictive dialogues of the utopian writings, from More to Bacon. These documents were circulated in dissenting circles and discussed by worried participants. The "General Observations" strove to quell such objections, acknowledging the woeful history of English colonization projects while still sustaining the dreams that the reforming tradition encouraged.

The upshot of this intense engagement with models both ideal and practical, hopeful and discouraging, not only among the Massachusetts Bay founders, but across the spectrum of English colonial ventures in the 1620s, was intense disagreement. Each group planning a new plantation had its own interpretation, its own way of melding idealistic dreams with the received wisdom on successful colonization. In the 1620s, puritan noblemen like the Earl of Warwick, Lord Brooke, and Lord Saye and Sele developed the Providence Island colony in the heart of the Spanish Caribbean. They shared the conviction of the Massachusetts organizers that the Protestant churches of England needed a refuge from the devastation of war and a corrupt English monarch. But these powerful grandees were also militantly anti-Spanish. They wanted to plant a colony where they could launch attacks on Spain's imperial stronghold. Their vision of colonial rule involved aristocrats like themselves dominating policy, not self-government by commoners. To compete with Spanish power, they would imitate Spanish models of colonial authority.[43]

By contrast, the chief figure in planting colonies on the coast of Maine, Sir Ferdinando Gorges, director of the Crown's Council for New England in the 1620s, wanted nothing to do with puritan refuges or reformed churches. Gorges envisioned his American colony as a return to feudal forms of authority, not an experiment in commonwealth government.[44] He imagined a city ("Gorgeana") at the center of his colony that would be the episcopal seat of the Church of England in America, with a resident bishop and cathedral, governed by aldermen and a mayor, and with many ceremonial offices ("two to four sergeants to attend on the said mayor . . . called forever sergeants of the white rod").[45] The Massachusetts Bay Company, with its middling investors and plans for self-government, differed dramatically from both of these contemporary alternatives.

Boston's founders were taking an enormous risk with no certain outcome. No single plan or version of colonial plantation had yet proven to be particularly effective. They were betting their lives and fortunes on a model of colonization for which they found an encouraging biblical precedent along with some successful examples from classical antiquity, but with no more guarantee of success than any of their predecessors. Not surprisingly, as Cotton came to the conclusion of his parting sermon on *Gods Promise to His Plantation*, he addressed a concern that was surely on the minds of his audience:

> "*Quest*. What is it for God to plant a people?"

In other words, what does this "plantation" metaphor really mean? What can we count on?

> *Answ*. When he promiseth to plant a people, their dayes shall be as the dayes of a Tree, *Isay* 65. 22. As the Oake is said to

> be an hundred yeares in growing, and an hundred yeares in full strength, and an hundred yeares in decaying.[46]

Cotton was offering a prophecy of remarkable prescience. *The City-State of Boston* follows his lead in dividing the history of the plantation of Boston in New England into three books, arranged along a chronology much like the days of the oak tree in Isaiah 65.

Book I, titled "Render unto Caesar," depicts Boston's rapid development in the seventeenth century. It focuses on Boston's expansion across New England, the hiving off of new colonies and their consolidation into a confederation, and the construction of an integrated political economy, linked to the markets of the West Indies and southern Europe. Boston began in the utopian dreams of dissident Puritans that a new kind of godly republic could be formed in the wilds of America, far from the decadent and corrupt power of European monarchs and state churches. But the challenge of survival pushed the infant colony into a fatal bargain: an economic alliance with the sugar islands of the West Indies. This effectively made Boston a slave society, but one where most of the enslaved labor toiled elsewhere, sustaining the illusion of Boston in New England as an inclusive republic devoted to the common good. To preserve the autonomy necessary to sustain its wide-ranging trade economy and egalitarian puritan culture meant that Boston was engaged throughout the century in a complex struggle with England's Stuart monarchs. Book I ends at a moment of vindication, when Britain's overthrow of James II and turn to constitutional monarchy seemed to ratify Bostonians' evolving vision of Protestantism, free trade, and political liberty.

Book II, called "The Selling of Joseph," begins after Britain's revolution of 1688 and Boston's simultaneous rebellion against James II's royal governor, which brought about a fundamental alteration of Boston's long antagonistic relationship with the Crown, and opened up new vistas for both commerce—rapidly growing trade in the Atlantic economy—and culture—the prospect that the city could play a major role in the creation of a Protestant International. But the hopes of the booming port city began to sour within the increasingly militarized British Empire of the later eighteenth century—a disturbing trend punctuated by Bostonians' forced participation in the 1755 ethnic cleansing and repatriation of the Acadians, the French population of Nova Scotia. The gradual deterioration of Boston's relationship with king and Parliament was marked by the ever-growing prominence of the "government of soldiers" in Britain's attempt to rein in the godly republic of New England, ending in rebellion and war, the city ravaged by military occupation and siege. Book II ends with Boston's liberty preserved, but with the older vision of an Atlantic world of liberty and commerce destroyed, and an uncertain future to be framed in its new relationship with a disparate group of other disaffected colonies.

Book III, "A New King over Egypt," resumes the story after the cataclysm of revolution had seemingly passed. Boston's independent commonwealth rebuilt its Atlantic commerce and negotiated new political relationships within the confederation of United States. Yet the arc of book III traces the dissolution of Boston as a city-state. The fateful decision to ratify the US Constitution began the slow demise of Boston's independence and regional power, as southern planters with continental ambitions dominated national politics, damaging Boston's interests and corroding its values. Additionally, the rise of New England's mechanized textile manufacturing, an economic shift made by Boston's merchants in response to Jefferson's trade embargoes and Madison's war, forged a new set of commercial relations with the American South. The rise of a powerful cotton interest within Boston's economy further divided the increasingly segregated city's population over the legitimacy of property in human beings. Despite efforts made by Boston's cultural leaders to reinvigorate its traditions of charity and cohesion, the city's internal divisions increasingly mirrored those of the American nation-state as both descended into violence and war. With the Union's triumph in the Civil War, Bostonians were at the forefront of seizing the spoils of victory and embracing the US imperial project. In that transformation, the centuries-old idea of Boston as an autonomous city-state, an idea that had been slowly deteriorating for decades, slipped away largely unnoticed.

Three centuries is an unusually deep time span for a book about an American place. But Boston's founders had a strong sense of time's depth; they understood their own project as a living extension of antiquity. Throughout this book, individual chapters attend to the layering effect of cumulative events over time, to the ways that lived experience built on, echoed, or rhymed with the past. Bostonians' awareness of the past often shaped the meaning of events through their understanding, consciously perceived or unconsciously felt, that the present moment was implicated in (though not determined by) the past and might be judged against the standards of history. By attending to the past's lingering echoes, I aim to convey a sense of the city-state of Boston's history as a slow and gradual emergence from the early modern world, rather than an impatient rush to find its place within a modern United States.

In structuring such a large work about a place so thoroughly documented from its beginnings, I have had to make choices about which events and people to focus on, and how to convey change across time and space, in order to construct what amounts to a biography of Boston in New England. But what does it mean to write the biography of a city-state? The story must attend to how this complex entity came into being and evolved over time—a story of growth, maturation, crises, and ultimate decline. That means following the actions of the emerging city's residents in their efforts to create durable connections with the region's hinterland, shape a self-sustaining political economy, and weather internal storms and stresses. This book dwells less on the internal development of the town and city of Boston proper—its political institutions and conflicts, population growth, built environment, and social and cultural life, or what is typically seen as the conventional materials of urban history—than on the life of Boston as lived beyond the boundaries of the city and region.

The life of a city-state takes place not only within the city's limits but also in its outreach to the hinterland to recruit talent and resources for the metropolis, and in the extension of its influence into the wider world. It would be absurd for a biography of an influential person to look only at the internal workings of that person's physical body, and ignore its subject's notable interactions with and significance in the world. So too this biography of the city-state of Boston is deeply concerned with the life that Boston led beyond its immediate boundaries, its struggles to define itself and sustain the autonomy and prosperity necessary to cultivate a distinctive identity within the Atlantic world.

Neither is this meant to be a complete narrative history of Boston. Even an internal history, focused only on events occurring within the city limits, would be an overwhelmingly large task, to which centuries' worth of dense historiography can attest.[47] The complexity of the task is compounded when it includes people from throughout the region who were recruited to join Boston's projects, reaches outward to the larger New England region that Boston shaped, and explores places around the Atlantic where Bostonians pursued their interests. As an antidote, the book's chapters are designed around particular moments, important problems, or significant passages in the history of Boston and New England. The chapters often focus on a relatively small number of Bostoners whose efforts to build and sustain the region's political economy, society, or culture, or whose connections in the larger Atlantic world are especially revelatory about the changing relationships between the city and its larger contexts. These individuals are not presented as typical Bostonians (it's hard to imagine what such a person might be) but instead as figures whose experience allows readers to develop an empathetic understanding of the public life of Boston in New England.

Boston's survival was precarious, and so were the qualities that sustained it as it grew: autonomy and security, material prosperity, self-governance, a commitment to commonwealth values, and a spiritual culture of reform and internal improvement. All these things were continually challenged and frequently in doubt. In each of them, the citizens of Boston in New England would sustain defeats, experience humiliating failures, and at times deal falsely with their god. Sometimes Bostonians chose life and good, and at other times death and evil. My inclination has been to call this story a tragedy. The city-state of Boston would be the noble hero of the drama, whose virtuous aspirations toward self-governing autonomy and an internal ethic of charity were eventually undermined by fatal flaws—an exclusionary social vision and a dependency on slave-based economies—that were present from New England's origins, aided its growth and prosperity, but ultimately destroyed both its autonomy and internal cohesion. And while that is the arc of the story to come, to call it a tragedy denies the open-ended choices that each generation faced in its efforts to create and sustain the city-state of Boston.

Book I

Render unto Caesar

> Then went the Pharisees, and took counsel how they might entangle him in his talk. And they sent out unto him their disciples with the Herodians, saying, Master, we know that thou art true, and teachest the way of God in truth, neither carest thou for any man: for thou regardest not the person of men. Tell us therefore, What thinkest thou? Is it lawful to give tribute unto Caesar, or not? But Jesus perceived their wickedness, and said, Why tempt ye me, ye hypocrites? Shew me the tribute money. And they brought unto him a penny. And he saith unto them, Whose is this image and superscription? They say unto him, Caesar's. Then saith he unto them, Render therefore unto Caesar the things which are Caesar's and unto God the things that are God's. When they had heard these words, they marvelled, and left him, and went their way.
>
> —Matthew 22:15–22

The city-state of Boston was Caesar's creature, by virtue of the Massachusetts Bay Company charter issued by King Charles I in 1629. Yet the charter granted the company's investors an unusual degree of autonomy in governing themselves. Boston's leaders stretched that autonomy still further, effectively creating an independent commonwealth, dedicated to promoting their vision for the kingdom of God rather than adhering to the decrees of England's Stuart monarchs.

The challenges of survival as a new colony were at least as great as the demands of the king. Unlike other colonies in the emerging Atlantic world, Boston's founders could not produce silver, gold, or any other high-value commodity to offset the expense of establishing a new society an ocean away from home, or provide employment for thousands of colonists. Left to their own devices, Boston's leaders produced their own "penny," designed to solve the challenges of political economy that their meager charter and scant resources created, bearing an image and superscription announcing their autonomy from Caesar. But their boldness required great efforts to determine what tribute they owed to Caesar and defend what they claimed as their own.

Chapter 1

Boston Emerges

From Hiding Place to Hub of the Puritan Atlantic

> If the Lord seeth it wilbe good for us, he will provide a shelter and a hidinge place for us and ours.
>
> —John Winthrop to Margaret Winthrop, 1629

In 1630, the year that Boston was founded, Governor Winthrop and the other leaders of the Massachusetts Bay Company's fleet of migrants looked for a likely place to settle among the islands and peninsulas in Massachusetts Bay. As the first ships arrived in July, the migrants crowded onto the Charlestown peninsula, between the Mystic and Charles Rivers as they met the harbor. But the heat, poor sanitation, and brackish water led swiftly to sickness. Dysentery and scurvy were common. Many people died, including Isaac Johnson, the largest shareholder and richest investor in the Massachusetts Bay Company, and his wife, the Lady Arabella, daughter of the Earl of Lincoln, after whom the flagship of the fleet had been named. In the first six months, two hundred of that year's fifteen hundred migrants perished.[1]

In August, the colonists began to disperse about the bay in search of healthier conditions and plentiful land. As they moved, they gave familiar English names to their new encampments: Watertown, Medford, Dorchester. In September, those leaders of the company still remaining in Charlestown and still alive—Winthrop, Thomas Dudley, and John Wilson (a clergyman who had already gathered a church among the Charlestown settlers)—crossed the river to the Shawmut Peninsula, planted themselves between the steep ridge of

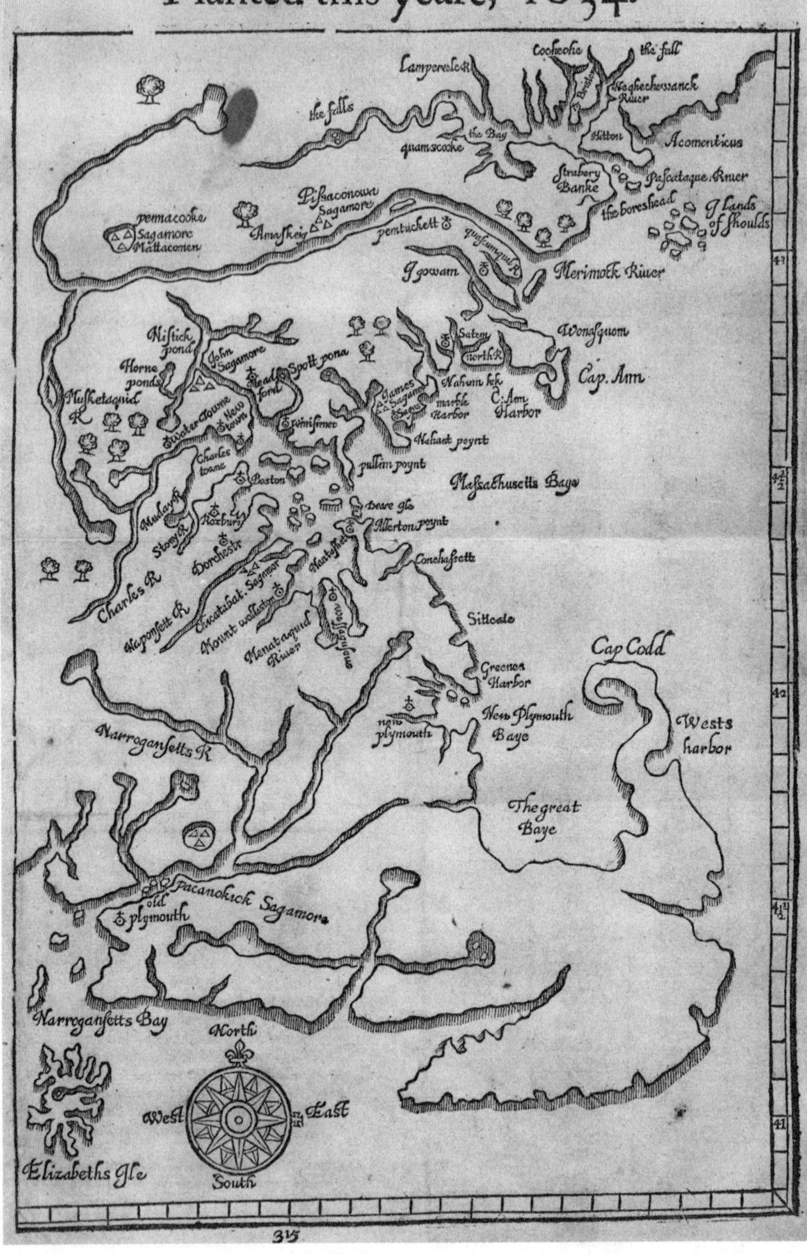

Map 1.1. *The South Part of New-England*, in William Wood, *New England's Prospect* (London, 1634). At this early date in the colonizing project, the cartographer's concerns were with bays, islands, and rivers. The shape and topography of the landscape are little noticed here.

three hills (the "Trimountaine") and shoreline, near a fresh water spring, and called their settlement Boston.[2]

There was no originating moment, no definable point at which the town of Boston came into being as a separate entity from the Massachusetts Bay Company. In September 1630, the Court of Assistants ordered "that Trimountaine shall be called Boston, Mattapan Dorchester, & the Towne vpon Charles River Waterton." Immediately following this naming exercise over the already-dispersed encampments, the court issued a general order that "noe p[er]son shall plant in any place within the lymitts of this Pattent, without leaue from the Govnr and Assistants."[3] In other words, the General Court, the colony's governing body consisting of the governor, his Council of Assistants or Magistrates, and later, the deputies sent by the towns who formed a lower house, would henceforth regulate the development of every future town within the jurisdiction of Massachusetts Bay. But no details about this system appear in the records until March 1636, when the General Court ordered that the freemen of the towns would have the power to distribute grants of lands to the town's inhabitants.[4] The earlier order of September 1630 merely recognized the de facto existence of several discrete settlements—Boston, Dorchester, and Watertown—but said nothing about their formal relationship to the colony, their boundaries, or under what terms they would hold or distribute land.

Meanwhile, the earliest extant town records of Boston begin in medias res with minutes of a 1634 meeting of the selectmen, a small group of officials elected by the town residents. It was clearly not the town's first. The selectmen were already dealing with mundane business, removing "stones and logges, . . . fish or garbage," near the town landing place along the inner harbor. Three months later at a town meeting, it was agreed that the selectmen "shall have the power to divide and dispose of all such lands belonging to the towne (as are not yet in the lawful possession of any particular person) to the inhabitants of the town according to the Orders of the Court."[5] But we do not know how particular persons had already acquired the "lawful possession" of land in Boston or even what land belonged to Boston. In addition to the Shawmut Peninsula, Boston's early

English inhabitants used various harbor islands and points of land from Muddy River in present-day Brookline to Mount Wollaston in Braintree for farms, animal grazing, and firewood.

In 1632, the General Court recognized "that Boston is the fittest place for publique meeteings of any place in the Bay." Boston thus became the colony's de facto capital, though no legislation ever made it so.[6] When the town of Boston used money from private donations to build a town house in the 1650s, with a public market on the ground floor and town meeting space upstairs, the General Court contributed funds for maintaining the upstairs space to host the quarterly sessions of the colony's government as well.[7] In the symbolism of its civic architecture and practices of government, it was impossible to separate Boston from Massachusetts Bay. This elision between capital and colony is part of what built and sustained Boston's character as a city-state. Boston was merely one town among many in Massachusetts, a part of the whole, and yet it represented the whole as well.

Boston was not a particularly auspicious name for this place. Other New World settlements bore the names of grander places or more hopeful sentiments: New London and New Amsterdam, Providence (there were several of these), Salem (like Jerusalem, from the Hebrew for peace), Eleuthera (from the Greek for freedom), Concord, and later, Philadelphia (brotherly love). Jamestown and Charleston honored Britain's monarchs. But old Boston, the new plantation's namesake, was notable mainly for the massive St. Botolph's Church in which John Cotton preached. That church, commonly called "Boston Stump" for its great tower, could be seen by ships far out at sea, plying the trade between Lincolnshire and the Netherlands that had once been the source of old Boston's prosperity, but had now fallen on hard times.

Boston in New England became the center of the puritan Atlantic by accident. It began as one part of a sprawling, complicated, and not altogether well planned effort to plant puritan colonists in the Americas. But within a dozen years of its founding, the new town of Boston began to acquire its defining characteristics, when the chaos of the first decade of puritan migration to the New World gave way to new patterns of settlement, trade, power, and authority. During that first decade, there was no obvious center of the puritan Atlantic or even of New England's small corner of this larger set of ventures. As merchants, members of the gentry, and influential clergymen arrived in America with followers in tow, they began to disperse along the coasts and rivers of New England from Maine to Long Island. Some explored the Delaware Valley, while others entertained offers to settle in Maryland and Virginia, Bermuda, Antigua, Barbados, and even Providence Island, deep in the heart of the Spanish Caribbean. But by the middle of the 1640s, among all these places, Boston emerged as the hub of this bumptious activity, the center of Atlantic Puritanism, a distinctive trading node and rising commercial power within the developing Atlantic economy, and the metropolis of the sprawling, quasi-independent composite state (Parliament, in a fit of absentmindedness, called it a "kingdom") of New England.[8]

I begin by tracing the story of Boston's unlikely emergence as the center of the puritan Atlantic, set within the context of many Atlantic colonial plantations attempted by England and its competing European imperial powers in the first half of the seventeenth century, and among the native American peoples they encountered in this process. This chapter examines the many ways in which Boston's origins, particularly with respect to its early political economy, were similar to other colonies, and the few ways in which it differed from most other plantations. It follows the attempts made in the first decade of colonization to turn various schemes for financial success into a permanent and stable economy, only to find these plans collapsing as the waves of new migrants that sustained the first decade's growth ebbed around 1640. From this point of desperation, when the survival of the colony was in doubt, it turns to examine a series of incidents in the early years of the 1640s, in which we can see the emerging trading connections and political relationships that allowed Boston to thrive economically, achieve political autonomy and authority over New England, and forge a distinctive identity in the Atlantic world. This chapter begins with high hopes and dreams of riches.

The Disappointments of Silver and Gold

The charter that King Charles granted to the Massachusetts Bay Company has a seldom-noted feature: its obsessive attention to gold and silver, mines and mining. At its upper-left corner appears a cartouche with a hand-drawn image of the king, bearing his royal scepter and orb, and looking somewhat demonic. Then in the first paragraph and repeated many times in subsequent ones, the charter states that the recipients of this gift from "CHAR. CAESAR" gain complete rights to "all Mynes and Myneralls, as well Royall Mynes of Gould and Silver, as other Mynes and Myneralls whatsoeuer," that they might discover within the lands granted. The charter promises that the company will forever hold title to all the lands in Massachusetts in the most unrestricted fashion known in England, with no quitrents, service obligations, or other contingencies, "as of our Mannor of East Greenwich, in the County of Kent, in free and comon Soccage, and not in Capite, nor by Knightes Service."[9] The one string attached to this otherwise-generous gift was that if the colonists actually did find any precious metals, then they would owe the king "the fifte Parte of the Oare of Goulde and Silver, which shall . . . happen to be founde, gotten, had, and obteyned in any of the saide Landes."[10] (See plate 4.)

One reason this feature is seldom noted is that we know, in retrospect, that no "Royall Mynes of Gould and Silver" have ever been found in Massachusetts. As a result, we tend to think that the New England colonies must have differed in their original purpose from, say, Virginia, where tradition has it that the cavalier founders were seeking nothing but riches. Those rapacious sons of the Elizabethan Sea Dogs modeled themselves after Spanish America, while puritan Boston was intended to be an exemplar of the superior values of industry and trade over the baser motives of lust for gold.[11] In this stereotypical rendition, we can ignore the boilerplate in the charter about mines and minerals because those things never mattered in Massachusetts. But in fact, New England was no different from Virginia or any other colonial project, whether English, French, Dutch, Swedish, Portuguese, or Spanish. Every New World colony needed to find some way to justify the expense of moving colonists across the Atlantic and sending ships to supply them. There was no simpler rationale than the discovery of precious metals that could be made into money.

The fabulous wealth in gold and silver that Spain's conquistadores plundered from Mesoamerica and Peru set such a prodigious model for a successful colony that no subsequent endeavors could shake themselves loose from this dream. From the 1570s onward, when Martin Frobisher's expeditions to Newfoundland shipped home tons of ore (that proved to be fool's gold), the patents given to Sir Humfrey Gilbert (1578) and Sir Walter Ralegh (1584) for their personal New World ventures, and subsequent charters of Virginia (1606), Bermuda (1612), Plymouth (1629), Providence Island (1629), Maryland (1632), Connecticut (1662), Rhode Island (1663), Carolina (1663), and Pennsylvania (1681), all included similar language about gold and silver mines and the royal fifth due to the king. So did the charter granted by King Gustavus Adolphus to the New Sweden Company (1626).[12] The royal officials responsible for drawing up these charters did not have a precise understanding of New World geography. They used blanket terms to cover all contingencies, making sure that the king and his heirs would always get an appropriate cut of any profits these speculative ventures might generate.

In this sense, Boston differed little from other colonial settlements. It was meant to be the end of yet another spoke emanating from a metropolitan hub, another plantation that might bring new wealth directly to the old country—if not silver and gold, then other high-value commodities in short supply at home. The high relative value of any colonial product was key to the economics of colonization. Throughout the age of sail, the cost of maintaining ships and crews made it prohibitively expensive to ship low-value goods to any place where they were already plentiful, as in "coals to Newcastle." As a new plantation grew, it might incidentally provide a market for manufactures from home. But at the time of Boston's founding, this aspect of colonial political economy had not been well conceptualized. It would take another century of growth before the consumer power of colonies made itself felt in the home country.[13]

In the meantime, the hunt for high-value goods began in Massachusetts. New England's early colonists scoured the countryside for "royal mines." The younger John Winthrop, a man of alchemical learning and an enterprising spirit, took the lead. By the early 1640s, he had located a "black lead" or graphite mine at Tantiusque, sixty-five miles west-southwest of Boston, that he hoped would also contain silver deposits. The site for the plantation that he founded at New London, along the Thames or Pequot River (in present-day Connecticut, but that he hoped to annex to Massachusetts), due south of Tantiusque, was chosen because this river gave easier transportation access to the mines.[14] Winthrop was not alone in these efforts; Roger Williams, exiled from Boston over theological disputes and founder of his own plantation on Narragansett Bay, occasionally wrote to Winthrop, sending "Bags of Oare . . . of Rode Iland where is certainly affirmed to be both Gold and Silver Oare upon Triall."[15] No one at the time knew that these efforts would be fruitless. Had the hills of Massachusetts held the mineral riches that the Spanish found in Peru in the 1540s or Californians found in the 1840s, then Boston's development would have been quite different—more like the model of Spanish America, or the plantations in Barbados and Virginia, where sugar and tobacco served as viable substitutes for precious metals.

In its earliest phase, the political economy of Boston differed from these other colonial plantations only in small ways. One was that the charter allowed the Massachusetts General Court to distribute land to colonists in simple and generous forms of ownership.[16] The colony's magistrates in Boston took advantage of this privilege, going beyond the letter of their liberties to establish townships that were, in effect, subcorporations of the Massachusetts Bay Company, usurping the king's exclusive power to create corporations. The magistrates gave these newly created town corporations the power to receive land grants from the General Court (as the company's governing body was called) and distribute the land equitably among the settlers.

No prior colony had done this, but then again, no prior colony had attracted the kind of settlers that the Massachusetts Bay Company was bringing to New England. The slow deterioration of the conditions in which Puritans could live comfortably as dissenters within the established Church of England pushed more and more families to abandon their homes and cross the ocean to the "shelter and hiding place" of Massachusetts.[17] As a result, the prospective planters that the Massachusetts Company recruited were likely to be landowning farmers, shop-owning artisans, or other prosperous middling sorts, with assets to convert into cash before they sailed to America.[18]

In most other English colonies, the settlers were essentially employees, often poor and rootless people with few economic options, shipped to the colony by investors who owned and operated the corporation from England. The colonists depended on the investors for supplies, while the investors expected profits, and the sooner the better. This system seldom worked well, especially in a plantation's early years, when expectations of rapid profits were unrealistic. Unaccustomed to the hardships of life in a strange land and unequipped with the skills needed to thrive there, most colonies' first planters could barely survive, let alone generate income for the investors who governed them.[19] By contrast, the Massachusetts planters had the advantage of being the investors in and governors of their own project. The assets that husbands and fathers sold off in England and brought to America, and the large families, including wives, children, and servants, that typically accompanied them, were the primary investment resources sustaining the new colony. The planters could use their money to buy what they needed to survive and their labor to stake out the farms that would sustain them.

So long as the migrant stream of prosperous settlers continued to flow across the ocean, bringing more cash and supplies in their transport ships, the Massachusetts Bay Colony could expect to flourish. The earliest arrivals frequently built farms on already-cleared land, cultivated not long before by Indians who had died in recent epidemics. On these farms, they produced simple foodstuffs that the next wave of newly arriving migrants would need until they, too, could reap the produce of their own farms.[20] Those who built homesteads in the new settlement at Boston had a more difficult time with this task. The Shawmut Peninsula was tiny, two miles long at most, a mile wide at its widest, and oddly shaped. At the time of the Winthrop fleet's arrival, it was nearly uninhabited. High rocky hills dominated its western half, while its low-lying land was often washed over by the sea at high tide, making it poorly suited for farming.[21] As a result, many of the early English settlers staked out farmland in nearby locations around the bay. From its earliest days, Boston could not supply its own food and timber, and relied on imports from the surrounding countryside. But the eastern-facing side of Shawmut, lying in a kind of natural amphitheater below the Trimount to the west, Fort Hill in the South End, and Copp's Hill in the North End, opened onto an excellent natural cove, deep enough for large ships to sail in close to shore, making Boston "fittest for such as can Trade into *England*, for such commodities as the Countrey wants, being the chiefe place for shipping and Merchandize."[22]

In Massachusetts, just like Bermuda and Barbados, Roanoke and Jamestown, Newfoundland and Plymouth, and the many other places where English colonies had already foundered, no gold and silver deposits were found within easy reach of first landing. The task of hunting or growing valuable commodities to produce export profits also proved to be difficult for inexperienced Englishmen. Sugarcane and tobacco did not flourish in New England's short growing season. Other exotic products, from wine grapes to silkworms, fared no better. Nonetheless, the Massachusetts Bay Colony planters did better than most of their English colonial predecessors. They did not starve, not much anyway, although there were high death rates in the first year, largely because of sickness and poor nutrition rather than outright starvation. To fend off hunger, the first colonists in the Winthrop fleet engaged one of the ship captains who brought them over, William Peirce of the *Lyon*, "to return to us with all speed with fresh supplies of victualls." They also purchased surplus corn from southern New England Indians, who "brought us 100 bushells of corne at about 4s. a bushell." The prices colonists paid for their imported "victualls," compared with their accustomed cost at home in England, shocked them: "The wheate we

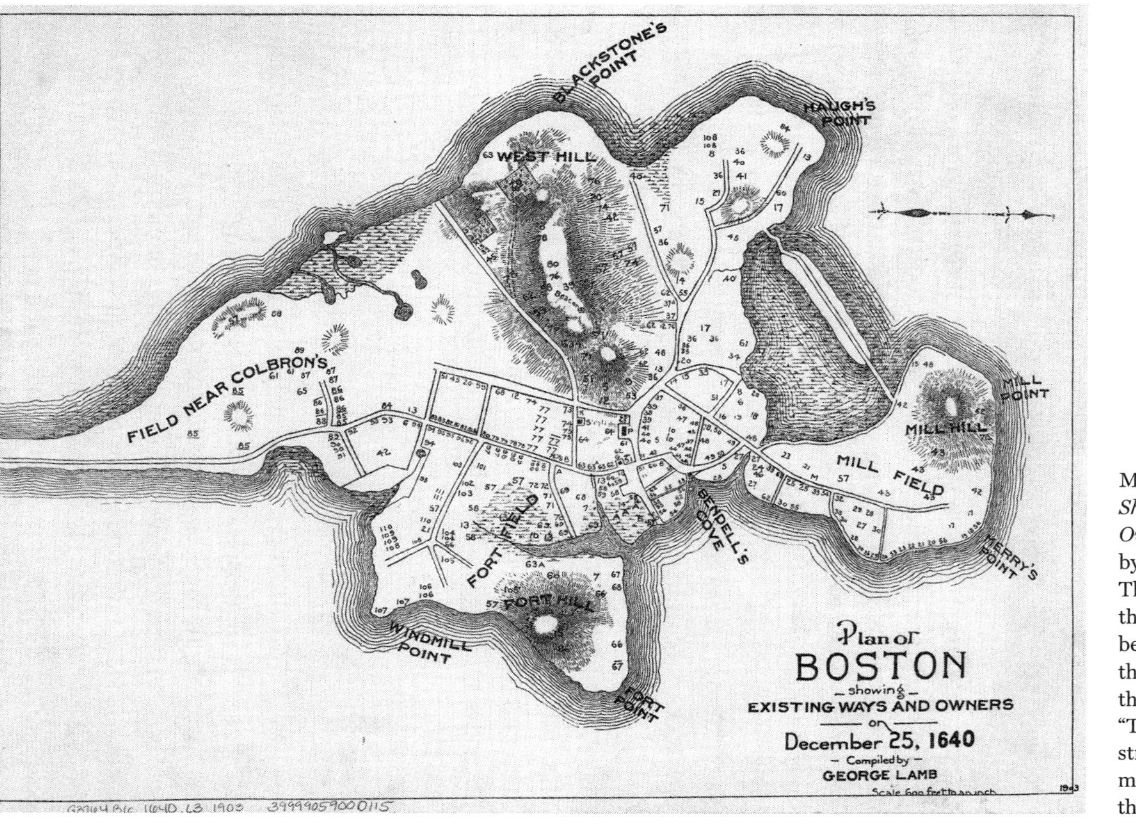

Map 1.2. *Plan of Boston, Showing Existing Ways and Owners on December 25, 1640*, by George Lamb, ca. 1903. The future Copp's Hill was then known as Mill Hill. The beacon atop Beacon Hill marks this point as the middle of the three-hill ridge making up the "Trimountain" or Tremont stretching westward across the middle of the peninsula. On this map, north is to the right.

received by this last shipp stands us in 13 or 14 shillinges a strike, . . . which is an higher price than I ever tasted bread of before."[23]

Nevertheless, the colony's frame of government proved adequate to the task at hand. It did not collapse in bitter contention between planters and investors, as did so many other joint-stock companies. But the economic system that sustained this success was inherently unstable. So long as new migrant investors and their money kept flowing across the Atlantic and into Boston, it did not matter that there was no gold, no silver, and not much else produced in Massachusetts that English merchants would accept as payment for the goods they shipped to Boston. And so long as the policies of "Char. Caesar" and his archbishop of Canterbury, William Laud, oppressed English Puritans, the migrant flow might continue indefinitely. But such schemes seldom last long. Whether foolhardy greed or fear and desperation, the conditions that cause investors to pour money into an enterprise with little hope of return are difficult to sustain.

To confront this problem, Boston's merchant leaders searched for a commodity, a substitute for silver and gold that would put the plantation's economy on a stronger footing. They staked their initial bets on fish and furs, the seafood for which Roman Catholic dietary practices created an inexhaustible market in southern Europe, and the pelts of exotic animals, such as beaver, seals, moose, and deer, that could be made into hats, collars, coats, and gloves for the gentlemen and ladies who defined fashions in European courts and cities.

The Insufficiency of Fish and Furs

The trade in codfish from the rich fishing banks off the coast of northeastern America went back long before permanent English colonization, to the Basque fishermen of northern Spain. For generations, the English West Country fishing fleets had also known about these aquatic riches. For much of the sixteenth century, English contact with the New World happened mainly at seasonal outposts along the Atlantic coast, where the fleets would salt and dry their spring and summer codfish catches before returning home in the fall.[24] But in the 1630s, changes in the relationship between Spain and England involving an entirely different commodity, wool, offered Boston's fledgling merchant community an opportunity to profit from its access to codfish.

Through the Middle Ages, England had produced and exported raw wool. But in the sixteenth century, English manufacturing of finished wool textiles expanded to absorb much of its domestic production of raw wool. In addition, new techniques in weaving finer wool cloth, the so-called new draperies, lighter than traditional broadcloth, increased demand in England for the finer-quality raw wool produced by Merino sheep raised in northern Spain.[25] English demand for fine Spanish wool increased rapidly, but English importation of Spanish wool suffered from a classic problem of long-distance trade: return cargoes. Shipping was slow, risky, and expensive in the age of sail; the cost of shipping often amounted to the greatest portion of the price of any commodity shipped across long distances.[26] Merchants wanted to make sure that their ships were filled with valuable cargo in both directions on any trading voyage. An empty voyage meant great expense with no returns to offset it. The problem with the growing English demand for Spanish wool was the limited array of English commodities in demand in Spain: it was hard to find English goods to fill the holds on the voyage to Spain.

Codfish solved this problem. In particular, the advantages provided by a North American colony with its own shipping capacity solved England's problem in a way that benefited Boston. The Roman Catholic prohibition on eating meat on Fridays and other religious holidays meant that for as many as 120 days per year, fish were a necessity in Spain. But this demand was not spread evenly throughout the year; Lent, in early spring, which called for six weeks without meat, was one of its high points. The codfisheries off Newfoundland and the Grand Banks of North America, however, so long as they were operated out of European seaports, were highly seasonal enterprises and not on a schedule that suited Spanish demand. British spring voyages returned in autumn with their catch of codfish, salted in the form of *bacalao* that Spanish consumers preferred, glutting the market between September and November, and lowering prices at a time of low demand. By the time the following spring and Lenten season came around, fish grew scarce and prices rose, but the quality declined; even salted fish only keep for so long. The solution was to base the fishing business on the North American coast. Instead of sending out an empty fishing fleet on a long and expensive voyage every spring to return full in the fall, the catching of codfish could be conducted year-round from the American mainland, and then good-quality fish could be sent to southern European markets by merchants, who timed their shipments to meet periods of higher demand.

The increase in English demand for fine wool from Spanish sheep developed most dramatically in the 1630s. Port records from Bilbao, in northern Spain, show a three- to fourfold increase in wool exports over this decade. At the same time, imports of *bacalao* in Bilbao also increased dramatically. Yet from the mid-1630s onward, most of the fish was arriving on ships not from England or Newfoundland but rather from Boston and its nearby settlements. As the first stable English plantation in America to include a substantial cohort of experienced Atlantic merchants among its founding colonists, Boston was uniquely well placed to take advantage of the new English and Spanish trade relationship.[27]

By organizing their access to the local fisheries that sprang up among the settlements of coastal New England, Boston merchants could ship their *bacalao* or "merchantable fish" just in time for the Lenten purchasing season in Spain. With the profits from the fish trade, they purchased Spanish wool from Bilbao merchants for export to England. And with the profits from selling Spanish wool in England, they returned home to Boston loaded with manufactured goods bought from English merchants to meet the steady demand of New England's growing population. English traders such as John Beaple, a West Country merchant who provided consumer goods to the early New England colonists, first pioneered this triangular solution. But soon Boston merchants perfected the trade themselves, taking advantage of direct access to local fishermen in New England and better knowledge of the English goods that Massachusetts settlers would buy.[28] Through the development of this initial triangle trade, Massachusetts merchants encouraged the growth of an indigenous shipbuilding industry and found a new source of credits for the purchase of English goods, augmenting the cash brought by new immigrants.[29]

Although the Spanish codfish trade would be a major factor in Boston's economy for generations to come, it could not solve the economic challenge faced by the large numbers of migrants arriving in Boston in the 1630s. Few farmers and artisans who made up the bulk of the puritan "Great Migration" had any experience as fishermen.[30] The actual business of catching cod fell to outliers, small groups of professional fishermen with little interest in the puritan commonwealth, who developed their own rather-lawless communities on the fringes of Massachusetts settlement, to the north and east of the covenanted communities of the bay. The merchants who purchased the fish and shipped it to Bilbao earned credits that benefited the entire colony. But the codfish trade could not provide employment or purchasing power for the great majority of the colony's migrant population.

Fur was the second commodity for which Boston's founders had high hopes. The merchant leaders of Massachusetts knew that furs could be lucrative, mainly because Dutch and French colonies were well ahead of them in exploiting these resources along the Hudson and Saint Lawrence Rivers. If Massachusetts merchants could use the rivers granted in their charter to access untapped forests, and form relationships with Indians who knew where and when to hunt the right animals, they might catch up with or even overtake their competitors.[31] But this meant relying on Indians who had the skills to hunt, clean, and prepare wild animal skins for export. Fur trapping and processing, even more than fishing, was completely unfamiliar to the artisans and farmers arriving in Boston throughout the 1630s.

In the end, both fish and furs shared the same problem for a colony consisting of large numbers of settler families. As items in demand in Europe, they could provide credits for the colony's merchants to conduct overseas trade, but they could not provide employment for the colonists themselves. Both were specialty trades requiring skills that most colonists lacked. No matter how lucrative they might be for merchants, they were the kind of enterprises that could only sustain *trading* operations such as those envisioned by the Dutch in New Amsterdam or French plantations along the Saint Lawrence. Fish and furs could never sustain a "New England" made up of tens of thousands of farming colonists. The continuous inflow of this unprecedentedly large migration through the 1630s disguised the problem by virtue of the resources brought by new settlers. But the migration's sudden end around 1640 with the outbreak of civil wars in Britain revealed the dilemma in the starkest possible terms.

During the Great Migration, as a thousand or more migrants disembarked in Boston every year, the grain and livestock raised by the first comers found ready markets among the new arrivals. The money that the new arrivals paid for their sustenance went to purchase English manufactured goods, such as clothing, shoes, tools, metal goods, glass, paper, and books—all the necessities of a new plantation. When the migration stopped, the flow of money stopped as well. Locally produced goods—Indian corn, wheat, salted beef, and pork—plummeted in price. Indian corn that sold for five shillings a bushel in 1640 literally could not be given away the following year; its price was zero.[32] Cattle prices dropped from the robust twenty to thirty pounds to an anemic four to five pounds per head—barely worth the cost to keep them, except that corn itself was going begging. The surplus produce of the first English farmers of Massachusetts Bay had been grown for the sake of these new arrivals; now there was no market for surplus goods. These commodities were no good to English merchants. No one in the home country would pay the transatlantic shipping costs, or tolerate the spoilage of grain or meat raised in America. With demand in New England saturated, prices fell to nothing. Now the problem of the merchant's empty voyage that had given Boston an opportunity with respect to Spain and the codfish trade snapped back against the new colony. It became a possibility that English merchant ships might no longer come to Boston at all—they would find no money there to buy their goods, and no goods to purchase worth the cost of shipping back home again.

The triangle trade between Boston, Bilbao, and London in fish, wool, and manufactured goods had effectively functioned without much need for money. Commodities were exchanged for commodities, with prices recorded in monetary figures for the sake of keeping the books, while little silver or gold changed hands. The New England fishermen who supplied Boston's merchants with cod were paid in the manufactured goods returning from the triangle trade; fishing was a commercial enterprise from the beginning. But Boston's merchants needed to encourage Indian hunters and artisans to kill and process animals beyond their own customary needs. To bring about this change in Indian behavior required the merchants to have something to trade with Indians for marketable furs that they could sell directly to England. Even before the arrival of Winthrop's fleet and the founding of Boston, the relationships among Dutch fur traders and their Indian suppliers had identified that something as wampum.

Throughout the seventeenth century, the growth of Boston's economy across New England's interior would come to depend heavily on the availability of money in various guises to lubricate and accelerate trade. As gold and silver had yet to be found in the hinterland, Boston's leaders would make a series of remarkable experiments in alternative ways to find or make money. This first took the form of wampum, and as experiments in money frequently do, it reconfigured social and political relationships in the region, dramatically altering the balance of power between Boston's colonists and New England's indigenous peoples.

Wampum Troubles

Wampum beads—white ones, that is—were little cylinders made from the inner spiral of the channeled whelk (*Busycotypus canaliculatus*), a snaillike shell. Black or purple wampum was cut from the dark edges of quahog clamshells (*Mercenaria mercenaria*). Black wampum beads were valued more highly than white ones.

Holes were drilled through the centers of these cylindrical shells, making them into tubes that were easy to string into fathoms, six feet in length, roughly the span of a man's arms. The strings could be woven into elaborate belts, with dark and white beads patterned to form images or meaningful shapes. Indigenous labor was key to the process of wampum production. Before European contact, Algonquian peoples living along the coasts of Long Island Sound, where the whelks and quahogs were readily available, made these strings and belts of wampum, using stone tools to drill holes in the beads. Indian populations throughout much of northeastern North America exchanged wampum, usually in ritual ceremonies controlled by sachems, the chiefs or headmen of Algonquian bands or tribes. The Iroquois or Haudenosaunee Confederacy had a particular fondness for wampum as a central element of its ceremonial culture. By the mid-seventeenth century, millions of these shell beads were circulating as far west as the Seneca Nation, in present-day western New York State.[33] (See plates 5a and 5b.)

Strictly speaking, wampum was not money, at least not before Europeans arrived. It did not bear a fixed exchange value that could be applied to any and all commodities, and it was not exactly a store of wealth. Its exchange value depended on the circumstances in which it was given and received. The possession of wampum marked its owner's power and prestige. Not just anyone could use it. When one community presented wampum in tribute to another, the exchange was made between sachems, who distributed it to their followers and dependents. Wampum was often worn as clothing or body ornamentation, as necklaces, bracelets, and belts that advertised the wearer's status.[34] Wampum could be presented as a sign of tribute or as ransom for a wartime captive. But it was also used as a mnemonic device to keep track of the provisions of treaties made among allies. Gifts of wampum demonstrated the power or authority of the giver over his or her followers, whose loyalty was signified by their labor in gathering and producing the shell beads. Before European colonization, the exchange of wampum resembled gift giving and diplomacy more than trade.[35]

If wampum was not money among northeastern Indians, it is nevertheless easy to see why Europeans thought that it was. As Daniel Gookin, a leader in Boston's Indian relations, saw it, "With this wompompeague they pay tribute, redeem captives, satisfy for murders and other wrongs, purchase peace with their potent neighbours, as occasion requires; in a word, it answers all occasion with them, as gold and silver doth with us."[36] Gookin's mistake was rooted in his vocabulary: "pay" and "purchase" were words that allowed the English to interpret Indian diplomacy as trade. For Indians, however, Gookin's words represented new concepts. According to Roger Williams, writing in the 1630s, the Narragansett words for "money" ("*Moneash*") and "I will pay you" ("*Cuppaimish*") were recent constructions borrowed from English.[37] This conceptual confusion between Indian wampum and European money might have been sorted out had Europeans not needed money so badly, and had they not relied so heavily on Indians in their pursuit of prosperity.

The Dutch fur traders of New Netherland were the first to mistake wampum (which they called "*sewan*") for money and thereby make it into money. In the 1620s, Dutch explorers moving up the Hudson River learned of the Iroquois demand for wampum (it was significantly more desirable than many European trade goods) and began to imagine wampum's monetary potential. By the mid-1620s, Isaak de Rasieres, the Dutch West India Company's commercial agent, acquired large amounts of wampum from eastern Long Island Indians in return for inexpensive Dutch goods. He then shipped wampum up the Hudson to exchange with the Mohawks for furs. The Mohawks may have understood this as a political alliance sealed with the exchange of gifts, but Rasieres took it to be a clever bargain made possible by this new form of money. Light in weight, durable, and easily portable, wampum was an ideal commodity for long-distance trade. Following Rasieres's model, the Dutch shipped boatloads of valuable furs to the Netherlands every year, averaging over two hundred thousand guilders' worth (roughly twenty thousand pounds) by the early 1630s, for a fivefold return on their investment.[38]

The Dutch traders' success led them to encourage both the rapid expansion of wampum production among coastal Indians, aided by the introduction of European iron awls, and the explosive growth in fur hunting among interior Indians, aided by European firearms. The Dutch supplied the Indians of Long Island Sound (the Pequots, Niantics, Mohegans, and Narragansetts) with a growing volume of trade goods in return for increased wampum production. These coastal Indians in turn became middlemen in the trade with the interior Indians of New England. Guns helped Indians bring in more furs, so guns joined wampum in the tribute the Dutch paid to the Iroquois. In 1627, Rasieres extended wampum's use to the Plymouth Colony for the first time, and Plymouth expanded the reach of wampum into northeastern New England. The Plymouth colonists used it to trade along the Kennebec River in present-day Maine, where wampum became far more popular than any European goods the impoverished Plymouth Colony had to offer.[39]

Thus by the time Boston was founded in 1630, wampum had already been monetized throughout much of New England. European merchants and their Indian partners had made it the predominant circulating currency in northeastern North America. High-status Indians no longer controlled wampum; anyone who had pelts to trade could now get their hands on it. In many ways, wampum seemed to possess all the qualities that Europeans expected money to have. Demand for it was high, and supplies were reasonably plentiful, but not *too* plentiful. Everyone wanted it, but it could not be found or made just anywhere. It was durable and easy to store, strong but not bulky. Counterfeiting proved to be impossible, though not for lack of effort. The Dutch experimented in producing their own wampum, but never managed to pass it off on Indian consumers as the real thing.

Boston's founders quickly realized the potential value of wampum for two strong reasons. First, the merchant entrepreneurs of the Massachusetts Bay Company, men like William Pynchon and Simon Willard, saw furs as the principle commodity on which to stake their prosperity, and by the 1630s, wampum was clearly the key to the fur trade.[40] But the Indian population of the area surrounding

Massachusetts Bay had been decimated by epidemics in the late 1610s and again in the first three years of Massachusetts' settlement. The main rivers within the territory granted to Massachusetts in its charter, the Charles and Merrimack, were disappointing as avenues to the interior; they were not navigable far enough to reach skilled Indians and fertile hunting grounds. So Boston's merchants and military leaders soon began to eye territories well beyond their patent, especially coastal Connecticut and Long Island Sound, to gain access to wampum and river routes to furs. Boston's imperialism started here, with the effort to stretch the boundaries of the Massachusetts Charter to control more of the resources of greater New England. A second reason for wanting wampum lay in Boston's own monetary troubles. English merchants demanded cash payments for the goods they supplied, so the money that crossed the Atlantic with the migrants tended to flow back across the sea just as quickly. Lacking currency, colonists were left to the cumbersome task of bartering among themselves and their Indian neighbors.[41]

The newly monetized wampum offered an obvious solution to the limitations of barter trade, and Bostonians quickly took advantage of this development. In 1637, the Massachusetts General Court made official what had already been happening for several years: it declared wampum to be legal tender for all transactions under the value of a shilling (twelve pence), exchangeable at the rate of six beads to a penny.[42] But by the geographic limits of the charter, Boston was poorly situated for access to wampum. The smaller English colony at Plymouth and the Dutch outposts along the Hudson and western Long Island were closer to wampum's sources, and had already established contacts with Indians there. In the words of William Wood, who returned to England in 1633 to report on the colony's progress, the Indians of coastal Rhode Island and eastern Connecticut were the "Southerne Mint-masters" from whom "the Northern, Eastern, and Western Indians fetch all their Coyne."[43] By the time of Wood's departure, Bostonians were planning to "fetch coin" there as well.

These plans had disastrous consequences for southern New England Indians, especially the Pequots, who lived at the lower reaches of the Connecticut and Pequot (Thames) Rivers in present-day southeastern Connecticut.[44] Even before Boston was settled, the Pequots and their neighbors to the east, the Narragansetts, were devoting their winter months to manufacturing wampum on an unprecedented scale to satisfy demand from New Amsterdam. The growing value of wampum led to violent conflict between the Pequots and Narragansetts, who each wanted to be the chief wampum brokers and middlemen of the interior New England fur trade. But with the expansion of the wampum trade to Plymouth in the late 1620s and the arrival of thousands of new colonists in Massachusetts Bay in the early 1630s, Dutch traders grew nervous about their continued access to wampum from Long Island Sound. In 1633, they established an outpost along the Connecticut River, near present-day Hartford, strategically chosen to link the coastal wampum resources to inland fur-trading Indians. They bought land from a group of Pequots, built a trading post, and called it "the House of Good Hope."[45]

By trying to keep the English out, the Dutch inflamed their already-tense relationship with the Pequots. In summer 1633, Dutch traders captured Tatobem, a Pequot sachem, and despite accepting wampum as ransom for his return, they murdered him. In customary fashion, Tatobem's supporters avenged his death by capturing and killing a European trader. Yet the man they killed turned out to be English, not Dutch, a trader named John Stone, a violent habitual drunkard who was none too popular in puritan Boston. Stone's troublesome personality was not much mourned, but Boston's leaders saw the advantage that his murder placed in their hands. A group of Pequots appealed to Boston for protection and support, as now neither the Dutch nor Narragansetts wanted to trade with the Pequots.[46] In October 1634, Pequot envoys went to Boston and worked out a deal. Boston would send ships loaded with European textiles to the Pequots, who in return would send Boston substantial amounts of wampum in tribute, turn over Stone's killers, and grant Massachusetts the rights to Connecticut Valley lands above the House of Good Hope. These rights were important to Boston. Colonists from the new settlements ringing Massachusetts

Bay were already moving overland to the Connecticut Valley, hoping to push aside the Dutch and Plymouth outposts, gain control over this avenue to the fur country, and farm the fertile lands along the river's banks. But Boston refused to give the Pequots what they wanted most: protection. As Winthrop described the agreement, "We should presently send a pinace with Clothe to trade with them, & so should be at peace with them, & as friends: to trade with them. but not to defende them."[47]

Instead, Boston's leaders hoped to reduce the Pequots' need for protection by negotiating peace between the Pequots and Narragansetts. Boston offered to share with the Narragansetts some of the wampum tribute that the Pequots promised to pay to them, if the Narragansetts would make peace with the Pequots. That is, Massachusetts brokered a transaction that would have dishonored the Pequots had it been conducted directly: the Pequots would never have *paid* the Narragansetts to make peace.[48] In the end, these agreements broke down over differing views of what the exchange of wampum signified. For the Pequots, payment of wampum as tribute to Boston was a matter of diplomacy, an act of submission, and they expected to gain protection from Massachusetts in return. Boston's offer of trade but not defense was unsatisfactory to the Pequots, who therefore refused to pay the wampum or turn over Stone's killers. From the Pequot point of view, the deal was off—a treaty that went unratified. But the Pequot interpretation did not stop Boston from acting as if the deal was still valid—a business contract that must be fulfilled. On the strength of the Pequots' initial offer, colonists from Massachusetts Bay poured into the Connecticut Valley in 1635 and 1636, displacing the Dutch and Plymouth traders and any Indians they found in the way, Pequot or otherwise.[49]

Diplomatic relationships in southern New England entered a descending spiral of violence. Massachusetts leaders still expected the Pequots to turn over Stone's killers when in July 1636, the murder of another English trader, John Oldham, made matters worse. In this case, the culprits were not Pequots but instead Indians from Block Island affiliated with the eastern Niantics or Narragansetts. Although Winthrop, Henry Vane, and other leading Bostonians were aware that the murderers were probably Narragansetts, blame for Oldham's death quickly shifted to the Pequots. News of Oldham's murder arrived in Boston at the same moment as the news that the Pequots refused to pay the wampum tribute and turn over the killers of Stone.[50]

In response, Boston organized a military mission to punish the Pequots. Captain John Endecott and his ninety soldiers sailed to Block Island, off the coast of the mainland opposite the mouth of the Thames River, where they hoped to catch Oldham's killers and seize stores of wampum. Failing at this, they put Indian houses and food stores on Block Island to the torch, then sailed into the river estuary and assaulted several Pequot villages. Pequot warriors repulsed these attacks, and then responded by targeting the English outposts in the Connecticut Valley, capturing and killing farmers in their newly planted fields and traders plying the river.

Boston now assembled a much larger expeditionary force and placed it under the command of Captain John Underhill, who had fought in the Dutch revolt against Spain. They recruited soldiers from the new Connecticut River villages as well, under the leadership of Captain John Mason, also a veteran of the Dutch wars. As rumors mounted that the Pequots were organizing a pan-Indian assault against all the English plantations, Boston's leaders were keen to pry other Indian groups away from supporting the Pequots. Uncas, leader of the Mohegans, supported the English colonists in the hope of expanding Mohegan power over southern New England. The Narragansetts were less eager, but in the end acceded to Boston's pressure and joined in an alliance to crush the Pequots.[51]

In May 1637, the combined English forces under Mason and Underhill's command, supported by Mohegan and Narragansett allies, surrounded the Pequots' fortified settlement near the Mystic River. They attacked its entrances, set the village ablaze, and mercilessly cut down the Pequots who attempted to flee. Having destroyed one of the two principal Pequot settlements, English and Indian forces proceeded to capture or exterminate as many of the remaining Pequots as possible over the next few months. Of the Pequots who survived these vicious assaults, most either melded quietly into the villages of the Niantics, Narragansetts, and Mohegans where they had relatives, or else were sold into slavery among the English and Indians of the region; some were put on ships and sold as slaves in Boston's first voyages to the West Indies.[52]

The violent destruction of the Pequots was not foreordained by an innate hostility between the races, or by a persecuting streak in puritan ideology or character. In other circumstances, English Puritans maintained lasting relationships of mutual respect with Indian allies, such as the Plymouth Colony's alliance with the Wampanoag under Massasoit, and John Eliot's and Thomas Mayhew's missions among the Massachusetts and Martha's Vineyard Indians. Rather, the conquest of the Pequots achieved precisely the dominance of the wampum supply, fur trade avenues, and land resources of coastal and riverine Connecticut that Boston's mercantile and political leadership began to covet in the early 1630s, when their own money supply, trade routes, and land resources had all run dry much sooner than expected.

From 1637 onward, the Indians of coastal Connecticut, Rhode Island, and Long Island Sound became client states of Massachusetts, Boston's tributaries. After Endecott's blundering mission to Block Island, the Block Island Indians began paying annual tribute in wampum to Boston to avoid further destruction. In the 1638 agreement that ended the Pequot War, all the former tributaries of the Pequots followed suit and agreed to send wampum directly to Boston.[53] The Narragansetts attempted to hold out against this pressure, but the humiliation and eventual execution of their sachem Miantonomi in 1643 at the hands of Uncas and the Mohegans, ordered and sanctioned by Boston's leadership, completed Boston's dominance over the wampum-producing Indians.[54]

The resulting tributary system proved to be lucrative for Massachusetts over the next three decades. In some years, as little as 30 or 40 fathoms of tribute wampum appear in the records, while in other years, amounts as large as 3,000 to 6,000 fathoms were paid. A fathom of wampum, 6 feet in length, held on average about 330 beads. At an exchange rate of 6 beads to a penny, a fathom was worth about 4.5 shillings, or a little less than one-fourth of a pound sterling (there were 20 shillings to a pound). In 1645, to take one example, the 2,000 fathoms of wampum Massachusetts received in tribute would have been worth around 460 pounds, a substantial sum of money, comparable to the total amount that the colony received in taxes from its own citizens in an average year. The most thorough analysis of this tributary system suggests that "about 5,000 pounds in English currency entered colonial coffers during this period, more if double-valued purple beads were included." All told, the Pequot War of 1637 resulted in "the partial underwriting of New England colonization costs by the conquered natives."[55] It was no accident that 1637, the year of the Pequots' destruction, was the year that Boston declared wampum to be legal tender throughout the region.

In addition to wampum payments received in tribute, Massachusetts demanded that the Narragansetts and Mohegans who adopted Pequot captives make annual payments to Boston for each captive they received. In effect, Boston used the Pequot War to become a slaving power not unlike coastal West Africa's indigenous merchants, who exchanged captive slaves taken in internecine wars for the cowrie shell money that circulated in the region. Just as in West Africa, some of the slaves taken in the Pequot War (mostly women and children) were redistributed within the region, while others (usually male warriors) were shipped out to meet demand in the growing labor markets of the Atlantic world. One difference, of course, was that if New England had perfectly resembled West Africa, the Pequots or Narragansetts would have been the conquerors and brokers, distributing the slaves to interior kingdoms like the Iroquois or selling them to offshore European merchants. But unlike European slave traders in West Africa who purchased slaves from Africans at trading forts or "factories" such as Elmina or Cape Coast Castle, Bostonians established a foothold on the continent first, and gained hegemony over the money and labor supply for themselves.[56]

In a remarkably short time, between 1633 and 1637, Bostonians exploited the potential value of wampum to achieve dominance over territory beyond their charter's limits, gain access to furs, and restructure political relations among Indians and colonists of the coastal Northeast. Yet in subsequent years, the political economy of wampum would collapse. After a decade and more of inflation and devaluation, in 1661 the Massachusetts General Court officially demonetized wampum, ordering that no one could be forced to accept payment in wampum against their will.[57] By contrast, the cowrie shell money collected in the Maldive Islands of the Indian Ocean, which became the small change of the West African slave trade, remained stable and reliable for centuries. Wampum seemed to have all the advantages of cowrie shells—decorative and ceremonial, lightweight, durable, uncounterfeitable, and available in large yet still limited supplies. What's more, European merchants did not have to transport wampum across thousands of miles of ocean or desert to reach the markets where it was most in demand, and they had far greater control over its production and acquisition than the Dutch and English East India Companies had over cowries.[58] Why, then, did wampum fail?

The answer lies in understanding the difficult challenge of integrating local economies and fiduciary moneys into international trade networks. When Portuguese traders first arrived in coastal West Africa, they discovered that cowries, despite the low individual value of each shell, were already part of an integrated, stable, and complex commodity trading economy that spread across North Africa to the Indian Ocean and beyond. Cowries had a long-established and fairly fixed relationship to the larger and more valuable forms of commodity money—silver and gold—that circulated in the Indian and Atlantic Oceans. Once Portuguese traders in the Indian Ocean gained access to cowrie shells, it was relatively simple to extend that economy a bit further, to use shells to buy slaves for the sugar-producing islands off the West African coast that they had recently colonized. As other European states moved into this trade network in the wake of the Portuguese, they simply followed the same pattern. By the late seventeenth century, a cowrie shell commodity exchange had appeared in Amsterdam, patronized by merchants from all over the Atlantic and Indian Oceans.[59]

The Dutch and English traders who entered Long Island Sound in the 1620s believed they had found something like cowrie shells, but they were wrong; wampum was different. Wampum was *not* already money. It was *indigenous* to the region, potentially *unlimited* in supply, *not* in demand outside the region, and had *no* fixed or practical relationship to other forms of commodity money. Nonetheless, the European traders wanted it to be money and assumed that it was money. In doing so, they transformed the regional economy of New England, with two immediate and disastrous consequences: overproduction of wampum, and overhunting of furs. The Pequot War marked the moment when Boston took control of the wampum supply and the rivers that promised untold wealth from furs. A decade later, the fur-bearing animals that could be reached by southern New England's rivers were disappearing. As more and more wampum chased fewer and fewer pelts, wampum's value as a currency collapsed. By 1649, it was no longer acceptable as payment to the General Court in taxes. By 1661, wampum was discontinued as legal tender for interpersonal exchange.[60]

Wampum would continue to circulate in New England for decades to come, especially in regions remote from Boston. Sarah Kemble Knight, a Boston woman traveling to New York in 1704, was surprised to find it among the forms of pay that rural Connecticut storekeepers still accepted.[61] But from Boston's point of view, its utility as money vanished when merchants could no longer rely on it to acquire furs for export. Demand for wampum existed only in eastern North America, centered on the Iroquois League. Although wampum could be produced in prodigious quantities, it could not be used as money in places outside eastern North America. In the 1630s, Boston's merchants saw only wampum's potential for earning woodland riches, but by the 1640s, as the promise of furs as a direct commodity link to European goods diminished, wampum's limitations became apparent. In the late 1640s, as the volume of silver money flowing into Boston began to grow, the city's merchants dumped as much of their wampum supplies as possible on the Dutch merchants, who had once taught them its value and from whom they had struggled mightily to wrest it only fifteen years before.[62]

The West Indian Solution: Triangle Trade for a Settler Society

Wampum's collapse and the failure of fur left Boston's merchants without a reliable means to connect New England's productive capacities to the wider world. But seafaring traders like William Peirce gradually discovered a solution. Peirce was a godly man and ship captain, a crucial figure in early Boston, though not a well-known name in the city's history. He saved the first colonists from starvation by arranging a quick voyage to Bristol and back, returning in spring 1631 with enough "victualls" to keep them alive. On all of his oceangoing voyages, Captain Peirce made a point of reading through the Bible "in course" with his crew, a chapter or two a day, just like many of the more sedentary folks among the godly. Peirce was seen as the fittest person by members of Boston's leading families to train their sons who wanted careers at sea.[63] Using his ship, the *Lyon*, Peirce delivered hundreds of English migrants to Boston, including some of the colony's leading lights—fugitives from Archbishop Laud's ecclesiastical courts.[64] Peirce's voyages supplied the new colony with the food and materials it needed to survive. And Peirce played a key role in solving the colony's problem of finding markets for the goods that its thousands of colonists were capable of producing from New England's rocky soil.

At the end of the Pequot War in 1637, Peirce agreed to take fifteen Pequot captives aboard his ship and sell them into slavery at the English colony in Bermuda. Missing his destination, he sailed on and eventually reached Providence Island, the new puritan outpost in the western Caribbean, where he exchanged the Pequot captives for "some cotton, and tobacco, and Negroes, etc." On the return voyage, he stopped at Tortuga, off the northwest coast of Hispaniola, acquired a load of salt, and thence returned, bringing the first African slaves to Boston. One of the "Negroes" became a maidservant to his wife. Judging by Bridget Peirce's pride in the family's collection of finely embroidered linen goods, Peirce's work as a ship captain was lucrative.[65]

On his trade mission to the West Indies, Peirce assessed the local demand for New England products, concluding that "dry fish and strong liquors are the only commodities for those parts." He also encountered two men-of-war, privateering ships outfitted by the Earl of Warwick, Lord Brooke, and Viscount Saye and Sele, English puritan aristocrats who backed the Providence Island colony and supported other puritan plantations in America, such as the short-lived Saybrook Colony in coastal Connecticut. Their men-of-war had captured several Spanish prizes under letters of marque issued by these so-called Lords of Providence. It was in these privateering raids that the African slaves Peirce acquired had been captured. Peirce had been a pivotal figure in Boston's first decade, and although he had done well there, by the late 1630s his interests were turning to the Caribbean and the risky but invigorating projects that powerful Puritans were projecting there. As Winthrop put it in spring 1640, "Many men began to inquire after the southern parts; and the great advantages supposed to be had in Virginia and the West Indies, etc." William Peirce was one of them.[66]

Among the other mainstays of early Boston now being pulled into the Caribbean orbit was John Humfrey. Like Winthrop, Humfrey was a lawyer and founding member of the Massachusetts Bay Company in 1629. Initially elected to serve as Winthrop's deputy governor, Humfrey delayed his migration until 1634. He stayed behind in England to protect the Massachusetts Charter from potential revocation and raise funds for the colony. Humfrey's ties to the puritan aristocracy were extremely helpful; he was married to the Earl of Lincoln's sister and closely connected to the Providence Island adventurers. On his migration to Boston, Humfrey immediately became a powerful figure in the colony, major general of Boston's Artillery Company, and assistant to the General Court. But his vision of the future of the puritan Atlantic was never confined to Massachusetts. In the late 1630s, he accepted the offer of the Lords of Providence to become the next governor of their Caribbean colony. By 1640, he had recruited several hundred New England colonists willing to move to Providence Island, much to the consternation of Massachusetts leaders like Winthrop and Endecott. Only a shortage of shipping prevented Humfrey from sending a fleet to the Caribbean that year.[67]

Here the interests of Peirce and Humfrey converged. In 1641, Captain Peirce set out from Boston in a New England–built ship, *Desire*, bearing the first forty-three settlers for Providence Island, with Humfrey and other colonists following in a separate ship. But the voyage was doomed to fail, even before the *Desire* set sail. Spanish forces overran Providence Island in May 1641, putting an end to the puritan nobles' experiment. While stopping en route at Saint Christopher, an island claimed by the English, the company heard rumors of a Spanish fleet on the move in the Caribbean. Peirce tried to persuade the Providence venturers to turn back and even volunteered to accept a share of the financial loss of the abortive journey. They refused his offer, to which Peirce responded, "Then I am a dead man."[68]

On the morning the *Desire* approached Providence Island, Peirce read to the crew from Genesis 50:24—the words of the dying Joseph to his brothers in Egypt: "And Joseph said unto his brethren, I die: and God will surely visit you, and bring you out of this land unto the land he sware to Abraham, to Isaac, and to Jacob." As the *Desire* neared the eerily quiet port of New Westminster and its fortress, a Spanish artillery piece swiveled on its moorings and fired a shot. Captain Peirce and Samuel Wakeman, a merchant who had gone to trade for cotton, were struck and killed. The guns continued firing, but the *Desire* managed to turn about and leave the harbor intact. Its sister ship, trailing behind, heard the cannon fire and avoided the fray. The surviving passengers spent two months, filled with self-castigation, on the watery deserts of the Atlantic on the return to their New English Canaan. Many openly acknowledged the error of their ways, and vowed never to leave a place of safety and refuge again.[69]

It seemed like a low point in the development of the puritan Atlantic: settlers abandoning the most populous plantation in the North, only to find its southern counterpart in Spanish hands and barely escape with their lives. Yet this event marked a turning point in Boston's rise to prominence. The following year, in 1642, when a group of puritan colonists in Virginia sought assistance for their struggling congregation, they turned not to Viscount Saye and Sele, not to the Earl of Warwick or Lord Brooke, but to Boston. The Virginians sent an agent to Massachusetts with a petition for ministerial assistance. Boston's magistrates and clergy were happy to oblige and recruited three ministers willing to leave for Virginia. In stark contrast to his concerns regarding the Providence Island migration of the previous year, Winthrop recorded that "we were so far from fearing any loss by parting with such desirable men, as we looked at them as seed sown, which would bring us in a plentiful harvest, and we accounted it no small honor that God had put upon his poor churches here, that other parts of the world should seek to us for help in this kind."[70] At the same moment, two long-awaited vessels arrived from the English colony of Barbados, where a sugar production boom was beginning, with similar letters seeking godly clergymen from Boston.

Something had changed about Boston's position in the puritan Atlantic. In the wake of the Providence Island fiasco, Boston looked less like a way station, a temporary refuge while grander plans were forming, and more like a source of stability and support to other uprooted transatlantic Puritans, especially those disappointed by the hopes of the grandees. Boston had resisted being drawn into the Caribbean scheme, and in that resistance lay a source of strength.

Confirmation of this newfound strength appeared the following July, in 1643, when a ship arrived in Boston from Trinidad. The ship had been outfitted by the Earl of Warwick, who hoped that his captain, John Chaddock, would be able to find New England recruits to plant a puritan colony in Trinidad; Humfrey had suggested this possibility. But Chaddock had no luck in Boston, for as Winthrop put it, "Here was not any that would enter upon that voyage, etc." The Providence Island disaster provided reason enough for caution, but another factor played a larger role. By 1643, Boston's economic prospects were improving from the dark days of 1640 when the Great Migration had ended, prices had plummeted, and the money supply had dried up.[71]

The reason lay in the growing opportunities for Boston merchants' ventures in the Caribbean and Atlantic world beyond. This success was born in fear: Boston's economic depression led many to believe that London-based ships would no longer bother to stop in Boston. In Winthrop's words, "The general fear of want of foreign commodities, now our money was gone, . . . set us on work to provide shipping of our own." Supported by the clergy and General Court, Boston merchants began building their own ships as the only means to prevent the ruin of themselves and the colony.[72] They were encouraged by the occasional appearance of privateering vessels, like that of Captain Jackson, commissioned by the Lords of Providence to attack the Spanish. In 1639, *Queen of Bohemia*, Jackson's ship, sailed into Boston Harbor laden with indigo and sugar. Jackson sold these tropical products in Boston for fourteen hundred pounds and used the profits to outfit himself for his next raid on the Spanish Caribbean so as to further avenge the real Queen of Bohemia. To Protestants everywhere, the Queen of Bohemia was an important figure; she was Elizabeth Stuart, sister of Charles I and wife of Frederick, Elector Palatine and "Winter King" of Bohemia, who had been driven from his throne by the Spanish Habsburgs in 1618, touching off the Thirty Years' War. In their attacks on Spanish wealth, privateers and their puritan sponsors hoped to advance the Protestant cause against the Catholic Habsburg Empire.[73]

Spurred on by these privateers, Bostonians launched several successful voyages in the late 1630s and early 1640s that demonstrated the value of Caribbean and Atlantic trade, among them Peirce's voyage that brought Pequot Indian captives to Providence Island in return for African slaves. Equally important was the voyage of "one John Turner, a merchant's factor of London," who left Boston for the West Indies in 1641 in a small pinnace and returned the following January with "great advantage in indigo, pieces of 8, etc." Although it was suspected that Turner had gained the Spanish silver by theft or privateering rather than fair trade, the results were still enticing.[74] Later that summer, a Boston-built ship of two hundred tons, aptly named the *Trial*, set sail with Thomas Coytmore, master, "and divers godly seamen in her," under the blessings of a sermon by John Cotton. A successful *Trial* it was. According to Winthrop,

> [Coytmore] sailed first to Fayal [in the Azores], where he found an extraordinarily good market for his pipe staves and fish. He took wine and sugar, etc., and sailed thence to [Saint] Christopher's in the West Indies, where he put off his wine for cotton and tobacco, etc., and for iron, which the islanders had saved of the ships which were there cast away. He obtained license also, of the governour, Sir Thomas Warner, to take up what ordnance, anchors, etc. he could, and was to have the one half; and by the help of a diving tub, he took up 50 guns, and anchors, and cables, which he brought home, and some gold and silver also, which he got by trade, and so, through the Lord's blessing, they made a good voyage, which did much encourage the merchants, and made wine and sugar and cotton very plentiful, and cheap, in the country.[75]

Coytmore's voyage proved that with the right commodities, the right markets, and some enterprise and luck, Bostonians could make fortunes in Atlantic trade. By using locally produced New England commodities (fish and pipe staves, carved boards used to make barrels) and branching out from Europe to include the West Indies, an alternative triangle to the one with Bilbao and London was possible. With the *Trial*'s success, others rapidly followed, and 1643 became a pivotal year in which Boston's economy turned definitively toward trade with the Iberian Peninsula, its nearby Atlantic islands, and critically, the Caribbean. In the words of historian Bernard Bailyn, "This year, 1643, seems to mark the real birth of New England's independent commerce, for no less than five New England vessels cleared port for the ocean routes."[76] The birth of independent commerce meant the creation of a sustainable political economy—a basis on which Boston's independence as a city-state and metropolis of the New England region could be built.

Trouble with Trade: Atlantic Commerce and Commonwealth Values

The rise of New England's independent commerce brought new challenges to Boston's moral economy—problems that threatened the nature of the commonwealth that Boston's founders hoped to build. In his meditation on *The City of God*, Saint Augustine had attempted to resolve the question of whether a commonwealth or republic could legitimately expand its size through the conquest of enemies. Augustine essentially said no. Even a just war, one fought against an aggressive enemy, involved sin and suffering—in this case, the sins of the foe—and therefore to build gains on the sins of others created moral peril. In that light, Augustine's opinion was contrary to the behavior of Thomas More's Utopians, who believed that it was legitimate to conquer neighbors who would not voluntarily join their regime. Perhaps the Pequot War had been, through a twisted logic that turned the Pequots into aggressors, justifiable on More's grounds, if not within an Augustinian framework.[77] But the new forms of trade in the Atlantic economy, and the sins and suffering this trade embraced, created new problems for the commonwealth.

In 1644, two mariners, Captain James Smith, like Peirce a godly man and member of the Boston church, and his first mate, Thomas Keysar, sailed in the ship *Rainbow* for West Africa. They met up with some London-based slave traders and became unwitting accomplices in a brutal conflict. The London slavers, claiming that they had "been formerly injured by the natives," kidnapped a number of Africans. When the Africans protested, the slave traders "assaulted one of their Townes and killed many people," using a small cannon to do their bloody business, "neare 100: slaine by the confession of some of the mariners."[78] After a meandering return trip, marked by complicated transactions in the West Indies during which Smith stayed behind in Barbados, Keysar arrived in Boston in May 1645, where he sold the two kidnapped Africans still remaining in his possession.

When Smith finally returned to Boston, he took Keysar to court to sort out their commercial disputes. In October 1645, the General

Court's magistrates took up the case, and after deciding who owed what to whom, took an extraordinary step. On the advice of Boston's clergy, the magistrates felt that they could do nothing to punish Smith and Keysar for "the slaughter committed" in Africa, "seeing it was in another Countrye, & the Londoners pretended a just revenge." With respect to the kidnapped Africans, though, "the magistrates tooke order to have those 2: sett at Libertye, & to be sente home." The court held that the Africans' captivity was clearly not the result of a just war (as compared, hypocritically, to their own recent war with the Pequots) but rather an instance of "manstealing." The Africans were returned to their homeland.[79]

At stake were the critical questions of what sorts of persons might be included in the godly commonwealth and under what terms. The earlier incorporation of African slaves into the community, as in the case of the "negroes" brought to Boston by Peirce, suggests that an English identity was not strictly necessary for inclusion, at least for people in a servile status. Two years earlier, the colony had published a pamphlet in London called *New Englands First Fruits*, which described the conversion and incorporation of Indians into the English community as well as the conversion and admission to the Dorchester church of a "Blackmore maid"—that is, an African woman.[80] But the method of acquisition clearly made a difference. The decision to return the Africans kidnapped by Smith and Keysar took place in the midst of an emerging argument within Boston about the colony's proper relationship to slavery, labor, commerce, and empire.

The labor shortage in Massachusetts exacerbated the problem. The civil wars in England were drying up the available pool of English servants, especially those with any inclination to go to a puritan colony. In Massachusetts, this made it difficult for masters to retain indentured servants once they had served their time, and wages for free servants rose to new heights. Winthrop records the story of a Rowley farmer who was forced to sell a pair of oxen in order to pay his servant's wages for the current year, but would not have enough money to employ him the following year. The servant offered to continue working in the future in return for the remainder of his master's cattle. "But how shall I doe (saythe the master) when all my Cattle are gone? The servant replyed, you shall then serve me, & so you may have your Cattle again." The general crisis of the 1640s in the British Atlantic was turning the world upside down; those in power struggled with how to right it. This incident struck Winthrop as potentially dangerous, accustomed as he was to being among those "high and eminent in dignity." At the same time, the servant's tale vividly illustrates the commonwealth model at work in a new environment. Regardless of who owned the cattle, the system could survive and even prosper as long as community members were mutually committed to sharing its resources in some fashion.[81]

In August 1645, members of two leading New England families, the Downings and Winthrops, corresponded about the potential for slavery as a solution to the labor problem in the puritan Atlantic. Emmanuel Downing was married to Winthrop's sister Lucy, and the Downings' son George, Winthrop's nephew, was a member of the first graduating class of Harvard College in 1642. Young George Downing traveled to the West Indies in spring 1645 as a chaplain on board a Boston vessel. His preaching was popular, and Downing received offers to remain as a clergyman on every island where he stopped—Saint Christopher, Nevis, Antigua, and Barbados. But he chose instead to go on to England with the ship, where he soon became chaplain to a parliamentary regiment in the war against the king.[82]

On his voyage to England, Downing paused to write a long letter to his cousin, John Winthrop Jr., describing the island colonies, emphasizing the significance of African slave labor to the islands' prosperity. He compared the sad economic decline of Saint Christopher with the rapid rise of Barbados, where "they have bought this year no lesse than a thousand Negroes; and the more they buie, the better able they are to buye, for in a year and a halfe they will earne (with gods blessing) as much as they cost." He encouraged the younger Winthrop to move to one of the islands and import English indentured servants for a span of "6 or 8 or 9 yeares time" to aid in beginning a plantation that would "in short tim be able with good husbandry to procure Negroes (the life of this place) out of the encrease of your owne plantation."[83] Even after the failures on Providence Island, the ideal of puritan colonies in the West Indies remained alluring to some of its promoters, especially now that sugar and slaves were bringing profits to islands like Barbados.[84]

At the same moment that George Downing encouraged the younger Winthrop to advance the puritan colonization of the Caribbean by means of slavery, his father urged the elder Winthrop to make Massachusetts Bay more like the West Indies. In a letter to Winthrop of August 1645, Emmanuel Downing evaluated local political conditions—military conflict with the Narragansetts loomed as a possibility—and suggested that a war against Indian devil worshippers might produce valuable captives:

> If vpon a Just warre the lord should deliver them into our hands, wee might easily haue men woemen and Children enough to exchange for Moores, which wilbe more gaynefull pilladge for vs then wee conceive, for I doe not see how wee can thrive vntill wee gett into a stock of slaves suffitient to doe all our buisines, for our Childrens Children will hardly see this great Continent filled with people, soe that our servants will still desire freedome to plant for them selves, and not stay but for verie great wages. And I suppose you know verie well how wee shall maynteyne 20 Moores cheaper then one Englishe servant.[85]

In plain and ugly terms, Downing envisioned with startling completeness the evolution of a racially based North American slave labor system, and imagined that New England would be fully enmeshed in it by means of Atlantic commerce and the exploitation of racial warfare. He offered a rigidly exclusive vision of the nature of the commonwealth, in which two large categories of human beings present in the Atlantic world, "hostile" Indians and captive Africans from "just wars," were by definition ineligible for inclusion within the social body, expendable objects within an economy rather than subjects in a polity. In both cases, human subjects would be transformed into objects by warfare—an exceedingly cynical manipulation of the doctrine of just war for the sake of solving a labor shortage.

We have no direct evidence of what the Winthrops thought of the Downings' letters; there are no extant replies. But neither one followed their kinsman's advice. The younger Winthrop remained in New England, where his schemes for economic success revolved around dreams of alchemical progress, silver mines, iron production, and skilled labor, not slave plantations, and where he nurtured mutually beneficial relationships with the Pequot Indians of the region.[86] The elder Winthrop endorsed the magistrates' decision to free the kidnapped slaves from the *Rainbow* and engaged in careful (if brutal) negotiations to avoid a potential Narragansett war, contrary to Emmanuel Downing's suggestion. Nevertheless, the conflict between the Winthrops and Downings was not a contest between Puritans and merchants, not a matter of moralistic landed gentry in opposition to cutthroat commercial interests. The Winthrops and Downings were in-laws and cousins; they came from the same English world of the lesser gentry who combined rural landholdings, commercial involvement, and legal training to maintain a tenuous hold on prosperity. They were encountering the opportunities and dangers of a risky new world of Atlantic commerce together, and all realized that Boston's economic future lay there, and there alone.

Although the issues at stake were moral ones, Bostonians were not deciding between the purity of isolation and taint of involvement; it was not a conflict between puritan isolationists and cosmopolitan, antipuritan merchants. Rather, the question was whether Massachusetts should become an approximate replica of these newly successful Caribbean colonies, or remain at a certain (albeit hypocritical) distance from the worst aspects of the West Indian colonies by supplying the island labor system through trade and commerce, while keeping open the prospect of a more racially inclusive society than the plantation colonies. One important aspect of this decision was whether to give up entirely on the possibility of incorporating New England's indigenous people into the commonwealth, or to expand efforts to bring Indians within the fold of its reformed churches and civil society. On both counts, in 1645, Boston made the latter choice, making peace with the Narragansetts, avoiding a full-fledged commitment to importing an African chattel labor source, and in 1646, beginning the missionary efforts of John Eliot and the development of Massachusetts' "praying Indian" town system.[87] In so doing, they revealed their ambidextrous approach to the Atlantic world. Boston was fully in it, but not completely of it.

Atlantic Competition and the Challenge of Diplomacy

The Narragansett war that loomed in 1645 was but one piece of the complex puzzle of Boston's diplomatic relations. A range of competitors threatened the fledgling Massachusetts Bay Colony's security. In the years between 1643 and 1645, just as Boston's unique position in the Atlantic puritan movement solidified and its commercial ties to the Atlantic community developed rapidly, Boston struggled to assert its political authority with respect to these competitors. These included a range of Indian communities, often in conflict with one another; a number of competing English settlements in the region, some Puritan, and some not, stretching from Long Island Sound to the Bay of Fundy; the Dutch West India Company's New Netherland colony and its claims to Connecticut and Long Island; the French colony in the Saint Lawrence Valley and its claims to Maine and Acadia; and finally, the rival claims made by the Crown and Parliament over England's colonies during the civil wars that began in 1639 and metastasized over the following decade to consume the three kingdoms of the British Isles. To understand the tangled web of Boston's external relations, we can begin almost anywhere. Every element of this intricate diplomacy was interconnected; tug any thread, and the others will follow. So let's return to the impending Narragansett war that made Emmanuel Downing greedy for slaves.

Narragansetts, Mohegans, and the Birth of the United Colonies

From almost the moment that Winthrop began keeping his journal/history of the colony, rumors and threats of war with New England's indigenous population were his constant concerns. One reason for this was the turbulence of Indian politics. Even before the invasion of English and Dutch colonists, the lands east of the Hudson River had been troubled by violent conflict. The Mohawks, the easternmost nation of the Iroquois League, pushed eastward from their homelands along the Mohawk River to assert their power over New England Indians.[88] The first rumor of Indian war in Winthrop's *Journal* appears in May 1631, when local Massachusetts Indians reported that "the mohockes were coming down against them and us."[89] The arrival of thousands of colonists over the 1630s intensified these conflicts. The English wanted land that belonged to Indians, and were willing to fight or connive in order to get it. But English colonization was not a monolithic venture, and disputes among English interests complicated these relationships.[90]

Many of these disputes were caused by the geographically narrow but legally open-ended patents, charters, and corporate structures on which various colonizing ventures based their claims to land. These patents were not merely flimsy and vague but their land claims overlapped in some instances and left other regions of New England unclaimed as well.[91] Into these contested areas and gaps came fur traders, land-hungry settlers, and malcontents who despised the religious or civil polity of Massachusetts Bay.

The Pequot War secured Boston's access to the Connecticut and Thames Rivers, drove the Dutch out of these fur highways, and reconfigured Indian relations in southern New England. To solidify these new conditions, Boston's leadership established tributary relationships with their Indian neighbors, expecting annual payments of wampum as evidence of Indian loyalty and submission to Massachusetts Bay, in return for military protection.[92] Governor Winthrop received annual visits and gifts of tribute not just from Boston's immediate neighbors, the Massachusetts Indians, but also the Narragansetts and Mohegans, who filled the vacuum left when the Pequots had been driven from coastal Connecticut. The Narragansetts and Mohegans occupied valuable land in Rhode Island and the interior of Connecticut that was not yet claimed by English colonists.

The other puritan colonies in the region—the older Plymouth and the nascent Connecticut and New Haven plantations—also attempted to extract tribute from Indians in return for protection. Even the scattered heterodox plantations at Rhode Island and Providence became involved, especially among the Narragansetts, their nearest neighbors, for whom Roger Williams served as negotiator with the Massachusetts Bay Colony. But Massachusetts Bay had the largest population, the greatest need to encroach on Indian lands, and the most power of any colony in the region. Boston aimed to gain hegemony over a larger region than the original Massachusetts Bay charter allowed through the exercise of power and diplomacy with southern New England Indians.[93]

By 1643, Indian diplomacy was on the verge of breakdown, in part because diplomacy among the puritan colonies had reached a new level of cooperation. In that year, Massachusetts Bay, Connecticut, New Haven, and Plymouth signed an agreement forming the United Colonies (or New England Confederation, as it was sometimes called), an organization for mutual defense among the orthodox plantations. The language of the confederation's charter made its dual purposes plain: first, to acknowledge that the settlements of Massachusetts Bay had indeed spread well beyond the bounds of the original charter, and second, that this wide dispersal among potential enemies created a need to defend the intended unity of the puritan colonial project.

> Whereas we all came into these parts of America with one and the same end and aim, namely, to advance the Kingdom of our Lord Jesus Christ and to enjoy the liberties of the Gospel in purity with peace; and whereas in our settling (by a wise providence of God) we are further dispersed upon the sea coasts and rivers than was at first intended, so that we can not ac-

> cording to our desire with convenience communicate in one government and jurisdiction; and whereas we live encompassed with people of several nations and strange languages which hereafter may prove injurious to us or our posterity. . . . We therefore do conceive it our bounden duty, without delay to enter into a present Consociation amongst ourselves, for mutual help and strength in all our future concernments: That, as in nation and religion, so in other respects, we be and continue one according to the tenor and true meaning of the ensuing articles.[94]

Pointedly excluded from the United Colonies were the English settlements to the north and east of Massachusetts in what became New Hampshire and Maine, though puritan grandees such as Warwick or Brooke sponsored some of these colonists. The problem was that the character of these other colonists and the construction of religious polities in these plantations did not mirror the requirements for puritan church organization that the confederation members expected.[95] They were not participants in the plan that had created Boston and its offshoots, and in many cases had deliberately avoided connections with the Bay Colony. Similarly excluded were the heterodox plantations of Rhode Island, comprised of exiles from Massachusetts. Williams, the most important leader among the dissenters from Massachusetts' church polity, had departed for England in 1643 seeking a patent or charter for his own colony. This potential for the increased political strength of Williams's Providence Plantation was enough to encourage the four orthodox colonies to join together in common cause.[96]

The New England Confederation reached this point of unity just when the tentative balance of power among southern New England Indians collapsed. After the Pequot War, the more powerful tribes such as the Mohegans, Pokanoket, and Narragansetts had served as go-betweens, client states for the larger English colonies, collecting tribute payments from smaller Indian tribes and bands, and offering tribute themselves in Hartford, Plymouth, or Boston. Of these groups, the Narragansetts were the most powerful in numbers but the most isolated politically. They hoped to keep Massachusetts settlers away from their lands west of Narragansett Bay, and their only ally was the weak support of Williams. Beginning in 1642, Massachusetts investors began to purchase land in the Narragansett country directly from local sachems rather than going through Miantonomi, the chief sachem of the Narragansetts. This aggressive approach to expansion received support from other southern New England Indians, particularly the Mohegans. Their leader, Uncas, saw Miantonomi as a rival, and he had his own aspirations for Mohegan hegemony in the region.[97]

Miantonomi attempted to assemble a pan-Indian alliance against all English encroachment on the region—or rumors to that effect began to surface late in 1642. But Uncas, with his close ties to Connecticut and Massachusetts, stood in the way. In 1643, Miantonomi allegedly hired an assassin to kill Uncas. The plot failed, and the would-be assassin was killed, possibly by Miantonomi, who then raised an army to attack Uncas and the Mohegans. In the battle, hampered by a heavy suit of European armor, Miantonomi was captured by Uncas. The desperate Miantonomi proposed an alliance with Uncas against the English, even offering to marry the daughter of Uncas and suggesting further marriages that would bring the Pokanoket of Plymouth into the league. Uncas rejected the offer and turned his prisoner over to the United Colonies.[98]

As a result, the first official business of the newly formed confederation was to decide what to do about the pan-Indian threat, insubstantial as it might be in reality. While Miantonomi was imprisoned in Hartford, the commissioners meeting in Boston voted to execute him for the murder of the assassin he had hired to kill Uncas. Uncas himself, under the supervision of United Colonies observers, then carried out the judicial killing of Miantonomi. Once Pessacus, Miantonomi's brother and successor, heard this news, he demanded a war of revenge against the Mohegans and Uncas. Fighting broke out between the Narragansetts and Mohegans. Pessacus sent Winthrop an otter-skin coat and girdle of wampum to request that Massachusetts not interfere with this war, which the Narragansetts saw as a matter of vengeance among Indians.[99]

This was the precise moment when Downing urged Winthrop to make war on the Narragansetts, take captives, and exchange them for African slaves. Instead, the United Colonies under Winthrop's leadership negotiated to maintain peace. It brought Uncas and the Narragansett representatives together to resolve their differences, and received assistance from Williams, newly returned from London with a patent for Rhode Island and Providence Plantations, in persuading the Narragansetts to avoid war. Although Rhode Island did not join the United Colonies, Williams's cooperation further advanced the organization's purposes. By July 1645, however, continuing Narragansett threats led the commissioners to decide that an armed force of three hundred men was needed to protect Uncas and the Mohegans. Edward Gibbon of Boston was named commander of the proposed expedition, comprised mainly of Massachusetts soldiers according to the terms of the United Colonies' covenant. The threat of force was enough to bring the leading Narragansett sachems to Boston, where a treaty was signed establishing a tributary relationship between the Narragansetts and Massachusetts Bay.[100]

The threat of war in summer 1645 was averted by means of diplomacy and negotiation. Not that tranquility now reigned. The Narragansetts resisted encroachments of Massachusetts Bay colonists in southern New England, often failed to make tribute payments, and continued to threaten the Mohegans. But the creation of a formal New England Confederation, dominated by Massachusetts in numbers and political power, had shifted the center of Indian diplomacy and negotiations to Boston. Before 1643 it had been scattered—conducted on the ground, at whatever point English colonists and Indians met and contested over the control of land. The events of 1643–45 marked the moment when Boston, as the leader of a newly united confederation, emerged as the focal point of diplomacy between the native people of the region and the sprawling bands of colonists moving steadily into their territory.

Boston and New Netherland

In addition, 1643 marked a turning point in Boston's relationship with the New Netherland colony, centered on Manhattan Island, spreading north up the Hudson Valley and east onto Long Island. The Dutch and English colonists shared similar religious beliefs. Many English colonists, such as John Davenport, New Haven's founder, had found safe haven in the Netherlands, and others had served in Dutch forces in military campaigns against the Spanish. But their similar religious outlook and shared hatred of Catholic Spain did not prevent Dutch and English colonists from fighting over control of American resources.

The English and Dutch colonies differed in ways that shaped their conflicted relationship. The Dutch were ambitious traders, but their settlers were nowhere near as numerous as the English. They spread thinly over a large expanse of territory, setting up trading posts for exploiting the fur trade of the interior. Their strategic location along the Hudson River gave them great advantage, for the Hudson was the deepest waterway into fur country in the Northeast, save for the Saint Lawrence.[101] The desire for access to these riches brought English settlers into territory claimed by the Dutch. Early in the 1630s, adventurers from Plymouth began exploring the Connecticut Valley, where the Dutch had built their trading fort at "Good Hope." Soon thereafter came settlers from Massachusetts Bay, seeking land for their growing population. In addition to these Massachusetts offshoots came independent colonies such as Saybrook, at the mouth of the Connecticut River, sponsored by Viscount Saye and Sele and Lord Brooke, and the New Haven Colony farther to the west at Quinnipiac, backed by prominent English merchants. Still more English colonists from Massachusetts chose to settle on eastern Long Island. Over time they moved westward near the Dutch settlements; on occasion the Dutch invited English settlers to come. English Puritans pushed into territory thought by the Dutch to be their own and threatened to overrun the isolated Dutch outposts. These unrestrained migrants revealed another important distinction between the Dutch and English ventures. The Dutch colony was ruled by a single authority, centered in New Amsterdam, under a system overseen by the Dutch West India Company in Amsterdam. The early English colonies were fragmentary, disputatious, and under no single political authority. (See plate 6.)

As a result, endemic conflict over land and furs that grew from English expansion was particularly frustrating for the Dutch, because the means for resolution of conflict with the English were difficult to locate. The immediate threat, from the Dutch point of view, came from the New Haven Colony. Not only was New Haven closest to the center of Dutch power in New Amsterdam, but New Haven in its early years was dominated by aggressive London merchants who wanted access to the fur trade.[102] Several New Haven merchants made direct inroads into the Hudson and even the Delaware River valleys, where they challenged not only Dutch control but also the New Sweden colony encamped along the Delaware. In 1641, a New Haven merchant, Captain Nathaniel Turner, purchased land on the upper Delaware River. The following spring, New Haven settlers began to move there, led by George Lamberton, an experienced trader, who built a blockhouse and attempted to organize a fur-trading station.[103]

In response, the Dutch sent two armed sloops, and with assistance from New Sweden, drove the New Haven colonists away. But this initial failure only led to further attempts by New Haven to reach into Dutch and Swedish territory. Similar efforts by Connecticut settlers to move into the Hudson Valley caused further conflict. In 1643, Dutch governor Willem Kieft (or William the Testy, as Washington Irving referred to him in *Knickerbocker's History of New York*) expressed these mounting concerns. By then the puritan colonies had formed the New England Confederation, which gave Kieft hope that a definitive resolution to the conflict could finally be achieved. Despite the fact that his dispute was with New Haven settlers, Kieft sent his letters (written in Latin) to Boston. He addressed them to the "governor and senate" of the "United

Provinces of New England," perhaps wishfully thinking that the government he was dealing with might be equal in authority to the United Provinces of the Netherlands.[104]

In a sense, Kieft was right. Boston and Massachusetts Bay played a dominant role, by virtue of their population, military might, and economic power, within the New England Confederation. And Boston's leading merchants and magistrates had much less interest than Connecticut and New Haven in competing directly with the Dutch. For that reason, the act of forming the United Colonies shifted diplomatic relations between the Dutch and English from scattered, on-the-ground conflicts wherever the two sides met, where heads and swords were often broken, to formal negotiations between leading representatives of the two sides, meeting in Boston, where cooler heads tended to prevail.

The shift of diplomatic relations to Boston did not entirely end the conflict with the Dutch; in fact, the immediate impact seems to have spurred some Bostonians' interest in exploring the Delaware for themselves. In 1644, the Massachusetts General Court commissioned Boston's William Aspinwall to examine "the western bounds of our colony" by sailing up the Delaware, but the Dutch prevented him from getting far.[105] Nevertheless, Bostonians were clearly thinking of all New England and even lands far beyond the limits of the 1629 charter as "our colony." In that guise, Boston's influence did have a restraining function. Through the 1640s and into the 1650s, as occasional conflicts with the Dutch continued, and as the Anglo-Dutch War of 1652–54 broke out in Europe, the New Haven and Connecticut colonies were constantly pressing for war with New Netherlands, while Boston and Massachusetts Bay held back. Even in 1654, when a British fleet arrived in Boston with orders from Parliament to join the conquest of New Netherland, the Massachusetts delegates to the United Colonies favored restraint.[106] The timely arrival of news that a peace treaty between England and the Netherlands had been signed meant that Boston's obstinacy was never put to the test. Just as Boston seized control of Indian diplomacy in the interior of New England in the mid-1640s, so the consolidation of Boston's political authority within the New

England Confederation in 1643 marked a turning point in New England's relationship with the Dutch.

Boston and New France

The ink was barely dry on the written agreement that formed the New England Confederation when Governor Winthrop and the town of Boston were shocked by the sudden arrival of a French ship of 140 tons, bearing 140 armed men. The ship anchored at Governor's Island, in the middle of the harbor, where Winthrop owned a pleasant garden and orchard. Winthrop's family was relaxing on a June day when they were surprised by Charles de La Tour, one of two rival claimants to the government of French Acadia, the northeastern end of the great coastal basin of which Massachusetts and Cape Cod form the southwestern counterpart. Much to his embarrassment, Winthrop realized that La Tour could easily have captured Boston. The provisional fort on Castle Island was deserted and in disrepair, and the town unguarded. But La Tour had come to Boston to barter, not to conquer. He needed the Massachusetts Bay Colony's help in his own conflict with a rival, Charles d'Aulnay, who was blockading La Tour's fort on the Saint John River and staking a competing claim to Acadia.[107]

Boston's interest in this northeastern region was stronger than its interest in the Dutch territories to the south and west. For several years, Boston merchants had been making expeditions to Cape Sable, on the southern tip of Acadia, in search of what they called "seahorse teeth" (walrus tusks) along with furs, skins, and whale oil, to extend the range of goods they could sell in Atlantic markets. The success of these voyages enhanced their desire to maintain good trading relations with the French.[108] In addition, Massachusetts kept its eye on the prospect of consolidating the scattered English settlements along the Maine coast under Boston's jurisdiction. Befriending the dominant power in Acadia would benefit that cause by enhancing the security of the lengthy coast between Massachusetts and Acadia. But the validity of these competing French leaders' claims to Acadia seemed to be just as ambiguous as the competing English claims to northern New England. La Tour claimed authority over Acadia by virtue of an appointment from Cardinal Richelieu, by way of Richelieu's cousin, Isaac de Razilly, the lieutenant general of all New France. But after Razilly died in 1635, his successor, d'Aulnay, refused to recognize La Tour's authority over Acadia.

As early as November 1641, La Tour had sent an emissary to Boston from his fort on the Saint John River, in present-day New Brunswick. La Tour asked for "assistance against D'Aulnay of Penobscott, whom he had war with," and suggested the possibility of free trade with New England. D'Aulnay had posed a threat to New England for several years. In 1635, d'Aulnay forcefully seized a Plymouth-owned trading post along the Penobscott River and asserted his claim to the Maine coast as far south as Pemaquid.[109] Bostonians favored La Tour, in part because he was from La Rochelle, the Protestant Huguenot stronghold on the coast of France, where Winthrop Jr. had taken part in England's futile effort to relieve the besieged city. Although not actually a Protestant, La Tour was vague enough about his loyalties and respectful enough of New England's religion to win sympathy in Boston. Initially, Winthrop responded to La Tour's emissary, "a Rocheller and a protestant," with ambivalence. He was happy to allow free trade between La Tour and Boston merchants, but not prepared to supply military assistance against d'Aulnay.[110]

In October 1642, La Tour tried again, sending a shallop with fourteen men to ask for assistance against d'Aulnay. They stayed a week, attended a service at Boston's church, but went away empty-handed, save for a French Protestant New Testament that one of the church elders gave to a "papist" among them. Yet several Boston merchants took this as another opportunity to trade with La Tour and sent a pinnace to La Tour's fort on the Saint John River that was "welcomed very kindly." On its return trip, the Boston pinnace was confronted at Pemaquid by d'Aulnay, who sent along forbidding letters to Winthrop, arguing that La Tour's claims were illegal and threatening to seize any future vessels that dared to trade with La Tour.

Having failed twice, the next year La Tour came to Boston in force. His heavily armed sloop made a strong impression on the nearly defenseless town. La Tour maintained the courtesy of his emissaries' earlier visits and showed his peaceable intentions by putting himself personally in the hands of Edward Gibbon, the Boston merchant adventurer who would later command the army raised to deter the Narragansetts. But La Tour and his men staged a display of military exercises on Boston Common, including a charge with drawn swords that frightened the crowd of onlookers: "They were very expert in all their postures and motions."[111] Honoring his commitment to the newly formed United Colonies, Winthrop was not empowered to offer direct military aid to La Tour without the consent of his fellow commissioners, who had already dispersed to their own colonies. Nor did he consult with the magistrates of the Massachusetts Bay Colony, but instead allowed La Tour to hire ships from any willing Boston merchant and recruit local volunteers as mercenary soldiers. In this way, La Tour raised four ships and seventy men to aid him in dislodging d'Aulnay from Acadia. By acting so freely, Winthrop angered a number of New England leaders, especially those from north of Boston who felt most vulnerable to the outcome of any conflict with the French. But he also moved boldly to establish Boston's independent trading connections, and potentially, a useful political link to Acadia and New France as well.[112]

Initially, Winthrop's bold move seemed to backfire. La Tour attacked d'Aulnay's settlement at Port Royal, but could not dislodge him. D'Aulnay wrote threatening letters to Boston, denouncing its aid to La Tour, and issued instructions for French privateers to capture Massachusetts ships in Acadian waters. After intensive negotiations, d'Aulnay accepted Winthrop's claim that La Tour had merely hired independent ships and men in Boston, and the colony had not officially joined La Tour's cause. But as Winthrop put it,

> Because we could not free Captaine Hawkins & the other voluntaryes, of what they had done, we were to sende a small present to mr Daulnye in satisfaction of that. . . . Accordingly we

> sent monsieur D'aulny . . . a very faire new Sedan . . . sent by the Viceroy of mexico to a Ladye his sister, & taken in the west Indiyes by Capt. Cromwell, & by him given to our Governour. This the Commissioners very well accepted.[113]

Winthrop happened to have an elegant sedan chair (worth forty to fifty pounds by his estimation), dropped in his lap by Captain Thomas Cromwell, a West Indian privateer, probably as a bribe to allow Cromwell to spend his booty freely in Boston. The sedan chair was useless to Winthrop, but it was just the right sort of tribute to assuage the ire of a vice-regent of New France.

Winthrop was voted out of the governor's office the year after this debacle, replaced by Endecott, a leader of the northern opposition to Winthrop's backing of La Tour. Endecott managed to work out a remarkably favorable treaty with d'Aulnay's emissary, a Capuchin monk named François-Marie de Paris who came to Boston in 1644 for negotiations. As long as Massachusetts would acknowledge d'Aulnay's authority over Acadia, then d'Aulnay would maintain peaceful relations with Massachusetts, including trade, "that it shall be lawful for all men, both the French and the English, to trade with each other." D'Aulnay even offered to sustain these open relations if France and England were to go to war—in effect suggesting colonial autonomy from imperial policy on both sides.[114]

Over the next few years, further negotiation extended the initial agreements to include free trade between New England and New France. D'Aulnay hoped to draw the large population force of New England into an alliance against the Iroquois, who constituted the principal threat to the success of Jesuit missionaries. Massachusetts and the United Colonies were unprepared to go that far. But the Massachusetts Council did agree to support d'Aulnay's idea that New England and New France could maintain peaceful relations even in the event of war between the home countries.[115] Grounded in these agreements, Boston's trade with Acadia and New France flourished in the late 1640s. Leading merchants such as Edward Gibbon, John Hawkins, John Leverett, Joshua Scottow, and younger members of the Winthrop family used their land claims in Maine as a base for trade with the French colonies. Boston managed the crisis in the mid-1640s by extending its economic power and maintaining an autonomous foreign policy—heedless of England's interests—that was rooted in its commercial connections in the Atlantic community and its desire to maintain peaceful relations with foreign neighbors.

The Challenge of England's Divisions

Boston's independence from the turbulent political situation in England was an essential feature of the way it handled the last of the interlocking diplomatic crises of the mid-1640s, when violent conflict between the Crown and Parliament spread across the Atlantic and washed up on the shores of Massachusetts Bay. The puritan colonists who fled from Charles I's repressive religious policies naturally sympathized with the parliamentary opposition. Yet the practical demands of diplomacy complicated these religious sympathies. For it was King Charles, not Parliament, who had granted Massachusetts Bay the charter on which its claims to autonomy rested. Moreover, the religious inclinations of Parliament's leadership may have been more congenial than the king's to Massachusetts Puritans, but the factionalism and dissent within English Puritanism, and the unpredictability of parliamentary rule, made Parliament an unsteady ally at best.

In the early days of the Long Parliament, Westminster looked fondly on Massachusetts. Parliament confirmed the colony's liberties according to its royal charter, lifted the restrictive orders that Charles I had placed on ships bound for the Bay Colony, and in March 1642, removed all customs duties on merchandise or goods shipped between England and New England in either direction. And in the order issued by the House of Commons, New England was described as a kingdom. Although perhaps merely a mistake of the House of Commons' clerk, the word suggests the extent to which New England's independence and consolidation were recognized facts. When the order was reissued two years later, the word "kingdom" was silently changed to "country." Even this correction implies the ready acceptance of the notion that "New England" was a single entity with Boston at its head.[116]

Parliament's approval was gratifying, but Boston's leaders were wary of the general trend in governance suggested by this order. If Parliament could assert its authority over New England, the independence guaranteed by the royal charter might vanish. As Winthrop put it, "If we should put ourselves under the protection of the parliament, we must then be subject to all such laws as they should make, or at least such as they might impose upon us; in which course though they should intend our good, yet it might prove very prejudicial to us."[117] This fear was put to the test in summer 1644. Captain Thomas Stagg, a Virginia merchant sailing under a privateering commission from the Earl of Warwick, now lord admiral of the navy, sailed into Boston Harbor in a heavily armed ship. In the harbor, Captain Stagg encountered a merchant ship from Bristol, laden with New England fish and about to depart for Bilbao, and seized it in the name of Parliament and the Earl of Warwick. His privateering commission gave him the right "to take all vessels in or outward bound to or from Bristol, Barnstable, Dartmouth, etc."; these ports were royalist strongholds in the Civil War. Although Boston favored the parliamentary cause, in this case a number of Boston merchants had invested in the outbound voyage of the Bristol ship that Stagg had seized. A Bristol merchant visiting Boston became incensed at the ship's seizure, and "began to gather company and raise a tumult." Winthrop put him under house arrest to avoid violence.[118]

The General Court and Boston clergy were divided on how to respond. Some of the elders argued that Stagg had violated the liberties of the people of Massachusetts under their charter, and that a parliamentary commission "could not supersede a patent" or royal charter. But the majority of the leadership supported Stagg's right to seize the ship from Bristol, largely for political reasons. As Winthrop argued, "The King of England was enraged against us, and all that party, and all the popish states in Europe: and if we should now, by opposing the parliament, cause them to forsake us, we could have no protection or countenance from any, but should lie open as a prey to all men." Winthrop also maintained that Massachusetts was similar to a variety of "special places" in England, such as the City of London or Duchy of Lancaster, created by royal charter with special privileges, but nonetheless subject to parliamentary authority, and represented in Parliament by burgesses or knights of the shire. Parliamentary rule had been favorable to Massachusetts, and now was not the time to oppose it, especially because other prominent colonies, notably Virginia and Barbados, were in rebellion against parliamentary rule. If Massachusetts were to defy Parliament, "it would grieve all our godly friends in England, or any other of the parliament's friends." In the end, Winthrop hoped that those Bostonians who lost their goods on the Bristol ship would be recompensed by Parliament in return for their loyalty and devotion.[119]

For the moment, the controversy was resolved, but the issue continued to upset local politics. The deputies, the lower house of the General Court, felt that the magistrates, the upper house, had been too lax in defending the charter liberties of the colony. In May 1645, the deputies proposed a bill protecting all friendly ships entering Boston Harbor from violence or seizure. The magistrates, however, pointed out that as in the case of Captain Stagg, this measure might force Boston's ships to engage in combat with parliamentary ships, "and so might weaken that Interest we had in the Parliament." On that basis the magistrates rejected the bill. In the end, a watered-down version was passed, in which Edward Gibbon and Robert Sedgwick were commissioned to keep the peace in the harbor, "and not to permitt any Shippes to fight in the harbor, without licence from Authoritye."[120]

In this fashion, Boston negotiated a middle position between defiance and submission to Parliament without actually offending Parliament or wavering in its support for the puritan cause. This was a delicate balancing act. Boston's leaders affirmed that while Massachusetts was not a "perfecta respublica" (a perfect commonwealth or independent state), neither was it the creature of Parliament. Should parliamentary regulation threaten real harm to Massachusetts' liberties, Winthrop and his fellow magistrates were prepared to argue that "parliament had taught us, that salus populi is suprema lex" (the welfare of the people is the supreme law), and "if we have strength sufficient, we may make use of salus populi to withstand any authority from thence to our hurt."[121]

In the charter of 1629, the Massachusetts Bay Colony's leaders had cleverly taken advantage of the king's power to grant liberties as a means to escape from the king's harm. That king continued to be in a rage against them. But now in the mid-1640s, Parliament represented the greater power and the greater potential threat. For the moment, Parliament's intentions seemed friendly enough, but Boston's leaders were careful to stake out a position in which Parliament's principles could be used as a basis for defense against parliamentary encroachment.

The Birth of the Commonwealth, 1643

At the end of the 1630s and beginning of the 1640s, Boston's future looked bleak. For several years, splinter groups of puritan colonists had been moving away from Massachusetts Bay. The center of gravity in New England seemed to be shifting south and west, to the warmer and potentially more productive lands on Long Island Sound and in the Connecticut River Valley, even perhaps to the Hudson and Delaware Valleys. Within the puritan movement, other colonies, like Providence Island in the Caribbean, beckoned with the promise of greater riches and nobler service for God's glory. With the outbreak of civil wars in England and end of the puritan migration, it was not clear that Boston would have any future at all. If supply ships had no incentive to come there, the new plantation would wither on the vine. Those colonists with the means to do so would return home to England or move to the Caribbean.

By 1645, the outlook was entirely different, and so was Boston's position within the Atlantic community. This chapter has explained the causes of these events topically, but if we look chronologically at the feverish activity in spring and summer 1643 alone, we gain a visceral sense of this dramatic change. In March 1643, Captain Coytmore and the *Trial* returned from their successful voyage to the Azores and the Caribbean, spurring on several more shipping ventures. In May 1643, commissioners from Plymouth, New Haven, Connecticut, and Massachusetts met in Boston to form the United Colonies, and then decided on the execution of Miantonomi. In

June, La Tour and his 140 men landed on Governor's Island in their quest for assistance against d'Aulnay. At the same time, reports from the three clergymen who had gone from Boston to Virginia the preceding year arrived, describing the success of their evangelizing ministry in the Chesapeake. Parliament's order exempting New England from customs duties arrived in June as well, along with its implicit recognition of the region as a quasi-independent kingdom. In July 1643, Governor Kieft's letters arrived from New Amsterdam, shifting negotiations with the Dutch to Boston for the first time. In the same month, the Earl of Warwick's ship arrived from Trinidad, seeking recruits in Boston, but failing to find them. In August 1643, La Tour's expedition returned from Acadia, with trouble from d'Aulnay following in its wake. In September, Miantonomi's successor, Pessacus, came to town, asking Winthrop and the United Colonies to stay out of the impending war between the Narragansetts and Mohegans, and touching off an intensive period of negotiations. Also in September, Winthrop received correspondence from Philip Bell, governor of Barbados, requesting aid from Boston in locating clergymen to gather congregations of the godly on that island. And Captain Gibbon received an offer from Lord Baltimore, granting him a commission as councillor, justice of the peace, and "admiral of Maryland," if he would consent to move to the new Chesapeake colony, with freedom of religion guaranteed to him and all those he would bring with him. Gibbon refused.

The events that brought Boston to this new position were in part the result of accident and circumstance. The failure of alternative puritan colonies in the Atlantic turned Boston and the peculiar Massachusetts Bay experiment from a backwater, a bystander in the puritan crusade against the Spanish foe, into a new transatlantic center of colonization to which other plantations looked for assistance. But in the main, Boston's sudden emergence as a significant node in the economy, politics, and culture of the Atlantic world was the result of commercial and political initiative from its leadership class. Boston's merchants exploited the emergent possibilities of the Atlantic economy, particularly the new profitability of trade in the West Indies and Iberian Peninsula. Its magistrates negotiated peaceable and favorable relations with the Indians, Dutch, French, and Parliament that would strengthen those commercial relations while recognizing Boston's authority over a large portion of New England.

The strategy, if strategy is not too dignified a word to describe it, that made this emergence possible was an ambivalent one—an attempt to balance interconnectedness with the powers and forces of the Atlantic world against independence from or resistance to the ways in which those powers could corrupt, dominate, or destroy. Boston had begun much like other colonies, other Atlantic plantations, hoping to find a commodity of sufficient value so that the colony could prosper as a conduit to the home country, a convenient gathering place for a particular kind of colonial production. Instead, it became something different, the metropolis of a region that had its own interests, an independent political economy framed within the Atlantic community, whose survival required connections to many points around the rim of that world, not merely a shipping lane to and from the metropole.

Typically, arguments for Boston's exceptionalism are the starting point for a larger narrative of American exceptionalism. Yet Boston's emergence and the framing of its identity was not, strictly speaking, an American story. Boston was exceptional in an Atlantic context, not because of its religious character or civic ideals, which were shared by other colonizing experiments, but because that character and those ideals were embodied by a large, homogeneous population of middling migrants, and funded by an aggressive commercial culture. In subsequent years, Boston's ability to sustain the identity that it discovered and assembled in the mid-1640s would be challenged by the problems that its assertive entry into the Atlantic world inevitably created.

Chapter 2

The World in a Shilling

Building the City-State's Political Economy

> The end of Coyning mony within this Commonwealth is for the more easy managing the traficque thereof within itself, & not Indended to make returnes to other Countrjes.
>
> —Massachusetts General Court, 1654

By virtue of its royal charter, the Massachusetts Bay Company appeared to be the creature of England's King Charles, much as Philippi had been the creature of King Philip of Macedon. But in its first two decades, Boston did not behave like the king's pet. In fact, the Crown tried to revoke the charter in the first decade because the new colony frequently acted as though it were an independent state, treating the charter as a malleable set of guidelines, open to interpretation by the governor and General Court.[1] By means of these free interpretations, the colony exceeded the charter's limits in many ways. The churches developed an organizational structure where each church gathered its own members and chose its own minister, contradictory to the hierarchical Church of England. The colony created incorporated townships and granted them colony lands (a usurpation of the Crown's power to create corporations), and created Harvard College in 1636 as a chartered corporation as well. The General Court, originally designed as a governor and his "assistants" to guide the company, expanded itself to include a house of deputies chosen to represent the freemen in the newly formed towns. And together with Plymouth, Connecticut, and New Haven, Massachusetts formed the United Colonies as an alliance for mutual defense.

All these actions generated arguments on both sides of the Atlantic about whether the commonwealth was a "perfect res publica" or a "free state." But nothing that Massachusetts did was quite as state-like as the creation of an independent circulating currency.[2] By issuing its own coins, Boston openly assumed the Crown's prerogative, and it used the economic power, trust, and credit that the coinage accrued to advance its own vision of political economy across the New England region and among the competing powers of the Atlantic world. This chapter explores Boston's role in developing and integrating New England's internal economy as well as the political consequences of these events, especially with respect to the colonists' relationship with New England's indigenous peoples. To do so, it takes a close look at Massachusetts' silver shillings, examining both the productive and destructive sides of these coins. This currency played a critical role in assuring the city-state of Boston's autonomy, and developing a stable, prosperous, and growing economy for the colonists who spread rapidly across the New England region, while providing the colony with the financial strength to overpower indigenous resistance to this expansion.

Scholarship on the political economy of early America tends to focus on the era of the American Revolution, when the British Empire's taxation reforms engendered violent colonial protests, and the independent United States struggled to shape its own economic future. The colonies' development in the two centuries before 1776 is often treated simply as background for the revolution, as though North America had a brief political economy moment in the late eighteenth century, but before that, a long period of preparatory, apolitical economics.[3] By contrast, the subject of political economy has a rich literature focused on the early modern British Empire, but its perspective tends to be distinctly metropolitan. The British homelands, usually England (and sometimes Scotland), constitute the polity whose economy the rest of the empire serves. The evolution of mercantilist doctrines that linked colonies to the metropolis, beginning with the Navigation Acts of 1651, takes center stage in these accounts. From the metropolitan viewpoint, the economic development of the colonies becomes the story of successes and failures in the production of commodities within a system run by London and Westminster, with variations suitable to the climates and conditions of the different colonial regions, but with little attention to the political ambitions of individual colonies.[4]

My aim here is different. By highlighting its capacity to act independently, this chapter concentrates on the political economy of the city-state of Boston itself. Rather than considering it as merely a subsidiary of England's empire, I proceed from the premise that Boston was for Boston—that it behaved as an autonomous entity pursuing its own political economy within the larger context of the Atlantic world.

What do I mean, then, by political economy? To use the definition that Adam Smith coined in *The Wealth of Nations* (1776), the two chief purposes of political economy are "to provide a plentiful revenue or subsistence for the people . . . and, secondly, to supply the state or commonwealth with a revenue sufficient for the publick services."[5] Chapter 1 introduced Boston's distinctive challenges in providing a "plentiful revenue or subsistence for the people"—in particular, the problem of finding employment for its many thousands of colonists in a manner that would produce marketable commodities for export and allow them to purchase necessary imports. By the mid-1640s, a solution began to appear in the growing markets of the Caribbean in the midst of the sugar boom. Although it remained uncertain how the productive capacities of the New England region would generate a plentiful revenue for its people, the West Indian markets offered a way forward. But what constituted the "publick services" of the state, the second part of Smith's definition, for which revenue was necessary? What were the goals and aims of the emerging city-state of Boston?[6]

The first and most necessary goal was to preserve the autonomy that allowed its merchants to trade freely in the Atlantic world. Boston's survival required it. Crown dependency and reliance on English merchants might have been acceptable for Virginia or Barbados. Their valuable crops made their utility to the home country easily visible within England's emerging empire. In the mind's eye of the metropolis, Virginia *was* tobacco, and Barbados *was* sugar.

The growing demand for these luxury goods in Europe meant that English merchant ships would readily supply the colonial planters with imports.

This definition of a colony's purpose was far too confining for Boston, which built its fortune on what economists refer to as "invisibles": the value derived from shipping goods from one place to another, and bearing the costs and risks of these ventures. When Boston merchants built their own ships, and then brought New England codfish to Bilbao, Spanish wool to England, and English manufactures back to Boston, they saved English merchants the cost of empty voyages to New England and Spain while increasing the flow and exchange of goods—real economic values, but difficult to see from the metropolis. For example, English merchant Sir Francis Brewster described New England as "that unprofitable Plantation, which now brings nothing to this Nation, but to the contrary buries Numbers of Industrious People in a Wilderness, that produceth nothing but Provisions to feed them." As one historian of New England's economy put it, "These invisible credits in trade—the value of which contemporaries consistently underestimated—constituted the region's single most valuable export."[7] "Export" is a curious word. In what sense can the activity of trade itself be considered an export? But it indicates the problem of pinpointing exactly *where* Boston's geographic limits were. It is ultimately impossible to say whether the carrying trade, Boston's invisibles, was "internal" or "external" to Boston. In terms of its economy, the pursuit of overseas trade *was* Boston, or at least an indispensable part of it, as necessary to its survival as tobacco was to Virginia or sugar was to Barbados. Boston required the freedom for its merchants to act as though Massachusetts were a free state, trading not just as a colonial dependency within England's mercantile system, but widely across the empires of the Atlantic world.

The second goal of Boston's political economy was to extend its territorial reach, political authority, and economic control beyond the narrow boundaries of the charter's original land grant, in order to gain access to new resources and settlement opportunities for its expanding population. Boston's success in pursuing this ambition also made the colony distinctive in seventeenth-century English America. Other colonies grew in population and spread out across the land as well, but their growth was usually confined within territory defined by their expansive charters. Virginia's charter created northern and southern boundaries hundreds of miles apart, initially defined by the 34th and 41st parallels, a distance of roughly four hundred miles. By contrast, the distance between the boundaries in the Massachusetts Charter, from three miles north of the Merrimack River to three miles south of the Charles, was less than fifty miles. The expansion of Boston far beyond these limits, the development of an integrated economy within this growing region, the extension of political authority and military control across New England, and the construction of durable commercial connections between the region and markets of the wider Atlantic all constituted formidable achievements, unparalleled in the Anglo-American colonial world, and the chief "publick service" provided by the city-state of Boston for its people.[8]

But to fully understand the challenges of the mid-seventeenth century, we need to go beyond Smith's definition and consider how these political economy measures influenced the colony's moral economy. Here I do not mean to resuscitate the once-prevalent view that the colony's commercial success undermined the religious zeal embodied in the first generation of puritan colonists, frequently called the "declension" narrative.[9] Instead, I aim to highlight the tensions between the colonists' aims to build a society on the principles of Christian charity and their encounters with the hard realities of their economic circumstances. Commercial engagement with the Atlantic world and its slave-based plantation economies, and territorial expansion with its destructive consequences for indigenous peoples, each held the potential to undermine the commonwealth ideal implicit in the references to Paul's colony at Philippi in the Great Seal of Massachusetts Bay. To understand these tensions, it is useful to explore the social and political functions of money in the early modern Atlantic world.

Two Dowries: Boston and Potosí

In 1676, two weddings took place at the opposite poles of European colonial settlement in the Americas—two weddings, more than four thousand miles apart, but connected by a silver thread. At the southern end of this thread, high in the Andes almost three miles above sea level, stood the city of Potosí in the Viceroyalty of Peru, then the largest city in the Western Hemisphere with a population comparable to Amsterdam's. Here, hundreds of thousands of Native American workers were employed in the heavy and sickening labor of digging silver out of the Cerro Rico, a giant mountain of silver that Spanish conquistadores had first encountered in the 1540s. Indian workers often developed black lung disease from breathing the mineral dust in the mines; the Quechua name for the Cerro Rico meant "man-eating mountain." In the century since its discovery, the Cerro Rico had disgorged many tons of silver. Potosí became the largest source of the stream of mineral wealth flowing to Spanish ports across the Atlantic. The giant flotas brought silver by the shipload

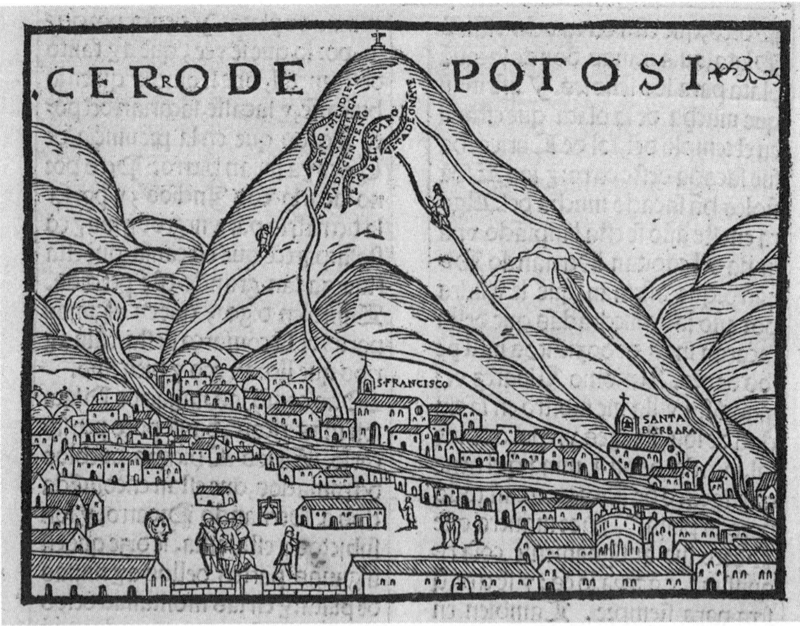

Figure 2.1. *Famous Woodcut of the Silver Mines of Potosí*, by Pedro de Cieza de Leon, 1553.

to Cadiz and returned to America laden with European goods. Meanwhile, the annual Manila galleon carried silver to the Philippines in exchange for the silks and spices of Asia.[10]

In Potosí, once the silver was dug out of the Cerro Rico, still more Indian workers refined it, using a mercury amalgamation process (also sickening, though in a different way). Then the Royal Mint transformed the purified silver into coins, the famous Spanish peso or eight reales piece, known as a Spanish dollar or "piece of eight." The master of the mint at Potosí was Don Antonio López de Quiroga. He was born in Galicia in northwest Spain, in the region where Boston merchants had already established a steady trade. It is not improbable to think that New England merchants were among the first foreigners Quiroga encountered as he made his way out from his Spanish homeland.[11]

In the late 1640s, Quiroga came to Peru in search of fortune, which the Cerro Rico and its forced Indian labor certainly provided. In the boomtown atmosphere of Potosí, poor Indian workers were forced to labor under the notorious *mita* system. Every year, Indian villages for hundreds of miles around sent roughly one-seventh of their adult male population to work in the mines. The Indians remained poor, sickened, and died, but the Spanish silver traders became *very* rich, none more so than Quiroga. His daughter, Doña Lorenza, set her wedding date for October 1676, and Quiroga supplied a handsome dowry to Lorenza's intended bridegroom, Don Juan de Velasco, another native Spaniard and aspiring bureaucrat in the colonial service. The official value of Lorenza's dowry was 100,000 pesos, an eye-popping sum.[12] Half of this treasure consisted of exquisite material objects imported from Spain: a gilded hardwood four-poster bed, a crimson damask bedspread embroidered in gold, a series of historical tapestries, a writing desk, a sedan chair, and a dozen paintings illustrating the months of the year as well as upholstered chairs, Oriental carpets, 7,000 pesos' worth of silverware and plate for entertaining, and another 6,000 pesos' worth of textiles ranging from tablecloths and napkins to handkerchiefs and dress gowns. Six African slaves (four men and two women) were also included in this "material" half of the dowry. But the remainder came in the form of silver coins, 50,000 pesos, twenty large sacks of the Spanish dollars produced in the mint at Potosí.[13] Each of those sacks would have weighed about 150 pounds, perhaps as much or more than each of the slaves. With each one of those twenty sacks, Velasco, the fortunate bridegroom, might have purchased five or six more adult male slaves.[14] (See plate 7.)

Far to the north, a small scattering of the silver that spewed forth from Potosí would occasionally wash up in Boston. In 1676, New England's capital was a town of about four thousand people, perhaps one-fiftieth the size of Potosí, lying at sea level on the shores of the Atlantic, or what the Spanish referred to as the *mar del Norte*. There the merchant John Hull, born in England but having moved to America in the 1630s with his family, was also Boston's leading silversmith. He had been employed since 1652 as master of the mint, occasionally using his craftsman's skills to turn miscellaneous pieces of silver into curious coins. These were the so-called pine tree shillings of the Massachusetts Bay Colony. In a good year, such as 1679, Hull produced about twenty thousand of these shillings, making for a face value of £1,000.[15] Over the thirty years in which he made them, perhaps 300,000 to 500,000 shillings were put into circulation.[16]

Like Quiroga, Hull was a pious and charitable man as well as a merchant and dealer in silver. Where Quiroga had founded the church and convent of San Francisco (pictured in figure 2.1 at the center of Potosí), Hull was among the founders of Boston's Third Church, with its meetinghouse dominating Boston's South End from a commanding position at the corner of Cornhill and Milk Streets (depicted in map I.1 at letter *C*). Throughout his life, Hull kept diaries of his spiritual experiences and notebooks from sermons he heard, alongside the ledgers and correspondence books in which he recorded his business affairs. And like Quiroga, Hull had a daughter, Hannah, who in February 1676 was planning to marry an aspiring merchant, public servant, and future judge.

From such a wealthy and generous father-in-law, Hannah's intended bridegroom, Samuel Sewall, could expect a substantial dowry along with his bride. Hull did not disappoint. In fact, Hannah's dowry became legendary in New England, with its value repeated and exaggerated by some of the region's finest authors. Nathaniel Hawthorne retold the story with inimitable flair in his children's history of New England, *Grandfather's Chair* (1850): "When the marriage ceremony was over, Captain Hull whispered a word to two of his men-servants, who immediately went out, and soon returned, lugging in a large pair of scales." In the story, the mint-master asks his daughter to climb into one of the scales:

> "And now," said honest John Hull to the servants "bring that box hither" . . . a huge, square, iron-bound, oaken chest . . . full to the brim of bright pine-tree shillings, fresh from the mint; and Samuel Sewall began to think that his father-in-law had got possession of all the money in the Massachusetts treasury. Then the servants, at Captain Hull's command, heaped double handfuls of shillings into one side of the scales, while Betsey remained in the other. "There, son Sewall!" cried the honest mint-master, resuming his seat in Grandfather's chair, "take these shillings for my daughter's portion. . . . It is not every wife that's worth her weight in silver!"[17]

Hawthorne got Hannah's name wrong, and we like to think that he must have invented the story or exaggerated the dowry. But he was not the first to do so. No less scrupulous a historian than Thomas Hutchinson recorded that Hannah's dowry amounted to £30,000, a preposterous figure (preposterous in Massachusetts, that is, though entirely believable in Potosí).[18] The face value of all the shillings Hull ever produced for the colony might have been £25,000 at most.

Given Hutchinson's exaggeration, Hawthorne's whimsical story turns out to be surprisingly close to the truth. In 1676, Hull was the treasurer of the Massachusetts Bay Colony; he did have his hands on all the money in the Massachusetts treasury. But he did not bestow it all on his daughter and her future husband. Hull's and Sewall's account books tell us the actual amount of Hannah's dowry: £500, paid in two separate transactions.[19] There was no dramatic moment when Hannah's weight could have been measured out in shillings. In all likelihood, Hull probably *never* had £500 worth—10,000 shillings—in his possession at any one time, given the small scale and sporadic schedule on which he produced the coins over the decades.[20] Yet the actual weight in English pounds and ounces of 10,000 pine tree shillings would measure out on a scale at roughly 105 pounds, perhaps not far from the real Hannah's actual weight.

The coincidence of the simultaneous weddings and mintmasters' dowries highlights two features of the relationship between Potosí and Boston—one a glaring contrast, the other a profound connection. Most obvious is the overwhelming difference in the scale of operations. The value of Lorenza's dowry was something like eighty times as large as that of Hannah's. Yet Hannah's dowry was thought to be a huge amount, large enough in New England's historical memory to become the source of legend. By any measure, the production of Potosí's mint dwarfs Hull's trivial output in Boston. This difference in scale reflects the different kinds of colonies that the Viceroyalty of Peru and Commonwealth of Massachusetts represented. With its fabulously rich silver mines, Peru was the ideal mercantilist colony: ruled from the metropolis, designed to extract commodity wealth for the home country and form a new consumer market for the products of the homeland.

Boston did not fit this model, despite the hopes of the first generation's explorers that New England, too, might conceal hidden veins of mineral wealth or at least provide some precious commodity for English consumers. Boston's fortunes were made not by extracting high-value commodities but by timely and ingenious forms of oceangoing trade, fueled by the humble, low-value commodities that New England farmers and fisherman could scrape together for sale. As a consequence, the social order created by the city-state of Boston, where even the most prosperous merchants lived modestly, was far more "middling" than that of Potosí, with its incredibly wealthy few served by hundreds of thousands of exploited Indians.

Nevertheless, despite the difference in scale of the minting operations, and because of the different models of colonial economy that Potosí and Boston represented within their competing empires, the two operations were connected, and not only by the coincidental weddings. The great majority of the silver that Hull worked into cups, spoons, buckles, and coins in his Boston shop was originally mined in Potosí. But the connection was still closer than this, for besides the royally supervised mints at Potosí and Zacatecas in Mexico, Hull's mint in Boston was the only other place in the Western Hemisphere where high-grade silver coins were being produced to European monetary standards. In fact, the decision by the General Court of Massachusetts to begin minting its own silver coins came in response to a crisis in Potosí in the 1640s. In monetary terms, the Atlantic world was already sufficiently interconnected by the mid-seventeenth century that events at one extreme influenced decisions at its polar opposite.

One of the most important things that independent states can do to advance their political economy is to create and maintain a money supply. This is why it was so unusual for Massachusetts, ostensibly a colony of another state, to begin creating its own high-grade silver coinage in 1652; no other British colony was ever so bold.[21] The right to mint coins was a royal prerogative going back to Roman times, and the penalties for uttering false coinage were those associated with lèse-majesté or high treason: "The punishment in Roman law and in early German law was the loss of one or both hands, but by the fourteenth century some form of gruesome death was the norm: hanging in England, burning in Venice, boiling in France."[22] In Potosí, atop a mountain of silver, the Spanish Crown had sensibly authorized a Royal Mint to supply currency for its global empire. But why was Massachusetts, a tiny colony with no silver deposits, and no authority to do so from the Crown or Parliament, engaged in this business at all? Why was Hull making silver shillings to serve as legal tender for "Massachusetts in New England"?

The Big Problem of Small Change

In the late 1640s, when wampum collapsed as a money supply for the interior of New England, the need to replace it with a reliable form of small change was urgent. Boston's merchants needed a plentiful currency that would promote local trade throughout the region and bear a stable relationship to the larger circulating moneys of the Atlantic world. This problem was not exclusive to colonial New England. For most of the Middle Ages and into early modern times, western Europeans had faced a "big problem of small change": a shortage of reliable, government-backed coins with stable values that were nonetheless small enough for the conduct of everyday commerce. High-value coins of precious metal, such as Venetian gold ducats (the coin loaned by Shylock to Antonio in Shakespeare's *Merchant of Venice*) or the nearly equivalent Florentine coin, the florin, circulated widely in long-distance trade (Antonio's ships were bound for Mexico, the Indies, England, and Tripoli). But the value of each coin was so large that individual consumers could not easily use them to buy daily necessities. For instance, in fourteenth-century Florence, a single unit of the *smallest*-available silver coin, the grosso, was enough money to purchase five liters of wine, a kilogram of olive oil, or pay an entire month's rent for a single working man—the Renaissance equivalent of trying to spend a $100 bill at a laundromat.[23]

When small coins became scarce, their value increased and the problem grew worse. In fifteenth-century England, a petition from the House of Commons to King Henry VI described the problem:

> Men travelling over countries, for part of their expenses of necessity must depart [i.e., divide in two parts] our sovereign lord's coin, that is to wit, a penny in two pieces, or else forego all the same penny, for the payment of a half penny; and also the poor common retailers of victuals, . . . for default of such coin of half pennies and farthings, oftentimes may not sell their said victuals and things, and many of our said sovereign lord's poor liege people, which would buy such victuals and

other small things necessary, may not buy them, for default of half pennies and farthings.[24]

Without readily available small change, small-scale commerce ground to a halt. In 1613, King James I recognized this problem when he issued "Farthing Tokens . . . to pass between Vintners, Tapsters, Chandlers, Bakers, and other the like Tradesmen and their Customers, whereby such small portions and quantities of things vendible as the necessity and use specially of the poorer sort of People doth oftentimes require . . . without enforcing men to buy more ware than will serve for their use and good end."[25]

Between the thirteenth century, when growing European trade networks began to spur production of a wider variety of coins, and the early nineteenth century, when western governments finally developed a reliable formula for solving this problem, most European states and their New World colonies suffered from a chronic shortage of small change. By small change, I do not mean fiduciary moneys—tin farthings, lead trinkets, or wooden or leather tokens—whose value depends on a community's confidence or trust that it will be accepted as a medium of exchange. These existed throughout Europe and its colonies, sometimes in enormous numbers and varieties. They circulated in narrowly confined areas (within a town, parish, or guild, for instance) and therefore had a local utility.[26] But with no stable relationship to the larger currencies of the state or empire, and no intrinsic value as coins, these fiduciary moneys did not work well to integrate local trade with larger regional, national, or international economies. Your local baker might accept your tin farthings for small amounts of bread, but not the baker on the far side of town or in the next town over. You could not buy expensive goods from an international merchant even with a wheelbarrow full of them, nor could you use them to pay your taxes. What was missing were good coins, with some appreciable intrinsic value (usually silver) and a reliable ratio to large coins, but in small enough denominations for everyday utility, good at your local bakery *and* for the big merchant or tax collector. We might think of this as money of moderate size, but economists call it small change—"small" because it's smaller than the big money coins, and "change" because it can be exchanged for big coins at a reliable rate.

In many parts of Europe, the small change shortage was a chronic problem that people simply endured. It meant that the integration of larger regional or national economies proceeded at a halting pace, because exchange was cumbersome and slow. As far as large-scale merchants and international traders were concerned, the problem was bearable. Their interests lay in corralling the few really valuable commodities produced in a given region—items expensive enough to make the costs of overseas shipping worthwhile, such as the fine woolen cloth woven in southeastern England, or sugar and tobacco produced in the colonies—and they generally used high-value commodity money of gold or silver, or bills of exchange denominated in commodity money values, in their transactions. Big merchants trading luxury goods tended not to care about humble foodstuffs and sundries bought and sold in local markets for local consumption. For these, fiduciary money sufficed.

Boston, as the emergent market hub of New England in the 1640s, was different. Boston's merchants faced the necessity of participation in the Atlantic economy, dealing in profitable and expensive goods like tobacco, sugar, and slaves. This meant that the humble goods New England's colonists could produce (grain, bread, salted meat, dried or salted fish, barrel staves, and potash) somehow had to serve as commodities for overseas trade. The big merchants of Boston needed steady, reliable access to modest goods not usually thought of as commodities in the early modern world, and for that they needed small change, a money of moderate size.

New England merchants had initially hoped that wampum would function as small change, because wampum could buy furs, and furs were like sugar or tobacco, commodities with a high value in European markets. Furs could be exchanged directly for desirable European import goods—the ultimate end point of Boston's Atlantic commerce. Had the wampum-to-fur relationship remained stable, New England might have become more like Virginia or Barbados, a staple-extracting colony with a direct trade relationship to the home country (although with little employment for its thousands of settlers). But when wampum could no longer reliably command furs, and as the supply of furs from New England diminished, the situation changed. In the 1640s, Boston merchants discovered that they could compete with metropolitan merchants for the carrying trade to the West Indies. Plantation owners in Barbados were using every available acre of the island to grow high-priced sugar. They needed low-priced food to feed their slaves, along with timber for barrels, building materials, and fuel—goods too cheap to waste their precious land and slaves in producing. Boston's merchants therefore looked for a reliable method to encourage New England farmers and fishermen to produce these cheap goods in large quantities necessary for a booming export market.[27]

From 1630 to the early 1640s, Massachusetts' colonists had strong encouragement to overproduce these humble goods, to generate more than their families consumed, because of the urgent demand from the stream of new migrants arriving by the thousands every year. New migrants desperately needed food to tide them over until they could start their own farms as well as timber to build and heat their houses. But when the outbreak of civil wars in Britain abruptly ended the persecution that had pushed puritan migrants overseas, the local market in New England for these goods bottomed out. When Boston merchants first attempted Atlantic voyages to vend these cheap commodities, they were risking little—selling an otherwise-useless surplus of not-very-valuable goods—and it turned out to be surprisingly successful. Yet that initial crisis around 1640, when local commodity prices fell to nothing, made farmers cautious about repeating this overproduction. How could Boston merchants encourage New England farmers to return to their industrious ways, and once again produce surpluses of food and timber for which there was no local market? Money provided a solution.

In a barter economy, farm families would have few incentives to spend idle winter months carving barrel staves, burning potash, or slaughtering and salting down meat, especially if all their neighbors are capable of doing the same thing. The local demand is limited to no more than what the locals themselves can use or consume. If too many people try to produce a surplus of these products, their local trade value becomes negligible. Producing them is a waste of time and effort. But if these goods can be sold for money to distant markets, and the money is of the sort that can be used to buy import goods not available locally, then the incentive to engage in extra production becomes much greater. The existence of a plentiful money supply, a stable small change currency, would be a great advantage to Boston's merchants. Money would flush humble commodities out of the countryside to sell in Atlantic markets and put buying power in the hands of New England's customers for European imports. For this reason, the collapse of the fur-wampum equation was especially dire for New England and the demand for alternative money was great.

The Trouble with Pieces of Eight

On the face of it, a solution to New England's monetary problem appeared to be at hand. With the inauguration of trade routes to the Caribbean, southern Europe, and the Atlantic islands, silver money started to appear in Boston. The holds of trading ships built in New England's seaports were bringing home Spanish silver. Some of these coins were acquired in legitimate trade, when Caribbean sugar, cotton, or tobacco growers, or wine merchants from the Azores or Madeira, paid for Boston's humble products in cash, as in Captain Coytmore's voyage with the *Trial* in 1641–42. Much of it was probably acquired in disreputable ways. Privateers or pirates captured Spanish or Portuguese trading vessels carrying silver, or stole slaves and sold them clandestinely to Spanish customers on the coasts of Central America, and then brought their tainted money to Boston for laundering. Such was the case when Captain Thomas Cromwell presented Governor John Winthrop with a sedan chair intended for the Viceroy of New Spain.[28]

The Spanish dollar, peso, or piece of eight might have been a solution to Boston's monetary problem. In the premodern era, money and its circulation were not "national." It was not generally expected that each kingdom or state should have its own exclusive monetary system. (This modern conception of the monetary world of nation-states did not fully develop until the nineteenth century).[29] If a steady supply of Spanish dollars could be had, there was no reason why they could not circulate throughout New England and fill some of the necessary functions of small change. Although it was a form of silver commodity money, the eight reales coin, weighing one ounce of silver, was not so large as to be useless in everyday situations. Its commodity value was only half that of the ducat, and in Massachusetts it was valued at six English shillings, or seventy-two pence. This was an inflated value, a "crying up" of these coins, which traded for only five shillings in England. The colony of Massachusetts authorized a higher local exchange value for Spanish dollars than they traded for in England, hoping to encourage people to keep them circulating within New England.[30]

Furthermore, the fact that this single round coin's denomination was "eight" reales (rather than, say "one" ducat) made it attractive to cut it, like pieces of pie, into two "four" reales halves, four "two" reales quarters, or eight individual real "bits" of smaller change.[31] But cutting coins is a risky practice (as any child who ever shared a cookie with a sibling knows)—too similar to other forms of manipulation like "clipping" or "washing" coins that deliberately debased their value. Herein lay the deeper problem with Spanish money as a solution to Boston's woes.[32] Premodern coin making's imprecision left the edges of coins less than perfectly round. All gold or silver coins were in jeopardy from clipping, washing, or shaving—practices that appropriated minute amounts of the valuable metal from the coin's edge while still passing the coin off at full face value. Inveterate clippers, especially those who handled great volumes of coinage, could accumulate large amounts of precious metal and seriously debase the coinage in the process. In his *History of England*, Thomas Babington Macaulay recounts the frequent hangings or burnings of convicted coin clippers on London's Holborn Hill; the Crown tried to make "terrible examples" by punishing the "wretches" guilty of "mutilating the money of the realm." Nonetheless, "some clippers were said to have made great fortunes. One in particular offered six thousand pounds for a pardon."[33] In the sixteenth and seventeenth centuries, new technologies, the screw and cylinder presses, were developed to improve coins' resistance to illegal debasement by making rings or markings around the edges of coins that would show off attempts to clip them. But these technologies were still imperfect and had yet to be fully implemented in the New World. At Potosí, huge numbers of silver coins were churned out annually using old-fashioned methods.

These coins made at Potosí were known as "cob" coins. Silver was rolled into long bars, a slice or "cob" of the bar was cut off, and then the cob was hammered or pressed into a coin. These were the most common coins circulating in the Atlantic world, and probably constituted the bulk of Spanish coinage arriving in Boston in the 1640s. The cob coins were crude, and the common practice of cutting these pieces of eight into smaller units threatened to debase them even further. In other words, there were already reasons to be suspicious of cob coins circulating in Atlantic trade routes and sea-lanes.[34]

In the 1640s, suspicion swelled into outright distrust as a consequence of scandal in Potosí. During this decade, while Boston's merchants were establishing their foothold in Caribbean trade, revelations at Potosí's mint undermined public trust in Spain's money supply. Since at least 1633, Spanish officials had begun to notice that Potosí coins were low in silver content. They warned the official assayers at the mint to mind their work more carefully. But the problem was endemic to the system. The minting of coins was farmed out to a dozen or more silver traders in Potosí, *mercaderes de plata*, who not only bargained with the miners and refiners to purchase silver but also oversaw the coining process, which included reserving one-fifth of all the silver produced for the Crown. The mercaderes had incentives to underreport the amount of silver produced so as to cheat the Crown, and also to skimp on silver in making the coins and skim the excess for themselves.[35]

By 1645, the problem had grown severe enough that the Viceroy of Peru agreed to the appointment of an outside inspector general. People in Spain had grown reluctant to accept Potosí coins because "there is not a *patacon* [piece of eight] of it that does not contain almost two *reales* of copper."[36] Spanish consumers had come to expect that Potosí coins might be as much as a quarter under their face value in silver. The inspector general, Don Francisco de Nestares Marin, a former inquisitor in Galicia, arrived in Potosí in December 1648. Even before his arrival, some of the mercaderes decided to improve the quality of their coins—in theory, a step in the right direction, though in practice a source of further confusion, since it was impossible to tell good coins from bad without an assayer's skill. Soon inspector Nestares identified the three most egregious offenders among the mercaderes, one of them, Francisco Gomez de la Rocha, a popular local benefactor who spread his ill-gotten wealth widely, and determined that they owed the Crown as much as a million pesos. When these three began to hide large sums of their money and then took refuge in the cathedral to escape from prosecution, Nestares turned to violent means. After luring them out of the church with promises of clemency, Nestares arrested and executed Gomez de la Rocha and left his corpse hanging in the plaza as an example to the town. (Note the image of a severed head displayed on a pike in the foreground of figure 2.1.) The assayer of the mint was executed as well, and other offenders were imprisoned. By 1652, only three of the dozen mercaderes remained in the coining business, and they now operated under a new regime designed to restore public trust in Potosí's coinage.

The new plan involved two stages: an effort to get people to bring underweight old coins into the mint for recoinage, and a timetable for restoring Potosí coins to their full 8 reales value. The inspector declared that from 1649 onward, all coins minted before that date would officially be devalued; they would circulate at only 6 reales, or three-quarters of their face value. Coins struck with a date of 1649 or later would temporarily circulate at 7.5 reales, or 93.75 percent of their face value. By October 1652, all the old coins were scheduled for remaking. The new coins, now of certified fine grade, would circulate at full face value. The old coins would no longer be recognized as having any value as money or legal tender, giving possessors incentive to turn them in for reminting. These draconian measures caused hardships, especially in Potosí, where most of the local fortunes were held in the now-devalued coins. Inspector

Nestares called in many debts to the treasury to be paid in full with the devalued currency in order to speed the recoinage. But the harsh measures restored widespread trust in Potosí's coinage throughout the Spanish Empire and Atlantic world.

Quiroga had the good fortune to arrive in Potosí well into the 1640s, untainted by the scandals, and to marry into one of the few local families that the scandal had not touched. His rise to wealth as master of the mint owed a great deal to the effective, if brutal, work performed by inspector Nestares.[37] The immense dowry that Quiroga presented to his son-in-law confirmed the stability that the production of reliable coins restored to Potosí.

From Spanish Silver to Boston Shillings

It is difficult to know how widely news of the scandal in Potosí and the Crown's reform measures spread beyond the Spanish Empire's boundaries.[38] But in the colonial world of scarce currencies, people everywhere paid close attention to those few coins that did pass their way. As Boston's early Atlantic traders, privateers, and pirates brought Spanish silver into the city, suspicion about its value and quality grew. Early in 1652, during the period when Potosí's coins had been discounted and were being called in for reminting, the Massachusetts General Court approached John Hull, one of the two trained silversmiths in Boston, with a proposal that he weigh, assay, and stamp all silver coins for authenticity and value. But Hull and his fellow silversmith, Robert Sanderson (the only two men in Boston with the skills to carry out the work), rejected the idea. In his diary, Hull confirmed the public's general awareness of the problem, noting that the General Court was motivated "upon occasion of much Counterfeit Coyne brought in the Countrey and much loss accruing in that respect (and that did occasion a stoppage of trade)."[39] This initial proposal failed because Hull and Sanderson had no incentive to take on the work of assaying and stamping the coins.[40]

Soon the General Court returned with a far more ambitious proposal: the creation of a mint for issuing new high-quality silver coins under the authority of the colony's government. On May 26, 1652, the House of Magistrates—the upper house or "council" of the General Court—enacted a measure allowing any person to bring Spanish coins or silver bullion to the new mint, "there to be melted & brought to the allay of sterling Silver by John Hull master of the sajd mint and his sworne officers." Hull would produce shillings (twelve pence) as well as six and three pence coins, "which shall be for forme flatt & square on the sides & stamped on the one side with N E." The law called for Hull to begin producing square (yes, square) coins of the plainest possible design, without any figure or image, simply its denomination in Roman numerals on one side, and the letters *NE* (for New England) on the other (the coin's design was yet another instance in which the entire region, New England, was used to designate the polity of which Boston was the head).[41] But Hull, the newly named mintmaster, was already undermining the concept of square coins, sketching various rough designs for round coins in the margins of the committee's minutes.

Before the first coins were minted, the General Court changed its orders. Even for Puritans given to iconoclasm, who would never think to put a graven image of God or Caesar on their coins, square pegs simply could not fill the round holes that legitimate money occupied in their imaginations. Square coins have always been rare, but before the Massachusetts General Court's brief flirtation with the idea, square coinage seems mainly to have been associated with fiduciary money.[42] In 1577, the Crown granted the city of Bristol permission to produce square farthing tokens made of lead, which may have been familiar to many of Boston's colonists including Hull, who migrated to New England on a ship leaving Bristol in the mid-1630s.[43] The General Court's decision to start coining sterling-grade silver shillings expressed a desire among the colony's leaders to bridge the crippling gap between fiduciary moneys, like wampum or musket balls, that might enhance the circulation of goods within New England, but were useless beyond the region, and the secure and reliable varieties of commodity money that were too rare and too high in purchasing power to function effectively as small change. The initial call for a square coinage may have reflected a latent

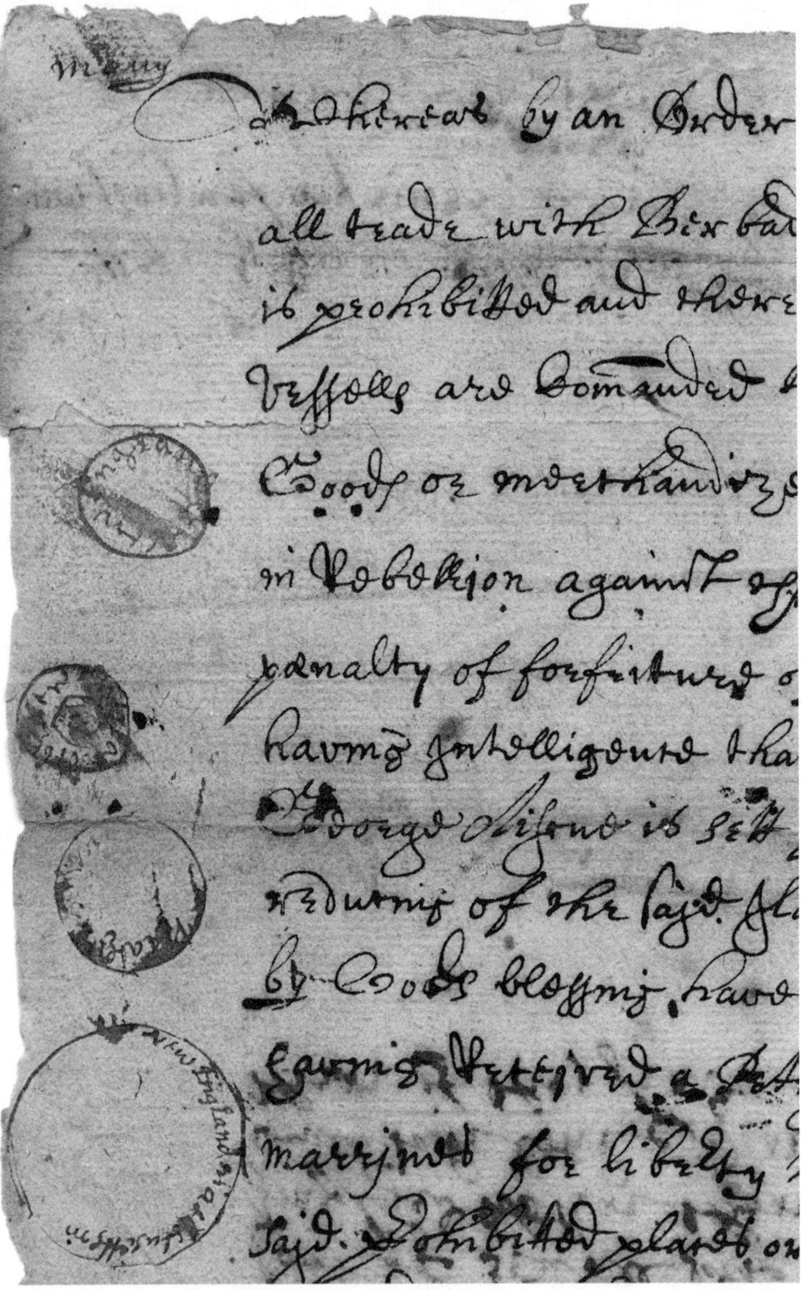

FIGURE 2.2. John Hull's sketches for Massachusetts coins, 1652.

uneasiness about making such a bold move. Perhaps the square design was meant to disguise the fact that Boston was linking its own coinage to the world of big money and challenging the prerogative of kings. But Hull and his fellow merchants knew better. They were making big money, not fiduciary tokens, and big money, commodity money, was round.

Nevertheless, the General Court hit on a plan to avoid some of the risks of challenging England's monetary authority, for the 1652 coinage act specified other distinctive features of this new coinage that unlike the square shape, were actually implemented. Hull was ordered to produce coins of the same quality alloy as English sterling, but only three-quarters the weight of their English equivalents.[44] Hull was to stamp the value of twelve pence, or one shilling, on a coin of fine sterling silver that actually weighed only the equivalent of nine pence in English coinage. A Massachusetts shilling would be lighter and smaller than an English one, though valued as the equivalent of an English shilling within New England. The lighter weight was to ensure that Massachusetts currency would stay in New England. Foreign merchants would be reluctant to accept underweight shillings—an intention supported by the order's claim that the new shillings would be legal tender "within this Jurisdiction only." Here was another marker of the conceptual slippage between Boston, Massachusetts, and New England. Clearly the General Court of Massachusetts issued the orders and produced the coins, but just as clearly the coins were meant to be legal tender throughout the entire New England Confederation.

The order creating the Massachusetts coinage bears a striking similarity to the plan in Potosí to refurbish the debased Spanish dollar, although for opposing reasons. In Potosí, an enormous profusion of coins with a face value of eight reales, but a commodity weight and value suspected to be only three-quarters of that amount, was seen as a serious problem, precisely because these plentiful coins were intended to circulate as widely as possible throughout Spain's expansive global empire and far beyond its boundaries as well. The common knowledge of the coins' corruption impaired that function. So to begin the remedy, the government temporarily reduced the effective face value of these coins from eight reales to six in order to get people all over the Spanish Empire to return them to Potosí for reminting. Boston's problem was the opposite of Potosí's. In Boston, silver was scarce, not plentiful. The objective was not to scatter this scarce coinage to the wider world—this happened readily enough in the general course of events as the colonists imported more goods than they had goods of their own to trade for them. Instead, the point was to keep the coinage circulating, but only within the region.

Boston's solution mirrored Potosí's problem. Hull deliberately issued coinage that like Potosí's, was debased. The face value was inflated above the "intrinsic" or commodity value of the silver contained in each coin, and by exactly the same amount. But there was a key difference. Potosí's problem stemmed from the fact that nobody knew the precise commodity value of any given coin because the dozen or so mercaderes in Potosí were not all equally corrupt. Boston, by contrast, made sure, through the well-remunerated skills of its sole mintmaster, that everyone could be certain of the precise commodity value of a Massachusetts shilling. The coin was underweight for its face value, but its alloy was of the same quality as English sterling. Therefore, the coins would circulate with great public confidence in the places where they were meant to circulate—the interior trade of New England—but would not be desirable beyond New England's borders, where merchants expected a shilling to weigh a shilling. (See plate 8.)

The initial coins that Hull produced, following the directives of the General Court, did not last long. The design was so plain and unembellished that it positively invited clipping and shaving. Few of these coins were made, and almost none have survived. To rectify the problem, the court issued an amended order on October 19, 1652, probably with Hull's direction, "ffor the prevention of washing or Clipping of all such peices of mony as shall be Coined within this Jurisdiction." Under this new plan, Hull produced coins with a double rim stamped around the edges on both sides of the coin, an inscription written inside each, and in the center, the image of a tree on one side and the date and coin's denomination on the other. The inscription itself read "Masathusets in New England," which aside from the curious spelling, neatly stated the position of the colony (Massachusetts) as the dominant political power within the larger geographic region (New England), and declared the intention of its makers that these coins would integrate and stimulate the economy of the entire region. (See plate 9.)

If these purposes were not clear enough in the design of the coins themselves, the General Court spelled it out two years later in an order limiting the export of Massachusetts coinage to twenty shillings per person and appointing searchers at ports to prevent smuggling beyond this small amount. The colony government did not want to go to the expense and trouble of creating a currency only to have merchants export it for its weight in silver bullion, and then charge their customers extortionate prices to make up for the fact that Massachusetts shillings were underweight.[45] The idea behind these coins was simple but ingenious and curiously modern in the fiscal world of the seventeenth century. As guaranteed sterling-grade alloy, the coins were trustworthy as commodities; when you had a Massachusetts shilling, you knew what you had.[46] And yet the face value stamped on the coin, the legal exchange value at which it circulated within the region, was deliberately higher than the commodity value of the silver it contained. These coins were a hybrid, neither pure commodity money (like a Venetian ducat) nor pure fiduciary money (like a square lead farthing), but something in between. If large Spanish dollars had already been officially "cried up" by the Massachusetts government from five shillings to six, trading at a face value higher than their intrinsic worth, then the new Massachusetts shilling was cried up still higher than the Spanish dollar—its face value was even higher, per ounce of silver, than that of the peso. This meant that Spanish dollars, rather than Massachusetts shillings, were more likely to be traded outside the colony because relatively speaking, the Massachusetts shilling had greater local purchasing power than the peso per ounce of silver. It also provided an incentive for New Englanders to convert their Spanish money into Massachusetts coins. Finally, although the coining of Massachusetts shillings would increase the money supply within New England, it still remained the case that silver was relatively scarce in the region. The colony was never in danger of an excessive production of coins (as it had been with wampum), especially given the legal commitment to issuing them at sterling grade.

What Hull and the General Court accomplished, motivated by the pressure of their distinctive commercial economy that demanded humble local commodities for the purpose of large-scale overseas trade, and by the doubtful value of Spanish silver coins, was to solve the big problem of small change almost by accident. The standard formula by which this problem was eventually resolved in Europe and North America was fully implemented only in the nineteenth century: "In England it was not applied until 1816, and in the United States it was not accepted before 1853." As economic historian Carlo Cipolla describes it, "Every elementary textbook of economics gives the standard formula for maintaining a sound system of fractional money: to issue on government account small coins having a commodity value lower than their monetary value; to limit the quantity of these small coins in circulation; to provide convertibility with unit money." Boston's shillings performed all three of these functions. Their commodity value was lower than their monetary value (although not as low as most small change in the modern era), the coins were necessarily limited in quantity by the scarcity of silver, and they were "convertible with unit money," be it the Spanish dollar or the English pound in which Boston's merchants recorded overseas transactions in their ledgers.[47]

The Virtues of Boston's Shillings

How did Boston's shillings work to expand and integrate New England's economy? The records Hull kept of his output at the mint, which occupied a small outbuilding near his house, a few steps down Cornhill from the Third Church, are incomplete.[48] Hull produced coins from 1652 to the early 1680s, but only the ledgers dating from 1671 to 1680 survive, limiting our knowledge of the output of shillings from the mint. The records reveal that during this decade Hull received consignments for coining money of 11,161.925 troy ounces of sterling silver. After accounting for wastage in the production process, this yields an estimate of 74,777 Massachusetts silver shillings produced.[49] We do not know how many Hull produced of each denomination of the coins, among the 12-, 6-, and 3-pence pieces authorized by the initial 1652 legislation, or the additional 2-penny piece added to the coinage in 1662. If they were all tuppences, then we are talking about over 400,000 coins, but that is extremely unlikely, as the smaller the coin's denomination, the more work and wastage there was in its production. At the time that the order to create the new 2-penny piece was issued "to answer the occasions of the country for exchange," the General Court ordered Hull to produce "the first year fifty pounds, in such small money [the tuppences], for every hundred pounds by him to be coined; and for after-time twenty pounds, in like small money annually for every hundred pounds that shall be coined."[50] The absence of mint records from the 1660s prevents us from knowing whether the court's orders were fulfilled or not, or whether tuppence production continued into the 1670s. Nonetheless, if we imagine a reasonable mix of the denominations, with half or more of the coins minted at the largest 1-shilling denomination, then it is likely that Hull produced over 100,000 coins in the 1670s.

Furthermore, the mint's production in the 1670s probably dropped below the rates of the two preceding decades. The turmoil of King Philip's War in the mid-1670s probably diminished the volume of internal trade and demand for new coinage. In addition, during the 1670s, the exchange value of the Spanish dollar within Massachusetts was increased by legislation from the General Court in response to similar measures being taken in other British colonies.[51] As a result, the value of Spanish dollars and Massachusetts shillings reached rough parity with respect to their face value as a ratio of silver content, which reduced the incentive to convert Spanish money into Massachusetts shillings.[52] In all likelihood, more Spanish money was reminted into Massachusetts coins in the 1650s and 1660s than in the 1670s. But even if we assume a constant rate throughout the three decades of protection, we can conservatively estimate that Hull produced 225,000 shillings' worth of sterling-grade Massachusetts money and as many as 300,000 individual coins.

How much is that? How does it compare with small change volumes elsewhere?[53] From 1650 to 1680, the settler population of Massachusetts increased from roughly fifteen to forty thousand. For the entire New England region, the same period saw growth from about twenty-five to seventy thousand colonists, including Massachusetts. Hull's production of shillings, presuming that most of them remained in New England, would have meant that on average, there was circulating about 3 shillings, or 36 pence, for every man, woman, and child in the region as a whole, or about 6 shillings per person if we only include Massachusetts proper. This turns out to be a fairly plentiful supply.

In 1682, the year in which Hull's Boston mint last made coins, the English political economist William Petty estimated what he believed to be the correct quantity of small change for England "by positing an appropriate per *household* figure of 12d. [1 shilling] and multiplying by his estimate of total population."[54] Given that Hull probably produced more than 1 shilling per *person* rather than per household, the Boston mint clearly produced a workable supply of small change for New England, even if we allow for the likelihood that substantial quantities of Massachusetts shillings were exported out of the region. These figures suggest that in the latter half of the seventeenth century, the average residents of New England, the farmers and fishermen who made up the great bulk of the population, may have been more deeply enmeshed in market enterprises, producing goods for overseas marketing and in need of ready cash to pay for imported goods, than their counterparts in England. Massachusetts coins played a significant part in the economic growth that Boston's merchants generated for the entire region.

What was good for Boston was also good for Hull. His account books, diaries, and correspondence show that the small change he produced, including the 1 in every 20 shillings that he was entitled to keep as "seigniorage," his fee for the work of minting coins, assisted Hull in building what we might call, for now, his personal fortune. A typical example of Hull's mercantile affairs is recorded in a letter to his Jamaican correspondent, William Pulford, on June 25, 1672:

> Sir I take the boldness to Consigne unto you 12 bbs of Porke & 52 bbs of mackrell now shipped in the seaflowr. Tho Smith mastr wch I intreate you to take care of & take yor best oppertunity to sell for my Advantage and as sold to invest ye mony in any good Comodytye for New Engld. viz loggwood, Caccoa, hydes, Span Iron or to send it in good silvr mony or plate in any vessell bound hither as opertunity Presents the bill of lading is here inclosed.

Most of Hull's business correspondence is more complex than this, but the exchange with Pulford is typical of the kinds of goods Hull shipped out from Boston and the kinds of returns he most wanted to receive. Barrels of salted pork and mackerel were standard products of New England's farmers, fishermen, and the forest industries necessary for barrel making—a crucial though somewhat-invisible part of Atlantic mercantile life in the seventeenth century. Mackerel was a low-grade fish, often called "refuse fish" in comparison to "good merchantable cod," and thus more suitable for the West Indian markets, where planters wanted cheap food for their slaves. Hull's letter does not tell us by what form of payment and from which producers he acquired the pork and mackerel; it would be of no interest to his Jamaican correspondent.[55]

Other contemporary Boston merchants' and New England farmers' account books offer examples of the diverse range of goods that merchants used to pay local producers for the products they sold in Atlantic markets. For example, the merchant Philip English arranged a West Indian voyage by acquiring pork, beef, codfish, rope, tar, and timber from Josiah Wilcott, in return for wine, cloth, buttons, rum, and "money paid."[56] The last item in the list, money paid, is important. The coinage produced by Hull was never extensive enough that we should expect money, sterling silver, to be used for entire transactions on a large scale. But the presence of money lubricated the system and made it easier to reconcile inevitable differences in value when goods of many kinds were exchanged for other goods. Ready money guaranteed that future exchanges would be easier as well—a fact that Hull reinforces when he suggests to Pulford that "good silver money or plate" might be among the "good Commodities for New England" that Hull might receive in return. Of the other commodities listed, logwood, used for making clothing dyes, would be "good for New England" in that it would be reexported to England for the textile industry, and Hull would earn credits from it to buy English manufactures. Cacao, hides, or Spanish iron might also be reexported to England, or perhaps used in New England, where there was local demand. But as for the good silver money or plate, Hull would recirculate it within New England to stimulate the local economy on which his overseas trade depended.

More than most merchants, Hull's unusual access to a steady money supply allowed him to build his business on a model that prefigured the modern corporate notion of vertical integration, combining under his own control the various stages in the production or collection of complex commodities. Hull tried to secure a reliable supply of the goods that he wanted for overseas trading ventures by encouraging New England producers to make and sell goods directly to him. Among the first enterprises Hull undertook after receiving the colony's mint contract was an exploration of profitable mining in New England, aided by the General Court's 1641 act "for incouragement of such as will adventure for the discovery of mines."[57] Instead of waiting for customers to bring him Spanish coins to melt down into Boston shillings, a successful mine would give Hull his own source of silver. In 1655, Hull drafted a charter for "a Companie for Mining," in which he, his partner Robert Sanderson, and a dozen other Boston merchants each invested £10 "as an Adventure tending to A search after metals—and upon discovery to get two or more men at worke, to dig into the bowells of the earth." This company never amounted to much because the rumored "royal mynes of gould and silver" never emerged from the bowels of Massachusetts.[58] Two years later, though, Hull joined four investors from Newport in a land venture known as the Pettiquampscut Purchase. They paid £151 to four Narragansett Indian sachems for a tract of land in southeastern Rhode Island, on the western shore of Narragansett Bay. Hull named parts of this region "Boston Neck" and "Point Judith" (after his wife), and initially hoped that it would produce valuable minerals, probably "black lead."

In the seventeenth century, black lead could mean a number of different minerals, including graphite, bismuth, and common lead. But its significance for Hull lay in the alchemical theory that metals were quasi-organic materials that grew in the ground from common "seeds," growing like the roots of plants along veins until they reached the surface of the earth. All metals grew from the same seeds, and different types of metals, and differing degrees of metallic purity, were signs of differing levels of growth and maturity in a vein or branch of metallic development. In particular, the relationship between black lead and silver was thought to be quite close; bismuth was sometimes called *mater argenti* (mother of silver) as it was often found atop silver deposits. In the Netherlands and Germany, metallurgists developed techniques for separating silver from black lead, and much of England's lead-mining industry shipped its products to the Netherlands for smelting. John Winthrop Jr. corresponded frequently with Dutch and German metallurgists, and visited both places on a trip to Europe in the early 1640s in order to learn these secrets for the lead mines he developed at Tantiusques, about sixty-five miles west-southwest of Boston.[59] The hope that black lead would produce silver drove Hull's investment in Point Judith.[60]

In 1662, Samuel Gorton of Rhode Island, a long-standing enemy of Massachusetts, informed Charles II's adviser, the Earl of Clarendon, of the existence of "a mine of black lead, the mint-master of Boston Allowes Six pounds p. tunn to them that did it, and we are informed it is easily comme by, and he keepes . . . eight or nine men at work about it privately in Boston and makes much plate."[61] Gorton was misinformed, or at least overly optimistic about the amount of silver that Hull's mine produced. Point Judith's mines never made a profit, but the investment did allow Hull to develop another aspect of his commercial portfolio.[62] Because Point Judith was a narrow peninsula, Hull suggested a plan to his fellow investors:

> If wee the partners of pointe Juda Necke did fence with a good stone wall at the north End thereof that noe kind of horses nor Cattle might get thereon . . . & procure a verry good breed of

> large & fair mares & stallions & that noe mungrell breed might come among them . . . wee might have a verry choice breed for coach horses some for the saddle some & for the draught others . . . & shipp them for Barbados nevis or such parts of the Indies where they would vend wee might have a vessell made for that service accommodated on purpose to carry of horses to Advantage.[63]

Unlike the mining schemes, this vision of integrated economic growth paid off. Hull had in mind a product (coach horses) with distinctive qualities (large, fair, and no mongrel breeds), prospective market (the rich planters of the West Indies), and special technology (a ship designed to carry horses). He even developed a plan for the charitable uses of the proceeds, consistent with his and the founders' vision of the commonwealth's purposes. Hull employed a manager named William Heiffernan to operate the horse farm at Point Judith, and shipped coach horses to Virginia and Barbados as part of the growing range of goods in his commercial portfolio. In addition, Hull encouraged the establishment of villages of English settlers in this region of Rhode Island and set aside three hundred acres of land, "the income or improvement thereof wholly for an orthodox person that shall be obtained to preach God's word to the inhabitants." This measure would guarantee the further plantation of Massachusetts' orthodox Puritanism in the otherwise-heterodox region of Rhode Island. Hull later donated the land to Harvard College to provide scholarships for boys, either English or Indian, whose parents were too poor to send them to college, especially boys from the Point Judith area.[64]

Hull organized a similar attempt at vertical integration by purchasing heavily timbered lands along the Piscataqua River at Salmon Falls, in present-day New Hampshire, and building a sawmill run by his partners in the venture, Roger Plaisted, Thomas Broughton, and Broughton's sons. By owning his own sawmill, Hull could arrange to have sawn timber floated on rafts down to Portsmouth and loaded directly onto his own ships bound for the West Indies markets.[65] Direct ownership removed the intervening step of buying timber from dealers or other sawmill owners, and Hull used the surplus that his mill produced to supply other overseas merchants at a profit. On October 17, 1673, Hull wrote to his manager, Broughton, saying that "about ten days since arrived Captain Thomas Clarke's ship & he hath earnestly spoken to me this week that he might have boards to load her delivered to him at the place engaged that he might get them rafted down speedily before the frost take the fresh river and I do most importunately request you that this may be attended by drawing all that you have already sawn speedily and by sawing day and night."[66]

The challenge of overseeing these operations often frustrated Hull. Many of his letters complain of slow communications, incompetent or self-serving managers, and the difficulties of coordinating the natural world with market expectations—rivers that froze too early or thawed too late, or prize animals that succumbed to mysterious diseases. But here, too, money, and access to money, eased these problems and gave Hull confidence to assume risks in order to gain rewards. In a letter to Plaisted, Hull pleaded with him to spare no expense to promote the sawmill operation: "These are therefore to Intreat you at this & at all such Seasons as that the laying out of a Penny will preserve a shilling to lay it out freely what ever be at any time. I hereby oblidge myself to be joint partner with you in charge to the valew of five ten twenty thirty pound or if need be fifty. The old proverb is to be minded we cast not loose a hog for a little tar."[67] Hull's curious proverb may no longer resonate today, but the concept it illustrated remains important. Secure access to reliable funding plays a crucial role in bringing stability and confidence to bear in the face of unpredictable market forces. It is this practice, simultaneously conservative and ambitiously expansive, that the pine tree shillings allowed the prudent Hull to pursue.

Captain Hull, "Entreprenour"

So what, exactly, was Hull pursuing? Earlier I described the advantages that silver coins gave Hull in seeking his "personal" fortune. Now I need to revisit this term to indicate the ways that Hull's commercial concerns were closely intertwined with those of the city-state of Boston. It is difficult to say where, or even if, a line between the "personal" and "public" might be drawn. Hull was an "entrepreneur," but in a different sense from what this word means today. Entrepreneur in the modern sense appears in English for the first time only in the nineteenth century. But an older version, sometimes spelled "entreprenour," appeared as early as the fifteenth century. At that time it meant "one who undertakes, a manager, controller," or more intriguingly, a "champion," in the sense that a knight could fight in single combat as a champion representing his realm, or as David slew the giant Goliath, the champion of the Philistines.[68] In the nineteenth century, when the word appears in its modern form, the earliest-recorded instances refer specifically to the manager of a musical institution, one who "gets up" public entertainments. This narrow definition precedes by a full generation the more capacious modern one of a person who owns and manages a business, and takes the risks of profit and loss.

Hull never approached the middle definition. Of all the ventures that Boston's Puritans were involved in, getting up musical entertainments was not among them. Certainly the third definition applies to Hull; he owned and managed many businesses, constantly risking profit and loss. But the archaic definition suits him best: a self-sacrificing undertaker of large enterprises, a champion not only of his own interests but also those of Boston in New England.

Hull began to intertwine his interests with those of the city-state of Boston even before he took control of the mint. In 1648, the Ancient and Honorable Artillery Company, a military organization in Boston, elected Hull as a member. Later that year, he joined the First Church of Boston. His eloquent description of the experience highlights the communal aspects of religious conversion, a process that is often erroneously understood as an individualistic experience:

> It pleased god, not to let me run on alwais in my sinfull way, the end of which is hell, but as he brought me to this good land, soe he planted me under choyse meanes, viz. in Boston under

> the minestrey of mr John Cotton, and in the end did make his minestrey effectual (by the breathings of his owne good spirit) to beget me to god, . . . through his abundant grace, he gave me roome in the hearts of his people soe that I was acepted to fellowship with his church.[69]

Although the pronouns in this statement are difficult to follow, Hull credits the *work* of his conversion to God, acknowledges the *means* through which it happened in the preaching of his minister, Cotton, and defines its *outcome* as a communal act in which the members of the church made room for Hull in their hearts and thereby brought him into church fellowship. Church membership made him eligible for the franchise, and the following year Hull became a freeman of the Massachusetts Bay Colony on May 2, 1649.[70] Hull was already fully vested in church and state when, three years later, his skills as a silversmith and merchant placed him at the vital intersection of personal and state interests as mintmaster.

Over the next three decades, the connections between Hull's personal fortunes and the interests of the state grew ever stronger and more difficult to distinguish one from the other. He gained more responsible offices, serving first as a selectman for the town of Boston, one of seven men chosen annually to administer the town's affairs. Soon thereafter he became the town's treasurer. By 1671, he had advanced from corporal to captain of the Artillery Company and was chosen to be one of Boston's deputies to the General Court, the lower house of the Massachusetts legislature. Later the lower house elected Hull to a seat on the council, the upper house of the colony's legislature, and he became the treasurer of the colony as well. In the early 1660s, the General Court chose Hull and two other men, John Norton, a prominent clergyman, and Simon Bradstreet, magistrate and husband of the poet Anne Dudley Bradstreet, to travel to London as the colony's agents to assess the relationship between New England and the newly restored monarch, Charles II. Essentially, Hull held every prominent office and position of authority in the colony with the exception of governor. Had he lived beyond his fifty-eight years, he would likely have gained that position too.[71] As his responsibilities expanded, Hull grew ever more willing to put his economic resources at the state's disposal because what was good for Boston was also good for Hull.

Perhaps the most difficult indigenous commodities for Boston's merchants to control were furs and hides. These products of the forest remained in steady demand in Europe, but merchants were dependent on Indian hunters and fur processors for their supplies. The vertical integration that Hull arranged for timber and livestock production was next to impossible with furs, given the difficulty of controlling the work habits and economic decisions of independent Indians.[72] Hull could develop a horse farm or sawmill operated by English workers, but not a beaver hunting enterprise, as "these beasts are too cunning for the English, who seldome or never catch any of them; therefore we leave them to those skillful hunters whose time is not so precious."[73] Historians of the fur trade suggest that most of the fur-bearing animals of southern New England were hunted to exhaustion in the first decades of colonization, and that the New England fur trade thus declined dramatically after the 1650s. According to Bernard Bailyn, "The eastern [Massachusetts Bay] fur trade like that of the west [Connecticut Valley] was quickly exploited and exhausted. Its drop in volume after 1660 was sharp; by 1675 it was entirely gone. . . . After King Philip's War the fur trade had no place in the economy of Massachusetts."[74]

The "Letter Book of John Hull" from the 1670s and 1680s tells a different story. Hull continued to ship large loads of forest animal products to his European trading partners. These furs and hides were quite varied, including not only beaver pelts and deerskins but also those of moose, elk, bear, and seals. Hull attended closely to patterns of European demand, noting that the "Russia merchants" wanted unusually thick-furred beaver pelts at certain times of the year and commenting on New England's cold winter conditions that produced these valuable furs.[75] Given the dire sense that furs had all but disappeared by the 1660s as a staple resource for Boston's overseas trade, how was this problem surmounted in later decades?

In the years after 1660, Hull and his fellow Boston merchants faced the challenge that fur-bearing animals within easy reach of southern New England had indeed been overhunted to the point of diminishing returns. It was common knowledge, however, that the neighboring French and Dutch settlements had access to untold quantities of furs by way of the Hudson, Saint Lawrence, and other interior waterways, and northern New England remained untapped as well. Two obstacles limited Boston's access to this trade. One was the native population of southern New England: Wampanoags, Narragansetts, Pocumtucks, Nipmucks, Sokoki, Abenaki, and other Indian groups that stood as middlemen, geographically, diplomatically, and economically, between English colonists and more distant interior Indians with access to furs. The other was the severe limitation that Massachusetts' geographic boundaries placed on Boston's ability to exploit new regions of economic opportunity in the fur trade and agricultural land.

Friends and enemies were equally aware of these obstacles, and of Boston's strategies for surmounting them. In 1661, Samuel Maverick, a critic of Boston after the Massachusetts Bay Colony founders had pushed him aside from his landholdings on Noddle's Island in Boston Harbor, wrote to the Earl of Clarendon following the Restoration of Charles II, with a program for punishing Boston's transgressions. Maverick's recommendations included "that they goe not beyond their just bounds, even those which for neare twentie years they were content withall."[76] Going "beyond their just bounds" describes precisely the strategic plans of Boston's leadership. Remember that in the vertical integration projects that John Hull undertook, both Point Judith and the Penobscot timber mills were located beyond Massachusetts' borders. In 1674, Daniel Gookin, a member of the Massachusetts Council and Superintendent of Indian relations, proposed a bold plan for sending a large and well-equipped expedition of at least fifty Massachusetts colonists, and an unspecified number of "our" praying Indians, to colonize the "great lake of the Iroquois." This quasi-mythical region, somewhere beyond the reach of French and Dutch settlements, was reported to be "not only very fertile, whereby provision is found for so numerous a people, but also they are otherwise furnished with furs and other desirable things." Such an adventure "will be a costly thing," but "may also be greatly advantageous unto the discoverers . . . in accumulating external riches, as well as honour, unto the first undertakers and perfecters of this discovery."[77]

In this light, it is worth considering whether King Philip's War, the bloody conflict between the United Colonies and a loose confederation of New England Indians led by the Wampanoag sachem Metacom, or "King Philip," was fought by the English and planned by Boston's leadership as a war of choice rather than one of necessity. In this ugly and disturbing way, Hull stood as a "champion" of Boston's interests as well. The historian Francis Jennings advanced a version of this argument thirty years ago, and was much criticized for his vitriolic attacks on puritan hypocrisy—or what he called "The Cant of Conquest." In the many subsequent studies of this conflict, few scholars have bothered to examine closely the material preparations that Boston made for fighting a major war in the New England interior without military assistance from the Crown.[78] But the fiscal power generated by the development of Boston's mint, which helped to integrate New England's settler economy with Atlantic markets, also prepared the colony for war with its indigenous neighbors.

Financing King Philip's War

Hull's papers reveal the ways in which the desire of Boston's leadership for access to land and furs may have led to deliberate warfare against indigenous peoples of New England. Hull's account books from his tenure as the Massachusetts treasurer contain detailed fiscal records of the war, including individual payments made to soldiers in militia units.[79] His "Letter Book," too, contains interesting revelations, including the fact that Hull and his fellow Boston merchant, Hezekiah Usher, began importing large numbers of military guns—upward of six hundred firelock muskets and cavalry carbines—eighteen months before the outbreak of war in 1675. In 1673, the

Massachusetts General Court sent orders to England for "five hundred new Snaphances or fire-lock Musketts, for the country's use."[80] On February 2, 1674, Hull wrote to his cousin, Edward Hull, a London merchant and one of his most frequent suppliers, asking for the usual mix of textiles (duffels, flannels, serges, and taffetas), and "alsoe the Country hath desired mr Usser and mee to send for some firelock musketts . . . to the number of one hundred or one hundred and forty such musketts I suppose they may be bought for aboute twelve shillings a piece or under."[81] It may be that the third Anglo-Dutch War, which started in 1672, prompted the purchase of these muskets and other guns. Boston stayed out of the first two Anglo-Dutch Wars, despite parliamentary and Crown efforts to encourage it to attack New Netherland. It was conceivable that this time the war might spread to New England, making military preparations wise. Even after news of peace between England and the Netherlands reached Boston, Hull reduced but did not cancel the orders for muskets.[82] In addition, the General Court placed another order, not from England, but from Bilbao, for sixty cannon or "great guns: twelve whole culverin, twelve demy culverin cutts, sixteen sakers, and twenty or thirty shott, proportionable for each gun." Some historians have assumed that these artillery pieces were meant for coastal defenses, not Indian war. But accounts of King Philip's War describe the English use of artillery to defend fortified inland towns against Indian assaults and in attacking Indian villages defended with palisades.[83]

Later that year, Hull began to include "lead and shott"—used for bullets and projectiles from firearms—among the commodities that he instructed his ship captains to purchase for the colony.[84] In August 1674, he wrote to a London merchant, Thomas Papillon, with ties to the East India Company, making this request: "Iff I have any monies in your hands when these come to your hands please to send it mee in good salt peter by any good vessel bound for Boston soe it exceed not the valew of £50 sterling because we are setting up a powder mill & I would not have them want peter."[85] Saltpeter was used in making gunpowder, which would reduce the colony's reliance on imported powder for self-defense or more aggressive purposes.[86] Hull ordered another fifty pounds of saltpeter from Papillon on January 4, 1675, and suggested that if Papillon could supply the best "Cleare East India peter, . . . good and as cheap as you may afford it," then Hull "may be induced to send for a larger quantity annual." The colony's demand for this critical gunpowder ingredient would be increasing for the foreseeable future.[87] By September 1675, with war now a reality, Hull did place a standing order with Papillon "that when soever salte peter may bee bought at the Cheap at hand to buy me a hundred pounds worth of that which is verry good."[88] As Papillon was not one of Hull's closest London contacts, Hull also wrote to two of his regular merchant factors in London, one of them his cousin Edward, instructing them to pay Papillon directly for the saltpeter with money that Hull had on account.[89] This was Hull's classic approach at work, protecting his credit and securing his purchase in a conservative manner for the sake of his own reputation, while promoting his own and the colony's interests by preparing for military conflict that might expand New England's economic reach.

By the mid-1670s, the potential for warfare among Indian and European competitors had been mounting for several years. In 1669, a group of Massachusetts Indians, with little support from Boston authorities, marched westward into New York territory and besieged a Mohawk village. The siege failed, and the Mohawks killed many Massachusetts Indians in the aftermath.[90] This event was part of a long-running war between the Algonkian Indians of the New England interior, many of whom had gradually come within the orbit of Boston, and the Mohawks, who sought to dominate and extract tribute from these regions. This war was finally resolved by negotiation in 1671. In that year, however, long-standing conflicts between the Wampanoags of southern New England and Plymouth Colony, whose population continued to expand into Wampanoag territory on the eastern shore of Narragansett Bay, stirred rumors that Metacom, the Wampanoags' headman, known to the English as "King Philip," was planning a pan-Indian uprising.

Metacom adopted the name Philip in 1660 as he and his people became ever more intertwined with the English colonists. He was the second son of Massasoit, the Wampanoag chief with whom the "Pilgrims" of the Plymouth Colony had maintained long-lasting and peaceable relations. Metacom's older brother took the name "Alexander"—yet another instance of the power of the Philippi metaphor in framing this colonial enterprise. Philip and Alexander were, of course, the names of the sons of King Philip of Macedon, the founder of the ancient city-colony of Philippi; Alexander went on to become the world-conquering Alexander the Great. By bestowing these classical names on Massasoit's sons, the puritan colonists were implying that Massasoit's Wampanoag people, like the original Philippians, were destined to become a Christian community and the seedbed for the conversion of a new continent. For a considerable period, Philip, who became headman after his brother Alexander died in 1662, cooperated with this project, wearing English clothes and participating in colonial commercial life by raising pigs, which he drove to market in Boston. Numerous Wampanoag people joined some of the fourteen praying towns organized by John Eliot and other puritan missionaries to inculcate English farming and lifeways among converted Indians. But the ceaseless encroachment of the growing colonial population on Indian lands created frequent conflicts—always adjudicated by the colonists' courts—that led to the steady deterioration of these relationships.[91]

When war did begin in 1675, the specific events that prompted it took place in Philip's home territory, Mount Hope, east of Narragansett Bay in what is now Bristol, Rhode Island, and involved mainly Plymouth and Wampanoag casus belli: the murder of an Indian named John Sassamon, who was friendly to the English and had warned them of Philip's potential hostility. There is every reason to believe that this initial outbreak of violence between Plymouth and Philip's Wampanoags grew out of the mounting tension between Plymouth's expanding population of farmers and the shrinking resources of their Wampanoag neighbors.[92] I am not arguing that Plymouth initiated war with Philip for larger strategic purposes; in fact, with the powerful rise of Massachusetts Bay to economic and political leadership of the United Colonies, Plymouth's own aims were limited to finding land for its settlers in the unpromising soil of Plymouth and Cape Cod.[93] Nevertheless, the immediate causes of the fighting did not dictate Boston's response to the fact that war had begun.

Instead of directing forces to the aid of Plymouth in putting down Philip's Wampanoag rebellion on the *eastern* shores of Narragansett Bay, Massachusetts took the lead in organizing the United Colonies for a general response to the situation. In late fall 1675, soldiers were sent from Boston to join Plymouth and Connecticut troops on the *western* side of Narragansett Bay. (See plate 10.)

There they attacked the homeland of the Narragansett Indians, not the Wampanoags, in a manner highly reminiscent of the Pequot War of 1637, destroying a major Narragansett settlement and killing more women and children than male warriors. For decades, leading Boston merchants and land investors, Hull among them, had been trying to gain ownership and political control of the Narragansett country. The outbreak of Indian war, regardless of its cause or original location, afforded them an opportunity.[94]

Once the war began, events quickly spun out of Boston's control. Philip succeeded in creating an unprecedented alliance among formerly competing Indian groups. The war spread in many directions—westward to the Connecticut Valley and beyond, and later north and eastward to the New Hampshire and Maine frontiers. Through late 1675 and into 1676, Philip and his allies repeatedly attacked the more distant settlements from Boston within Massachusetts proper, burning and destroying dozens of English towns. English armies likewise ravaged dozens more Indian villages and fields. Thousands died on all sides of the conflict (probably far more Indians than English), which dragged on for almost four years, including two years beyond August 1676, when English forces under Benjamin Church killed Philip. Philip's death brought the fighting in southern New England to an end, but shifted the theater of warfare to the north and east.[95] Remarkably, despite the unprecedented danger and expense of the war, and despite (or perhaps because of) the intense scrutiny of the Restoration monarchy, Boston and the United Colonies never petitioned the Crown for assistance. Instead, the Massachusetts General Court created the

Committee for the War to direct military operations and underwrite their expenses, naming Hull as its treasurer.[96]

The credit networks built by Hull over his thirty years as a merchant, augmented by his access to silver, made an enormous difference in Boston's capacity to conduct the war. By the terms of the charter of the United Colonies, Massachusetts' contribution of soldiers and material to any military effort was substantially larger than those of Plymouth or Connecticut (the formerly independent New Haven had been subsumed under Connecticut's authority in a patent that Winthrop Jr. negotiated with Charles II). Massachusetts' larger population provided the rationale for this distribution, but with numbers came power, and Boston's fiscal leadership therefore had considerable decision-making authority as well. In September 1675, in preparation for the Narragansett assault, the United Colonies voted to raise 1,000 soldiers for the mission (527 from Massachusetts, 315 from Connecticut, and 158 from Plymouth). Hull negotiated the complex arrangements for purchasing and distributing the weapons, food, clothing, and transportation necessary to put an army in the field. Two months later, in November, a second 1,000-man army was called up. Two thousand soldiers, from a population of roughly 70,000, was a high percentage by European standards, putting perhaps 1 out of every 8 men of military age in the field. The demand for troops required that the colonies shift from volunteer soldiers to a system of impressment, whereby each town was responsible for sending an assigned number of soldiers to serve in each colony's contingent.[97]

As his account books reveal, Hull personally managed the payment of the soldiers. In addition to this meticulous work, Hull put his personal resources, both credit abroad and cash at home, at the colony's disposal. Along with the guns and saltpeter described above, his "Letter Book" shows orders sent to London for "two or three tuns of lead" along with "three pair of choice moulds to cast bullets," and "flat steel Pinzcers to trim ym when out of ye Mould."[98] Hull's correspondence with John Flint of Concord, one of the commissaries for the war, describes the distribution network for moving the goods that he imported into the soldiers' hands and the accounting system for charging soldiers the cost of equipment out of their military wages. Flint was ordered to distribute food for the troops "with what prudence you can, yt no waste may be made thereof." With respect to the soldiers' clothing, Hull ordered Flint that "you must in an Alpabetical order set down each souldier's name, & what he hath of you, & under whose Command he is, yt they may have it deducted out of their wages."[99] A similar correspondence developed with John Pynchon of Springfield, a leading merchant and power broker in the Connecticut Valley. Hull sent Pynchon large shiploads of clothing, weapons, barrels of gunpowder, and "twenty hundred of leade" for the soldiers, saying, "Good sir by all means take care that the westcoats drawes shoes stockings etc d[elivere]d to the souldiery may bee carefully by an officer for that end appointed put down to each man that when they come to receive their money for wages they may be deducted."[100]

Hull's accounting practices were not those of modern commerce. Although double-entry bookkeeping had been invented long before by European merchants and bankers, Hull was self-trained and kept simple accounts, essentially a running tab with each of his clients, recording his debts and credits with each of his many correspondents, near and far. For the duration of his term as treasurer, Hull simply added the colony of Massachusetts and the various merchants and suppliers from whom the colony purchased goods as another set of clients on his list, mingling his "private" mercantile affairs with those of the "public" trust he now served.[101] This mingling was not, in any way, a dishonest attempt to use public funds for his personal gain. Rather, it was a simple extension of the fact that in Hull's mind, and in his commercial practices, the distinction between his personal fortunes and those of the state was blurry at best, and in the larger scheme of things, relatively meaningless.

Hull's credit, and that of a handful of other Boston merchants, financed the war effort. At the war's beginning, the colony was already in debt to Hull for about £700. By the end of 1675, after the organization of the thousand-man army for its assault on the Narragansett country, the colony's debt to Hull had increased to nearly £1,000. By the end of the southern phase of the war in summer 1676, it was over £1,300. Indeed, by Hull's reckoning, from the time he became the treasurer of the Committee on the War, the colony's debt to him was "seldom less than 15 or £1600."[102] Some of this debt arose as direct payments Hull made to the soldiers to keep armies in the field.

Beyond these direct payments, Hull supervised the collection of the "country rates" or taxes on the towns that the Massachusetts General Court imposed to fund the war. Despite the thousands of shillings that Hull had produced over the years, it was inevitable that large amounts of these wartime taxes (exceptionally high by historic Massachusetts standards) would be paid not in money but in farm products.[103] Part of Hull's duties involved the marketing or redistribution of these in-kind payments to finance the war. Hull absorbed some of the war's costs through the "invisible" work and the credit relationships necessary to convert bushels of corn, barrels of salted meat, or even large and unruly animals into cash or credit on London markets.[104] All this took time away from his ordinary business, as he wrote to Philip French, a fellow merchant, explaining his seeming neglect of commercial affairs: "Wee haue had trouble with the Indians & my time hath bene most taken up to provide for and pay souldiers & when it will be over wee cannot as yet see."[105] The work came with frustrations known to quartermasters and supply chiefs throughout history. A large order for muskets and carbines from his cousin Edward Hull "came competently safe only sundrey of them were Crooked in the b[arrel]s and slight, theire breech pins loose, their screw pins not big enough, & all or most of them old locks, the lock smith with faire words I am afraid cheate you."[106] By January 1677, as the war moved from southern New England to the northeastern frontier, Hull wrote to his cousin Daniel Quincy in England that "I fear I shall not be able to send you anything before you come away, for my own Money is exhausted for the Countrey."[107]

Dealing in the Spoils of War

Among the disturbing tasks that Hull undertook as treasurer for the Committee on the War involved managing the Indians captured by English forces. In some cases, women and children captives were placed as indentured servants or slaves in the homes of English or loyal Indian families. More often than not, especially when the captives were adult male warriors, Boston sold its prisoners to slave or labor markets in distant places around the Atlantic world.[108] This was a common practice based on the assumption that the deracination of captured soldiers would limit their potential for destructive violence and maximize their labor value. It echoed an English practice from earlier decades when, during Britain's civil wars, Scottish prisoners of war were sold into indentured servitude in the colonies both as punishment and to remove these dangerous enemies from Britain.[109]

But in the case of New England Indians during King Philip's War, English colonists' abilities to distinguish between "friend" and "enemy" Indians tended to blur. While the United Colonies ordered that captive enemy Indians be held in internment camps, in other cases friendly Indians were similarly grouped together in encampments. One such camp on Deer Island in Boston Harbor was ostensibly for the safety of friendly Indians from the threat of indiscriminate English retaliation. Yet it was not uncommon for slave kidnappers, unscrupulous profit seekers in the Atlantic labor market, to snatch from the camps any Indians they could get their hands on, friend or foe, for sale to Bermuda, Barbados, Jamaica, or other places of high labor demand. In at least one instance, Massachusetts legislation that prohibited "manstealing" allowed a group of Indian petitioners to demonstrate that several Englishmen had kidnapped friendly Indians and sold them as slaves in the Azores. In a measure reminiscent of the *Rainbow* case of the mid-1640s, when Massachusetts ordered the return of two kidnapped Africans to their homeland, the General Court sent agents to the Azores to try to redeem the kidnapped Indians and restore them to Massachusetts.[110]

The only defense that can be made of Hull's engagement in this practice is that it may have been the least bad of his options. As the war grew in geographic reach and ferocity, most of the New England colonies passed legislation making it illegal to keep captive Indians, especially males of military age, as household servants within New England. At the same time, many of West Indian colonies, including the larger slave markets such as Barbados and Jamaica, began to prohibit the importation of captives from King Philip's War. Eventually, the only legal option remaining was to send captives to destinations such as Spain, Portugal, the Azores, and Madeira, well out of the orbit of England's colonies. The few people who possessed the shipping capacity, logistical know-how, and commercial connections to these destinations were large-scale transatlantic merchants like John Hull.[111]

An early instance of this practice surfaces in the letter to fellow merchant Philip French cited above. Hull told French that he was outfitting a ship under the command of one of Hull's regular captains, Mr. Richard Sprague, for a "venture to Cades [Cadiz] and Malaga to get a fraite home & shall have above one hundred Indians to carry there to a market."[112] Hull's account books from the following year reveal the extent of this trade in greater detail. On two occasions, August 24 and September 23, 1676, Hull recorded the sale of Indian captives to various Boston purchasers; as treasurer, these were among the colony's accounts that Hull supervised.[113] There were at least thirty-two different purchasers, among them a woman, Ann Shepcutt. In the first of these two lists, Hull recorded details about the Indian captives: their sex, their age, and sometimes their size or physical condition, such as the "4 Squawes, 3 girls, 2 infants" purchased by Samuel Shrimpton, or even names, such as the "2 Lads, Viz. Pomham & Matoonas," purchased by Thomas Smith.[114] Of the 77 captives sold on August 24, 48 were listed as women or girls, and another 15 as "infants" or "small children" with no mention of their sex. This leaves only 14 of the 77 definitely listed as male. Of these 14, 9 are called "boys" or "lads," and another is described as an "old man," which suggests that only 4 of the 77 were healthy adult males. Most of these sales were to buyers purchasing 1 or 2 slaves, making it likely that this lot was destined for slavery as domestic or small-scale agricultural workers. These were mainly women and children who posed little threat of insurrection, and who could be put to work in homes, gardens, or other forms of domestic manual labor.

But other merchants had different aims, looking to enter the Atlantic slave trade on a larger scale. Smith purchased 29 slaves in this lot, including 3 of the 4 adult men listed as well as the 2 named "lads," Pomham and Matoonas. In the next sale of captives on September 23, Smith purchased another 41 captives. In recording this second sale, Hull did not list the personal qualities of the captives, merely the numbers sold to each purchaser. Here many of the purchases were larger. In addition to Smith's 41 captives, other Boston merchants such as James Whitcomb, Richard Wharton, and Benjamin Gibbs bought lots large enough—respectively, 13, 8, and 8—to suggest that these captives may have been adult male warriors to be sold into Atlantic markets in places such as Cadiz or Malaga, where Hull had sent "above one hundred" Indians the year before.[115] Although smaller in scale, Boston was thus not altogether different from the slave-trading stations of West Africa such as Cape Coast Castle. Captives from King Philip's War were sequestered at the fortress on Castle Island in Boston Harbor, visible from the town. When purchase arrangements were made onshore among merchant brokers and ship captains, the slaves for export were loaded on ships and sent out of the harbor, never to return. Altogether, the colony took in £333, 3s for the sale of 185 captives in 1676. Perhaps some of its debt to the colony treasurer, John Hull, may have been reduced from these sales. (See plate 11.)

Thomas Smith, the largest purchaser and distributor of slaves, was the same Captain Smith who painted seventeenth-century Boston's most famous self-portrait. Smith was one of Hull's peers in Boston; Hull brought his young son-in-law, Samuel Sewall, to meet Captain Smith and "see the manner of the Merchants" when Sewall was first considering a commercial career.[116] Perhaps more significant, Smith had considerable experience in trade along the coasts of North Africa, West Africa, and the Iberian Peninsula. The naval battle raging in the background of Smith's self-portrait appears to depict Dutch and English ships fighting in the vicinity of a Muslim port city, indicated by the yellow and white crescents visible in the red flags above the fortress.[117] Among Hull's and Smith's other merchant colleagues was Captain Thomas Savage, who also sat for a Smith portrait, and who as a major general in King Philip's War, played a major role in acquiring the captives that Hull sold and Smith shipped out into the Atlantic. The silver thread that decorated the lace collars and cuffs that Smith, Savage, and Hull wore around their necks and wrists was intimately linked to the metalwork—chains and handcuffs—around the necks and wrists of the captives they sold in the Atlantic slave markets, and to the coins they made and used in the transactions that smoothed the way for these brutal and exploitative purposes.[118]

Insofar as Hull and merchants like him on the Massachusetts General Court were responsible for crafting the legislation that made keeping adult male Indian captives within the region illegal, this defense of the trade in Indian captives is really no defense at all. The fact of the matter is that there was little here to distinguish Boston's behavior from that of the so-called Barbary pirates feared throughout the Atlantic world for enslaving their victims or the West African slave traders who sold captives of African warfare into the Atlantic plantation complex. King Philip's War and its aftermath brought a devastating defeat to the commonwealth ideals of Boston's founders, and an end to the utopian dreams of John Eliot, Daniel Gookin, and other advocates of Indian inclusion in the city-state of Boston.

As destructive as the war may have been to the English and Indians of southern New England, the immediate postwar period saw a boom in the fur trade. In that sense, Boston's commercial leaders got what they wanted out of this strategic plan. Gookin's idea for a joint Anglo-Indian project to colonize the Great Lake of the Iroquois was never realized. But the human and territorial impediments to accessing the trans-Hudson and northeastern fur resources were removed by the destruction of the military capacity of central New England's Indians and by the advance of Boston's interests on the northeastern frontier of New Hampshire and Maine. After 1676, beaver and hides began to appear far more frequently in Hull's overseas export cargoes. In September 1678, he sent one of his regular London merchant correspondents a cargo that included 479 moose skins and several barrels of beaver and other furs.[119] In January 1679, Hull wrote to a correspondent in New York asking that an outstanding debt be paid directly in beaver pelts rather than in money as "I haue had more occasion for Beavrs then ordinary in this two yeares past."[120]

Boston's money, the silver shilling, had done its job. The coins had been a critical element in expanding the geographic reach and economic power of Boston into the hinterland, and that expansion was yielding its reward. Beaver was what Hull wanted for his overseas trading partners, and now beaver was once again something that he could get as a result of the colony's gains in King Philip's War, financed through the careful management of New England's cash and credit. New England's silver currency and the trade relationships across the region that it fostered had been designed to stimulate ever-greater production from the countryside, including a far more wide-ranging fur-gathering economy than in the colony's early years. Beaver furs were better than Boston shillings to send to England, and now that the war had been won, beaver were again within reach.

Independence and Allegiance in the Land of the Shilling

Hannah Hull's wedding to Samuel Sewall took place on February 28, 1676, at the height of King Philip's War, to which John Hull committed his resources and personal credit. The wedding occurred just two weeks after the raid on Lancaster, Massachusetts, in which Mary Rowlandson, wife of the town's minister, was taken captive, famously memorialized in Rowlandson's narrative of her ordeal. After nearly three months in captivity, she was ransomed on May 2 and returned to her family, and expressed her gratitude that the twenty pounds that the ransom cost was "raised by some Boston gentlemen and Mrs. Usher, whose bounty and religious charity I would not forget to make mention of."[121] It's likely that John Hull would have been among those Boston gentlemen. Mrs. Usher was the widow of Hezekiah Usher, Hull's friend and fellow merchant, with whom he had worked to purchase munitions before King Philip's War. Usher was a fellow founder of the Third Church of Boston, and at Usher's death, Hull had inscribed a silver cup with

Usher's initials as a gift to the Third Church's collection of communion silver.[122]

There would be no ransom money forthcoming from King Philip and his fellow Indian warriors to redeem their own captives taken in the war. Three months later, Hull would oversee the sale of another two hundred captives into the labor markets of Spain—Cadiz and Malaga—two stops among the myriad links in an expanding chain of Atlantic commercial contacts that Hull and his colleagues had forged over the preceding three decades. The silver thread that linked Potosí to Boston through places like Cadiz and Malaga, Barbados and Jamaica, had been spun into a network of credit among overseas merchants operating at a distance, based on faith and trust as much as on reserves of silver. The trickle of silver flowing into Boston had been melted down and remade into the small change that accelerated the domestic economy of New England. Economic growth made it possible for the city-state of Boston to develop internally at the same time as it expanded its external reach. This process linked the interests of the farmers of Boston's hinterland and the fishermen of its remote coastal regions into a unit of political economy remarkable for its internal solidarity and resilience.

In 1676, the same year of the twin weddings that began this chapter, the English colony at Virginia tore itself apart over Bacon's Rebellion, borne of issues quite similar to those Boston faced: conflict between settler expansion and Indian landownership. But in Virginia, what began as violent attacks on Indian settlements turned to an internal rebellion when Governor William Berkeley denounced Nathaniel Bacon and his backcountry supporters as rebels. Bacon's and his men's desire for land ran counter to the policies of Berkeley and the Virginia Tidewater elite, who already had large plantations and secure incomes from tobacco, and saw no reason to conduct expensive and dangerous Indian wars on the frontier. Named a rebel, Bacon became one, leading his army of supporters to Jamestown, where they burned the capital, destroyed Berkeley's estate, and forced the governor to flee to the eastern shore. King Charles II sent a force of a thousand soldiers along with three royal commissioners to restore the peace and resolve the internal conflicts in Virginia. It took them several years to fully suppress the resistance.[123]

Bostonians knew about these events in the Chesapeake. Hull had to change his plans for trade there, writing to one of his correspondents, "Here is newes come in from Virginia that they are more furiously engaged one against another then formerly. They tell us James's town is burned, and sundrey slain, so yt several intended for those parts do intend to lay aside the beginnings of such a voyage."[124] Bacon's Rebellion exposed deep conflicts between the planter elite of Virginia and laborers whom they wished to exploit—a division that would grow deeper as African slave labor slowly replaced English indentured servants in the decades to come.[125]

King Philip's War in New England was probably more brutal than Bacon's Rebellion in terms of the level of violence between Indians and English, and in the destruction done to human lives and property.[126] And the war did expose fault lines among the colonists over the status of Indian converts to puritan Christianity and whether English Christian identity could really be extended to the indigenous population. But King Philip's War also demonstrated how tightly integrated the interests of New England's colonists had become as a result of the deliberate development of a regional political economy that linked the productive success of the region's farmers to the mercantile interests of Boston's commercial leaders.

Not only was there nothing in New England comparable to Virginia's backlash of poor and disenfranchised white workers against Virginia's elites, but King Philip's War actually strengthened solidarity among colonial groups within New England. The United Colonies successfully ran a conscription campaign, recruiting the poor from towns all over the region to fight in its cause and raising taxes to pay their salaries. Rhode Island's support for the war and the United Colonies' willingness to fight on behalf of Rhode Island mark other examples of this solidarity. When Providence was attacked and burned by Philip's forces, Boston rescinded its banishment of Roger Williams from four decades earlier, so that the venerable Rhode Island patriarch could take refuge in the Bay Colony.[127] Most significant, despite the fact that the violence and potential for destruction of the entire colonial enterprise was considerably greater in New England during King Philip's War than in Virginia under Bacon's Rebellion, the authorities in Boston never turned to the Crown for assistance during the crisis. Instead, the challenge of Philip and his Indian alliance was defeated entirely by homegrown soldiers, both volunteers and conscripts, led by local generals (some of them experienced in England's wars *against* the king in the 1640s) and financed by the colony's own resources.

The sacrifice of thousands of indigenous people to the internal expansion of the city-state of Boston was the dark and bloody outcome of this process. This was the most flagrant and indefensible violation of the commonwealth principles that Boston and the United Colonies otherwise espoused. Boston's leaders committed gross injustices to loyal Christian Indians, many of whom were interned on Deer Island during the war, ostensibly for their safety, but greatly to their misery. The bloody fighting inspired growing hatred of Indians among many of the English. Despite all these outrages, there were nonetheless substantial numbers of Christian Indians who had adopted English ways and fought for the English colonies during the war, demonstrating the extent of their own integration into the political economy of Boston.[128]

FIGURE 2.3. (a and b) Peace medal, Massachusetts Bay Colony, bronze alloy, 1676.

During the war, longtime supporters of Indian missions such as Eliot, Gookin, Thomas Danforth, and John Cotton Jr. worked diligently to maintain distinctions among Indian groups and protect those loyal to English ways.[129] Of course, it could often be difficult to tell friend from enemy Indians, especially for those English colonists who encountered Indians infrequently.[130] To solve this problem, the Massachusetts General Court turned to lessons well learned. On June 20, 1676, it held a council at Charlestown, across the river from Boston, and presented a brass medallion, made to resemble a sort of coin, to the Christian Indian soldiers fighting in its cause. On one side, the coin had an image of an Indian, based on the Great Seal of the Massachusetts Bay Company, and on the other, a vaguely poetic inscription signed by Edward Rawson of Boston, the colony's secretary: "In the present Warr with the Heathen Natives of this Land / They giving us peace and mercy at their hands." This was a sad commentary on the hopeful image of the Macedonian who summoned Paul to "Come Over and Help Us"—a phrase nowhere to be found on this medallion. Perhaps Hull and his fellow Boston merchants might have justified their actions with the thought that like Paul in Philippi, New England's Puritans had located the few potential converts among the Indians, and that the rest of the native population were like so many Roman soldiers, whose customs could not be reconciled to Christian ways. But to the Christian Indians who received them, the medallion sent a clear message: to identify yourself with the city-state of Boston, it was good to wear its coin around your neck.

Chapter 3

Boston Pays Tribute

The Political Trials of an Expanding City-State

> It is ordered, that ye two very large masts now on board Capt Peirce his ship . . . be presented to his maj[es]ty . . . as a testimony of loyalty and affection from ye country, & that all charge thereof be paid out of the country treasury.
>
> —Massachusetts General Court, 1666

Boston's desire for territorial expansion, driven by the perception that its charter boundaries were too small to provide land for its colonists and resources for its economy, caused violence among the competing political forces within the New England region. The Pequot War of 1637 and King Philip's War in 1675–78 were products of this same expansive impulse. But Boston's drive to expand created conflict in other spheres as well. The original charter of the Massachusetts Bay Company was in every way ideal for promoting the colony's autonomy, except for the amount of land that it granted. Sustaining this autonomy remained a goal throughout the seventeenth century. Although the charter had been the gift of Charles I, Boston viewed it as a license to evade the authority of the king, and after the Restoration of the monarchy in 1660, the authority of his sons, Charles II and James II, as well. Had the land grant defined in the charter been large and rich enough to furnish the productive hinterland that Boston needed, evading royal authority might have been easy. Instead, other plantations whose settlers saw the Stuarts as their benefactors and did not share Boston's desire for independence bounded the Massachusetts Bay Colony to the north and east. Whenever Boston risked conflict with its neighbors for the sake of expansion, it also risked the political consequences that Crown intervention in the dispute might bring.[1]

During the 1640s, English royal authority was distracted by civil war and then collapsed altogether. The execution of Charles I left Parliament and Oliver Cromwell to rule from 1649 to 1660. Boston took advantage of the absence of Crown oversight to solve some of the problems caused by its narrow charter limits. The creation of the United Colonies in the mid-1640s united most of southern New England into a confederation of allies with Boston in the dominant political, military, and economic role.[2] This achievement was fostered by the fact that the southern New England colonies of Connecticut, New Haven, and Plymouth shared most of Boston's fundamental religious and political allegiances; Connecticut and New Haven were themselves, at least in part, colonies of Massachusetts, and graduates of Harvard College soon began to fill church pulpits in the older Plymouth Colony. The political organization of Rhode Island was so chaotic as to pose little threat to Boston's hegemony. As a result, Boston settlers and investors gained access to land and resources in southern New England in the years after the Pequot War, even when political control remained out of their hands. King Philip's War further enhanced these territorial gains, as the previous chapter described.[3]

This chapter turns from Boston's economic and political integration of the southern New England hinterland to its efforts to expand its political influence to the north and east. The previous chapter focused on Boston's efforts at internal economic integration and their destructive consequences for Indian relations through the cataclysm of King Philip's War in the 1670s. Here I first circle back in time to trace Boston's early external relationships with its competitor colonies to the northeast, and then follow the escalating conflicts that emerge between colony and Crown in the wake of the Restoration of 1660. The region beyond Massachusetts' boundary north of the Merrimack River proved to be a difficult challenge in the era of the Stuart Restoration. An overlapping patchwork of patents and land grants held by various English aristocrats and colonial promoters predated the claims of Massachusetts Bay. The holders of these earlier claims, some with close ties to the royal court, shared few of Boston's sympathies for religious dissent and independence from the Crown. During the civil wars and interregnum, Massachusetts took advantage of the demise of royal authority to extend its influence deeply into these regions, asserting itself as an independent city-state more strongly than ever. But after the Restoration of Charles II to the throne in 1660, the former claimants to these northeastern regions attempted to reassert their authority in the expectation of royal support. Consequently, the quarter century following the Restoration saw the rise of a complex political contest—a delicate dance around the issues of economic control, territorial authority, and governmental autonomy that led to a major crisis in the 1680s.

In effect, two of the principal goals of Boston's seventeenth-century political economy, its need for autonomy and its desire for expansion, did not sit well together. The best way for Boston to remain free of Crown interference or conflict with neighboring powers would have been to remain quiet, not to expand. But that would have been destructive of the economic and political autonomy that this Atlantic trading state needed to survive. Consequently, Boston dealt with the notoriety and opposition that arose from its expansionist policies through the use of the twin tools of diplomacy and tribute—by rendering what tribute was necessary unto Caesar, while maintaining its authority over the godly commonwealth. The Crown's attacks on Boston's autonomy grew more and more strident in the three decades after the Restoration, testing whether Boston's tribute money could keep Caesar at bay.

Absorbing the Eastern Frontier

The confused and overlapping legal claims for the territory northeast of Massachusetts were the product of the haphazard workings of the New England Council. This was an organization of a small group of noblemen and colonial organizers, created in 1620 by King James I to administer the northern parts of England's extensive claims to the Atlantic Seaboard, a region that was then still referred to generally as "Virginia."[4] The most dynamic figure on the Council was Sir Ferdinando Gorges, an Elizabethan courtier and soldier, friend and contemporary of Sir Walter Ralegh. Gorges saw northern "Virginia" as a place to develop new overseas domains on a feudal model, imagining the settlers working the lands and seacoasts of present-day Maine as tenants providing revenue to their noble patron.[5] In 1622, the council granted Gorges and his ally, Captain John Mason, a patent for the province of Maine, the region between the Merrimack and the Kennebec Rivers. In 1629, Gorges and Mason divided this region, with Mason taking title to the area south and west of the Piscataqua River. Mason's portion was called New Hampshire, while Gorges renamed his portion, north and east of the Piscataqua, New Somersetshire.[6]

Mason's and Gorges's patents, however, conflicted with the territory granted to Massachusetts in its own charter, which defined the Bay Colony's northern boundary as a line three miles north of the Merrimack River. At a minimum, both Massachusetts and New Hampshire claimed this three-mile-wide strip lying north of the Merrimack. But the exploration of New England soon revealed that the Merrimack's course, roughly east-west for the first forty miles from the coast, turns at that point sharply northward for nearly one hundred miles to its source in present-day northern New Hampshire. This discovery of the Merrimack's northern origins became the basis for Boston's subsequent claim that it was entitled to expand northward far into the territories also claimed by Mason and Gorges. If the northern boundary of the Merrimack is taken to be at its *source* in the New Hampshire hills rather than its *mouth* at the Atlantic Ocean, thirty-five miles north of Boston, then the northern boundary of Massachusetts would lie much farther north than originally believed, beyond even the Kennebec River where the Gorges patent reached its northern end. In short, legal title to the northern New England coast was deeply contested because of these confusing patents and charters. (See plate 12.)

The numbers and allegiances of the colonists who settled the Gorges and Mason plantations would prove to be far more powerful than lines on maps or paper charters in the ultimate determination of authority over the region. The rapid settlement of

Massachusetts Bay in the 1630s and the concentration of a large portion of its initial population on the coast north of Boston quickly put pressure on the trans-Merrimack territory as an outlet for newcomers seeking land, and Boston-based colonists moved northward. Massachusetts also created an attractive structure for land distribution. Its incorporated towns gave colonists freehold title to their lands, free of any rents or obligations due to the Crown or landlords. By contrast, Gorges and Mason retained restrictive control on the land grants they issued to settlers in their territories, acting more like feudal proprietors who expected annual fees or quitrents from their subjects, and they also expected to retain a strong hand in governing their colonies from afar.[7]

Their approach to the northeastern settlements might have succeeded had conditions in England remained stable enough for Gorges and Mason to attend to colonial affairs. But the intensifying struggles between King Charles and Parliament in the 1630s, descending into civil war in the 1640s, prevented these courtier-proprietors from asserting their authority, and developing the economies of New Hampshire and Maine. As a result, the motley groups of colonists that occupied the Gorges and Mason patents gradually came to embrace the idea that government by Massachusetts was in their best interests. The death of Captain Mason in 1635, just as he was preparing his first voyage to his colony, left the inhabitants of New Hampshire rudderless. They formed their own voluntary governmental associations in the four towns or "plantations" that had emerged in the region: Dover, Portsmouth, Exeter, and Hampton. By 1641, all four towns had agreed to incorporate themselves with Massachusetts, gaining all the rights and privileges of other Massachusetts towns, including representation at the General Court in Boston and inclusion in the judicial system of the Bay Colony.[8]

Similar events led to the absorption of Maine's settlements by Massachusetts, though the details were more complex and the process was slower.[9] After Mason's death, Gorges arranged for the New England Council to grant him a new patent for the entire province of Maine (including Mason's New Hampshire). But his supervision of the settlers of this region faltered as he grew distracted by

England's civil wars. In the power vacuum of the late 1630s, some ambitious settlers of the Maine territory attempted to establish their own colonial project called the province of Lygonia. Conflict between these upstarts and Gorges's agents over land and authority ensued. Through the later years of the 1640s, with Parliament and the Crown at war, these feuding plantations in Maine turned increasingly to Massachusetts and its reliable courts as the only authority available to resolve their disputes. Encouraged by agents sent from Boston who helped local land claimants settle their conflicts, the Maine plantations one by one voted to accept government under Massachusetts. By 1658, the last holdouts in Lygonia agreed to join the city-state of Boston as well.[10]

The General Court in Boston now had direct (if ad hoc) authority over the entire region from Massachusetts Bay to the Kennebec River, complementing the influence that it had gained over southern New England through the formation of the United Colonies. Massachusetts had already been the dominant partner within the New England Confederation, and the acquisition of these new regions made it all the more powerful. By the late 1650s, the city-state of Boston had expanded the territory of its hinterland, and gained control of the resources that it needed for growth and prosperity. It had also extended its commercial power even further than its territorial control. The English fisheries as far off as Newfoundland were by this time essentially commercial outposts of Boston, not of English ports: "They chiefly consume the products of New England, ye Shipping of which Country furnishes them with French Wine and Brandy, and Madeira Wines in exchange for their Fish without depending for any supply from England."[11] As the prior claims of aristocrats like Mason and Gorges receded, Boston's independent authority over the northern New England coast grew stronger.

Restoration, Rendition, and Tribute

If Boston's 1652 decision to coin its own high-grade silver money stands out as one claim to sovereignty, this expansion to the northeast reveals another. As Massachusetts established authority over the Maine and New Hampshire region, the colony required all landowners who wished to be freemen in the commonwealth to swear an oath of allegiance, not to the Crown or Parliament, but to the General Court of Massachusetts.[12] Parliament enacted the first of its Navigation Acts in 1651, insisting that colonial trade be confined to English or colonial ports, and conducted by English or colonial ships, preventing the free trade with ships of other nations. Boston ignored it, refusing to enact the law within the colony. Even in the face of severe pressure from the Crown in later years, the General Court continued to maintain

> that for the acts passed in Parliament for incouraging trade and navigation, wee humbly conceive, according to the usuall sayings of the learned in the lawe, that the lawes of England are bounded wthin the fower seas, and doe not reach America. The subjects of his majte here being not represented in Parliament, so wee have not looked at ourselves to be impeded in our trade by them.[13]

Far from condescending to obey Parliament's Navigation Acts, Massachusetts created its own system of mercantile inspections and customs duties, charging excise taxes on imported wine, rum, and other goods, including those imported directly from England.[14]

During the interregnum between the execution of Charles I in 1649 and Restoration of Charles II in 1660, the de facto sovereignty of Massachusetts over most of New England went unchallenged, as openly proclaimed by John Hull's shillings; their superscription of "Massachusetts in New England" identified the "Caesar" to whom these coins belonged. But after 1660, Charles II demanded a reckoning of the conduct of his colonies. This was the moment at which Boston's many enemies, especially those whose land and authority the Bay Colony had usurped, petitioned the new king for redress of their grievances. Chief among these claimants were Robert Mason and Ferdinando Gorges the younger, each a grandson of the original proprietors of New Hampshire and Maine, respectively. For the next two decades, they would strive to reclaim their ancestral holdings.[15]

Sir Thomas Temple represented Massachusetts' interests at the Restoration court. He lived in Boston in the late 1650s, as he attempted to confirm land rights and extend English authority over the French colonies in Acadia. In 1656, Temple had entered into an agreement with Charles de La Tour, the French combatant for control of Acadia who had come to Boston in 1643, seeking help for his conflict with Charles d'Aulnay. The Temple–La Tour agreement claimed Acadia, the region northeast of Maine, for English rule under a patent issued by Parliament. Temple moved to Boston and used the city as his base for establishing forts and settlements along the Saint John River in present-day New Brunswick and on both sides of the Bay of Fundy in what are now New Brunswick and Nova Scotia.

As he assimilated to Boston society, Temple's interests in Acadia attracted Boston's merchants, such as Thomas Lake and Edward Tyng, who used their new connections with Temple to establish

MAP 3.1. *A Map of New England, and Nova Scotia*, by Thomas Kitchin, 1758. Kitchin's map clearly depicts the basin from Cape Cod to the Bay of Fundy that generated both trade and conflict between Massachusetts and Acadia.

trade with Acadia's settlers, and sponsor fishing and seal-hunting ventures off the coast of Cape Sable, on the southern tip of the peninsula. In return, the General Court rewarded Temple with monopoly rights to all trade in furs from "Acady and Nova Scotia."[16] Typically for this chaotic region, Temple's claims were contested by rivals, both French and English.

With regime change at home in 1660, Temple returned to England to petition the Restoration Crown for a more authoritative patent for his claim to Acadia. By this time, the experience of the New Hampshire and Maine settlements had clearly demonstrated the power of Massachusetts in the region. To develop authority over territory in the Northeast, it was useful to have Boston's interests aligned with your own. Despite his royalist sympathies and dislike for the Puritans' religious and political persuasion, Temple willingly defended the colony, as the support of Boston would help him to pursue his own interests.[17]

In 1662, King Charles II questioned Temple closely about various aspects of Massachusetts government, including the currency issued by John Hull's mint. Charles was concerned that his royal prerogative had been usurped. In an episode that became legendary, reported over a century later by Boston clergyman Andrew Eliot, Temple explained to the king that the colony had been ignorant of the law and had meant no harm in coining money strictly for its own local use. And as he explained, Temple pulled a Massachusetts coin from his purse and presented it to his majesty:

> Charles inquired what tree that was? Sir Thomas informed him it was the royal oak; adding, that the Massachusetts people, not daring to put his majesty's name on their coin, during the late troubles, had impressed upon it the emblem of the oak which preserved his majesty's life. This account of the matter put the king into good humor, and disposed him to hear what Sir Thomas had to say in their favor, calling them a parcel of honest dogs.[18]

In this dexterous act of verbal tribute, Temple insisted that Massachusetts had usurped nothing. With its coinage, the colony had

FIGURE 3.1. (a) Massachusetts "oak tree" two-pence coin, obverse, silver, ca. 1662. (b) Charger, by Thomas Toft, slipware, ca. 1680. Images of Charles hiding in an oak tree at Boscobel Wood to escape Oliver Cromwell's soldiers after the 1651 Battle of Worcester became popular after Charles's restoration to the throne.

symbolically rendered a form of tribute unto Caesar—a hidden, nearly invisible tribute, appropriate for a temporarily hidden monarch, and for a colony whose chief exports were invisibles.

The wording of this dialogue between Charles and Temple may be apocryphal, but later testimony by the Massachusetts General Court indicates that the encounter between Temple and the royal court did indeed take place.[19] Temple's ingenious gesture highlights the characteristic response that Boston developed to ward off imperial meddling. Again and again, Boston's leaders turned to forms of tribute payment to keep the Crown at bay, acknowledging allegiance to the new king (whose father had given them their charter) and yet sustaining their independence.

Paying tribute is not the same as paying taxes. To be taxed is to be counted as a subject or citizen in relation to the state, a member of the body politic. In the King James Version of the Gospel of Luke 2:1, Mary gave birth to Jesus in Bethlehem because Joseph had brought Mary there in response to the decree from Caesar Augustus "that all the world should be taxed." The word "tax" connotes a sense of burden, obligation, censure, or even punishment. Etymologically, tax is essentially the same word as "task." In premodern times, taxes were often paid in tasks, by rendering labor rather than money to one's lord. Taxpayers expect some return on their payment in the form of protection or other services. Tribute, by contrast, more frequently involves a relationship between states or governments, and its connotations have more to do with honor and respect than with burden or censure. Tribute payment also offers greater opportunities for ceremonial relationships of subservience. Taxes could be collected in various ways, often farmed out to intermediaries, so long as the king or lord got his share in the end. Tribute, by contrast, requires ceremonial contact, gestures of allegiance and obedience, for the act to be effective. In paying tribute, a weaker state acknowledges submission to a stronger one, and expresses its respect, fear, or affection. But tribute's connotations tend more toward exclusion than inclusion. People pay tribute in order to be left alone. In the wake of the Pequot War, Boston had been extracting this kind of tribute payment for several decades from the Indian nations of southern New England, including the Narragansetts, Niantics, and Mohegans, in the form of wampum or persons. Now, in response to closer scrutiny and potential interference from the Restoration monarchy, Boston developed its own forms of tribute payment to mollify the Crown.

Fending Off the Crown's Agents

If Temple's ready wit avoided a challenge to Massachusetts' coinage in 1662, the inquisitory commission that Charles sent to New England two years later took a more sober approach to colonial usurpation of royal authority. The king's four commissioners, Richard Nichols, Samuel Maverick, Robert Carr, and George Cartwright, arrived in Boston in summer 1664, and spent the fall and winter touring southern New England.[20] They heard grievances from Indians and from other colonies, particularly Rhode Island, the colony excluded from the New England Confederation, before returning to Boston in spring 1665. Having perused the Massachusetts laws, the commissioners addressed the General Court and freemen of the colony on the annual election day, May 24, 1665, when hundreds, if not thousands, of leading citizens assembled in Boston. In their judgment, twenty-six articles in Massachusetts' "booke of the Generall Lawes & liberties" required amendment to bring them in line with royal authority. Twenty-second on the list was "the law yt a mint house, &c, be repealed, for Coyning is a Royall prerogative."[21]

The commissioners' concern was not with the mint's economic utility but rather that the coinage undermined royal authority, as did numerous other laws on the books. The commissioners also complained about "undecent expressions & repetitions of the word 'commonwealth,' 'state,' & the like," and proposed that the phrase "his majesty's colony" should be substituted for them in every case. They further noted that Massachusetts had no right to join in confederation with other colonies—a clear assault on the United Colonies and Boston's leadership role within this organization.[22] What the king's commissioners objected to was that Boston acted like an independent city-state, holding unlimited and unchallenged authority over its own territory and regional hegemony over its neighbors, English and Indian alike. They demanded that Boston send agents to London in order to defend its past behavior and, if necessary, negotiate terms for a revision to its charter.

The colony's response was remarkable for its effrontery, but characteristic of the depth of its commitment to autonomy. The General Court neither complied with the demand to revise its laws nor sent representatives to Whitehall. Instead, it offered tribute to the king. The court voted to acquire goods "in the best Commodity that may be procured in this his Colony, meete for transportation & accommodation of his Majesty's Navy to the value of five hundred pounds," with provisions to repeat this gift over the next several years.[23] In his diary entry on September 12, 1666, John Hull indicated that the General Court understood these gifts as a substitute for the king's requests to send an agent: "They [the General Court] concluded to write, and send a present, two brave masts, but sent no person to answer in our behalf." Indeed, in the General Court's records, "it is ordered, that ye two very large masts now on board Capt Peirce his ship . . . be presented to his maj[es]ty . . . as a testimony of loyalty and affection from ye country, & that all charge thereof be paid out of the country treasury."[24] Two years later, Hull's diary repeats: "The Generall Court sent a shipload of masts as a present to the king's majesty."[25] Even disgruntled outliers within Boston who had long reviled the haughty independence of the puritan leadership were fully aware of the purpose of these gestures. Maverick, who had nursed a grudge against the colonists since 1630 when their arrival forced him out of his secluded homestead on Noddles Island, mentioned that Boston's leaders "boast of the gracious letters they have received from His Majesty and of his kind acceptance of the Masts they sent him." In an allusion to the Book of Samuel, Thomas Breedon, another royalist newcomer in Boston, referred to the tribute of masts as "Sacrifice, not Obedience."[26] But given the king's positive response in the form of these "gracious letters," tribute seemed to be obedience enough.

Notwithstanding its show of "loyalty and affection" to the king, Boston continued to produce the coins that filled the "country treasury" with silver. In 1667, in the midst of these annual tributary gestures, the General Court formed a committee to negotiate with Hull and Sanderson about the costs of running the mint house. They asked Hull and Sanderson to make incremental payments over the next seven years for the "aediffices" that the colony had built on Hull's property to house the coining operation. Almost to the end of Hull's life in 1683, the General Court made occasional adjustments in matters such as Hull's minting fees, showing no signs that the Crown's objections in 1665 had diminished Boston's commitment to issuing its coinage.[27]

Repeated gestures of tribute kept Boston free from royal interference through the late 1660s, but the situation on the northeastern frontier became more complicated in these years.[28] In addition to the Mason and Gorges heirs pressing the king about their claims to New Hampshire and Maine, the king's brother, James, Duke of York, had been granted title to the region beyond Gorges's Maine patent, northeast of the Kennebec River. This grant was part of the settlement of New Netherland on the Duke of York, in the wake of the English conquest of the Dutch colony in 1664.[29] Through various commissions and reports, the Crown attempted to restore the Maine territory to Gorges's heirs and to colonists on the site who had received land grants from Sir Ferdinando. But Boston's leaders, the governor and council, continued to ignore these claims and even increase their authority over the Maine region by way of the Massachusetts court system. The Crown's great distance from the site, the difficulty of communication and control from afar, and the local political and economic power of Massachusetts meant that Boston had little to fear from Crown interference.

King Charles's wars with France and the Netherlands, especially the third Anglo-Dutch War of 1672–74, in which the Dutch momentarily recaptured New York, allowed Massachusetts a free hand on its frontier to the east. By the mid-1670s, Boston's control over Maine was stronger than ever. Massachusetts circuit courts headed by Boston magistrates such as Richard Waldron met regularly in Maine to keep order and resolve disputes. The Maine towns sent deputies to the General Court in Boston, granted land to local inhabitants on the freehold Massachusetts model, paid their taxes based on rates set in Boston, and sold land to Boston speculators such as Joshua Scottow. Boston's strength in the region was such that even new settlements beyond the Kennebec in the Duke of York's patent were incorporated into a new Massachusetts county: Devon.[30] Nicholas Shapleigh, a local proprietor loyal to Gorges and the Crown, complained that Massachusetts colonists "drew away most part of the people to petition the Government of the Bay of Boston to Governe and Rule over them."[31] As John Evelyn, famous diarist and member of King Charles's Council on Plantations, noted in 1671, the government of Boston was "very independent as to their regard to old England, or his Majestie, rich and strong as they now were. . . . We understood they were a people al most upon the very brink of renouncing any dependence of the Crowne."[32]

Despite its power in the Northeast in the early 1670s, the long and costly Indian wars starting in 1675 sapped Boston's riches and strength. When peace on the northern frontier was finally established in 1678, it was not through a decisive confederation victory over Indian forces. On this northeastern front, where violence escalated after the defeat in 1676 of Philip's southern Indian alliance, the strength of the Abenaki Indians was such that Boston, fighting without aid from the other members of the United Colonies (Connecticut and Plymouth were reluctant to send soldiers so far from home), now had to pay tribute to the Abenaki in return for a negotiated peace; corn, not coin, was the form of payment.[33] At the same time, a new round of royal investigation further tested Boston's "very independent" will. By 1676, just as the first phase of King Philip's War was ending, the problems that plagued Charles II's reign (among them, literally, bubonic plague in London) had abated enough for a new royal commissioner to be sent to New England. Edward Randolph, a cousin of New Hampshire claimant Robert Mason, arrived in Boston in June 1676.[34]

The potential threat of this second royal commission was considerably greater than the first one in 1662. In addition to pressing his cousin's New Hampshire claims, Randolph renewed the critique of Boston's independence. According to Randolph, the coins Hull had been minting for years demonstrated the colony's unlawful claim to be a free state: "And, as a mark of sovereignty, they coin money stamped with inscription Mattachusets and a tree in the centre, on the one side; and New England, with the year 1652 and the value of the piece, on the reverse." Randolph actually overstated the relationship between the coinage and the colony's autonomy: "All the money is stamped with these figures, 1652, that year being the aera of the commonwealth, wherein they erected themselves into a free state, enlarged their dominions, subjected the adjacent colonies under their obedience, and summoned deputies to sit in the generall court, which year is still commemorated on their coin."[35] Although Boston had indeed accomplished all these things, they did not all happen in 1652, nor did the date on the coins commemorate them.

Randolph also sent the Lords of Trade and Plantations new information to apprise the Crown of Boston's violation of the Navigation Acts. In his "Narrative of the State of New England," Randolph listed the many merchant ships recently returned to Boston from foreign ports in France, Spain, the Canaries, the Azores, the Netherlands, the Hanse cities in the Baltic, "Scanderoon" (Iskanderun in the Ottoman Empire), various African ports from Madagascar to Guinea, and several Caribbean locations as well: "There is no notice taken of the act of navigation, plantation, or any other lawes made in England for the regulation of trade. All nations having free liberty to come into their ports and vend their commodities, without any restraint; . . . that government would make the world believe that they are a free state and doe act in all matters accordingly."[36] In Randolph's eyes, this unrestrained trade had an extremely deleterious effect on England's commerce with its New World possessions. He lists the commodities that Boston merchants supplied to other American colonies "as brandy, Canary, Spanish and French wines, bullion [i.e., silver], salt, fruits, oyles, silkes, laces, linen of all sorts, cloath, serges, bayes, kersies [varieties of woolen cloth], stockings, and many other commodities." Randolph complains that "there is little left for the merchants residing in England to import into any of the plantations, those of New-England being able to afford their goods much cheaper than such who pay the customes and are laden in England. By which meanes this kingdome hath lost the best part of the western trade, . . . and Boston may be esteemed the mart town of the West Indies."[37] Although he exaggerated the extent of Boston's intentions in creating these conditions, most of what Randolph reported was true. The remarkable expansion of Boston's trade throughout the Atlantic world had given the city a dominant position within all British American trade. Randolph's aim was to make Boston's achievements look like defiance of Crown authority.

Despite the severity of Randolph's threat and in the midst of the sea of troubles the colony now faced, the General Court responded much as it had a decade earlier by presenting the king with still more tribute. Pursuant to the court's order, John Hull, now the colony treasurer, consigned aboard his own ship *The Blessing* a handsome gift consisting of 1,860 codfish (about 700 of them "very large fish, between two and three feet long") along with 10 barrels of cranberries and 3 barrels of samp—cornmeal mush.[38] Whether the king received these presents as a "blessing" remains unknown. The utility of the masts is obvious, as a proven tribute commodity and an essential element in the naval expansion that Charles II pursued in commercial wars against the French and Dutch. But what Boston's leaders thought Charles would want with cod, cranberries, and samp is harder to fathom, unless one imagines that these humble commodities somehow *represented* the Massachusetts economy to the king. They were tangible symbols of what the colony's coins served to circulate, the equivalent for New England of Virginia's tobacco or Jamaica's sugar. It seems unlikely that the king acknowledged these gifts as adequate tribute. But from Boston's point of view, these gestures worked. Hull continued to make pine tree shillings to the end of his life. Only when the Massachusetts Charter was revoked in 1684 did the mint stop producing coins. Even then, his majesty's treasury seriously considered the idea of reestablishing Boston's mint, based on arguments for economic utility that Hull had been making for thirty years.[39]

The continuity that the coinage brought to Boston's political economy remained important through the 1670s and into the 1680s. Randolph challenged the legality of Boston's expansion to the Northeast, and economic and fiscal power proved vital in resisting this threat. The Crown ordered Randolph to act as its agent, presenting the complaints of the heirs of Gorges and Mason to the governor and magistrates "of our town of Boston in New England" (even the king addressed the city-state of Boston in these terms). Randolph alleged that Boston had usurped Gorges's and Mason's rightful authority and title to Maine and New Hampshire, and demanded that the colony send agents to London to respond to these charges.[40] After delivering this message in Boston in June 1676, Randolph toured the northeastern towns and settlements, notifying New Hampshire residents that Mason's heirs were reasserting their claims and contesting Boston's authority, and spreading a similar message to Maine.[41]

A reprise ensued of the initial struggle for territorial control that had ended in Boston's favor in the 1650s. Only now the situation was complicated by warfare between Massachusetts, the Abenaki Indians, and their French allies. The outbreak of violence in the Northeast began in September 1675, when Abenakis attacked the town of Falmouth, then one of the most distant English communities from Boston, on the edge of Casco Bay. The scattered pattern of Maine's settlements, spread along the intricate coastline, made defense and communications difficult. The long duration of the war in this region and the intensity of violence on both sides eroded settlers' willingness to remain in this exposed territory. The political argument over the future of Maine and New Hampshire took place while the English settlements themselves were crumbling.[42]

Financing the Colony's Agents

In this turbulent context, the General Court changed its strategy and decided that it was now time to send agents as well as tribute to appease the Crown. Along with the customary gifts, the court selected two leaders, Peter Bulkeley, speaker of the House of Deputies, and William Stoughton, a councillor and one of Boston's wealthiest merchants, as agents for the colony. Hull consigned the codfish, cranberries, and samp directly to Bulkeley and Stoughton to present to the king when they sailed aboard *The Blessing*. Their instructions encouraged them to emphasize the colony's readiness to obey the king's command, to diminish the significance of Mason's and Gorges's "pretensions and accusations," to underplay the value of the Maine territory even if Mason's and Gorges's claims turned out to be valid, and finally, "yet notwithstanding, if yow finde a sume of mony will take them [Mason and Gorges] off from further prosecution of their pretensions, and that they are willing & doe resigne & release all their interest to those parts unto us, and that that may be a fynall issue, yow shall engage in that way as yor discretion shall direct."[43] This was the strategy: make the claims of Mason and Gorges look doubtful, make the Maine land look worthless, and then try to buy it at a good price.

The purchase of Maine from the younger Gorges required complex negotiations, and it was almost two years before a deal was made. The king's ministers verbally roughed up Bulkeley and Stoughton in the process. The Committee for Trade and Plantations pressed the Massachusetts agents on the colony's violations of Crown prerogatives, including the coining of money. Bulkeley and Stoughton, however, claimed that they had no instructions from the General Court to deal with any issue besides the Mason and Gorges claims. To this the committee insisted that "His Majesty did not think of treating with his own subjects as with foreigners and to expect the formality of powers."[44] But this was how Boston thought of treating with His Majesty. It would render Caesar his due, but Boston's godly commonwealth was its own business. The Crown seemed fed up with Massachusetts and was on the verge of deciding the matter of legal title to Maine in favor of Gorges when a Boston merchant residing in London, John Usher, the son of Hezekiah Usher, Hull's friend and business partner, negotiated the purchase of the title from Gorges. In the end, the General Court's instructions to Bulkeley and Stoughton proved to be prophetic; a "sume of mony" did the trick. Usher agreed to pay Gorges some £1,250, but only had access to a little over £500 himself.

By now the question of *where* Bulkeley and Stoughton might find such a large "sume of mony"—the £750 that Usher needed was more than seven times the annual salary that Increase Mather would earn as president of Harvard College—ought to be obvious.[45] Indeed, if we turn to Hull's "Letter Book," the answer is readily available. On November 26, 1678, Hull wrote to John Ive, a frequent London correspondent, with the following unusual request:

> Sir . . . I understand the countreys occasions to bee such that mr Stoughton & mr Buckly haveing bought the province of Main will need seven hundred pound to compleat the payment thereof. . . . I desire you to doe mee that favr to take up soe much mony at interest on behalfe of the countrey as shall make up what money of mine you have in yor hand seven hundred pound if sd mr stoughton and Bulkly have not taken it on their own Creddit. . . . I doe oblidge my Selfe that through the Goodness & favr of god what ever I my Selfe should suffer by it you shall not loose one peny.[46]

Hull was prepared to raise this large sum at his own risk.[47] But with the Indian wars he had helped to finance barely at an end, and many Massachusetts towns still in arrears on their back taxes from the war, Hull feared that his credit was stretched thin—perhaps to the breaking point. He hoped that Bulkeley and Stoughton, each a prosperous merchant in his own right, might bear the burden of the Maine purchase themselves, as Hull had so often done for the colony.

On the same day that Hull wrote to Ive, he wrote separately to Bulkeley and Stoughton, urging them to do their best to assume the costs themselves: “Therefore if you doe not herein need my Creddit I beseech you spare it for I am almost afraid least I should crack it.”[48] In the end, when Bulkeley and Stoughton failed to arrange the payment on their own credit, Hull made the sacrifice himself. He arranged for a shipment of high-value goods (“sixteen hogsheads of good muscovado Sugers”) and bills of exchange (“for £500 on Mr: John Paige and Comp”) to pay off his debt to Ive. This meant that Hull’s own orders from Ive would have to wait until he had further resources: “I wold have noe debt of the Countreys left unpaide which they descire I might so discharge though I shold be dissapointed of what I wold have for my selfe. Publique Concerness must be prefered before private.”[49]

The purchase of Maine, which gave Boston control over this extensive hinterland (control that would endure for the next 140 years) and also improved the colony’s future access to resources in Acadia, would be the last major victory for Boston’s strategy of political economy in the era of the first charter. In 1679, efforts to make a similar deal to secure New Hampshire failed. The attorney general in England declared that Mason’s proprietary title to the *land* in New Hampshire was valid, but that Mason’s patent had not come with *governmental* rights over the region. To resolve this discrepancy between the New Hampshire towns’ voluntary political allegiance to Massachusetts and Mason’s valid land title, the Crown separated the four New Hampshire towns (Portsmouth, Exeter, Dover, and Hampton) from Boston’s political control and created a new province under royal authority.[50] Randolph, who had returned to England in 1677 to report on the outrages of Massachusetts, came back to Boston with the revised New Hampshire commission and resumed his vendetta against the Bay Colony. He was now backed more strongly by a policy of Charles II and, after Charles’s death in 1685, James II to undermine independently chartered forms of power everywhere within the king’s dominions.

The magistrates on the General Court, and merchants and ministers who supported them, did their best to fend off these threats using well-tested methods: tribute to the king, bribery in Whitehall, agents sent to the Lords of Trade and Plantations, and any combination of defiance, negotiation, delay, flattery, appeasement, prayer, and luck that might work. But the Crown's desire for a new program of imperial organization grew increasingly obvious, and not just in Boston. In England, a concerted attack on town corporations, boroughs that sent Parliament members to Westminster where they might challenge the power of the king, led to the revocation of many municipal charters including the City of London that were similar in structure to the colonial charters. Other forms of corporate privilege, from oyster monopolies in Kent to the Stationers Company, which licensed the press in England, were challenged as well. In April 1683, the Crown seized London's charter through a writ of quo warranto, a legal device for challenging corporate authority, and it remained in limbo until the revolution of 1688.[51] Among the king's overseas colonies, in addition to Massachusetts, the charters of Connecticut, Rhode Island, Bermuda, the Bahamas, Maryland, Delaware, and East and West Jersey came under scrutiny or were revoked in the 1670s and 1680s.[52]

John Hull and his fellow members of the General Court fought against Randolph with the same methods that had worked to gain title to Maine. The colony chose two new agents, John Richards and Joseph Dudley, both Boston merchants, to argue its case in Whitehall. Again Hull was ready to supply them with the financial power they needed. Although another Boston merchant, James Russell, had succeeded him as treasurer, Hull still expected to lend his credit for the colony's interests. In June 1683, as Richards and Dudley negotiated to save the Massachusetts Charter from the Crown's challenge, Hull wrote to Thomas Glover, another London merchant with whom he did business, in a familiar manner:

> Sir if the agents of this colony mr Joseph dudly & mr John Richards should . . . find that the having some quantity of money in London would be of anny considerable advantage unto this poor country These are to Intreat you to take up five

> hundred pound In my behalf at as low Interest as you can & supply them with it. . . . It is not for theire ordinary expences for that the Treasurer of the country mr James Russell will take effectuall care about but as I may Impart to you privately what yo can easly there guess at whether it will be advisable or If so whether feasible to buy our peaceable enJoiyments.[53]

But in the climate now prevailing in Whitehall, the peaceable enjoyment of Massachusetts' charter rights were no longer for sale, either through formal negotiations or bribery of the sort that Hull hinted at. When met with intransigence from the Massachusetts agents, whose instructions from Boston prevented them from endorsing any revisions to their charter rights, the Committee on Trade and Plantations ordered the attorney general to prepare a writ of quo warranto against the Massachusetts Charter—the same tactic that had been used to undermine London's charter. In Randolph's letter to the committee listing the "Grounds for Revoking the Colonial Charter," the first charge read, "1. They have erected a Publick mint in Boston and Coine money with their Own Impresse."[54] On October 23, 1684, the charter under which Boston had formed an independent city-state was vacated, and the colony's future was left in limbo.[55]

These last years of independent government were disheartening ones for John Hull, and for many other Bostonians who had invested their lives and fortunes in the Commonwealth of Massachusetts. Even as Hull wrote to London correspondents to raise money for Boston's efforts at expansion, his letters revealed these worries. His desire to "give [Ive] as much Ashurance as I was Capable that what Ever I suffered he shold not looss one peny by it," and his promise to Glover to "oblige my self my heirs my excecutors & administrators" to pay the debts he was now incurring, reflected the fact that Hull lived "in a place of such mortality." He feared that he might not survive to pay the debts himself.[56] Boston suffered through a smallpox outbreak in 1678–79: "Wee have had two verry sicke Townes Charlestowne first & then Boston. I suppose about foure hundred in both have dyed of the small pox in little more then one yeare & yet it contineweth."[57] Hull's son-in-law, Samuel Sewall, contracted smallpox during this outbreak, and Hull himself feared that he was vulnerable. The following year, on August 8, 1679, a massive fire struck Boston's North End, destroying some of the city's most valuable property: "About midnight began a fire in Boston, an alehouse, which, by sunrise, consumed the body of the trading part of the town: from the Mill Creek to Mr. Oliver's dock, no one house nor warehouse left."[58] Through all this, the financial crisis brought on by the Indian wars continued. Several Hull letters from the early 1680s are addressed to Massachusetts towns such as Salisbury, Dedham, and Lynn that were badly in arrears for the taxes levied during the war. The town of Salisbury alone owed Hull some £650.[59]

On October 25, 1681, Hull addressed a plaintive letter to the General Court in Boston, describing the financial difficulties in which his contributions to the state had left him. In explaining his willingness to put his own money and credit at the colony's service, Hull wrote,

> My encouragement was that God had called me to the place and had given me what I had for such a time,—that it was for a good people as (I hoped) such would be just & righteous if not also grateful. Gent. I am willing to lose freely one hundred Pound out of my own estate, & if it were indeed needful, much more. . . . I do count it my duty to spend and to be spent for the public welfare but I think it (with all Humility) also your duty, Honoured Gentlemen, not to suffer me to lose more than needeth.

The hardships that his colony suffered even led Hull to fantasize about a monarch more benevolent than Charles II or his brother James would ever be. While writing to Bulkeley and Stoughton about his credit problems, the difficulty of raising money for the colony, and the damage caused by Indian wars and smallpox, Hull fell into a reverie, imagining what a truly generous king might do for his people:

> I am thinking Some times the king's maj[es]ty is a father to this Country and he hath here for quantity of Subjects as obedient

> Children as any in his dominion. And though they are represented a rich People yet they are really a poore people and yet deeply in debt for the late Indian wars & many of them made more poore by the Sickness since. Why might he not please to Conferr upon these his poore Children ten thousand Pound to helpe them out of theire debts?

Hull briefly gripes about how little the city-state of Boston has cost the Crown in its half century of development, especially when compared with other colonial projects. He bewails the unfairness of the Navigation Acts to a trading society like his own, which has "not Occasioned any charge to him [the king] by shiping and men as Virginia and other plantations. If they [New Englanders] have Gotten a little Shipping it is by great diligence and Industry. And pitty such industry shold be discouraged by being obliged to such a Corse as must of necessity Crush them. I doe not see how it is Possible the Acts of navigation Can be attended to here. The Mercht People will be occationed to bid farwell to the Country and Com to England."[60]

In this moment of despair, the only alternative Hull could imagine to the pitiful end of everything that he and his fellow Bostonians had been striving for was a radical one: rustic simplicity and self-sufficiency. Hull offered a puritan variant on the utopian musings of Shakespeare's Gonzalo in *The Tempest*. If only the colonists could apply themselves "to all sorts of manufacture and forbeare trading by sea" so as not to be dependent on expensive goods from overseas, "to Eate noe fruit, sug[a]r, Spice and drinke noe wine but o[u]r owne Cyder and weare noe Clothing but of o[u]r owne making," then they could surely be "as he[a]lthy and as warme as we are now," and "may be more holy righteous and humble."[61] Then, just as quickly as the reverie came over him, Hull snapped out of it. He returned to the details of life as a colonial merchant operating in the shifting currents of Atlantic trade and politics. He made plans to protect the colony's and his own resources should the worst happen and Randolph's threats become reality. He arranged for scribes to record the details of a group of Boston investors' claims to land in the Narragansett Country should Rhode Island's charter be attacked.[62] He raised still more money to ransom captured Boston seafarers in the hands of Algerian pirates.[63] He wrote to Sir Henry Ashurst, London alderman and treasurer of the New England Company, offering to put his own credit at Ashurst's disposal in order to resume Indian missionary work in New England, even while he still struggled to collect debts owed to him from the recent ghastly Indian war.[64] And intriguingly, he and his longtime merchant friend Eliakim Hutchinson explored a new prospect, or rather, a new version of an old prospect: getting their hands on Spanish silver.

The Lure of the "Wracks"

In the 1670s and 1680s, rumors circulated around the English Caribbean about sunken Spanish treasure ships whose silver had never been recovered. Notions of this sort had been a staple in the English Atlantic from the time of the settlement of Bermuda, early in the seventeenth century. They increased with the colonization of the Bahamas in the 1640s by Puritans from Bermuda who settled on islands that they named Eleuthera ("freedom" in Greek) and New Providence. Bermuda and the Bahamas lay along the route taken by Spanish treasure fleets as they returned to Spain from the Caribbean through the straits between Cuba and Florida. The notoriously dangerous weather and hidden undersea coral reefs of this region made shipwrecks common. In 1648, a Bermudan named William Berkeley wrote to John Winthrop Jr. about "a Spanish ship of three hundred and fifty tonnes cast away uppon our rockes . . . the richest ship that hath bin cast away there since the iland was inhabited."[65]

Although this particular ship was never recovered, over the years Bermudans scavenged a certain amount of silver from the remains of Spanish wrecks. They were aided by the invention of a diving bell, known as the "Bermuda Tub," reportedly developed by a local pirate named Richard Norwood. This was essentially an oversize wine cask, inverted and weighted around its edges so that it could be lowered into the sea with air trapped inside. Divers exploring the ocean floor could enter the tub, breathe for a few minutes, and then return to work without having to swim to the surface. In 1642, such a device was used in Boston Harbor by Edward Bendall to salvage a ship that exploded while bringing munitions to the city. According to Winthrop Sr., Bendall "could continue in his tub near half an hour, and fasten ropes to the ordnance, and put the lead etc., into a net or tub."[66] By the early 1680s, the Bermuda Tub had become a standard device in places like the Bahamas where "fishing" for Spanish wrecks began to show signs of success. Sailors on provisioning ships sent by Boston merchants to the Bahamas, Jamaica, and other Caribbean islands began to return with gossip, centered on stories about two or three unusually rich Spanish wrecks of the mid-seventeenth century. One of these, a ship with the elegant name of *Nuestra Señora de la pura y limpia Concepción* went astray during a storm in 1641 and wrecked on coral reefs in shallow water, somewhere east of the Turks Islands, north of Hispaniola, and within striking distance of the Bahamas and Jamaica. It was reputed to have carried 140 tons of silver, worth £1,000,000.[67]

In 1683, this prospect for windfall profits led John Hull and his sometime business partner Eliakim Hutchinson to outfit the ship *Endeavor* for a salvaging expedition, commanded by Richard Rook, Peres Savage, and ship captain Francis Lester, to whom they offered these instructions:

> You will make all speed to the wrack where when the lord shall bring you we desire; this as your dayly constant to love & assist & to your utmost help each other, be united your selves & do your utmost to keep your wholl company. . . . [B]e careful to maintain his maiesties peac[e] & to break no law of nature nor nations especially of old england & new. In attending to the law of god & making his word your rule you will keep all which that you may be helped to doe.[68]

The odd juxtaposition here, the excessive emphasis on mutual love, keeping the peace, and obeying the law of God while treasure hunting, are the product of the sensibilities of two puritan traders now applying themselves to a business commonly associated with pirates and buccaneers. Indeed, in a second letter to Rook, Hull and

Hutchinson alluded to some nefarious practices that previous New England "wrackmen" had engaged in, including enslaving Indian labor. They warned Rook, "We fear the taking Indians by force is man stealing and to kill any of them in that designe will Involve in the guilt of blood which I would have you & us keep far from." Yet at the same time, given the desperate straits that New England's finances (and their own personal investments) were facing, Hull and Hutchinson envisioned that a successful salvaging voyage would bring the treasure "home hither" to share.[69]

Most other contemporary English salvaging projects included the Crown directly in plans to salvage the wrecks, with the king receiving a substantial cut of the proceeds.[70] This is not to say that if Rook and company had brought home the *Concepcion*'s millions, the Boston merchants would have tried to deny the Crown its share. Rather, following the habits formed over a half century, Hull and Hutchinson characteristically saw this salvage operation as yet another project stemming from the independent interests of their own political economy. Like the first trading voyages to the Caribbean of the 1640s, the coinage of silver shillings in the 1650s, and the expansion of their territory through politics, purchase, and warfare in the 1660s and 1670s, this new venture was intended to solve Boston's problems, not the Crown's. It seemed ever more obvious to Hull that Charles II was not a benevolent father who might grant his "poor children" £10,000 to ease their economic suffering. So the poor children would have to find it on their own.

Rook and the *Endeavor* failed to bring the *Concepcion* or any other wreck home hither to Boston. Likewise the expedition of the colony's agents, Richards and Dudley, to salvage the Massachusetts Bay charter failed as well. Hull did not live to see either disappointment. His health began to decline in summer 1683, and he died on October 1. The writ of quo warranto against the charter named Hull among those called to account for violations of royal authority, but Hull was dead before Randolph arrived in Boston bearing the writ.[71] Over the next few years, in a process delayed by the death of Charles II and the succession of his brother James II to the throne, the charters of Connecticut and Rhode Island were also revoked. James II created a new monster of a colonial entity, ruled by the Crown through an appointed governor, uniting all the colonies from New Jersey to Maine under a single government, known as the Dominion of New England.[72]

Fighting the Dominion's Kleptocracy

The history of the Dominion of New England and its eventual overthrow, prompted by news of William of Orange's invasion of England and James II's flight, is a story that has been told many times over and need not be repeated here at length.[73] James II's appointed governor of the Dominion, Sir Edmund Andros, a soldier and experienced colonial administrator, was viewed by most Bostonians as tyranny embodied. Andros and the Dominion government threatened the practices at the heart of the city-state of Boston: political autonomy and self-governance, freehold land title that created equity throughout the commonwealth and encouraged market production, free trade throughout the Atlantic world for Boston's merchants, and the communitarian ethos grounded in the religion of the puritan churches. When Boston's rebels rose up on April 18, 1689, and arrested Andros (and Randolph), the Dominion's assault on these practices constituted their chief grievances. But most accounts of the Glorious Revolution in America neglect an important feature of these events: the distinctively unified quality of Boston's rebellion within the larger British Atlantic world—a unity that stemmed from the political economy of the city-state of Boston and from the moral economy of the commonwealth.

The last quarter of the seventeenth century witnessed a series of colonial rebellions against royal authority in British America. Boston's uprising in 1689 was one among a number of such events precipitated by the downfall of James II and the invasion of William of Orange. Other rebellions occurred in New York, Maryland, and Antigua. Further uprisings were narrowly averted in Virginia by the governor's rapid proclamation of William as the new monarch, and in Jamaica by the sudden death of its governor, Christopher Monck, Second Duke of Albemarle, who had overindulged in food and drink in celebrating the birth of an heir to James II. But these other rebellions and near rebellions differed from Boston's, because in all these other colonies, the overthrow of royal government was either caused by or unleashed internal tensions within the colonies. In each of these other colonies, conflict between local elites (merchants or plantation owners) and common folks who resented the rule of local aristocrats and the support they received from the Crown led to outbreaks of violence. In some cases, such as Leisler's Rebellion in New York and the rebellion led by John Coode in Maryland, ethnic and religious differences within the colony exacerbated the conflict as well—Dutch versus English in New York, and Catholic versus Protestant in Maryland.[74]

Boston was different. Although thousands of common soldiers, members of town militias who had fought in the Indian wars, marched into the city with the aim of arresting Governor Andros and his small group of supporters, they met no resistance from local elites in Boston. Quite to the contrary, the merchants, ministers, and magistrates of the city put aside minor differences over tactics for resisting royal control, and embraced the common cause by demanding the surrender of Andros and his henchmen, including the despised Randolph. In the words of Randolph's biographer, "The revolution was entirely conservative. And it was, as near as anything could be, unanimous."[75] Cotton Mather concurred; he called it "the most Unanimous Resolution perhaps that ever was known to have inspir'd any People."[76]

Historians across subsequent centuries have spilled much ink in trying to distinguish among various factions in Massachusetts politics in the later decades of the seventeenth century. They tend to settle on a split between "moderates" who favored some accommodation with the Stuart monarchs as the best way to retain most of their original charter privileges and the "popular" party that favored complete resistance to any change as the best approach. But seen in the wider context of the British Atlantic and the revolution in the metropolis, these small differences in tactics seem far less important than the remarkable consensus expressed in Boston's uprising against Andros and in the provisional restoration of charter government until a new settlement could be made with King William. After the arrest of Andros, the elderly former governor Simon Bradstreet, who avoided public service during the hated Andros regime, stepped forward as acting governor until instructions from the new king arrived. Even among the fifteen gentlemen who arrested Andros, a deliberate balance was struck between those who had favored total resistance to charter revisions and those who had wanted to accommodate the Crown in order to retain their overall autonomy.[77] Both symbolically and actually, the overthrow of Andros and the Dominion was perhaps the most unanimously acclaimed political act in the history of Boston.

This unanimity was fostered by the consensus among the city's denizens and the people of the New England hinterland that the political economy of the region, together with its thick religious culture and the moral economy that it sustained, knit the population together into an integrated set of interests. It was exactly the interconnections among varied interests, from rural farmers to Atlantic merchants, fostered by the coins that Hull had minted over these decades and by the reliable government that the currency symbolized, that held the city-state of Boston together in the face of divisive forces. This is not to say that the region was without conflict, or that the interests of city merchants always aligned perfectly with those of farmers or fishermen. But compared with the other colonial regions of British America, the degree of mutually self-sustaining integration within the region that Boston controlled is extraordinary. Different groups within Boston's ambit might have emphasized different aspects of their grievances against Andros and the Dominion of New England, but collectively their commitment to unrestrained Atlantic trade, freehold land titles within the Massachusetts town system, political self-rule through an assembly of elected deputies and councillors, and a puritan religious culture supported by the state were the foundations of a political economy they badly wanted to keep. It was this integrated system that royal government under Andros had threatened at every level.

The unanimity of opposition in Boston was enhanced by the widespread feeling that the king's appointees, Andros and his military supporters, were rapacious usurpers, stealing the wealth, profiteering from the trade, and banking on the political stability that the city-state of Boston had built over the course of a half century. At the time of the creation of the Dominion of New England, there were already two other royal colonies in British North America: Virginia and New York. In the case of the former, the Crown had rescued a failing colonial project, taking it over in the aftermath of Opechancanough's Rebellion in 1622—an Indian assault that was the last nail in the coffin of a floundering colony.[78] In the case of New York, the Crown's army and navy had seized New Netherland, a Dutch enterprise that was likewise suffering from fading fur supplies and conflict with Indians.[79]

But the city-state of Boston was not a failed state. The "Bostoners" (as Randolph referred to them) saw no need for the Crown to create a Dominion of New England because Boston had already created its own successful dominion of New England.[80] Starting from the independence of their strong but geographically confining charter, Boston had hived off new colonies in southern New England along Long Island Sound and up the Connecticut River, and then built a political, military, and economic confederation to bring this region under control. The "government of Boston Bay" had expanded to the northeast, and incorporated large new regions in New Hampshire and Maine. Boston's merchants had forged a vigorous and wide-ranging commercial network, stretching to the far reaches of the Atlantic world and beyond, and they used this skill to become the "market town of all British America."[81] From their point of view, the imposition of royal authority, especially in the persons of crypto-Catholic soldiers and rapacious political appointees like Andros and Randolph, the chosen agents of England's Roman Catholic king, was the imposition of a useless kleptocracy on a successful colony, which in the document that justified their uprising against Andros, they referred to as "Boston, and the Countrey Adjacent."[82]

During the three miserable years of Andros's rule and in the aftermath of the rebellion, the grievances expressed by Bostonians against Andros and his men repeated these accusations. They argued that Andros neglected the interests of the people and instead "govern[ed] by the advice only of a few others, . . . Strangers to the Countrey," with no stake in the community, "persons of known and declared Prejudices against us," with "Designs and Hopes to make unreasonable profit of this poor People."[83] Strong evidence supports this accusation. Randolph stood foremost among those seeking unreasonable profits. In addition to promoting the bizarre idea of bringing Roman Catholic priests into New England, Randolph spent much of his time during the Dominion trolling for land on which to build an estate and seeking lucrative offices that would provide fees to build his fortune.[84] On several occasions, Randolph petitioned Andros's handpicked council (of which he was a member) for grants of "a certain tract of vacant and unappropriated land," usually about five to seven hundred acres, near enough to Boston for building a country manor house from which he could keep an eye on his lucrative city contracts.[85] But land that in Randolph's eyes appeared vacant and unappropriated was actually common land at Nahant, used by the residents of the town of Lynn, "the whole fenced as a common field & . . . a grazing field with great benefit to the body of the whole town." They believed that if Randolph were to seize their commons, "it will . . . impoverish the body of ye inhabitants of Lynn who live not upon Traffique & trading as many seaport townes doe, . . . but upon husbandry & raising such stocks of Cattle & Sheep as they are capable." Finally, they argued, "if the pasture be alienated from us . . . we shall be rendered very uncapable . . . to contribute such dues & duties to his Majesty's Government sett over us."[86]

Here in a nutshell was the political economy of the city-state of Boston. The farmers of towns like Lynn were dependent on the land that they shared as a corporate community, and the stocks they raised were necessary to the merchants in the seaport towns engaged in overseas trade. From the land distribution within its country towns and villages to its overseas trade in the humble commodities these towns produced, the city-state of Boston had created a successful commonwealth. Its virtues were invisible to Randolph, Andros, and their cronies, seeing them as they did from an imperial perspective.[87] The Dominion kleptocrats were no commonwealth men. So alien to Randolph were the practices of the Massachusetts political economy, to which Hull had devoted much of his fortune, that he simply could not recognize them for what they were. When Randolph observed the large pools of collective wealth gathered for public services, like the endowment of Harvard College or the funds raised for Indian missions by the New England Company, and saw that these funds were administered by "private" individuals such as Hull, Stoughton, or Daniel Gookin, he could only assume that "they have possessed themselves of the money of the Colledge converting it to their private benefitt."[88] That, after all, is what Randolph tried to do whenever he could.

Most of Andros's Boston entourage had moved with him from New York, where Andros had been the governor chosen by the Duke of York, now King James II. Andros and his cronies saw the richer New England colony as another opportunity to line their pockets. Andros was to be paid "the princely salary of twelve hundred pounds a year," far beyond anything that Boston's elected governors in the charter period had ever received. Many of the early colonial governors, from John Winthrop forward, were "volunteers, governing without pay from the people."[89] The Declaration of Grievances issued on the day of the revolt against Andros, probably written by Cotton Mather and signed by the fifteen "Gentlemen" who led the uprising, claimed that "of all our Oppressors we were chiefly squeez'd by a Crew of abject Persons fetched from New York . . . nor could a small Volume contain the other Illegalities done by these Horse-leeches in the two or three Years that they have been sucking of us."[90] Andros and his crew came to colonial service from the military, and in addition to the fees of office and the prospects of land grants, Andros thought that Boston needed a greater military presence, from which he might personally profit. Andros introduced two new "companies of souldiers," infantry companies under the governor's command, paid for by taxes on the local population, that would transform the traditional system of self-defense by local militia that had served Boston well since its founding.[91]

Everything that Andros and the Dominion stood for opposed the city-state of Boston and its commonwealth tradition. Even the consolidation of all the colonies from Delaware to Maine in the omnibus Dominion of New England demonstrated this. The process of expansion that the Bostoners had conducted in their first fifty-five years was also a process of exclusion. They had deliberately kept the Dutch colony of New Netherlands from encroaching on Boston's access to Connecticut. They had excluded heterodox Rhode Island (founded by Massachusetts exiles) from the United Colonies. In expanding to incorporate New Hampshire and Maine, they had fought to rid these regions of rival claimants whose royalist values and proprietary land rights conflicted with their own vision of their commonwealth.[92] They had made considerable efforts to include the native population of southern New England within their commonwealth, but when these efforts collapsed in violence in the 1670s, their exclusionary response had been brutal—and effective. The city-state of Boston had created the dominion of New England that it wanted, even if it failed to live up to its highest ideals for a commonwealth. Its citizens saw no reason to be yoked together under a single government with other colonial projects they had fought to exclude. And they suspected that "an horrid Popish plot" lay behind this "Design," that "Popish Commanders" in the king's army and "papists" among Andros's council were stealing the wealth and security that New England Protestants had created for themselves.[93] For all these reasons, their rebellion against Andros and Randolph was overdetermined. The news of William's invasion and James's flight from England gave impetus to their rebellion, but the country militia and gentlemen of Boston rose up and arrested Andros *before* William's triumph was confirmed, and without evidence that the new king would look with favor on a colonial rebellion against royal government.

Once King William's coronation took place, the settlement he made with the Massachusetts Bay Colony offered neither complete approbation nor outright rejection of the rebellion. Over a period of three years, from 1688 to 1691, Increase Mather, Boston's leading minister, negotiated a new charter. Mather began with personal interviews with James II before his dramatic downfall and then continued with William after the Glorious Revolution.[94] Many of the defenders of Boston's old regime would have preferred to restore the original charter of 1629, but this was not to be. Yet in many ways, the city-state of Boston had outgrown its original charter. The new charter issued in 1691 ratified many of the remarkable gains that Boston had made during its half century of relative independence. The new charter confirmed that the territory of Maine, its ownership and allegiance contested for so long, did indeed belong to Boston. It added the region of the old Plymouth Colony, including Cape Cod and the islands of Nantucket and Martha's Vineyard, to Massachusetts' jurisdiction, giving the Bay Colony effective control of the entire coastline from Cape Cod to the Bay of Fundy.

In this sense, the new charter was better than the old one, confirming gains that Boston had won over a half century of struggle. The new charter restored the rights and liberties that Andros and Randolph had threatened, including land titles granted under the original charter, restoration of town governance, religious liberty (which in Boston meant the right to sustain the Puritans' established churches so long as tolerance of other Protestants was allowed), and the right to elect an assembly, both the lower house of deputies and the upper council of magistrates, whose consent was necessary for all taxation measures. The major difference between the new charter and the old, the trade-off that Mather accepted in return for the guaranteed title to Maine and Plymouth along with all the other original liberties that Massachusetts Bay enjoyed, was the Crown's assertion of the privilege to appoint a royal governor. And in the remarkable story of the man whom the new king chose as the first royal governor of Massachusetts, this account of the political economy of Boston comes full circle, back to the search for silver and the making of local money.

The Apotheosis of William Phips: Silver Makes a Bostonian

John Hull and Eliakim Hutchinson's 1683 expedition to the shipwrecks off Hispaniola ended in failure. But this did not mean the end of fishing projects to the "wracks." The odds against success seemed ludicrous, rated by Daniel Defoe as "a Lottery of a hundred thousand to one odds."[95] But shipwreck salvaging remained an obsession of many Atlantic seafaring men, among them, William Phips of Boston.

Actually, Phips was not "of" Boston. He was born in Maine in 1651, where Boston's religious culture was thin, and Boston's political hold still tenuous. According to the biography of Phips written by Cotton Mather, his birthplace was "at a despicable Plantation on the River of the Kennebeck, and almost the furthest Village of the Eastern Settlement of New England."[96] As a youth, Phips learned the skills of a shepherd and ship's carpenter, but he was barely literate. He grew to be a large, powerful, and violent man, coarse and wild in his manner. But if Boston's political and religious control of Maine was weak, its economic influence was strong. Phips was drawn to Boston in search of greater fortunes and adventures than shepherding and joinery could win him in Maine. In 1673, Phips moved to the city and married the widow of a local merchant. Although he began to establish himself as a shipbuilder, he set his eye on becoming a ship captain and perhaps a substantial merchant. As Mather described Phips's ambition, "He would frequently tell the Gentlewoman his Wife, That he should yet be Captain of a King's Ship . . . and, That he should be Owner of a Fair Brick-House in the Green-Lane of North-Boston."[97]

For Phips, as for Hull, the key to achieving success involved silver, but the path Phips took to wealth was different. The Phips family had obscure connections to English nobility—not an uncommon trait among the settlers of early Maine. Land grants often came through the hands of aristocrats such as Gorges, who favored their lesser relations with these speculative gifts.[98] These connections gave Phips the idea—a rare notion among Bostonians, but more common in the 1680s as the possibility of royal government loomed—that noble patronage offered the best route to worldly success. After trying his hand in a minor salvaging voyage off the Bahamas, where he heard about Spanish treasure ships still undiscovered in Caribbean waters, Phips went to London in spring 1683—at the same time that Hull and Hutchinson were sending their own ship to the wracks—to search for patrons to mount a substantial expedition.

In London, Phips met two naval officers, Sir John Narbrough and Sir Richard Haddock, who had served in the Caribbean and were also interested in salvaging. Through their support, and with his blustering self-confidence, Phips secured the loan of a Royal Navy frigate for his expedition. The ship was called *The Rose*, or sometimes *The Rose of Algiers* or *Algier-Rose*. It had been a vessel in the naval forces of Algiers, captured by the English in a battle off the Barbary Coast, and outfitted with twenty guns by the Royal Navy. Phips's first duty as its commander was to sail to Boston, where he delivered his quarrelsome passenger, Edward Randolph, bearing the writ of quo warranto against the Massachusetts Charter. At this moment, Phips seemed to care not at all about Boston's politics and its fate at the hands of the Crown. All that mattered to him was that in Boston, he could supply the ship with diving tubs and other necessities for his expedition.[99]

His first venture failed to find the *Concepcion*, but Phips picked up enough additional information during the voyage to convince his English supporters to try again. Phips also proved capable of withstanding his frustrated crew's entreaties to turn from fruitless wreck hunting to lucrative Caribbean piracy, and this enhanced his reputation as well.[100] He gained some new patrons, including the Duke of Albermarle, soon to be Jamaica's governor, and set off in 1686 in a larger ship, the *James and Mary*, armed with better information, a larger crew, and richer backing.

This time, Phips and his crew succeeded beyond their fondest imaginings. On January 19, 1687, divers from one of Phips's companion ships located the wreck of the *Concepcion*. A salvage operation began that "brought up Thirty Two Tuns of Silver." Cotton Mather recorded Phips's reaction: "Thanks be to God! We are made."[101] To Phips's credit, he managed the delicate feat of salvaging the treasure and then sailing it back to London. The ship's crew had signed on for fixed wages, but now declared that "they knew not how to bear it, that they should not share all among themselves, and

FIGURE 3.2. Gold medal commemorating Sir William Phips's salvage of the wreck of the *Concepcion*, 1687. On the reverse face, the Latin inscription "Navfraga Reperta" translates as "wreck recovered," and "Semper Tibi Pendeat Hamus" means "always let your hook be hanging."

be gone to lead a short Life and a merry."[102] By promising the men a share in the profits, "which if the rest of his Employers would not agree unto, he would himself distribute his own share among them," Phips staved off mutiny. He brought the *Mary and James* back to England with the largest treasure since Sir Francis Drake had seized a Spanish fleet more than a century before.

All told, the silver that Phips recovered was valued at £210,000 sterling. King James II claimed his share, the royal "tenth." The various investors took their cuts, but honored Phips's promise to reimburse his crew. In the end, Phips received a sixteenth share of what remained after the king's tenth was taken, worth roughly £11,000, plus a series of gifts from the grateful patrons who sponsored the voyage. These included a golden cup for his wife reportedly worth £1,000 and a medal cast in his honor, with King James and Queen Mary on one side, and an image of the eponymous ship salvaging the wreck on the other, affixed to a golden chain to wear around his neck.[103] King James knighted Phips in June 1687, making him henceforth "Sir William," the first New England native ever to earn this honor. In August, Phips was awarded the title of provost marshal of New England, a newly invented position under the Dominion of New England that would have charged Phips with naming and overseeing the county sheriffs—a new judicial system that the king and Governor Andros had envisioned to replace the county courts of the charter period.

The immensity of Phips's treasure and the popular notoriety it received in England set off a wave of speculation in treasure seeking, joint-stock corporation forming, and other financial adventures that influenced the formation of the Bank of England in the following decade.[104] In his *Essay upon Projects*, Defoe singled out the extraordinary success of the Phips venture as the key to launching the projecting spirit that had taken hold in Britain.[105] A second venture to the *Concepcion* was immediately planned to salvage the remainder of the treasure; estimates suggested that Phips had recovered only one-fourth of the total. The master of the Royal Mint was among the lead investors in this return voyage, as England faced a specie shortage in the late seventeenth century.

At this point, many an enterprising colonist might have continued along the path that Phips was already on, perhaps buying a country estate in England, living off his fortune, and making friends among other gentry who had prospered in military or colonial service. This was the pattern of many West Indian planters who made fortunes in the sugar industry, received knighthoods as a reward for their wealth, and retired to England, where they lived as absentee landlords.[106] According to Mather, Phips was offered "a very Gainful place among the Commissioners of the Navy, with many other Invitations to settle himself in England." Instead, he returned to Boston to take up his position as provost marshal in the Dominion of New England.[107]

The reasons for this choice are obscure, although several possibilities exist. First, Phips joined the return expedition to the wreck of the *Concepcion*, but this time not as its commander. His earlier patron and one of the major investors, retired admiral Sir John Narborough, took charge of this much-larger expedition, which despite its greater size and resources turned out to be far less lucrative. After Phips's initial success on the *James and Mary*, word of the wreck's location had spread, and small parties of local scavengers from the Bahamas, Jamaica, and Hispaniola hauled up still

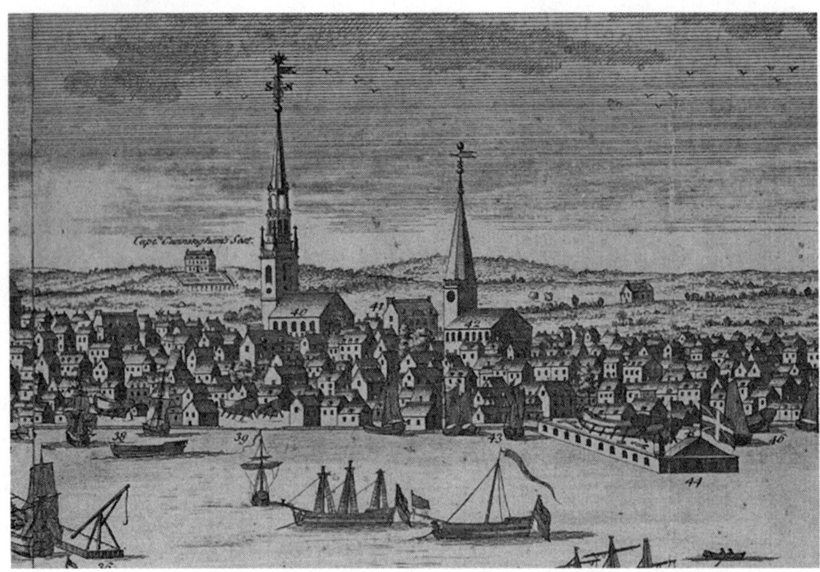

FIGURE 3.3. *A South East View of the Great Town of Boston in New England in America*, by William Price, 1743. Detail. The mansion that had belonged to William Phips in the 1690s is labeled "41," visible between the steeples of Christ Church and the New North Meeting House.

more treasure before the Narborough expedition returned in 1688. Little remained to be found, and Narborough soon died of a contagious fever, so Phips decided to return to New England. He had been away from his wife for five years, and now he had the money to buy her the promised grand brick house in the North End. In addition to losing his most prominent patron in Narbrough, his other major supporter, the Duke of Albemarle, now the governor of Jamaica, died later in 1688, cutting Phips off from his strongest connections in England.

His alienation from imperial advancement further hardened on his return to Boston. Andros, Randolph, and other members of the Dominion government were openly disdainful of Phips and his claim to gentry status. They ignored his appointment as provost marshal, as Andros had already appointed one of his own clients to this lucrative position. They excluded Phips from the honors that he felt he deserved. Mather even suggests, and Randolph's letters confirm, that Andros and Randolph attempted a bureaucratic double-dipping from Phips's fortune; they tried to assess the royal share of the treasure in Boston even though this had already been done in London after the initial return voyage.[108]

In the meantime, leading Bostonians of the old guard saw an opportunity in Phips's arrival. They slowly drew Phips into their circle and groomed him for the role of champion so as to serve the interests of the state while serving his own purposes, much as Hull and others had done before him. The role that Boston's traditional leaders cultivated for Phips, an image that Mather's biography would set in print, drew on the commonwealth tradition. Mather made much of Phips's honest commitment to the sailors and salvagers who had signed on for wages, but were rewarded by Phips with shares of the silver. According to Mather, when Phips was faced with mutiny on the return voyage to London, "he made his Vows unto Almighty God, that if the Lord would carry him safe home to England with what he had now given him, to suck of the Abundance of the Seas, and of the Treasures hid in the Sands, he would for ever Devote himself unto the Interests of the Lord Jesus Christ, and of his People, especially in the Country which he did himself Originally belong unto." Mather also repeated a story that Phips had refused any reward from King James, save "that New-England might have its lost privileges restored."[109]

A decade earlier, the £11,000 in silver that Phips brought home to Boston would have answered the dreams of John Hull, who had longed for cash from the king to relieve the colony's troubled fiscal state. But now it seemed strangely irrelevant; silver was not what Boston needed most in 1688. Hull was dead, the mint was shut down, and the oppression of Andros's government weighed heavily on the local economy and public spirit. Still, according to Hull's son-in-law, Samuel Sewall, Phips's arrival turned out a large crowd, as "many of the Town . . . [went] to complement him." At the Harvard commencement that summer, the speaker, the Reverend William Hubbard, took special care to honor Phips and "compared Sir William to Jason fetching the Golden Fleece."[110] Phips's new North End mansion stood near Boston's Second or North Church, where Increase and Cotton Mather shared the pulpit. The father and son clergymen quickly cultivated their rich new parishioner. On his first Sunday back in Boston, Phips ostentatiously attended Cotton Mather's sermon at the North Church, deliberately avoiding the upstart Anglican service that Andros and Randolph had recently initiated.

Over the next two years, Phips would go through the intensive process of baptism and full membership in the Mathers' church, a rigorous religious education that no matter what the state of his inward piety, served to link Phips closer to the Mathers and the old guard of Boston's leadership. Later in 1688, Phips sailed to London again, where he joined Increase Mather in attempting to persuade King James to dismiss Andros and restore the Massachusetts Charter.[111] These hopes were more realistic than they might at first seem, as James was cultivating the support of Protestant dissenters in London for his own reasons. James wanted reforms that would bring toleration to all English nonconformists, including his fellow Roman Catholics, for which support from other dissenters might be useful. As a result, Increase Mather had already initiated a series of meetings with James. When Phips arrived, Mather brought the celebrity treasure hunter into the game; James tended to look with favor on anyone who had brought him a gift of £21,000. Despite the turbulence of the later months of 1688 and early 1689 in England, with William's invasion and James's flight, Mather and Phips managed to ride the wave of change adeptly. They picked up negotiations with William where they left off with James and petitioned for the restoration of the old charter.[112]

Phips returned to Boston in spring 1689, sailing from London in March bearing a definitive proclamation that William and Mary had been crowned as England's new monarchs, and ordering the temporary reinstatement of the old charter government until a final determination could be made. The new king had been about to order the reappointment of all standing colonial governors, simply as an expeditious measure for continuity, but Phips and Mather had urgently petitioned him to exclude Andros from this command. Phips's slow journey across the Atlantic meant that by the time he arrived, Boston's rebellion had already occurred. Instead of encountering the hostility he expected from Andros, Phips was met with a different crisis, which had been one of the precipitants of the rebellion.

Over the winter of 1688–89, violence had erupted on the northeastern frontier. Abenaki Indians in league with French supporters from Canada attacked the villages and towns of Maine. Andros had attempted to quell the violence early in 1689, but suspicion that Andros and his fellow officers were part of a French Catholic conspiracy to overthrow New England's liberties had undermined his support among the New England militiamen sent to the front.[113] The mutiny of some of these soldiers in spring 1689 initiated a rising tide of anger against the Dominion government throughout the New England hinterland. It was this anger that eventually sent thousands of men marching on Boston in April. The rebellion restored a more acceptable government, at least until further word from the Crown, but it left the problem of frontier violence unresolved. Although Boston's leaders could not have known this, royal instructions from Louis XIV to the new governor of Canada, Count Frontenac, ordered him to encourage the Abenaki to continue their attacks on New England's frontier. What Boston did know was that the attacks kept coming, amid rumors of French soldiers and priests aiding the assaults. In response, the provisional General Court devised a plan to attack the French fort at Port-Royal in Acadia. The seizure of this fort might undermine French encouragement of Indian attacks. And if Port-Royal were easily taken, then the expedition might move on to the Saint Lawrence Valley and seize the center of French American power: the city of Quebec.[114]

But old habits die hard. In making these invasion plans, Boston followed its long military tradition as an independent city-state. The General Court and Boston's local leadership organized the expedition, raised the troops and ships, supplied the arms and equipment, and funded the enterprise on their own without applying to the Crown for assistance, despite the knowledge that the new king was himself going to war with France. Although it took time for the realization to sink in, the necessity for this remarkable degree of independence from the Crown, ingrained among Bostonians since

1630, was changing. The traditional goals of Boston's political economy were suddenly and for the first time congruent with the foreign policy of England's monarch. William III, unlike his Stuart predecessors, would likely have supported Boston's desire to conquer Acadia and even Quebec.[115] Louis XIV's instructions to Frontenac to harass New England's frontiers began a new phase in relations between New England and New France. They were issued in direct response to William III's fiercely anti-French policy, which would lead Europe into a quarter century of Anglo-French warfare that spilled over into North America.[116]

In its long years under the first charter, Boston's many military ventures had seldom included amphibious assaults. Combining naval and ground forces was a notoriously difficult feat to coordinate in the age of sail.[117] Now an assault on Port-Royal, and perhaps Quebec as well, required a greater degree of coordination and expenditure than Boston had ever managed before. Much as in King Philip's War, the General Court appointed a committee of merchants and magistrates to oversee the logistics, including old hands like John Richards and Elisha Hutchinson, and younger magistrates like Samuel Sewall. William Phips was named the commander of the expedition.[118]

The assault on Port-Royal was an easy victory. The French fort, it turned out, had few defenses. Phips and his men reaped considerable plunder from the local population, and Acadia fell under English control. But the assault on Quebec did not go well. Phips and his naval expedition entered the Saint Lawrence River as autumn was approaching, with little time to mount an attack on the fortified city before snow came and the river started to freeze. A hoped-for but ill-planned second attacking flank coming from western New England never materialized. After a brief, fruitless bombardment of Quebec's stone walls, and an embarrassing encounter between Frontenac and Major Thomas Savage, who demanded a French surrender to the New Englanders' laughably inadequate forces, the expeditionary fleet retreated. Many of the soldiers and sailors fell ill and died of smallpox on the miserable return voyage. The expedition had momentarily shored up the colony's frontier defenses by undercutting the French in Acadia, but it had been enormously expensive for its slight gains. Cotton Mather reported that the General Court was now in debt to the amount of £40,000 "and [had] not a Penny in the Treasury to pay it withal."[119]

From Silver to Paper: Moving the "Mountains of Peru"

In this moment of fiscal crisis, with only a provisional government in place, a large debt to be paid, and nothing in the treasury to pay it, the General Court drew on the lessons learned in its many decades of fiscal experimentation, first with wampum, then with the "small change" of the pine tree shillings, and took the process a step further. It issued paper money,

> printed from Copper-Plates, a just Number of Bills, and Florished, Indented, and Contrived them in such a manner, as to make it impossible to Counterfeit any of them . . . all Signed by the Hands of Three belonging to that Committee. These Bills being of several Sums, from Two Shillings, to Ten Pounds, did confess the Massachuset-Colony to be Endebted unto the Persons, in whose Hands they were, the Sums therein Expressed.[120]

But whereas the pine tree shillings had claimed to be a full shilling, even though everyone knew they only contained three-quarters of a shilling's worth of silver, this paper money was based on nothing. Nothing but faith, that is, in the promises made by an ad hoc provisional government with not a penny in its treasury to honor its obligations—promises based on taxes that it vowed to collect sometime in the future.

This was a bold experiment, a "project," to use Defoe's term, with almost no precedent in the history of government in Europe or its colonies. It may have been prompted by the appearance in London in 1688 of an anonymous pamphlet titled *A Model for Erecting a Bank of Credit . . . Adapted to the Use of Any Trading Countrey, Where There Is a Scarcity of Moneys: More Especially for His*

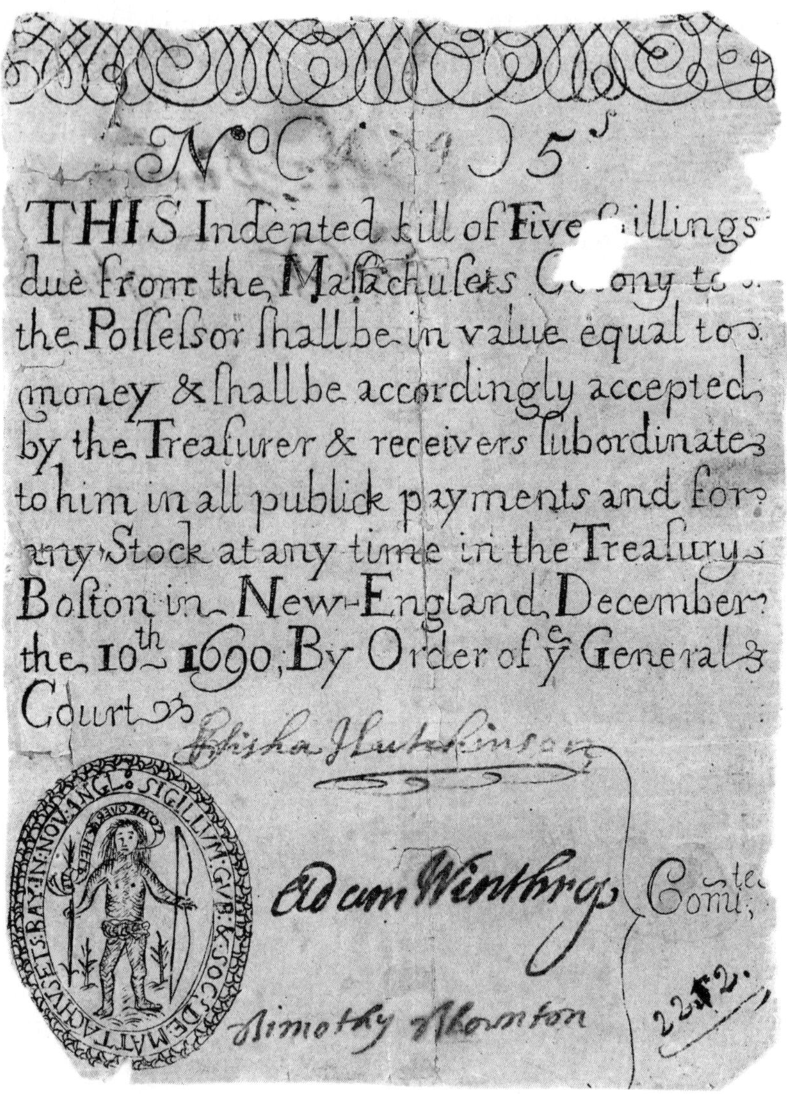
No 5s

THIS Indented bill of Five [illegible]illings due from the Massachusets Colony to the Possessor shall be in value equal to money & shall be accordingly accepted by the Treasurer & receivers subordinate to him in all publick payments and for any Stock at any time in the Treasury. Boston in New-England December the 10th 1690, By Order of ye General Court.

Elisha Hutchinson

Adam Winthrop Comte

Timothy Thornton

SIGILLUM GUB: & SOC: DE MATTACHUSETS BAY IN NOV: ANGL:

FIGURE 3.4. Massachusetts five shilling note, 1690. Note the continued use of the Great Seal of the Massachusetts Bay Company, even though the 1629 charter had been revoked four years earlier and the colony's government was in limbo until the second charter of 1691.

Majesties Plantations in America. This pamphlet described in glowing terms a bank of credit developed in Venice, where the bills issued, originally backed by specie (silver coins), became so useful and desirable as to rise in value above that of specie itself. With public trust and demand for these bills of credit so high, Venice issued even more of them and began to spend the specie it had kept in reserve to pay down the state's debt. In essence, the Venetian Bank of Credit offered a method to issue money based only on faith in the state, "for there is not one Ducket for them in Bank."[121] Cotton Mather had clearly read this pamphlet, for his own account of Boston's paper money system follows it closely: "The Massachusetts Bills of Credit had been like the Bank Bills of Venice, where though there were not, perhaps, a Ducat of Money in the Bank, yet the Bills were esteemed more than Twenty per Cent. better than Money."[122]

Where Boston failed to match Venice was in the trust that common people had in the government's fiscal promises. At this moment of transition and uncertainty, with the colony under a provisional government pending negotiations between Increase Mather and King William's councillors, faith in "the State's Word" was difficult to sustain. The paper money issued by the General Court did depreciate significantly—but not disastrously. It fell to "Fourteen or Sixteen Shillings in the Pound," roughly three-quarters of the face value (a pound was twenty shillings), oddly similar to the ratio of intrinsic to stated value of the pine tree shillings. Only now, the intrinsic value was not measured in silver but rather in faith in the state. The bills were used to pay the soldiers and sailors who participated in the Canadian expedition and the merchants who supplied them, and despite the depreciation, "this Method of paying the Publick Debts, did no less than save the Publick from a perfect Ruin." The reason for the limited depreciation was familiar from Boston's commonwealth tradition. The paper money's value was supported by the willingness of Boston men of wealth to accept the bills at face value. In Cotton Mather's words, "General Phips was in some sort the Leader; who at the very beginning meerly to Recommend the Credit of the Bills unto other Persons, cheerfully laid down a considerable quantity of ready Money [i.e., silver coins] for an equivalent parcel of them."[123] Phips's treasure did support the political economy of Boston after all; its value as specie encouraged greater faith among the public in the provisional government's monetary promises.[124]

Mather, for one, was certain that if the government had not been in such an unsettled state, with the people unsure whether orders from Whitehall might undermine the tax measures on which the paper money promises were made, that "the Bills of Credit had been better than so much ready Silver." The image he used to emphasize this point is striking and bears close attention. It demonstrates how far the city-state of Boston had come in the forty years since the crisis at Potosí led the General Court to commission Hull to make silver coins: "Yea, the Invention [of paper money] had been of more use to the New-Englanders, than if . . . the Mountains of Peru had removed into these Parts of America."[125] Mather's analogy is, on the surface, the sign of an amazing conceptual transformation in the space of a few decades. In 1650, Bostonians were seeking desperately for any way to fetch silver from the "Mountains of Peru" and to devise a plan for keeping silver coins circulating within the colony in the belief that reliable small change was essential to stimulate the internal economy. By 1690, many Bostonians were ready to give up on the need for silver to do this work and instead attempted an experiment to see if obviously worthless paper—worthless in an intrinsic sense—could function as a substitute—nay, an improvement—on silver as a trading currency.

But it would be a mistake to see this change simply as a leap from medieval to modern conceptions of money in one concentrated forty-year period. In 1690, and for many decades thereafter, resistance to the idea that paper money could retain its face value without backing from silver (or other commodities of reliable worth) remained a feature of life in Boston and everywhere throughout the Atlantic world. The fact that one of the government's chief supporters, Phips, happened to be sitting on a large pile of Spanish bullion helped give the General Court the confidence necessary to issue paper currency. Because of the striking combination of a limited supply of valuable commodity resources with an incredibly vigorous trading economy, Bostonians were compelled to be more creative in the way that they thought about money than many other places in the Atlantic world. Yet they had by no means shaken off all older customs. The conceptual leap from silver coins to paper was an important shift—part of a larger trend in experimental political economy that had been part of English political and religious improvement schemes from the mid-seventeenth century onward.[126] But it was not the most striking development in Boston's political economy in the seventeenth century.

Rather, the key to understanding the changes in this period is to grasp the actual development of the overall political economy of the city-state of Boston. It began as a small experimental corporate colony in the 1630s, unclear on the direction of its political and economic future. Within a decade, Bostonians realized that the advance plans made at the time of settlement were not going to work. From there, by way of the deliberate actions of Boston's merchants and political leaders, and with the cooperation of its thousands of colonists, it transformed itself into an entity—expansive, integrated internally, well-connected externally, fiscally sound, militarily strong, and socially stable—that might sustain public faith in its financial promises, even in the absence of silver.

Boston was not Venice, not in the strength of its government, the power of its navies and armies, the reach of its commerce, the wealth of its merchants, or the glory of its artists. No one would ever mistake the home of the bean and the cod for the Lion City of the Adriatic. But as Mather's citation of the Venetian example for the Bank of Credit suggests, Venice was a model for the kind of place that Boston had become. In that sense, the silver coins that Hull issued for over thirty years, from 1652 to his death in 1683, had been a great success: they played an integral role in the development of a city-state's political economy. Its mercantile interests and proven powers of self-government were now strong enough that the coins themselves were no longer necessary; they had served as a fiscal scaffolding that could be kicked away, now that the political economy had been built.

The growth and expansion of the city-state of Boston in the seventeenth century was a remarkable accomplishment. It was also at times a brutal and exclusionary one. The definition of who might be included in the commonwealth shifted with time and circumstances, but the commitment to the ideal of commonwealth remained steady throughout. The model for this Atlantic commonwealth drifted from the definition favored by Saint Augustine's *City of God*, and in the end become more literally "Utopian," devastating to the native populations of southern New England that would not commit themselves to joining the city-state of Boston, and aggressively elbowing aside rival English, French, and Dutch claimants to the territories, resources, and trade routes that Bostonians needed to make their commonwealth succeed.

Succeed it did, and no better mark of this success could be found than the Crown's agreement to appoint Phips, the cultivated ally of Increase and Cotton Mather, a Bostonian made, not born, and made by turning Spanish silver toward New England commonwealth ends, as the first royal governor of the province of Massachusetts under the new charter granted by King William. The creation of the city-state of Boston was all the more remarkable for the fact that it had been done in the face of the hostility of the Stuart monarchs and their colonial agents. Now that Boston had found, at last, a Caesar it could love, the prospects for a glorious future in the cooperation between the city-state of Boston and the new British Empire seemed limitless.

Book II

The Selling of Joseph

> And it came to pass, when Joseph was come unto his brethren, that they stript Joseph out of his coat, his coat of many colours that was on him; And they took him, and cast him into a pit: and the pit was empty, there was no water in it. And they sat down to eat bread: and they lifted up their eyes and looked, and, behold, a company of Ishmeelites came from Gilead with their camels bearing spicery and balm and myrrh, going to carry it down to Egypt. And Judah said unto his brethren, What profit is it if we slay our brother, and conceal his blood? Come, and let us sell him to the Ishmeelites, and let not our hand be upon him; for he is our brother and our flesh. And his brethren were content. Then there passed by Midianites merchantmen; and they drew and lifted up Joseph out of the pit, and sold Joseph to the Ishmeelites for twenty pieces of silver: and they brought Joseph into Egypt.
>
> —Genesis 37:23–28

Jacob's sons saw that it was better for their pockets to sell their brother than to slay him. They met merchants, distant cousins from another of the nations descended from Abraham, engaged in the long-distance luxury trade. The Ishmaelites seemed willing enough to add human merchandise to their wares. Their ready silver bought Joseph, and they brought him to Egypt and sold him to one of Pharaoh's officers.

Despite the crime of his brothers and the callousness of the slave traders, Joseph prospered by virtue of his talents and godly spirit. He rose to become Pharaoh's viceroy and made Egypt prosper. Later when his brothers came to Egypt to buy food, he reconciled with them and brought all of Jacob's descendants, the children of Israel, into Egypt to save them from famine and starvation.

Joseph's story, a critical passage in the establishment of the nation of Israel, posed a critical question for the city-state of Boston: Are evil actions justified by the good that may come of them? The question was essential because the eighteenth-century British Empire was built on practices that Joseph's brothers and their Ishmaelite trading partners would have recognized. The Atlantic slave trade that Britain came to dominate as well as the colonial production and far-flung distribution of sugar, coffee, tobacco, and other luxury goods, the early modern equivalents of "spicery and balm and myrrh," were premised on acts of "manstealing," the expropriation of labor from violently uprooted workers. It was an enormous system for the generation and circulation of commodities, governed by king and Parliament, defended by the king's soldiers and the Royal Navy, and organized by merchants who moved people and things to their places of greatest utility and demand. From the time of the Glorious Revolution in Britain and the overthrow of the Dominion of New England in 1688–89, the city-state of Boston embraced this system wholeheartedly, and therefore had to reckon constantly and in many different guises with the moral challenge of the selling of Joseph.

Chapter 4

Theopolis Americana

Boston and the Protestant International

> Tis *Aelian*, a Grecian Writer, who sayes, That in Times long preceding his, there was a Tradition, that *Europe* and *Asia* and *Africa*, were encompassed by the Ocean; But without and beyond the Ocean, there was a *great Island*, as big as *They*. And in that Other World, there was an huge CITY, called, *Theopolis*, THE GODLY CITY. . . . I know not what well to make of a Tradition so very *Ancient*, and yet having Such an *American* Face upon it. . . . There are many Arguments to perswade us, That our Glorious LORD, will have an HOLY CITY in AMERICA; a *City*, the STREET whereof will be *Pure* GOLD.
>
> —Cotton Mather, *Theopolis Americana*, 1710

On the night of January 1, 1686, Samuel Sewall, Boston merchant and aficionado of apocalyptic speculation, had a dream. Earlier that day, he had finished reading a four-volume commentary on the Book of Revelation, written in the 1610s by David Pareus, professor of divinity at the University of Heidelberg.[1] That night, his head filled with millennial thoughts, Sewall dreamed "that our Saviour in the dayes of his Flesh when upon Earth, came to Boston and abode here sometime, and moreover that He Lodged in that time at Father Hull's"—that is, at the South End home of John Hull, Sewall's late father-in-law. The next morning, Sewall remembered two reflections that he had during this dream: "One was how much more Boston had to say than Rome boasting of Peter's being there. The other a sense of great Respect that I ought to have shewed Father Hull since Christ chose when in Town, to take up his Quarters at his House. Admired the goodness and wisdom of Christ in coming hither and spending some part of His short Life here."[2]

More than fifty years after Boston's founding, the shadow of Philippi, the puritan colony's aspiration for continuity with apostolic Christianity, still lurked powerfully in Sewall's dream life. If Rome had Peter and Philippi had Paul, Boston had Jesus Christ himself, wisely lodging at Hull's house just steps down the street from Sewall's beloved South Church and conveying his blessings on Hull's little "mint house" that stood nearby. But on that first night of 1686, Boston's purpose and identity were in danger as never before. Edmund Andros and the Dominion of New England, the latter-day equivalent of Caesar's Roman legions who ruled Philippi, and rejected the strange religion and commonwealth practices of Paul and his Christian followers, threatened to dismantle the accomplishments of Boston's founders.

For most of the period from its founding in 1630 to the revocation of its charter in 1685, Boston had suffered the distant authority of governments it despised. In 1686, the Stuart government was no longer distant. The Stuart monarchs' affinity for Roman Catholicism and their admiration of Bourbon absolutism were anathema to Bostonians, who refused to join in any of their projects, and resisted the Stuarts' efforts to rein in Massachusetts' republican polity and independent churches. Even during the long decade of parliamentary rule in midcentury, when Oliver Cromwell and his Puritan allies governed on principles more sympathetic to Massachusetts, Bostonians avoided involvement in the protector's overseas ventures, steered clear of Cromwell's Western Design to conquer the Spanish Caribbean, and hemmed and hawed over the prospect of joining an assault on New Netherland until a peace treaty ended the first Anglo-Dutch War.[3] Bostonians under the first charter showed no lack of imperial ambition, but their aggressive assault on the territory of New England's native population, their participation in new colonial ventures from Connecticut to New Hampshire and Maine, their construction of the New England Confederation, and their development of Atlantic trading networks from Acadia to Africa were do-it-yourself projects, unaided and frequently opposed by the English Crown.[4]

In the few turbulent years that followed Sewall's dream, all this changed. As we saw in book I, the people of Boston and New England rose up in arms, arrested Andros and sent him back to England. Their rebellion was spurred by rumors that James II had fled to France and Parliament had invited William of Orange to succeed him. But after an anxious period of waiting and negotiation, William's favorable reaction, in the form of a new charter for Massachusetts, opened new vistas for imperial cooperation and wider opportunities for Atlantic commerce for those Bostonians able to comprehend the magnitude of the revolution.

By forming an alliance between England and the Protestant kingdoms of northern Europe, and by implementing an aggressive strategy to thwart the ambitions of France's Louis XIV, King William made it possible for Bostonians to believe that their own ambitions might no longer be limited to their remote corner of the Atlantic world. For decades they had imagined themselves to be a saving remnant of Protestantism, on the run from tyranny, Catholicism, and the Antichrist in Europe, Africa, Asia, and Spanish and French America. Now, with a militant Dutch Protestant patriot on the throne of the united kingdoms of Britain, they might finally align their own aspirations with a powerful political and military force that they could imagine turning dreams into reality.[5]

This chapter explores what Bostonians made of these new opportunities, and how contact with this widening world reshaped Boston in New England in the half century after 1689. The preceding chapters focused on the growth of Boston's political and economic power across New England; now we turn to cultural power, and how Britain's new monarchy and reconstructed empire in the wake of the Glorious Revolution generated challenges and possibilities for Bostonians trying to envision their place in the Atlantic world. For a new generation of the city's leaders, the Dutch and German lands offered prospects for new political alliances, new opportunities in trade and industry, and new models of religious and cultural reformation to which Bostonians could aspire, and to which they could contribute their own ideas and examples, as they claimed a place in the Republic of Letters and the Protestant International. The evidence for these new connections forms an intricate web, spun out through a series of transatlantic journeys, mutual friendships, and correspondence networks maintained across the early decades of the eighteenth century. To attempt to replicate the entire network would be hopelessly confusing. But the general outline can be seen clearly through the experiences and ideas of three men who played as large a part as any in these new movements: Samuel Sewall, Jonathan Belcher, and Cotton Mather. All three men were sons (or sons-in-law) of powerful fathers who had played important parts in the formation of Boston's political economy and the preservation of its autonomy in the seventeenth century.

Until his death in 1683, John Hull largely overshadowed his son-in-law, Samuel Sewall, who dreamed of Christ in Boston. Then Sewall came into his own, first as a merchant taking over the family business, but also as a magistrate, a member of the council (the upper house of the General Court), a judge riding circuit on the Massachusetts Superior Court, and a leading layman in the South Church of Boston. Belcher, an ambitious merchant and politician, and heir to his father Andrew Belcher's fortune, was one of the wealthiest and most powerful figures in Boston during the first half of the eighteenth century, but his role in shaping the city and commonwealth has long been underappreciated.[6] Mather was equally ambitious, and his role in Boston's religious life has never been underestimated, though often misunderstood. Unlike Sewall and Belcher, Mather never managed to step out fully from his father's shadow; Increase Mather lived a long time, predeceasing Cotton by only a few years.[7] Nevertheless, as the generation of New England leaders dominated by men like their fathers began to give way in the eighteenth century, Sewall, Belcher, and Mather stood at the center of an expansive network of people whose contacts and experiences in the Atlantic world gave a new cast to Boston's cultural ambitions.

They moved through their networks in different ways, motivated by different forces. Sewall, as a circuit riding judge and member of the governor's council, knew Boston and its New England hinterland in minute detail, and saw its troubles and contentions pass before him from his seat on the bench. But Sewall was also an overseas merchant, profoundly attuned to the wider Atlantic context, and he made deliberate efforts to understand the local in terms of the global. Belcher, compared with either Sewall or Mather, was no intellectual. He went where fate, his interests, and his connections led him, with the result that his experience has a haphazard, accidental quality. The best way to understand his Atlantic connections is to follow his footsteps, which the detailed journal he kept of his voyage to the Netherlands and Germany makes possible. Mather, by contrast, was a systematic thinker who seldom left Boston and never crossed the Atlantic. Unimpeded by confusing encounters with the messiness of external reality, Mather could contribute to the construction of an organized, imaginative Protestant Atlantic network. Rather than immediate experience, what allowed Mather to perform this imaginative construction was one of the most remarkable material artifacts of the early modern Atlantic world: the library amassed over several generations by the extended Mather family, housed in their North End of Boston home.

The following pages explore Samuel Sewall's encounter with the problem of slavery—a problem first brought before him on the judicial bench in Boston, but that he pursued imaginatively to the ends of the earth and across the span of human history. We then follow Jonathan Belcher on his tours through the Netherlands and Germany, where he encountered a surprising, and surprisingly appealing, alternative world of politics, religion, and economy that shaped his own ideas about what kind of place Boston might become. Finally, we turn to Cotton Mather, following his mental journey across much of the same territory traveled by Sewall and Belcher—a journey that requires an excursion through the Mather family's enormous library in order to explain the shape, dimensions, and meaning of Boston's new connections to the Atlantic world in the early eighteenth century.

Samuel Sewall and *The Selling of Joseph*

On June 24, 1700, Samuel Sewall published *The Selling of Joseph*. This pamphlet offered one of the first significant arguments against African slavery and the slave trade ever published in North America.

Sewall's reasoning is simple and direct: "*Liberty* is in real value next unto Life: None ought to part with it themselves, or deprive others of it, but upon the most mature Consideration." He uses scripture to defend the proposition that human beings are by nature self-possessed, citing chapter and verse to decry "Man Stealing" as an atrocious crime. He asserts that African slaves make poor servants because they are always pining for their lost freedom. He challenges the common defenses of African slavery at the time, finding none of the arguments convincing, and concludes his tract with a plea to honor the common humanity of all people under a universal deity: "These Ethiopians, as black as they are; seeing they are the Sons and Daughters of the First Adam, the Brethren and Sisters of the Last ADAM, and the Offspring of God; They ought to be treated with a Respect agreeable."[8]

The Selling of Joseph has usually been seen as an aberration, a peculiar product of Sewall's sensitive puritan conscience, spurred by his unusual reading habits and by a petition that came before his court "for the freeing of a Negro and his wife, who were unjustly held in Bondage."[9] Its immediate reception was hostile. A year after its publication, Sewall's fellow judge on the Massachusetts Superior Court, John Saffin, attacked it in print. By most accounts, Saffin got the better of the argument, refuting each one of Sewall's objections to slavery by accepted social and legal standards of the day.[10] *The Selling of Joseph* subsequently fell into obscurity. Only a single copy of the original edition is known to have survived. It was reprinted only once in the eighteenth century, and not again until 1864. Sewall's efforts failed to create a persistent antislavery movement in eighteenth-century Massachusetts, and there is no direct line of influence to be drawn from Sewall to William Lloyd Garrison and nineteenth-century abolitionism.[11]

But if we expand our horizons to consider the contexts, both local and global, in which Sewall wrote *The Selling of Joseph*, a different picture emerges. In the closing decade of the seventeenth century and first third of the eighteenth, rapidly changing circumstances within Boston, the British Empire, and the larger Atlantic community brought slavery to the forefront of public concern. If

Sewall's pamphlet was not the start of an antislavery movement, it was an early statement in a circuitous conversation on slavery and related subjects that spread far beyond Boston. The full meaning of *The Selling of Joseph* can only be understood if we follow this conversation out into the complex world of the changing Atlantic community. (See plate 13.)

In Sewall's own words, his pamphlet was prompted by his observation that "the Numerousness of Slaves at this day in the Province, and the Uneasiness of them under their Slavery, hath put many upon thinking whether the Foundation of it be firmly and well laid."[12] The number of slaves in Massachusetts more than doubled between 1676 and 1708, from roughly 200 to about 550, and three-fourths of these 550 slaves were concentrated in the city of Boston.[13] These are small numbers compared with the many thousands of enslaved Africans imported into the Chesapeake, Carolina, and above all the West Indies in this era. Yet the roughly 400 enslaved Africans in Boston constituted about 6 percent of the city's population in 1700, which means that an enslaved African may have dwelled in as many as one in four of Boston's households. From the perspective of Boston, Africans were visibly more numerous in the province in 1700 than they had been in the 1670s, when Sewall (b. 1652) came of age.[14]

Sewall's pamphlet appeared at the end of a decade of extraordinary unease in Boston. During the 1690s, local trafficking in human bodies and souls reached unprecedented levels, and concerns about coerced labor and the forced migration of unwilling populations seemed particularly urgent. Africans constituted a substantial part of this traffic. In 1696, Parliament suspended the Royal African Company's monopoly on the slave trade within the British Empire, allowing more Boston merchants than ever to enter the "Guinea trade" directly, which accounts for the increased number of slaves in town.[15] But enslaved Africans were not the only human commodities routinely bought and sold in Sewall's Boston.

Since 1689, the war that King William initiated against Louis XIV's France had spilled over into New England. The war against New France and its Indian allies, known as King William's War in the colonies, created a lively market in captives on all sides. The exchange of prisoners of war and the enslavement of prisoners were not new to Boston. During the Pequot War of 1637 and King Philip's War of 1675–78, as we saw in book I, captive Indians were sold into slavery in the West Indies, and exchanges for English prisoners were made with their Indian captors. King William's War brought a new dimension to these colonial conflicts, involving the deliberate strategy of raiding enemy settlements and seizing captives for the purpose of exchange.[16] Sewall's diary for September 10, 1699, records a typical example: "There is a press in Boston, of 32 Men, four out of a Company, to goe to the Eastward, by reason of the fears and dispersions people there are under. It seems 10 or 11 English persons are taken away as hostages till those Indians sent into Boston, be return'd."[17] The town of Boston, divided into eight wards or "companies" for the sake of military conscription, raised a troop of thirty-two soldiers to send to Maine "to the Eastward" in the hope of preventing further hostage-taking raids. The raid on Deerfield, Massachusetts, in 1704, in which the Reverend John Williams and his family were captured and brought to New France, is just the most notorious example of this common approach to warfare that emerged in the 1690s. One of its most appalling features in the eyes of many Bostonians was that French and Indian captors separated English children from their parents in order to destroy their personal and religious allegiances, in much the way that slave owners dealt with African slave families.[18] Consequently, the separation of families was one of the cruel aspects of slavery that Sewall addressed in his pamphlet: "It is likewise most lamentable to think, how in taking Negroes out of Africa, and Selling of them here, That which GOD ha's joyned together men do boldly rend asunder; Men from their Country, Husbands from their Wives, Parents from their Children."[19]

All through the 1690s and into the eighteenth century, Indian or French captors held English colonists, while French and Indian prisoners languished in Boston jails. The prices on the captives' heads were negotiated, measured against their personal qualities, their professed allegiances, and their value as bargaining chips. Was a French Indian held in Boston who had "publicly abjured the popish religion"—renounced Catholicism—worth trading for a Boston merchant, captive in Quebec, who had suspicious French sympathies and Anglican religious affinities?[20] Questions like these loomed large in Boston's moral economy. In the 1670s, few had doubted whether Indian prisoners in King Philip's War could be sold into slavery on Atlantic islands; in the eyes of the English colonists, the Indians' military "savagery" made it unthinkable to keep them in the colony. In the 1690s, Bostonians now had to ponder the morality of selling "civilized" French soldiers captured from the Port Royal garrison into servitude in Barbados.[21]

In addition to moral questions raised by New England's brutal warfare with the French colonies in Quebec and Acadia and their Indian allies, the turn of the eighteenth century marked a high point of piracy in the English Atlantic, and this raised ambiguous ethical issues too. A year before the publication of *The Selling of Joseph*, the infamous Captain Kidd, who had plundered a Mughal merchant ship in the Indian Ocean, had been seized and imprisoned in Boston. The privateer-turned-pirate's treasure, "the Iron chest of Gold, Pearls, &c," was entrusted to Sewall and four other members of the council for safekeeping. It was an enormous relief to Sewall when Kidd and his booty were finally shipped off to London for trial in February 1700. But not all of Boston's problems with pirates could be so easily exported.

The threat of privateering and piracy heightened Bostonians' awareness of the trade in human souls. Sewall's pamphlet challenged the notion that African slaves were "lawful captives taken in Wars" by this analogy: "I am sure, if some Gentlemen should go down to the Brewsters [on Cape Cod] to take the Air, and Fish: And a stronger party from Hull [a town at the southern end of Massachusetts Bay] should Surprise them, and Sell them for Slaves to a Ship outward bound: they would think themselves unjustly dealt with."[22] This was no mere hypothetical example. Boston's sailors and fisherman were commonly drawn into similar situations. New Englanders on Atlantic voyages were frequently taken captive and held as slaves by privateers operating out of North African ports such as Tripoli, Tunis, and Algiers, the so-called Barbary Coast Corsairs; Sewall had put time and money into redeeming friends from "Algerian captivity."[23] Hull had done a great deal of this too, but had not seen the moral conflict that Sewall did between selling Indian captives from King Philip's War and ransoming English captives from Algerine privateers.

New England's homegrown pirates also dragooned coastal fishermen and sailors into criminal enslavement.[24] This practice raised a difficult question: If servants or slaves were forced onto voyages that turned from privateering to piracy, were they responsible for their crimes? Privateers were merchant ships operating under license from a government to prey on enemy shipping, while pirates were unlicensed predators robbing ships of all nations. In a notorious case that Sewall adjudicated in 1704, Captain John Quelch commanded a ship with a mixed crew of both free and enslaved sailors that some Boston merchants had commissioned as a privateer against the French off Acadia; France and Britain were once again at war, making privateering attacks against French shipping legal. Quelch instead sailed to Brazil and preyed on Portuguese shipping. Given that a treaty of amity had been signed by England and Portugal the year before, Quelch and his crew had committed piracy. For their complicity, the free white sailors on Quelch's ship were hanged alongside their captain, while the African slaves were set free—a rare instance in which it was advantageous to be defined as property rather than independent moral agents.[25]

Beginning around 1690, then, Boston's public life was challenged by an unprecedented rise in the number of people whose status and condition raised moral and legal quandaries. Even refugees, whether survivors from the devastating frontier wars or Huguenots fleeing persecution following Louis XIV's 1685 revocation of the Edict of Nantes, contributed to the change. Money had to be raised, homes and food provided, and occupations found for these forced migrants and victims of unjust wars. In 1686, Sewall was one of two council members appointed to distribute relief to Huguenot refugees from the West Indian islands of Saint Christopher and Eleuthera. Unless refugees had particular skills, they were usually placed as servants in private homes, or set to work alongside African or Indian slaves. The most notorious instance of this practice occurred in the early 1690s, when refugee girls from war-ravaged Maine settlements were placed as servants with families in Salem Village, where they encountered other servants, including the Afro-Indian slaves Indian John and Tituba, and became principal figures in the witchcraft crisis of 1692, an episode that caused Judge Sewall years of personal distress and moral anguish.[26]

The uneasiness that Sewall felt in 1700 over the numerousness of slaves was part of his larger sense of rapid dislocation in Boston. Until the 1680s, the city had been a small, homogeneous English community with strong isolationist instincts, resisting involvement in England's imperial projects. But after 1689, with the restructuring of the provincial government, the rapid growth of commercial contacts around the Atlantic rim, and the advent of imperial warfare, the city saw an influx of new and unfamiliar kinds of people. Their arrival coincided with an increase in poverty, crime, and religious heterodoxy, with the latter mandated by the new charter's toleration for all Protestants. The status, condition, and numbers of these newcomers forced Bostonians to consider the moral and social costs of involuntary migration, coerced labor, and human commodification—the challenges posed by the selling of Joseph.[27]

Behind these changes lay major transformations in the Atlantic world. The "Protestant Wind" of 1688 that allowed William of Orange's invasion fleet to land uncontested in Britain breathed fresh air into the sails of a resurgent Protestant International. In addition to restructuring England's overseas empire and making way for the creation of Great Britain, William's Glorious Revolution inaugurated more than a century of warfare rooted in profound religious and ideological differences.[28] Britain and France were the principal combatants, but William and his successors managed to link the Protestant powers of northern Europe in a more stable set of alliances than the seventeenth century had seen.[29]

Boston's transformations in the 1690s can be attributed to this major restructuring of the British Empire and the coming of global warfare. The Royal African Company's monopoly on the British slave trade was suspended in part because the hated Stuart monarchs had founded the company.[30] New England's war with New France was the North American manifestation of the War of the League of Augsburg, the Protestant alliance that William led into combat against the ambitions of Louis XIV. The image of Louis XIV loomed large in Bostonians' fears; the town was frequently swept by wishful rumors of the Sun King's demise.[31] The piracy that plagued Boston's shipping was the natural spillover of a military strategy that used privateering as an extension of naval warfare; during the intervals of peace between wars, seafaring men who had served in the navy or as legitimate privateers now turned their idle hands and plundering skill to piracy. The morally complex issues surrounding piracy in Boston stemmed from cases where privateers, like Captain Quelch, had crossed the line into piracy by attacking ships from friendly countries instead of enemies.[32] The settlement of refugees was another by-product of heightened Catholic-Protestant conflict. What began in 1685 with the Huguenots diaspora continued into the eighteenth century, as Bostonians aided in the relocation of the "poor Palatines," the Salzburg exiles, and other victims of Catholic repression on the European continent.[33]

Sewall's *The Selling of Joseph* represents the most original voice in Boston's local conversation about how to respond to this new set of internationally inspired problems. Sewall's pamphlet denounced the trade in slaves on moral grounds, contesting the common religious defenses of slavery. He rejected the notion that Africans suffered under the "curse of Cham," doubting whether "Ethiopians" really were the descendants of the cursed son of Noah. Even if they were, Sewall was skeptical that it was up to modern Europeans to act the part of "Executioner of the Vindictive Wrath of God." He dismissed the claim that the slave trade was justified because it brought pagans to the Gospel, taking a definitive position on the moral dilemma of the selling of Joseph: "Evil must not be done, that good may come of it." He cast doubt on the premise that Africans were captives taken in just wars: "Every War is upon one side Unjust. An Unlawful War can't make lawful Captives."[34] And even if Abraham had owned slaves, Sewall reminds his readers that "Israelites were strictly forbidden the buying, or selling one another for Slaves," and that "Christians should carry it to all the World, as the Israelites were to carry it one towards another."[35] This was Sewall's restatement of the fundamental premise underlying the spread of the Christian gospel beyond Israel, at the heart of the original Massachusetts Bay enterprise.

In Sewall's eyes, slavery was wrong because "all Men, as they are the Sons of *Adam*, are Coheirs; and have equal Right unto Liberty, and all other outward Comforts of Life." At the same time, Sewall's moral objections to slavery were paired with a racial belief that whether slave or free, Africans would never blend into English society and "will remain in our Body Politick as a kind of extravasat Blood." With respect to the labor force, Sewall argued (in opposition to what Emmanuel Downing had suggested in dialogue with John Winthrop in 1645) that "it would conduce more to the Welfare of the Province, to have White Servants for a Term of Years, than to have Slaves for Life." Regarding military affairs, Sewall believed that "as many Negro men as there are among us, so many empty places there are in our Train Bands," as the Massachusetts government dared not risk arming the enslaved. Sewall even feared for the colony's reproductive potential, claiming that imported African workers take the places of "Men that might make Husbands for our Daughters. And the Sons and Daughters of New England would become more like Jacob, and Rachel, [i.e., the progenitors of a great nation] if this Slavery were thrust quite out of doors."[36]

All of Boston's participants in the debate on slavery in this era shared some of Sewall's equivocations, and consequently, Boston's response to the problem of slavery moved in several directions at once. Sewall and a few allies tried to discourage the slave trade as much as possible. In 1702, Boston's representatives to the General Court introduced a bill to promote the importation of white indentured servants and propose an end date for slavery in Massachusetts, but nothing came of this measure.[37] Meanwhile, local and provincial legislation responded to the perception of social disorder by enacting measures to control servants and slaves more carefully. Between 1690 and 1720, town governments and the General

Court enacted legislation that linked slavery to the maintenance of a racial color line of the kind that the Chesapeake colonies had developed several decades earlier. These included laws prohibiting miscegenation, limiting the access of blacks to firearms and participation in militia training, imposing curfews, and defining slaves as personal property (rather than persons) for taxation purposes.[38]

While the racial definition of slavery and its legal debilities were being drawn more sharply, a contrasting effort was made to ameliorate the condition and treatment of the enslaved. The General Court passed manumission restrictions, which on the face of it would seem to entrench slavery more deeply. Yet their purpose was to prevent masters from using manumission as a way to abandon elderly slaves who were no longer productive workers. Similarly, Sewall worked to soften the worst effects of the antimiscegenation law, as he feared the bill "will promote Murders and other Abominations" by giving mixed-race couples incentive to abort or kill offspring who would be living evidence of their "crime."[39] As originally written, "an Act for the Better Preventing of a Spurious and Mixt Issue" barred any sexual relations between whites and either Indians or Africans. Blacks who broke the law were to be sold out of the colony. Sewall removed Indians from the bill and inserted a clause that recognized the legitimacy of marriage among enslaved people—something that was never achieved in the southern British colonies. In the end, the miscegenation law also included a provision that shipmasters had to pay a four pounds impost on each imported slave—a fee designed to encourage a preference for white servants over enslaved Africans.[40]

In addition to these conflicted legislative efforts, Boston's religious community began to acknowledge its responsibilities to the souls of those in bondage. Mather led the way, organizing neighborhood prayer societies for slaves as well as free blacks in Boston, and holding meetings for the North Church African society in his own home. In 1706, Mather published *The Negro Christianized* to encourage similar efforts throughout New England at the same time that his own congregation presented him with the gift of an African slave to assist with household chores. Following his own principles, Mather educated his slave, whom he named Onesimus after the biblical runaway slave who became Saint Paul's servant (and in some traditions, the bishop of Ephesus). Mather encouraged Onesimus to work outside the household and earn an independent income—a practice not uncommon in colonial Boston, where in the absence of a plantation labor system, the labor of enslaved people was put to a widely varied range of tasks in the urban seaport. Yet even as Mather reminded his neighbors that slaves are "Men, and not Beasts," *The Negro Christianized* argued that slavery was not inconsistent with Christianity, and baptism and Christian instruction would not force masters to free their bond servants.[41] Mather's position offered an unfortunate compromise on Sewall's dictum that "Christians should carry it to all the World, as the Israelites were to carry it one towards another."

None of these measures concerning slavery in Boston, contradictory as they seemed, occurred in isolation. Sewall's challenge to the slave trade as well as the colony's attempt to define slavery and control slaves were part of a general movement to counter a rapid rise in social disorder and human dislocation. The participants were well aware that their concerns were linked to escalating conflict and change in the wider Atlantic world. Alongside this flurry of activity regarding slavery, Boston's leaders in the post-1689 era undertook a parallel set of reforming endeavors: a renewal of missionary work among New England's Indians; the formation of religious societies for young people, sailors, and servants; the creation of new social institutions for the sick, the poor, widows, orphans, and refugees; and the regulation of public markets in Boston.[42]

Just as Boston's new set of social and cultural problems was rooted in transformations happening throughout the Atlantic world, so this local reform program found inspiration in the newly resurgent Protestant International. First in 1689 with William III, and then fifteen years later when Parliament placed the royal succession on the electoral house of Hanover, British interests were knit together with those of Dutch and German Protestants. William's "Northern Alliance" encouraged evangelical Protestants, dissenters, and Pietists throughout northern Europe to strengthen their international ties. Reforming societies emerged among dissenters in Britain in the 1690s, and together with the newly founded Society for the Promotion of Christian Knowledge, worked to reform the manners and morals of every social class. These activist societies in Britain reached out to forge strong connections with like-minded Dutch, German, and Danish reformers. From 1690 onward, as Bostonians vigorously addressed their local concerns in new ways, their actions were influenced by new connections to a resurgent Protestant International.

Boston's contribution to these developments can be traced in an extensive paper trail of legal records, pamphlets, newspaper controversies, and diary entries; reformers are inveterate scribblers. The publication of reforming pamphlets was itself part of the effort. The realization that the press could be used to promote social change encouraged the publication of dozens of polemical and exhortatory pamphlets, mostly by the clergy.[43] But to assess the origins and development of Boston's reform movements and understand their influence, we need to look beyond the Shawmut Peninsula and follow the paths, both literal and figurative, that leading citizens took through a newly emerging version of the Atlantic world in the wake of the Glorious Revolution.

Jonathan Belcher's Wanderjahr

Belcher's father, Andrew, started life as a tavern keeper in Cambridge, across the river from Boston, but built a fortune in the 1670s by provisioning the colony's militia during King Philip's War and later outfitting expeditionary fleets during the wars of the 1690s. By 1699, when Jonathan graduated from Harvard College, his father was a leading Boston merchant and seeking to become still grander.[44] He sent Jonathan to England in 1704 after the outbreak of the War of the Spanish Succession, hoping that his son could secure profitable military contracts. At the age of twenty-two, Jonathan set sail for London, where he proved to be adept at advancing his father's interests.[45] Mission accomplished, the son went on holiday, and from July through October 1704, visited the principal cities

FIGURE 4.1. Portrait of Jonathan Belcher, mezzotint engraving by John Faber, 1734, after a painting by Richard Phillips.

of the Netherlands, and then traveled eastward across the Rhine to Hanover and Berlin. Throughout this trip, Belcher kept a journal that reveals how this young man's travels shaped his developing sense of identity as a Bostonian in a wider Atlantic context than his father had known and foreshadowed the issues that would be central to his subsequent career.[46] Over the course of that career, Belcher would become one of Boston's most important merchants and political figures, and eventually the royal governor of Massachusetts and New Hampshire. His formative experiences exploring the newly accessible Dutch and German realms of the Protestant International would have a profound influence on the city-state of Boston.

Belcher's Dutch tour began at the port city of Rotterdam, and proceeded from there to Delft, The Hague, Leiden, Haarlem, and finally Amsterdam. In his experience of urban life in the Netherlands, three principal themes emerge: a strong desire for an imaginative association with Dutch Protestant Patriotism, curiosity about the practice of religion in a Calvinist yet tolerant state, and interest in the moral and social problems of commercial cities. None of these interests was unique to Belcher; his sightseeing agenda fell squarely within a well-established itinerary followed by many travelers from England to the Netherlands.[47] But as a Bostonian, Belcher's cultural baggage was different, and so the meaning of his Dutch experience would be different as well.

Unlike some contemporary English travelers, Belcher was unencumbered by any ambivalence toward the House of Orange. His visits to Dutch historic sites were occasions for outbursts of Protestant patriotic emotion.[48] Belcher was only seven years old when news of William III's triumphal entry into Britain had prompted Boston's rebellion against Andros, the tyrannical royal governor of James II's Dominion of New England, in which his father had played a significant role, and it was through supplying expeditions in King William's War that the Belcher fortune was made.[49] Belcher dutifully visited and admired the late king's palaces, but his strongest connection to the House of Orange was forged at Delft, where he was inspired by the monument to "the great Nassau," William the Silent, great-grandfather of the late king and champion of the Dutch revolt against Spain. Belcher visited the palace where William was assassinated in 1584 and vividly recounted the details of the death of "this glorious prince, . . . the first deliverer of the Dutch from Popery," done in by the "cursed villany," the "folly and madness" of a "Frenchman" who "recd money from the Spaniards" to commit murder "on so great, so good a man."[50] On his return to Boston, Belcher would name a street that he laid out through his family estate, "Nassau Street." Fifty years later, as governor of New Jersey, he named the main building of the fledgling college at Princeton "Nassau Hall."[51] This powerful identification with Dutch Patriotism would stay with Belcher throughout his life and was emblematic of Boston's position in conflicts among Atlantic empires. Even if the religious and ideological charge of the wars among Britain, France, and Spain diminished across the eighteenth century, from Boston's viewpoint they remained a contest between Protestant patriotism and Catholic tyranny.

Dutch Protestantism and toleration were also among Belcher's major concerns. Belcher grew up during the transitional period when the new Massachusetts Charter of 1691 mandated toleration for all Protestant denominations. Staunch Puritans like Belcher's father put up a united front of hostility toward Anglican newcomers to Boston, fearing that contact with lax forms of worship would corrupt New England's traditions.[52] Andrew Belcher even commissioned the minister of Boston's South Church to preach a private family sermon for Jonathan on the eve of his departure, warning him to cling to his ancestral faith throughout his travels.[53] But Belcher's Dutch experience transformed his religious opinions in unexpected ways. He attended services of many different faiths, noting the novel things that pleased or upset him. Unlike New England's churches, Dutch Calvinists sang hymns accompanied by an organ "play'd very delightfully"—and Belcher liked the music. Yet they used a "form of prayer not altogether unlike the Church of England"; Belcher disliked worship according to a liturgical ritual.[54] At no point during his excursions through Dutch churches (and synagogues) did Belcher seem remotely in danger of wavering in his beliefs. After his journey, when he reflected on the advantages and disadvantages of travel, he did see the main drawback of life on the road to be its danger to religion, but not in the way that his father and minister had feared. It was not doctrinal heterodoxy but rather waywardness in the "duties of religion" that a transient life encouraged. Being away from home and associating with strangers who were also uprooted tended to undermine the steady habits necessary to maintain a vital faith.[55] Belcher had seen firsthand a range of confessional routes to attaining such a faith and came to believe that the *practice* of piety within any one of them was the essential basis for salvation. His encounter with the varieties of Dutch religion set Belcher on the way to becoming an ecumenical Protestant Pietist.

In addition to Patriotism and Protestantism, Belcher explored a third feature of Dutch life: the ethical and social obligations of a commercial society. Boston at the time was rapidly expanding its involvement in the Atlantic economy to the point where it stood among the leading provincial ports in the British Empire, and its population had doubled since the time of Belcher's birth.[56] This boom brought unfamiliar problems—those that plagued merchants most, like commercial risk (especially in wartime), bankruptcy, chronic currency shortages, and the absence of banking as well as poverty, crime, and the dependency of widows, orphans, and the chronically ill.[57] Belcher kept a watchful eye on Dutch approaches to these problems. In Amsterdam, he visited the "Great Change" in the main square, which he compared favorably to the London Exchange. But what impressed him most was the "civility" of the Dutch merchants who entertained him at dinner.[58] On his return to Boston, Belcher would become a leader in the movement to regulate and introduce greater civility to Boston's chaotic market practices, where unregulated commerce took place at all hours in every corner of the city.[59] He also toured the Bank of Amsterdam in the magnificent Stadhuys (a "glorious pile," he called it) and remarked on its value to the city: "The money of their bank is much better than their curr[en]t coin, in that they receive no money into the bank but what is the best silver and of such a weight." Here, perhaps, is the beginning of Belcher's development as an opponent of paper money, framing the position he would maintain in the endless controversies over currency and banking schemes that dominated his political career in Massachusetts.[60] Belcher also admired the absence of poverty and misery in the cities that he visited, for which he gave credit to Dutch advances in philanthropy. He was impressed by the hospitals at The Hague and Amsterdam, including huge establishments for orphans and widows, where the inmates lived with great civility amid gardens and orchards.[61] His subsequent career in Boston would lead Belcher to take part in the establishment of similar institutions.[62]

Belcher visited Dutch palaces and courts as a tourist, making little contact with the country's rulers. But while stopping by the English embassy at The Hague, a chance encounter changed his fortunes. He met Baron Johann Kaspar von Bothmar, envoy from Hanover, who gave Belcher a letter of introduction to Princess Sophia of Hanover, the presumptive heir to the English throne and mother of the future George I.[63] When Belcher set out eastward from Amsterdam for Hanover, his expectations were high for a direct encounter with courtly society. Reality exceeded his fondest hopes. At Hanover he would meet with nobility on intimate terms, learn the rituals and manners of courtly life, and assess at close hand the glories and ravages of royal power.

Belcher's letter of introduction brought him to the center of Hanoverian courtly life, the Electoral Palace at Herrenhausen, where he was swept away by his meeting with Princess Sophia, who became his ideal of a pious, educated ruler. Sophia spoke six languages fluently, loved painting, music, and history, and raised a Calvinist, was especially sympathetic toward the Pietists.[64] During his two weeks' stay, Belcher frequently dined at Sophia's table, accompanied her on long walks through the palace gardens, and played cards with her in the evening. Coming from Boston, where cards were played only in disreputable taverns, Belcher needed etiquette lessons. "When one gives the cards to the Electress, you rise & give them with Ceremony, but they that play often, do it only the first 2 or 3 dealings." Belcher lost, of course, "the game being new to us," and then learned "tis the custome here never to give the money you loose the same night, but the first after."[65] It was uncouth for the loser to pay up immediately; a gentleman waited until the next day to make good his losses.

Not all courtly customs seemed so gracious. Belcher enjoyed the twice weekly "Consort of Musick" that the elector sponsored until he heard an appalling story:

> One of the hautboyes, a young boy and the best player had run away . . . , which was the 4th time he had done so. The 3d he was taken, he was kept 15 dayes in prison and fed on bread and water, and now the Elector sent him word if he would promise to run away no more, he'd only cut off 2 of his fingers. His answ: was he wd run away a thousand times, if he did not hang him. The hautboyes are all slaves, the Elector buyes 'em from one at Cassel, who breeds them up and sells 'em afterwards.[66]

Yet these same musicians performed beautifully in a service in the court chapel "to give thanks for the victory" at the Battle of Blenheim, a decisive victory in the War of the Spanish Succession that maintained the Grand Alliance arrayed against Louis XIV. The news of the Duke of Marlborough's triumph was received at court the day that Belcher arrived, and it became for Belcher not merely a general moment of pride in a Protestant victory but a personal event as well; he was there to witness Princess Sophia fretting over the fate of her son on the battlefield.[67] Life at court presented extremes of feeling and sensibility: the brutality of the future George I toward the musician-slaves, mixed with the tender regard of George's mother toward her younger rebellious son.

Belcher relished his chance to mingle with power and wealth. He enjoyed the dizzying sense of favor and would profit from it in the long run. He also marveled at the curiosities of the far-flung world brought to a European court, taking note of the two dark-skinned Turkish slaves kept by the elector, one of them a wartime captive.[68] His admiration of Princess Sophia never wavered. On his departure, she presented him with her portrait, which was henceforth prominently displayed in the Council Chamber of the town house in the center of Boston.[69] But he was not without ambivalent feelings about the moral effects of royal power and the wealth that it

FIGURE 4.2. Portrait of Sophia, electress of Hanover, by Andreas Scheitz, ca. 1701.

commanded—feelings that his further travels in Germany would bring out more strongly.

As he continued his journey on to Berlin, Belcher stopped to visit a Benedictine monastery that had become a refuge for English Catholic gentry. Here Belcher had an encounter with learned and devout Catholics—a rare experience for a Bostonian, but one that became something of a set piece for many pious Bostonians who ventured into the Atlantic world.[70] It took the form of a debate with the "fathers" in the monastery's library, where Belcher found "none of the best works" of the Pietist writers, whereupon "the fathers fell out against the Pietists at a most prodigious rate & told us several stories of their madness & folly." Ever the patriotic Protestant, Belcher also observed with disdain several relics that the monastery had been given, including a skirt that Charles II had allegedly worn to disguise himself in his flight after the Battle of Worcester. Nor did Belcher think that monastic life weaned the monks from worldliness: "They live retir'd from the world, but for ought I saw, their concern & care for it, is as great as if they liv'd in it."[71] Belcher's direct encounter with Catholicism reinforced the limits of his toleration. His ecumenical impulse would be confined within Protestant boundaries.

The next stop on the way to Berlin was a visit to the famous silver mines in the Harz Mountains, where guides took him down into the enormous underground city, with "towns and streets below as well as above ground and every mine has a name." Belcher watched the dangerous drilling and blasting, and then paid close attention to the intricate process of refining silver. The use of "great quantities of wood to increase the heat" made "some of these fires . . . frightful and terrible to look at, [and] brought to mind the fire of Hell, *and who can dwell in everlasting burnings*." He was equally dismayed by the disparities in wealth that the labor system created. Most of the silver went directly into the elector's coffers, and the mine's director lived like a prince. The workers, by contrast, "are at prodigious labour, but it is for others, not themselves tho they have the silver in their own ground, & dig it with their own hands." More curious still, when the miners were finally paid, they behaved just like debauched noblemen "in that they spend all the time they have to themselves in gaming and drinking." From witnessing the brutal labor required to extract silver as well as the profligacy with which it was spent by lords and laborers alike, Belcher concluded that "nothing is harder come at, and nothing easier parted with, yet would make a man a miser to be a month or so at the mines."[72] From the Amsterdam exchange to the Harz silver mines, Belcher's progress was an education in the value of commodity money. It also inspired his future endeavors, such as in 1714, when he became a principal investor in a copper-mining company in Simsbury (now East Granby, Connecticut) and brought German metallurgists from Hanover to run the refining operation in the hope of creating a potential source of mineral wealth for New England.[73]

When Belcher finally arrived in Berlin, he met with further examples of lavish courtly wealth, and with the aid of a letter from Princess Sophia, he was soon on familiar terms with her daughter, the Queen of Prussia.[74] But his most intriguing encounter in Berlin occurred by chance while touring the royal library, "where we met with one Mr. Leibnitz." This "mighty civil and obliging man," the philosopher and polymath Gottfried Wilhelm Leibniz, was serving as president of the Academy of Sciences in Berlin. Belcher tells us that "we chanc'd to fall upon the subject of Chymistry," and Leibniz told him a story "that lately hapned at Berlin" of an apothecary's apprentice who had discovered the secret of producing gold from lead. The King of Prussia had tried to capture the apprentice, who fled, only to be seized by the King of Poland and imprisoned at Dresden, "where he now continues" making gold for the King of Poland, "but not enough for him."[75] Alchemy, or "chymistry," as it was interchangeably called, was still prevalent in the scientific world, and Leibniz's curious story was told in earnest. It reflects the philosopher's ambivalence over his hopes for experimental science as a transforming power in the world, a kind of alchemical utopianism, set against the concern that such power might be perverted by Europe's feuding monarchs.[76]

From Berlin, Belcher retraced his steps to the Netherlands, crossed the channel, and returned to Boston, where his experiences made him an instant celebrity. He dined out on his adventures for months and circulated his manuscript journal in polite Boston society. Four years later his father's interests sent him back to London, and once again, having accomplished his necessary business, Belcher set off for the continent.[77] He had promised to send Princess

Sophia an indigenous product of the New World, and now he made good on it. He brought (along with some green candles) an Indian slave, a boy named Io, probably a captive from New England's Indian wars, whom he presented to Sophia as a gift. The princess was overjoyed: "She took a great liking to the boy, she kept him at Court in his own habit, and [he] always stood with a plate behind her chair at table." In addition, she "immediately put him to school to learn to speak and write high Dutch and French and told me would have him instructed in the Christian religion." Belcher's comment on the Indian's fate is telling: "If he behaves himself well, his fortune is made for this world."[78]

Princess Sophia now had her own exotic servant to match the two Turks her son possessed. And like his Indian slaves, Belcher's worldly fortune was made; the royal family thoroughly embraced him. The next day he dined with the princess and her family, dandling on his knee her great-grandson, the infant Prince Frederick, "who doubtless will be King of Great Britain."[79] When Belcher finally departed, Sophia gave him a medal bearing her likeness, along with the promise that "it may sometime be in my power or some of mine to do you some service, when you may be sure you will not be forgot-

FIGURE 4.3. (a and b) Silver medal commemorating Parliament's nomination of Sophia, electress of Hanover, to the British succession, 1701. The obverse face depicts Mathilda, daughter of England's twelfth-century king, Henry II, who married the Duke of Saxony and Bavaria, uniting England and Germany, as the succession of Sophia's line to the British throne would reprise.

ten."[80] By internalizing the political logic of the British Empire and its newly widened European world, Belcher seems to have inverted the moral logic of the selling of Joseph. Io, the Indian slave boy, occupied the position of Joseph, but it was Belcher, the Ishmaelite merchant, who now expected to receive the future Pharaoh's favor.

The Local Politics of Universal Truth

Cotton Mather was no traveler. Unlike Jonathan Belcher, he never crossed the Atlantic, never left New England, and rarely ventured outside his native Boston. For his entire career, he served as minister of the same church in Boston's North End, over which his father had also presided. Nevertheless, Mather's theology, personal piety, intellectual life, and vision of social and moral reform were as profoundly shaped by new elements emerging in the British Empire and Protestant states of northern Europe as if he had joined Belcher on his Dutch and German journeys. Mather brought a powerful organizing intelligence to his own Atlantic connections, and through it constructed a vision of Boston's future that Belcher's experiences had only vaguely foreshadowed—a vision that required mastery of the most recent intellectual developments along with a tenacious will to adapt them to Boston's history and circumstances.

Imagination and intelligence alone would not have been enough to sustain Mather's efforts. In the absence of direct experience with peers in England and continental Europe, contacts of the sort that his father had sustained through repeated transatlantic journeys, Cotton fed his mind and built his world on what he read in books. To understand Mather's approach to the emerging Protestant International and Republic of Letters, we need to know more about the Mather family library, the cultural capital on which powerful relationships were built.

The American Antiquarian Society in Worcester, Massachusetts, possesses the largest-surviving portion of the library assembled by the Mather family over two centuries: roughly two thousand volumes of what may once have been seven to eight thousand, among the largest private libraries in early British America. The library has

FIGURE 4.4. Portrait of Cotton Mather, mezzotint engraving by Peter Pelham, 1728.

posed a challenge to scholars; it is not the writings *of* the Mathers (which are dauntingly voluminous in their own right), nor is it a set of books *about* the Mathers, but rather a possibly random subset of the books owned by the Mathers. We do not know what process winnowed the Mather volumes down to a quarter of their earlier number. Only recently has the Antiquarian Society systematically catalogued the collection, which sat ceremoniously for two centuries on its shelves. The collection was built over four generations, beginning with Richard Mather, who arrived in Massachusetts Bay in the 1630s, the emigrant patriarch of a clan of puritan clergymen. His sons, grandsons, and great-grandsons fanned out from Boston across New England, and back across the Atlantic to the British Isles. Increase Mather, Richard's most prominent son, acquired the largest number of volumes in the collection during several extended trips to England, where he haunted the London book markets.

We may be tempted to call the library "private," but private is not really the word to describe the functions served by the Mather library in early Boston.[81] The marginalia written on the flyleaves and endpapers of these volumes, together with the diaries and correspondence of various family members, reveal that this was a circulating library, its volumes available to members of the greater Boston community, depending on the station of the borrower and the social or cultural capital that such lending and exchange might bring. The endpapers often bore signatures, dates, places of exchange, and other evidence that many hands thumbed these books, including manuscript poems, jokes, and hand-drawn illustrations. The books' margins were filled with notes, and their pages show evidence of the inevitable underscoring. During the library's heyday, from the time Increase Mather returned to Boston after the Restoration of Charles II to the death of Cotton Mather in 1727, Boston was the dominant entrepôt for cultural relations between Europe and British America. If one lived in early America and wanted European books, chances are that they would come by way of Boston.[82] An essential function of this library was its strategic importance in organizing and disseminating knowledge that was critical to the construction of authority in early America. The Mather family home in Boston's North End became the de facto capital of the Republic of Letters in its North American provinces.

In using the phrase Republic of Letters, the network of people engaged in scholarly pursuits in the early modern era, I want to call particular attention to the significance of the word "republic." It was not an Empire of Letters or Kingdom of Letters; there was no centralized hierarchy to it, no single metropole or court. The learned world was an open elite, ready to accept participation from many regions. But neither was it a Democracy of Letters. Different communities, regions, or provinces had influential figures, power brokers, and leaders who dominated local affairs and represented their region to the larger world, all the while acting, by their own lights, for the good of the whole.[83] In England, the nabobs of the Royal Society took on this self-appointed task. In Boston, in New England, and for colonial British America, the Mathers occupied the role of power brokers in the Republic of Letters. As the intellectual and moral leaders of one of Boston's largest and most prominent churches, and for Increase Mather, as president of Harvard College for sixteen years, the Mathers served as gatekeepers and authority figures in shaping the culture of their city and region and connecting it to the wider Atlantic world's Republic of Letters, much as the city's merchants did for Boston's material interests. And their library was both an asset and tool that helped them maintain this position.

Yet to say that it was a republic is not to say that the world of scholarly authority was egalitarian or uniform. Some people and places were more powerful and richly endowed than others. The Mathers came from the Protestant evangelical wing of this republic, and they represented a small, poor, and remote district, with limited resources but high aspirations. These conditions are crucial in order to understand why questions of temporality, continuity, knowledge, and authority were constructed differently in early America than they were in the capitals of contemporary Europe. All politics is local, even when the political prizes at stake are thought of as universal truths and eternal verities. The Mathers were connected to a circum-Atlantic conversation among fellow intellectuals, but this does not mean that the world of knowledge was uniform or consistent throughout the Atlantic world.

The Mather library was a conglomerate artifact of Atlantic culture from the fifteenth through the eighteenth centuries. At the same time, it was a distinctive one, shaped by the interests and connections of the family that assembled it, and the region where they played a leading role. A sampling of the shelves on which the volumes were organized reveals some striking features. First is the sheer size of the collection. When examined shelf by shelf, the Mather library conveys the overwhelming physicality and weight of books: they would have lined the walls from floor to ceiling in the second-story study of Increase Mather's North End home—an impressive reminder to visiting parishioners of the depth of learning behind his clerical authority. In 1679, when their house caught fire, father and son rescued hundreds of volumes from the flames, with the teenaged Cotton throwing armfuls of enormous tomes down the stairs to his father's waiting arms. The Mather library was big, but at the same time personal. The books and pamphlets were a form of extended and distributed personhood: they helped make the Mathers who owned them larger, weightier, and more extensive and ubiquitous in Boston.[84]

Another important feature is the breadth of the collection. One shelf, for instance, containing forty volumes, bears titles that range from a Latin Bible printed in Venice in 1476, barely into the Gutenberg era, to English pamphlets of the 1720s, spanning the first quarter millennium of European printing history. Of these forty random volumes, eighteen titles are British imprints (London, Oxford, and Edinburgh), while another eighteen are from continental Europe, including Frankfurt, Amsterdam, Leyden, Paris, Basel, Rotterdam, Westphalia, Antwerp, and Hamburg. Four have no printing place indicated (sometimes printers left this out or invented fictitious places if they were publishing unlicensed works). There are no American imprints. In subject matter, the Mather books cover a wide spectrum, from systematic divinity and ecclesiastical politics to travel guides and geographic gazetteers, from the published volumes of European royal societies to alchemical and hermetic medical manuals, from commercial handbooks and treatises on Semitic languages to British political tracts, Niccolò Machiavelli's *The Prince*, Latin and Greek classics, and the early church fathers.

A striking feature of this large collection, less obvious at first, is the impression it creates that for this family of clergymen, intellectuals, and political leaders, there were no periods, no distinctive breaks or turning points, between their experiences as Europeans in North America and the continuous past of Western Christendom. The Mathers still lived in the world of Philippi; their Christian intellectual tradition required ongoing engagement with the ancient and medieval world. The holdings and patterns of usage of three of the most prominent genres or categories of knowledge found in the Mather library convey this clearly: works on science, medicine, and natural history and philosophy; works on controversial divinity and church history; and works on politics in the turbulent British kingdoms under the Stuarts.

In the constellation of subjects that we might categorize as science, the Mather library contains many works published from the sixteenth to eighteenth centuries. Between the covers of these volumes are marginalia along with other odds and ends (buttons, dead bugs, and notes pinned to flyleaves) that demonstrate remarkable continuity over time in the use of these works, despite dramatic developments in theory, method, and practice that historians of science have often described as revolutionary. Medicine provides a useful example. The Mathers were avid medical practitioners, learned men to whom New Englanders turned in the absence of university-trained physicians. They collected titles that would aid their efforts, from practical guidebooks of general practice such as Jean François Fernel's *Universa Medicina* (orig. pub. 1554; Mather copy a Utrecht reprint, 1656) to recent works such as Robert Boyle's *Memoirs for the Natural History of Humane Blood* (1684), which Increase acquired in London in the late 1680s.

It seemed not to matter to them that some authors (like Fernel, who specialized in the study of ancient Greek physicians) prescribed medical practices defined by the humoral theory of medicine known since the ancients, while other titles, such as Jean Baptiste van Helmont's *Ortus Medicinae* (Amsterdam, 1652) or the Danish Ole Borch's *Hermetis, Aegyptiorum, et chemicorum sapientia* (Copenhagen, 1674) offered alchemical and hermetical theories on the causes and cures of disease that challenged the Galenic humoral system. This apparent indifference to changing theory and practice

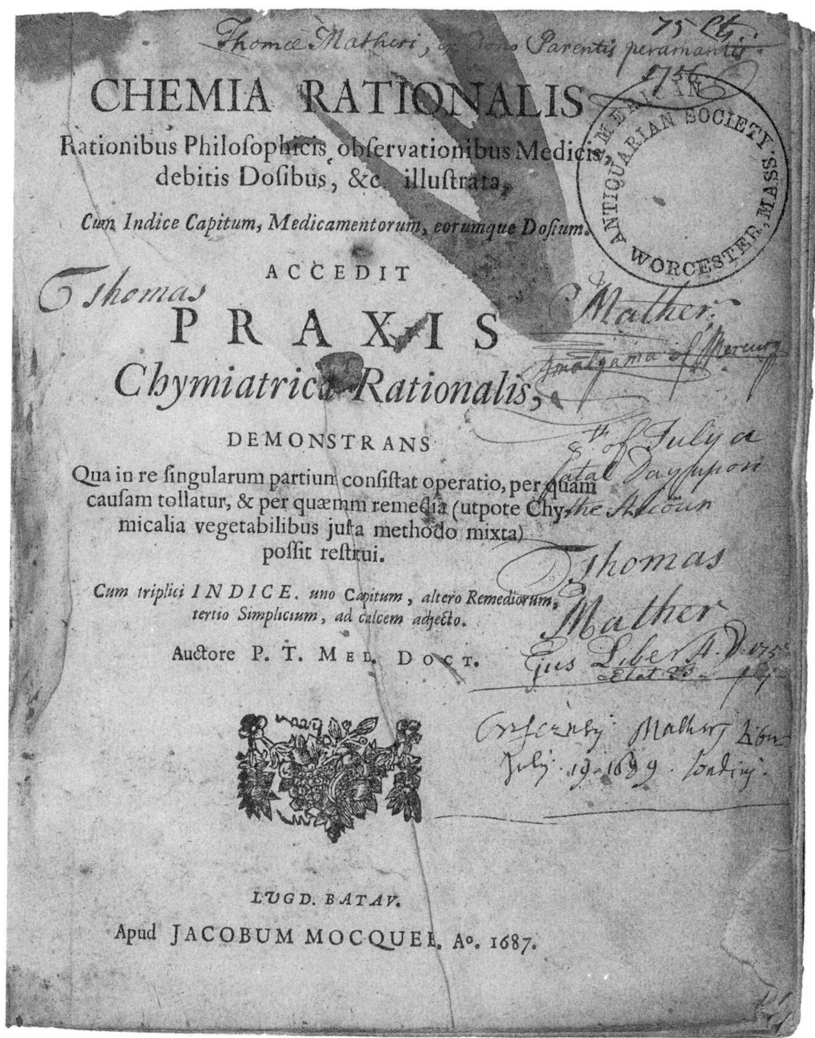

CHEMIA RATIONALIS
Rationibus Philoſophicis, obſervationibus Medicis, debitis Doſibus, &c. illuſtrata,
Cum Indice Capitum, Medicamentorum, eorumque Doſium.
ACCEDIT
PRAXIS
Chymiatrica Rationalis,
DEMONSTRANS
Qua in re ſingularum partium conſiſtat operatio, per quam cauſam tollatur, & per quæmm remedia (utpote Chymicalia vegetabilibus juſta methodo mixta) poſſit reſtitui.
Cum triplici INDICE. *uno Capitum, altero Remediorum, tertio Simplicium, ad calcem adjecto.*
Auctore P. T. Med. Doct.
LUGD. BATAV.
Apud JACOBUM MOCQUEL, Aº. 1687.

FIGURE 4.5. Title page with manuscript autographs of Increase Mather, Cotton Mather, and Thomas Mather, in P. T. Med. Doct., *Chemia Rationalis*, vol. 1 (Leiden, 1687), copy in the Mather Library, American Antiquarian Society, Worcester, MA.

is most clearly evidenced in those texts—such as *Chemia Rationales* (Leyden, 1687) by the mysterious "P. T., Med. Doct."—that several generations of Mathers indexed in their own hands on the flyleaves, creating a working palimpsest of pharmaceutical recipes, methods of treatment, and signs for recognizing unusual symptoms or dangerous diseases.

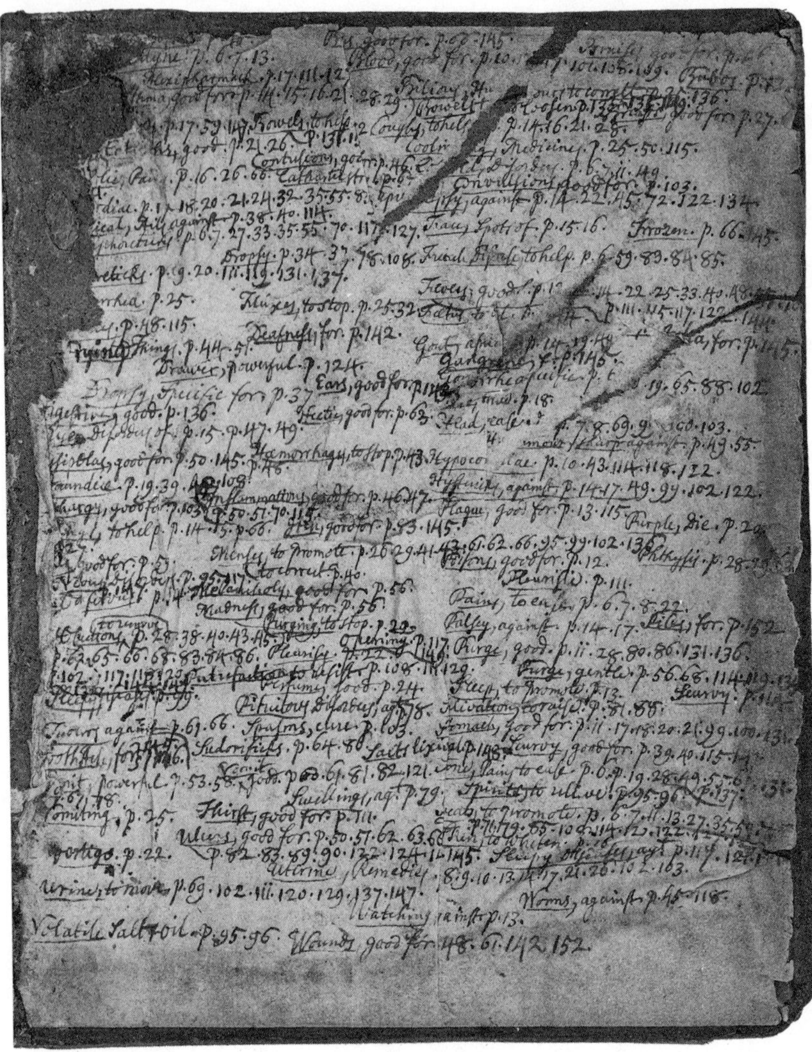

FIGURE 4.6. Manuscript index, rear endpapers, P. T. Med. Doct., *Chemia Rationalis*, Mather Library. This working index on the back flyleaves was constructed by several generations of the Mather family who used *Chemia Rationalis* as a practical medical guide.

The Mathers were not merely passive recipients and distributors of knowledge created and tested elsewhere. They saw themselves as active participants in an international scholarly world, and their books were the tools that made such participation possible. Their copy of Robert Hooke's *Lectures and Observations on Comets*

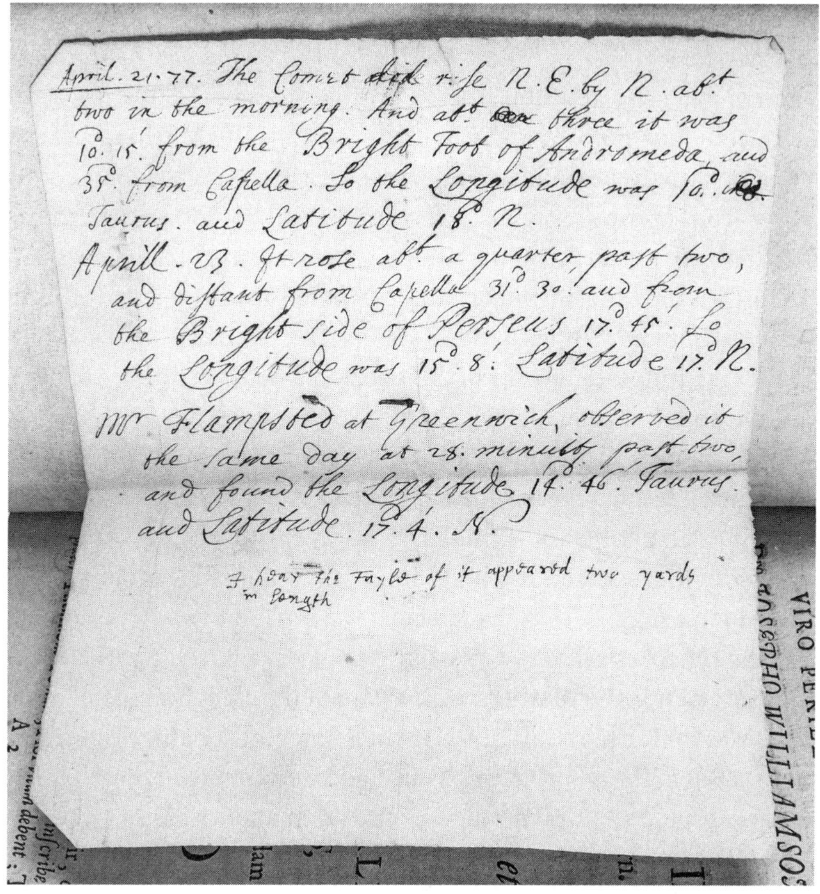

April. 21. 77. The Comet rise N. E. by N. abt two in the morning. And abt three it was 10°. 15′. from the Bright Foot of Andromeda, and 35°. from Capella. So the Longitude was 10°. Taurus. and Latitude 18°. N.

April. 23. It rose abt a quarter past two, and distant from Capella 31°. 30′. and from the Bright side of Perseus 17°. 45′. So the Longitude was 15°. 8′. Latitude 17°. N.

Mr Flampsted at Greenwich, observed it the same day at 28. minuts past two, and found the Longitude 14°. 46′. Taurus. and Latitude. 17°. 4′. N.

I hear the Tayle of it appeared two yards in length

FIGURE 4.7. Manuscript notes of Cotton Mather and Increase Mather, pinned to reverse of title page, Robert Hooke, *Lectures and Observations on Comets*, Mather Library. The single sentence at the bottom is in the hand of Increase Mather. The remaining notes were written by Cotton Mather, who was fourteen years old in 1677, when these observations were made.

(London, 1678) contains, pinned into the inside cover, a manuscript copy of Increase's and young Cotton's observations of a comet seen in Boston in April 1677—the same comet that Hooke had observed as a source for his treatise. Together, Hooke's published text and the Mathers' notes create a scholarly dialogue. Building on this dialogue and future observations, such as the 1682 visit of the comet that we know as Halley's, Increase went on to write and publish his own treatise, *Kometographia, . . . Wherein the Nature of Blazing*

Stars Is Inquired into, with an Historical Account of All the Comets Which Have Appeared from the Beginning of the World unto the Present Year (Boston, 1683).

In religious politics and Christian history, the Mather library's most striking feature is its collective depiction of Christian continuity from apostolic times to the unfolding present. Although the Mathers obviously favored authors in the reformed tradition, from John Calvin, Martin Bucer, and Heinrich Bullinger to William Ames, Richard Sibbes, and Richard Baxter, they also owned, read, and annotated works of their ecclesiastical enemies (Anglican archbishop Richard Hooker), English Catholics (Sir Kenelm Digby), leading figures in Roman Catholicism (Cardinal Bellarmine), and the church fathers stretching back through Saint Thomas Aquinas to Saint Augustine and Irenaeus. The works that they owned and favored with repeated readings define their allegiances clearly, but they do not suggest that the Mathers were given to stark periodization or rigid divisions in Christian history or church politics. Like all Protestants, the Mathers were aware of the cataclysmic upheaval that Martin Luther, Calvin, and other sixteenth-century reformers began. But in the way that they collected, used, and read their library, and presented their own religious tradition and its history, there is little sense of Reformation as a sharp break, a bright dividing line, in the history of Christianity, so much as an ongoing struggle to preserve true Christianity from the worldly powers in every era that corrupt and diminish it.

No single reformer is unduly favored or singled out as the standard-bearer of religious truth; in this sense, the word "Calvinist" is a misnomer for New England's Puritans. Rather, many different reformers were read as champions of the godly cause, though all were human and fallible. As in the realm of the sciences (a distinction the Mathers themselves would not have made), the emphasis in their collections on Christian history falls on gradual revelation, the slow accumulation of truth, the sufferings of martyrs in defense of the faith, and the correction of Romish errors.[85] This attitude was similarly reflected in Belcher's statement in 1704, while visiting the palace where William the Silent was assassinated, that William had been "the first *deliverer* of the Dutch from Popery." It conveyed the notion that Roman Catholicism had been a millennium-long captivity during which true faith lay bound and hidden, but true believers (like themselves), the saving remnant of the saints, had always managed to preserve it.[86]

This emphasis helps explain the purpose in the library of a work in French by Antoine du Pinet, published in Lyon in 1564, that describes the church polity of reformed congregations in a series of French cities. Appended to this text are dozens of pages of manuscript notes taken at Huguenot synods held on the Channel Islands of Jersey and Guernsey in the late sixteenth century. Increase Mather may have acquired the book and sewn in the manuscript notes during the late 1650s when he served as minister to an English garrison on Guernsey.[87] Although there are few French books in the library, this work fits the collection perfectly as part of the Mathers' compendium of knowledge of the historical revelation of the true church as well as their desire to preserve the cultural remnants of a threatened branch of international Protestantism. As citizen power brokers of the Protestant wing of the Republic of Letters, the Mathers' scholarly practices contributed to sustaining the health and strength of the whole.

One of the few works in the collection that does reveal an intense concern among the Mathers with historical periodization is a title that makes a mockery of orthodox schemes of providential history, Catholic or Protestant. Isaac de La Peyrère's *Men before Adam, A System of Divinity*, was published in London in 1656 during the radical religious ferment of the interregnum. La Peyrère, originally a French Calvinist from Bordeaux, was a fellow traveler in the Republic of Letters, if one of its more disreputable citizens. An autodidact, he had big ambitions, but no scholarly training. La Peyrère was a polymath, ranging widely across natural, human, and historical spheres, and deeply interested in reconciling the Bible with other ancient texts, not only Greek and Roman, but also the "Caldeans, Egyptians, Scythians, and Chinensians."[88] This desire inspired *Men before Adam*, an attempt to argue that the two versions of human creation offered in the first two chapters of Genesis actually describe

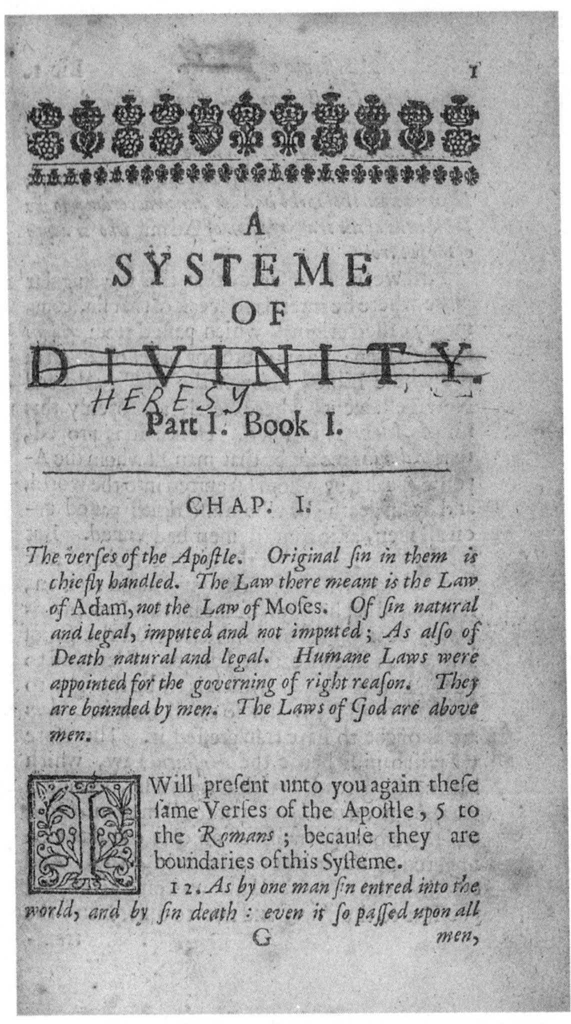

1

A

SYSTEME

OF

~~DIVINITY.~~ HERESY

Part I. Book I.

CHAP. I.

The verſes of the Apoſtle. Original ſin in them is chiefly handled. The Law there meant is the Law of Adam, *not the Law of* Moſes. *Of ſin natural and legal, imputed and not imputed; As alſo of Death natural and legal. Humane Laws were appointed for the governing of right reaſon. They are bounded by men. The Laws of God are above men.*

I Will preſent unto you again theſe ſame Verſes of the Apoſtle, 5 to the *Romans*; becauſe they are boundaries of this Syſteme.

12. *As by one man ſin entred into the world, and by ſin death: even it ſo paſſed upon all men,*

G

FIGURE 4.8. Cotton Mather manuscript emendation, chapter 1, book 1, of La Peyrère, *Men Before Adam*, Mather Library.

two separate creation stories—the first of humanity in general, and the second of the Jews as God's chosen people—meaning that there were many men and women long before Adam and Eve.[89]

La Peyrère's pre-Adamite claims so troubled Cotton Mather—like Peyrère, a polymath, but with proper academic training and credentials—that on page after page of the text, Mather crossed out the word "DIVINITY" from the running heads and replaced it, in ink, with "HERESY." He also took the time to create at the end of the text an index of subjects that he could then systematically refute. Peyrère's heresy challenged a belief that Mather in particular, and the founders of Boston in general, took seriously: all people were Adam and Eve's descendants, encompassed under God's plan for humanity, and therefore suitable subjects for evangelization and potential conversion. Peyrère's fundamental assault on Mather's sense of Christian history and purpose was what provoked this visceral refutation.

If we turn from Christian history to secular politics (not that the Mathers would have acknowledged such a stark division), a brief glance at a single volume reveals a similar approach. The Mather library contains dozens of examples of composite books, collections of small pamphlets on related political subjects stitched together and bound to create a kind of homemade magazine for a running conversation among numerous authors on a single theme. What is striking about these compilations is the fact that the publication dates of the individual pamphlets are often widely dispersed across time; titles from the reign of James I in the 1620s are sewn in beside works published under James II in the 1680s. The impression conveyed is that although individual rulers come and go, and the godly's fortunes ebb and flow with dynastic shifts, the universal human condition and its relationship to worldly power continues on essentially unchanged.

How do we explain the Mathers' insistence on the unbroken unity of the world of knowledge in all its separate realms, and unbroken continuity of the past with the present, when we have become accustomed to believe that the era in which they lived was one of scientific revolution and intellectual enlightenment—in short, of a dawning modernity, led by pioneers who were the Mathers' associates and correspondents, fellow delegates to the Republic of Letters?

An answer can be found in understanding the power of local conditions to shape the politics and sociology of knowledge. In Restoration London, scientific investigators such as Robert Boyle, Isaac Newton, and Robert Hooke framed a social and political context in which they could present their work as a revolutionary change from past practices. For Boyle and his contemporaries who founded England's Royal Society, it was politically useful to demand a purification of knowledge that required a sharp break with the methods and sureties of the past. In particular, to retain the favor of the restored king, Charles II, it was essential for these natural philosophers to distance themselves in their pursuit of knowledge from the kind of speculation about the role of divine providence in human affairs that had been so prevalent among their predecessors in the era of Britain's civil wars.[90]

In addition to being a leading light of the Royal Society, Boyle was closely connected to the world of the Mathers. He was in age a near contemporary of Increase Mather, and the two men became friends during Mather's sojourn in England. Boyle's work in chemistry was strongly influenced by George Starkey, an early Harvard College graduate and secretive alchemist.[91] Boyle served for many years as a commissioner of the New England Company, responsible for raising funds to promote Indian conversion and education in Massachusetts. The Mathers read and absorbed Boyle's works, from *The Usefulness of Experimental Natural Philosophy* (1663) to *The Christian Virtuoso* (1690).

But Boyle's London was quite different from the Mathers' Boston. In London, under the careful scrutiny of Crown authorities, the claim to a distinctive discontinuity between past and present methods in science made it easier to distance inquiry into the natural world from contentious disputes about religion and providence that had plagued English politics. The general crisis of authority that marked the bloody first half of the seventeenth century in Britain, ending in regicide, religious anarchy, and finally counterrevolution, all encouraged Boyle and his cohort of Royal Society founders to make science something new and different, to reconstitute its authority on experimentally produced facts, and to downplay the interpretation of nature as a method for reading the purposes of God in human affairs.

Christianity still held an essential place in the cosmology and mental universe of Boyle and his cohort. The world was as much God's book of nature as the Bible was His revealed word. Furthermore, the personal authority on which scientific practitioners like Boyle rested their claims to speak the truth about God's nature lay as much in their demonstration of an irenic and charitable godliness as in their gentlemanly honor and integrity. Yet in the wake of the violence and fanaticism fostered by religious belief in portents and providence in the mid-seventeenth century, Christian virtuosos and natural philosophers in England tended to leave wonders, signs, and marvels of nature aside as they assembled their natural histories into a new philosophy.[92] In the context of Restoration England, Boyle and his Royal Society cohort found it effective and powerful to do this, and the chief proponents of the new method used it to gain positions of power. It was no accident that Newton spent his later years holding two offices: president of the Royal Society and director of the Royal Mint, any more than that he published his mathematical and mechanical philosophy, but kept his alchemical and religious speculations to himself.[93]

To understand the distinctive politics of Boston's participation in the Republic of Letters, it is vital to remember the significance of both time and place in politics, even the politics of knowledge. As we saw in book I, Restoration Boston, with three thousand miles of ocean discouraging Crown oversight, could continue to act in defiance of the king's authority, and sustain its political autonomy and culture of puritan dissent. In this context, as intellectual leaders of a colony far removed from the politics of Restoration London, there was no incentive for the Mathers to break away from the past, to claim a newfound purity in the knowledge that they were absorbing and helping to create, and to distance natural philosophy and scientific inquiry from revealed religion and biblical authority. To the contrary, they had every reason to sustain the idea of continuity. Their possession and absorption of the volumes of scholarship that contained the knowledge of past ages and distant regions was, in the circumstances of colonial Boston, the source of their power and authority as cultural brokers, as delegates for New England to the Republic of Letters. They knew their constituency well, knew its devotion to biblical truth and its belief in an active God who intervened in human affairs to show his pleasure or dismay at the behavior of his chosen people.[94] Absent the revolutions that shook English life, the covenanted society of Massachusetts had not lost its faith in the civil authority of godly magistrates. Given such a constituency, it would have been folly, even intellectual treason, to announce that scholarly advances, new experimental methods, or strange new facts required a scientific revolution that must discard providential interpretations. The Mathers did not embrace the concept of a scientific revolution because nothing in the world where they lived gave them any incentive to do such a thing. This makes them not lesser thinkers than Boyle, Newton, Hooke, and the other luminaries of the Royal Society but instead the same kind: scholars who knew their own circumstances and interests, and shaped their research and conclusions to comport with those needs.

The local importance of the Mathers' claim to intellectual continuity and authority can be seen in the politics surrounding the 1721 introduction of smallpox inoculation in Boston, when the contest over knowledge and authority erupted into a violent public controversy. The deadly scourge infected thousands of people, and hundreds died. In the midst of it all, Cotton Mather and his colleague, a self-trained doctor named Zabdiel Boylston, best known as a "stone-cutter," a surgeon adept at removing gallstones, began experimenting with inoculating the not-yet infected with live smallpox matter. Inoculation might prevent the disease, or it might deliberately spread the deadly infection to otherwise-healthy folks. Some applauded and embraced these efforts, others denounced them. One opponent threw a bomb into Mather's window, others mobbed Boylston's house.[95]

To reach the decision to try inoculation, Mather followed the methods that his family had developed over the generations. He read about inoculation from reports sent in by trained physicians working in Italy and the Levant to the *Transactions* of the Royal Society; as a corresponding fellow of the society, Mather received its volumes.[96] He also read reports of inoculation in Denmark's medical community's publications, including an account of a smallpox epidemic in Copenhagen in 1656.[97] Cotton Mather had been charting the course of smallpox epidemics in Boston and New England for years. He knew that the region's children, including his own, lay in danger of devastation when the next epidemic came. The previous epidemic had been almost twenty years earlier, leaving children born since then without immunity from exposure. Beyond his reading and timetables, he spoke to his sometime slave, Onesimus, who had been inoculated in his West African homeland, where it was a common practice, and described the process to Mather.

Boylston and Mather's opposition came from several quarters. The poor and frightened crowd was one, and that could be expected; it seemed ludicrous, for those without the esoteric knowledge that Mather derived from his learned tomes, to spread deadly disease deliberately to healthy people. But opposition also came from Dr. William Douglass of Edinburgh, the only physician in New England with training at a European university, and from Boston's new satirical newspaper, the *New England Courant*. James Franklin, the paper's founder and older brother of Benjamin Franklin, consciously adopted the coffeehouse wit and the tone of sophisticated discernment and secular mockery of clerical earnestness first advanced by fashionable London magazines such as Addison's *Spectator* and Steele's *Tatler*.[98] Taken together, Douglass and the *Courant* (where Douglass published his diatribes) represented voices of the so-called Enlightenment. They had imbibed the culture that had developed in London in the decades since the Restoration, during which amateur medical practitioners and self-trained stone-cutters were ridiculed, and experimental philosophy had supposedly made folk medicine and pious clergymen obsolete. But in truth, Douglass and Franklin, for all their attitude of cosmopolitan superiority, backed by the fashionable trends of London culture, knew no more about the causes and prevention of smallpox than did Mather and Boylston.

In Boston's smallpox crisis, although Mather and Boylston were hewing more closely to the practice of experimental medicine than their critics, they were losing the political authority to sustain their claims because a new form of challenge had entered the local picture. In the eyes of Douglass and the *Courant*, Mather's authorities and credentials were no longer good enough. The Royal Society reports came from physicians in ungodly and exotic places: Italy and the Levant. An African slave's testimony was obviously beneath contempt, and Douglass openly derided it in his critiques in the *Courant*. Douglass, the *Courant*, and their Boston audience refused to credit such disreputable authorities, and would not "buy" the pox inoculation, as the slang of the time described it.

Mather was willing to risk what Douglass denounced because it was consistent with his practices as a delegate to the Republic of Letters. He was fully convinced that knowledge could be discovered in the provinces just as well as in the metropolis. What had changed was not the standards of science but rather the politics of science. A new mode of authority to speak scientific truth had triumphed in London for reasons distinctive to London. In post–Glorious Revolution Boston, far more open to European intellectual currents and a wider variety of people than it had been before 1689, this new form of cultural authority had now been introduced to New England, taking hold where it had been out of place before. The political and intellectual culture of the empire's metropolis had diverged sharply from that of provincial Boston. As new metropolitan viewpoints were imported into Boston, latter-day Puritans like Mather faced new attacks on their authority and therefore looked to new resources to shore up their vision of Boston's distinctive cultural identity.

Cotton Mather's Journey to Pietism

The challenge for Mather, and intellectuals like him seeking to link their local traditions and circumstances to the new potential for an integrated Protestant Atlantic, was to find like-minded people with whom to organize their parallel intellectual projects into a strong and coherent whole. Their task was as much a political as an intellectual one, and if the fashionable world of London aristocrats and coffeehouse sophisticates belittled their aspirations, there were other places to turn for allies. And so like Belcher, but through the medium of books and correspondence rather than immediate experience, Mather found connections in other centers of cultural power that were opening up in the post-Stuart era, and found his interests and ambitions mirrored in German Pietism.

The Pietist movement in Lutheran Germany, beginning in the later decades of the seventeenth century, was something of a parallel to what Puritanism had earlier been in England, with a strong emphasis on the authority of scripture and the necessity of individual spiritual rebirth as a foundation for social reform.[99] Around 1709, evidence appears of Mather's awareness of the Pietist institute at Halle, in Saxony, developed by the Lutheran minister August Hermann Francke. Versions of Francke's works published in London in 1707 had found their way into Mather's hands, and the following year Mather resolved to send some of his own recent publications, which he described as "the true American Pietism," to "Dr. Franckius, in Saxony."[100]

Francke and his works were a revelation to Mather, and a challenge as well. The two men were exact contemporaries—born a month apart in 1663, they died eight months apart in 1727—and they were extraordinarily similar. Both were sons of prominent, highly educated, and devoutly pious families. They shared an intense devotion to the practice of piety and were equally extravagant in their ambitions, with wide-ranging interests, massive correspondence networks, and unbounded energy. In Francke, Mather had finally discovered someone whose intellect, ambition, piety, and energy surpassed his own, which fascinated him and brought out his competitive instincts. He began an eager correspondence with Francke and his Halle connections that would last through his lifetime.[101]

Before his discovery of Francke, and unbeknownst to him, Mather's connection with German Pietism had already been decades in the making. In 1687, Increase had corresponded with Johannes Leusden, professor of Hebrew at Utrecht, to whom he sent a description of John Eliot's efforts to convert the Indians of Massachusetts.[102] At the time, Cotton used his father's letter as an outline for his own considerably longer biography of Eliot, published in Boston and London in 1691 under the title *Triumphs of the Reformed Religion in America*.[103] The younger Mather's Eliot biography received wide acclaim among dissenters in Britain. It influenced the work of a fellow of the Royal Society named Patrick

Gordon, whose *Geography Anatomiz'd* of 1693 was revised in 1699 in order to promote missionary activities, like those of Eliot, throughout the expanding global empires of Europe's Protestant nations.[104] Gordon's *Geography* was, in turn, an inspiration for the establishment of the Society for the Promotion of Christian Knowledge (SPCK), a voluntary organization formed in 1699 to promote missionary endeavors and the publication and distribution of Bibles and pious tracts.[105]

In its early days, the SPCK, seeking to extend its influence throughout the Protestant world, made Francke a corresponding member.[106] When Queen Anne came to the English throne in 1702 (after the death of King William, brought on by a fall from his horse), her husband, George, Prince of Denmark and a great supporter of Lutheran Pietism, installed a Francke protégé, Anton Wilhelm Böhme, as court chaplain in London. Böhme became the principal conduit between Halle Pietism and its British sympathizers.[107] In 1705, Henry Newman filled the SPCK's leading position, serving as its secretary for the next forty years and becoming intimate friends with Böhme.[108] Newman, as it happens, was a Bostonian, Harvard College class of 1687, son of a puritan minister and grandson of Samuel Newman, among the most venerable of New England's founding clergy.[109] Although Henry Newman was drawn to the Church of England, he never lost his New England connections, maintaining lifelong friendships with Bostonians like Cotton Mather, Jonathan Belcher, Benjamin Colman, and Thomas Prince. Through Newman, Böhme, and the SPCK, the links between Francke in Halle and Mather in Boston were forged, and over the next two decades the network would grow wider and more elaborate.[110]

Mather's earliest letters to Francke went awry in the transatlantic journey, but a later effort in 1714 received a gratifying response. Francke wrote Mather (in Latin) a seventy-page account of the history and accomplishments of the Halle institute, which Mather then summarized in English and published in Boston.[111] Francke mentioned that he possessed a copy of a letter to Johannes Leusden written by one "Crescentius Mather," whom he guessed (correctly) to be a relative of his correspondent. He described how Eliot's work among the Massachusetts Indians had influenced Halle's missionary work in India, which must have been enormously gratifying to the Mathers.[112] In response, Mather sent off to Francke, by way of Böhme in London, "a large Number of Packetts, which had in them scores of American Treatises, besides a few small presents in Gold" for Francke's orphanage; the gold was a gift from Belcher, whose interest in Germany remained strong. Mather urged Böhme to hurry these on to Halle and send some of his tracts to the "Malabarian missionaries; And if you can do it, send them into France; yea, excuse me, if I say, procure them to be translated into as many Languages as you can."[113] Not content to rely on middlemen, Mather then corresponded directly with Halle's missionaries at Tranquebar on the southeast coast of India, the Lutheran ministers Bartholomäus Ziegenbalgh, Henry Plutscho, and Ernst Grundler. Mather then used this correspondence as the basis for a 1721 pamphlet titled *India Christiana*, a lengthy discourse outlining principles for the conversion of pagan peoples in both the East and West Indies.[114]

During these first two decades of the eighteenth century, as his contacts with German Pietism increased and the works of its leading figures, Johann Arndt, Philipp Spener, Böhme, and Francke, became available in English, Mather read them intensively, and urged his family, church, and members of the religious societies he organized in Boston to do the same.[115] But the influence of these connections went beyond personal piety. For Mather, German Pietism complemented and confirmed a range of ideas that he had independently been developing. This was the period in which Mather's interest in practical piety, reform, and social benevolence was at its height. His most famous work in this vein, *Bonifacius: An Essay upon the Good* (1710), refers to Halle Pietism in its penultimate chapter.[116] In *Bonifacius* and other works of this period, Mather laid out a plan for social and religious reform that was reinforced by the works of other contemporary Bostonians, both clergy and laymen. The interlocking array of issues and subjects for pious reform constituted a developing vision of an ideal society that Boston could come to represent—a vision shaped by the transatlantic conversation with German Pietism.[117]

Foremost in this constellation of concerns came individual conversion, the experience of the "new birth," which for Mather and all Pietists constituted the essential foundation for social action. Only those whose hearts, through a kind of divine alchemy, had been converted from love of sin to love of God could be expected to persevere in the Lord's work. This belief underlay Pietism's intense commitment to evangelical efforts; increasing the number of converts was a necessary step in the creation of a godly society.[118] Missionary work among pagan peoples on Christendom's frontiers was obviously part of this concern, and the transatlantic conversation on this subject was an issue on which Bostonians made the greatest contribution to the Pietist movement, though it did not stop there. Another issue embraced by Mather and other Boston Pietists was opposition to the slave trade. Although Mather, who promoted efforts by masters to convert slaves, did not attack slavery per se, the slave trade as a system that ignored or perverted the missionary imperative became a common target.[119]

In addition to pagans of the East and West Indies and the plight of African slaves, Mather's concerns extended to those suffering persecution within the Christian world, especially refugees from Catholic tyranny. At the time that Mather began thinking in this vein, the Huguenot population fleeing from Louis XIV's 1685 revocation of the Edict of Nantes was the main concern, but in the eighteenth century the plight of various German refugee groups would move to center stage.[120] Together with the desire to aid the afflicted came a vitriolic anti-Catholicism, which included a fierce devotion to the Protestant succession in Britain and constant awareness of the fate of Protestant forces in the wars of the eighteenth century.[121] Yet amid the intellectual currents swirling about the North Atlantic, these seemingly disparate subjects could become oddly entangled. A peculiar document in this vein was written by Boston's Paul Dudley, whose *Essay on the Merchandize of Slaves and Souls of Men* combined a rabid critique of Roman Catholicism with a diatribe against trafficking in human merchandise.[122]

The intense passion of this opposition to popery was fueled in part by envy. Mather and his Pietist colleagues coveted the success of the Jesuit missionaries, and the doctrinal and practical unity that Roman Catholicism could enforce.[123] Therefore, another major aim of the evolving Pietist program was to counteract Protestantism's divisive tendencies toward divided national churches and sectarian schisms in order to compete with Roman Catholic efforts. The chief subject of Mather's conversation with the Halle missionaries in India was his attempt to reduce the tenets of Christianity to a few simple principles that all Protestants, Lutheran or Reformed, might agree on as a way to overcome national and confessional differences—principles that would be easily grasped by people unfamiliar with Christian doctrine.[124]

The final linchpin in the promotion of an expansive Protestant ecumenism came in the realm of language and communications. Mather and his Pietist colleagues sought new ways to make their ideas universally known and understood.[125] The aspect of Francke's work that Mather found most breathtaking was Halle's translating and publishing business. As Mather put it, "Within a few Years, and since the light of Evangelical Piety thus breaking forth in the Heart of Germany, there have been more Volumns of the Scriptures vended, than in the whole Period of the Time, from the Reformation until Now; and never were they so cheap since the World began."[126] Halle's success became a model for Mather's own efforts to publish and broadcast his American Pietism as widely and accessibly as possible.

Still another element in this constellation of concerns was the need for reform at home in order to construct model communities at the centers of Protestant Christianity that would be examples to the unconverted world as well as training centers for missionaries. For Mather in Boston, this meant attending to immediate social problems, for which Halle again provided a useful model—orphanages, homes for widows and destitute women, hospitals, poor relief, and schools where poor as well as rich could learn Christian piety and be trained for missionary work. But Mather's idea of a perfectly reformed society went beyond these customary forms of charitable activity to include a range of things that we would call, roughly, scientific, including medicine (Halle's hospitals and pharmaceutical business were particularly important in this light), and alchemy, which was intimately linked to the healing arts.[127] Still another of Mather's favorite notions, supported by friends and colleagues, was a belief in commercial and market reform. For Boston to become a model community, its commercial transactions would have to be conducted in a fair, open, and charitable manner so that commerce would be a benefit to all, rather than a means for the rich to cheat and oppress the poor.[128]

This last position was not a diatribe against commerce itself but instead a collective vision of commercial friendship and prosperity that Mather advanced in a pamphlet titled *Theopolis Americana: An Essay on the Golden Street of the Holy City*, preached before the Massachusetts General Court in 1709. This essay, based on the Book of Revelation and built around an explicitly alchemical metaphor, explored the question of how the streets of a godly city might be converted into "pure gold." Here, in a single text, Mather combined all the issues just described—the importance of individual conversion, the need for market regulation (according to the golden rule), an attack on the slave trade, virulent anti-Catholicism, the urgency of missionary activities, the quest for ecumenical Christianity (including apologies for Massachusetts' earlier persecution of Quakers and suspected witches), and the promotion of education—with the ultimate purpose of suggesting the millennial potential of this work. He concluded by paraphrasing a pagan writer of ancient Greece:

> Who sayes that in Times long preceding his, there was a Tradition, that Europe and Asia and Africa, were encompassed by the Ocean; But . . . beyond the Ocean, there was a great Island . . . [where] there was an huge City, called Theopolis, the Godly City. In that City, Sayes he, they enjoy all Possible Peace and Wealth, and Plenty, and . . . have God marvellously coming down among them. I know not what well to make of a Tradition so very Ancient, and yet having such an American Face upon it. [But] there are many Arguments to perswade us, That

> our Glorious Lord, will have an Holy City in America; a City, the Street whereof will be Pure Gold.[129]

Mather was not so bold as to identify Boston directly with that luminous place, but the implications for his audience must have been obvious. What Mather had done, in conversation with other Bostonians and in his correspondence with German Pietism, was to take the jumble of issues and concerns that Sewall had fretted over in *The Selling of Joseph*, and Belcher had stumbled his way through in his Dutch and German travels, and assemble them into a coherent program for ushering in a Protestant millennium, with high hopes for Boston's role in the process.

Mather was not alone among turn-of-the-century Bostonians in drifting into millennial reveries, inspired by the reconstructed British Empire and upsurge in international Protestantism. In 1697, his friend Sewall published *Phaenomena Quaedam Apocalyptica . . . or, Some Few Lines towards a Description of the New Heaven . . .*, in which he endeavored "to prove that America's Name is to be seen fairly Recorded in the Scriptures; particularly, in the Book of Psalms, in Daniel, and the Revelation. . . . I propound the New World . . . stands fair for being made the Seat of the Divine Metropolis."[130] For Sewall as for Mather, this belief had direct implications for local policy, especially Indian missions.[131] Sewall compared the American Indians before the Gospel's arrival to Joseph, thrown by his brothers into a pit with no water: "These Inhabitants were exactly in the circumstances of *Joseph*; out of which they could by no means get; being Prisoners there; or *Persons bound*." Sewall urged his Boston readers to take action: "For Love, or Shame, Get Up! . . . What is done or prepared by Papists among Indians, is not to be despised; but improved by Protestants. . . . Let Protestants now, for shame, arise, and shew that they have some breathings of a true Apostolical Spirit in them."[132] In another millenarian pamphlet published in 1713, Sewall reiterated his belief that "something of a Local consideration" with respect to New England was implied in the Gospels' parables about sowing the seeds of faith. In a world where the churches of Asia, the first to receive the Gospel seed, were now "trodden down and devoured," and the churches of Africa were now "scorch'd and dryed up by persecution," and the churches of Europe were "choaked" by the thorns of "Worldly Hypocritical Interest, . . . Why may we not . . . hope that the *Americans* shall be made the good Ground that shall once at last prove Especially, and Wonderfully fruitfull?"[133]

Theopolis Americana

These millennial ambitions, partially homegrown but greatly amplified by Bostonians' dialogue with German and Dutch sources, provide a context for the social, political, and religious reform movements that occupied Boston in the late seventeenth and early eighteenth centuries. Though the millennium did not arrive in Boston when Sewall or Mather had hoped it would, Mather did note as the year 1715 drew to a close that Louis XIV had finally died. He wrote to the Halle Pietist Böhme in London that "I apprehend the Time is now coming on apace, for the Empire of Antichrist and Satan . . . to come unto its promised period, and the Kingdome of our Saviour to be Exhibited wth glory to God in the Highest, and on earth Peace, thro' Good Will among Men."[134] The integration of Boston and Massachusetts into the cultural realm of international Protestant Pietism as well as the reconfigured British Empire and its strengthened continental alliances was for Mather becoming a powerful reality.

During these years, Belcher, though not so given to millennial speculation, pursued his parallel interests, developing his mining ventures in the New England interior, expanding his overseas trading business, taking a seat on the Council of the General Court, fighting against the spread of Anglicanism in Boston, and working to implement market reforms in the city. In 1730, Belcher's longstanding relationship with the House of Hanover finally paid off: George II appointed him royal governor of Massachusetts.[135] The following year, the Roman Catholic archbishop of Salzburg, trying to suppress a Pietist revival within his principality, ordered the expulsion of all Protestants, sending some twenty thousand refugees north into Germany, where the Halle Pietists organized their wide-ranging resettlement.[136] Halle reached out to its English connections at the SPCK, and through the guidance of its secretary, Henry Newman, late of Boston, several hundred Salzburgers were transported to the new British colony at Georgia (named for Britain's German-speaking monarch).[137] With Newman as go-between, Belcher and Colman, minister of Boston's Brattle Street Church, began a correspondence with Halle's missionaries to Georgia and their superintendent, Samuel Urlsperger, the Lutheran senior of Augsburg.[138] Had Mather lived to see this day, he would have relished the opportunity to develop new links in the chain of Pietist connections.

On their journey to Georgia, the Salzburg refugees were accompanied by Baron Philipp von Reck, a young Hanoverian nobleman and ardent Pietist who served as a commissioner, overseeing their settlement. Once the plantation of Salzburgers in Georgia had taken shape, von Reck set off overland through British America to drum up support for the refugees. In his tour of the colonies, he was repeatedly shocked by the depredations of the slave system, particularly the slaves' ignorance of Christianity, for which he rightly blamed their masters. But of all the places that he visited, including Philadelphia and New York, von Reck was most impressed by Boston, "the largest and most imposing commercial city in all of English America, . . . as favorably situated for commerce as any city in the world." He was entertained, of course, by Belcher, whom he described as "Jonathan Belcher, Knight, Commander-in-Chief and supreme Governor of New England . . . who can be put before all people in America as an example of honesty, good conduct, and love."[139] Belcher was extremely flattered by the visit, especially by the way that it mirrored his own experiences thirty years earlier.

Here was the young Hanoverian nobleman come to Boston, paying flattering attention to the same things that Belcher, the young merchant prince, had observed in his German travels. In particular, von Reck noted that in Boston,

> Many Christian provisions have been made here for the poor and the orphans. There is, for example, a corn house in which a large quantity of corn is stored every year when prices are lowest and where, when food gets expensive in the winter and people begin to starve, they can buy the corn they need for the price at which it was bought. There are, likewise, a hospital, four schools for poor orphans, etc. Four English miles from Boston is the University of Cambridge [Harvard College] where 200 students are enrolled.

The baron also admired the beauty of the streets, especially "Hanover Street, so named by the governor," and the quality of religious life in the city. By the time he left, von Reck, laden with gifts and correspondence for his German contacts, had received promises from Belcher for two sloops loaded with wood to be sent to Georgia for the construction of an orphanage, and he had formed elaborate plans with a group of Boston merchants for the further settlement of Salzburg refugees in America, extending the circles of benevolence that Mather and Francke had projected in their attempts to promote ecumenical Protestantism.[140]

It is easy to be dismissive of the aspirations of Sewall, Mather, Belcher, and their naive fellow Bostonians. We might compare their dreams with the "Rosicrucian Enlightenment" described by Frances Yates in her speculative history of an incipient movement that never fully materialized—a moment of extraordinary intellectual, religious, and political ferment centered around the electoral court at Heidelberg in the 1610s. Indeed, there are connections between Heidelberg and Boston: the alchemical theme in Belcher's and Mather's experiences; the relevance to Sewall, dreaming of Christ coming to Boston and reading David Pareus, a theologian at Heidelberg during that utopian interlude in 1612 when Princess Elizabeth, daughter of James I of England, mother-to-be of Sophia of Hanover, and grandmother of the future George I of Great Britain, married Frederick, the elector palatine.[141] At the "chymical wedding" of Elizabeth and Frederick, the marriage of the Thames and Rhine, a new alliance between leading Protestant powers of Europe gave rise to dreams of a unified Christianity, the revival of piety, and a flourishing of the arts and sciences, emanating from a European courtly center that would be a model of Christian charity for the world to emulate.[142] Those dreams, of course, were crushed by Frederick's defeat at the Battle of White Mountain and the thirty years of brutal warfare that followed. For like-minded people in England, the portentous rise and disastrous fall of Cromwell's commonwealth, and the creeping Catholicism of the later Stuarts, crushed their fervent millennial aspirations as well. Only faint traces of that earlier utopian moment remained, traces that Yates detected in the early enthusiasm for alchemy, cabbalism, and hermetic science among the founders of the Royal Society—an enthusiasm that was suppressed after the Restoration of Charles II.[143] The course of imperial state building in Europe left these earlier dreamers skeptical, if not cynical, about the possibility that earthly kingdoms could be made to serve the kingdom of God.

But people in Boston, spared the experience of defeat in their provincial isolation, found it possible to harbor utopian dreams longer than their European counterparts. Throughout the seventeenth century and well into the eighteenth, New England remained a hotbed of alchemical studies and millennial speculation, and the dream of a holy city remained alive there as well.[144] When the crisis in 1688 that placed a Dutch Protestant on the throne of England was followed in 1701 by an Act of Parliament settling the royal succession on Belcher's future patron, Sophia of Hanover, the last surviving child of Princess Elizabeth and Palatine Elector Frederick, there were people in Boston who imagined that at the moment of this remarriage of the Thames and Rhine, the Charles River could also add a small trickle to the rising tide of an emerging Protestant Atlantic community.[145] And so they reached out to that world, attempting to solve problems that the ocean delivered to their doorstep (as in the case of Sewall), moving through it directly and with unbounded ambition (as in the case of Belcher), or enveloping themselves in it through reading, correspondence, and imagination (as in Mather's case), until they made contact with those elements that were congenial to their way of thinking, reinforcing the cultural identity that Bostonians had been developing for a century.

Dreams of a utopian Protestant International no longer lay at the center of European state politics, if indeed they ever had, despite the occasional illusion created, for instance, by the Duke of Marlborough's victory over the Catholic forces of France and Bavaria at Blenheim, announced on the day that Belcher arrived in Hanover. But there was still sufficient encouragement, indeed growing encouragement, for such beliefs on the margins of Europe's centers of power in voluntary societies like the SPCK, in quasi-independent organizations like Francke's institute at Halle, and in the revivalist Protestant Pietism that they promoted beyond the bounds of state churches and confessional orthodoxy. In these circles, Bostonians felt the most at home and had the most to contribute, for their century-long history as a marginal community, a voluntary society dedicated to the promotion of evangelical Christianity, built on a highly independent commercial foundation, gave them a wealth of experience to contribute to the growing transatlantic conversation. As Cotton Mather contemplated this world opening before him, he exclaimed, "O wide Atlantick, Thou shalt not stand in the way as any Hindrance of those Communications! Verily Our Glorious Lord will have Dominion from Sea to Sea."[146] That was the hope of the Bostonians who imagined the Charles River joining the Thames, the Rhine, and the Elbe, all flowing together to form a Protestant Atlantic world, where *Theopolis Americana* would prosper with a glory that would give Boston more to boast about than Rome had ever had.

CHAPTER 5

"God Deliver Me and Mine from the Government of Soldiers"

> About 3 oClock this after Noon I ordered the whole to be Drawd up in a Bodey and bid the french men march of[f] and sott fire to their Buildings and Left the women and children to Tack care of themselves with grate Lementation which I must Confess itt seemed to be sumthing shoking.
>
> —Captain Abijah Willard, *Journal*, 1755

From 1730 to 1741, Jonathan Belcher served King George II, the last British monarch to lead an army into battle, as the royal governor of Massachusetts. The son of a merchant who made his fortune from military contracts, Belcher was no pacifist. But he had a profound sense of the proper role of the military in the government of his commonwealth. He firmly believed soldiers should be subordinate to civilian authority, as had been the case throughout all but three years of the colony's first century: "[Soldiers] are good & proper in their places, but not to be at the head of a civil polity."[1] Massachusetts differed from most of Britain's other royal colonies in that few of its appointed governors were military men. From 1691 onward, though, when the commonwealth became a royal province, the people of Massachusetts always feared that their next governor might be a soldier—like Sir Edmund Andros, who ruled for the infamous three years over the Dominion of New England—a soldier who would threaten the liberties framed by their charter.

In 1733, Belcher wrote to a political confidant in England, discussing a curious situation. Massachusetts' neighboring colony, the royal province of Nova Scotia, had recently offered large tracts of land for settlement by Protestant colonists, but few New Englanders had taken up the generous offer. This seemed strange to Belcher, who as we have seen in the previous chapter, had recently taken part in relocating Protestant refugees from Salzburg to the new British colony at Georgia, where they had eagerly taken up similar land grants. The reason, Belcher conjectured, why Nova Scotia attracted no one from Massachusetts was that the former French colony, under British authority since the conquest of 1710, was ruled by military governors and vice admiralty courts. Nova Scotia lacked the town governments, civilian courts, jury trials, and representative assembly to which Massachusetts had always been accustomed—institutions that Bostonians in the seventeenth century had spread north and eastward up the coast of Maine to the Nova Scotia boundary. What right-thinking Massachusetts citizen would move to such a place, lose his liberties, and give up his right to self-government? Belcher concluded his epistle with a prayerful admonition: "God deliver me and mine from the government of soldiers."[2]

Belcher's career in New England government took place during the "Long Peace," a period marked by the relative absence of warfare among Indian nations and colonists in eastern North America, as the Iroquois or Haudenosaunee Confederacy signed treaties of neutrality with both the French and English colonies. These were also the years between the Peace of Utrecht (1713) that ended the War of the Spanish Succession, which pitted Britain and its allies against Louis XIV's France, and the outbreak of the War of Jenkins' Ear between Britain and Spain (1739), a quarter-century period when the military powers of the Atlantic world were in a tranquil phase as well.[3] During this era, Belcher's prayer held true. The Boston of his mature years was a city that aspired to be, in the words of Cotton Mather, a "Theopolis Americana." Boston had the luxury of peace in which to pursue its dreams of commercial prosperity, charitable benevolence, and exemplary religious and social reform. Yet the end of Belcher's term as Massachusetts governor coincided with the resumption of imperial warfare among Britain, Spain, and France. For the next four decades, Boston would be involved in military conflict more often than not, culminating in the Revolutionary War from 1775 to 1783.

With the end of the Long Peace, however, the British Empire's aims became increasingly militarized; the "government of soldiers" played an ever more prominent role as Britain acquired additional overseas territory. This shift in policy slowly began to alienate the Crown's most autonomous province. Boston in New England had shown the strongest devotion to the eighteenth-century empire's success, so long as it had leeway to bend some of the empire's most stringent rules. As military plans and military rulers came to shape colonial policy and make greater demands on the king's subjects, it became increasingly difficult to avoid the fact that manstealing, the violent seizure and movement of people from one place to another against their will, was central to Whitehall's emerging vision of the empire. The increasing role played by the military in governing the empire also undermined the Crown's and Parliament's toleration for the complexity that Boston's Atlantic world was built on. Military rule frequently meant the disruption or perversion of the free circulation in commodities, persons, and ideas that had made Boston's Atlantic world profitable and enriching. If the generation before 1740 had experienced the British Empire as a champion of Boston's causes, and had fantasized, like Sewall, Mather, and Belcher, that the pursuit of their own utopian projects coincided with the interests of a truly Protestant empire, then the post-1740 generation became profoundly disillusioned.

Boston's Atlantic connections were many and far-flung, from the silver mines of Peru to the commercial cities of the Netherlands and the courtly palaces of Germany, from the slave-trading factories of West Africa to the sugar plantations of the West Indies. Nearer to home, but equally important, was Boston's commerce with the region to its north and east, in the territory called Acadia (or *Acadie*) by seventeenth-century French colonists. By 1710, Britain had taken tenuous hold of this region (which it called Nova Scotia) through the conquest of Port Royal.[4] The British Army renamed this flimsy fortress Annapolis Royal, but the settlers in the region remained French Catholics. They and their Mi'kmaq Indian allies, with whom the Acadians traded and intermarried, remained largely independent of British control. But the Acadians' relationship with Boston was multivalent and complex, and continued to grow to the benefit of both parties through the subsequent decades.

In the following pages, I will explore the lives and careers of people who were profoundly shaped by the fraught relationship between Acadia and Boston. As in the preceding chapter, the focus here will be on three exemplary figures within a wide and complex story: a professional soldier named Paul Mascarene, a politician named William Shirley, and an ordinary farmer from Boston's hinterland named Abijah Willard. Their fortunes and fates reveal the severe damage done to the relationship between Boston and Acadia, and the perverse dislocations visited on the people of Nova Scotia and New England, when the empire's military policies came to insist that there was no middle ground between British and French allegiances, and no room for dissenting autonomy under the Crown's military authority. The militarization of the British Empire and its governance of the colonies forced Bostonians to take sides on these questions, either to persist in supporting Boston's nuanced relationship with a friendly enemy, as Colonel Mascarene would do; to embrace the empire's military logic, as Governor Shirley would do; or to have their lives torn apart by the conflict, as would be the fate of Captain Willard.

Boston and Acadia: *Nos Amis, les Ennemis*

The coastal region that stretches from Cape Cod in the southwest to the Bay of Fundy in the northeast makes for a natural trading area. The coastline is indented with thousands of inlets, streams, and rivers, and thousands more coastal islands, creating endless small harbors and safe havens where ships and boats of all sizes can travel and anchor in safety. This region, roughly four hundred miles long as the crow flies, but with many more miles of coast along its bays and estuaries, is broken up by a half-dozen major rivers, from the Saint John in the northeast to the Merrimack in the southwest, that afford access to inland products, from fur and timber to grain and livestock. In addition, the coastline is indented with remarkably good natural harbors, from Boston Harbor in Massachusetts Bay to Annapolis Royal on the eastern side of the Bay of Fundy, and many more between.

In the north, the Nova Scotia peninsula, stretching from Canso Island to Cape Sable, affords the region some protection from harmful Atlantic storms, especially the dreaded winter nor'easters. Similarly, the southern coast of New England, reaching eastward out to Cape Cod, protects the region from hurricanes brought northward by the Gulf Stream in late summer. The northerly latitudes and rocky soils prevented this region from developing the plantation commodities that fueled colonial projects in the Caribbean, the Chesapeake, and Carolina. But there were stretches of fertile lands at both ends of the region, in the Minas Basin of Nova Scotia and along Massachusetts Bay and Cape Ann, that caused its early colonists to dream of Arcadia or a "New English Canaan" when describing their new homelands. No natural barriers, mountain ranges, diverging ocean currents, impassible shoals, or hostile prevailing winds separated this coastal region into distinctive parts. Its greatest resources, the fishing banks of St. Georges and the smaller banks off Cape Sable, were equally accessible from almost anywhere in the region.

With all these advantages, this maritime region lent itself to commercial integration. And over the course of the long century between 1630 and 1740, that is essentially what Boston accomplished. Most of Acadia's colonists were French Catholics who owed their political allegiance to France's kings, but Boston nonetheless became the transshipment point for imports and exports of the region, and the center of news and information. Boston's commercial hegemony was so complete that it even buffered Acadians from epidemics prevalent in other Atlantic regions, as Massachusetts' strict quarantine regulations prevented the New England traders who dominated the region from accidentally introducing infectious diseases to their Acadian customers.[5] A 1737 map of the region made by Cyprian Southack, a Boston-based trader, depicts this hegemony graphically. Southack's map shows the "New England Coast" extending all the way through Nova Scotia, and includes an inset map of Boston to emphasize its dominance over the region. If

Map 5.1. *A Map of the Coast of New England*, by Cyprian Southack, 1737.

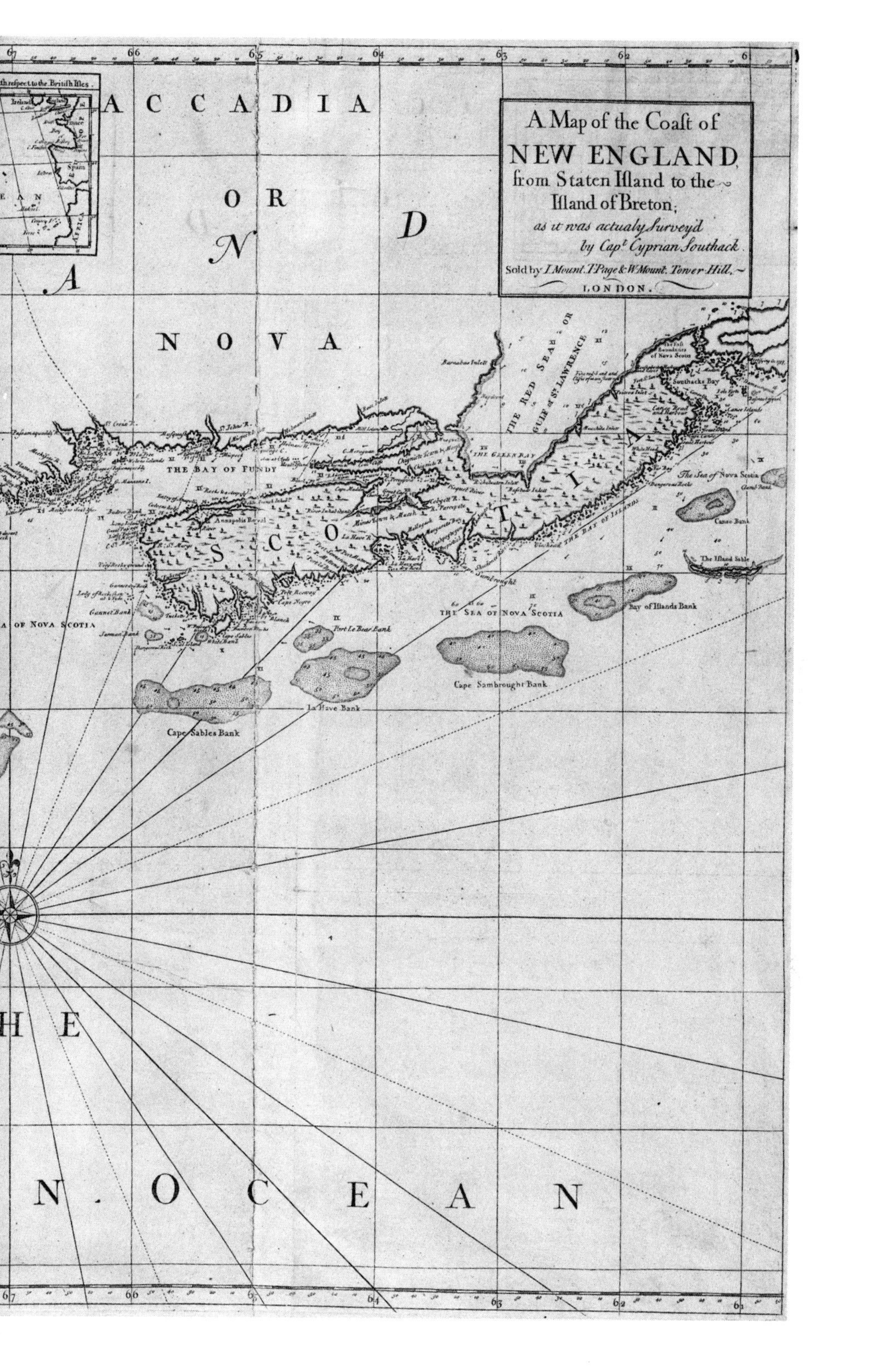

A Map of the Coast of
NEW ENGLAND
from Staten Island to the
Island of Breton;
as it was actualy Surveyd
by Capt. Cyprian Southack.
Sold by I. Mount. T. Page & W. Mount. Tower Hill,
LONDON.
ACCADIA
OR
NOVA SCOTIA
THE BAY OF FUNDY
Annapolis Royal
THE SEA OF NOVA SCOTIA
The Sea of Nova Scotia
THE GREEN BAY
THE RED SEA OR GULF of St. LAWRENCE
Southacks Bay
THE BAY OF ISLANDS
Canso Bank
The Island Sable
Bay of Islands Bank
Port Le Bear Bank
Cape Sambrought Bank
La Have Bank
Cape Sables Bank
Gannet Bank
Cape Sambrought
THE OCEAN

natural conditions encouraged the trade that linked the entire basin together, what divided the region was not natural but rather man-made: politics and religion, nations and cultures.

For early European colonizers, this region was among the more remote and undesirable places on the Atlantic Seaboard, which helps to explain how it came to be divided. Even for the English and French, who lagged behind their Iberian competitors, their initial colonial ventures had steered clear of this region. The English focused much farther to the south, from the Chesapeake to the Caribbean, where they could challenge the hegemony of Spain, and the French developed the Saint Lawrence River Valley as an avenue deep into the interior of North America. From both perspectives, the basin from Cape Cod to the Bay of Fundy was an afterthought, a region peopled by social and religious outliers: radical dissenters in the English case, and Huguenots, fishermen, and poor farmers among the French. The propensity of the latter to intermingle with the local Mi'kmaq Indian population and form mixed or metis households and communities further distanced them from the mainstream of New France.

From the earliest days of colonization along this stretch of coastline, the competing parties respected no boundaries. The borders were artificial, overlapping lines drawn on makeshift maps by courtiers and investors who never visited the lands they claimed. The Plymouth colonists, whose settlements hugged a narrow stretch along Cape Cod Bay, established fishing stations and trading posts far to the north along the Maine coast, well beyond the bounds of their patent.[6] In the 1640s, as discussed in chapter 1, two captains, Charles d'Aulnay and Charles de La Tour, each with commissions from competing French authorities, laid claim to the same Acadian territory, fought pitched battles for it, and recruited ships and soldiers from Boston for assistance. On the coastline of present-day Maine and New Brunswick, between the Massachusetts outposts in Casco Bay and the Acadian settlements along the Saint John River, no one could really say where New England ended and Acadia began.[7] Nothing about the region's geography guaranteed that any particular settlement would come to dominate the whole. But the emergence of Boston's Atlantic trade in the 1640s provided advantages that other settlements lacked.[8] Over the next century, as Boston grew to be a commercial powerhouse in the Atlantic world, its success made it the dominant trading partner throughout this maritime region.

When the conflict over Acadia between d'Aulnay and La Tour ended in the former's favor, d'Aulnay and John Winthrop agreed that their French and English colonies would trade freely with one another, even if France and England went to war. This was prescient in seeing that valuable commerce could be disrupted by imperial conflicts that bore little relation to local circumstances. Let England and France fight over the big prizes in faraway places—sugar islands, plantation colonies, and precious metals—so long as the trade in furs and fish, barrel staves, salt pork, and Indian corn continued up and down the nearby coast. But when this agreement was made in 1644, neither d'Aulnay nor Winthrop could imagine what a big business trade in small things would become. Nor could they foresee the demands for imperial uniformity that France and Britain would make in the following century, as these rival states expanded their overseas territories and developed the fiscal, administrative, and military capacity to exert greater control over their subjects. The early North American plantations were often motley societies, "English," "French," or "Dutch" more in name and the location of their governing bodies than in the ethnic identities of their settlers. But this pattern began to change in 1710, when British military forces seized the Acadian peninsula from French control during the War of the Spanish Succession.

The British conquest of Acadia in 1710 was launched from Boston, but it was not planned or encouraged by Bostonians. Over the preceding two decades, war between France and England had spilled into North America in what colonists called King William's War (1689–97) and Queen Anne's War (1702–13). Boston's chief aim in these conflicts had been to punish its Catholic enemies for brutal frontier raids and regain New England prisoners held in New France.[9] New England volunteer soldiers, recruited to capture Port Royal in Acadia in spring 1707, mutinied and returned to Boston when they discovered that their commanders had been instructed to keep the fort and seize the territory around it, rather than simply to burn it and destroy the surrounding crops. Revenge, not conquest, is what motivated most New England violence against their French neighbors. The Boston merchants who had the most to gain from this relationship did not need to rule Acadia's territory in order to profit from its trade, as long experience in trading with the West Indies had taught them.[10]

Rather, the 1710 conquest of Acadia emerged from within the British Army, promoted by a Scottish officer named Samuel Vetch. Vetch had earlier been involved in Scottish colonizing ventures, such as the disastrous Darien project in 1698 on the Isthmus of Panama, where he had been elected to the governing council, and was among the few survivors of the poorly planned and disease-ridden venture. After the Act of Union of 1707 that fused England and Scotland together under the rule of the Parliament at Westminster, Vetch's energies were directed into British ventures. Vetch hoped to develop a New Scotland to the north of New England, creating a colonial parallel to the newly united Great Britain.[11] Together with Francis Nicholson, another experienced colonial administrator, Vetch brought Massachusetts royal governor Joseph Dudley into their plans and used his influence to recruit New England soldiers for the 1707 capture of Port Royal. And it was Vetch's order to occupy the fort that the New England volunteers had refused to obey.

In the aftermath of this initial failure to hold Acadia, Vetch expanded his plans. He dreamed of conquering not only Acadia but the entirety of New France.[12] In Vetch's view, by seizing Acadia and the Saint Lawrence Valley, Britain would gain more resources to supply the Caribbean sugar islands, and the New England colonies would no longer waste money and men fighting French competitors. Vetch also believed that Protestant missionaries could convert New France's Indian population from Catholicism and displace the Jesuit priests who held sway over them. Protestant settlers, preferably Scotsmen, would be recruited to supplant the Acadians.[13]

With these plans in mind, and in light of the mutiny of the New England volunteer soldiers, Vetch and his military collaborators turned to New York and its prominent Livingston family to recruit troops and supplies for their next assault on Canada. They also lobbied Whitehall to gain support from the Royal Navy and Army. The British government authorized an attack—not a full assault on all of French Canada, but a more limited conquest of Acadia—and promised Vetch that he would become military governor of his New Scotland should the venture succeed. With the added support of the Royal Navy and British regulars, the conquest was accomplished with little difficulty. By offering strong economic incentives, Vetch and Nicholson managed to recruit some New England soldiers for the expedition, but the troops once again refused to garrison the fort at Port Royal (now renamed Annapolis) under Vetch's command and insisted on having a New Englander for a commanding officer. By 1711, they were replaced by English, Scottish, and Irish soldiers; few of the New Englanders showed any interest in remaining in Acadia or submitting to imperial authority.[14] Britain had now acquired a new colony, but its population and government differed dramatically from its English and republican southern neighbor.

An Accidental Bostonian: Paul Mascarene

Acadia, now Nova Scotia, lay in British hands, and its government would henceforth be led by British imperial soldiers—exactly the form of government that Boston and New England had overthrown twenty years earlier in the rebellion against Andros and the Dominion of New England. The conquest of Acadia provides the background for understanding how a young Huguenot exile named Jean-Paul Mascarene came to Nova Scotia, and from there to Boston, where he became a leader in forging beneficial relationships between the Acadians and New England's metropolis.

Jean-Paul Mascarene was born in winter 1684–85 in Castres, in the Languedoc region of southern France, closer to Barcelona than to Paris. His father, Jean Mascarene, was a Huguenot. When Louis XIV revoked the Edict of Nantes in 1685, which for nearly a century had given Protestants in France a measure of toleration and civil rights, Jean was banished from France and moved to the Netherlands. Relatives raised the infant Jean-Paul and smuggled him to the Netherlands at the age of ten to reunite with his father, but the elder Mascarene died shortly before his son's arrival. The boy was educated at Utrecht, where the treaty ending the War of Spanish Succession would be signed in 1713. This treaty would shape young Mascarene's future by setting the terms of peace between his native and adoptive countries.

On reaching maturity in 1706, Mascarene moved to England and was commissioned a lieutenant in a British Army regiment made up of exiled Huguenots.[15] In 1708, Mascarene was among the troops chosen for the expedition planned by Vetch and Nicholson. In April 1709, he first set foot in Boston, at just about the time that Belcher returned from his second trip to the Netherlands and Germany. Mascarene joined the 1710 expedition to conquer Acadia as the captain of a company of grenadiers. He distinguished himself in the siege of Port Royal, gained promotion to major, and received the honor of taking formal possession of the fort from the French. With Vetch in command as military governor, Paul Mascarene (he dropped the "Jean" from his name) became the chief liaison between the British Army and the Acadian population. His command of French made him the natural interpreter of British military policy to the Acadians and eventually the Acadians' favored intermediary with British authority as well.

Under Vetch's plan, Mascarene, a victim of Louis XIV's demand for religious uniformity in France, was ordered to enforce a similar policy over the Acadians. Vetch's plan had included the conversion of Acadia to Protestantism, either through missionary work or by replacing Acadians with Protestants, and deporting the Acadians to French colonies in Martinique or Newfoundland.[16] When Vetch received no support for this from the British government, he instead treated the conquered Acadians as prisoners of war, in the words of embittered Acadians and Vetch's subordinate officers, "keeping us like negroes" and "using the people more like slaves than anything else." At this point, Mascarene, despite his French origins and loyalty to the British Crown, began to demonstrate what we might call a Bostonian sensibility: an intuitive grasp of the Acadians' plight and an awareness of their potential role within the wider ambit of the city-state of Boston. His manuscript account of the conquest explained that Vetch's abusive treatment of the Acadians "caused a great deal of clamour and noise," and generated resistance against their new British overlords.[17]

Over the next four decades in the military government of Nova Scotia, during which he would become lieutenant governor of Annapolis Royal, Mascarene's sympathy for the Acadians and respect for their commercial relations with Massachusetts would continue to grow. It began immediately, in November 1710, when Vetch sent him sixty miles eastward to treat with the Acadians at Minas Basin, Chignecto, and Cobequid, some of the region's most populous and prosperous settlements. Vetch insisted that the eastern Acadians should pay tribute of six thousand livres in return for his mercy in letting them continue to farm their lands (similar to Andros's demand for quitrents from Massachusetts landowners in the 1680s). Mascarene, in negotiation with his fellow Francophones, began to realize how excessive Vetch's demands were and how harmless the Acadians were to British interests. Like Belcher and every other Boston merchant, Mascarene understood that a settled and peaceable population of Acadian farmers producing goods for export and consuming imports was a boon for Boston's economy. On his own initiative he agreed to reduce the tribute by half, which the Acadians paid in furs they acquired from their Mi'kmaq allies.[18] Nevertheless, a portion of the Acadian population chose to move out of Britain's jurisdiction. Some went to French settlements on neighboring Cape Breton Island, near the new French fortress being constructed at Louisbourg to defend the Saint Lawrence River. Others moved to Ile Saint-Jean (Prince Edward Island) just north of Acadia. Those who remained in Nova Scotia posed a persistent problem from the viewpoint of the British military government (if not for Boston's merchants) because they preferred to remain subjects of the French king.

Vetch's successor as Nova Scotia's governor, Colonel Richard Phillips, tried to solve this problem by enforcing an oath of allegiance on the Acadians. Phillips promised them freedom to worship as Roman Catholics and the civil rights of British subjects, but threatened those who refused with deportation. After a long struggle, the

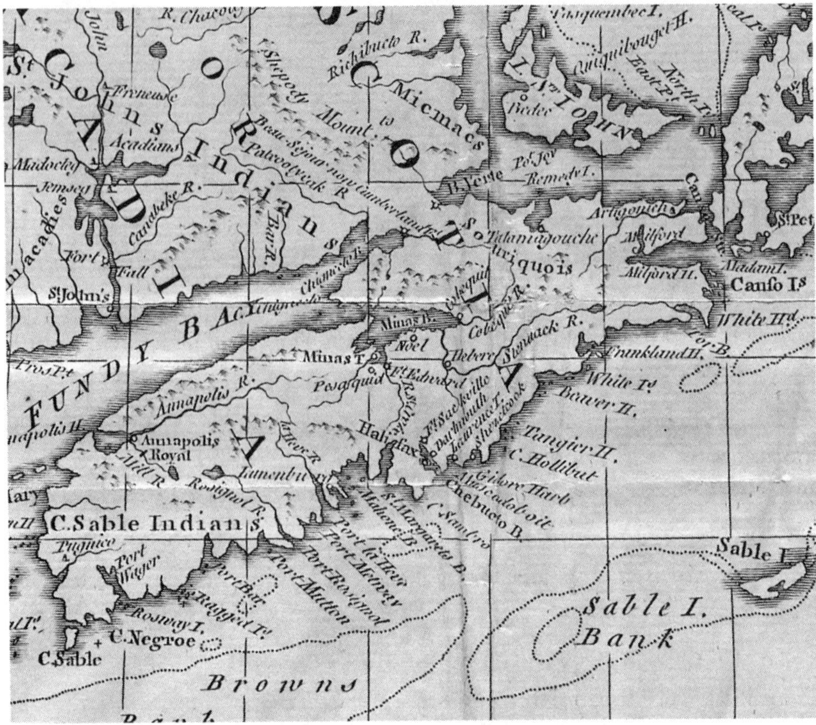

MAP 5.2. *A Map of New England, and Nova Scotia*, by Thomas Kitchin, 1758. Detail. Made during the Seven Years' War, Kitchin's map depicts the principal areas where the Acadian removal took place, from the Minas and Chignecto basins across the peninsula to "Tatamagouche" south of the Ile St. Jean, soon to be renamed Prince Edward Island.

Acadians gained a compromise by agreeing to remain neutral while the British military fought a brutal war against the Mi'kmaq Indians. The Acadians agreed in 1730 to swear allegiance to George II so long as they would never be required to fight for Britain against their French kinsmen.[19] British officials commonly referred to them, sometimes appreciatively, and sometimes with suspicion, as "the French Neutrals." Mascarene shared this skepticism about the Acadians' neutrality. He feared that their Catholicism and the fact that their priests also served the Catholic converts among the hostile Mi'kmaqs meant that their subjection to British government remained in doubt. But his response to these doubts was shaped by his growing involvement in the social and cultural life of Boston, and his adoption of Boston attitudes toward Acadia.

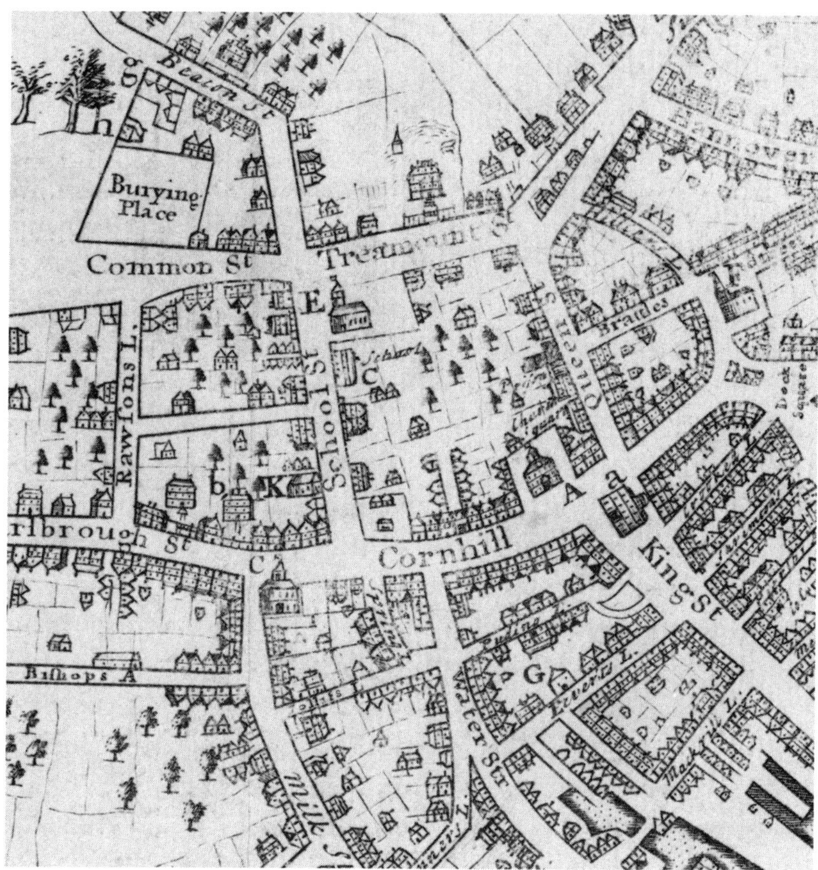

MAP 5.3. *The Town of Boston in New England*, by John Bonner, 1722. Detail. Paul Mascarene's house is across School Street from the French Church, marked "K," just down the hill from King's Chapel, "E," and close by the royal governor's residence at the Province House, "b," the Old South Meetinghouse, "C," the Old Brick Meetinghouse, "A," and the town house, "a."

Like most of Nova Scotia's officer corps, Mascarene spent his winters in Boston. The garrison at Annapolis Royal was bitterly cold and often short of food. Boston offered warmth, plenty, and the hospitality of a community of exiled Huguenots. In 1714, after a long stay in Boston, Mascarene married Elizabeth Perry, the daughter of a prominent Boston merchant and cousin of John Nelson, a minor English aristocrat who had promoted eastward trade between Boston and Nova Scotia. Paul and Elizabeth had four children, and built a two-story brick house on School Street in the heart of

Boston, just a few steps from King's Chapel, the city's oldest Anglican Church, where Elizabeth's family were members. Within a few years, the Huguenot community built its own church on School Street adjacent to Mascarene's house.[20]

His association with Boston's Huguenot refugees shaped Mascarene's thinking about the French Neutrals in Nova Scotia. He came to believe that a settlement of French Protestants in the vicinity of the Catholic Acadians, under the guidance of a Protestant clergyman, would gradually convert the Acadians. As Protestants, they would then swear the oath and become reliable British subjects.[21] In the late 1720s, he recruited Andre Le Mercier, the pastor of Boston's Huguenot church, to select one hundred French Protestants from Boston to settle in Nova Scotia, and advertised in the *Boston Gazette* that "large tracts of land are to be granted in fee-simple" to those willing to migrate. But none of the Boston Huguenots took up the offer. Many Huguenots had been in Massachusetts for four decades, with a second generation coming of age, anglicizing their names, and assimilating to the community. Andre Faneuil's nephew, Pierre, relocated from New York to Boston and became Peter Faneuil (pronounced "Fannel" by Boston Anglophones), the future donor of Faneuil Hall, the colonial city's most iconic building. Apollos Rivoire's son by his English wife was christened Paul Revere. The Huguenots' unwillingness to abandon comfort, security, and a voice in their own government was not hard to understand. It was their refusal to accept the offer of free and fertile Acadian land that Jonathan Belcher explained by reference to the province's military rule: "God deliver me and mine from the government of soldiers."[22]

Mascarene abandoned the idea of resettling Protestants in Acadia, but not the hope of converting the Acadians. In the 1730s, he began to correspond with Claude de la Vernede de St. Poncy, a Catholic priest in Annapolis Royal. Mascarene aimed to convince St. Poncy to convert to Protestantism and lead his flock along with him.[23] St. Poncy remained unswayed. While Mascarene persisted in his conversion efforts, he also became more involved with Acadian commerce. At some point in his education, Mascarene had learned engineering skills. In that capacity he was assigned to repair the fort at Annapolis Royal, working with Boston's contractors and suppliers. Building on these relationships, Mascarene proposed a plan to develop a coal mine in Acadia, on the eastern shore of the Chignecto Basin, north of Minas, about seventy miles from Annapolis along the Bay of Fundy. Mascarene gained the support of Henry Cope, a Boston merchant and former British Army officer, who helped raise the capital and supervised the opening of the mine in 1731. The profits from the mine augmented Mascarene's military salary and maintained his family comfortably in Boston. With these religious and commercial projects, Mascarene was joining the long-established Boston practice of drawing ever more of the greater New England region under its cultural and economic sway, even if Nova Scotia's government lay beyond Boston's reach.

The success of these projects helped to make Mascarene a fixture in Boston society. In 1728, he commissioned John Smibert, a Scottish-born artist who specialized in portraits of Boston's elite, to paint his likeness, depicting Mascarene dressed in armor and gesturing toward an idealized image of Annapolis Royal.[24] Boston newspapers printed verses in praise of the likeness, to which Mascarene responded in kind—for in his spare time, Mascarene translated Molière into English.[25] Although Mascarene's wife died young in 1729, his daughters would marry leading Boston citizens, including Foster Hutchinson, Superior Court judge and brother of Thomas Hutchinson, the future royal governor. His only son, John, married Margaret Holyoke, daughter of the president of Harvard College. Mascarene's proliferating connections solidified his place within the tight network of mercantile and clerical authority that dominated public life in mid-eighteenth-century Boston. The closer he came to this circle, the more he began to think as they did about the Acadians. (See plate 14.)

By the mid-1730s, Mascarene's duties came to include protecting the fishing and trading station that New Englanders had long maintained on Canso Island. Canso lay at the northeastern tip of Nova Scotia, along the narrow channel that separated the peninsula from Cape Breton Island, where the French fortress at Louisbourg stood.

As it was close to the mainland, Canso was endangered by the ongoing warfare in this region between the British military and the Mi'kmaq. In supervising Canso's defenses from his base in Boston, Mascarene also forged connections with Boston's merchant and fishing communities on the island. Much of the commerce from Boston *to* Canso also involved commerce *through* Canso, to the Louisbourg fortress. This trade, of course, was illegal, violating the Navigation Acts' restriction on interimperial commerce, and after Britain joined the War of the Austrian Succession in the 1740s, it constituted trading with the enemy. But the French at Louisbourg had come to rely on Boston for food and other supplies. Goods from Boston were cheaper, better, and more plentiful than French imports. Boston merchants made a profit, and the strategically valuable Canso station remained stronger than it otherwise might have been. Mascarene, now as much a Bostonian as an imperial military officer, turned a blind eye to the illegal trade.[26]

In December 1739, the lieutenant governor and military commander at Annapolis Royal, Lawrence Armstrong, a melancholic soldier, frustrated by the intractable Acadians, the hostile Mi'kmaq, and the grim winters on the Bay of Fundy, committed suicide in a grisly fashion with "five wounds in his Breast" made by his own sword. Mascarene was Armstrong's replacement. Through thirty years of service to the province, and equally long exposure to life in Boston and its complex relationship with Acadia, Mascarene, unlike his predecessors in the office, had come to value "mildness" toward the French Neutrals. As he assumed authority over the province, his main goals were to make peace with the Mi'kmaq and preserve peace with the Acadians. His long-standing relationship with their Catholic priests proved useful, keeping open channels of communication that his predecessors had lacked. Still more useful was his conviction that most Acadians wanted "to live at peace and in submission to the King." To encourage this peaceful relationship, Mascarene built on an informal process established in earlier years in which the Acadians sent self-selected deputies to convey their interests to the ruling council of Nova Scotia. Mascarene "committed himself to recruiting responsible deputies and utilizing them to the limits of their capacity." In a note to himself, he described such prospects as "upright men of property, having the good of the community at heart, and sensible to the duty to which they are bound by their oath of allegiance."[27] Essentially, Mascarene's plan was modeled on the deputies in the lower house of the Massachusetts General Court, modified to suit the conditions of the Acadians in their curious position as French Neutrals. Perhaps without knowing it, Mascarene's approach mimicked the one that Bostonians had used in the seventeenth century to bring the Maine coast settlements into the fold of Massachusetts government.

Mascarene's irenic policy in Nova Scotia served the larger interests of the empire and the city-state of Boston. But just as Mascarene assumed authority over Nova Scotia in 1740, Britain went to war with Spain, shattering the relative peace among Atlantic empires that had lasted a quarter century. From this time forward, the Crown began to call on its North American colonies to join its overseas military expeditions on a large scale, recruiting thousands of colonial soldiers for amphibious assaults against Spanish strongholds in the Caribbean. For the preceding half century, Boston and New England had come to believe that their interests, and those of the empire, were one. Starting in 1740, New Englanders joined the Spanish War, and later war with France, with an enthusiasm and military prowess unmatched by the other British colonies. With this rash embrace of imperial warfare came surprising victory and elation, then disillusion, and finally destruction.

A Soldier by Convenience: William Shirley

Shirley, who came to play the leading role as Boston embraced Britain's imperial wars, was an unlikely candidate for the position, neither a military man by training nor a Bostonian by birth or inclination. He was born in England in 1694, a decade later than Mascarene, and in much more promising circumstances. Shirley came from a cadet branch of a distinguished Sussex family, and his parents planned to improve their fortunes through their son's education: the Merchant Taylors' School in London, Pembroke College,

Cambridge, and then the Inner Temple at the Inns of Court to study law. A modest inheritance allowed Shirley to purchase a clerkship in London government, and his legal training gained him admittance to the bar. Although he married well, he and his wife, Frances Barker, produced eight children in a dozen years, and then the South Sea Bubble of 1720 wiped out the remains of his inheritance. A large family, high aspirations, and limited funds. What to do?

Among Shirley's Sussex connections was the Duke of Newcastle, master of patronage throughout the British Empire. Newcastle granted Shirley an audience and suggested that he try his luck in the colonies, where ambitious men with legal skills, government experience, and personal charm might gain preferment. With a letter of reference addressed to Belcher, the newly appointed royal governor of Massachusetts, Shirley and family set sail for Boston in summer 1731.[28] Over the course of the next decade, Shirley built a successful practice in the bustling commercial city.

In the 1730s, Boston was the largest and most prosperous city in colonial British America, but it still had no bar association and no formal legal training of any kind. Aspiring local practitioners might read a bit in Sir Edward Coke's *Reports* and *Institutes* under the guidance of a self-trained magistrate. But English immigrants with bona fide formal training rose rapidly to the top of the profession and tended to lord it over the local courts. So Shirley did well, and rapidly made clients of some of Boston's greatest merchants and landowners. In 1733, Governor Belcher appointed him advocate general of the Vice Admiralty Court in Boston, thereby deepening his connections to Boston's maritime commercial world, enhancing his salary, and advancing his political prospects. Shirley moved his family into a brick house on Queen Street, conveniently adjacent to the courthouse, one block over from the Mascarene residence on School Street (see map 5.3).

From his position as advocate general, Shirley had a good vantage point on the issues that troubled the colony's politics: conflict between the legislature and royal governor over the governor's salary; conflict between the governor's favorites, who wanted access to timber-cutting contracts, and the king's surveyor general, charged with protecting the white pines of the north woods for the Royal Navy; conflict between overseas merchants who controlled the colony's money supply, and farmers and artisans, always starved for cash, who pressed for the creation of a Land Bank to issue paper money. During the late 1730s, as Governor Belcher became embroiled in one after another of these controversies, Shirley kept his eye on the main chance. He quietly befriended Belcher's opponents without giving obvious affront to Belcher. He solidified his alliances among Boston's merchant elite. Shirley sent his ambitious wife back to London, where she could lobby the Duke of Newcastle for her husband to be Belcher's successor, whenever the incumbent might fall from favor.[29]

But Shirley never became a Bostonian, at least not in the way that Mascarene did. His biographer put it this way:

> The Shirleys still had no roots in native society. Their associations were mostly confined to the British spoilsmen of Boston, people of the admiralty court, Americans relying for a living upon British contracts, and members of King's Chapel. Although Shirley loved books and respected academic training, his sons were not being prepared for Harvard College. He feared the influence of Congregationalism upon them and their contamination by colonial ideas. It is not surprising, then, that Frances Shirley spoke of Boston as a "Foreign Country" and that William Shirley after five years was willing to leave Massachusetts if something better was offered in another part of America.[30]

In short, Shirley, though trained as a lawyer and not a soldier, had an imperial point of view and was drawn to Boston only for its potential to advance his career within the empire. By contrast, Mascarene, a soldier sent to America in service of the empire, was drawn to Boston for its own sake, out of sympathy for its people, its culture, and the advantages that it offered him as a refugee Huguenot within the Protestant International.

War changed everything for Shirley. In the late 1730s, he slowly mounted an attack on Belcher, quietly undermining the governor's support in New England and Whitehall. He had no quarrel with Belcher's policies or person; he simply wanted his office. On every local political issue, from forestry conflicts to smuggling, Shirley sided with Belcher's opponents and tried to make the governor look bad in his correspondence with London. The beginning of war with Spain in 1739 gave Shirley an opportunity. His patron, the Duke of Newcastle, led the faction in Parliament pushing for war. Newcastle wanted to use New England soldiers in the Caribbean expeditions and asked Shirley to be Belcher's chief aide in recruiting. Shirley went behind Belcher's back, using the influence of his mercantile clients and fellow imperial officials to recruit soldiers, not only in Massachusetts, but in New Hampshire and Rhode Island as well.[31]

One of the locals Shirley relied on was John Winslow, a young man descended from one of Plymouth's oldest families (both his grandfather, Josiah, and great-grandfather, Edward, had been governors of the Plymouth Colony) now working as a trader out of Boston to the Maine and Acadian coast. With the help of men like Winslow, Shirley burnished his reputation as an effective colonial administrator, readily taking credit for his work in his letters to Newcastle. Three thousand North American troops volunteered for the Caribbean expedition—two thousand of them from New England. Many of them saw the expedition as an opportunity to liberate the West Indies from Catholic oppression and force open more Caribbean trade for Boston merchants. The colonial soldiers augmented eight thousand British regulars assigned to the expedition, and with tropical diseases decimating the ranks of the regulars, the assaults on Cartagena and Havana could not have happened without the arrival of the colonial troops.[32] Frances Shirley, waiting in London, delivered her husband's reports on his successful recruiting directly to Newcastle himself. In return, Newcastle arranged that William Shirley would succeed Belcher as the next royal governor of Massachusetts.

The moment finally came in 1741. Belcher's support in Whitehall collapsed over the partisan position that he took in the conflict between competing banking schemes. The Land and Silver Banks were meant to solve New England's chronic monetary shortage, but each represented a different social faction. Belcher, a believer in hard money, sided with the Silver Bank, a plan to issue paper currency backed by silver deposits, but was blindsided when Parliament declared *both* banks to be illegal under the Bubble Act of 1720, which forbade the creation of any joint-stock company without a royal charter. At the same moment, the Board of Trade in London recalled Belcher and declared that Shirley would henceforth be the new governor of Massachusetts.[33]

Shirley was not a soldier. He had never sought a commission in the military, and had never worn a uniform or seen battle. Yet he quickly learned the political value of supporting British military aims. In his career as governor from 1741 to 1756, longer than any other governor in Massachusetts' history, he remade himself as a military leader by expanding the scope of his imperial vision and by seizing the opportunities of an era in which warfare lay at the center of imperial policy.

On taking office, Shirley renewed his support for the War of Jenkins' Ear, so called because a British merchant ship captain, Robert Jenkins, had lost an ear in a scuffle with Spanish coast guards who boarded and searched his ship for contraband. The incident was used as a pretext for British forces to attack Spain's Caribbean holdings, in an effort to expand the empire's trading opportunities and defend its contract to supply slaves to Spanish America. British forces had failed in their attempt to take Cartagena and Havana from Spain, but were gearing up for a second assault on Cuba. Shirley reappointed Winslow as the chief recruiter of colonial troops. Winslow enticed New England recruits with advertising descriptions of Cuba's balmy tropical breezes and fertile lands, but the reality was far different.[34] The British Army encamped at the eastern end of the island, near Guantanamo Bay, and the soldiers died rapidly from heat, poor nutrition, malaria, and yellow fever. Of the two thousand New England men and boys sent on the expedition, fewer than two hundred made it back to their homes. Despite the military fiasco and great loss of life, colonial administrators like Shirley had developed a workable system for martialing resources: young men who would volunteer to fight far from home;

ship captains who would transport troops and supplies; and Boston merchants such as Thomas Hancock and Samuel Auchmuty who would supply the necessities for wars of conquest.[35]

In 1744 and 1745, Shirley put these logistical capacities to work in response to a mounting crisis in Nova Scotia. The War of the Austrian Succession had spilled over into North America. French priests and their Mi'kmaq allies, led by Father Le Loutre, a leader of resistance to British military rule, seized the fishing station on Canso Island, then swept across the Acadian Peninsula, targeting Annapolis Royal as well. Mascarene, now the lieutenant governor and commander of Fort Anne, led the effort to stave off the attack. A hastily dispatched squadron of ships and soldiers from Boston, organized by Shirley and his merchant associates, arrived to relieve the garrison. It was rare in British America for one colony to come to the military aid of another, especially when the endangered province was a military establishment to begin with. Yet Shirley's action, unremarked in the historiography, suggests how normal it seemed, after a century of growing regional power, for Boston to express and defend a hegemonic interest over the entire region.[36] But the French-led aggression was nonetheless ominous. Mascarene's informants on Canso convinced him that the impetus for these new attacks came from the French military command at Louisbourg, not from the local Acadian population. He feared that Nova Scotia would not be safe until the fortress at Louisbourg had been taken from the French.

Louisbourg's formidable reputation stemmed from its strategic location near the mouth of the Saint Lawrence River, and from the great expense of building the fortified town and its thick stone walls.[37] But Mascarene knew that its impressive facade concealed a garrison that was poorly trained, inadequately armed, ill nourished, and undermanned. This view was seconded by John Bradstreet, a man whose Yankee name masked a complex past typical of the hybrid world of New England–Acadian relations. Bradstreet's mother was Agatha St. Etienne de La Tour, granddaughter of Charles de La Tour, the French captain who had recruited troops from Boston in the 1640s. His father was an Anglo-Irish officer stationed at Annapolis Royal. Like his father, Bradstreet joined the British Army, and saw no contradiction between its position as the ruling power in Nova Scotia and his relationship with his French Catholic relatives and friends. Bradstreet traded with the French on Cape Breton Island, and had been taken captive there by the French when they launched their attacks on Canso Island. By the end of 1744, a prisoner exchange freed Bradstreet and a number of other soldiers, who like Mascarene, knew how weak the fortress at Louisbourg actually was.[38]

Bradstreet and Mascarene convinced Shirley that an assault on Louisbourg stood a good chance of success, if the Royal Navy could support the besieging troops and prevent relief from the French Navy. As the information brought by Bradstreet and the other released prisoners leaked out, excitement about the potential conquest spread. An anonymous author in the *Boston Evening Post* claimed that "*Delenda est Carthago* [Carthage must be destroyed] had all the Year past been in everybody's Mouth"—echoing words that Cato the Elder is reported to have used to convince his fellow Romans of the mortal threat posed by their Mediterranean competitor.[39]

The city's resources coalesced around the project to destroy the Carthage of New France. Boston's merchant and fishing communities supported the plan. Shirley pledged to seek repayment for the mission's expenses from the Crown and naval support from the convoy led by Peter Warren, commander of British naval forces in American waters. Shirley enlisted William Pepperell, a merchant from Maine experienced in the eastward trade, to organize the expedition and raise the troops for the siege. At Shirley's bidding, the General Court authorized funding for three thousand soldiers. The officers appointed under Pepperell were leading figures in Massachusetts politics and society. Facilities for housing and feeding the recruits were built in Boston and the neighboring towns. Over the winter of 1744–45, preparations for the assault slowly came together. Despite the memory of the banking troubles that had unseated his predecessor, Shirley pushed several emissions of paper money through the legislature to finance the expedition. The city-state of

Boston began to emulate the fiscal-military state that British government and finance had perfected under Robert Walpole and his successors.[40]

By the beginning of spring 1745, all was ready except for Captain Warren, cruising with the Royal Navy fleet in the West Indies, who had yet to respond to Shirley's pleas. Word finally came in late March, but not the news that Shirley wanted to hear. Warren had received no authority to support the Massachusetts plan since it had not been organized by the admiralty. Shirley, with the support of Pepperell, gambled that a makeshift navy of converted Boston merchant vessels would suffice. The fleet sailed from Boston on March 28. This was a bold decision for a man with no military experience, but it succeeded. Within a week, new orders had granted Warren the authority to harass French shipping throughout the Atlantic, and Warren interpreted this to mean that he could support the Louisbourg assault. Together, the New England soldiers and the Royal Navy besieged the undermanned fortress. On June 17, 1745, Louisbourg surrendered to Pepperell and his men.[41]

The victory met with ecstatic responses all around the British Atlantic. The Crown made Pepperell a baronet, the only North American ever so honored. Shirley's leadership was celebrated throughout the colonies, and the navy promoted Warren to admiral. The Boston clergy interpreted the victory as a sign of God's providential hand in action. Thomas Prince, minister of Boston's Old South Church, published his sermon from the colony-wide day of thanksgiving, titling it *Extraordinary Events, the Doings of God . . . Occasion'd by Taking the City of Louisbourg*. It was accompanied by dozens of similar reveries, including some very bad poetry:

When Christian Lewis comes to hear what's done,
  With his strong fortress on the Isle Breton,
He'll swear the valour of the British breed,
  In Western climes their grandsire far exceed.[42]

Charles Chauncy, minister of Boston's First Church, quarreled with Prince on the spiritual meaning of many events, including the recent religious revivals that had swept through the region. But on the matter of Louisbourg, Chauncy shared Prince's view: "I scarce know of a conquest since the days of Joshua and the Judges wherein the finger of God is more visible."[43] Chauncy notably compared the Louisbourg conquest to those of the Israelites before the advent of kings. He chose biblical texts for his sermon from the book of Judges, thereby emphasizing the specifically republican aspect of Boston's military efforts, much like the earlier comparison with republican Rome and its conquest of Carthage. With classical and biblical allusions alike, the popular Bostonian interpretation of Louisbourg was a decidedly republican one, in which Boston's interests were supported, but not dominated, by the power of the British Empire.

But conquest can bring harsh rewards, particularly when it raises impossible expectations of millennial glory. Over the following winter, the garrison experience of the New England soldiers left behind to hold Louisbourg was nearly as grim and deadly as that of the men who had gone to Cuba and Cartagena. The expense of sustaining the remote fortress and the loss of soldiers to disease, malnutrition, and the tedium of garrison duty, alongside growing levels of hostility between the British regulars and New England volunteers sharing occupation duties, created an unbearable sense of futility for many New Englanders. These emotions erupted into violence in November 1747, when three days of severe rioting brought chaos to the streets of Boston in response to the efforts of Admiral Charles Knowles to "impress" local Boston sailors into the Royal Navy against their will.[44] The following year, the Treaty of Aix la Chapelle returned Louisbourg to France in exchange for French concessions of territory in the Netherlands, bringing yet another moment of disillusion; the common belief among Bostonians that the British Empire and its military ambitions were in sync with the city-state of Boston was shaken by the reality of imperial diplomacy. And yet the treaty also acknowledged the growing significance of American events to European affairs. If an American military victory could offset European losses, then strategically, the colonies were now important—a fact that presaged more imperial warfare in America.[45]

The War of the Austrian Succession had been less than triumphal from Britain's imperial point of view, but it was a great personal victory for Shirley. It convinced him that the way forward, for himself and for the empire that he served, involved larger and more elaborate plans for the complete conquest of New France. In the aftermath of the Louisbourg conquest, Admiral Warren deported four thousand French colonists from Cape Breton Island to France and other French colonies. A similar attempt was made with the small settlements on Ile Saint-Jean, but there the local inhabitants, together with French soldiers who had fled Cape Breton and the Mi'kmaq Indians, drove off the British squadron that tried to round them up.[46]

The Acadians presented a larger problem. Over the three decades since the Treaty of Utrecht put the province in British hands, the Acadian population had grown rapidly, from roughly two thousand in 1713 to perhaps as many as twenty thousand in 1745.[47] Yet Shirley imagined that a properly organized military force could remove the entire population of French Neutrals from their homeland and replace them with loyal Protestants. The governing council of Nova Scotia concurred. Although the Acadians had not fought alongside the French in the recent war, they had "refused to supply the British with adequate warning and intelligence . . . [and] they had furnished the invaders with provisions, horses, boats, and even guides."[48] After thirty years as British subjects, their military rulers still believed that the Acadians' loyalty could not be relied on. Over the course of the next decade, Shirley worked to make the council's proposal a central element in a larger scheme to drive the French entirely out of North America.

The campaign began in 1746, when Shirley, together with some of the more aggressive merchants from Boston and New York, planned a second and larger assault on French Canada. Already they were starting to see diminished enthusiasm from Massachusetts, where the dismal garrison experience at Louisbourg had soured many soldiers on the glories of war. Yet the bigger shock to Shirley's plan came from events in Britain. The Jacobite rebellion of 1745, led by the Young Pretender, Charles Stuart, grandson of the exiled James II, had shaken Britain's Hanoverian monarchy. The demand for troops to put down the rebellion and pacify the

Scottish Highlands dampened the ministry's willingness to commit forces overseas. Shirley's plans for 1746 were canceled. The soldiers he had begun to recruit were sent home, and a similar plan for 1747 met the same fate. Although the Young Pretender's rising delayed Shirley's hopes for a second conquest of Canada, its result would prove critical to the empire's long-term plan for Canada in general and Nova Scotia in particular. Many British officers who organized the pacification of the Scottish Highlands and deported Highland soldiers to the West Indies went on to take leading roles in Britain's later imperial wars. One of them, Edward Cornwallis, was appointed military governor of Nova Scotia in 1749.[49]

Even before Cornwallis arrived, Shirley had further developed his scheme for remaking Nova Scotia as part of a plan to drive France out of North America. In 1749, he published, anonymously, an eighty-page pamphlet, *Memoirs of the Principal Transactions of the Last War . . . Containing in Particular an Account of the Importance of Nova Scotia or Acadie, and the Island of Cape Breton to Both Nations.* The pamphlet, dedicated to his patron the Duke of Newcastle, went through multiple editions, enjoying a second run almost a decade later during planning for the Seven Years' War. Shirley presented the "importance of Nova Scotia" from an entirely imperial point of view and thus badly distorted the long history of Boston's relations with Acadia.

For Shirley, Nova Scotia's value lay solely in its strategic importance to the ongoing conflict over North America. If Britain were to conquer the region, including Louisbourg and Cape Breton, then "the Command it gives them of the Navigation of the Gulf of St. Lawrence and Bay of Funda, puts it into their Power to cut off the Communication between France and Canada, . . . and consequently in such Case she [France] must hold them at the Will of Great Britain." But if the French were to retake Acadia, its fertile soil would provide enough agricultural production to sustain a standing army on the continent without the need for supplies from France. In addition, the French possession of Acadia "puts it into their Power . . . to deprive Great Britain of the Naval Stores, which are now drawn from the King's Woods there for masting the Royal Navy." Not only would French control of Acadia be dangerous to the empire's interests, but it would renew an unhappy history of the region as a hazard to New England: "The New England Colonies, in every Period of this Province's Subjection to the French, continually felt most pernicious Effects from it, in Depredations upon their Trade, and Incursions into their Territories."[50] Shirley's claims were exaggerated, grossly overstating the power of Acadia's small population to threaten New England and raising fears of French assaults on the maritime coast that had never materialized in the past. Above all, Shirley's tract ignored the long history of commerce and cooperation between the two regions.

Shirley's first and most important argument, that a firm British hold on Nova Scotia and Cape Breton would make it impossible for France to sustain its colonies from the Saint Lawrence to the Great Lakes, did make sense from an imperial point of view. It ran counter, though, to the interests that Bostonians had developed in Acadia over more than a century. Critical to Shirley's vision for how this might be accomplished was the removal of the twenty thousand French Neutrals from their homelands. In a 1747 letter to Newcastle, Shirley asserted (falsely) that the Acadians "seem to have been so deeply engaged on the Side of the Enemy as to make 'em forfeit all pretense of right to hold their Posessions." He begged Newcastle's leave to raise a New England army of a thousand men so that the Acadians could "be transplanted into New England and distributed among the four governments there"—Massachusetts, Connecticut, New Hampshire, and Rhode Island—and their land given to the Protestant soldiers who displaced them.[51] (See plate 15.)

Over the next six years, Shirley devoted himself to convincing the British ministry to implement his design. At one point, he confessed in a letter to Newcastle that "you must think I have no other thoughts than those on Nova Scotia." His expertise in these matters led Newcastle to appoint him to a peace mission to Paris from 1750 to 1753—a boundary commission to negotiate mutually acceptable borders between French and British North American possessions. For Shirley, the mission was pure torture. He saw every French effort to extend its holdings, from the Saint John River in present-day New Brunswick to the Ohio River Valley in western Pennsylvania, as an affront to Britain that could easily be thwarted if only the Crown would implement his military schemes.

On his return to Boston in 1753, Governor Shirley expanded his plans. He now wanted to include, in addition to the deportation of the Acadians and seizure of Cape Breton, a simultaneous westward assault from the Hudson River Valley against the French fort on Lake Ontario at Oswego. This second force would then move from the west down the Saint Lawrence Valley toward Montreal and Quebec, and meet another British force sailing up the Saint Lawrence toward Quebec from the east. Shirley was already envisioning the strategic plan that British military commanders would ultimately implement in the Seven Years' War. As of 1753, these possibilities were unimaginable to all but a few imperial visionaries, which is what Shirley had become. The rest of the Boundary Commission in Paris, Shirley aside, had agreed to a policy of containment and rapprochement, not invasion and conquest, between Britain and France in North America.[52]

But events in the Ohio Valley, beyond the influence of officials in Whitehall or Versailles, turned these agreements upside down. In May 1754, a lost and confused detachment of Virginia militia, led by their twenty-two-year-old lieutenant colonel, George Washington, stumbled on a French patrol in the woods of western Pennsylvania. The ensuing massacre of the French commander, Joseph Coulon de Jumonville, and a number of his men by the frightened Virginians and their Indian allies touched off a global war. Over the following winter and spring, Britain sent an expeditionary army of two regiments to America under the command of Major General Edward Braddock. With Braddock as commander in chief, Shirley and several other colonial governors met in Alexandria, Virginia, in April 1755 to plan a coordinated attack on French positions across the continent. Their plan essentially melded Braddock's orders for a direct conquest of the headwaters of the Ohio with Shirley's scheme for a three-pronged invasion of Cape Breton and the Saint Lawrence Valley. Shirley's imperial vision and detailed plans for the northern expeditions, now six years in the making, so impressed Braddock that he appointed Shirley to be his second in command. On July 13, 1755, French and Indian forces routed Braddock's army along the Monongahela River, and Braddock was killed in action. William Shirley, governor of Massachusetts, was now Major General Shirley, commander in chief of the largest British military force ever assembled in North America.[53]

Something Shocking: The Ordeal of Abijah Willard

This unexpected rise to military supremacy vaulted Shirley's plan for the deportation of French Neutrals to the forefront of British military strategy. With Governor Shirley himself leading the expedition westward to Crown Point, on Lake Champlain, then on toward Oswego and Lake Ontario, oversight of the Nova Scotia plan was given to Charles Lawrence, the military governor of Nova Scotia. Lawrence appointed Lieutenant Colonel Robert Monckton, Mascarene's successor in command of the Annapolis Royal garrison, to head the military operations. Lawrence sent Monckton to Massachusetts to recruit soldiers, equipment, and naval support for the expedition. The reliable Boston merchants Thomas Hancock and Charles Apthorp agreed to outfit the troops and supply the ships that would transport them to Acadia. Hancock and Apthorp also arranged for additional vessels, fitted out in the manner of slave ships for the large numbers of expected deportees, to carry the Acadians to wherever British authorities might choose to send them.[54]

To aid the recruiting efforts, Shirley announced that Monckton's second in command for the expedition would be John Winslow, the Boston trader who had organized the recruitment of Massachusetts troops for Cuba in 1740–41. Winslow had since then served at the conquest of Louisbourg and as an officer at Annapolis Royal in the early 1750s. In 1754, he led eight hundred New England soldiers up the Kennebec River in present-day Maine in response to a rumor that the French aimed to seize the harbor at the river's mouth. Shirley appointed Winslow major general of the Massachusetts militia, adding authority to Winslow's considerable skills at turning out New

England recruits for British expeditions. By late spring 1755, Winslow had enlisted two thousand volunteers, the bulk of them from Massachusetts. But the purpose of this expedition remained vague, at best, to the men and boys who signed on.[55]

Winslow's method for recruitment, developed over fifteen years and two wars, involved selecting captains from across the commonwealth—young men with strong local reputations and military experience. Each captain received orders to sign up one hundred men from the town or region in which they lived. Of the twenty captains Winslow commissioned, one was Abijah Willard of Lancaster, Massachusetts.

The Willards were a sprawling family in Massachusetts with various branches, all of them stemming from the early colonist and land speculator Simon Willard. A century earlier, Simon, a "Kentish soldier" and fur-trading merchant with a head for business, had developed towns west of Boston in the 1630s through the 1660s, including Concord and Lancaster, about thirty-five miles northwest of Boston. This archetypal Massachusetts town father also fathered seventeen children by three wives during his long life.[56] For much of the seventeenth century, Lancaster stood at the western edge of settlement spreading westward from Boston. In 1676, Indian forces under Metacom (King Philip) attacked and destroyed Lancaster and took many captives, including Mary Rowlandson, whose narrative of her experience became one of the best sellers of colonial New England.[57]

The most prominent branch of Willard's descendants became leaders in Boston society. His son, Samuel, a prolific theologian, served as president of Harvard and minister of one of Boston's largest churches. Samuel Willard's monumental collection of sermons, *A Compleat Body of Divinity*, was the largest publishing project ever undertaken in the colony. Samuel's son, Josiah Willard, held an important position as secretary of the council of the General Court.[58] But the various branches descended from Willard's seventeen children distributed their land and wealth in different ways. If Samuel and Josiah devoted themselves to learning and public service, the rest of the Willards focused on farming and craftsmanship (one branch became the leading clockmakers of New England). The Lancaster Willards were husbandmen who made the most of the rocky soil of Worcester County, annually driving their cattle to the markets of Boston and Cambridge.

Young men from small town New England often made a name for themselves and earned money to set up their own households by volunteering for military service. The rapid increase in Britain's overseas expeditions after 1739 expanded these opportunities dramatically. In cash-poor, land-poor New England, the promise of a few pounds and shillings in sterling beckoned many young men to war, despite the grave risks. Abijah Willard's father, Samuel, had advanced his fortunes this way. In 1745, as a prosperous Lancaster landowner, he took his place among the officers of the Massachusetts forces in the victorious siege of Louisbourg. Colonel Samuel Willard commanded a Worcester County regiment at the siege, and his son Abijah, age twenty-one, served as a captain under his father, along with his younger brother Levi.[59]

A decade later, Abijah, now married and with children of his own, took up the call. He accepted a captain's commission from Winslow and recruited his hundred men: thirty-five from his hometown of Lancaster, and the other two-thirds from the neighboring towns and villages of Chelmsford, Lunenburg, Marlborough, Petersham, and Shrewsbury.[60] He marched his men down the cattle trails from Lancaster to Boston, where they met the other nineteen companies and prepared to sail for the Bay of Fundy. This was how the city-state of Boston operated in service of the Crown, much as it operated as an economy, drawing the resources of the countryside into the metropolis for export by its merchants.

Abijah Willard is notable among the thousands who served in this expedition for the journal that he kept of his experiences. Willard's journal offers intimate details about his interactions with the people of Acadia, and the impact of the orders that he received, months into the expedition, to round up the French Neutrals, destroy their crops and livestock, and burn their villages to the ground. Like his father before him, Willard was more than willing to serve the interests of a king to whom he was profoundly loyal.

But like his father and the other New England men and boys who laid siege to Louisbourg, and like the New England Huguenots who refused the earlier offers of free land in Acadia, he had no interest in leaving his Massachusetts home to settle in Nova Scotia, and no particular reason to want to make Acadians leave theirs.

When the expedition fleet of Thomas Hancock's forty-one ships left Boston Harbor in May 1755, under the protection of three Royal Navy gunships, Willard and his fellow soldiers imagined their goal was to capture a fort called Beausejour, at the remote eastern end of the Bay of Fundy, which the French Army had recently seized from the British. Engagements like this had happened dozens of times before, going all the way back to the time of Winthrop, La Tour, and d'Aulnay in the 1640s. Winslow had led the most recent of these the year before at the Kennebec River. Only Governor Lawrence, Shirley, Colonel Monckton, and his two lieutenant colonels, Winslow and George Scott, knew that this expedition aimed for something different.[61]

Willard's account, *A Journal on the Intended Expedition to Novicotia*, begins as many early modern journals do, on the day the author left home, April 9, 1755.[62] As the title suggests, Captain Willard had an imperfect grasp on the finer points of capitalization, spelling, and grammar. But he wrote with a vivid sense of the remarkable as well as the mundane in military service. Many of the initial days' entries contain the words "Nothing Remarkable &c." Some consist of no more than that. Even better is April 17: "Nothing Strange Happins." We learn much about the weather (April 25: "Cold weather for the time of year and snowd"). We learn how an eighteenth-century provincial army ate ("they Complaind had nothing but french porke to Eate which I am Certain is non pleasant"), how they dressed ("very mean & scandelus"), and how they worshipped ("Sunday ordereed all to go to meeting"). The excitement and pageantry of a military expedition comes through, as does the tedium: "April 21st, a generall Train[in]g in Boston where their was a vast number of people"; "May ye 1 1755, . . . we waid anchor aboute 3 oClock and Came Down to King Roade and gave three whozaws when we past the Casell and then came Down 12: or 14 and Dropt anchor against Dear Island

and their waite till further orders." Church and state combined to sustain military discipline: "May 4th, Sunday orders Came on board for to go on to Dear Island to hear preaching which we was Entertaind a Discourse be Content with your wagers."[63]

When the expedition finally sailed for the Bay of Fundy and approached the part of Acadia, Chignecto Harbor, where Fort Beausejour lay, Willard's journal entries grew progressively longer; the "nothing remarkables" fell away. The ostensible task of the expedition, the recapture of the fort at Beausejour, happened quickly. The two thousand New England soldiers, backed by heavy artillery, made easy work of the defenses put up by a few hundred French soldiers and their Mi'kmaq allies. By mid-June, the expedition had reestablished British military control over all the forts in the region. Up to this point, Willard's experiences had been exciting and even "remarkable," but still familiar from his previous engagement in the Louisbourg expedition ten years earlier. Now, with the siege of Beausejour completed, the farmer-soldier from rural Massachusetts began to encounter Acadian people for the first time.

For years, military and religious propaganda had led rural New Englanders to believe that the Acadians were half-savage devils. Here is what Willard actually experienced:

> June 20th this Day a number of the french came and Deliverd themselves up as prisoners.
>
> June 21st the french people Come into the Camps for to Sell provition Such as milk and Eggs & fowlis and Straberys.
>
> July 2d this Day nothing Remarkable but after Dinner I went to 2 or 3 veliges along with Capt Stevens and Mr Philips [the chaplain] with aboute 20 Souldirs wher I Saw a grate many french women and gorls their Faces Loock well but their feet Loock very Strange with wooden Shoos which they all wore but I Caried sum Rum and sugar and had Severall Nogens of milk punch and Returnd to ye Cam[p] aboute Sundown.[64]

The reason that Willard met so many "women and gorls" among the Acadians is that British policy had begun to drive away the men and boys. The army initially tried to trick Acadian men onto the waiting British ships. British commanders announced meetings of all the heads of households to be held in the Acadians' churches. Once the men from a village had entered the church, soldiers were stationed to surround the churches ("mass houses," the English called them) and imprison the men, until their women and children agreed to join them. Then all would be deported.[65]

After the army's first few attempts to implement this plan, and in the midst of wild swirls of rumor, the men of Acadia's villages began to flee into the woods, joining Mi'kmaq allies and relations where they would be safe from British patrols. The British Army was unable to maintain secrecy or pursue its deportation policy by stealth because of the extensive intermarriage, commerce, and cooperation among the English and Acadians. John Bradstreet, for instance, the British Army officer who informed Shirley of Louisbourg's vulnerability in 1745, had joined the planning for the Acadian expedition of 1755, only to learn that while he was serving in Shirley's planned attack on the French at Oswego on Lake Ontario, the Acadian forces would be rounding up and deporting his cousins, the nephews and nieces of his mother Agatha de La Tour.[66]

With the failure of the original plan, Colonel Monckton issued new orders on August 5. Willard described them: "This Day orders Come for a hundred men to be Deteacht from both battalions to be Ready to March to morrow morning att six oClock with Eight Days Provitions this after noon. Coll munckton sent a Letter to me to Know wether I would Command this party and Joyne Capt Lewies att Cobequit." He accepted, chose his brother, Ensign Levi Willard, as one of two junior officers for this newly made company, and off they went: "100 privates 3 s[argents] 3 c[orporals] 2 Drums and marcht from the fort aboute 9 oClock this morning and all the men in high spirits had 2 french men for my Pilots and marcht abote 2 miles." Drums and high spirits, but neither Captain Willard nor his men knew where they were going, or what they would do when they got there.[67]

The next day, "Coll Munckton sent a Frenchman with a Letter to me and he wrote to me he had News from Halifax and he gave me further orders which I was not to open till I Come up with Capt

Lewis who went 2 Days before me." For the next several days, Willard led his hundred men through the Acadian countryside, heading for his wilderness rendezvous with Captain Lewis. Along the way, he and his troops encountered, again and again, the remnants of Acadian families—women, children, and old men—who treated Willard and his soldiers with kindness:

> Agust 9: I march on aboute 5 miles and a half upon the Bank to a plase Called Canomi wher we found 2 french Familys and Severall Houses Deserted And got their aboute 10 oClock att Night wher the french was very Kinde Agust 10: Sunday This morning marcht from this velege Upon Marsh aboute 9 miles to vilege Coled Pintepeak [Portapique] In Cobequid a Large number Of Inhabitants Staid their and Refrshed our selves and marcht on aboute 7 mils to another vilege to an old french mans house and their Loged wher we was Kindly Entrtaind with milk and Buter August 12 1755: this Day Rested and Refreshed My People with good Beefe & mutton which the french Brought in to us.

Finally, on August 13, Willard's company met up with Captain Lewis at "Tatmagosh, . . . and then I opened My orders which was suprising to me for my orders was to burn all the houses that I found on the Road to the Bay of verts against the Island of Saint Johns."[68]

The "news from Halifax" that Colonel Monckton had conveyed in his sealed orders was that the chief justice of Nova Scotia had approved the military's request to conduct a scorched-earth policy across the northern reaches of Acadia. From Chignecto Bay, across the isthmus to the "Bay of verts," opposite the near shore of "the Island of Saint Johns" (Prince Edward Island), the combined forces of regular soldiers and New England recruits from the "Boston Army" of John Winslow were to destroy any possible means of survival for the Acadian families left behind by their husbands and fathers who had fled to the woods. The Nova Scotia chief justice who approved this plan was none other than Jonathan Belcher Jr., son of the Massachusetts governor who twenty years earlier had prayed for the preservation of his own family from the "government of soldiers."

By threatening the "women and gorls" with starvation and exposure in the oncoming winter, the British military government believed it could coerce the Acadian men to surrender, then deport the whole population with ease. Willard described some of the nightmarish scenes that ensued:

> August ye 16: 1755. This Day Capt Lewis and Ens willard [Abijah's brother] Returd with the party from Ramshack with 3 fa:milys and Burnt Severall Houses about 12 oClock upon their Return I went with a Small party of men over a Large River Tatmagoush wher I Burnt 12 Buildings one of which was a Storehouse with Rum and malosas and Iron ware and another of Rum sugar & molasas & wine and a masshouse. I ordered the men to Draw as much Rum as they had Bottles to Cary which they Did and sot fire to the Rest burnt all their vessels and Cannoos. . . . [A]boute 3 oClock this after Noon I ordered the whole to be Drawd up in a Bodey and bid the french men march of and sott fire to their Buildings and Left the women and children to Tack care of themselves with grate Lementation which I must Confess itt seemed to be sumthing shoking.[69]

The brutal story of the Acadian removal has been told many times over. Without question, New England's soldiers played an active and willing part in this ethnic cleansing. Boston's leaders, from William Shirley to Thomas Hancock to John Winslow, were deeply engaged in and expected to profit from the expedition. But retelling this episode through the eyes of Abijah Willard can reclaim the ways in which the experience was "sumthing shoking" for men like Willard as well for their Acadian victims.

The shock came in part from encountering the Acadians as kind and generous farm people more or less like themselves, give or take some wooden shoes. Some of the Acadians, like the elderly owner of a fine farm, Francis Boyes, could even "Talk Good English."[70] In this context, the order to burn all their houses and threaten them with starvation might have felt almost as shocking if they had been told to do the same to their own villages in Massachusetts. But another shocking aspect emerged in the plans that the British government under Shirley and Lawrence made for the Acadians' future. Knowing the experience of the Huguenots from as far back as the 1680s and of sectarian groups from all over Europe that had blended into the motley British American ethnic scene, Shirley believed that dispersing the Acadians in small groups—extended families at most—across the colonies of British America would separate the Acadians from their Catholic priests and convert them into good Protestant subjects.

As a lesser officer in a large operation, Willard lacked the big picture of the plan that his superiors were implementing. Yet some of his superiors shared Willard's shock and dismay. Winslow concluded his own journal of the expedition—a journal devoted much more than Willard's to the logistics of a complex military operation—in the following way:

> I have made out a Summary of this Unplesant Business upon which I, Lieutenant-Colonel John Winslow of the Army of Boston, was Detailed. I caused to be Burned the following in the region around the Basin of Minas:
>
> Barns 276
> Houses 255
> Mills 11
> Churches 1
> Total 543
>
> I shipped one thousand five hundred and ten inhabitants from Grand-Pre on certain Vessels to Strange Parts, where these French will needs find themselves Houses. . . . Winter will be coming on apace to this Camp and the Sea beats desolately against the Shore.[71]

As the soldiers rounded up Acadians by the thousands and loaded them onto Hancock's converted slave ships, the vessels were dispatched to destinations along the Atlantic Seaboard from Georgia to Massachusetts. More than a thousand Acadians arrived in Boston over the winter of 1755–56 (Boston's total population at the time was about fifteen thousand). The General Court made hasty plans to house them temporarily in the city and then disperse them to towns across the commonwealth. By the time that Willard, his brother Levi, and the thirty-odd other soldiers from Lancaster returned via Boston to their hometown after a year's service, they were stunned to find their neighbors playing reluctant hosts to thirty-odd Acadian deportees.

If New Englanders had been unwilling to settle under Nova Scotia's government of soldiers throughout the eighteenth century, then Acadians had certainly never expressed any desire to become New Englanders. Yet on February 12, 1756, the town records of Lancaster note that "the Lancaster Selectmen received in charge two families of French Neutrals: a farmer from Grand Pre, Benoni Melancon age 38, his wife Marie Benoit age 37, their seven children; and a demented farmer from Canard, Godfrey Benoit, age 36, brother to Benoni's wife, his wife Madeleine Bain age 36, their four children."[72] As town records from across Massachusetts demonstrate, people like Godfrey Benoit became "demented" as a direct result of the trauma of removal. These fifteen Acadians were sent to live in the households of two Lancaster men, Myles Cooper and William Phelps, and put to work in service. In many cases like this, the Acadians were treated badly by their new masters. The General Court records are filled with petitions from Acadians complaining of mistreatment.[73] In the case of these two Lancaster families, we know little about their experience, except that the town record's description of Benoni Melancon was inaccurate. He was a fisherman, not a farmer. He languished in rural Lancaster, thirty-five miles from the sea, with neither the skill nor desire to work outside his lifelong profession. Many Acadian fishing families clamored to be resettled in Boston, Salem, Marblehead, Gloucester, or in the case of Melancon, Weymouth. But during the Seven Years' War, which continued until 1761 in New England, public fear of French Catholics in the port towns was so great that few Acadian fishermen were granted their wishes. Melancon would never fish for a living again. He died in Lancaster in 1766, at the age of forty-eight.[74]

The story of these forced exiles repeated itself a thousand times over throughout British America. The initial plan for redistribution had spread the Acadians across all the continental colonies south of Nova Scotia. But especially in the southernmost colonies, from Georgia through Maryland, the Acadians were desperate to escape their exile. The southern colonial governments, far removed from the generations of conflict between New England and New France, and in some cases barely brushed by the tumult of the Seven Years' War, saw little reason to spend any effort to keep these French Catholic aliens among them. Shirley, who returned to Boston in 1756 from the failed expedition to take Oswego from the French, narrated one version of the story himself:

> Upon my return to Boston I found here Ninety Acadians which Governor Lawrence had sent to Georgia to be distributed in the Country there, from whence having obtained a let pass from the Governour, they coasted it in Boats to South Carolina, where they obtained another pass from Governor Glenn, and with that they coasted quite to New York, where Sir Charles Hardy gave them another with which they coasted it to this Province where their progress is stopt and I have ordered them to be distributed in the Country Towns and provided for. The next trip they had taken would have been to Nova Scotia, where they would have prov'd to that Government worse than Indians, and I suppose after this voyage they must be exceedingly good Pilots to every part of the English Coast for any French ships of War.[75]

From his perspective, now embedded deep within the imperial war administration, Shirley could only see the Acadians as a threat to his plans, not as deportees desperate to return to their homes. But because Shirley and Governor Lawrence of Nova Scotia refused to accept returning refugees, most of the Acadians who managed to flee the southern colonies ended up in Massachusetts and Connecticut, washed up by the Gulf Stream in their makeshift boats on the southern shores of New England.

Despite the original plan for widespread dispersal, New England became the center of this first Acadian exile. Of the roughly seven thousand Acadians deportees for which clear records exist, at least twenty-seven hundred of them ended up in Massachusetts and Connecticut—more than two thousand in Massachusetts alone.[76] For the five years after the removal in 1755, the Massachusetts Archives contain "hundreds of bills and vouchers" that show how the selectmen of the towns "supplied Acadians with abundant and varied food, some implements and tools, much firewood, transportation for each family, available housing, soap, and in hundreds of instances medical care from physicians."[77] As news spread of their decent treatment from the government in Boston (especially once Thomas Hutchinson, brother-in-law of Mascarene's daughter, became lieutenant governor in 1758), what had been unthinkable only a few years before became increasingly common. Acadian holdouts, families that had escaped the military dragoon and were hiding in remote locations across Nova Scotia, began to petition the Massachusetts governor and council for the privilege of being removed from their homeland:

> December 4, 1758, His Excellency having communicated to the Board an application which he yesterday received from Joseph Landry dated Cape Sable September 15, 1758 in behalf of himself and about forty French families settled there, praying that they may be quieted in their possessions as they are willing to take the oaths to the Government, and to help maintain the war against the French king or that if that may not be, that they may be permitted to come and settle in this Government.[78]

In 1733, Belcher had blamed "the Government of Soldiers" as the reason for his fellow Protestants' reluctance to move to Acadia, even for free land. Now, twenty-five years later, French Catholic Acadians begged for deliverance from the government of soldiers in Nova Scotia, even if it meant voluntarily committing themselves to lives of servitude, so long as it was in the civilian hands of "le Gouvernement de Baston."

The Government of Soldiers and *The Selling of Joseph*

Many of the principal figures in the fraught relationship between Massachusetts and Nova Scotia died before the rebellion of thirteen colonies finally broke Britain's American empire apart. Paul Mascarene, relieved of command in Nova Scotia in 1751, retired to his Boston home on School Street, where he died in 1760. William Shirley, after the early fiascos of the Seven Years' War, fell from grace with his Whitehall patrons, but was eventually rewarded with the governorship of the Bahamas—not a lucrative post, but suitably sleepy for his declining years. During his tenure in the Bahamas, Shirley spent his summers in Roxbury, just outside Boston, where he built a country estate. He retired there permanently in 1768, and died in 1771. John Winslow retired from military service after 1757. The Acadian expedition was his last time recruiting New England troops for the Crown. He returned to his native Plymouth County, but continued to serve as a deputy to the General Court in Boston. Winslow died in 1774.

Abijah Willard was young enough to suffer through one more episode of severe displacement, once again driven by military conflict. After the Seven Years' War, where he took part not only in the Acadian deportation but also in 1759–60 as a colonel under General Jeffrey Amherst in the Saint Lawrence Valley campaigns that sealed the fate of New France, Willard again returned home to Lancaster. Having proven himself in two major campaigns and risen to as high a rank as a colonial soldier could expect, Willard retired to his farm and hoped to live out his life in the peace that his service had helped to win. Yet the emerging postwar conflict between Massachusetts and the royal government, in which Willard seems to have expressed no interest whatsoever, would alter these plans.[79]

In 1774, Parliament passed the Coercive Acts (or Intolerable Acts, depending on one's viewpoint) to punish Boston and Massachusetts for the destruction of East India Company tea in December 1773. The Boston Port Act suspended all trade until the city agreed to reimburse the East India Company, and the Massachusetts Government Act disbanded the legislature and replaced it with a military government in the hands of General Thomas Gage. Gage was instructed to choose thirty-six Massachusetts citizens to form an appointed or "mandamus" council, as a replacement for the elected council and house of deputies that the commonwealth had always enjoyed. In choosing his councillors, Gage looked to men of local distinction, loyal to the Crown, with distinguished records of military service to prove it. Abijah Willard was one of the thirty-six.

Unaware of the dubious honor coming his way, Willard was visiting friends in Connecticut when this news became public. He was immediately seized by a local mob (Connecticut strongly supported Boston during the crisis and felt equally aggrieved by the punishment aimed at New England's metropolis). The mob dragged Willard to jail and set him free only when he agreed to renounce his appointment to the mandamus council. The other thirty-five appointees all faced similar threats. Some acceded; others, closer to the protection of the army in Boston, defied the crowd. The following April, when war broke out at Lexington and Concord, Willard happened to be traveling again, on the way from Lancaster to Beverly on the north shore. He immediately changed course for Boston, where General Gage appointed him captain of the first company of the "Loyal American Associates" raised in the city. The British Army, however, never managed to break out of the siege imposed by the New England militia. Willard waited in Boston and watched its slow destruction until the great evacuation on March 17, 1776, when Gage and his troops left for Nova Scotia with thousands of loyalists in tow.[80]

Willard never saw his Lancaster, Massachusetts, home again. Instead, he served during the Revolutionary War as commissary to loyalist militia and regular soldiers, mainly on Long Island in New

York. In 1783, at war's end, he returned to Nova Scotia and petitioned the Crown for one of the grants of free land being given to loyalists who had served the empire's cause. He was awarded a thousand acres in the town of Saint John, about forty miles across the Bay of Fundy from Chignecto Harbor where, thirty years before, he had found his orders to destroy the Acadian villages "sumthing shoking." In 1786, the parish where he settled was named "Lancaster," and there Abijah Willard died in 1789.[81]

The relationship between Acadia and New England had been forged by Boston's merchants, traders, and fishermen, and cultivated by people like Paul Mascarene, who were capable of accepting or overlooking differences in language, religion, and political allegiance when commerce proved to be mutually beneficial. The city-state of Boston's commercial relationships throughout the Atlantic world had followed this pattern from its earliest days of trading salt cod to the wool merchants of Bilbao. But the government of soldiers and the demands of imperial warfare made the ambiguity on which these relationships depended no longer tenable. By enforcing a brutal logic of authority and allegiance, and imposing a vision of ethnic and religious uniformity on the polities that it governed, the British Empire destroyed the relationships and deranged the lives of people who had been usefully but loosely connected by threads of commerce.

Through no fault of his own beyond loyalty and service to the empire in which he was born, Abijah Willard was forced from his home, and exiled to the land where he had once been sent to uproot and deport others. One of the victims of that expedition, Benoni Melancon, through no fault of his own, was forcibly exiled and sent to live and die in Willard's hometown, alienated from his profession and homeland. Their tangled and battered lives laid bare the injunction that Sewall had made in *The Selling of Joseph*: "Evil must not be done, that good may come of it. The extraordinary and comprehensive Benefit accruing to the Church of God, and to Joseph personally, did not rectify his brethrens sale of him," nor did it justify "such Wars . . . as were between Jacob's sons and their brother Joseph."[82] As the Long Peace gave way to decades of perpetual war and the government of soldiers, many citizens of "le Gouvernement de Baston" would question whether the British Empire really provided such extraordinary and comprehensive benefits after all.

Chapter 6

Cutting Off the Circulation

Phillis Wheatley and Boston's Revolutionary Crisis

Boston's a town, polite and debonair,
To which the beaux and beauteous nymphs repair.

—Phillis Wheatley, "An ANSWER to the Rebus," 1772

Columbia mourns, the haughty Foes deride,
 Her Treasures plunder'd, and her Towns destroy'd:
Witness how Charlestown's curling Smoaks arise,
 In sable Columns to the clouded Skies!

—Phillis Wheatley, "Liberty and Peace," 1784

By the early 1760s, two decades of warfare had profoundly disturbed Boston's relationship to Nova Scotia and to other connections around the shores of the city's Atlantic world. Two thousand soldiers sent to the Bay of Fundy from Boston had taken part in deporting more than ten thousand Acadian men, women, and children from their homes. More than two thousand Acadians were shipped to Boston and then dispersed across the New England countryside. At the same time, thousands more Massachusetts men and boys were recruited into His Majesty's provincial army, and then sent off to fight against French and Spanish foes, including a second expedition to Cuba in 1762. Unlike its predecessor in 1741, this mission succeeded in conquering the mighty fortress of Havana. But as with Louisbourg in the 1740s, the victory was reversed by the 1763 Treaty of Paris that ended the Seven Years' War and restored the Caribbean's largest fortress to its original Spanish owners, making the deaths of many New Englanders in far-flung places seem yet again for naught.

Through the long war fought to drive the Gallic foe out of North America, New Englanders had once more demonstrated their martial spirit, their willingness to sacrifice themselves for the cause of British Protestantism, liberty, and trade, not just in defense of the city-state of Boston, but wherever His Majesty King George II needed them. Fully a third of the Bay Colony's men and boys, ages sixteen to sixty, served in some military capacity in the Seven Years' War—a war of global scope that drew Spain, Austria, and Russia into France's coalition, and Prussia on the side of Britain.[1] Their avid service offered a definitive demonstration that the city-state of Boston, more than any other place in British America, was a full and equal participant in the British Empire's global aims. After the British Army under General James Wolfe defeated the French at Quebec in September 1759, Bostonians of every rank were unrestrained in celebrating the decisive and providential victory. There was no reason to think that when George II died in 1760 and his young grandson, George III, succeeded him as king, Boston's loyalties would change.

As the war's North American phase drew to a close, a young girl, captured somewhere in West Africa and sold into slavery, also arrived in Boston among the waves of unwilling migrants and bound laborers that washed up on the city's shores. She was what slave traders sometimes called a "refuse" slave, not the sort of strong and fully grown person well suited to strenuous labor who would fetch a good price in a plantation colony's slave market. In July 1761, the wealthy Wheatley family purchased her; they named her Phillis, after the ship that brought her from Africa to America. The arrival of yet another enslaved African on American shores was nothing unusual for this era, when the Anglo-American slave trade reached flood levels. But Phillis was not a typical slave, and the Wheatleys were unusual masters.[2] She was purchased not as a productive laborer—a small, sickly, seven-year-old child was more of an expense than an asset—but as something exotic, a luxury good rather than a practical investment, meant to enhance a rich family's domestic life in their Boston mansion. Under the tutelage of Susannah Wheatley and her daughter, Mary, Phillis became a literary prodigy. By her late teens, she was an accomplished and published poet with admirers on both sides of the Atlantic. As the first published African American female poet, Wheatley has come to be seen as a founding figure in African American literature, with her work anthologized in canonical collections and taught in college courses.[3]

Through these decades of Boston's growing involvement in imperial warfare, beginning around 1740, many of the city's residents worked to keep the dream of *Theopolis Americana* alive, continuing to cultivate Boston's connections to international Protestantism and the Republic of Letters, and building on the movements for social reform and cultural improvement that earlier generations had initiated. In the 1740s, Boston and New England were swept by the Protestant revivals that followed in the wake of Pietism's rise in Europe. George Whitefield, the famous English evangelist, made his first tour through North America in 1740, and touched off a series of powerful revivals in Boston and the surrounding region. Whitefield's work was continued by homegrown followers such as Joseph Sewall, Samuel Sewall's son and the minister of Boston's Old South Church, and his colleague in the pulpit, Thomas Prince. Waves of spiritual enthusiasm revitalized religious life in the city, and spawned the development of many new churches, devotional groups, lecture series, and pious publications.[4] Connected to these revivals were renewed efforts by clergy and lay reformers to teach the poor, minister to the enslaved, convert New England's Indians, and build new hospitals and institutions for poor relief, especially since the great expansion of warfare left many widows, orphans, and crippled veterans in its wake. Anglo-American humanitarianism was a coat of many colors, patched together from many different approaches to alleviating human suffering, but sharing a common commitment to Protestant Christianity that was easy for Bostonians to embrace as an extension of their commonwealth tradition, an essential part of the moral economy promoted by the founders and their commitment to Christian charity.[5]

The Wheatley family was immersed in this world of evangelical religion and social reform. They were connected to influential Protestant reformers throughout New England and in Britain, and they took a strong interest in the continuing efforts of these groups, inaugurated in earlier decades by Samuel Sewall and Cotton Mather, to ameliorate the evils of slavery and the slave trade in the colonies, Britain, and even Africa. In that sense, the seven-year-old girl who became Phillis Wheatley was fortunate in her purchasers: she landed among as sympathetic a group of English enslavers as a captive African was likely to find. In this relatively supportive context, by making the most of her remarkable talents, Wheatley transformed herself from an exotic object of household adornment into an active subject, a valuable participant in a cause dear to her mistress's heart, and presumably dearer to her own.

This chapter traces the fate of this young Bostonian who arrived at the end of the Seven Years' War. It explores how the subsequent political and military crisis that tore apart the British Empire also devastated the city-state of Boston, including its ties to the transatlantic circuits of benevolence and reform in which Phillis Wheatley came to prominence. Because she was a child, and female, and enslaved, Wheatley's direct engagement in these events was limited, but her poems reveal that she was an avid observer of Boston's rapid and jarring transformations. During her young lifetime, the militarization of imperial policy that had reshaped and traumatized many of Boston's Atlantic connections, from Havana to Nova Scotia, came home to roost in the city itself.[6]

In August 1765, when Wheatley was about eleven years old, the city witnessed violent protests and rioting over Parliament's Stamp Act, a new form of direct taxation intended to alleviate the expense of keeping the king's army in America after the Seven Years' War ended in 1763. Mobs opposed to the act threatened the life of Andrew Oliver, the Crown's designated distributor of the stamps, attacked his home and demolished a building that he owned on Oliver's Dock, within view from the nearby Wheatley residence, a block away on King Street.[7] Three years later, in October 1768, when Wheatley was fourteen, the king's occupying army would arrive to enforce further customs duties under the Townshend Acts, with the troops marching up Long Wharf and King Street past the Wheatley family's home to take possession of the city and quell the violence against Crown customs officers.

Map 6.1. *A New Plan of the Great Town of Boston in New England in America,* by William Price, 1769. Detail. John Wheatley's house stood at the corner of Kilby Street and King Street, roughly two hundred yards from Oliver's Dock, where the Stamp Act rioters destroyed Oliver's warehouse, and from the town house on King Street, where the Boston Massacre took place.

For the next several years, these four regiments, two thousand soldiers, would occupy a city of fifteen to sixteen thousand people. Boston in 1770 held a total of two thousand families—a soldier for every family in town. In the city's close quarters, conflict between occupying soldiers and the local men and boys with whom they competed in their spare time for menial labor generated endemic violence. In March 1770, when Wheatley was sixteen, soldiers gunned down five civilians—working men, sailors, and apprentices—in

"The Bloody Massacre in King Street," as Paul Revere's famous engraving called it, two blocks from the Wheatleys' home.[8] Although the troops were subsequently withdrawn from the city, they returned in force several years later, when Wheatley was nineteen, after the destruction of shiploads of East India Company tea in December 1773 by an organized crowd protest against another parliamentary measure.[9]

The Coercive Acts that Parliament passed in 1774 as punishment for the "Tea Party" shut down Boston's economy by closing the port, deprived Massachusetts of its cherished self-government, suspended the authority of local courts over royal officials, and enhanced the power of the royal governor to quarter soldiers in public buildings. The new royal governor appointed to rule Massachusetts was precisely what Jonathan Belcher had forty years earlier dreaded: a soldier, General Thomas Gage, since 1763 the commander in chief of all British regular forces in North America. With four thousand troops under his command, Gage initiated a series of forays into the countryside in vain attempts to suppress the mounting rebellion, which exploded into mass violence in April 1775, when militia resisted and repelled the column of nearly a thousand regulars sent to Lexington and Concord to seize munitions, killing or wounding hundreds of redcoats.[10]

For the next eleven months, Boston lay under siege from thousands of militia men who gathered from across New England—troops that were formed into the Continental Army under the command of the Virginian George Washington. Although Gage and his men attempted to break the siege, including the brutal assault and burning of Charlestown in June 1775, with hundreds more killed, they were at last forced to evacuate Boston the following March, when artillery installed by Washington's soldiers on the Dorchester Heights, south of the city, made Gage's position untenable. The British evacuation left behind a city in ruins.[11] Phillis Wheatley was twenty-two.

There are many excellent accounts and analyses of the coming of the rebellion against Crown rule in Boston, and the War of Independence that spun out across the continent and Caribbean from this starting point. My aim is not to retell this familiar story but rather to highlight how this intense eight-year period, from 1768 to 1776, of military occupation by King George III's army and navy was experienced by Wheatley as the rapid destruction of a world that had been many decades in the making. Boston's rebellion against the Crown's military occupation dismembered the lives of the powerful elites into whose circle the young African poet was drawn and by whom she had been promoted. Historians have demonstrated the destructive force of the revolution in Boston; Bernard Bailyn's *The Ordeal of Thomas Hutchinson* evokes the tragic fate of the last royal governor of Massachusetts, a fifth-generation Bostonian deeply devoted to the welfare of his native city who died in exile from the country he loved.[12] But as Hutchinson was one of Boston's richest and most privileged citizens with a near monopoly on the highest offices that the Crown could distribute, it remains difficult for many readers to sympathize with his downfall, particularly given his obtuse response to the resistance movement's grievances. By turning our focus to Wheatley, we can better appreciate that the dream of *Theopolis Americana* engaged Bostonians at all levels of society. The city's connections to British and international Protestant reform circuits created advantages and aspirations for many of its citizens, and the destruction unleashed by the rebellion tore apart the rich Atlantic fabric into which Boston had woven itself. In the subsequent chapter, I will examine the experiences of another Bostonian, a near contemporary of Wheatley's, who engaged more directly in the events of the rebellion and for whom its outcome was far more beneficial. But for now, in Wheatley's life and eloquent testimony, we can measure some of what was lost, the price paid in human suffering, when the government of soldiers came to Boston.

Locating Phillis Wheatley in *Theopolis Americana*

Phillis Wheatley was unique. It should be no surprise that the scholarship devoted to interpreting her poetry focuses on her singular qualities. Unlike most published poets of her day, Wheatley was young (around nineteen when her first book of poems was published in London), female, born in Africa, sold into slavery, transported to America, and purchased by a merchant and put to work as a slave in his household. The attention that scholars pay to these unusual attributes is both natural and justified. Wheatley herself emphasized these singular qualities in some of her most famous poems, and her more unsurprising characteristics as an eighteenth-century Anglo-American author are often associated with the more conventional aspects of her poetry. If every eighteenth-century English author was influenced by Alexander Pope, then why should we bother to dwell on Pope's impact on Wheatley when there are these other distinctive qualities to discuss?[13]

Nevertheless, it may be useful to set aside for a moment the sophisticated scholarship that explores Wheatley's singularity as an Anglo-American poet, especially her race and enslaved status, and instead concentrate on those aspects of her life that she shared with others: her connections throughout the British Atlantic world among whom she found her way to prominence in the early 1770s, when the prospects for Wheatley and her associates were both heightened and precarious. In many ways, we know Wheatley and her poetry better than we know her world. By attempting to understand the shape and strength of her Atlantic connections, and the benevolent hopes and ambitions the members of this community cherished, we can better see the tragic aspects of the violent rift that began in Boston, tore Britain's empire apart, and created the American imperial republic. The creation of this new republic destroyed an old order, and this destruction brought about, both literally and figuratively, the death of Wheatley.

To read a selective sampling of Wheatley's poetry without knowing anything about her identity, background, and circumstances, her work would seem typical of an eighteenth-century writer who was a devout member of Britain's commercial empire, akin to that of poets such as Isaac Watts (1674–1748), the composer of hymns, or James Thomson (1700–1748), whose "Rule Britannia" became the unofficial anthem of the far-flung seaborne empire. Other examples might be a poet like Elizabeth Singer Rowe (1674–1737), a pious and popular writer in eighteenth-century England, or Wheatley's Boston neighbor, the clergyman Mather Byles (1706–88), nephew of

Cotton Mather, a poet of minor distinction who corresponded with both Pope and Watts.[14] Wheatley's work, like theirs, embraces Britain's eighteenth-century imperial ideology, the common belief that Britain stood for Protestant Christianity, liberty, and commerce, sustained by oceangoing trade and representative government, and stabilized by an ancient and venerable hierarchy.[15]

But in 1761, at the moment of her first appearance in the historical record, Wheatley was at the absolute bottom of this hierarchy. A small child, sickly, barely clothed (she was wrapped in a dirty bit of old carpet), female, African, and enslaved, she lacked even a recorded name. Her place of origin is thought to have been somewhere in the region stretching from Gambia to Ghana, possibly along the Senegambia coast, and she may have been a native Wolof speaker.[16] But these are the most imprecise of guesses. Essentially, she was nobody, from nowhere, as lowly as it was possible for a person to be in mid-eighteenth-century Boston.[17]

The moment of her arrival was a time of triumph for the empire and Boston's place within it. Wheatley's early and unknown African years coincided with the North American experience of the Seven Years' War. Judging by the fact that she was missing her front baby teeth, the Wheatley family thought she was about seven years old, which would place her birth near 1754, the year the war began in America. In 1761, Bostonians still basked in the reflected glow of General Wolfe's triumph over Louis-Joseph de Montcalm at Quebec in 1759, and the campaigns led by Jeffrey Amherst and supported by Massachusetts provincial troops that captured Montreal the following year and finally swept the French enemy from the continent. Among the many works of celebration and thanksgiving for the victory over France published in Boston that year, more than one author turned to verse to express their sentiments. Here is one, by Joseph Fisk:

To CANADA they march again;
In order that King GEORGE might reign
Over the *French* and *Papist* powr;
And now we see the day is ours. . . .

And now their Fighting they do cease;
The Indians too do sue for Peace:
For they do bow unto our King,
Which is the most delightful Thing.[18]

Fisk's doggerel is sadly representative of the patriotic effusion that poured forth from Boston pulpits and pens in the wake of Britain's military triumph over France. Although Wheatley entered this self-congratulatory world at its bottom, within a decade she would be vaulted to a place of wide recognition among the highest. What brought her from the bottom to within sight of the top were the same things that made anyone in the British Empire: connections.[19]

Phillis Wheatley's Connections: The Making of an Eighteenth-Century Celebrity

Phillis was the ship that brought her to Boston from Africa. When the man who purchased her named her after the ship, he marked her with an indelible connection to transatlantic commerce.[20] Wheatley was his name, John Wheatley, a merchant tailor of Boston, whose home on King Street, in the heart of the city near the Long Wharf, placed Phillis in the midst of the flowing traffic that connected Boston to the Atlantic world.[21] But it was primarily his wife, Susannah, and their daughter, Mary, who recognized the remarkable talents of their young slave and began to treat her as something closer to an adoptive daughter than a servant. In doing so, Susannah and Mary Wheatley played a part common to women within the empire. Though excluded from most official positions of power and authority, women filled a central role in conveying and embodying the tenets of the faith, both civic and religious.[22] Susannah was a devout evangelical Christian and member of Boston's New South Church. Mary, also a New South member, would marry the Reverend John Lathrop, minister of Boston's Second or Old North Church, the church of Increase and Cotton Mather in earlier generations.[23] Their education of Phillis focused on the Bible and the doctrines of the Westminster Confession, supplemented by the classical poets and works of modern history and polite letters, from Milton to Pope.

Gradually, as Phillis became literate, she became a Christian as well, and in this way her circle of connections began to extend beyond the immediate family. She became a favorite of the Boston clergy, who oversaw the development of Wheatley's religious education. Samuel Cooper, minister of the Brattle Street Church, baptized her in 1771. Other clergy included John Moorhead, minister of the Long Lane Presbyterian Church; Joseph Sewall of the Old South Church; and Mather Byles, grandson of Increase and nephew of Cotton Mather, and a poet who strongly influenced Wheatley's work. Samson Occom, to whom Wheatley wrote her first-known composition, was a Mohegan Indian minister who journeyed to England to raise money for missionary work and Indian education in America. Occom was an occasional houseguest of the Wheatleys when he preached as substitute for John Moorhead. The Reverend Moorhead was himself the owner of a slave, Scipio, who became a talented painter, and about whom Wheatley wrote an important poem. In August 1771, Phillis joined Sewall's Old South Church in full membership.[24]

Through these clergymen, who ministered to Bostonians of all ranks in their capacious meetinghouses, and through the social circle that the Wheatleys entertained on King Street, where Phillis waited on table, she encountered literary, political, and mercantile leaders of the town. As her reputation grew, Susannah took Phillis on rounds of visits to other genteel families. During these visits, servants in these households found themselves serving tea to a slave as she entertained their masters and mistresses with her poetic talents.[25] The enthralled circle included Thomas Hutchinson, friend to the Acadians, and by 1760 the acting royal governor of Massachusetts, and his lieutenant governor and brother-in-law, Andrew Oliver, the two main targets of the Stamp Act riots in summer 1765. When Oliver's wife died in 1773, Wheatley wrote a moving elegy, "To His Honour, the Lieutenant Governor." Her acquaintances also numbered other amateur poets and literary benefactors, such as the merchants Joseph Green and Richard Carey, and merchant politicians such as John Erving, Harrison Gray, and James Bowdoin, the future governor of Massachusetts.[26]

Bowdoin is thought to be the author of a poetical rebus addressed to Phillis, which Phillis solved in verse of her own. Together, rebus and reply, placed by Phillis at the conclusion of her published volume of poetry, display how committed she and her circle were to their vision of Boston's place in a triumphal British Empire. Bowdoin's clues combined biblical and classical allusions with pride in the colony's accomplishments, and Wheatley readily picked them up:

To Bowdoin's clue:
A town of gaiety and sport
Where beaux and beauteous nymphs Resort
And gallantry doth reign?
Wheatley responded:
Boston's a town, polite and debonair
To which the beaux and beauteous nymphs repair.

The first initial of each of the six words that answer Bowdoin's clues spelled out the hidden word "Quebec" (the *B* was for Boston)—and so Wheatley concludes in her answering poem:

Quebec now vanquished must obey,
She too must annual tribute pay,
To *Britain* of immortal fame,
And add new glory to her name.[27]

What this circle of worthies surrounding Wheatley shared was a faith in the liberating and ennobling power of Britain's empire. If the world were not yet perfected, then the conditions promoted by the empire—liberty, property, the Protestant religion, and free commerce among diverse peoples from around the globe—offered the prospects for future perfectibility. Did this common faith include opposition to slavery, and make these men (and a few women) protoabolitionists? Well, yes and no. All were opposed to the kind of "slavery" that at least from the time of the Stamp Act and reaching back to the overthrow of Edmund Andros, had been a watchword in Boston against encroachment on their liberties. An overweening imperial government could threaten to make them the kind of slaves that, in the words of Thomson's "Rule Britannia," Britons never will be. But so long as Parliament restrained itself, and the king's benevolence continued to favor them, then the Royal Navy's rule over the waves would guarantee British subjects' commercial freedom and make them masters of their own property. Tribute payment was for conquered enemies, not the king's loyal subjects.

In addition, they were all believers in "liberty," but their definition of the term, a Protestant Christian liberty, was complex. This liberty was not license to do what one lists, but freedom to know what is right and to do good. This was a freedom rooted in submission to an omnipotent God's authority and acceptance of Christ's love, demonstrated in his substitutionary atonement for humankind's sins, which transformed believers from the slaves of sin into free and active servants of God's divine purpose. Sarah Osborn, an evangelical Christian from Newport, Rhode Island, with whom Phillis made contact by way of the Wheatley family, and through whom Phillis became acquainted with the antislavery clergyman Samuel Hopkins, ably made the connection among these ideas.[28] In the wake of Parliament's repeal of the Stamp Act in 1766, Osborn had written, "O that Liberty, precious Liberty were used for the Glory of God. . . . Let us not be entangled with the yoke of Bondage, Lord; free us yet more from the bondage of sin."[29] The best government was one, like Britain's, that freely circulated the Protestant gospel as widely as possible, and as with the Stamp Act, could correct itself when it went astray and trampled the interests of the free people it governed. As chief beneficiaries of the commercial prosperity that Bostonians wrung from Atlantic trade, the members of this circle shared the luxury to treat the people they claimed to possess as privileged servants—like Phillis or Scipio—rather than as field hands.

In these circles, the practice of African chattel slavery was a serious but murky problem. As we have seen, as early as 1700, Samuel Sewall argued that the slave trade was inherently wrong, legalized manstealing, and no more justified than the selling of Joseph by his brothers. Other eighteenth-century Bostonians justified slavery on the grounds that it was wrong to leave a continent in darkness, untouched by Christianity, and neglect the souls of those unfortunates already captured into slavery and deposited on American shores. Some, like Harrison Gray, Joseph Sewall, and Andrew Eliot, minister of the New North Church, were actively opposed to slavery, refused to own slaves themselves, and spoke out against the institution.[30] Others—John Wheatley and John Moorhead among them—saw no contradiction between owning slaves and treating them humanely as Christians, just as they would servants in less permanent forms of bondage. Phillis Wheatley was surrounded by an influential group that generally believed the best principles of the British Empire would certainly ameliorate the conditions of slaves, bestow Christian truth on Africans, and eventually eliminate an institution inconsistent with and ultimately unnecessary within the empire's benevolent domains.[31] These positions were closely linked with similar beliefs that Christian missionary efforts toward the indigenous populations of the Americas, Africa, and Asia would spread the light of civilization and the truth of the gospel throughout the world—the Philippi impulse writ large. The support of these Boston worthies, including the Wheatleys, for Occom's Indian missionary work was intimately connected to their championing of Phillis and their hopes to ameliorate the problem of slavery.[32]

Through her connections to this circle in Boston, Phillis became acquainted with and then celebrated by an even wider range of contacts around the Atlantic, with larger and more immediate ambitions for addressing the problem of slavery. It began with George Whitefield, the celebrated itinerant preacher, whom Wheatley encountered in her own Old South Church, where he preached four times in August 1770. Whitefield probably lodged with the Wheatley family in Boston shortly before his death in Newburyport the following month.[33] Moved by his preaching and sudden demise, Wheatley wrote a funeral elegy, noting Whitefield's prominence in bringing Christian instruction to enslaved African Americans.[34] The elegy was addressed to Selina Hastings, Countess of Huntingdon; Whitefield had been her chaplain. Susannah played host to a series of evangelical missionaries sent to America by the countess, who took note of Phillis when the Whitefield elegy was published to wide acclaim in both London and Boston in 1771. This was the beginning of Phillis's international fame.[35]

The Countess of Huntingdon played a distinctive role within British religious and public life. Although married to a titled peer of the realm, her early conversion by Whitefield to his brand of Calvinist Methodism allied her with the sorts of people among whom the nobility did not ordinarily mix: tradesmen, the laboring poor, and even the urban destitute. Her mission in life became to heal the ills that Britain and its empire suffered, using religion as her chief tool. She founded a series of missionary and educational institutions that she called "the Connexion," aimed to bring Christian education to the poor and unlearned. The countess took an interest in missions to India and America that the connection between Cotton Mather and the Halle Pietists had promoted in the 1720s. She was a major contributor to the orphanage in Georgia that Whitefield founded, and she sponsored his evangelical tours and the publication of his diaries to promote the good works that followed in their wake.[36] In the course of these pursuits, she became interested in the problem of slavery and the conversion of Africans as well, thanks in no small part to Wheatley's remarkable qualities. The countess, like some of Wheatley's Boston circle, did not think that all slaves should be immediately freed—she inherited a number of slaves in Georgia and never manumitted them—but she was committed to bringing Christianity to Africans and treating slaves humanely. Missionaries trained in the countess's "Connexion" became leading figures in the British West African colony of repatriated former slaves in Sierra Leone.[37]

The Countess of Huntingdon became Wheatley's patron, sponsored her visit to London in 1773, and assisted in publishing Wheatley's volume of poetry in London. Wheatley dedicated the book to her. Through the countess, Wheatley met the wider circle of antislavery activists in Britain. Among these were John Thornton and Granville Sharp, who took Wheatley on a tour of London including the Tower of London's zoological collections.[38] Most significant of all was William Legge, the 2nd Earl of Dartmouth. Dartmouth, like

Huntingdon, was born into the titled nobility. His father died at an early age, and his widowed mother married Francis, Lord North, father of the future British prime minister. Dartmouth and his stepbrother were educated together, and both took their expected places of power within government. Yet Dartmouth, like the Countess of Huntingdon, was peculiar in his religious preferences. Huntingdon introduced him to Whitefield's preaching, and Dartmouth became a devout evangelical, ready to mix with fellow believers of all ranks. When attending Methodist meetings, he insisted on being called "Brother Earl," a cause for ridicule from his peers in the House of Lords. But Dartmouth took the ribbing in stride. He believed that through faith and service, the rifts that separated human beings in matters of religion, class, and race—or even in the late controversies between the colonies and home country—could be overcome.[39]

In 1772, Lord North appointed his stepbrother as secretary of state for the colonies. In the wake of the disasters of the Stamp Act, the Townshend Duties, and the "massacre" in Boston, it was hoped, especially by American evangelicals, that Dartmouth's appointment portended the restoration of friendly relations between the Crown and colonies. New Englanders looked forward to "the full enjoyment of civil and religious liberty."[40] With this hope as inspiration, Wheatley wrote one of her best poems, "To the Right Honourable WILLIAM, Earl of DARTMOUTH," comparing the slavery under a domineering government that the American colonies feared to her own experience of enslavement:

No more, *America*, in mournful strain
Of wrongs, and grievance unredress'd complain,
No longer shalt thou dread the iron chain,
Which wanton *Tyranny* with lawless hand
Had made, and with it meant t'enslave the land.

Should you, my lord, while you peruse my song,
Wonder from whence my love of Freedom sprung,
Whence flow these wishes for the common good,
By feeling hearts alone best understood,

I, young in life, by seeming cruel fate
Was snatch'd from Afric's fancy'd happy seat:
What pangs excruciating must molest,
What sorrows labour in my parent's breast?
Steel'd was that soul and by no misery mov'd
That from a father seiz'd his babe belov'd:
Such, such my case. And can I then but pray
Others may never feel tyrannic sway?

Wheatley plucks Dartmouth's heartstrings by offering her own parents' grief at the loss of their stolen child as an example of what Dartmouth must have felt to see his fellow Christians in New England robbed of their liberties by an unfeeling Parliament.[41]

Circulation and Salvation in Wheatley's British Empire

A prevalent but seldom noticed theme in Wheatley's writing is central to understanding the trust that she and her fellow colonists placed in the British Empire as an agent of benevolence. Running through Wheatley's poetry is a belief in the efficacy of circulation to right wrongs, restore order, recover lost health, bring light to darkness, and salvation to sinners. This idea was not new to Boston's intellectual world; it was implicit in the founding image of the Great Seal of Massachusetts, borrowed from Saint Paul's vision of the man of Macedon, of an Indian saying "Come Over and Help Us." From the belief that the message of the Christian gospel must circle the globe to usher in a millennial paradise, to the idea that overseas trade would properly distribute the world's material riches to its dispersed populations, Europe's colonizing projects since Columbus had been rooted in similar convictions. But from the Glorious Revolution onward, the British Empire's power to rule the waves had intensified the concern for the proper, ethical, and benevolent circulation of ideas, persons, and commodities in the imagination of visionaries like Wheatley. Many of Wheatley's most powerful poems, including those that explore her own condition as an enslaved

African, rely on the concept that the movement and distribution of people and goods throughout the circuits of the Atlantic world, both metaphorically and literally, was the central purpose of Britain's empire, and formed the basis for her optimism about the empire's future.

In Wheatley's poems, circulation appears in many guises and might as easily be described as translation, in the early modern sense of the removal or transference of something from one place to another. In 1597, Anglican archbishop Richard Hooker had asserted that "ascension into heauen is a playne locall translation of Christ," and in 1760, Whitefield learned of the death of a friend as "the news of dear Mr. Polhill's sudden translation." In the dominant humoral theory of medicine, translation or circulation of fluids and matter in the body was both the cause and cure for disease; in 1665, Robert Boyle described the causes of "madness . . . by the translation of the Humours into the Brain."[42] This way of thinking need not mean circulation in the sense of a single item or element performing a complete circuit, as a planet's orbit around the sun or in the circulation of blood from heart to lungs, through the body and back to the heart again. Rather, it involves thinking of the entire British Empire, from Europe to Africa, India, and the Americas, as a circuit in which goods and people move along ocean currents, with the object of finding the right and appropriate place for each to flourish. The key is motion from one place, one environment, to another, and this applies not only to earthly happiness but to the soul's eternal life as well. The story of Joseph is the great biblical exemplar of this phenomenon. By selling their brother into slavery in Egypt, the sons of Jacob unwittingly set in motion a circulatory process that leads to their own migration to Egypt to escape famine, the eventual enslavement of the Israelites by the Egyptians, their ultimate liberation led by Moses, and their triumphal return to the land of Canaan.[43] In her poetry, Wheatley would turn repeatedly to such images, and many similar instances of circulation and translation.

Although Wheatley wrote many of her individual poems for specific occasions over the course of several years, the 1773 publication of *Poems on Various Subjects, Religious and Moral* arranged them into a coherent sequence. The story of human sin and redemption, often repeated throughout Wheatley's work, is cast as exile from the innocence of the garden, followed by eventual restoration and salvation, described as a physical translation to a heavenly abode, as in her "Hymn to Humanity" or the many elegies in which the subject, like Joseph Sewall, is seen as a "saint ascending to his native skies," with "native" emphasizing the circularity of the soul's journey.[44] Even Dartmouth, though years away from giving up the ghost in 1772, gets the same imagined treatment:

> But to conduct to heav'ns refulgent fane,
> May fiery coursers sweep th' ethereal plain,
> And bear thee upwards to that blest abode,
> Where, like the prophet, thou shalt find thy God.[45]

The two poems following the "Ode to Dartmouth" translate this metaphor into earthly terms. They focus on travel or circulation around different places within the British Empire as a source of restoration for lost health, and by implication, a form of saving grace as well. The voyage of her mistress, Susannah, from Boston to England in 1772 was undertaken to restore Susannah's failing health. Wheatley composed an "Ode to Neptune, on Mrs. W—'s Voyage to England," in which the raging ocean god is calmed by prayers to ensure Susannah's safe voyage:

> The Pow'r propitious hears the lay,
> The blue-ey'd daughters of the sea
> With sweeter cadence glide along,
> And *Thames* responsive joins the song.

Wheatley duly praises the restorative powers of Britain's climate for her mistress's health:

> To court thee to *Britannia's* arms
> Serene the climes and mild the sky,
> Her region boasts unnumber'd charms,
> Thy welcome smiles in ev'ry eye.[46]

A similar theme is set forth in Wheatley's next poem, "To a LADY on Her Coming to North America with Her Son, for the Recovery of Her Health." Here the voyager leaves Jamaica's "fervid" and "malignant" shore to cross "Neptune's wat'ry realm" and find her health in "the Northern milder climes."[47] The theme is given still fuller treatment in yet another ode, "To a GENTLEMAN on His Voyage to Great-Britain for the Recovery of His Health," where the power of circulation in the form of ocean travel is celebrated directly:

O thou stupendous, earth-enclosing main
Exert thy wonders to the world again!
If ere thy pow'r prolong'd the fleeting breath,
Turn'd back the shafts, and mock'd the gates of death,
If ere thine air dispens'd an healing pow'r,
Or snatch'd the victim from the fatal hour,
This equal case demands thine equal care,
And equal wonders may this patient share.[48]

The power and depth of this concept, the importance of the beneficial value of circulation within Wheatley's worldview, is best revealed in the poems where she addresses her own condition. In "A Farewell to America," written on her departure for England, Wheatley emphasizes that she, like her mistress, is leaving New England's springtime charms for England in order to restore her health:

In vain for me the flow'rets rise,
  And boast their gaudy pride,
While here beneath the northern skies
  I mourn for *health* deny'd. . . .
While for *Britannia's* distant shore
  We sweep the liquid plain,
And with astonish'd eyes explore
  The wide-extended main.
Lo! *Health* appears! Celestial dame!
  Complacent and serene,
With Hebe's mantle o'er her Frame,
  With soul-delighting mein.

Hebe was the Greek goddess of eternal youth, a popular image in portrait painting in Wheatley's era (Marie Antoinette was painted "en *Hébé* in 1773). Hebe's powers were often symbolized as freeing men from their bondage and chains (she was also worshipped as the goddess of pardons), thus tightening the metaphorical links that Wheatley forged between health, liberation from slavery, and salvation.[49]

A more profound, if more troubling, variation on this theme appears in the poem for which Wheatley is most famous, "On Being Brought from AFRICA to AMERICA." This poem has stimulated much fraught criticism by modern literary scholars, brought on by the fact that in it, Wheatley seems to be accepting and even celebrating her own enslavement:

> Twas mercy brought me from my Pagan land,
> Taught my benighted soul to understand,
> That there's a God, that there's a *Saviour* too:
> Once I redemption neither sought nor knew.[50]

The presence of this seeming false consciousness within the work of a poet whom many scholars regard as a founding figure in African American literature has created a major challenge for contemporary literary critics.[51]

Yet Wheatley's wholehearted embrace of New England's version of British imperial culture may best be understood not as a denial of slavery's brutality but rather as akin to the experience of Eunice Williams, the English puritan girl taken captive in 1704 by Roman Catholic Caughnawauga Indians in the raid on Deerfield, Massachusetts. Like Williams, who was similarly captured, torn from her family, and taken to an alien world at around the age of seven, Wheatley adopted her captors' language, culture, and religion. She had no other choice and no context for resisting. Her captors offered her a new name and identity, lavished attention and concern on her, and treated her as one of their own (the latter highly unusual within the Anglo-American slave system).[52] Not surprisingly, Wheatley, like Williams, later refused the opportunity to "return" to her native African shores. When British abolitionists suggested that she become a religious missionary in Sierra Leone, Wheatley declined the offer, arguing that her poor health prevented it. But she also asserted that New England was her home, and that she would seem "like a Barbarian" to Africans, "being an utter stranger to the language of Anamaboe."[53] Only the year before, the introductory preface to her published works of poetry, written by John or (more likely) Susannah Wheatley, had described Phillis as "an uncultivated Barbarian from Africa" at the time she arrived in Boston.[54] By her original translation from Africa to New England, the purpose of transatlantic circulation had, from Phillis's perspective, been achieved. From "uncultivated Barbarian from Africa," she had made herself into a cultivated member of New England society and was now loath to reverse the process.

If we set aside the anachronistic concern among scholars about Wheatley's problematic status at the beginning of an African American literary canon and instead consider Wheatley within the context of eighteenth-century British Atlantic writers, then in this poem, the "mercy" that brought her from Africa to Boston functions much like the other forms of translation, relocation, and movement throughout her work: as an agent of grace. This reading is reinforced by the fact that "saviour" in this poem is italicized, just as "health" is italicized in her "Farewell to America"—italics marking the appearance of the redeeming qualities that emerge in new places when imperial circulation brings souls that have been suffering elsewhere into a beneficial environment.

This reading of the power of circulation is reinforced by Wheatley's ode to the Earl of Dartmouth. Here, the "Fair *Freedom*" portended by Dartmouth's appointment as secretary of state for the colonies is cast in the figure of the rising sun, whose absence has until recently left New England in darkness: "Long lost to realms beneath the northern skies / She shines supreme, while hated *faction* dies." With the return of Freedom's light, New England "no longer mourns, / Each soul expands," while destructive faction, by contrast, "sick at the view, she languish'd and expir'd."[55]

So far, the poem is consistent with Wheatley's general table of metaphorical equivalences, aligning light, truth, freedom, health, grace, and salvation, against darkness, ignorance, slavery, sickness, and death.

Then, while she claims the power to speak for all New England ("For favours past, *our* thanks are due"), Wheatley personalizes the poem's narrative. Addressing Dartmouth directly, she explains that if Dartmouth wonders "whence my love of *Freedom* sprung," the source of this feeling, which Dartmouth's sympathetic heart presumably shares, derives from the fact that "I, young in life, by seeming cruel fate / Was snatch'd from *Afric's* fancy'd happy seat." Wheatley has already informed the reader in her earlier poem, "On Being Brought from AFRICA to AMERICA," why this fate was only "*seeming* cruel"—it was ultimately an act of mercy—and why "Afric's" seat is only "*fancy'd* happy"—because in Africa she neither sought nor knew Christian redemption. So it is not her own sufferings that bring her the sympathetic capacity to long for freedom but rather her contemplation of her *parent's* feelings:

What pangs excruciating must molest,
What sorrows labour in my parent's breast?
Steel'd was that soul and by no misery mov'd
That from a father seiz'd his babe belov'd.[56]

Wheatley's rhetorical position here rehearses the story of Joseph from the book of Genesis, sold into slavery by his brothers, but raised up through his talents to become Pharaoh's servant, lord protector of all Egypt. Although Joseph must have suffered when his brothers stripped him of his multicolored coat, cast him into a pit, and sold him to passing merchants, the text of Genesis does not dwell on Joseph's suffering, passing over it in silence. Instead, Genesis shows the reader how Joseph eventually benefited from his brothers' evil deed. But Genesis does depict the suffering of his father, Jacob, who mourned his lost son, tore his clothes, wore sackcloth, and refused to be comforted. Jacob's suffering could only be remedied, in the end, by Joseph's revelation of the freedom, power, and glory to which he had ultimately been elevated.

From at least the time of Sewall's *The Selling of Joseph*, this story had been a critical narrative for thinking about the problem of slavery in New England. Wheatley herself had this connection in mind when she described America's slaveholders in a letter to Occom as "our modern Egyptians."[57] Devout Protestant evangelicals were strongly conditioned to think that bringing Africans to Christendom meant translating them from darkness to light, from sin to salvation—a gift of value beyond measure. But neither could those of tender conscience endorse the method—manstealing—as anything but tyranny itself. To reconcile this tension, Wheatley's feelings about the meaning of freedom had to be cast in terms of the suffering of her parents, the true victims of her theft, rather than her own. Her hopes, in light of Dartmouth's elevation to the Crown's chief minister for the colonies, are for a world in which the blessings of circulation—light, truth, knowledge, health, redemption, and salvation—can be achieved without the crime of tyranny and enslavement, which can "from a father seize his babe belov'd" as easily as it can "enslave the land" with an "iron chain."[58]

Wheatley revealed the depth of her humanity to her erstwhile enslavers by publishing a book of poems—turning her thoughts and talents, her poetic inspiration, into a commodity that could be bought and sold. In other words, with the act of publishing her *Poems on Various Subjects, Religious and Moral*, Wheatley coined herself; she put herself into circulation among her enslavers, but in a way that did not compromise her liberty.[59] Even the book's original frontispiece—a portrait of Wheatley in the shape of a medallion—suggests as much.[60] Surrounding her, like the circumscription on a coin's edge, are words declaring that she belongs to an earthly master: "Phillis Wheatley, Negro Servant to Mr. John Wheatley, of Boston." (Recall that in Jesus's encounter with the Pharisees in the temple, he had referred to the tribute money's circumscription to identify its true owner, Caesar). But here the image belies the circumscription, for Phillis Wheatley—not Caesar, not John Wheatley—is depicted with the pen of authority in her hand. Her eyes, gazing beyond the servile circumscription toward the heavens, demonstrate that the source of her inspiration, her only true master, is divine.[61]

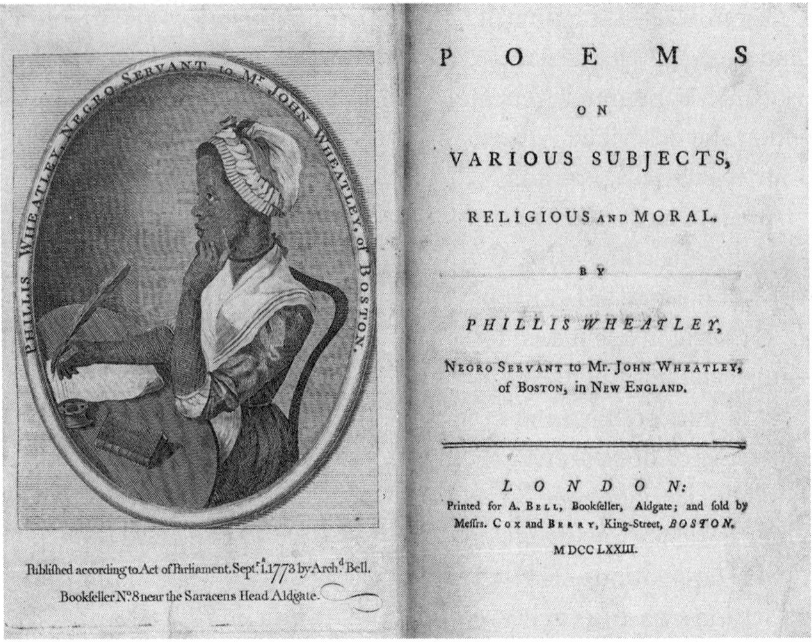
PHILLIS WHEATLEY, NEGRO SERVANT to Mr. JOHN WHEATLEY, of BOSTON.

Published according to Act of Parliament, Sept. 1. 1773 by Arch.d Bell. Bookseller N.o 8 near the Saracens Head Aldgate.

POEMS

ON

VARIOUS SUBJECTS,

RELIGIOUS AND MORAL.

BY

PHILLIS WHEATLEY,

NEGRO SERVANT to Mr. JOHN WHEATLEY, of BOSTON, in NEW ENGLAND.

LONDON:

Printed for A. BELL, Bookseller, Aldgate; and sold by Messrs. COX and BERRY, King-Street, BOSTON.

MDCCLXXIII.

FIGURE 6.1. Frontispiece and title page, Phillis Wheatley, *Poems on Various Subjects, Religious and Moral* (London, 1773).

To prove that this coin is no counterfeit utterance, the text reprints the signed testimony of eighteen of "the most respectable Characters in Boston, . . . to assure the World, that the Poems . . . were written by Phillis, a young Negro Girl, who was but a few years since brought an uncultivated Barbarian from Africa, and has ever since been . . . a slave in a family in this Town."[62] First among the signatories was the royal governor, Hutchinson, attesting that "none might have the least Ground for disputing" the poems' authenticity, much as his grandfather, Elisha Hutchinson, had signed each of the Massachusetts paper money bills of 1690 to guarantee their value (see figure 3.4).

If Wheatley's book of poems represents the translation of her thoughts and sentiments, her poetic self-representation, into a commodity for sale, then the contents of her poems themselves pay tribute to the better angels of Boston and the British Empire. She writes poems of praise to her late minister, Joseph Sewall, to the promising youth of Harvard College, and to the recently deceased

Whitefield, whose unceasing circulation through Britain's colonial possessions had accelerated the Christianization of African Americans.[63] She also offers tribute to her patron and Whitefield's, the Countess of Huntingdon, and to the Earl of Dartmouth. There is even a poem to the greatest of Caesars, King George III. Not to let the point slip by unnoticed, the collection begins with an "Ode to Maecenas," the great Roman patron of poets under Caesar Augustus—a poetic tribute to the ideals of patronage and tribute.[64]

In all these poems, and especially in the ode to Dartmouth, Wheatley demonstrates that she has the author's power, despite her subservient relationship to her patrons. She assumes the part of the biblical Joseph, raised up from slavery by his remarkable abilities and the favor of God's grace to become Egypt's effective ruler, with the power of life and death over the brothers who had sold him. Wheatley accepts the argument that although her kidnapping, like Joseph's, was a crime, it nevertheless brought her the benefit of redemption in Christian Boston.[65] On this basis, she refuses to allow her enslaved status or racial difference to separate her from New England's birthright of British liberty. When Wheatley addresses the Earl of Dartmouth, she speaks confidently as the voice of New England's freedom. She assumes that the current defense of liberty in Boston's resistance movement against Parliament and the Crown is part of an expansion of the ideal of liberty throughout the empire that Dartmouth will embrace.[66] Enslavement gives her special access to the emotional value of liberty. Yet like the mature Joseph thinking of the sorrows of Jacob, it is not her own suffering that moves her but instead that of her bereaved parents. By refusing, as Joseph did, the part of the victim, Wheatley denies the power of the crime of manstealing to determine her destiny. Her poetry, although it follows the attack against slavery articulated by Sewall in *The Selling of Joseph* (1700), does so not by denouncing slavery in so many words, and certainly not by accepting Sewall's idea that "Negroes" must remain an "extravasat blood" in the body politic, forever separate from the white majority. Rather, her poetic self-rendition as a circulating commodity makes manifest the truth of Sewall's maxim that there is no proportion between twenty pieces of silver and liberty. The commodity itself, Wheatley, is the claimer. The refined value of her poetical self-coinage is incomparably greater than the price of her original sale.[67]

Circulation Interrupted: The Destruction of Phillis Wheatley's World

There is tragic irony in the timing of Wheatley's remarkable self-rendering. Samuel Sewall made his arguments against manstealing in 1700, when Bostonians were newly hopeful that Britain's expanding realm could be an empire of godliness and liberty. Seventy years later when Wheatley performed the same arguments, that faith was on the verge of disintegration. Three months after the London publication of Wheatley's *Poems*, the ship *Dartmouth*, loaded with East India Company tea, entered Boston Harbor, forcing the city to make a final decision on whether to pay tribute to Caesar in the form of the tea tax. The deliberate destruction of the tea shipment by an organized and disguised crowd of protesters decisively set in motion the chain of events that ended in war.[68] The "respectable characters" who authenticated the value of Wheatley's literary tribute included both loyalists and rebels—Hutchinson, Oliver, and Gray, on one hand, and Hancock, Bowdoin, and Cooper, on the other. (More of them were loyalists than rebels; eleven of the eighteen had clear Tory sympathies, and six died in exile.) This was perhaps the last time this group of Bostonians would agree to endorse anything. The ensuing revolution broke Boston's ties with those elsewhere in the Atlantic world who were beginning to consider an empire without slaves. British supporters of schemes for slave emancipation believed that it would require enlightened imperial governance, not colonial self-rule, to bring about such a dramatic change in the empire's political economy.[69]

Wheatley's poetic self-coinage also came at a moment of seeming high promise for the future of enslaved persons in the British Empire, when it looked as if the forces that she embraced might prevail. In summer 1772, when the eighteen Boston worthies attested that Wheatley was, indeed, the author of her poems, another slave who had recently come from Boston, James Somerset, had his fate decided in a British court by the Earl of Mansfield, lord chief justice of Great Britain. Somerset had much in common with Wheatley. He, too, had been enslaved as a youth in Africa and purchased by an Atlantic merchant, Charles Stewart, who went on to become the paymaster general of the American Customs Board in Boston. Like Wheatley, Somerset was brought by his master to London. Unlike Wheatley, he escaped from his master's service, only to be recaptured. His owner had then attempted to ship Somerset in chains to Jamaica for reenslavement. But during his extended time in London, Somerset made friends with antislavery activists, including Granville Sharpe, who brought his case to court. There Lord Mansfield decided that because Parliament had passed no laws expressly legalizing slavery within Britain itself, it was unlawful to enslave a man there. Mansfield's statement from the bench reads, "The state of slavery is of such a nature that it is incapable of being introduced on any reasons, moral or political, but only positive law. . . . It is so odious that nothing can be suffered to support it but positive law." Even if custom and colonial legislation justified the institution elsewhere within the empire, "I cannot say this case is allowed or approved by the law of England, and therefore the black must be discharged." Colonial lawmakers, in other words, did not have the power to legislate for Parliament in England.[70]

The Somerset case seemed to mark a moment of triumph and spurred British antislavery activists to new efforts. But it had an ominous undertone. It threatened to cut off the circulation between colonies and imperial center. The news of Mansfield's decision spread quickly throughout the Atlantic world, causing colonial slaves to long for England, but making masters wary of bringing slaves there for fear of losing the power to bring them back home. The decision created a legal rift between colonies and home country.[71] In 1768, in her ode to King George III, Phillis had thanked the king for repealing the Stamp Act, which had threatened to cause a similar rift by insisting that Parliament had the right to legislate for the colonies. She offered this future hope for the king's gracious rule: "And may each clime with equal gladness see / A monarch's smile can set his subjects free."[72] After the Somerset decision, it appeared that in

England's clime, the monarch's smile did set his subjects free, but colonial climes were different. Phillis Wheatley was emancipated on her return to Boston, late in 1773, but only because John Wheatley's smile, not Mansfield's decision, set her free.

Shortly after her manumission came the destruction of the tea on the East India Company ship, *Dartmouth*, on December 16, 1773. Bostonians would not accept Parliament's revised Tea Act, which gave the company a monopoly on distribution rights and levied a small tax on imported tea, and so they refused to allow the tea to be unloaded. Governor Thomas Hutchinson, whose sons were among those named by the company as consignees of the tea, insisted that Parliament's law be enforced. He would not allow the *Dartmouth* to leave the harbor without unloading its cargo. The "Tea Party" settled the matter, cutting off Boston's imperial circulation once and for all.

As punishment, Parliament passed the Boston Port Bill, the first of the Coercive (or Intolerable) Acts of 1774, which closed the port down entirely. Within another year, virtually all legal transatlantic commerce between Britain and America had ceased. The second of the Coercive Acts, the Massachusetts Government Act, in a single stroke dismantled the commonwealth's hundred-fifty-year history of self-government by abolishing the elected assembly and council of the General Court, and replacing it with the government of soldiers: military rule under General Gage and his handpicked council. The transformation of Massachusetts from a self-governing commonwealth into a military autocracy was sudden, abrupt, and devastating. In response, the people of the New England countryside rose up in defense of occupied Boston and their own political rights, just as they had done in 1689 against Andros, and launched an open rebellion. If Mansfield had decided that the colonies could not legislate for Parliament in the matter of slavery, now Massachusetts colonists asserted that Parliament could not legislate for them without making them slaves.

The ensuing warfare, the siege of Boston begun in April 1775, and lasting until the evacuation of the British military in March 1776, destroyed the community that had created Wheatley, the world that she had embraced and in which she raised herself to a precarious prominence. Her former master, John Wheatley, remained loyal to the Crown, abandoned Boston, no longer a town of "gaiety and sport," and went into exile in England. So did many other members of her circle of supporters; Governor Hutchinson, Lieutenant Governor Oliver, Colonel John Erving, and the poet Joseph Green as well as some of the most outspoken antislavery voices from earlier and happier days, such as Harrison Gray. Other supporters who remained in Boston, like the clergymen Mather Byles, Ebenezer Pemberton, and Andrew Eliot, were effectively silenced by their Tory inclinations, or in Eliot's case, his inability to decide which side to support. Susannah Wheatley, Phillis's closest friend and supporter, died shortly before the crisis, never recovering the health that the voyage to England had been meant to restore. Mary Wheatley and her only brother, Nathaniel, died during the war as well. In this context, manumission was at best a mixed blessing. It cut Wheatley off from the means of support, both material and moral, that had sustained her early years in Boston, leaving her to fend for herself in a city ravaged by war.[73]

She made a valiant effort to embrace the new direction that her adopted city was taking. The Continental Congress meeting in Philadelphia commissioned George Washington to assume command of the army of militiamen besieging Boston, transforming it into the Continental Army. After Washington's arrival in Cambridge in July 1775, Wheatley wrote an ode in his honor, not unlike earlier ones she addressed to imperial dignitaries. She wrote to the "Generalissimo," as she called him, enclosing her poem, and was rewarded by an invitation to meet with Washington in his Brattle Street headquarters, but may have been unable to accept.[74] Otherwise, the Revolutionary War did not inspire a poetic outpouring. Wheatley wrote (but did not publish) only two other poems during the war: one on the capture of Charles Lee, a Continental Army general, by British forces, which she sent to her old mentor, James Bowdoin; the other concerned another general, the Connecticut merchant David Wooster, with whom she had corresponded before the war about selling her book. Wooster was killed in battle, and Wheatley addressed her ode to his widow, enclosed in private correspondence. Though she made various proposals for book projects, her publications largely ceased with the onset of the revolution.[75]

When the war ended, Wheatley celebrated by writing a poem titled "Liberty and Peace." For Wheatley, the chief benefit of the war's end was the return of the free circulation of commerce and people throughout the Atlantic world: "To every Realm her portals open'd wide, / Receives from each the full commercial Tide."[76] Despite the bitterness, violence, and destruction of war, symbolized in her description of how "Charlestown's curling Smoaks arise / In sable Columns to the clouded Skies" during the Battle of Bunker Hill, Wheatley hoped that "E'en great *Britannia*" will resume its part in transatlantic commerce:

> Britain, whose Navies swept th' Atlantic o'er,
> And Thunder sent to every distant Shore:
> E'en thou, in Manners cruel as thou art,
> The Sword resign'd, resume the friendly Part!

She enumerates how "every Kingdom on Europa's Coast" can now take part in the free commerce that a liberated America champions. But she does not—and cannot—celebrate any sense of personal liberty for herself or her fellow Africans resulting from the revolution's settlement.[77]

For Wheatley personally, despite her limited efforts to redeem the war's destruction and restore a sense of order to her world, the damage brought on by the rebellion could not be repaired. In 1778, she married John Peters of Boston, a free black man and grocer. The couple had two children, both of whom died in infancy. John Peters was jailed for debt on at least one occasion, and Wheatley worked as a maid in a boardinghouse to make ends meet. She did not live long beyond the war, dying shortly after giving birth to a third child in December 1784.[78]

Even before her death, she had been appropriated by the makers of new American national narratives in ways that undermined her past as a distinctive but fully coherent voice for New England's imperial aspirations. In his *Notes on the State of Virginia*, Thomas Jefferson cruelly used Wheatley as evidence in a conversation with the French philosophe the Marquis de Barbé-Marbois regarding the innate physical and mental capacities of Africans and their prospects for self-government. Jefferson infamously claimed that "religion, indeed, has produced a Phillis Whately [*sic*]; but it could not produce a poet. The compositions published under her name are below the dignity of criticism"—in other words, counterfeit literary coin, not suitable for circulation in the "State of Virginia."[79] On both sides, this argument between slave owners presumed an American exceptionalism, stark differences between America and the rest of the world. Barbé-Marbois believed, following the French naturalist Comte de Buffon, that the Americas produced diminished and degenerate versions of Old World species. Jefferson maintained the opposite: that America was by nature more vigorous and productive than Europe.[80] All of Wheatley's poetic efforts had been written to oppose such a binary distinction. Her work consistently promoted the idea that the free circulation of people, goods, and Christianity throughout an interconnected Atlantic world would balance out and correct any accidental differences among various climes, and distribute grace, health, knowledge, and virtue equally and everywhere.

Thomas Jefferson rejected this position out of hand. His cruel mockery of Wheatley's talent, his intimations that Wheatley and all Africans were innately inferior to Europeans and Euro-Americans, inaugurated an unenlightening argument that has gone on for two centuries. This argument has shaped the history of African American literature in ways that have made Wheatley a discordant figure—an embarrassing beginning to African American literature in the eyes of many critics.[81] Phillis Wheatley, who, like Abijah Willard, was a latecomer to the fantasy that Boston's interests and the empire's were one and the same, witnessed the destruction of her world when the violent rebellion in Boston destroyed the circulation on which her idealized vision of the British Empire depended. The destruction of Wheatley's world meant the end of Boston's participation, as *Theopolis Americana*, in a system of transatlantic Protestant evangelical reform that the British Empire promoted—a vision that went back to the century's first night, when Samuel Sewall dreamed of Christ coming to Boston.

CHAPTER 7

John Adams, Boston's Diplomat

Apostle of Balance in a World Turned Upside Down

> It was a settled Point at Paris . . . that I was not the famous Adams, and therefore . . . that I was a Man of whom Nobody had ever heard before, a perfect Cypher, a Man who did not understand a Word of French—awkward in his Figure—awkward in his Dress—No Abilities—a perfect Bigot—and fanatic.
>
> —John Adams, on being confused with Samuel Adams, his better-known cousin, 1779

In the early 1760s, at the time that Phillis Wheatley arrived in Boston, another young person was drawn into the city. A provincial boy from a middling farming family on Boston's South Shore, an ancient family that had been in Braintree since the Great Migration of the 1630s, he had attended Harvard College, graduating in 1755 at the age of twenty. Like many a Harvard student from the rural hinterland, he ranked nearer the bottom than the top of his Harvard class, as class rank was then a measure of social standing rather than scholarly accomplishment. His family was neither rich nor mercantile, so his future lay in the professions: clergyman, lawyer, doctor, or perhaps soldier. The timing was right for soldier, with the French War heating up just as he finished college. But his lack of connections or military experience made it unlikely that he could get an officer's commission, even in Massachusetts' Provincial Army, and the life of an enlisted man was no life for a young man with ambition. John Adams had ambition.

In 1755, Adams moved to Worcester, a county seat of perhaps fifteen hundred villagers forty miles west of Boston, where he took a position as a schoolmaster. This was neither an auspicious place nor an auspicious job, but he had no better offers. Keeping school, despite the tedium of training boys and girls to do sums and parse Tully, could serve as a stepping-stone to the clergy or law.[1] The pay was bad, but the work was light, giving a young single man time for the study and preparation needed to enter a learned profession. In Worcester, Adams came under the wing of a local lawyer, James Putnam, and resolved to study law under his guidance. By 1758, he was prepared for an interview with Boston's leading attorney, the great Jeremiah Gridley. After an afternoon of anxious conversation with Gridley, Adams was admitted to the Massachusetts Bar.

Adams moved back to his parents' home and began a legal practice, which involved riding circuit along with Superior Court judges. Lawyers had to go where there was lawyering to be done, and a quiet village like Braintree could not exhaust the time and aspirations of the energetic Adams. As he made the rounds with the court, Adams slowly became a familiar figure in Boston's courtrooms, though he was generally overawed by the judges, king's counsels, and splendid orators of the city's legal establishment. His "arrival" in Boston, if we can call it that, roughly coincided with that of Wheatley. Adams was certainly far higher on the social scale than Wheatley, and his prospects were far rosier than hers. But in 1761 he was nothing special, just another instance of a common pattern. The city was a magnet for young talent, drawing on the ambitions of the people in its hinterland just as it drew on the countryside's food, fuel, and building materials for sustenance and growth.

Whereas war and revolution dismantled the world that fostered Wheatley's talents and advanced her unlikely fame, the same crisis served unexpectedly to promote Adams's career, in part by dislodging many leaders of the legal and political establishment that he held in awe. Because Adams, unlike Wheatley, was free, white, adult, male, educated, property owning, and a professional, he could engage directly in Boston's resistance movement and eventual rebellion, which rapidly transformed Adams from a provincial farmer-lawyer into a national politician and international diplomat. The rebellion enabled Adams to play a guiding role in remaking the governmental framework of Massachusetts after a decade of violence and destruction. And it provided Adams with the opportunity to engage with political leaders from the other colonies who joined the rebellion, and with the rulers and diplomats of Europe's imperial powers, playing the part of an evangelist for New England's political principles and practices—a civic equivalent of the apostle Paul preaching Christianity to Philippi.

Like Wheatley, Adams wholeheartedly embraced Boston and New England's traditions, but he emphasized somewhat different aspects of this usable past. For Wheatley and her connections among the city's merchant elite, Boston was *Theopolis Americana*, a vision articulated early in the eighteenth century by Cotton Mather and his contemporaries, who saw the city as a cosmopolitan participant in Britain's Protestant commercial empire. For the more provincial Adams, however, it was the seventeenth-century image of New England as a godly, virtuous, and autonomous republic—resisting the tyrannical encroachment of the Stuart monarchs—that was more compelling. This tradition powerfully shaped his response to the imperial crisis that began in the 1760s, just as he gained a foothold in the city's legal and political cultures.

The young Adams was, and would always remain, somewhat eccentric to Boston proper. He was never a permanent resident of the city, and only lived there for about five years, from 1768 to 1770, and again from 1772 until 1775, when he left for the Continental Congress and service to the nascent United States. Though he became the city and region's spokesman and champion in national politics and on the international stage, and while he was deeply imbued with an understanding of its political and religious history, as a farmer-lawyer, Adams was neither closely connected to nor particularly expert in Boston's mercantile traditions. In 1772, as Adams took a seat representing Boston in the General Court, William Shirley, former Massachusetts governor of long standing and deeply immersed in Boston's political culture, could not figure out who Adams was or where he came from.[2] Four years later, Adams was

Boston's delegate to the Continental Congress, lobbying for independence and preparing to represent the United States in France.

Like Wheatley, Adams was a singular figure in Boston's history. He was the only Bostonian of the revolutionary generation to play a major part in the national government and international relations of the new United States. While John Hancock's flamboyant signature adorns the signed copy of the Declaration of Independence, most Americans, then and now, might find it hard to say what Hancock actually did to promote independence or shape the new nation. Most of the major figures in Boston's resistance movement and Massachusetts' newly independent government—Hancock, Samuel Adams, James Otis, Thomas Young, James Warren, Thomas Cushing, William Molineux, Paul Revere, James Sullivan, Robert Treat Paine, and James Bowdoin—played a limited role, or no role at all, on the national stage. These are generally not household names in contemporary America.[3] By contrast, the large part played by Adams in national politics as a leading figure in the Continental Congress arguing for the Declaration of Independence, as the first US minister to Great Britain, and first vice president and second president of the United States, has made Adams part of the cult of the founding fathers encouraged by popular historians. Adams is the subject of best-selling biographies and multipart television series, which focus their attention on the later part of Adams's career, when he occupied the national stage and engaged in political battles with other celebrated figures such as Thomas Jefferson and Alexander Hamilton.[4]

But if, as with Phillis Wheatley, we set aside John Adams the national icon and instead focus on his early years, we can see how his early writings brought New England's history as an autonomous republic to the forefront of Boston's resistance movement, and gain fresh insight into the collapse of Boston's imperial relationship with Britain and the remaking of Massachusetts as a fully independent republic. Unlike Wheatley, whose strong ties to transatlantic reform, antislavery, and evangelical movements discouraged any interest in breaking with Britain, Adams enthusiastically supported Boston's rebellion as a defense of the commonwealth's republican liberties against a tyrannical Parliament and king. He played a central role in the internal project of sustaining the city-state of Boston's traditions through the turbulence of rebellion, independence, and the re-creation of Massachusetts as a sovereign state.

The rebellion against Britain elevated Adams's career, but his efforts to advance New England's political principles on the national and international stage would prove to be profoundly disillusioning. Adams's political service at the Continental Congress in the 1770s, and then as a US ambassador in France, the Netherlands, and Great Britain in the 1780s, can collectively be seen as a kind of diplomacy, negotiating first as one of Massachusetts' representatives in the "congress" with the other colonies in rebellion against the Crown, working out a collective strategy of effective resistance and eventually independence, and then later representing the confederation as a whole in its relations with foreign governments. The principles of political economy and republican government that had long guided the city-state of Boston served as his lodestar throughout, the gospel of independence that he would preach. Yet the other states in the new confederation, and the foreign governments and diplomats that Adams encountered, generally refused to adopt or accept Adams's claims for the superiority of New England's political traditions and social values.

The conflicts that he encountered on the national and international stage, including the challenges of his one-term presidency from 1797–1801, when both foreign and domestic opponents attacked his vision of government, have made John Adams into a discordant figure—a prophet without honor in his own country—seemingly out of step with the direction taken by the new republic. The historian Gordon Wood has described this as the "irrelevance" of John Adams, arguing that Adams's understanding of republicanism may have been suitable for a colonial society resisting imperial authority, but had no place in the new conception of a continental republic envisaged by James Madison and his fellow framers of the Constitution of 1787.[5] But Adams's supposed irrelevance stems from the way in which Wood (and virtually every other historian or biographer of Adams) frames the question in hindsight, as if the direction that the United States took in the nineteenth century as an expansive "empire of liberty" was necessary and inevitable, rather than contingent and political—as if Madison's and Jefferson's vision of America is the only context in which relevance can be measured.

By examining Adams's political and intellectual career in his earlier years, focusing on the period between 1761 and 1788, and his unlikely transition from provincial lawyer to international diplomat, we can better see that what Wood called Adams's irrelevance was really a sign of deep fissures between the city-state of Boston and the other British colonies that rallied to Boston's cause in 1775 and joined its rebellion against the king. Adams's political position and republican philosophy, which made enormous sense from a Bostonian viewpoint, helped Massachusetts to weather the transition from royal colony to independent commonwealth with its republican traditions intact. But it would fail to convince the other states outside New England to remake their constitutions on a Massachusetts model. And Adams, like many of his fellow Massachusetts citizens, would oppose the idea of the concentrated national government created by the Philadelphia Constitutional Convention of 1787. Boston's and New England's ideals for republican government failed to gain political traction in a national contest eventually dominated by other regions, even while it remained a successful form of political economy for Boston and its hinterland.

The disappointments of Adams's later career were the result of the tragic mistake that Adams made in believing that the "cause of Boston" would ever really be adopted as the "cause of all America." Adams's profound devotion to the republican tradition of New England and the seeming centrality of its tenets to Boston's rebellion against the Crown led him to overestimate its capacity to influence the other member states of the new confederation assembling itself in Philadelphia. These disappointments did not make John Adams irrelevant; they foreshadowed a rocky relationship between the ancient city-state of Boston and the newly emerging United States.

The Limited Reach of John Adams's Connections

The connections into which Adams was born in 1735 would not have been bad ones if his goal had been simply to lead a prosperous life as a civic-minded farmer in Boston's hinterland.[6] His father,

"Deacon" John Adams, the fifth generation of Adamses in Braintree, owned a farm conveniently near the South Shore of Boston Harbor, along the main road from Plymouth into Boston. During his lifetime, the elder Adams (1691–1761) filled every office expected of a head of household in a Massachusetts town: church deacon, town officer, and lieutenant in Braintree's militia—a solid and useful citizen. Adams's mother, Susannah Boylston Adams, was the great niece of Zabdiel Boylston, the doctor who joined Cotton Mather in Boston's earliest experiment in smallpox inoculation. They were a socially respectable and materially comfortable family, evident not least in Deacon Adams's ability to send his most talented son to Harvard College.[7] But their circle of influence did not extend far beyond their ancient Braintree homestead.

Adams's strongest family connections were acquired ones. With his 1764 marriage to Abigail Smith, whose mother was a Quincy, Adams gained ties to an equally ancient but much grander Braintree and Boston family. Abigail's cousin, Dorothy Quincy, had married John Hancock, heir to one of Boston's richest merchants. Two branches of the Quincy family in Braintree sat atop the local hierarchy—one headed by Colonel John Quincy (Abigail's grandfather), and the other by Colonel Josiah Quincy, who together with his older brother Edmund (Dorothy's father) won a fortune through privateering in the War of the Austrian Succession. Colonel Josiah built the grandest house in Braintree and maintained strong political ties to Boston, where his brother Edmund continued to operate as a merchant. The Quincys were good connections, but as a relation by marriage to a lesser branch of the clan, Adams could not expect them to vault him to the forefront of Boston society.[8] The Quincys paled in comparison to the grandees of Boston (let alone those of London) who patronized the young Wheatley. But as a free white Englishman and the oldest son of a landowning family, Adams could rely on the certainty of his inheritance and the liberties that the charter of Massachusetts guaranteed. Without better connections, Adams knew, as he wrote in his diary, that it was "my Destiny to dig Treasures with my own fingers. No Body will lend me or sell me a Pick axe."[9] What went unspoken was his confident assumption of the right to dig and to keep whatever treasures he found. If Wheatley coined herself in a brilliant and audacious act of literary self-rendition, Adams would slowly excavate the soil of New England's past and Britain's legal traditions, and refine the ore that he found there into a political philosophy.

Adams's most important tool for digging treasures would be his training in the law. Yet as he set out on his own practice, he "found reason to complain" of how provincial and insufficient his preparation had been under Putnam, the Worcester lawyer: "I feel the Disadvantages of Putnams Insociability, and neglect of me. Had he given me now and then a few Hints concerning Practice, I should be able to judge better at this Hour than I can now."[10] Even as his skills improved and his practice drew him into influential circles in Boston courtrooms, his inward insecurities followed him. Adams's self-revealing and voluminous diaries are filled with anxious expressions ("I used to dread J[ames] O[tis] and B[enjamin] K[ent] because I suspected they laughed at me") of awe and inadequacy ("[Jeremiah] Gridleys Grandeur consists in his great Learning, his great Parts and his majestic Manner") as he encountered the titans of the Massachusetts Bar.[11]

Chief among these lordly exemplars was Timothy Ruggles, who embodied everything that Adams longed to be: a successful lawyer and judge, a decorated military officer, a rich man, and a leader in Massachusetts politics. Ruggles represented the South Shore town of Sandwich in the General Court for many years. As an attorney in Boston, Ruggles acquired a fortune that allowed him to develop an enormous estate in Hardwick, west of Worcester. There he lived the life of a country gentleman, hosting grand dinners and riding to hounds in the deer park that he created. During the Seven Years' War, Colonel Ruggles recruited a regiment of Massachusetts volunteers, and rose to brigadier general in charge of all the forces from Massachusetts and Rhode Island. He served as second in command to Jeffrey Amherst in the 1759 assault on Fort Ticonderoga—part of the strategic plan that would culminate in Wolfe's victory over Montcalm at Quebec later that year. After the war, Ruggles's star continued to rise; he was granted a handsome sinecure (surveyor general of the king's forests), became chief justice of Worcester's Superior Court, and in 1762, speaker of the house in the Massachusetts General Court. In April 1759, Adams assessed his hero's character in the midst of this stratospheric rise: "Ruggles' grandeur consists in the quickness of his apprehension, Steadiness of his attention, the boldness and Strength of his Thoughts and Expressions, his strict Honour, conscious Superiority, Contempt of Meanness &c. People approach him with Dread and Terror."[12]

Adams eventually overcame his dread and terror, and approached Ruggles, Gridley, Benjamin Prat, Oxenbridge Thatcher, and other great legal figures of Boston, gradually winning their respect through his legal acumen. With Thomas Hutchinson and his circle, it was different. In Ruggles, Gridley, Prat, and Thacher—even in the flamboyant young James Otis—Adams saw versions of himself. All were sons of established but modest New England families, men whose talent and training in the law, more than their personal connections, had advanced them to prominence in Boston. But Hutchinson and his circle––the brothers Andrew and Peter Oliver along with their intermarried families and commercial connections that included Rowes, Fosters, Belchers, and other major figures from Boston's past—were different.[13] They were merchants of long-standing wealth, raised in some of the grandest houses in Boston, with their families attended for generations by slaves of the sort Phillis Wheatley would have become had her prodigious talent not emerged.[14] These men assumed high positions in the government of Massachusetts almost by birthright; their fathers and grandfathers had done so before them. Nevertheless, they augmented their authority by forming close connections to imperial officials who played an ever-greater role in the making of power and wealth in Boston, beginning with William Shirley in the 1740s. In their attachment to Shirley and his ilk, Hutchinson and his circle took on something of Shirley's character as an accidental Bostonian. Their attachments to the empire and its promise of advancement threatened to overshadow their local ties.[15]

As Adams found his place and dug his treasures in Boston's legal and political culture, the Hutchinson-Oliver clan was engrossing a remarkable degree of power and authority, consolidated under the administration of a new royal governor, Francis Bernard, who arrived in 1760. With their mercantile wealth (grand town houses in Boston and country estates for summers), tightly interconnected family networks, and intimate ties with Whitehall, the Hutchinson-Oliver clan seemed out of reach to the ambitious young Adams. Members of this elite circle were awarded the lucrative administrative positions that the Otises, Gridleys (and distantly, young Adams) coveted, such as the chief justiceship of the Massachusetts Superior Court, simply because of who they were and who they knew, not because they were learned in the law, as Gridley was and Adams aspired to be. To Adams, Hutchinson's clan represented a profound corruption of his ideal of republican Massachusetts, the corrosive intrusion of royal patronage into a system that had once been framed to reward talent, toil, and virtue. The same Boston circles into which Wheatley arrived by happenstance were to Adams a closed world of power bounded by corruption, and he nurtured a visceral hatred of them.[16]

John Adams Reads History

There is no small irony in the fact that Adams's hatred of Hutchinson was rooted in a quality that he shared with his nemesis: a profound immersion in the history of the Bay Colony. Hutchinson wrote a three-volume history of Massachusetts—a feat made possible by his lifelong access to extraordinary collections of the colony's records.[17] Hutchinson's sister Hannah had married Samuel Mather, Cotton Mather's son and heir to the Mather family's immense library. In addition, Hutchinson had access to documents collected by the Reverend Thomas Prince of Boston's Third Church, including the manuscript of William Bradford's *History of Plimoth Plantation*. Adams lacked this immediate access to the paper trail of the colony's founders. But as a Harvard student and avid reader, he nonetheless became well versed in the history of New England and its relationship to Britain, and in the biblical and classical models of ancient republics that influenced Boston's founding.

For Hutchinson, and for his kinsman Peter Oliver, the chief justice of the Massachusetts Superior Court who later wrote a history of the "American Rebellion," the colony's puritan origins were faintly disreputable. For them, New England puritanism was tainted by excessive religious "enthusiasm" and the colony's ties to Parliament's rebellion against Charles I, "that Catastrophe, which will ever disgrace the english Annals," and left "too great a Sympathy of Soul between the Brethren of Old and of New England."[18] But for Adams, both Massachusetts' godly republicanism and the puritan revolution in England had been noble experiments—the former an extraordinary success, the latter defeated only by the many forces arrayed against it. In Adams's view, the strongest advocates of republican government were the English writers whom he cited avidly, defenders of England's commonwealth in the 1650s and promoters of the Glorious Revolution—"Sidney, Harrington, Nedham, Neville, Burnet, and Hoadly"—even if "a man must be indifferent to the sneers of modern Englishmen" to advocate their ideas a century later.[19] These writers supplemented Adams's pride in the traditions of Massachusetts town government, the courts, and the colony government at large. Together, New England history and the English Whig tradition lay at the heart of his convictions throughout his lifelong exploration of political theory and practice.[20]

When Deacon Adams died in 1761, John inherited the family land in Braintree. Real property brought responsibilities in town government, beginning with a position as Braintree's surveyor of roads. Adams also used the money that his growing legal practice yielded to buy books—lots of books. As a member of a learned profession, like the clergymen in Boston's Mather family before him, Adams viewed a library as a cross between a gentleman's estate and an artisan's tools. He spent freely to get a good one.[21] In 1775, looking back on his financial history, with the city of Boston occupied by the king's soldiers and the house that he recently bought there inaccessible to rebels like himself, Adams complained, "Of the little acquisitions I have made, five hundred Pounds sterling is sunk in Boston in a real estate, four hundred sterling more is completely annihilated in a Library that is now wholly lost to me."[22] But what he had learned in his two decades of intense postcollege reading had by then vaulted him to a position of prominence in the Continental Congress.

The importance of his reading is evident in Adams's earliest public writings, prompted by the crisis over the Stamp Act in 1765. Later published under the daunting title *A Dissertation on the Canon and Feudal Law*, these thoughts first appeared as anonymous essays in the *Boston Gazette* in August 1765—the same month that Stamp Act rioters attacked Andrew Oliver's and Thomas Hutchinson's houses.[23] For Adams, the canon and feudal law of medieval Europe constituted "the two greatest systems of tyranny" in the history of Christendom. The canon law of the "Romish clergy" and the feudal law of "the Princes of Europe[,] . . . originally a code of laws for a vast army in a perpetual encampment," had been joined together in "a wicked confederacy" of church and state authority so that "the people were held in ignorance," and "liberty, and with her knowledge and virtue too seem to have deserted the earth." What finally rescued humanity from the clutches of this twin tyranny was God's "benign providence," which "raised up the champions who began and conducted the Reformation," allowing an increasingly enlightened populace to understand its oppression and overthrow its oppressors. In seventeenth-century England under the Stuart monarchs, James I and Charles I, this "struggle between the people and the confederacy aforesaid of temporal and spiritual tyranny, became formidable, violent, and bloody," ending in the beheading of King Charles.[24]

To this world-historical narrative, Adams applied a distinctly local twist: "It was this great struggle that peopled America. It was not religion alone, as is commonly supposed; but it was a love of universal liberty, and a hatred, a dread, a horror, of the infernal confederacy before described, that projected, conducted, and accomplished the settlement of America. It was a resolution formed by a sensible people—I mean the Puritans—almost in despair." As early as 1765, Adams already had the habit of positing the city-state of Boston as synecdoche for "America."[25] He also put the historical learning of its puritan founders at the center of Massachusetts' republican foundations: "To many of the [founders] the historians, orators, poets and philosophers of Greece and Rome were quite familiar."[26] Adams believed that the genius of New England's origins stood in diametric opposition to the tyranny of the canon and feudal law—a genius rooted in a combination of sacred and secular wisdom still accessible to contemporary readers.[27]

Adams's views in the 1760s aligned with John Cotton's image from 1630 of the typological essence of Massachusetts colonization: the founding by the apostle Paul of the church at Philippi.[28] For Adams, as for Boston's founders, the planting of Philippi as the first Christian colony in the Greek and Roman world, the marriage of "revelation and reason too," was the biblical type for the planting of Massachusetts and England's colonization of America.[29] While Britain, with its Glorious Revolution, Bill of Rights, Protestant settlement, and Hanoverian succession, had followed Massachusetts' lead in rolling back the forces of canon and feudal law, the twinned beast was not dead yet: "The canon and feudal systems; though greatly mutilated in England, are not yet destroyed." To Adams, the passage of the Stamp Act signified exactly this. The act levied taxes on newspapers, pamphlets, books, even college diplomas—all attempts to reforge the chains of superstition, ignorance, and dependency that had enslaved the mind of medieval Europe.[30]

Two months after Adams made these arguments in his *Dissertation on Canon and Feudal Law*, the townspeople of Braintree appointed him to write instructions for their representative to the General Court to address the Stamp Act crisis. Adams's instructions, also published in the *Boston Gazette*, rehearse familiar complaints against Parliament's infringement on colonists' right to consent to their own taxation. But Adams's most vivid criticism aimed at the act's attempt to institute feudal tyranny in the form of Vice Admiralty Court judges: "In these courts, one judge presides alone! No juries have any concern there! The law and the fact are both to be decided by the same single judge. . . . What can be wanting . . . but a weak or wicked man for a judge, to render us the most sordid and forlorn of slaves?"[31] Adams cites the exact language of Magna Carta that the Stamp Act violates: "No freeman shall be taken, or imprisoned, or disseized of his freehold . . . but by lawful judgment of his peers." By providing military judges to preside over a law that violates an Englishman's right to consent to taxation, the Stamp Act seemed perfectly designed to resuscitate feudal tyranny. (See plate 16.)

Parliament repealed the act in spring 1766, but in the following months, Massachusetts royal governor Bernard's sympathy with the Stamp Act's tyrannical principles continued to roil the Boston press. To this controversy Adams contributed two more anonymous letters, adopting the pen name of "Governor Winthrop," writing to "Governor Bradford," to lament that royal placemen like Bernard were violating the principles of "our favorite enterprise of planting America. We were Englishmen; we were citizens of the world; we were Christians. . . . [I]t was the unwearied endeavor of our lives to establish a society on English, humane, and Christian principles."[32] Adams here reveals his conviction that the founding principles of Massachusetts were not merely in accord with English liberties but had actually surpassed them. As "citizens of the World" and true Christians, John Winthrop, William Bradford, and their ilk had established a "supremely happy" independent commonwealth beyond anything that Britons to that point had known.

Following a year of relative peace in the wake of the Stamp Act's repeal, the resistance movement in Boston sprang back to life with Parliament's passage of the Townshend Acts in 1767, and Adams's engagement in it grew more direct. These laws placed new duties on imported goods and added enhanced enforcement measures, including the creation of an American Board of Customs Commissioners with a much-expanded bureaucracy. The year 1768 began with Adams questioning himself about his own ambitions: "I am mostly intent at present, upon collecting a Library. . . . But when this is done, it is only a means, an Instrument. . . . [M]y End will not be answered. Fame, Fortune, Power say some, are the Ends intended by a Library. The Service of God, Country, Clients, Fellow Men, say others. Which of these lie nearest my Heart?"[33] Political events would provide the answer, granting Adams fame, fortune, and power by way of service to his country and fellow men.

Adams moved his young family from Braintree into a rented house in Boston so that he could be closer to his legal practice and at the center of politics in the province. His legal skills and deep learning earned him a more prominent role in the city's turmoil, in clear opposition to Hutchinson and his circle. He continued to focus on military authority and the dangers of an established church—feudal and canon law—as the direst threats to New England's liberties. Adams declined an appointment as advocate general for the Admiralty Court (William Shirley's stepping-stone to power and military authority) as his "political Principles" and his "Connections and Friendships" set him against it. In May 1768, he published another anonymous essay in the *Boston Gazette*, decrying the Church of England's proposal to introduce an American bishop as "so flagrant an Attempt to introduce the Canon Law, or at least some of the worst Fruits of it, into these Colonies, . . . that every Friend of America ought to take Alarm."[34] In June, Adams drafted instructions for Boston's representatives to the General Court, much as he had done three years earlier for Braintree, to protest the new Customs Board's use of naval warships to enforce customs regulations, putting military authority above civil law. Adams's instructions similarly denounced the Royal Navy's impressment of Boston's civilian sailors and the rumored introduction of royal troops into the city to enforce the new customs duties. All these new measures provided reason to fear that the feudal as well as canon aspect of the design to enslave the colonies, seemingly defeated with the Stamp Act, had reemerged in the Townshend Acts.

When the king's soldiers did arrive in October 1768, the friction generated by two thousand troops stationed in a densely populated peninsula of two thousand families exploded in the so-called massacre of March 5, 1770. A detachment of soldiers under the command of Captain John Preston discharged its muskets point-blank at an angry and threatening crowd, killing five workingmen. Adams stepped further into the political fray. He served as defense attorney for the accused soldiers in their trial. Crucially for Adams's political position, this allowed him to defend the concept that Massachusetts remained a government of laws, not of men, even if Britain did not. He meant to demonstrate that the city-state of Boston was every bit Britain's equal in defense of English rights and liberties, and had no more need for soldiers to enforce the law than did the homeland.[35]

The aftermath of the massacre brought another temporary quiet to Boston's politics, during which Adams moved with his family back to Braintree. Three intense years in the political cockpit had worn on his health and his nerves. But even in rural retirement, Adams wrote an "Oration on Government" for the Braintree town meeting in spring 1772, and later that year moved back to Boston to rejoin the conflict. Renewed strife followed a declaration from Whitehall that the Massachusetts governor's salary, along with those of the colony's judges, would henceforth be paid by Crown revenues, not by the people of Massachusetts as had long been the custom, eliminating the people's last measure of control over otherwise-unaccountable royal officials.[36] Adams, now one of Boston's representatives in the General Court, responded in typical fashion, denouncing Governor Hutchinson's defense of the royal salary and composing anonymous articles for the *Boston Gazette* on the need for independent judges, not paid lackeys of the Crown.[37]

Adams was not involved in the destruction of the East India Company's tea shipments on December 16, 1773.[38] But he applauded the gesture: "This is the most magnificent Moment of all. . . . This Destruction of the Tea is so bold, so daring, so firm, intrepid and inflexible, and it must have so important Consequences, and so lasting, that I can't but consider it an Epocha in History." At the same time, Adams worried; "What Measures will the Ministry take[?] . . . [W]ill they punish Us? How? By quartering Troops upon Us?—by annulling our Charter?—by laying on more duties? By restraining our trade? By sacrifice of Individuals, or how?"[39] Answers came soon in Parliament's Coercive Acts of 1774. The Boston Port Act did punish the city by restraining its trade in the strictest manner possible, closing the port altogether until the city repaid the cost of the ruined tea. The Massachusetts Government Act did annul the colony's charter, transforming the council into an appointive body under Crown control, eliminating the autonomy of the House of

Representatives, and suspending town governments for anything but Crown-mandated business. The Administration of Justice Act, which allowed trials of customs officers accused of violating local rights to be removed to England for hearing before Admiralty Courts (the so-called Murder Act), did open the way to the "sacrifice of individuals" of all sorts. And the Quartering Act, rounding out the quartet, did grant the governor, soon to be a soldier, General Thomas Gage, a freer hand in quartering troops in Boston.

Adams's only fear that did not come to pass was the "laying on more duties." But the duties had always been the least of Adams's concerns. Once the principle of consent to taxation had been violated, the number or amount of such taxes was inconsequential. The game was lost already. Accompanying the four Coercive Acts, however, was something worse than a new tax: the Quebec Act. With its enormous expansion of the province of Quebec (nearly as large now as all the other mainland colonies combined), and its allowance for Roman Catholicism as Quebec's state-sponsored church and for Catholics to serve in the provincial government, the Quebec Act was the most blatant move yet in the ministerial design to force canon law on the colonies—a popular view among Bostonians that Paul Revere's "Mitred Minuet" print reinforced.

The destruction of the tea, the Coercive Acts, and the Quebec Act transformed Adams's life, just as they had Wheatley's, but in different ways. For Wheatley, the ensuing crisis tore apart the circuit of transatlantic connections in which she had risen to fame, and in which her poems made a coherent argument and found an appreciative audience. In the midst of the crisis, Adams had predicted that "the Town of Boston . . . must suffer Martyrdom: It must expire: And our principal Consolation is, that it dies in a noble Cause."[40] Wheatley's experience exemplified that destruction, although she would reap none of the benefits of the wealth, splendor, and power that Adams imagined might rise from the city's ashes. For Adams, the crisis pushed him outward, away from Boston and the role that he had only recently won for himself among the city's political leaders. From this point on, Adams would have little direct role in the government of Massachusetts, the formative center of his political

FIGURE 7.1. *The Mitred Minuet*, engraving by Paul Revere, *The Royal American Magazine* 1, no. 15 (1774). The bishops are dancing their minuet around a copy of the Quebec Act on the floor, with Lord North, Lord Bute, the devil, and a bag-piping Scotsman looking on with approval.

imagination. For the next phase of his career, he would serve as a diplomat to foreign congresses and courts (beginning with the Continental Congress), and an apostle of the city-state of Boston as a republican model. His vision of his home colony's government had been forged by his reading of history, and by the writings it inspired him to compose in defense of Massachusetts' resistance to canon and feudal tyranny. Now he was ready to spread the news.

The Search for Stability within Crisis

As the imperial crisis neared its climax, Adams continued to argue in favor of the traditional charter government of Massachusetts, its autonomy from Parliament, and eventually its independence from the Crown. By the time he wrote his *Novanglus* essays in late 1774 and early 1775, royal authority was collapsing. In Massachusetts, an ad hoc provincial legislature was meeting in Concord as the de facto government. The king's government, now in the hands of General Gage, barely reached beyond occupied Boston. Adams likened

Gage's predicament to the Dutch Revolt against Spain in the sixteenth century: "We are in this Province . . . at the Brink of a civil War. Our Alva, Gage, with his fifteen Mandamous Councillors, are Shutt up in Boston, afraid to Stir, afraid of their own shades, protected with a Dozen Regiments of Regular soldiers, and strong Fortifications, in the Town, but never moving out of it."[41] In December 1774, the loyalist Daniel Leonard, Adams's former legal colleague and now one of Gage's handpicked councillors, launched a series of essays in the Boston press under the awkward pseudonym of "Massachusettensis." Leonard's essays called on the colony to draw back from the brink of rebellion. Adams responded under his own pseudonym, "Novanglus," arguing that New England's republican tradition and Britain's departure from government by law justified the colony's move toward independence.

Like Wheatley just a few years before in her "Ode to Dartmouth," Adams turned to the biblical story of Joseph to think through the problem of political "slavery." Leonard's essays had attempted to pin the blame on the Whigs, the resistance movement, for the "present calamity." Adams responded by referring to "another story, which I have read in the Old Testament. When Joseph's brethren had sold him to the Ishmaelites for twenty pieces of silver, in order to conceal their own avarice, malice, and envy, they dip the coat of many colors in the blood of a kid, and say that an evil beast had rent him in pieces and devoured him." Adams casts Massachusettensis, in company with Hutchinson, Oliver, and former royal governor Bernard, as Joseph's brothers, hoping to disguise their guilt for having sold Joseph—the colony and its resistance leaders—into slavery. But Adams reminds the Tory writer that "what the sons of Israel intended for ruin to Joseph, proved the salvation of the family," and expresses his belief that Boston's resistance leaders will have the magnanimity, "like [Joseph], to suppress their resentment, and the felicity of saving their ungrateful brothers."[42] A little more than two years earlier, in a more hopeful moment, Wheatley had imagined herself as Joseph in exactly this magnanimous state, able to feel the pangs of a parent whose child had been snatched away into slavery, but capable of forgiveness when proper order was restored to Israel.[43] By February 1775, Adams's hope that righteous Whigs could be charitable toward chagrined Tories was rapidly dissipating.

In his seventh *Novanglus* letter from March 6, 1775, with civil war in Massachusetts looming, Adams revisited the histories of colonies and parent states, from ancient Greece and Rome down to the present, focusing on Massachusetts and Britain. Here, Adams offered a simple definition of a republic: "If Aristotle, Livy, and Harrington knew what a republic was, the British constitution is much more like a republic than an empire. They define a republic to be a *government of laws, and not of men*. If this definition be just, the British constitution is nothing more nor less than a republic, in which the king is first magistrate."[44] In Adams's view, the essence of a republic was this: that laws, not men, be the ultimate source of authority, regardless of the state's institutional organization. Adams's purpose for introducing this definition was not to demonstrate that Massachusetts was a republic but instead to show that Britain was not really an empire in order to clarify Boston's proper relationship to British authority.

For Adams, "an empire is a despotism, and an emperor a despot, bound by no law or limitation but his own will."[45] Leonard had addressed his Massachusettensis letters "To the Inhabitants of the *Province* of Massachusetts Bay." In eighteenth-century terminology, the word "province" implied that Massachusetts had been annexed to the realm of Britain and was therefore subject to Parliament's laws. In the same sense, Scotland was, since the 1707 Acts of Union, a province of Great Britain. By contrast, Adams deliberately chose to address his Novanglus letters "To the Inhabitants of the *Colony* of Massachusetts Bay," reverting to the seventeenth century's terminology to emphasize his point that the Bay Colony had never been annexed to England or Great Britain by any formal statute or agreement. Massachusetts' only connection to the present government of Britain was through the person of the king, the descendant of Charles I who had granted the original charter. Parliament, Adams argued, had played no role in constructing this relationship. The only authority that Massachusetts and the kings of England had ever recognized for Parliament over Massachusetts was in the Navigation Acts. Even these, the Massachusetts General Court had freely agreed to adopt of its own sovereign volition, by voting the Navigation Acts into Massachusetts law in the General Court.

Adams applied exactly the same logic to parliamentary dominion over Massachusetts that Lord Mansfield had recently used to decide the question of a slave owner's dominion over James Somerset. Parliamentary taxation without consent was tantamount to slavery, depriving people of the fruits of their labor without permission. As Mansfield had argued, slavery was so "odious" as to require a "positive law" to make it valid. But since Adams could find no such positive law granting Parliament dominion over Massachusetts, he judged that the colony, like Somerset, must be discharged from any such odious dominion as well. Adams had rehearsed this reasoning earlier in the crisis, in his 1772 draft for the House of Representatives' reply to Hutchinson's defense of Parliament's sovereign authority over the colony. There, he cited a 1676 case from Massachusetts history, cleverly drawn from a volume of historical papers that Hutchinson himself had published: "That no Law is in Force or Esteem there, but such as are made by the General Court; and therefore it is accounted . . . a Betraying of the Liberties of their Commonwealth, to urge the Observation of the Laws of England."[46]

In *Novanglus*, Adams went on to show that throughout European history, colonizing powers had often allowed their colonies to govern themselves. When the Greeks planted colonies, they "neither demanded nor pretended any authority over them, but they became distinct independent commonwealths." Adams cited James Harrington's *Oceana* (1656), a utopian model commonwealth with a similar vision of widespread land distribution, to show that the Roman Republic planted colonies in Italy that "were always allow'd all the rights of Roman citizens, and were govern'd by senates of their own."[47] Adams rejected Massachusettensis's claim "that when a nation takes possession of a distant territory, that becomes a part of the state equally with its ancient possessions." In Adams's learned judgment, "The practice of free nations, and the opinions of the best writers, are in general on the contrary."[48] Here, as throughout his career, Adams defended the principle that from its first charter onward, Boston in New England was autonomous, like the city-states of the ancient world.

So long as the charter government of Massachusetts continued to function, even with a royally appointed governor, the colony had been capable of defending its autonomy in exactly these terms, as an independent commonwealth with a "senate" of its own. *Novanglus 6* argued that in the 1760s, Parliament's attempts to subvert these rights with the Stamp Act and Townshend Duties "had been defeated. The charter Constitution of the Massachusetts Bay, had contributed greatly to both these defeats." Note how clearly, even before the outbreak of war and Declaration of Independence, Adams identifies the colonial charter as the "Constitution" of Massachusetts: "By this constitution the people had a check on every branch of power, and, therefore, as long as it lasted, parliamentary taxation, &c. could never be enforced."[49] But events after 1770, beginning with the controversy over the governor's and judges' salaries, and extending through the tea crisis and Coercive Acts, all showed the Hutchinson junto's plan to undermine the Massachusetts Charter. To Adams, it was obvious that "the port bill, charter bill, murder bill, Quebec bill, making altogether such a frightful system, as would have terrified any people, who did not prefer liberty to life, were all concerted at once."[50] With the Massachusetts Charter now in ruins, there was no longer a legal basis on which to resist the canon and feudal tyranny threatened by the Coercive Acts. In a measure as "desperate" as that of the puritan founders of Massachusetts who fled the tyranny of Charles I and Archbishop Laud, delegates from the Bay Colony turned to their fellow British colonies for support in a Continental Congress.

From here, events moved swiftly. A month after *Novanglus 6* and *7* appeared, General Gage's troops attacked Lexington and Concord on April 19, 1775. The Second Continental Congress soon transformed the New England militias that turned out in the tens of thousands to defend their towns into a Continental Army. Boston lay under siege. On June 17, Gage's soldiers, in concert with Royal

Navy warships, attacked and burned Charlestown across the river from Boston, giving the Continental Army its first brutal defeat. Fifteen hundred men were killed or wounded on both sides. As summer gave way to a long cold winter, conditions in the city deteriorated, with smallpox and starvation looming. Adams's younger brother, Elihu, died of dysentery while serving as a captain in the Braintree militia laying siege to the city.[51]

Adams returned to the Continental Congress, but its "Olive Branch" petition to the king was brushed aside. On August 23, George III declared the colonies to be in open rebellion. On December 22, Parliament passed the Prohibitory Act, or as Adams described it, "The Act of Independency. . . . It throws thirteen Colonies out of the Royal Protection . . . makes us independent in Spight of all our supplications and Entreaties."[52] In Adams's view, the colonies had been forced into independence through the open hostility of Britain's government. If the king was now making war on the colonies, endorsed by his government in Parliament, then any pretext of dependency must be abandoned. To encourage the recalcitrant colonies (New York, Pennsylvania, South Carolina, and Georgia) to act on the Crown's "gift" of independence, Adams turned his pen to the task of describing an ideal form of republican government that other colonies might adopt as independent states.

This pamphlet, *Thoughts on Government*, published in Philadelphia in spring 1776, formalized ideas that he had been developing in private correspondence and diaries for some time. Yet as it was grounded in New England's tradition of republican government, Adams's model was blind to the varied political economies and governing traditions of other colonial regions, where the populations were far more divided between rich and poor, free and bound, and much less devoted to participatory self-government than Massachusetts. The other colonies would not, in fact, want Adams to "come over and help us." *Thoughts on Government* was doomed to fail.

On November 15, 1775, Adams had written to Richard Henry Lee, delegate from Virginia to the Continental Congress and fellow proponent of independence, who had been "polite enough to ask me for this model." The main points of his hasty sketch are worth quoting in full, as they spell out Adams's ideal of a republic, a civic Sermon on the Mount:

> A legislative, an executive, and a judicial power comprehend the whole of what is meant and understood by government. It is by balancing each of these powers against the other two, that the efforts in human nature towards tyranny can alone be checked and restrained, and any degree of freedom preserved in the constitution.
>
> Let a full and free representation of the people be chosen for a house of commons.
>
> Let the house choose, by ballot, twelve, sixteen, twenty-four, or twenty-eight persons, either members of the house, or from the people at large, as the electors please, for a council.
>
> Let the house and council, by joint ballot, choose a governor, annually, triennially, or septennially, as you will.
>
> Let the governor, council, and house, be each a distinct and independent branch of the legislature, and have a negative on all laws. . . .
>
> Let all officers and magistrates, civil and military, be nominated and appointed by the governor, by and with the advice and consent of his council. . . .
>
> Let the judges, at least of the supreme court, be incapacitated by law from holding any share in the legislative or executive power; let their commissions be during good behavior, and their salaries ascertained and established by law.
>
> Let the governor have command of the army, the militia, forts, &c.
>
> In this way, a single month is sufficient, without the least convulsion, or even animosity, to accomplish a total revolution in the government of a colony. . . . [H]uman nature would appear in its proper glory, asserting its own real dignity, pulling down tyrannies at a single exertion, and erecting such new fabrics as it thinks best calculated to promote its happiness.[53]

This sketch closely echoes an account Adams wrote a decade earlier describing the actual government of Massachusetts, as should be no surprise.[54] The "model" that Adams casually dashed off to Lee was a generalized version of Massachusetts' colonial constitution, combining the best features of its first and second charter eras.[55]

During the early months of 1776, prospects for colonial independence lurched rapidly forward. In January, Thomas Paine's *Common Sense* demolished conventional wisdom about the king as the people's protector and the colonies' dependence on Britain. Paine convinced many readers that the continental colonies were ready to be self-sustaining. Adams agreed, but he abhorred Paine's design for the government of a free American nation, especially its unicameral popular national legislature, which would subvert the integrity of the individual colonies. Amid the more temperate conversations within the Continental Congress, where several colonies remained reluctant to discuss independence at all, four other delegates, in addition to Lee, asked Adams for a written statement that they might use in drafting constitutions for their home states.[56] In response, Adams published *Thoughts on Government* in April, just weeks before Congress resolved that each colony should create its own independent constitution.[57]

Thoughts on Government reiterated the description of a model republic that Adams had offered in his January letter to Lee. But Adams added elements designed to make the Massachusetts model more appealing to other colonies. During the first half of 1776, prompted by Paine's *Common Sense*, many colonies, including Massachusetts, had heard proposals for unicameral legislatures in the new state governments. Adams addressed this (to him, horrifying) possibility head-on. He admitted that many different forms of republics had existed in the past,[58] but using examples drawn from seventeenth-century English and Dutch history, he described the vices that plague all republics that adopt a "single assembly."

Adams also drew from Massachusetts history to recommend measures to promote the security and virtue necessary for a republic, including "a militia law, requiring all men . . . to be provided with arms and ammunition, to be trained at certain seasons," as well as "laws for the liberal education of youth, especially of the lower class of people, . . . [and] no expense for this purpose would be thought extravagant."[59] He knew these ideas would never be adopted by the "Bashaws" of the South. Universal male military service and lavish spending on public education for the poor would not appeal to slave-owning planters, as they had to Boston's puritan founders.

Adams also recommended a collective frame of government for the thirteen colonies. He supported the sovereignty and self-determination of each colony: "They should be left entirely to their own choice of the forms." But once the states had made their own constitutions, "if a continental constitution should be formed," Adams believed that "it should be a congress . . . and its authority should sacredly be confined to these cases, namely, war, trade, disputes between colony and colony, the post-office, and the unappropriated lands of the crown, as they used to be called. These colonies, under such a form of government, and in such a union, would be unconquerable by all the monarchies of Europe."[60] Adams's argument appeared in print months before the Continental Congress drafted the Articles of Confederation, which would closely resemble his outline.

Adams had strong faith in his model for a confederation, as it too had an antecedent in New England history. The United Colonies, or New England Confederation, formed in 1643 with Connecticut, New Haven, and Plymouth, and led by Massachusetts, had been a military alliance that successfully defended the interests of the city-state of Boston for most of the seventeenth century. As we saw in book I, the martial republican culture nurtured across the region defeated French, Dutch, and Native American rivals for New England's territory, and deposed a British military tyrant in 1689.[61] By April 1776, when Adams's pamphlet was published, the strength of New England's military resistance had forced Britain's high command to abandon Boston and give up on crushing the American rebellion at its New England source. Adams was no soldier, but why wouldn't he imagine that thirteen independent states, each framed on the Massachusetts model and joined together after the fashion of the New England Confederation, would be equally unconquerable?

This was an exhilarating moment. Adams closed his *Thoughts on Government* with a peroration to the fictive colleague whom the pamphlet addressed: "You and I, my dear friend, have been sent into life at a time when the greatest lawgivers of antiquity would have wished to live. . . . When, before the present *epocha*, had three millions of people full power and a fair opportunity to form and establish the wisest and happiest government that human wisdom can contrive?"[62] As Adams looked ahead, determined to be an apostle for just such a wise and happy government, two primary goals shaped his hopes for the future. The first was to assure that Massachusetts would cross the divide from royal colony to independent state with its republican legacy intact. The second was to promote his vision within a new, as yet unknown configuration of national and international power, where the republicanism that the city-state of Boston embodied would hold greater sway. Both tasks were challenging. The first required correcting the imbalances left behind when the weight of nearly a century of royal government was lifted. The second involved persuading other new states to adopt New England's republican principles, building a durable confederation among these states, and representing the interests of the confederacy at large in the fierce world of international diplomacy.

The Massachusetts Constitution: Restoring Balance to the Kingless Commonwealth

Adams's part in the making of the Massachusetts Constitution happened almost by accident, as a momentary diversion from his work in national and international diplomacy. From 1775 onward, the Continental Congress kept Adams away from Boston and its politics, although as a dedicated correspondent he was never uninformed.[63] Congress commissioned Adams as an American diplomat, first in France in 1778–79, then later to the Netherlands and Britain, keeping him overseas for most of the next decade. Nonetheless, a brief interlude during Adams's foreign service allowed him to intercede in drafting the Massachusetts Constitution. The constitutional process in Massachusetts took far longer than most of the other states because Adams's fellow citizens took their task so seriously. In 1778, the towns rejected a first attempt, written by the Massachusetts legislature in 1777, in part because a frame of government drafted *by* a sitting legislature lacked sufficient independence *from* the legislature to be considered fundamental law.[64] Legitimacy to the structure of government under the old charter had been conferred by the power of the king. What could confer such legitimacy now that there was no king? In 1779, Massachusetts answered this question by calling for a separate convention of the people (not the legislature) to draft a constitution. This method would represent the will of the sovereign people as something separate from the actions of a sitting legislature. Just at that moment, Adams returned home from France. Braintree chose Adams as a delegate to the convention, which met in Cambridge in September and appointed a subcommittee to prepare a draft. The subcommittee turned the task over to Adams, and it fell to him to address the imbalance created in the structure of Massachusetts government by the removal of the royal governor—a powerful element in place since 1691.

From the moment in May 1776 when the former colonies began constructing independent governments, there had been agitation in many states to eliminate executives altogether. The rapacity of royal governors, their lack of accountability to the colonial population, and the disfavor into which the king had fallen created a sharp backlash against anything that smacked of monarchical authority. Across the colonies, royal portraits were taken down from public buildings, and crowds destroyed royal statues in public squares. In Boston, the main thoroughfare from the town house to the Long Wharf, formerly called King Street, became State Street. In Massachusetts, the loudest opposition to governors came from rural districts where popular uprisings in the wake of the Massachusetts Government Act in 1774 had resisted the royal appointment of mandamus councillors, judges, and sheriffs, and the suspension of town meetings.[65] The town of Petersham, in the western part of Worcester County, wanted no governor for fear that the people would be "Droved into parties By the influence of Rich and Powerful Men."[66]

Adams understood these sentiments. No one had hated the royal sycophants who had dominated colonial offices more than he. But the intensity of these feelings in summer 1776 made him fear for the stability of the commonwealth.[67] His political vision, grounded in his assessment of humanity's sinful nature, convinced him of the need for a government balanced among the one, the few, and the many. This was not an endorsement of hereditary monarchs and aristocrats, as Adams made plain time and again: "Rulers are no more than attorneys, agents, and trustees, for the people; . . . the people have a right to revoke the authority . . . and to constitute abler and better agents, attorneys, and trustees."[68] Adams also opposed highly stratified or hierarchical societies, writing to Patrick Henry of Virginia in June 1776 that the age of "the Dons, the Bashaws, the Grandees, the Patricians, the Sachems, the Nabobs" was at an end: "The Decree is gone forth . . . that a more equal Liberty, than has prevail'd in other Parts of the Earth, must be established in America."[69]

Nevertheless, Adams believed that some degree of inequality was inherent in the human condition; it was the social equivalent of a Newtonian law in physics, "as infallible a Maxim, in Politicks, as that Action and Re-action are equal, is in Mechanicks. . . . [T]he Ballance of Power in a Society, accompanies the Ballance of Property in Land." For Adams, this meant that the availability of land for people at every level of society was essential to reducing the extremes of inequality that could destabilize a republic: "I believe these Principles have been felt, if not understood in the Massachusetts Bay, from the Beginning."[70] The greatest danger to a successful republic came from the aristocratic element in society, accumulating excessive amounts of land and power when left unchecked by an executive charged with protecting the common people's interests and rights. In Adams's view, this had caused the breakdown of British government because a weak young king, George III, had been unable to prevent the great lords of Parliament from plotting with the local Boston aristocrats—Hutchinson and his circle—to deprive the colony of its rights. This was likewise Adams's fear for the future of Massachusetts without a strong executive endowed with veto powers to check the schemes of Boston's grandees.[71] Adams insisted that the legislature of a republic must have *three* balanced elements within it: a lower or democratic house, an upper or aristocratic house, *and* a popularly elected executive to protect the people's interest, each with a veto on the other two.

In preparation for the Constitutional Convention, Adams reread his own *Thoughts on Government*, along with Harrington's *Oceana*. Then in the space of a month, he turned out a draft that included a bicameral legislature, along with a powerful governor, "whose Title shall be—HIS EXCELLENCY," yet accountable to the citizens by means of annual popular elections.[72] Adams's draft contained a striking innovation in the composition of the Senate and its manner of representing the interests of "the few."[73] In some of the other new states, and in Massachusetts' charter tradition, the lower house elected the upper house. But since independence, in the absence of antagonistic royal governors, this method of selection made the upper house overly dependent on the lower house, unable to check the whims of the more popular branch.[74] To remedy the problem, Adams returned to the logic of Harrington's *Oceana* and the example of early Massachusetts in his belief in the "infallible" axiom that "power always follows property."

Adams devised a scheme to confine aristocratic power to a single house within the legislature by linking the Senate to the interests of property. In contrast to the House of Representatives, where delegates would be elected in proportion to the population in the state's various districts, Adams designed the Massachusetts Senate to represent not people but property. The Senate would consist of "forty persons" chosen by the inhabitants of districts laid out so that "the numbers to be elected by the respective districts" depended on "the proportion of the public taxes paid by the said districts."[75] The General Court would assess the property values for each county and proportion the number of senators by the relative value of each county's taxable property. Wealthy Suffolk County, where Boston lay, would be entitled to elect six senators. Poor and remote counties like Lincoln and Cumberland in the district of Maine would get only one senator, or in the case of the island counties of Nantucket and Martha's Vineyard, half a senator each.

By Adams's logic (ratified by the Massachusetts towns with relatively little discussion), this method guaranteed representation for an inescapably powerful element within any society, the interest of property, but confined it to a single house. The conflict between the few (in the Senate) and the many (represented in the lower House of Representatives) would be transparent for all to see. This conflict could be balanced and adjudicated by a powerful governor, elected annually by the people, with at least a partial veto on all laws.[76] This striking innovation in the formation of the Senate, the most important deviation of the new Massachusetts Constitution from the colonial charter, was intended to solve the problem of adjusting the balance within government among competing elements in society now that independence had removed the power and influence of the Crown. But in his efforts to solve this problem, Adams inadvertently created two new ones that would erupt in violent conflict after the new constitution's ratification in 1780.

Shays's Rebellion: The Massachusetts Regulation of 1786–87

The first problem stemmed from Adams's insufficient understanding of the role of commerce in the political economy of the city-state of Boston. The concept of property embodied in the Senate was rooted in land. The equitable distribution of land had indeed been a strong element creating a stable polity in early New England. But commercial wealth and movable property had come to dominate the economy of the Bay Colony over its first century and a half, and Adams's republican theorizing did not account for this. Adams's political beliefs emerged from his experiences as a rural yeoman farmer trained in the law and as a reader of history. He had never grappled directly with overseas commerce, as had been common among leading figures of the seventeenth century such as John Hull and Samuel Sewall, or the eighteenth, including royal governors Jonathan Belcher and Thomas Hutchinson. Even through his visceral hatred, Adams could admit that no one had a better grasp than Hutchinson on the complexities of "coin and commerce."[77] Adams drew on older writers such as Harrington for his belief that "the Ballance of Power in a society, accompanies the Ballance of Property in Land"—not an unreasonable position in the context of mid-seventeenth-century England.[78]

By contrast, commerce was for Adams something more frivolous and dangerous within a republican government. In October 1775, with the port of Boston closed by occupying soldiers and New England's overseas trade stifled, Adams wrote to James Warren, asking, "How long will or can our People bear this? I Say they can bear it forever—if Parliament Should build a Wall of Brass, at low Water Mark, We might live and be happy."[79] From the perspective of most Bostonians, this was an eccentric definition of happiness, to say the least. The merchant John Hull had entertained such a notion at a particularly glum moment in the 1680s—and then promptly dismissed it. Adams persisted. Six months later, after the British evacuation of Boston, he wrote to Mercy Otis Warren, expressing his fears for the future: "The Spirit of Commerce, Madam, . . . is incompatible with that purity of Heart, and Greatness of soul which is necessary for an Happy Republic."[80] Adams's new colleague in the Continental Congress, the plantation-owning Thomas Jefferson, would have agreed. But John Hull knew better. Commerce was the lifeblood of Boston. It brought value to the land and generated the revenue of the commonwealth. Commerce had always been essential to Boston's happy republic. Without the benefits of overseas trade and the internal circulation of goods, the productive capacities and consumer demand of New England would collapse. But Adams, swayed by French physiocrats, political economists such as François Quesnay and Anne-Robert-Jacques Turgot who believed that agriculture was the only true source of wealth, and who influenced Jefferson and the Virginia dynasty's nineteenth-century American expansion, failed to appreciate the role of commerce in the political economy that Boston's merchants and New England's farmers had together developed over the previous century and a half.[81]

In his desire to craft a frame of government that restored a proper balance between people and property (conceived primarily as land),

Adams failed to account for how Massachusetts' independence would influence commerce in all its manifestations of credit and debt, money and goods, and their fluid forms of circulation. In its first decade as an independent state, the Commonwealth would experience a crisis of a sort that it had never encountered during the colonial period: a deep schism between Boston and the countryside. This division was not reducible to the interests of the many versus the few in the terms that history taught Adams to fear. Rather, the division was created by the new government's inability to regulate the commercial challenges of money, credit, debt, and taxation.

A second problem engendered by Adams's innovative design for the upper house involved the way that it altered the influence of local elites throughout the commonwealth, and increased tensions between Boston and the hinterland. Under the old charter system, when the lower house elected the council, men held in high esteem for their wealth, wisdom, family connections, and service to the commonwealth were commonly chosen regardless of their place of origin, and returned again year after year. Because the upper house was selected by the lower, it tended to underrepresent Boston and the wealthier towns of the east, as these towns were underrepresented in the lower house as well. Boston sent four deputies to the House of Representatives, often referred to as the "Boston Seat." A few other large towns like Salem would send two deputies, but most other towns in the commonwealth sent one apiece. Boston's population was in many cases tenfold or more larger than that of country towns. Collectively, the rural towns' population was vastly overrepresented in the lower house compared with Boston and therefore elected a disproportionate number of non-Bostonians to the council.[82] In addition, the colonial council's twenty-eight members always included, by rules of the 1691 charter, eight men from regions that were once the separate colonies of Plymouth and Maine, even though these sparsely populated areas held far less than a quarter of the colony's population. This anomaly meant another avenue into the upper house for rural elites. Ultimately, where the councillors came from mattered less than the kind of citizens they were. The old system tended to favor regional power brokers, such as the grandees of the Connecticut River Valley (the so-called River Gods) or the Otis clan from Barnstable County on Cape Cod, members of prosperous families of good standing in their own regions.

The Massachusetts Constitution of 1780 provided a more systematic version of the idea of selecting elites for the Senate by creating defined electoral districts based on property. But it altered the older structure by creating a formal geographic quota—a cap on the number of senators from each county. The wealthy eastern counties of Suffolk, Essex, and Middlesex were now guaranteed to have six, six, and five senators, respectively. The poor and remote counties such as Barnstable, Cumberland, and Lincoln were now confined to one senator apiece.[83] The quotas allowed far fewer opportunities for local elites from these poorer regions to serve in the upper house, no matter how long or how well they served their communities, no matter how prominent they were in regional affairs, no matter what connections they had in Boston.

These two new problems, the failure of the state constitution to account for the power of commercial wealth, and a restructured upper house that limited traditional elites' access to power, generated a violent crisis. In 1774, when Parliament's Massachusetts Government Act had mandated the replacement of an elected council with one handpicked by the royal governor, rural Massachusetts erupted in mass protest and intimidated the mandamus councillors into resigning their positions. At that time, the protesters believed that a corrupt cabal of conspirators, in league with the king's ministers and their lackeys in Parliament, were seeking to create "lordships" over the small landowners of rural Massachusetts.[84] A decade later, the urban and commercial Senate sponsored new tax laws, designed to pay off the state's war debt and stabilize the state's currency for the sake of restoring overseas trade. These taxes, requiring payment in specie (silver coin), oppressed the farmers and landowners of the rural interior, and a similar eruption occurred for nearly identical reasons. The demand for payment in silver (just as the Stamp Act had required) threatened to ruin land-rich but cash-poor farmers to the benefit of Boston's moneyed men. The county courts were the instrument of enforcement for the hated foreclosures that took men's farms in lieu of their taxes. The ensuing insurrection, labeled "Shays's Rebellion" by its enemies but more often called the "Regulation" by its supporters, articulated the fear that now "lordships" over the state's farmers would be created, not by a guilty cabal of Tory aristocrats, but by the transparent designs of financial speculators and moneyed interests in the Senate, through legislative control over the state's newly independent fiscal policy.

The eastern interests called this rebellion "Shays's" in order to discredit it. One of its ostensible leaders, Daniel Shays of Pelham, was a nobody—a recent arrival in his western Massachusetts town with no family, no history, and no connections. But the reality was quite different. The bulk of the participants and most significant leaders were not poor and isolated, like Shays. Rather, the Massachusetts Regulators (so named because "Regulation" was an eighteenth-century term for a public uprising against legislators who failed to satisfy popular demands) were led and supported by close-knit families of long-standing importance in the rural towns of Massachusetts, often headed by power brokers who were now excluded from the upper ranks of government in Boston. Examples include Amherst's Moses Dickinson, who "had been elected selectman, town moderator, and state representative more times than most townsfolk could remember," Colonel Benjamin Ely of West Springfield, "a wealthy landowner and easily the most popular man in town, elected selectman seven times, town moderator six times, state representative five times," and Job Shattuck, a selectman, war veteran, and the largest landowner in Groton. None of these men became a member of the post-1780 Senate. The choice to call this a rebellion and to name it after Shays was meant to distract attention from the fact that the Regulation's leaders were public spirited men of substance with a stake in the commonwealth.[85]

The moneyed interests of Boston put down the Regulation with force. Governor James Bowdoin, who fifteen years earlier entertained Wheatley with rebuses about Boston as a town of "gaiety and sport," now hired Benjamin Lincoln, the former revolutionary general, to lead a mercenary army (not the state militia) to suppress the insurrection. In so doing, they drove a divisive wedge into the integrated political economy of Massachusetts, which the seventeenth-century leadership of Boston had been so careful to construct, and that had held together through the turbulence of the eighteenth-century imperial conflict. When the redcoats under General Gage occupied Boston and attacked its neighboring towns, the militiamen from all over New England turned out to defend their liberties and liberate Boston from the king's army of oppression. A dozen years later, these same rural soldiers and their sons prepared to fight against a mercenary army paid for by Boston's homegrown speculators and bankers, who could no longer be seen as simply a corrupt extension of alien royal and aristocratic interests.[86]

The constitutional structure that Adams devised and the people ratified inadvertently promoted this rift in the commonwealth's political economy by keeping the rural spokesmen of the old order out of the newfangled Senate, and giving the Senate's concentrated wealth the power to block the House's efforts to ease the people's burdens. But other aspects of the new constitution helped to heal this division. Many scholars view the so-called Shays's Rebellion as a political disaster because fervent proponents of the US Constitutional Convention in 1787, such as James Madison of Virginia, chose to view it that way: as a sign that republican government within even the most carefully governed state was disintegrating without a powerful national government that could intervene in a crisis.[87] But unlike the violent rupture of 1774 that it seemed to resemble, the Massachusetts Regulation of 1786–87 was a success for exactly the reasons that Adams had shaped the constitution to promote. The critical factor that prevented this crisis from cleaving a permanent split in the commonwealth's political economy was the constitution's mandate for annual elections. In the aftermath of the military defeat of the Regulators, Governor Bowdoin, who organized the mercenary army at the behest of Boston's speculators, was defeated by a three-to-one margin in the next year's election by a more popular candidate, John Hancock. The newly elected legislature radically revised both the tax policy and the enforcement mechanisms for its collection, to the enormous relief of the state's debtors.[88] Plans to retire the state's war debt and stabilize the currency were put on a more gradual schedule. This "Regulation" of the government by the people when the workings of the legislature failed, together with a republican constitution designed to give voters frequent opportunities to replace their representatives, resolved this crisis without the need for external intervention.

The transformation from a royal colony to a fully independent commonwealth was traumatic for Massachusetts. John Adams, and the thousands of Massachusetts voters who endorsed the constitution he drafted, collectively endeavored to restore the best features of the autonomous republic that the city-state of Boston had created in the seventeenth century. But eighty-five years of royal government, from the charter of 1691 to independence in 1776, had upset the political balance and economic integration created in the seventeenth century under the first charter. King and Parliament had prevented Boston from coining its own money or creating its own banks, depriving it for eight-five years of the fiscal power it needed to regulate its own economy. The commonwealth was economically far less equal in 1776 than it had been in 1691, and that too added to the trauma of independence. Yet in the end, the state's efforts to restore its republican traditions weathered the storms of this first decade of independence.

Adams was already overseas in 1780 when the Massachusetts convention completed its deliberations on the draft constitution he produced. In fact, he had left the convention for Braintree and was preparing his return to France when on November 9, 1779, a delegate to the convention made a motion that the word "Massachusetts" in the first paragraph of the constitution be removed, "and that the word 'Oceana,' be substituted in its stead."[89] The motion was defeated—the commonwealth kept its ancient name—but the debt that Adams's draft owed to English republican thought was nonetheless obvious.

Adams would devote the years from 1776 to 1788 to promoting his model of republican government to the other new states in the American confederation and representing the interests of that confederation in negotiations with the great powers of Europe. But as a cranky apostle for the New England way in the larger world,

Adams would not achieve the same success he had in preserving the republican government of Massachusetts. He began his diplomatic career hopeful of the potential to remake the world beyond New England. He ended it deeply disillusioned about the once enthralling notion that the "cause of Boston" had ever really been the cause of all America.

Diplomat to the American Republics: Fear of the "Eternal Yoke"

It is common to think of the Continental Congress and Articles of Confederation that formalized its operations as poor precursors to the US Constitution—faulty rough drafts for a permanent national government. But it would serve us well to remember that as the delegates from a dozen distressed colonies gathered in Philadelphia in 1774, their Congress was more like the subsequent Congress of Vienna in 1815, a diplomatic meeting among sovereign states of differing characters and constitutions, than a consolidated national government. We should think of John Adams's *diplomatic* career as beginning in summer 1774, when he left New England for the first time as part of the Massachusetts delegation to a congress of some (but not all) of the quasi-sovereign states from across the American continent. It was exactly in this sense that Adams outlined his vision of a future union of these states in *Thoughts on Government*: "It should be a congress, containing a fair and adequate representation of the colonies, and its authority should sacredly be confined to these cases, namely, war, trade, disputes between colony and colony, the post-office, and the unappropriated lands of the crown, as they used to be called."[90] These "cases" were all those issues beyond the scope of any one colony's authority and therefore subject to negotiation among them all.

Adams imagined that this new confederation would resemble the New England Confederation of the seventeenth century in which Massachusetts was the dominant partner over Connecticut, New Haven, and Plymouth—smaller, weaker colonies with flimsier patents or charters, which nonetheless shared Massachusetts' commitment to godly republicanism. Over the next year and a half in Congress, Adams realized that Massachusetts would have to contend with a set of stronger and far more diverse sovereign equals in this new confederation. Massachusetts would not be the biggest and strongest member, and Boston would not be the confederation's metropolis, even if its plight had been the cause that called the congress into being. His private correspondence soon revealed mounting skepticism, even pessimism, that the southern states could become republics comparable to those of New England.

On November 25, 1775, Adams wrote from Philadelphia to a Massachusetts colleague, Joseph Hawley, who was worried that the Continental Army would disintegrate without sufficient "Encouragement to the Privates" in the form of "Some Small Bounty given them, on the Inlistment." Hawley's concern launched Adams into a revealing discussion of the differences between New England and southern traditions of military and public service, and the differing characters of the societies and constitutions of these regions:

> An opinion prevails among the Gentlemen of the Army from the Southward, and indeed throughout all the Colonies, excepting New England, that the Pay of the Privates is too high and that of the officers too low. . . . Gentlemen in the other Colonies, have large Plantations of slaves, and the common People among them are very ignorant and very poor. These Gentlemen are accustomed, habituated to higher Notions of themselves and the Distinction between them and the common People, than We are, and an instantaneous alteration of the Character of a Colony, . . . cannot be made without a Miracle. I dread the Consequences of this Dissimilitude of Character. . . . [I]t is very hard to be linked and yoked eternally, with People who have either no opinions, or opposite opinions, . . . at the same Time that you have all the Monarchical superstitions and the Aristocratical Domination, of Nine other Colonies to contend with.[91]

Here, Adams is disparaging "monarchical" not in the constitutional sense of an executive power but instead with respect to the "superstition" necessary to believe that particular families are hereditarily endowed with superior governing abilities.

Four months later, even as he carefully delineated his public position for *Thoughts on Government*, Adams's private view remained unchanged, as he revealed in a letter to the English-born Continental Army general Horatio Gates:

> All our Misfortunes arise from a Single Source, the Reluctance of the Southern Colonies to Republican Government. . . . The Difficulty lies in forming Constitutions for particular Colonies, and a . . . Continental Constitution for the whole, each Colony should establish its own Government, and then a League should be formed, between them all. This can be done only on popular Principles and Maxims which are so abhorrent to the Inclinations of the Barons of the south, and the Proprietary Interests in the Middle Colonies, as well as to that Avarice of Land, which has made upon this Continent so many Votaries to Mammon that I Sometimes dread the Consequences.[92]

"I dread the Consequences" became Adams's steady refrain as he contemplated the union of New England's republican traditions with the barons of the South and their boundless hunger for land.

The South's response to *Thoughts on Government* further discouraged Adams's hopes. Virginia began its Constitutional Convention immediately after the May 15, 1776 resolution. Carter Braxton, an extremely wealthy plantation owner and Virginia delegate to the Continental Congress, published a pamphlet in direct response to Adams's *Thoughts on Government*, which he denounced as utterly unsuitable to the history, temperament, and society of Virginia's leaders:

> Schemes like these may be practicable in countries so steril by nature as to afford a scanty supply of the necessaries and none of the conveniences of life: But they can never meet with a favourable reception from people who inhabit a country to which providence has been more bountiful. They will . . . gather estates for themselves and children without regarding the whimsical

impropriety of being richer than their neighbours. These are rights which freemen will never consent to relinquish.

Braxton recommended a government for Virginia extraordinarily different from what Adams had suggested, including an elected executive who would serve under "good behavior" and an upper house that would serve for life, a plantation equivalent of a constitutional monarch and House of Lords. Although similar in cameral structure to the Massachusetts model, Braxton's proposal promoted an oligarchy unrestrained by frequent popular elections.[93]

Here, spelled out in full, were Adams's fears about the "inclinations of the Barons of the south" whose "higher Notions of themselves" created a "Dissimilitude of Character" between New England and the rest of the states. He tried to make the best of the situation, writing to Virginians like Patrick Henry whose notions of themselves were not quite so high as Braxton's, the grandson of Robert "King" Carter, Virginia's largest slave owner. Adams hoped that Henry's influence on the Virginia Constitution might soften Braxton's aristocratic pretensions, even if some features of the Massachusetts model (annual elections) were "too frequent, for your Colony. . . . The Usages and Genius and Manners of the People, must be consulted." Regardless of Virginia's differences from New England, Adams confirmed to Henry his aspirations: "For every Colony to institute a Government—for all the Colonies to confederate, and define the Limits of the Continental Constitution—then to declare the Colonies a sovereign State, or a Number of confederated Sovereign States—and last of all to form Treaties with foreign Powers." Having done what little he could to influence the first of these steps, Adams now turned to the last two.[94]

International Disappointments: Constitutions in Need of Defense

In the task of declaring the colonies to be a sovereign state, Adams became one of the most vocal advocates for independence in the Continental Congress. Although Virginians' reason for promoting independence differed from those of Boston, Adams happily cooperated with Virginia delegates such as Richard Henry Lee to achieve their common goal.[95] Adams joined the drafting committee, and although Jefferson composed the text, the logic of the Declaration of Independence followed precisely the argument that Adams had spelled out in his *Novanglus* essays of 1775.[96] Adams had asserted that the American colonies had never been formally annexed to the realm of England and therefore had never fallen under the authority of Parliament. Their connection to Great Britain came only through the person of the king, by way of the charters or proprietary patents that the king's royal ancestors had granted. Therefore, when the current king declared those colonies out of his protection and made war on them, independence was already an established fact. The Declaration of Independence merely served to confirm to a candid world the reasons for formalizing this separation, with a lengthy indictment of the king's efforts to destroy the ancient political bands that his ancestors had forged with the colonies.

If declaring the former colonies to be a league of sovereign states was conceptually a simple task, forming treaties with foreign powers was far more complicated. Within the new American confederation, there were widely varying opinions about what kinds of foreign alliances would best suit the United States. Nor could the foreign powers of Europe be expected to accommodate easily this infant confederation. Britain's traditional enemy, France, was the obvious ally for the colonies' war against Britain, and sometime in March or April 1776, Adams sketched some brief "Notes on Relations with France":

> Is any Assistance attainable from F[rance]?
> What Connection may We safely form with her?
> 1st. No Political Connection. Submit to none of her Authority—receive no Governors, or officers from her.
> 2d. No military Connection. Receive no Troops from her.
> 3d. Only a Commercial Connection, i. e. make a Treaty, to receive her Ships into our Ports. Let her engage to receive our

> Ships into her Ports—furnish Us with Arms, Cannon, Salt Petre, Powder, Duck, Steel.[97]

Once again, Adams based his policy ideals on his understanding of the glorious New England past. His notes coincide precisely with his descriptions, from the *Dissertation on the Canon and Feudal Law* to the *Novanglus* essays, of the way that Boston and the New England Confederation had dealt with imperial authority. The seventeenth-century Bay Colony had accepted no governors and no troops from the Crown, and had acknowledged Parliament's Navigation Acts only by passing them in its own legislature, as though ratifying a treaty.

If France were to become an ally in winning American independence, it would be pointless to gain French aid by replicating the very terms that had forged the shackles of dependency under British rule. Adams rhetorically interrogated his friend James Warren on precisely this point in April 1776: "But We ought to form Alliances. With Whom? What Alliances? You don't mean to exchange British for French Tyranny. No, you don't mean to ask the Protection of French Armies. No. We had better depend upon our own. We only Want, commercial Treaties."[98] In June 1776, Congress appointed Adams to a committee "to prepare a plan of treaties to be proposed to foreign powers." Adams took over the task personally, transforming his brief notes into a fully formed plan for a treaty with France.[99] This so-called Model Treaty offered the king of France little more than access to the markets of the new American confederation in exchange for opening France's markets (including the French West Indies) to American merchants. If this commercial alliance drew France into America's war against Britain, then the United States would promise neither to assist Britain against France nor to make a separate peace with Britain. France in turn would promise not to invade or conquer any territory of the United States, or any British territories on the North American continent adjacent to the United States, such as Florida or Nova Scotia. Congress adopted Adams's Model Treaty in September 1776, and sent the first US diplomatic commission, consisting of Benjamin Franklin, Arthur Lee of Virginia, and Silas Deane of Connecticut, to France to begin negotiations.

Over the course of the next year, a dispute between Lee and Deane undermined the US commission, and Congress selected Adams to replace Deane. But by the time Adams arrived in Paris in April 1778, Franklin, Lee, and Deane had signed both a commercial treaty *and* a treaty of political and military alliance. France pledged its military and naval power in support of the war effort until American independence was won. Adams's diplomatic vision for the American confederacy had been defeated before his work had even started. The United States was already encumbered by a military alliance that "might embarrass Us in after times and involve Us in future European Wars."[100] Here, Adams was at his most prophetic. The French alliance created entanglements for the United States that would later be the undoing of Adams's own term as president. But at the moment of his arrival in France, the fact of these new treaties rendered the purpose of his mission moot.

Despite this initial disappointment, overseas diplomacy remained central to Adams's career for the next decade. He returned to France in 1780, moved on to Britain to begin possible peace negotiations in 1781, served intermittently in the Netherlands, where he secured loans to support the American war effort, and finally became the first diplomat of the United States to the Court of Saint James. Compared with the remarkable eleven years from 1765 to 1776, though, when the obscure country lawyer from Braintree vaulted into national prominence, the eleven years from 1777 to 1788 were ones of disappointment and frustration. Much of the time he was separated from his wife, Abigail. Adams's anxious personality, social awkwardness, and limited skill in modern languages all made a diplomat's life uncomfortable.[101] Before his first arrival in Paris, Paine's *Common Sense* had been published there in an abridged edition (removing much of its antimonarchical tirades) and mistakenly attributed to an "M. Adams" (the French confused Paine with Boston's radical leader, Samuel Adams). When John Adams turned out to be neither of these, and more conservative than both, his reputation plummeted. Among the self-styled radical political thinkers that he encountered in Europe, he found his most cherished notions about the nature of republican government disputed and scorned.[102]

In particular, Adams was stung by criticism of the new American state constitutions from Turgot, former French minister of finance, physiocrat, and radical philosophe. In 1778, Turgot wrote to the English radical, Richard Price, disparaging the bicameral legislatures and executive powers in many of the new American constitutions—exactly those things Adams had fought to preserve for Massachusetts. Turgot, Condorcet, and other French republican thinkers had met Franklin in Paris in 1777, and had much admired the unicameral legislature and absence of a governor in the constitution that Pennsylvania adopted in 1776. Unicameral democracy accorded with their notion that a truly representative government would dispense with the ancient royal, aristocratic, and clerical orders, and place the power of the nation directly in the hands of the people. As Adams later remembered these events, when he arrived in France for the second time in 1780, "I carried a printed copy of the report of the Grand Committee of the Massachusetts Convention, which I had drawn up; . . . Mr. Turgot, the Duke de la Rochefoucauld, and Mr. Condorcet and others, admired Mr. Franklin's Constitution and reprobated mine. Mr. Turgot, in a letter to Dr. Price, printed in London, censured the American Constitution as adopting three branches, in imitation of the Constitution of Great Britain. The intention was to celebrate Franklin's Constitution and condemn mine. I understood it, and undertook to defend my Constitution, and it cost me three volumes."[103]

Twenty years after the fact, Adams misremembered the sequence of events. Turgot had written his letter to Price in 1778, the year before Adams drafted the Massachusetts Constitution. But Adams did not mistake the spirit of Turgot's critique, which was indeed aimed at the mixed republican forms that Adams had promoted in *Thoughts on Government*. In his letter of 1778, Turgot condemned the state constitutions: "By most of them the customs of England are imitated, without any particular motive. Instead of collecting all authority into one center, that of the nation, they have established different bodies; a body of representatives, a council, and a Governour, because there is in England an House of Commons, a House of Lords, and a King."[104] Turgot's letter reveals how little he understood the deep roots of Adams's design for the frame of government that the philosophes disparaged. The Massachusetts Constitution was not a slavish imitation of English political institutions but rather the expression of more than a century of successful republican government in New England.

To Turgot's challenge, Adams responded in characteristic fashion: he read, studied, and wrote. The "three volumes" that Turgot's challenge "cost" Adams appeared as *A Defence of the American Constitutions*, his longest published work. Adams assembled a vast array of sources on the history of republics, from ancient Greece through recent times, to write a commanding rebuttal of Turgot's attack. Although he would later misremember this detail as well, Adams was *not* prompted to write the *Defence* by Shays's Rebellion or the US Constitution, as he was immersed in its composition before news of the Massachusetts Regulation reached him.[105] The first two of the three volumes were published in London before Adams would learn the results of the 1787 Constitutional Convention, and he finished the third volume before leaving for Boston in April 1788. Together, these volumes offer a sprawling survey of the history of Western republics in all their variety: modern republics, ancient republics, opinions of philosophers, opinions of historians, and so on, ad infinitum. Adams's essential message, repeated again and again, is neatly summarized in a passage on medieval Florence: "So simple an invention as a separate executive . . . is a full remedy against the fatal effects of dissensions between nobles and commons. [W]hy should we still finally hope that simple governments [i.e., unicameral legislatures] or mixtures of two ingredients only, will produce effects which they never did and we know never can?"[106] That Turgot and Condorcet were incorrect to favor a "concentrated" government in a single legislature, Adams never fails to point out. But the gospel of balance that preserved Massachusetts' independent republic failed to persuade the French philosophes, and its apostle returned to his home shores. (See plate 17.)

On his arrival in Boston in June 1788, Adams found that the world at home had changed dramatically. Four months earlier, a convention representing the people of Massachusetts had ratified the US Constitution written in Philadelphia the summer before. The vote was close: 187 in favor, 168 opposed.[107] The Constitution's many opponents had expressed exactly the objections implicit in Adams's earlier writings. His *Thoughts on Government* had called for a confederation of states with its authority "sacredly confined to . . . war, trade, disputes between colony and colony, the post-office, and the unappropriated lands."[108] These were the powers to which the Articles of Confederation had limited the Continental Congress. During his absence in Europe, he had come to believe that these powers should be slightly expanded, especially to raise a national revenue through customs duties and to strengthen the nation's diplomatic corp. But Adams stopped short of advocating anything like what the Philadelphia convention recommended: a representative continental republic with sovereign power over the people.

From the time of his first encounters with southern delegates in the Continental Congress, Adams had dreaded the consequences of the "Dissimilitude of Character" between New England and the rest of the union, fearing it would be "very hard to be linked and yoked eternally, with People who have . . . opposite opinions." In Adams's absence from the Massachusetts ratifying convention, other Bostonians expressed comparable sentiments. James Winthrop, the son of Adams's favorite college professor and lifelong correspondent John Winthrop, made the same argument: "It is impossible for one code of laws to suit Georgia and Massachusetts. They must, therefore, legislate for themselves. Yet there is, I believe, not one point of legislation that is not surrendered in the proposed plan."[109] Under the new constitution, not only were Massachusetts and Georgia yoked together, but the powers granted to the national legislature vastly exceeded the "sacred" few that Adams had countenanced a

1

Plate 1.
The Bloody Massacre Perpetrated in King Street, engraving by Paul Revere, 1770.

Plate 2.
The Engagement at the North Bridge in Concord, engraving by Amos Doolittle, 1775.

2

Plate 3.
Rendition of Anthony Burns, pencil sketch by George DuBois, 1854. Detail. Burns is the figure in the center of the cavalry-led column, wearing a top hat with hands clasped and cuffed. The marines' horse-drawn artillery is at the rear of the column, nearest the Old State House.

Plate 4.
Royal charter of the Massachusetts Bay Company, 1629. Detail.

3

kinge of England Scotland
Royall ffather kinge Frances
Raigne Hath given and
England in America and
from the Equinoctiall Line
Landes from Sea to Sea.
Mynes of Gould and Silv
ffraunchises and preheminen
That the saide Ilandes o
Christian Prince or Stat

4

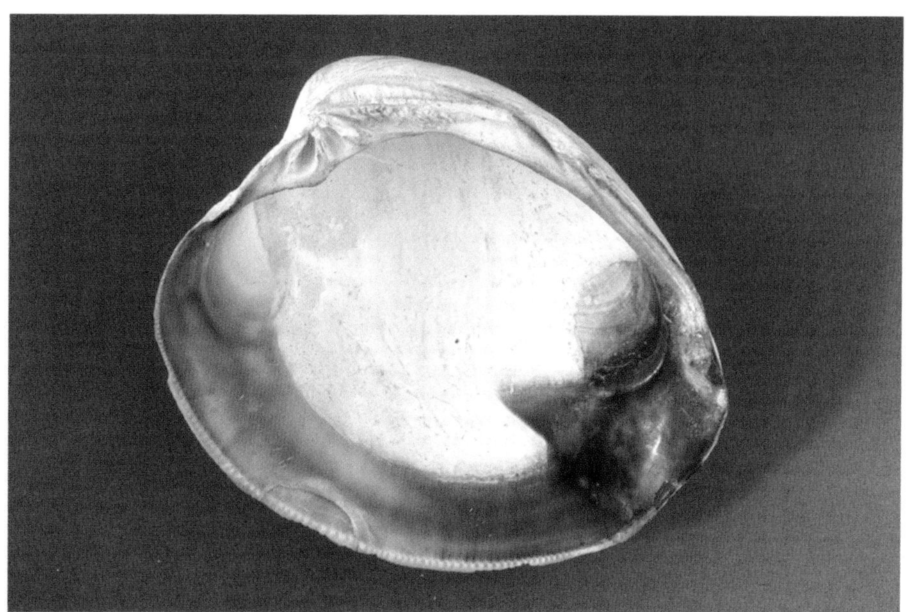

a

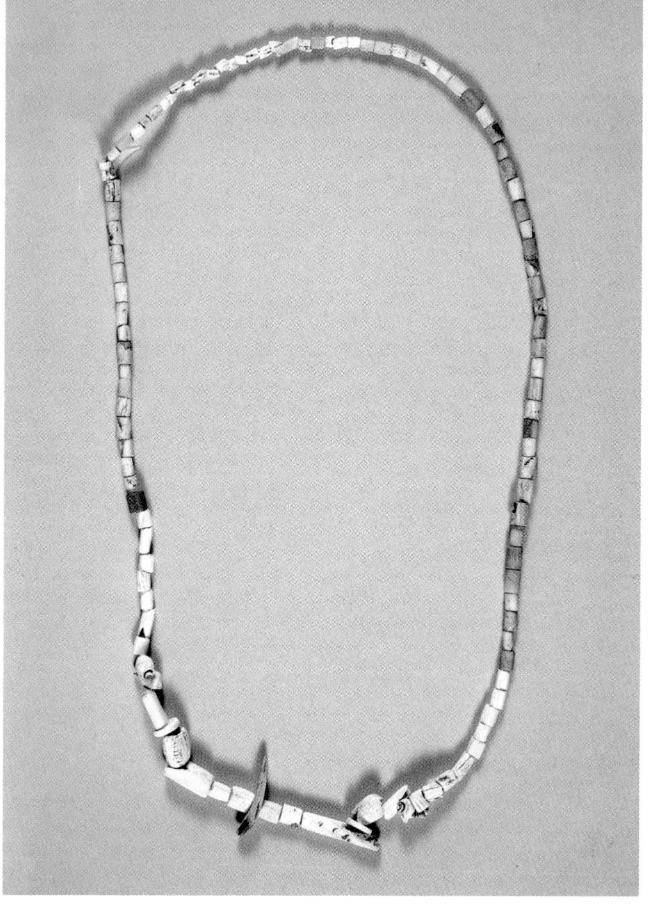

b

Plate 5.
(a) Quahog shell for making wampum.
(b) String of white and purple wampum, ca. 1650, excavated from Seneca Powerhouse site, Lima, New York, likely made by Long Island Sound Indians for the Dutch Hudson River trade.

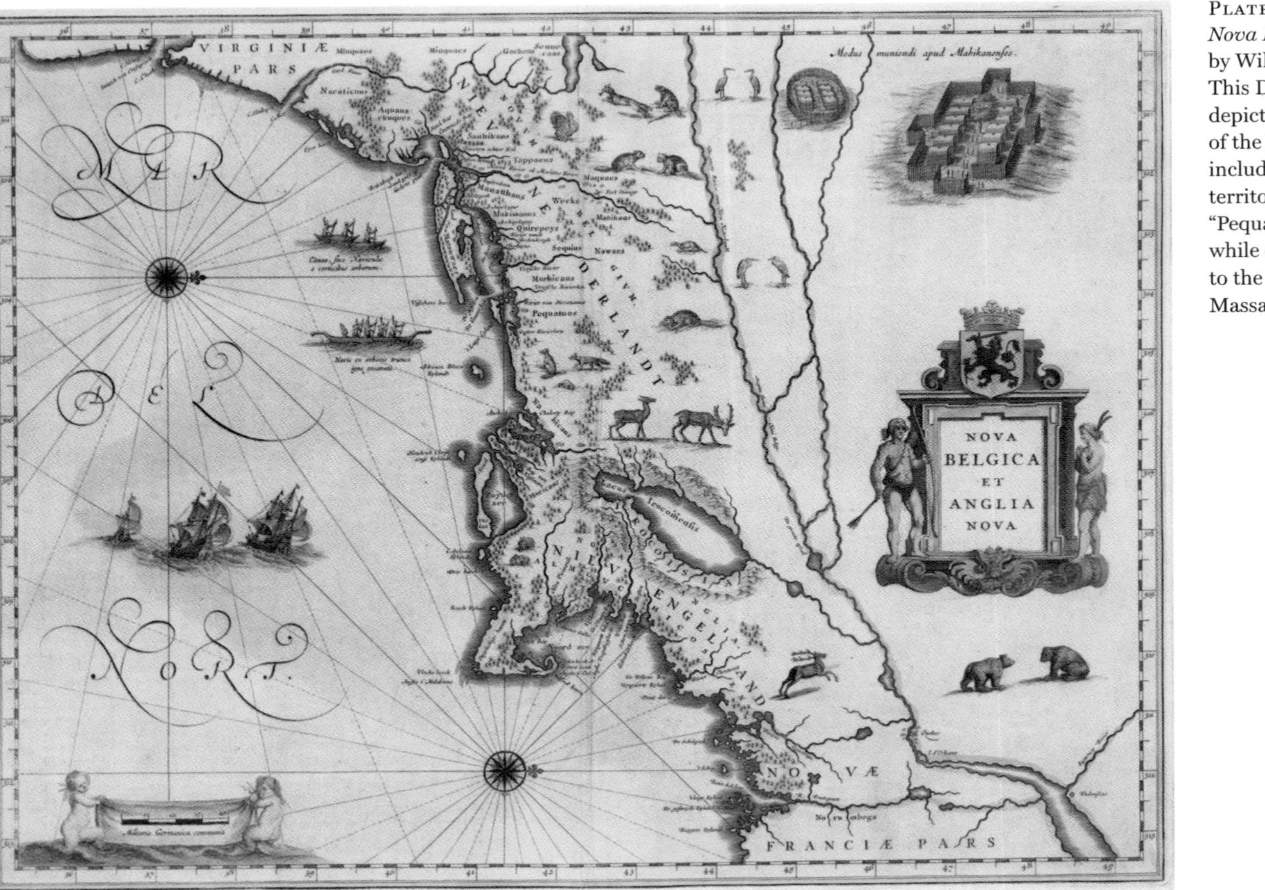

Plate 6.
Nova Belgica et Anglia Nova,
by Willem Janszoon Blaeu, 1635.
This Dutch cartographer's map depicts the extensive land claims of the New Netherland colony, including the wampum-producing territory of the "Morhicans" and "Pequatoos" on Long Island Sound, while confining "Niev Engeland" to the coastal regions along Massachusetts Bay.

Plate 7. Spanish eight reales coin of Philip II, silver, 1595.

Plate 8. Massachusetts shilling coin, silver, 1652.

Plate 9. Massachusetts pine tree shilling, silver, 1652. The "pine tree" designation was the invention of later collectors and numismatists—nothing in the colony records indicates any specific types of trees as the intention of the mint under Hull's direction.

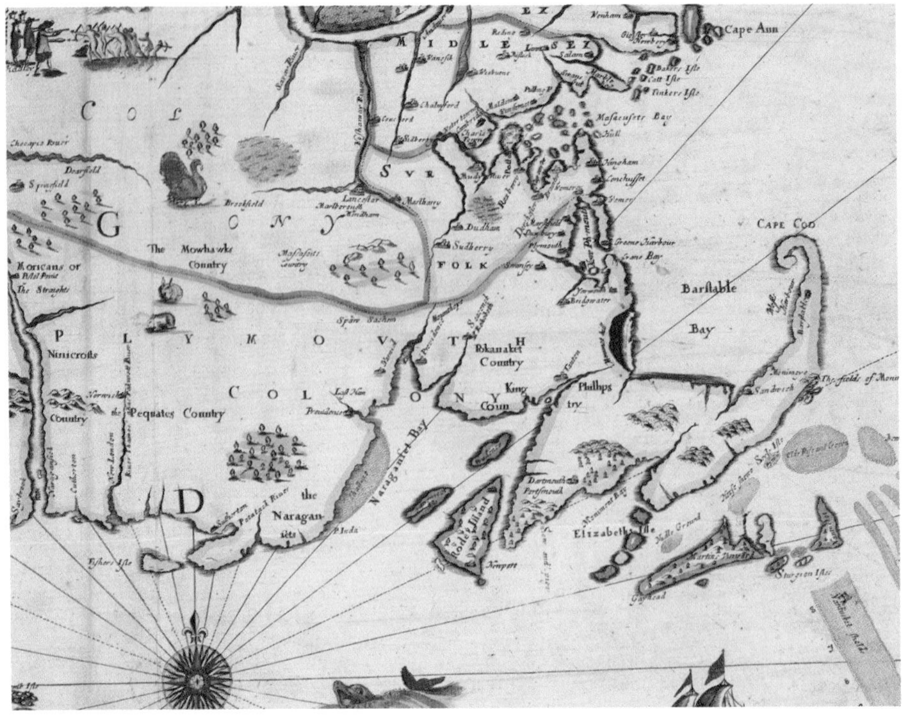

PLATE 10. *A Map of New England*, by John Seller, 1675. Detail. Seller's map depicts "King Phillips Country" on the east side of Narragansett Bay and puts "the Naragansets" on its far southwestern edge.

PLATE 11.
Captain Thomas Smith, self-portrait, ca. 1680.

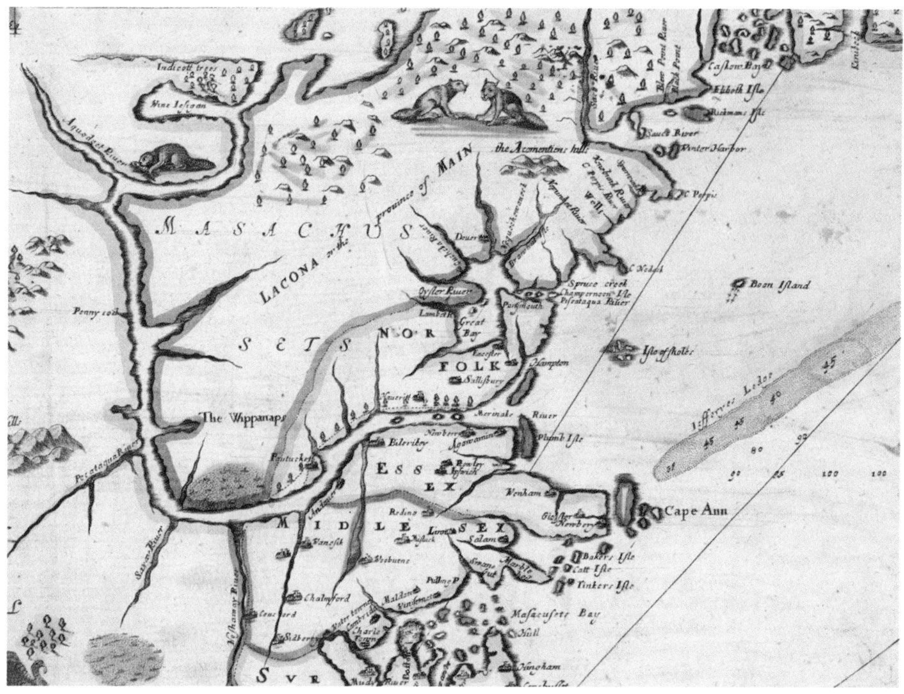

Plate 12. *A Map of New England*, by John Seller, 1675. Detail. Here, Seller's map labels all the territory north of the Merrimac River, outlined in pink, as part of "Massachusets," regardless of the Mason and Gorges claims.

Plate 13.
Portrait of Samuel Sewall,
by Nathaniel Emmons, 1728.

Plate 14.
Portrait of Paul Mascarene, by John Smibert, 1729.

Plate 15.
Portrait of William Shirley, by Thomas Hudson, 1750.

Plate 16.
Portrait of John Adams,
by Benjamin Blyth, ca. 1766.

Plate 17.
Portrait of John Adams,
by John Singleton Copley, 1783.

PLATE 18.
Portrait of Fisher Ames,
by Gilbert Stuart, ca. 1807.

PLATE 19.
Portrait of Josiah Quincy III,
by Gilbert Stuart, 1806.

Plate 20.
Portrait of Daniel Webster, by Francis Alexander, 1835.

Plate 21.
Portrait of George Ticknor, by Thomas Sully, 1831.

Plate 22.
Unfinished Portrait of Edward Everett, by Gilbert Stuart, 1820.

Plate 23.
Portrait of George Gordon, Lord Byron, in Albanian Dress, by Thomas Phillips, 1813.

PLATE 24.
Portrait of Samuel Gridley Howe, in the dress of a Greek soldier, by John Elliot, ca. 1822.

PLATE 25.
Portrait of Thomas Handasyd Perkins, by Thomas Sully, 1831–32.

Plate 26. *Bird's Eye View of Boston*, by John Bachmann, 1850. Detail. Bachmann's image shows Bulfinch's new Massachusetts State House looming above the old town house of colonial times, which had served as a meeting place for both town and colony governments. The older building clearly faces east, toward Long Wharf and the sea, while the new State House faces the land.

PLATE 27. *Brook Farm*, by Josiah Wolcott, ca. 1846.

PLATE 28. *Prospekt von Boston gegen der Bucht am Hafen*, by Francois Xavier Habermann, ca. 1776.

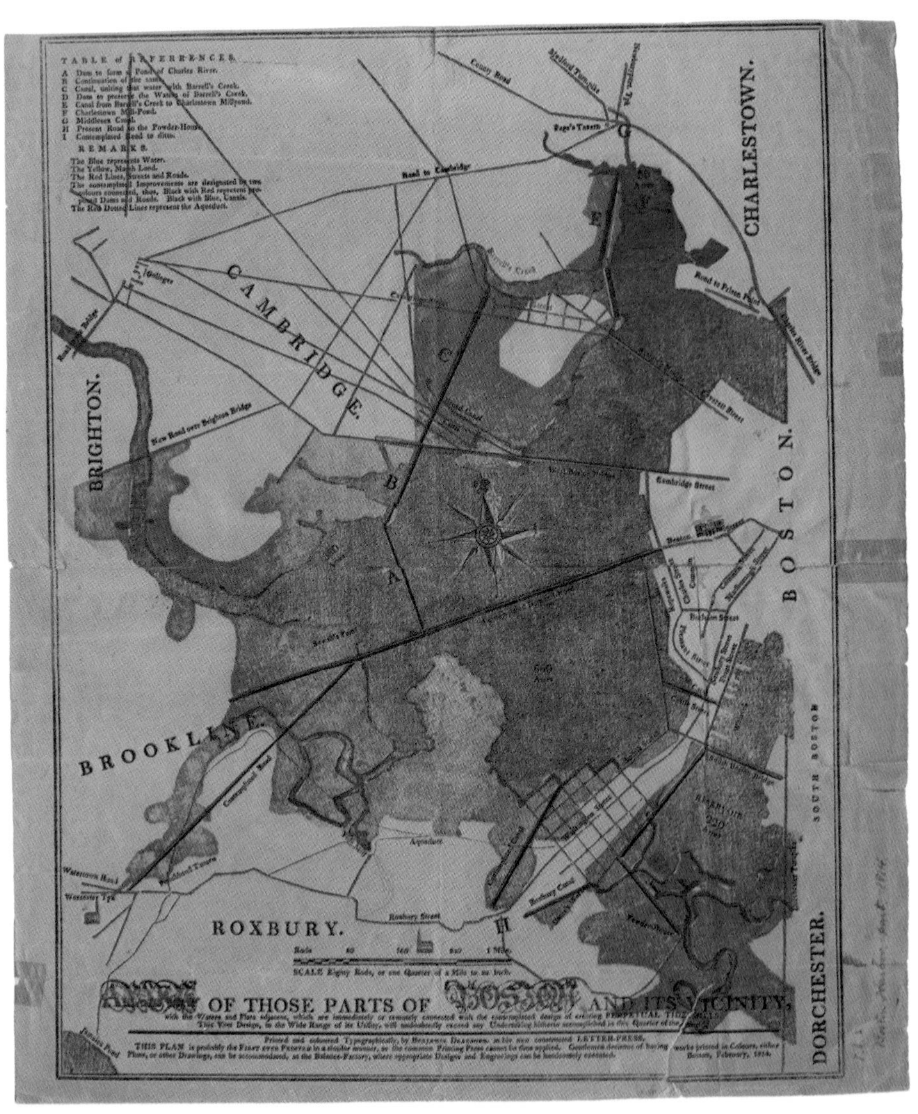

PLATE 29. *A Plan . . . of Boston*, by Benjamin Dearborn, 1814.

decade earlier. Winthrop proposed that the Philadelphia Constitution be rejected out of hand, and the powers of the existing confederation instead be expanded to include an impost and a strengthened system of diplomacy.[110] In the end, its Massachusetts opponents were unable to defeat the US Constitution outright. But they did achieve consensus around a recommended set of amendments for the first Congress to consider, should the remainder of the states vote to ratify.

Adams returned to Massachusetts in 1788 to a fait accompli, much as he had arrived to one in Paris in 1778. As in Europe, he accommodated himself to a change he had not welcomed. The fact that the US Constitution mandated a bicameral legislature and a strong executive, with a (limited) veto over legislation, assuaged some of Adams's fears. At least this was not Paine's unicameral national legislature. Furthermore, the intricate method that the convention devised for the electoral college required that the electors from each state, with two votes each for president, must cast one of their votes for a candidate from a state other than their own. Because of the virtual certainty that Washington would receive one vote from every delegate, a non-Virginian was likely to finish second and become vice president. So it went for Adams: he was swept into high office in a continental republican government that he had never hoped to see.

In this context, Adams's newly published *Defence of the Constitutions of America* was interpreted as something it was never meant to be: a defense of the US Constitution of 1787. By accepting the position as the first vice president, Adams seemed implicitly to endorse this interpretation. Yet he had further private criticisms of the new national constitution. The scale of the republic alarmed him, as did the "southern yoke." In his eyes, the office of the president was not powerful enough to fully check the legislature. Adams would have preferred an absolute veto for the executive, just as he recommended in drafting the Massachusetts Constitution. And he thought that the Senate had been given too much power over what should have been the president's executive appointments. To remedy these perceived defects, he embarked on a rhetorical campaign to elevate the status of Washington by insisting on grand, quasi-monarchical titles such as "His Excellency"—exactly the same title he had proposed for the governor of Massachusetts.

Although it may be difficult to recall in the era of the modern imperial presidency, the term "president" for a head of state had little precedent in the 1780s. The word sounded lowly, like the moderator of an occasional meeting, compared to a distinguished term like "governor." Adams thought elevated titles might make up for the formal powers the president lacked. But when General Washington rejected this language for fear of being seen as a tyrant, a Caesar in the making, Adams looked foolish, as though his years in Europe had turned him into a monarchist, transformed by his experience among crowned heads and aristocrats from the radical republican he had been in 1776. In this perceived change, and in the failures of Adams's presidency in the later years of the 1790s in the wake of the French Revolution, his enemies' assessment of Adams as a backward-looking monarchist took hold—an assessment that culminated in Wood's description of Adams as "irrelevant" after 1787.

John Adams had not changed his position on the nature of republican government. What had changed was the political context in which he attempted to project this vision. In the heady days of 1774 to 1776, when nine other British American colonies beyond the nation of New England had somehow come to agree for the moment that the cause of Boston was the cause of all America, Adams had been beguiled into believing that the republican strategies of early Boston, laid out in the first charter of the Bay Colony, shaped by the Massachusetts General Court in its relationship with the Crown and united into the New England Confederation with its satellite colonies, could be projected onto all of America and create "such a union" as to "be unconquerable by all the monarchies of Europe." In 1780, he had succeeded in refashioning the constitution of the Commonwealth of Massachusetts in line with his vision of republican government.

But the other states of the union, and especially Virginia, did not want Massachusetts to "come over and help us." They failed to see the need to remake themselves on the egalitarian principles that Adams recommended. Harrington was not for them; no proposals to adopt the name "Oceana" were made in Virginia's constitutional convention. Instead, Virginia and its allies proposed a new union that consolidated the states into a single national government with direct powers of taxation over the people, much like Parliament asserted in the 1760s. In his *Novanglus* essays of 1775, Adams had staked his entire political philosophy on the claim that Parliament had no such authority, that nowhere in common law, statute, or diplomatic agreement had Massachusetts ever been "annexed to the realm" of Great Britain where Parliament ruled. But as of February 1788, Massachusetts had annexed itself to the realm of the United States. By a narrow vote, and with an appended list of amendments that it earnestly hoped the new government would adopt, Massachusetts had performed its own positive act of self-annexation, just months before Adams returned from his decade of diplomacy. That John Adams, the most important theorist and the most effective practical advocate for the independence of republican Massachusetts, a man whose preparations for seizing such an opportunity had made his career, was now so discordant within the national government as to be labeled a monarchist by the barons of the South, did not bode well for the city-state of Boston's ability to preserve its identity and thrive under the authority of the United States of America.

Book III

A New King over Egypt

> Now these are the names of the children of Israel, which came into Egypt; every man and his household came with Jacob. Reuben, Simeon, Levi, and Judah, Issachar, Zebulun, and Benjamin, Dan, and Naphtali, Gad, and Asher. And all the souls that came out of the loins of Jacob were seventy souls: for Joseph was in Egypt already. And Joseph died, and all his brethren, and all that generation. And the children of Israel were fruitful, and increased abundantly, and multiplied, and waxed exceeding mighty; and the land was filled with them. Now there arose up a new king over Egypt, which knew not Joseph.
>
> —Exodus 1:1–8

Much of the heritage of colonial Boston and New England survived the exodus from the British Empire, and found safety and comfort in the new confederated nation created by the rebellious former colonies to support Boston in its plight. The Commonwealth of Massachusetts retained a form of republican government derived from the best aspects of its colonial traditions. The church of the puritan founders remained its established religion. Although many of Boston's leading merchants departed in the Loyalist exile of 1776, they were quickly replaced by new men, new families, replicating their patterns of overseas commerce in light of new opportunities. Names such as Winthrop, Mather, Leverett, Dudley, Cotton, and Quincy were joined by Cabots, Lowells, Higginsons, Lawrences, and others new to the city. The city of Boston recovered from the destruction of wartime, rebuilt and prospered; the New English Israelites were fruitful and increased abundantly, and multiplied, and waxed exceedingly mighty.

The national government found its footing and moved from New York to Philadelphia on its way to permanent residence in the new federal city of Washington. But it became evident that the preponderance of its power lay in the hands of people who no longer recalled the time when the cause of Boston was the cause of all America or that the union had been founded by the collective states to prevent the destruction of any single member. Although Boston's representatives promoted a politics based on consensus around measures of mutual benefit to all, they found themselves instead under the thumb of persistent majorities, presided over by the Virginian dynasts, who were willing to promote policies as destructive to Boston as those of past Parliaments and kings. The city's merchants and manufacturers, too, discovered that a new king arose over the nation's commercial life, King Cotton, a monarch that demanded bound labor as the price of its own prosperity and insisted that all the confederation's members honor its right to slaves. Faced with the oppressive power of these new kings over Egypt, Bostonians once more confronted the question of whether exodus would be necessary to preserve their lineage.

Chapter 8

The Failure of Federalism

Boston's French Years

> The power attained in the House of Representatives by the effect of the slave ratio is twenty votes. The State of Massachusetts has but twenty. So that this great and ancient and once proud, but now, constitutionally speaking, humbled Commonwealth, has absolutely no more weight in the national scale than a species of beings in fact as destitute of political rights as the brute creation. Upon theoretical principles, can anything be more shameful?
>
> —Josiah Quincy, "Oration before the Washington Benevolent Society of Boston," 1813

For its first century and a half, the city-state of Boston's concerns about maintaining its autonomy in the face of imperial authority had usually been framed in a British context: Britain acted, and Boston reacted. But from the time the Continental Congress declared independence and began negotiating alliances with foreign powers, France moved to the forefront of Bostonians' consciousness as a critical factor in shaping their place in the Atlantic world. The ratification of the Philadelphia Constitution and the beginning of American national government in 1789 coincided with the outbreak of the French Revolution, auguring a quarter century of turbulence in France's relationships with Europe and America. Now it was France that acted, while Britain, the United States, and Boston reacted.

Historians of the early American republic often presume a solidity and uniformity to the nationhood of the United States, as though diversity and conflict among the colonies had suddenly been erased by the Declaration of Independence or the Constitution.[1] This tendency is particularly prominent in histories of US foreign relations in the revolutionary era. It is far more convenient to imagine a unified "America," or to see conflict within the United States over foreign affairs as a simple division between national political parties, than it is to explain how the independent states pursued their separate interests and contemplated dissolving the national union long after its formal confederation. This chapter therefore focuses not on Boston's committed nationalists like John Adams (of whom there were few; his son John Quincy Adams was another) but rather on Bostonians who were more deeply enmeshed in the long tradition of Boston as an independent city-state that protected its interests, preserved its cultural identity, and conducted its own foreign policy in the larger Atlantic world.

From the earliest days of government under the Constitution, it became clear that Boston in New England held a radically different vision of the political economy of the United States than that of Virginia and its many allies. The southern states, and the new western states rapidly admitted to the union, imagined that land and its exploitation rather than overseas trade held the key to the country's future prosperity. The emerging conflict that these divergent visions created within the US government became rapidly entangled with the emerging conflict between Britain and France as the French Revolution caused waves of turbulence across Europe and beyond. As Napoléon's empire swept across Europe and gobbled up small self-governing states and republics, Bostonians saw in it a counterpart to the American continental aspirations of the Jeffersonians and feared for their own survival as a consequence.

These challenges dominated the careers of the two Bostonians who played the leading roles in representing the city-state's interests in national government during the French Revolution and Napoleonic Wars. Fisher Ames and Josiah Quincy repeatedly attempted to persuade their fellow members of Congress to pursue a federative political process, honoring the needs of all the union's individual member states and acting as a whole only when consensus could be reached on beneficial measures for all. But they were persistently defeated, and Boston's interests were repeatedly punished, by the ability of southern and mid-Atlantic majorities in Congress to pass measures that benefited themselves and left Boston's merchants, fishermen, and farmers to suffer the consequences. As the United States developed a national politics far different from what Massachusetts had anticipated when it ratified the Constitution, the pressing question emerged, not for the first time: Could Boston afford to remain in a compact that had become so detrimental to its interests?

Federalism and federalism

Though they may seem like one and the same word, "Federalism" and "federalism" are really far more than two words. Each version of this word—capitalized and lowercase—has multiple and internally conflicting definitions. Each of them also changed its meaning over time amid the shifting politics of the early American republic. Certain people who were anti-Federalists in the late 1780s became Federalists in the 1790s without changing their political views, and vice versa. Because these words were used by contemporary actors, it is impossible to dispense with them altogether and substitute simpler or better terms. Yet each of them has also been distorted by subsequent developments in history, which have layered on top of the words themselves the later meanings that concepts such as "party," "nation," and "union" have come to signify. To gain a better understanding of Boston's prospects for making its way in the complicated new world that began to unfold in 1789, it will be helpful to peel away some of these interpretive layers to see what federalism meant to Boston's Federalists.

In his *Two Treatises of Government* (1689), John Locke identified the fundamental powers of a government as the legislative, the executive, and *not* the judicial but the "federative" power. Regarding the last of these, he wrote, "The power of war and peace, leagues and alliances, and all the transactions with all persons and communities without the commonwealth, . . . may be called *federative* if any one pleases. So the thing be understood, I am indifferent as to the name."[2] For Locke, the federative power was a necessary consequence of the fact that "in a common-wealth the members of it are distinct persons still in reference to one another, and as such are governed by the laws of the society; yet in reference to the rest of mankind, they make one body, which is, as every member of it before was, still in the state of nature with the rest of mankind."[3] Until such time as a universal government over the world's nations exists, every polity must fend for itself among all others. Therefore one of the chief duties of government is to work out its relationships with external polities. This was the federative power.

Locke was not alone in drawing attention to this fundamental power of government. Earlier in the seventeenth century, political philosophers such as Grotius and Pufendorf had advanced various theories of federalism in describing the United Provinces of the Dutch Republic and the German principalities of the Holy Roman Empire. In the eighteenth century, the French philosophes Vattel and Montesquieu wrote approvingly of the virtues of a division of authority within a system of federated states.[4] In the arguments that arose after 1763 when Parliament asserted its power to tax American colonists, alter colonial charters, and impose military authority, it was obvious that competing concepts of federalism existed side by side in the political theory of the Atlantic world.

The US Constitution, though it supplanted the Articles of Confederation, by no means solved all the problems of federalism. Rather, in the degree of interpretive ambiguity that the Constitution left open, it simply offered new ground on which these old questions could be contested yet again. Compared with the Articles of Confederation, which defined the relationships of the states to the federal union quite precisely, the new Constitution created a governmental machinery with many moving, interlocking, and overlapping parts, designed to avoid facing questions of ultimate authority that had sparked conflict and violence in the 1760s and 1770s.[5] In ratifying this new Constitution, the citizens of Massachusetts were not accepting a fixed definition of "federalism." Even the terms of Massachusetts' ratification, in which a narrow victory became possible only with the addition of "recommended" (though not mandatory) amendments, indicate the ambiguity present at the creation of this new version of federated government. By calling for immediate modifications to the document, Massachusetts announced that the "more perfect union" to which the Constitution's preamble aspired was still obviously imperfect.

Ratification therefore meant something more like an agreement to continue the argument under a new set of rules than an expression of final approval. To put it in Lockean terms, the city-state of Boston's "federative" powers, its "transactions with all persons and communities without the commonwealth," were reframed, but not fully determined, by its ratification of the Constitution. This reframing meant, at the very least, Boston's loss of hegemony over the New England region—a hegemony that stemmed from the fact that the bulk of the region's territory and coastline as well as its strongest economy and largest population were within the boundaries of Massachusetts, over which Boston was the capital. Now, each of the fictively equal states would need to work out its own federative relationships with the others within a union where the states were actually quite unequal in real power.

The process of ratification generated our other problematic term, "Federalist," and its similarly capitalized variants—Federalism and Anti-Federalist—as labels for political factions or parties.[6] Initially, "Federalist" was the name seized on by those who argued vigorously in support of the new US Constitution drafted in Philadelphia in 1787. *The Federalist* is what Alexander Hamilton, James Madison, and John Jay called their subsequently famous series of newspaper essays written to persuade the skeptical citizens of New York to ratify the Constitution. Objections were made at the time (and by subsequent historians) that these constitutional proponents had wrongly usurped the name. The true "federalists" were those who preferred the original confederacy of states under the Articles of Confederation rather than a consolidated national republic with direct power over private citizens. But the name "Federalist" stuck to the Constitution's advocates.[7] The meaning of this term, however, began to change almost immediately.

Within months of the inauguration of national government under the new Constitution, a rift emerged between two of the most ardent "Federalists" of the ratification period, New York's Hamilton and Virginia's Madison, over their competing visions of the future political economy of the United States. From this rift, two mutually hostile factions or parties in national politics emerged. Hamilton's faction, because it had the ear and backing of President George Washington and the new federal government's administration, continued to be called "Federalists." Consequently, the word now meant something different than it had just months before. A major group of former Federalists, led by Madison, had now distanced themselves from Hamilton's faction that embraced the term. Nor did this transformation end the word's protean political career. With the election of 1800 and the rise of Jefferson and Madison to national executive power, "Federalist" could clearly no longer be synonymous with those holding the reins of the federal government. It thus became, as of 1800, the designation for the party in opposition to the elected federal administration, and as such, a name for the sort of thing whose very existence "Federalists" had once denounced.

At no time did the term "Federalist," as a label for a political faction or party, actually comport with a consistent philosophy regarding "federalism" in the Lockean sense: the relationship of the individual states and their powers to the collective government of the United States. For example, in 1788, while writing one of the *Federalist* papers to persuade skeptics of the Constitution's virtues, Madison argued that the new union would be a *compact* among the states: "Each state in ratifying the Constitution, is considered as a sovereign body independent of all others, and only to be bound by its own voluntary act."[8] A decade later, Madison reiterated precisely this point in the Virginia Resolution of 1798, written in opposition to Congress's Alien and Sedition Acts: "In case of a deliberate, palpable, and dangerous exercise of other powers, not granted by the said *compact*, the states, who are parties thereto, have the right, and are in duty bound, to interpose, for arresting the progress of the evil."[9] However, Madison was no longer defending a "Federalist" party position, but arguing *against* the party in power known as the Federalists. Yet another decade later, in 1808, it was the Federalists, now out of power, who followed Madison's logic in arguing for the authority of states to nullify national legislation (Jefferson's Embargo Act) and even to withdraw from the union altogether to arrest the progress of evil. Madison's administration and party now rejected this position outright.[10] To know that a person or group was identified as "Federalist" tells us nothing certain about their position on "federalism" at any given moment in the early republic's history.

But even this caveat fails to explain the problem caused by thinking of Federalists, or at least Boston's Federalists, in terms of national party politics. It is certainly the case that from 1789 to 1815, Boston's interests were often identified with Federalist positions in national politics, and the great majority of Boston's politicians in this era embraced the term. Less clear is the extent to which this common designation of Boston politics as "Federalist" misleads modern readers into assuming that Boston was actually engaged in a contest for long-term dominance *of* the national government of the United States as opposed to negotiating an ongoing relationship *with* the national government of the United States. The too-easy acceptance of "Federalist" to describe Boston's political stance obscures our ability to see that the city and its region were still working out a successful form of "federalism," still trying to find the best way to exercise their federative powers, within the United States and with the array of other powers of the Atlantic world.

To understand this process better from a Bostonian point of view, the following pages trace the political careers of two politicians, Boston's longest-serving members of the US House of Representatives in the years between 1789 and 1815, Fisher Ames and Josiah Quincy: Ames as a supporter of the Washington administration, Quincy in opposition to the administrations of Jefferson and Madison.[11] Ames held national office from 1789 to 1797, or rather, served as an "ambassadour," as he once put it, representing Boston and New England to the US Congress until chronic ill health forced his retirement.[12] Ames then took up writing political essays for the Boston press until his death in 1808 at the age of fifty. Quincy, like Ames, entered Congress as a young man, and he too retired from national office after serving four terms, from 1805 to 1813, but then continued a long career of public service, first as mayor of Boston and then as president of Harvard University.

Both Ames and Quincy have been accused by modern historians of behaving perversely while in Congress, playing the game of national politics poorly, losing touch with larger trends in American political development, and willfully clinging to a hopeless cause to the point of madness. Josiah Quincy's modern biographer sums up his career in Congress: "Quincy had been badly miscast as a national legislator, particularly as a member of a hopeless minority in a period of sharp ideological conflict. His self-righteousness rendered him ineffective as a politician and his intense sectional loyalties restricted his capacity for statesmanship. Denied an opportunity to put his talents to use in shaping national policy, he frittered away his eight years in Congress chasing bogeymen of his own creation."[13] Fisher Ames has been described in even more strident terms as "emotionally unstable," a politician whose "writing seems to be so thoroughly infected with hysterical and paranoid symptoms that it is difficult to believe that he represented a sane body of thought."[14] The key words in these critiques are "national," "statesmanship," and "sane body of thought." They collectively assume that Ames and Fisher were attempting to be effective statesmen within an American nation-state that in fact barely existed, and that a sane body of thought would abandon sectional loyalties and get down to the preordained business of continental nation building.

Ames and Quincy made no such assumptions. They were neither hysterical nor paranoid. But their sanity can best be seen by considering their roles in the proper context, not as perversely inept players in a game of national politics, but as Boston's ambassadors in a federative process (re)inaugurated by the Philadelphia Constitution and profoundly shaken by the earthquake of the French Revolution. Ames and Quincy were schooled in the historical traditions of the city-state of Boston. They knew what Boston's interests were and went off to Congress to pursue a federative brand of politics that would promote those interests. In this, they followed the footsteps of Boston's earlier leaders, as when John Winthrop and Thomas Dudley went to Hartford in 1643 to create the New England

Confederation, when Increase Mather went to London in 1688 to negotiate with James II (and later William III) for a new charter, and when John Adams went to the Continental Congress as an apostle for the cause of Boston. The quality of their statesmanship, the effectiveness of their protests against the growing power of other regional interests within the United States, needs to be measured and judged in the context of the city-state of Boston, and not just against the standards of the nation-state that Jefferson and Madison wanted to create.

Fisher Ames and the Frenchified Politics of the American Confederation

In background and experience, Fisher Ames resembled John Adams, his predecessor in representing Boston at a congress of American states. Like Adams, Ames was born into an ancient Massachusetts family situated in a rural town outside Boston. The Ames family, like the Adamses, became farmers and artisans, and held important offices in town, militia, and church affairs, but were more peripatetic than the Adamses. Ames's ancestors migrated through the region south of Boston, from Braintree to Bridgewater in Plymouth County, until Nathaniel Ames, his father, settled in Dedham, about ten miles southwest of the city. Here Nathaniel made his modest fortune by publishing British America's first almanac in 1725, which he continued for the next forty years, selling as many as sixty thousand copies a year.

Fisher was born in 1758, the third son of Nathaniel's second marriage (both marriages were coincidentally to women with the surname of Fisher).[15] A bright boy, he was sent early to Harvard College, graduating in 1774 at the age of sixteen. For the next few years, he kept school intermittently in towns around Boston, served for a few weeks in the Massachusetts militia, saw one of his brothers die from disease while serving in the siege of Boston, and then began to read law. His education and early career mirrored that of Adams, and the lawyer under whom Ames studied, William Tudor, had himself been trained by Adams a decade earlier.[16] A generation younger than Adams, Ames replicated the familiar pattern by which young men of talent were drawn into Boston and became champions of its interests.

Like Adams before him, he emerged from his youthful training a strong believer in the virtues of the nation of New England. In a letter home from his first term in Congress, Ames wrote, "I believe that the New England people are better taught than any other, and Boston better than any other city. Since I have been here [New York], I have thought of the advantage of our town corporations and town schools. I do not believe that any country has such judicious expedients for repelling barbarism, supporting government, and extending felicity. Boston might be an Athens, and I would wish to make it a London."[17] Ames may have lacked the insatiable hunger for historical and legal knowledge that Adams possessed, but his training equipped him well to be Boston's ambassador in the post-revolutionary federative process. In studying with Tudor, Ames read Pufendorf's *De Jure Naturae et Gentium* (On the law and nature of nations), Grotius's *De Jure Belli ac Pacis* (On the law of war and peace), and Vattel's *Droit des Gens* (Law of nations)—key texts in defining federal relationships among sovereign states.[18] (See plate 18.)

Like Adams, Ames became a figure on the national stage after only a brief time in Boston. He was admitted to the bar at the end of 1781, shuttled back and forth between Dedham and Boston building a legal practice, and was admitted as an attorney before the Massachusetts Supreme Judicial Court in 1784. As his practice grew, Ames turned his attention to politics. He published his first essays in Boston's *Independent Chronicle* in 1786, denouncing the violence of the Massachusetts Regulators whose protests were then reaching their height.[19] The following year, Dedham selected Ames, not yet thirty years old, as one of its delegates to the state convention on ratifying the Constitution.

Like many opponents of the Shaysite Regulation, Ames strongly favored the new US Constitution as a defense against instability within the states and conflict among the states, while still preserving the sovereignty of the states from being fully "consolidated" in a national government. He spoke many times and with compelling force during the convention, most notably following John Hancock's proposal to ratify the Constitution with a set of recommended amendments attached. The Federalists' narrow victory and Ames's brilliant summation speech made him famous throughout the commonwealth. Three months later, Dedham's voters chose Ames for a term as one of their two representatives to the Massachusetts General Court—his only term, because six months later Dedham's voters, together with Boston and other towns in Suffolk County, elected him as their first representative to the US Congress.[20]

The temptation is strong to describe this as a meteoric rise. Ames did make a rapid ascent from local to national office, and the man he defeated in the election was Samuel Adams, a formidable figure in Boston politics. But service in the national government was not necessarily considered a high honor in 1788. The reputation of the Continental Congress had plummeted during the 1780s, partly a result of gridlock caused by fierce sectional conflict, partly a consequence of sovereignty remaining with the states. High office in state government was the more desirable place for most American politicians, and the ratification of the Constitution did not immediately alter these sentiments. Samuel Adams was willing to stand for Congress because of his lack of local success; his aspirations to the Massachusetts governorship had been blocked by more popular figures like James Bowdoin and John Hancock. In addition, Samuel Adams was sixty-six years old in 1788 and had not been a particularly strong supporter of ratification. This left Fisher Ames, the youthful, dynamic supporter of the new Constitution, as the likeliest candidate for a national office that most of Boston's leading politicians had not bothered to seek.

When the eager Ames arrived in New York City for the scheduled opening of the First Congress on March 4, 1789, he was met by only twelve other representatives—three of these were fellow delegates from Massachusetts.[21] Not until April 1 would even half the fifty-nine members of the House (enough to make a quorum) arrive at Federal Hall on Wall Street to begin the work of government. All the while the old Confederation Congress continued to conduct the nation's business in Philadelphia, leaving Ames "doubtful whether the old government is dead or the new one alive." The First United States Congress did not burst onto the world stage as a great center of power. Aside from one prominent figure, James Madison of Virginia, the remaining fifty-eight representatives are names seldom thought of as America's "founding fathers." As Ames put it, "There are few shining geniuses." But Ames did credit his new colleagues for being "sober, solid, old-charter folks, as we often say"—Boston's code for devotion to traditional republican government—"nor are they, for the most part, men of intrigue."[22] Much like John Adams in his early days in the Continental Congress, Fisher Ames hoped that the newly configured federal government could align the interests of the city-state of Boston with those of the nation: "I believe the individual interest of each part is compatible with the general interest. . . . On this principle our existence as a nation depends."[23] In a letter to George Minot, his closest friend in Boston, Ames reported that some New England representatives had voted for a measure simply because it favored local economic interests. Ames asked, "Is that a just principle of action? It is little and mean, as well as unwise and unsafe, to discriminate. I wish I may never sacrifice national principles to local interests." As Ames's biographer put it, "He did not regard nationalism as incompatible with loyalty to New England since he could not conceive of the success of any government which neglected the interests of his region."[24]

Ames's enthusiasm for the Constitution was grounded in the powers that it gave Congress to regulate trade, raise revenue, and negotiate treaties with foreign trading partners. These were vital elements to Boston's mercantile interests, and issues on which Parliament's assertion of ultimate authority had damaged New England's autonomy. Ames's vision of republican government was rooted in New England's understanding of the body politic's interrelatedness; a republic could no more do without one of its vital elements than a healthy body could do without a head or heart, hands or feet. To that end, he believed that a legislator in a republican federation needed to represent the interests of his home constituents *and* consider the good of the confederation as a body. A city and region that devoted itself to international trade, marketing commodities produced domestically and importing desirable goods from afar, was clearly a vital element in the union. Ames was shocked, then, by how rapidly it became evident that other members of Congress, especially from the southern states, viewed New England's interests as narrowly local and superfluous to the American body politic—and that some of them turned out to be men of intrigue after all.

The need to raise a national revenue to honor the obligations of the United States, especially its war debt, was a top priority for the First Congress. Under the Articles of Confederation, the union had lacked any taxing power. Fiscally minded members of the Continental Congress had proposed various forms of customs duties on imported goods, but they never gained the unanimous support necessary to amend the articles. Federalists, the initial supporters of the new Constitution, saw these enhanced powers as one of its obvious strengths. Madison took the lead by introducing a new revenue plan during the first week of the Congress. Madison proposed specific duties on common imports that might be thought of as luxuries or at least not necessities: rum, molasses, wine, tea, pepper, sugar, cocoa, and coffee. In addition, he called for "tonnage" duties, taxes proportional to the carrying capacity of ships entering American ports: low taxes for American ships, higher duties for ships from countries with trade agreements with the United States (such as France), and *much* higher duties for foreign ships from countries without such agreements—notably Britain.

In principle, Ames and the New England delegation, Federalists all, supported Madison's plan as the best way to raise a national revenue. The Constitution provided for a variety of methods for taxation, including direct taxes in which the proportion due from each state would be based on the state's free population, plus three-fifths of its enslaved population. But direct taxes would be cumbersome to execute, whereas the collection of customs duties was easy and familiar, and the Constitution guaranteed that any customs duties would be uniform throughout the nation. Every state imported the goods that Madison's bill enumerated, and despite the fact that New Englanders engaged in shipping to a far greater degree than the southern colonies, the tonnage fees were designed to encourage southern exporters to patronize American rather than foreign merchants to handle their carrying trade. For New England merchants, the increased business would offset the additional cost of the tonnage duties. In theory, this revenue plan could have been beneficial to all the nation's states and regions.

Ames, however, pointed out one problem in Madison's proposal. The duty on molasses, at eight cents per gallon, was too high. In his first major speech in Congress, Ames argued for the distinctive importance of this commodity in New England's political economy.[25] First, molasses was essential to making rum, New England's most lucrative industry and a major export commodity. At eight cents per gallon, the molasses duty would raise the price of New England rum higher than the price of imported French or British rum even after the import duties were paid. Second, molasses, more than many of the other enumerated goods, was a crucial aspect of the diet of the poor in New England. Third and most significant, West Indian molasses was the principle item of exchange that New England merchants received for one particular commodity, low-grade fish, that was unmarketable anywhere else, but that Caribbean plantation owners bought to feed their slaves. As Ames put it, "We exchange for molasses, those fish that it is impossible to dispose of anywhere else; we have no market within our reach, but the islands from whence we get molasses in return, which again we manufacture into rum. These circumstances form a material link in our chain of navigation, and upon our success in navigation the most important interests of the United States depend." Finally, given the history of widespread smuggling that arose after Britain implemented the Molasses Acts of 1733, Ames also warned that Madison's proposed high duties would be unenforceable. "The State of Massachusetts [including Maine] has a prodigious extent of seacoast, of near one thousand miles in length, indented with innumerable bays and rivers, forming the finest, most accessible, and securest harbors in the world. It must be impossible to guard them all."[26] A lower, more reasonable duty would actually raise more revenue for the government, which was precisely Parliament's reasoning when, in the

Sugar Act of 1763, it reduced the molasses duties from six pence to three pence per gallon. Ames and his New England colleagues were certain that the molasses duty proposed by Madison would harm the economy of their region, and therefore damage the interests of the nation as a whole. From Ames's perspective, this was an obvious point, consistent with the federative politics that he and his colleagues were seeking to promote as the norm for the new nation.[27]

After making what he considered to be a small amendment to a bill that he generally approved, Ames was taken aback by the response from Madison, Thomas Fitzsimmons of Pennsylvania, and other congressmen from outside New England. They accused Ames and the New England delegates of a "littleness injurious to their reputation" by making "arguments unworthy of their national character."[28] Madison waxed sarcastic: "Are the Northern people made of finer clay? Do they respire a clearer air? . . . Are they the chosen few? Are all others to be oppressed with accumulated burthens, and they to take their course easy and unrestrained? No; I trust the General Government will equally affect all."[29] It is hard to know quite what Madison meant here. Ames was arguing for an adjustment of the molasses duty that would apply equally to all the states. Madison offered no example of how the duty on any of the other enumerated commodities unfairly burdened some other region. Eventually, through bargaining in the House and revisions in the Senate, the duties on molasses were reduced to Ames's satisfaction. But Ames was disturbed by how rapidly his argument for a regional interest with national implications had been attacked by opponents as local special pleading, disparaging the republican and federal motives that Ames defended. By assenting to an impost on commerce rather than other possibilities open to the national government under the plausible tax regimes of the later eighteenth century, such as a property tax, poll tax, or excise tax, New England was accepting the form of taxation that affected its own economy most directly. Yet in trying to adjust the rate on this one item, Ames and his colleagues were accused of special pleading in the face of the "national" interest.

When Ames suggested alternatives such as an excise tax on the sale of goods produced within the United States, Madison and

Fitzsimmons objected that excise taxes weighed unequally on the states. As Ames explained to Minot, "The southern people dread it, and say the excise is an odious, unpopular tax, and will fall unequally on them. They are afraid for their whisky."[30] Even more portentously, Ames's Massachusetts colleague George Thatcher argued that the duty on molasses was just as much a tax on the productive labor of Massachusetts as it was on an imported consumer good. Because the brutally difficult work of North Atlantic fishing was necessary to acquire the fish that were traded for molasses, "[molasses] becomes the produce of their industry, as much as the rice and tobacco of Virginia and Carolina become the staple articles of the labor of those States. Can any reason be assigned why the industry of Massachusetts should be imposted, while that of the other States goes free?" To answer his own rhetorical question, Thatcher pushed into dangerous territory: "Suppose a member from Massachusetts was to propose an impost on negroes, what would you hear from the Southern gentlemen, if fifty dollars was the sum to be laid? And yet this is not more than the proportion laid upon molasses."[31] Madison chose to overlook this comment, as if Thatcher were deranged and could not possibly have meant it: "I do not conceive it expresses either the deliberate temper of his own mind, or the good sense of his constituents."[32]

In fact, the Constitution itself, in Article I, Section 9, had explicitly set a maximum import tax of ten dollars per slave, singling out enslaved humanity as the only commodity to receive such protection. Thatcher, Madison, and all the other members of Congress knew this. What Thatcher really meant was that if a fifty dollar duty on slaves was unconstitutional, a proportionally large tax on a commodity vital to New England's productive capacity should be equally out of bounds. But the southern delegates to the Constitutional Convention had carefully written defenses of their vital interest in slave labor into the document. The delegates from the "carrying states" (as New England was often called) had understood the Constitution's powers to raise revenue, regulate trade, and form commercial treaties as advantages to their own interests, but they had failed to foresee that their own countrymen from competing regions might use these powers as a weapon against them. In the first month of the Congress's first session, the sharp regional differences between the interests of Boston and those of the southern states were laid bare in these arguments over molasses. The precarious position of Boston under this government was immediately exposed.

The "tonnage" duties were potentially even more ominous than the molasses debate. Ames objected to the differential Madison proposed between the duties charged to nations with favorable treaty relations and those without such agreements. To Ames, this policy deliberately insulted Britain, historically the colonies' dominant trading partner, for the sake of favoritism toward France; Ames described Madison as "Very much Frenchified in his Politics."[33] To Ames, American commerce would best be served by simply charging one (low) rate to American ships, and another (high) rate to all foreign ships, regardless of origin. Such a policy would promote domestic shipping and invite all foreign trade on an equal basis. As a representative of Boston, Ames saw his duty to include negotiating the federative relationship within the United States in Congress, while at the same time maintaining New England's relationships with Britain and France, as both of these Atlantic powers were critical to Boston's overseas commerce. In Ames's view, the power granted to the United States by the Constitution was designed to make it easier to pursue the purely commercial vision of diplomacy that Adams had envisioned in 1776.

Madison's proposal for differential tonnage duties advanced an altogether-different view of the role of commerce in national and international politics. For Madison, the overseas trade of the United States could be used as a tool or even a weapon to coerce foreign competitors to make more favorable agreements with the United States. In the face of such arguments, it began to dawn on Ames that Madison was "not a little of a Virginian, and thinks that State the land of promise."[34] For Madison and his supporters, overseas commerce, the economic foundation of the city-state of Boston, had only negligible value for the United States' political economy as a whole. More than one Virginia plantation owner in Congress saw the carrying trade as extrinsic to the American economy, claiming not to care "who carries my tobacco to market." From this perspective, New England's commerce was not one among many essential elements in the American body politic but an expendable weapon for waging conflict against international enemies. There was no fear that damage to overseas commerce would result in lasting damage to the body itself.[35]

By contrast, the southern states, aware from the time of the Somerset decision in 1772 of a growing international antislavery movement, had taken care in forming the Constitution that slavery and slave importation could not be used as a political weapon or made expendable. In addition to the Constitution's ten dollar impost limit on slaves, the institution of slavery was fundamental to representation in the legislative and executive branches by virtue of the three-fifths ratio. And the power of Congress to regulate the importation of slaves was expressly exempted for twenty years from its general powers to regulate commerce. Faced now with a southern strategy that aimed to use commerce as a weapon against other nations rather than treating it as a vital American interest, Ames and his colleagues began to see that they, too, should have provided against the danger that national commercial regulation could be used destructively against New England. Worse was yet to come.

For Ames, these arguments over impost duties and tonnage were alarming, but at least they were conducted openly on the floor of Congress. What emerged next was more disturbing: a series of conflicts over major issues in which backroom deals by "men of intrigue" shaped the future of the new republic's politics and defeated the federative approach that Ames promoted.

The Constitution empowered Congress to create a national capital, "such District (not exceeding ten Miles square) as may, by Cession of particular States, and the Acceptance of Congress, become the Seat of the Government of the United States." Yet like so much else in the Constitution, the location of the capital was left undetermined. In August 1789, discussion of the issue began on the floor of the House (still meeting at Federal Hall in New York). But from the time Congress first assembled in April, various members had engaged in clandestine negotiations. In addition to the need to find a convenient meeting place for representatives from across the enormous new union, larger than any republic in history, it was obvious that a new federal city would augment the economy and enhance the access to power of the region where it was built. No one imagined that the geographic extremes of the union, New England in the north or Carolina in the south, would be a convenient site. But among the centrally situated states, possibilities ranged from the Hudson River to the Potomac, and the Susquehanna and Delaware in between.

Various Congressmen made proposals to award a temporary site for a decade or so to an already-established city or town, allowing time for another location to be developed as a permanent site. Virginians strongly favored a permanent site on the Potomac near Chesapeake Bay, but were willing to grant Philadelphia temporary rights. Delegates from New England and New York preferred that New York City remain the temporary capital, and suggested a permanent site in Philadelphia or along the Susquehanna River in Pennsylvania. But in the eyes of Ames, the real problem lay with the intrigue itself. As he wrote to Minot in Boston, "We are caballing about the permanent residence of Congress . . . and in such dark intrigues, the real designs of members are nearly impenetrable."[36] By late September, it looked as though Pennsylvania held the balance of power, and Congress would approve a site near Philadelphia (on the Delaware) or somewhere along the Susquehanna. At the last minute, Madison, through a series of parliamentary maneuvers, deferred a final resolution until Congress adjourned with the matter still undecided.

By the time Congress reconvened for a second session in January 1790, a new issue had arisen. The treasury secretary, Alexander Hamilton, submitted his *Report on the Public Credit of the United States.* During the ratification debates, the Constitution's supporters, Ames among them, anticipated that the national government would assume the states' debts still remaining from the war. As the national government now had exclusive authority over imposts and barred the states from levying customs duties, it was ludicrous to expect that the states could raise the money to repay their war debts on their own. In addition, Federalists argued that the state war debts were really "national" in character. The purpose of the debts had been to secure the independence of all the states collectively and therefore should be shared equitably by the nation as a whole.[37] Hamilton's *Report* supported this view. It proposed the consolidation of outstanding state debts with the national debt, provided a fund supported by national taxation to pay the interest on the consolidated debt, and called for a subsequent balancing of state and national accounts. Neither states that had already retired their debts nor states that had paid a disproportionate share of the costs of war would be injured by the consolidation plan.

Massachusetts possessed one of the largest outstanding state debts, in part because it had been "exceptionally zealous in raising troops for the Continental army," offering bounties for enlistment even higher than the Continental Congress had recommended. Massachusetts had also absorbed much of the cost of the rapid depreciation of the currency issued by the Continental Congress. The value of the "Continental" in Massachusetts remained much higher than in the rest of the United States, and consequently Continentals flowed there and were retired in payment of state taxes.[38] Both of these elements were consistent with Boston's long history of raising troops for distant service from its vigorous militia system and sustaining the value of fiat money through careful fiscal policies.

When Congress reconvened in 1790, Madison immediately declared his opposition to Hamilton's *Report*. Madison's Virginia constituency opposed the federal assumption, as Virginia had already retired its own war debt, which was proportionally small; little of the war had been fought in Virginia. Madison opposed the prospect that "speculators" and "monied men" would reap rewards from Hamilton's plan of assuming the debt at face value. Instead, Madison offered a complex and unworkable "discrimination" plan that would reward multiple holders of the debt.[39] Ames gave speeches in Congress on February 15 and May 19, 1790, denouncing Madison's amendments and supporting Hamilton's *Report*. Despite vigorous debate over the plan in Congress, Ames feared that the "dark intrigues" of private negotiations would settle the matter: "The world ought to despise our public conduct, when it hears intrigue openly avowed, and sees that great measures are made to depend, not upon reasons, but upon bargains for little ones."[40]

Resolution came through exactly the sort of intrigue that Ames feared. In late June, Secretary of State Jefferson hosted a private dinner, where Madison and Hamilton agreed to a compromise.[41] The permanent national capital would be granted to a site on the Potomac (despite the strength of support in Congress for a site in Pennsylvania), as a concession to Madison who would drop his opposition to Hamilton's *Report*.[42] Over the course of the next few weeks, both bills passed through Congress. With the passage of the debt assumption bill, which "The New England States demand[ed] as a debt of justice," the specter of disunion was momentarily dispersed.[43] But Ames was aghast at the means by which the result had been reached: "If such jobbing, such shameful jockeying is to be the common mode of carrying private points in our public councils . . . I think we may safely predict a speedy end to our existence as a nation."[44] By the time the Federal Congress ended its first term in August 1790, the Boston Congressman and his fellow New Englanders' intentions to coordinate their city's and region's interests with the nation's collective good had been reduced to "jobbing" and "shameful jockeying."

The disappointments of Fisher Ames in the first Federal Congress resembled those of John Adams in the Continental Congress fifteen years earlier. Ames learned, as Adams had before him, how alien the South's character and interests were from New England norms. That different regions preferred different measures from the national government was not news. Yet Adams had worked in a system where consent among all the states, or at least a supermajority among them, was required for any major action, thereby highlighting the need for a politics of accommodation. Ames now found himself confronting something much different: a legislature that conducted its business in ways that resembled Britain's Parliament, with ministers of state (not even elected officials in the case of Hamilton and Jefferson) concocting deals in secret and then funneling them through Congress based on bare majorities they controlled. Parliament had at least upheld the fiction that each member acted for the good of the whole nation and not just the local interests of his constituency. The US Congress seemed to offer no such illusions. Over the course of his remaining three terms in Congress, Ames's vision of the prospects for his New England homeland within the American union would become progressively darker, as the French Revolution shaped every aspect of Boston's federative relationships.

The French Revolution and Greater Virginia

During the 1790s, events in France took unpredictable turns. As Bostonians followed these developments, their interpretations of the French Revolution often led them to find connections between its aims and those of their American antagonists. The sectional conflict in American politics therefore took on a persistent ideological slant. That Boston's interests conflicted with those of Virginia, the most powerful competing force within the United States, was clear long before the execution of the French king, the reign of terror, or the rise of Napoléon Bonaparte. But the willingness of Jefferson, Madison, and their Democratic-Republican followers to embrace revolutionary France as a model in their own pursuit of an American "empire of liberty" created an increasingly rigid ideological framework in which Boston's conflict with Virginia would play out. If Ames and his colleagues sought to defend the political economy of the city-state of Boston as one vital part within the body of an American confederation, then Jefferson's party, by contrast, sought to capture the American confederation in its entirety and remake it as a consolidated national entity in Virginia's image.

Well before the United States secured its independence from Britain, Jefferson had sketched out a vision of Virginia as the center of an American continental empire. In 1780, Jefferson composed his *Notes on the State of Virginia* in response to the queries of Marquis de Barbé-Marbois, secretary of the French delegation in Philadelphia. Barbé-Marbois had asked about Virginia's "rivers, rivulets, and how far they are navigable." Jefferson replied with an extraordinary list. It included the major rivers of tidewater Virginia where the great plantations lay, the James, the York, the Rappahannock, and the "Patowmac," as well as smaller ones such as the Elizabeth, the Rivanna, and the Piankatank. But Jefferson also placed the "Ohio, the most beautiful river on earth" along with the Tennessee, the Cumberland, the Wabash, the Illinois, the Mississippi, and the Missouri among Virginia's principal rivers. He noted in the published edition of 1787 that "the Missouri, since the treaty of Paris, the Illinois and Northern branches of the Ohio since the cession to Congress, are no longer within our [i.e., Virginia's] limits. Yet having been so heretofore, and still opening to us channels of extensive communication with the western and north-western country, they shall be noted in their order."[45] Prompted by the virtually limitless reach of Virginia's original colonial charter, which had fixed its western boundary only at the "South Sea," Jefferson's imagination ranged across an American continental empire, a Greater Virginia extending past the Mississippi to the Rocky Mountains.

To Jefferson's imagined empire, the city-state of Boston and its interests were at best superfluous and at worst a cancerous excrescence. In another famous passage from *Notes on the State of Virginia*, Jefferson wrote, "The mobs of great cities add just so much to the support of pure government, as sores do to the strength of the human body." Although Jefferson's politics, like Madison's, were already "very much Frenchified" before the storming of the Bastille, the French Revolution provided encouragement, opportunity, and direction to Jefferson and his nascent party in their pursuit of an empire of liberty on this ideological model.[46] Late in 1792, the revolutionary National Convention sent Edmond Charles Genet, "Citizen Genet," as he became known, as France's minister to the United States, bearing hopeful, if unrealistic, expectations for what a mission to America might accomplish. The convention's instructions to Genet show that France's aspirations for America corresponded closely with Jefferson's vision of the American future, and not at all well with Boston's conception of the federative nature of the American republic. Genet was instructed to encourage the peoples living adjacent to the United States in Canada, Florida, and Louisiana to cast off the oppression of Britain and Spain, the revolution's monarchical enemies. This feat was to be accomplished by recruiting American citizens, especially the "habitans du Kentucky" (Kentucky, admitted to statehood in 1792, was the preferred French term for the entire trans-Appalachian west), to organize expeditions against Spanish Louisiana to open up "la navigation du Mississippi, à délivré nos anciens frères de la Louisiane du joug tirannique de l'Espagne," at the same time reuniting Canada, "la belle étoile du Canada," to its rightful connection with the remainder of "la Constellation Americaine."[47] With help from Americans, Genet aimed to create a Franco-American revolutionary republic, uniting Canada, Florida, and the trans-Mississippi west to encircle the Anglo-American republic of the United States.

In addition, the convention instructed Genet to pursue a new treaty with the United States, expanding the alliance made in 1778: "A national pact in which the two peoples would mingle their commercial and political interests and establish an intimate accord to assist in every way the extension of the empire of liberty, guarantee the sovereignty of peoples, and punish the powers that still hold to an exclusive colonial and commercial system, by declaring that the vessels of those powers shall not be admitted to the ports of the two contracting nations."[48] The contradiction between guaranteeing the sovereignty of peoples and encouraging American adventurers to invade Florida, Louisiana, and Canada seems not to have troubled Genet. This vision of diplomacy was obviously far removed from the purely commercial strategy that Adams and now Ames favored from the perspective of Boston. But over the course of the next twenty years, Genet's aims were precisely the actions that Jefferson and Madison would pursue: purchasing Louisiana from Napoléon by extraconstitutional measures in 1803, overrunning the Gulf Coast and Florida through military adventures led by Andrew Jackson, and invading Canada in the War of 1812. The blundering Citizen Genet failed to negotiate a new treaty with the United States. But in the eyes of Bostonians, these dismaying events made it appear as though "*un concert intime*," an "intimate accord," had indeed been established between revolutionary France and, if not America as a whole, then Greater Virginia.

Ames, the French Revolution, and the Rise of Bonaparte

Initially, Boston's political leaders and merchants welcomed the news of the French Revolution and the rise of a sister republic as the best possible outcome of the alliance of 1778. When France's citizen armies defeated the Duke of Brunswick at Valmy in 1792, abolished the monarchy, and declared France to be a republic, Fisher Ames joined in the raucous celebrations organized by some of the city's leading merchants. But the blunders of the subsequent Genet mission, by putting the interests of Boston in danger, began to turn Ames against the more radical direction that the new French Republic was taking. High on Genet's list of goals was encouraging American merchants to turn privateer and attack British shipping. After the execution of Louis XVI in January 1793, France declared war on Britain, but the Washington administration maintained US neutrality and opposed Genet's efforts, not wanting to be dragged into war with Britain again.

From Boston's viewpoint, the French problem was as much economic as political. Even with French receptivity to American trade and despite Britain's restrictive trade policies, Boston merchants' overseas trade with Britain remained ten times as large as their trade with France.[49] Nationwide, American demand for British-made goods far outstripped the desire for French manufactures. British demand for American grain and other products, even with high tariffs, created better prices for American exports than France could pay. In Boston's recovering postwar economy, merchants had little incentive to become privateers and attack their best customers.

Ames and his New England colleagues in Congress were therefore gratified when Washington's administration asked the French Republic to recall Citizen Genet. The French National Convention, now ruled by the Jacobins who had overthrown Genet's Girondin supporters, willingly obliged. By August, Ames wrote from Boston to his friend Thomas Dwight, informing him that "the town is less frenchified than it was. Citizen Genet is out of credit; his rudeness is as indiscreet as it is extra-ordinary, and everybody is provoked with him."[50] For Jefferson and his growing legion of followers forming Democratic-Republican Clubs all over the United States, the setback of the Genet affair did not diminish their support of France and hatred for Britain.[51] In private correspondence, Jefferson began to use terms like "monocrat" to describe his Federalist opponents, when in actuality, the nature of Boston's republicanism, as expressed by Ames and his New England colleagues, remained unchanged. Their reluctance to make an enemy of Britain was rooted in their political economy, not in any love for British monarchism. But the more their Jeffersonian opponents took ideologically charged positions in defense of revolutionary France, the more the critiques of Ames and his New England colleagues focused on France as well.

By 1796, Ames's failing health could no longer stand the rigors of travel from Boston to Philadelphia, where Congress had met since 1790. After one final sublime speech ("My God, how great he is! Bless my stars I never heard anything so great since I was born," said Supreme Court Justice James Iredell of North Carolina) in which he supported the Jay Treaty as a commercial alliance between the United States and Great Britain, Ames announced that he would not seek reelection and retired to his law practice.[52] He turned his dwindling energy to writing political essays for the Boston press, even helping to found new publications like the *Boston Repertory* and *New England Palladium*, where Federalists' voices could compete with the organizational strength of the Jeffersonian Republican press.[53] With Napoléon's rise and the coup d'état that made him first consul of France late in 1799, Ames launched a series of dozens of essays over the next eight years.

Now that he was no longer Boston's ambassador to the US Congress, Ames's intended audience changed. The four essays he published in February 1801 were addressed "To New England Men," as if he were no longer a spokesman *for*, but a counselor *to*, his native country.[54] That Ames thought of New England as a "country" is clear: "In consequence of our extraction and the institutions of our ever to be remembered ancestors, New England has a distinct and well-defined national character, the only part of the United States that has yet any pretensions to it."[55] The pen names he chose for other essays, such as "Laocoon" (who warned the Trojans against the dangers of Greeks bearing gifts) or "Phocion" (the fearless Athenian assemblyman who defended his city after Macedonian kings had gained control over it) convey the cautionary quality of these works, as Ames reported on the growing dominance of Jefferson, Madison, and Virginia, the Macedon of American politics to Boston's Athens. Ames's essay titles convey the subjects that gripped his attention: "The New Romans" (i.e., France), "Prospect of a New Coalition against France," "The Successes of Bonaparte," "Dangerous Powers of France," and "Duration of French Despotism."

Grounded in his extensive knowledge of ancient history, these essays dwell on how France had become the most highly militarized state since the Roman Empire: "No modern nation has, however, come so near being, like the Romans, all soldiers, as the French." Ames argued that regardless of who controlled its government at any given moment, France's *spirit* is essentially "Jacobin," displaying a tyrannical willingness to throw the entire force of its people into violent military conquest. "Her government, ever changing hands, was ever the same in spirit. Like Rome, who extended her conquests, while she was convulsed with civil war, every change has breathed new fury into the military enthusiasm of France."[56]

Ames pointed out that despite its republican rhetoric, the actual conquests of revolutionary and Napoleonic France either destroyed or absorbed into the French Empire the remaining small republics of Europe. This left only monarchical empires like Great Britain, Austria, and Russia to oppose France's aspirations to universal dominance: "Before this boasted revolution, Europe had many free republics. Alas! they are no more. France, proclaiming war against palaces, has waged it against commonwealths. Switzerland, Holland, Geneva, Venice, Lucca, Genoa are gone, and the wretched

Batavian, Helvetian, and Italian republics are but the faint images, the spectres, that haunt the sepulchres where they rot. So far has France been from paying exclusive regard to republics, that she has considered them, not as associates, but as victims."[57] Ames's argument reinforced the predictions that Adams made fifteen years earlier in his *Defence of the American Constitutions*. Adams had insisted that balanced bicameral legislatures and strong executives were essential ingredients of durable republics, which French philosophes of the 1780s had scorned. Ames now argued that the French Revolution's imperial aftermath demonstrated the truth of Adams's analysis. Without a balanced republican constitution, the French experiment had degenerated into imperial tyranny.

Ames attributed France's conflict with Britain to French hostility to commerce and manufacturing and love of honor and military glory: "The passion to acquire is characteristic of the English; the passion to rule is predominant with the French; the one seeks gain, the other glory."[58] For Ames, America's Jeffersonian "democrats," if not themselves actual "Jacobins" (although he uses that term for them constantly), were enthralled by France's revolutionary democratic rhetoric. The Virginians' hostility to commerce and manufacturing and their desire for territorial expansion made them France's ideal allies, the junior partners of Napoléon's effort to create a universal monarchy under the banner of liberty: "Mr. Madison's famous commercial resolutions were grounded on the idea of making America useful as a colony to France."[59] As Ames concluded in yet another essay, "[France's] triumphs are terrible. A voice seems to issue from the tombs of the fallen republics for our warning."[60]

By October 1802, when this last passage was composed, Ames had fixated on the growing likelihood that Bonaparte would reestablish the French claims to North America that Citizen Genet had attempted to revive a decade earlier. At this point, the news emerged that in a secret treaty of 1800, Spain had ceded Louisiana to France, and France had given Tuscany, Parma, Florence, and Piombino to the Spanish infanta and transformed them into the newly created kingdom of Etruria. Former republics were made into a puppet kingdom in return for vast American land cessions.[61] Ames believed that Napoléon was "ready to make the United States the tool of France," and "revive the famous resolutions of Mr. Madison, and the report of Mr. Jefferson on the privileges and restrictions of our commerce with foreign nations," in order to separate American commerce from Britain. The fact that Napoléon's foreign minister, Charles-Maurice Talleyrand-Périgord, had recently claimed that America was of no greater "consequence to them [the French Directory] nor ought to be treated with greater respect than Geneva or Genoa," city-republics that Napoléon had already swept up, lent support to these concerns.[62] What was more alarming, Ames feared, was that "France will soon have Louisiana. A formal treaty has already given it to her, and all our papers have published its contents. She only waits for a more convenient season; she waits to conquer the islands."[63] By this Ames meant the reconquest of Saint-Domingue and Napoléon's plan to reestablish the slave system that the Haitian Revolution had overthrown.

Napoléon's attempt to reenslave Haiti failed, and without Haiti's slaves as a market for food and timber, Napoléon lost interest in Louisiana. The following year, President Jefferson negotiated an extraconstitutional purchase of the Louisiana Territory, doubling the land claims of the United States in a single stroke. Jefferson then established a provisional government over this enormous territory as "essentially a presidential dictatorship, in which he or his appointees would administer the territory without a legislature," much as Britain had done with Quebec after the Seven Years' War. To justify unrepresentative government in the Louisiana Territory, Jefferson claimed that the inhabitants of Louisiana were "as yet as incapable of self-government as children."[64]

These events made Ames all the more fearful that Jefferson, Madison, and the Republican Party aimed to transform the United States into a consolidated empire with Virginia at its center—a fear he spelled out in "The Dangers of American Liberty" in 1805. Ames returned to his earlier analogy from the "Phocion" essays, describing how the Amphyctionic League of ancient Greece, "the most illustrious federal republic that ever existed," had been overwhelmed by the predominance of Thebes, "as . . . Virginia now does in congress." Then Philip of Macedon, who flattered Theban vanity, "turned his arms against those very Thebans whom he had before assisted. They had no refuge in the federal union which they had helped to enfeeble." To drive home his unsubtle analogy, Ames added, "Here, let Americans read their own history. Here let even Virginia learn how perilous and how frail will be the consummation of her schemes." Switching then from a Greek to Roman analogy, Ames continued:

> Is Virginia to be our Rome? And are we to be her Latin or Italian allies, like them to be emulous of the honor of our chains on the terms of imposing them on Louisiana, Mexico, or Santa Fe? . . . [D]emocratic license leads not to a monarchy regulated by laws, but to the ferocious despotism of a chieftain, who owes his elevation to arms and violence and leans on his sword as the only prop of his dominion. Such a conqueror, jealous and fond of nothing but his power, will care no more for Virginia, though he may rise by Virginia, than Bonaparte does for Corsica. Virginia will find, that, like ancient Thebes, she has worked for Philip, and forged her own fetters.[65]

In 1805, Ames might not have imagined that these fears would someday be embodied in the likes of Andrew Jackson, James Knox Polk, and Jefferson Davis rather than Napoléon and his marshals. But Ames's warnings were nonetheless remarkably prescient about America's future direction under the consolidated leadership of King Cotton, and how Virginia's scheme would eventually redound against Virginia itself.

Josiah Quincy and the Lure of Secession

By the time that Ames died in 1808, his successor as Boston's representative to Congress, Josiah Quincy, had established himself as Ames's equal in hostility to Jefferson and the imperial ambitions of the Virginia dynasts. As Quincy himself wrote, "I came to Washington with an abhorrence of Jefferson's political character."[66] After fifteen years of fiercely partisan factional conflict in the national government, embittered by the effects of the French Revolution on international relations, Quincy lacked the optimism for the success of federative politics that Ames had displayed at the beginning of his congressional career. But Quincy's focus differed from the issues that obsessed Ames. As his son Edmund put it years later, Quincy early on saw the dangers to which "an oligarchy, resting on ownership of human beings, as a constituent part of our national polity, exposed the future of the young Republic; . . . this . . . prevailing feeling gave the keynote to his fiercest utterances."[67] Ames used the word "slavery" in the sense common to the revolutionary generation, as a capacious term to describe unwarranted political dominion.[68] For Quincy, rhetorical slavery often meant actual chattel slavery, and this fatal flaw in America's composition doomed its hopes for successful republican government. This outlook shaped all of Quincy's efforts to represent Boston in the national confederation.

It can be difficult to keep the Josiah Quincys straight, for there were so many of them in eighteenth- and nineteenth-century Massachusetts history. This Quincy line constituted the more prosperous and prominent branch of the family that John Adams married into. Our Quincy (Josiah Quincy III) was the grandson of the Josiah Quincy who captured a Spanish treasure ship in 1748 carrying 161 chests of gold and silver. This first Josiah Quincy, who liked to be called "Colonel," sold his house in Boston and left the merchant business to his brother, retired to Braintree, built the largest mansion in town, and lived out his life as a local patriarch. The Colonel's son, also named Josiah, became a brilliant lawyer; he and Adams were cocounsel in the "Boston Massacre" trials. Like Adams, Quincy Jr. staunchly supported the resistance movement. In 1774, he sailed for London on behalf of the Continental Congress to gain firsthand information on Parliament's intentions in the wake of the Coercive Acts. But the younger Quincy had never been in good health. He was overtaken by "a consumption" and died on April 26, 1775, on board the homeward-bound ship.

In his will, he left the following to his son: "When he shall reach the age of fifteen years, Algernon Sidney's works in a large quarto, John Locke's Works in 3 Vols. in Folio, Lord Bacon's Works in 4 Vol.

in Folio, Gordon's Tacitus in 4 Vol., Gordon's Sallust, Cato's Letters by Gordon and Trenchard and Mrs. Macauley's History of England. May the Spirit of Liberty rest upon him."[69] It did. Josiah Quincy III was only three when his father expired, but his mother, Abigail Phillips, was the daughter of another wealthy Boston family, and she sent her son to boarding school at the Phillips Academy in Andover, Massachusetts, founded by her cousin.[70] Josiah recoiled at the school's severe discipline, but developed a lifelong interest in Greek and Latin. Harvard College further developed these interests, which along with the library of Whig writers bestowed on him by his father and a deep commitment to the honor of one of New England's oldest families, confirmed Quincy in his devotion to the ideals of New England republican government shared by his late father, the young Adams, Ames, and Boston's Federalists.[71] (See plate 19.)

One other literary legacy reinforced these beliefs. The year before his fatal trip to England, Quincy Jr. had taken an extended tour of the southern colonies, hoping that a milder climate would restore his health. He kept a journal of his observations, recording his dismay at the conditions for slaves on southern plantations and the detrimental effect of slavery on the masters themselves: "The brutality used toward the slaves has a very bad tendency with reference to the manners of the people." These concerns made him doubt the South's capacity for republican government: "The luxury, dissipation, life, sentiments, and manners of the leading people naturally tend to make them neglect, despise, and be careless of the true interest of mankind."[72] The "defective" quality of South Carolina's "constitution" worried him further: "It is true they have a house of Assembly, but whom do they represent? The labourer, the mechanic, the tradesman, the farmer, or yeoman? No,—the representatives are almost wholly rich planters. The planting interest is therefore represented, but I conceive nothing else, as it ought to be."[73]

Like the father he never knew, Josiah Quincy III read law in a Boston office, the office of William Tudor where Fisher Ames had trained not many years before. Although his career trajectory resembled that of Adams and Ames—childhood education in the hinterland, Harvard College, then reading law and practicing in

Boston—the bounty of his family's fortunes meant that Quincy did not have to dig treasures with his fingers. Quincy, more than Adams or Ames, deliberately chose politics as a profession and Boston as its center. In 1796, at the age of twenty-four, he took his place as a member of the Boston town meeting and was soon selected town orator by Boston's selectmen—a position of honor in this speech-loving town. After a failed run for Congress in 1802, when he lost to William Eustis, a popular Revolutionary War veteran, Quincy ran again in 1804, this time taking a larger portion of the Boston vote and winning the seat that Ames had occupied.[74]

Although Ames was older by only fourteen years, Quincy revered his predecessor as a legendary figure from his own youth, when politicians such as John Lowell and George Cabot would gather with Ames in Quincy's grandfather's house. Quincy remembered listening to "the brilliant conversation of Ames, so full of imagery, drawing similes to illustrate the topics of his discourse from everything about him."[75] As he prepared to join Congress on his election in 1804, Quincy "diligently applied himself to the study of the French language . . . to converse easily with foreign ministers, and other European visitors whom he met at Washington." Quincy's preparations also included studying "American history and politics, especially . . . between the adoption of the Federal Constitution and [the present]." He scoured the published debates, newspapers, and pamphlets to "obtain a command of all the topics which then or before had divided the American people. . . . I opened a folio commonplace-book, on John Locke's plan, embracing abstracts and researches into the history of the United States."[76] Quincy prepared for his position as congressman from Boston to the US Congress as though he were assuming a diplomatic role. He readied himself to converse with Europeans who were critical players in the making of US policy and tried to form not a provincial political view as an agent for his congressional district alone, but a truly empathic understanding of the issues that "had divided the American people" in order to make the government of the national confederation succeed.

Yet even before he went to Washington, Quincy embarked on a political trajectory that would make the success of these national aspirations impossible. Before the congressional election of 1804, Quincy represented Boston in the Massachusetts state senate, where he promoted "a movement for eliminating from the national Constitution the clause permitting the Slave States to count three fifths of their slaves as a part of their basis of representation." This was known as the Ely Amendment, as it was drafted by Massachusetts congressman William Ely.[77] In the presidential election of 1800, Jefferson's narrow victory over Adams was attributable to the fifteen additional electoral college votes that the three-fifths clause, commonly called the "Federal Ratio," had given to the Virginian.[78]

On this issue, Quincy's opinion would never waver. In a later speech before the Washington Benevolent Society of Boston, he outlined the Federal Ratio's effect on Massachusetts' interests:

> The States of Virginia and Georgia together possess a white population but a little exceeding that of Massachusetts. Yet, through the effect of the slave ratio and the principles of the Constitution, while Massachusetts possesses in the Senate and the House of Representatives twenty-two votes, they possess thirty-three! . . . I state one other fact. The power attained in the House of Representatives by the effect of the slave ratio is twenty votes. The State of Massachusetts has but twenty. So that this great and ancient and once proud, but now, constitutionally speaking, humbled Commonwealth, has absolutely no more weight in the national scale than a species of beings in fact as destitute of political rights as the brute creation.[79]

The southern states' intransigent commitment to the slave ratio helped explain the futility of Massachusetts' political efforts in the national congress. Had Ames's federative style of politics succeeded in shaping the operations of the national congress, then the slave ratio might not have troubled New England. But in the winner-take-all politics that emerged in the first years of national government, these numbers mattered enormously, and Quincy was prudent to count them carefully.

Through eight years in congress, Quincy saw slavery as part of a larger set of problems. What seized Quincy's attention was the fundamental difference between the political economy of the city-state of Boston and its confined New England hinterland, and the vision that Jefferson and his presidential successor, Madison, projected for an American empire of liberty (and slavery) extending from the southern states to the ever-expanding west. Three interrelated issues, each grounded in these conflicting visions, dominated Quincy's congressional career: the embargo of 1807–9 in which Congress prohibited all American overseas trade, the political disposition of the Louisiana territories, and the War of 1812. Each of these issues raised serious questions about the value of the union to Boston.

From the time Quincy entered Congress, the possibility of Boston leading the New England states in secession was in the air. In 1803–4, Senator Timothy Pickering of Massachusetts was part of a "conspiracy" among several New England congressmen to withdraw from the union and create a "northern confederacy."[80] Conspiracy, however, is a term applied to these events seventy years later by the historian Henry Adams. Although the supposed conspirators, which included Senator William Plumer of New Hampshire and Congressman Roger Griswold of Connecticut, did not trumpet their conversations in public, neither did they keep them secret, for what they were doing was political, not treasonous. They were motivated by their opposition to the Louisiana Purchase, Jefferson's impeachments of federal judges, and Jeffersonian constitutional amendments that favored the repeated election of Jefferson and his chosen successors to the presidency. The Twelfth Amendment, by requiring electors to designate separate votes for president and vice president, allowed parties to run presidential "tickets" for the first time, preventing the possibility that a president elected from one party would have to work with a vice president from an opposing party, as happened in 1796 when Jefferson became Adams's vice president. (Massachusetts rejected ratification of this amendment in 1804, and did not ratify it until 1961.) Napoléon's recent self-elevation from Consul to First Consul for Life to Emperor of the French pushed these concerns to the forefront of the contemporary political imagination.[81]

Pickering's secession plan failed to win overwhelming support in the New England states, in part because it conflicted with the simultaneous efforts of Quincy and others to support the Ely Amendment that would eliminate the three-fifths clause. By the time Quincy took his seat in Congress, Pickering's scheme had faded. But during his four terms in office, with the Jefferson and Madison administrations advancing measures ever more destructive to Boston's political economy, Quincy experienced a growing sense of desperation not unlike that of Pickering and his collaborators. Over these eight years, Quincy's hope that the state legislatures could be used to amend the Constitution gave way to serious contemplation of withdrawing Massachusetts from the union.

The Embargo

In 1802, the Treaty of Amiens created a year's truce between Britain and France, but with the truce's end, the United States found it increasingly difficult to maintain official neutrality between the combatants. President Washington had instigated the neutrality policy in 1793, permitting the wide-ranging foreign trade that had been the mainstay of Boston's commercial prosperity through much of the 1790s. Boston's recovery from the destruction of 1775–76 had been accelerated by its merchants' ability to exploit overseas markets free of domestic restrictions. But the resumption of warfare in 1804 led to renewed attempts by Britain and France to use embargoes, blockades, and trade restrictions to prevent the United States (and other neutral countries) from trading with their respective enemies. The Jefferson administration's responses generally favored France and harmed Britain. During Quincy's first term, the overwhelmingly Jeffersonian Congress (113–26 in the House, 27–7 in the Senate) passed a bill prohibiting the importation of an extensive list of goods from Britain.[82] Given that this act of Congress resembled the nonimportation agreements made by the Continental Congress in 1774 and 1775, the prospect that it would likewise provoke Britain into war was a serious threat.

Quincy made his first major speech in Congress to address this danger. His choice to come forward was prompted by the way this moment resonated with his late father's most famous political work, *Observations on the Boston Port-Bill; with Thoughts on Civil Society and Standing Armies* (1774). Quincy's father had called for Boston to resist Britain's military power by quoting Plutarch's *Life of Brutus*: "'On the ides of March,' said the great and good man to his friend Cassius, just before the battle of Philippi,—'on the ides of March I devoted my life to my country, and since that time I have lived a life of liberty and glory,'"[83] Like the ancient city-colony of Philippi in the age of Cassius, Brutus, Octavius, and Mark Antony, Boston was now squeezed between competing military threats: Britain, on one hand, and Napoleonic France, seemingly allied with the Jefferson administration, on the other.

The younger Quincy's objection to nonimportation lay not in the danger of war itself. Boston's merchants were willing to defend their commercial rights, with force if necessary, as Ames had argued since the Anglo-French Wars began in the 1790s. Rather, Quincy protested that Jefferson's administration had virtually eliminated the US Navy, and had failed to defend American coasts and seaports, leaving the United States badly exposed should war with Britain erupt. Quincy believed that the Jeffersonian majority in Congress simply failed to appreciate how vital overseas commerce and the security of port cities were to New England, and thus to the union: "It may be sport to you, gentlemen, but it is death to us."[84] He also reminded his opponents that the commerce of the "eastern states" generated the revenue of the United States as a whole.[85] In the corporal metaphor favored by Bostonians, death to a necessary part meant death to the whole.

Quincy's moving speech took pains to explain (to his uninformed southern colleagues) the nature of the integrated commercial and agricultural economy that Boston and New England had developed: rural farmers and urban merchants were linked by commercial bonds, easily taken for granted until something like a war disrupted overseas trade. At such times, "the country is associated with the city in one common distress, not merely through sympathy, but by an actual perception of a union in misfortune." For Quincy, this traditional New England relationship was no idle or changeable thing: "The true tap-root of commerce is found in the nature and character of the people who carry it on. They and their ancestors, for nearly two centuries, have been engaged in it." He warned Congress that the people of New England would not permanently submit to a national government that raised its revenue from taxes on overseas trade but failed to defend this commerce against threats, foreign or domestic.[86]

At this point, early in his congressional career, Quincy believed that reconciliation would triumph over nullification or secession. In that spirit, he advised his southern colleagues to show their appreciation for New England's commercial interests, "to give them a due share of the national revenue for their protection. Show an enlightened and fair reciprocity." But should they continue to pursue a "narrow, selfish, local, sectional policy," then conflict within the union would result "in either a change of the system of government or in its dissolution."[87] With a few changes in vocabulary, substituting "enlightened" and "reciprocity" for "Christian charity," Quincy's speech could have been written by John Winthrop; with fewer changes, by John Adams or Fisher Ames. Quincy articulated a philosophy of political economy essentially unchanged from Boston's colonial past as a countervailing position to that of Greater Virginia. Like Adams and Ames before him, Quincy promoted federative politics as the only means to sustain a confederation containing such different political economies. During his remaining years in national office, his position would not change, but the desperation with which he advanced it grew, crisis by crisis.

The first crisis emerged directly out of the nonimportation measure of 1806. Lord Horatio Nelson's decisive naval victory at the Battle of Trafalgar in October 1805 established Britain's dominance of the seas, leaving the French Navy crippled. Napoléon responded with the Berlin Decree of 1806, establishing his "Continental System" across conquered Europe. It forbade the importation of British goods, regardless of the carrier's nationality, anywhere in continental Europe under French authority, from Prussia on the Baltic to Italy in the Mediterranean, and all points westward with the exception of Portugal and Denmark. Britain responded with its own Orders in Council (1807), declaring commercial warfare against any country, neutral or aligned, that traded with France and its dependencies, putting the Royal Navy to work blockading ports and seizing ships that violated these orders.

American merchants were left in a quandary. President Jefferson, still supported by an overwhelming majority in Congress (roughly four to one), responded to this assault on America's neutral trade by declaring an absolute embargo. In December 1807, Congress passed Jefferson's Embargo Act, prohibiting all American merchant ships from leaving US harbors for foreign destinations. Exceptions were allowed only from President Jefferson's hand. From New England's viewpoint, this was the Boston Port Bill all over again, now imposed by King Thomas and his Congress rather than King George and his Parliament.

Through month after month of 1808, the embargo devastated Boston's commerce. Ships rotted at the docks, the fisheries and their Caribbean trade went dormant, unemployment skyrocketed, and New England fell into depression.[88] By contrast, southern production of goods like tobacco and cotton went relatively unimpaired, as the Embargo Act actually permitted British ships to carry these items as exports. For the embargo's first three months, British imports of American cotton barely declined at all. After further legislation tightened restrictions on exports, twelve million pounds of American cotton were nonetheless imported by Britain in 1808. This was a significant decline but not an utter decimation of the trade, and southern planters could hold this nonperishable crop for future sales after embargo-induced prices had risen.[89] In short, the embargo punished Boston without harming southern cotton planters.

When Congress reconvened in the fall, Quincy attacked the embargo. Although he formally represented only Boston's congressional district, he adopted a rhetorical position familiar to Boston's political leaders, speaking to and for the nation of New England. Much as Ames had done in his political essays, Quincy explained to his fellow congressmen the nature of the city-state of Boston's political economy: "Our people are not scattered over an immense surface, at a solemn distance from each other. . . . They are collected on the margin of the ocean, by the sides of rivers, at the heads of bays, looking into the water or on the surface of it for the incitement and the reward of their industry."[90] Quincy's address was occasioned by the distorting effect of the language used by Jeffersonians in Congress. The Committee on Foreign Relations had resolved not to submit to "the edicts of Great Britain and France."[91] Quincy initially took this to be good news, thinking that the embargo would end and Americans would finally fight to defend their trading rights.[92] But no; the committee report went on to argue "that therefore the Embargo should be continued."[93] To Quincy, this bizarre logic proved that the Jeffersonians simply could not recognize New England's value to the union, and he lashed out against their ignorance. He compared New England's commerce to a force of natural law: "Should this House undertake to declare that this atmosphere should no longer surround us, that water should cease to flow, that gravity should not hereafter operate, . . . just as utterly absurd and contrary to nature is it to attempt to prohibit the people of New England, for any considerable length of time, from the ocean."[94]

Nathaniel Macon, a Jeffersonian congressman from North Carolina, challenged Quincy and New England to show more of the "spirit of '76," by which he meant unity among the states against an external enemy. Quincy snapped back, reminding Congress of the causes for rebellion against Britain: "*Unnecessary restrictions upon trade; cutting off commercial intercourse between the Colonies; embarrassing our fisheries; wantonly depriving our citizens of necessaries; invasion of private property by governmental edicts; the authority of the commander-in-chief, and under him the brigadier-general, being rendered supreme in the civil government; the commander-in-chief of the army made governor of a Colony*"—all measures implemented by the Embargo Act and the act for administering the Louisiana Territory.[95] For Quincy, the national government under Jefferson and his Congressional supermajorities had become no less "external" to Boston's interests than King George and his Parliament had been in 1776.

Quincy also attacked the distorted reasoning behind the Foreign Relations Committee's desire to continue the embargo: "Let me ask; *Is Embargo Independence?* Deceive not yourselves. It is palpable submission. . . . Gentlemen say, Great Britain is a robber, she '*takes our cloak*.' And what says Administration? '*Let her take our coat also*.' France and Great Britain require you to relinquish a part of your commerce, and you yield it entirely. Sir, this conduct may be the way to dignity and honor in another world, but it will never secure safety and independence in this."[96] Here, Quincy seems to have departed from Winthrop's "Christian Charity," which used the counterintuitive injunctions of the Sermon on the Mount as a model for the compact among Boston's founders. But on closer look, Quincy was flinging the hypocrisy of Jefferson's dream of universal free trade without the power to defend it back at the Republicans in Congress. Quincy meant to show that the Jeffersonians had never treated Boston and New England as equal partners in the corporate body of the federal compact. When Britain wants to steal an American cloak, Jefferson's administration gives her Boston's coat, sacrificing New England's overseas commerce, but preserving Virginia's interests by leaving tobacco exports open to Britain's carrying trade. In the topsy-turvy moral world of Jeffersonian politics, enemies like Britain are treated as friends, while fellow members of the same body are sloughed off as needless appendages.

Nine days later, Quincy turned his oratory from the logic of the embargo to the nuts and bolts—or rather, potatoes and cabbage—of political economy. Quincy insisted that New England's merchants were not intimidated by British and French threats, and would fight to defend their right to trade. A Jeffersonian congressman, George Troup of Georgia, interrupted Quincy to ridicule New England's "paltry trade in . . . potatoes and cabbages" compared with the south's high-value plantation commodities.[97] Quincy's response defended his native country's political economy and brought the lurking issue of slavery to the fore. Yes, New England farmers raised modest goods for sale, but Quincy swore that he would rather represent them than "to be the representative of all the growers of cotton, and rice, and tobacco, and indigo, in the whole world. Sir, the men whom I represent not only raise these humble articles, *but* they do it *with the labor of their own hands,—with the sweat of their own brows.*" In addition to denigrating the southern use of slaves, Quincy promoted the intelligence and martial prowess of New England's working men, whose "hardy industry" made them perpetually ready to defend their rights.[98]

Quincy here touched on a seldom-spoken truth. New England had long enjoyed the strongest martial reputation of any part of British America. Its disciplined system of town-based government sustained a strong militia, and during Britain's imperial wars, Bostonians were effective at recruiting soldiers and sending them to fight on distant fields. By contrast, the predominance of slave labor was a severe handicap to the southern states' fighting power. Both the threat of slave insurrection (with the example of Haiti on plantation owners' minds in 1808) and the underdeveloped structure of local government, taxation, and public service weakened the South's military capacities.[99] The War for Independence had clearly borne this out. Proportional to wealth and population, New England sent more soldiers and spent more money on the war than the other states.

On behalf of his Boston constituents, Quincy was appalled by Jeffersonian schemes to exploit New England's martial spirit and its free laboring men. As the potential for war mounted, the Democratic-Republican Congress passed a bill offering bounties for the military enlistment of minors without parental approval. In another dramatic speech on the House floor, Quincy explained that this bill effectively bribed the sons of New England farmers and artisans away from their parents by playing on the region's martial culture. The promise of "false glory" would lure New England's free laborers to war, while southern slaves would continue to toil in their masters' fields. Quincy accused southerners in Congress of promoting, for their own benefit, a version of mass military service on the French revolutionary model, from which their own enslaved labor would be exempt.[100]

These speeches made Quincy widely hated by southern congressmen, who began to pour vitriol on him, aiming to force him into a duel; "false," "malicious," "defamatory," "cowardly," "base detraction," "dastardly act," "old Tory," "friend to Great Britain," and "Nero" were among their ad hominem attacks. Quincy framed his refusal to fight in the language of New England nationalism: "It is a disgrace, *in my country*, to avenge wrongs of words in the way which is here, in a manner, necessary."[101] His resolve was strengthened by support from Boston colleagues, including Harrison Gray Otis, who had served two terms as Boston's congressman between Ames and Quincy, and was now president of the Massachusetts Senate. Otis assured him that Massachusetts was ready to support Quincy's defiance of the embargo.

Any action to nullify the embargo or separate from the union would require cooperation across the country of New England. In December 1808, Otis called on Quincy to sound out the Connecticut delegates to Congress to see if they were ready to declare the embargo unconstitutional and call a convention of New England states, "at Hartford or elsewhere," to discuss their options. The suggestion of Hartford as the site for such a convention echoed the reason why the New England Confederation of 1643 was framed in Hartford as well. Massachusetts was New England's dominant power, and Boston was its center of authority. But a convention in Hartford rather than Boston, called by Connecticut's legislature and congressional delegates, would demonstrate that the historic integration of New England's economy still supported the region's independence.[102] It was a disturbing fact, however, unintentionally revealed by Otis's letter, that Washington, DC, was now the place best suited for planning such a strategy for New England. Two decades of national government had created an alternative locus of power besides Boston.

As the embargo continued to depress New England, ambivalence hung in the air, reminiscent of the period in 1774 after the Coercive Acts. Was it better, asked Otis, to "sit down quietly and count the links of our chains," or was the Jeffersonian stranglehold "so monstrous, so unprecedented, so ruinous," as to "make resistance a duty"?[103] Other local measures in Boston pushed for separation from the union. In January 1809, a group of merchants led by

Thomas Handasyd Perkins called for a town meeting to discuss resistance to the enforcement of the embargo, much as they had done in the 1760s and 1770s with the Townshend and Tea Acts. The New England *Centinel* described the meeting as the "Second Rocking of the Cradle of American Independence." Perkins presented a resolution calling those who complied with the embargo "enemies of the Constitution of the U.S., enemies of the State of Massachusetts and hostile to the liberties of the people," deliberately echoing Patrick Henry's Stamp Act Resolutions in the Virginia House of Burgesses. Perkins's resolution (unlike Henry's) carried the meeting by an overwhelming majority—more than 85 percent of the vote.[104]

But unlike in 1774, over the next several months the pressure eased. The 1808 elections saw a Federalist resurgence in the House of Representatives, reducing the Jeffersonian majority. In the presidential election, the New England states stood solidly against Madison, depriving him of a landslide comparable to Jefferson's. These results convinced Madison that the embargo should be repealed, and Congress dutifully complied. As New England's economy began to recover, discussions of secession lapsed until the next major crisis: the debate over the admission of the state of Louisiana. For the moment, membership in the federal compact seemed to provide New England with advantages that subordination to Parliament had lacked.

Louisiana and the Breaking of the Federal Compact

When Quincy arrived in Washington, DC, for his first session of Congress in 1805, the Louisiana Purchase was already a fait accompli. Nonetheless, in Quincy's later recollection, it "filled me with inexpressible disgust and apprehension." Quincy recognized the valid national interests that prompted the Purchase: "The people of the Western States were clamorous for the free opening of the Mississippi. . . . Had Jefferson confined his policy to that object, it would have received the approbation even of the Northern States."[105] When reckoned in the manner of federative politics long characteristic of the city-state of Boston, the navigation of the Mississippi and the use of the port of New Orleans were legitimate concerns of western states like Kentucky, Tennessee, and Ohio, just as Atlantic trade was for New England. These new western states had been formally admitted to the union by the time that Quincy arrived in Congress, under explicit provisions in the Constitution for the admission of new states from the nation's western territory.[106] All this was part of the original pact that Massachusetts had ratified in 1788. The Constitution, though, had (and has) no provisions for the acquisition of new territory beyond what was granted to the United States in the Treaty of Paris of 1783. Therefore, it also lacks any provisions for the admission of new states from territory that had not originally been part of the United States. Here lay the source of Quincy's apprehension and disgust.

Jefferson's Louisiana Purchase extended the president's diplomatic power beyond the letter of the Constitution, but Quincy agreed that the Louisiana Purchase itself was demonstrably in the interest of some of the member states. In that regard it was no different from Hamilton's proposals for a national bank or funded debt—not expressly granted as a power in the Constitution, but consistent with its principle for promoting the union's general welfare. The Louisiana Purchase was not the problem. Rather, Quincy's objections were grounded in his understanding of the federal compact itself and in his commitment to the federative process.[107] The form of government imposed on the immense Louisiana territory by Jefferson, in which all power lay in the hands of appointees chosen by the territorial governor, had been troubling in its own right—reminiscent of Britain's Quebec settlements or Nova Scotia. The Boston *Repertory* declared that "the establishment of a monarchy over a large country appertaining to the United States is a gross violation of the spirit of the Constitution." Massachusetts clergyman and congressman for Essex County Menasseh Cutler was even more caustic, comparing the Louisiana territorial governor to the despotism of "the Grand Turk. Every officer is appointed by him, holds his commission during his pleasure, and is amenable only to him. He is the executive, the legislature, and the judicature." Cutler had assisted in drafting the 1787 Northwest Ordinance, which had prohibited slavery in the Northwest Territory and provided for a representative assembly for territorial residents before admission to statehood. He abhorred the striking departure that Louisiana made from earlier precedent.[108] Even the Jeffersonian William Eustis, Quincy's predecessor in Boston's congressional seat, admitted that this territorial government was a "new thing in the United States," but defended it on the grounds that Louisiana's Spanish population was accustomed to despotism.

Quincy's position on the constitutional questions followed Cutler and the *Repertory*, but in one sense, he agreed with Jefferson and Eustis. Like many New Englanders, including Adams and his own father, Quincy had been dubious about the prospect that all of the British North American colonies, different as they were in character and political economies, could be governed collectively as a single republic. But at least the "thirteen colonies" had long experience of internal self-government through their colonial legislatures. As independent states, they had expressed their commitment to republican government in the compact made by the US Constitution (Article IV, Section 4). None of these conditions were true for the residents of the Louisiana Territory, whom Quincy described as "a population alien to [the Constitution] in every element of character, previous education and political tendency, . . . French and Spanish subjects whose habits, manners, and ideals of civil government are wholly foreign to republican institutions."[109] From Quincy's viewpoint, the future disposition of the Louisiana Purchase threatened to pull the already-stretched capacities of the United States for self-government to the breaking point, extending the "southern yoke" that Adams had feared to include the yoke of Spanish despotism.

After the admission of Ohio in 1803, the union held steady at seventeen states; Vermont, Kentucky, Tennessee, and Ohio, formed out of territory granted to the United States under the Paris Treaty of 1783, plus the original thirteen. Despite the rapid movement of American citizens to the trans-Appalachian west (and their displacement of Indian peoples), enormous stretches of US territory remained just that—territories administered by the federal government. Fully 40 percent of the land under US authority had appointed territorial governments.[110] But in the legislative sessions of 1810–11, the Madison administration pushed for the admission of Louisiana, then known as the Territory of Orleans, as a new state in the union. Its valuable land west of the Mississippi was rapidly filling up with new plantations. During the deliberations on January 14, 1811, Quincy rose to address the House "with an anxiety and distress of mind with me wholly unprecedented." He based his adamant opposition on constitutional grounds:[111]

> Mr. Speaker. . . . The friends of this bill seem to consider it as the exercise of a common power, as an ordinary affair, a mere municipal regulation which they expect to see pass without other questions than those concerning details.[112] But, Sir, the principle of this bill materially affects the liberties and rights of the whole people of the United States. To me it appears that it would justify a revolution in this country, and that in no great length of time it may produce it. . . . I am compelled to declare it *as my deliberate opinion, that, if this bill passes, the bonds of this Union are virtually dissolved; that the States which compose it are free from their moral obligations, and that, as it will be the right of all, so it will be the duty of some, to prepare definitely for a separation; amicably if they can, violently if they must.*[113]

At this point, the nonvoting delegate from the Mississippi Territory interrupted Quincy and called him out of order. Quincy appealed to the House, which voted its approval for him to continue, as his observations were meant as "no low intrigue; no secret machination." He wanted his constitutional objections heard "on the people's own ground; to them I appeal concerning their own rights, their own liberties, their own intent, in adopting this Constitution."[114] This was no conspiracy or cabal; it was Quincy's open attempt to defend Boston's understanding of the federal compact.

The Jeffersonian arguments for the constitutionality of Louisiana's admission had not been persuasive, and Quincy attacked them directly. Representative John Rhea of Tennessee had drawn an analogy from the agrarian mythos of Jeffersonian expansionism: "If I have a farm, have not I a right to purchase another farm in my neighborhood and settle my sons upon it, and in time admit them to a share in the management of my household?" Quincy clarified the difference between Rhea's patriarchal metaphor and his understanding of federal government:

> Are these cases parallel? Are the three branches of this government owners of this farm called the United States? I desire to thank Heaven they are not. . . . [N]either the gentleman from Tennessee, nor his comrades, . . . nor of the other branches of the Legislature, nor the good gentleman who lives in the palace yonder [he meant Madison], nor all combined, can touch these my essential rights, and those of my friends and constituents, except in a limited and prescribed form. No, Sir. We hold these by the laws, customs, and principles of the Commonwealth of Massachusetts. . . . I beg gentlemen not to act upon the principle that the Commonwealth of Massachusetts is their farm.[115]

Quincy insisted that Congress must only act under the principle that the Constitution was a compact, made by the people through their sovereign states. This compact was made for the mutual benefit of all the states that joined it, and carefully designed to balance and accommodate the obvious inequalities that existed among the contracting parties.

To make this argument, Quincy cited Washington, who had described the Constitutional Convention's proceedings in these terms. For Washington, it had been difficult to draw "the line between those rights which must be surrendered [to the national government] and those which may be reserved [to the states]; and . . . this difficulty was increased by a difference among the several States as to their situation, extent, habits, and particular interests."[116] The Ely Amendment of 1803–4, proposed in the Massachusetts legislature and promoted by Quincy, had claimed that the Constitution's initial balance had been thrown off by the rapid expansion of the southern slave population and Congress's failure to use direct taxation methods equalized across the states, as opposed to customs duties that heavily burdened the commercial states. The Constitution needed amending to restore a proper balance of these interests.[117] Yet now, Quincy argued, the admission of the territory of Orleans to statehood and the prospect for the admission of many more states (six? nine? fifteen?) from the vast Louisiana Territory, all potentially slave states, made a mockery of the careful balance crafted by the Constitution's authors: "They were not madmen. They had not taken degrees at the hospital of idiocy. They knew the nature of man and the effect of his combinations in political societies. They knew that when the weight of particular sections of a confederacy was greatly unequal, the resulting power would be abused; that it was not in the nature of man to exercise it with moderation."[118]

On the basis of the sovereignty of its ratifying bodies—the people in the states—Quincy insisted that the Constitution was a compact, a legal contract, and asserted, as any lawyer would, that "the violation of a contract by one of the parties may be considered as exempting the other from its obligations." He compared the Constitution to a business partnership: "Suppose in private life thirteen form a partnership, and ten of them undertake to admit a new partner without the concurrence of the other three, would it not be at their option to abandon the partnership after so palpable an infringement of their rights?" A political partnership was far more dangerous, however, "where the admission of new associates without previous authority is so pregnant with obvious dangers and evils!"[119] In Quincy's view, the admission of Louisiana to statehood, to equal status in the compact, and the precedent that it would set for the admission of untold future "partners" from unlimited future territories, brought the constitutional compact to an end: "I oppose this bill from no animosity to the people of New Orleans, but from the deep conviction that it contains a principle incompatible with the liberties and safety of my country. I have no concealment of my opinion. The bill, if it passes, is a death-blow to the Constitution."[120] On the day after Quincy's speech, the bill passed the House by a vote of seventy-seven to thirty-six. This was certainly a large majority, but not the three-quarters supermajority that had been necessary under the Articles of Confederation or the three-quarters majority of states necessary to amend the Constitution. Yet from Quincy's perspective, it was hard to see how the Louisiana Purchase and the admission of innumerable new states within it was not a dramatic amendment to the Constitution's fundamental balance. On April 30, 1812, Louisiana became the eighteenth member state of the United States, while two-fifths of the nation's original territory still lay under appointive government.

In the careful, legalistic way in which Massachusetts had always used its charters to defend its autonomy, Josiah Quincy's 1811 argument in Congress aligned precisely with the case that John Adams made in his *Novanglus* essays against Parliament's encroaching authority over the Massachusetts General Court. Adams had acknowledged the authority of the Crown because the king's charter had been accepted by the people as a valid compact. But he rejected Parliament's claims to authority because nowhere in the charter, or in any positive law passed in England or Massachusetts, was Parliament's right to legislate for Massachusetts ever granted by the king or accepted by the people. To suffer Parliament's dominion without consent was slavery. In the same vein, Quincy acknowledged Massachusetts' obligations to the other states it had joined in ratifying the Constitution and the new states added to the union out of the original territory for which the Constitution provided a formal process. But for Massachusetts to be placed under the potential authority of Louisiana's representatives, and those of unlimited future states that might someday be added to the union without Massachusetts' consent, and with no express language in the original compact providing for such expansion, was likewise slavery. It was a condition, as Lord Mansfield had said in the Somerset case, too odious to be tolerated.

In the conclusion to his Louisiana speech, Quincy declared his ultimate political allegiance. "I confess it," he said, "the first public love of my heart is the Commonwealth of Massachusetts. . . . The love of this Union grows out of this attachment to my native soil, and is rooted in it."[121] Before his speech on the admission of

Louisiana, he had already been elected to a fourth term in Congress from 1811–13. His support from Boston was strong, and his margins of victory had grown with each election, but Quincy would not run for national office again. Now that a ruling majority of the union had abandoned the principles on which he had understood it to operate, he could no longer serve in Congress. As Quincy later explained, "Seven years of observation and experience in the national Legislature had brought my mind to the conclusion that the *Southern*, as then called, but now *the Slave-holding States*, were omnipotent in this Union. That their influence was not temporary, but *permanent*."[122]

The War of 1812 and Pressure for Separation

Quincy's last two years in Washington were dominated by the slow run-up to war against Britain pursued by the Madison administration and the war hawks in the Democratic-Republican Congress.[123] To the prospect of war itself, Quincy did not object. He had long argued that New Englanders would gladly fight to defend their right to pursue overseas commerce. But the war that Madison sought seemed unlikely to serve that purpose. Once war was declared, Quincy spoke out against the act to enlist minors since it discriminated against New England's free labor and protected slave labor. He also denounced the US military invasion of Canada, which did nothing to oppose the Royal Navy's depredations on the high seas, the declared purpose of the war.[124]

When he retired from Congress, Quincy did not retire from politics. On returning home in 1813, he was immediately elected as one of Boston's senators in the Massachusetts General Court, where he took up the task that Otis had suggested in 1808, forging a consensus that could orchestrate a separation from the United States. A year of war had already damaged New England's economy, as the Royal Navy's dominance at sea made commerce hazardous. The absence of defensive preparations by the Jefferson and Madison administrations left the New England coast exposed to British invasion. Quincy's wife, Eliza, reported from Braintree that she "anxiously watched" the "ships in the harbor, especially those of a warlike character."[125]

Quincy's political context was now different as well. He had left the hostile environment of Washington, and was surrounded, both in Boston and the Massachusetts General Court, by an overwhelming majority of Federalist supporters among the clergy, the press, and political leaders. The general public seemed well ahead of its leaders in the violence of its opposition to "Mr. Madison's War."[126] In his first major speech to a Boston audience, Quincy repeated that the constitutional compact had now been violated and that to remain by choice under US rule, Virginia's rule, would be to admit that "we are slaves; and I add,—for I know the natures of the predominating influences of those States,—slaves to no very desirable masters." There was now but one way to fix this: "Out from your councils, and out from your confidence, be every man who will not maintain the old foundations of New England prosperity. . . . Contend earnestly for the commercial faith delivered by your fathers."[127]

Quincy faced the challenge of reconstructing the political unity across New England in 1813–14 that had prevailed in 1774–75 in order to make separation from a hostile government an attainable goal. The widespread resistance across New England to the war made this seem possible. Before leaving Congress, Quincy had denounced the invasion of Canada as an unjust war of aggression, so much akin to Napoléon's conquests in Europe as to ally the United States with France against Britain. Quincy singled out the "Three Virginians and a Foreigner"—Jefferson, Madison, Monroe, and Treasury Secretary Albert Gallatin, a native of Geneva, as the conspirators in this plan for military conquest to ensure that Monroe would follow Madison into the presidency, "that James the Second shall be made to succeed, according to the fundamental rescripts of the Monticellian dynasty."[128] Madison's war was different from the defensive commercial war against British *and* French restrictions that Quincy had formerly advocated. Support for this position in Boston was strong, indicated by pamphlets such as John Lowell Jr.'s *Mr. Madison's War* (1812), which argued that Madison had allied the United States with France by drumming up war against

Britain on false pretenses.[129] Lowell's claims were supported by Madison's continued pursuit of his war plan, despite the fact that Britain had withdrawn its Orders in Council restricting American neutral trade five days after Congress declared war.

Quincy took the lead in the Massachusetts Senate, and joined with James Lloyd (who had similarly resigned from the US Senate and returned to Massachusetts state politics) and Harrison Gray Otis in the lower house to propose a remonstrance against the war "as impolitic and unjust after the repeal of the Orders in Council,—as having the color at least of being waged in alliance with France against England."[130] The other state legislatures in New England followed suit. When the US Army sent national forces on expeditions to invade Canada, the chief military officer of New England, General Henry Dearborn, called for New England's state militias to man the defensive forts that the regular soldiers had left behind. Governor Caleb Strong of Massachusetts and his counterparts in Connecticut and Rhode Island refused to comply on constitutional grounds. They maintained that the nationalization of state militia was only to be undertaken for defensive emergencies, when US territory was in danger of foreign invasion, not to support the unwarranted invasion of neighboring countries. Amid the growing fear that state militia forces would also be marched to Canada, New England militia officers and enlisted men refused to comply with Dearborn's order.[131]

In December 1813, the Madison administration reimposed an embargo on all American seagoing trade, including the internal coasting trade within the United States, to prevent smuggling by New England's merchants. In response, towns throughout the region petitioned their state legislatures seeking relief, and much as in 1774, began to organize themselves spontaneously into county conventions to promote resistance from the bottom up.[132] By spring 1814, the Sixth Coalition of European allies had driven Napoléon's forces out of Germany and Spain, and forced the emperor's abdication and exile to Elba. With the European war seemingly at an end, Britain's military forces turned with greater strength to the American conflict.

The British Navy blockaded the Massachusetts coast, and conducted raids on harbors and exposed coastal towns. Although the state militia initially cooperated with federal troops under Captain William Bainbridge to protect the US warships stationed at the Charlestown Navy Yard, soon the General Court advised Bainbridge to move the ships to a remote part of Boston Harbor, to spare the city of Boston from bombardment by the Royal Navy. Bainbridge not only refused to comply but also warned that if Boston were to surrender to the British without a fight, "*he should certainly Fire upon the Town.*" The Boston town meeting then rallied under the leadership of Harrison Gray Otis in support of the state militia to defend the town against either Bainbridge's or Britain's threats.[133] But the prospect that Bainbridge, a US naval officer, might act on his threat, that as in 1775, Boston might be occupied and attacked by the armed forces of its own government, was not lost on the city.

In addition to ongoing resistance to military participation, the fiscal demands of the war created further opposition in Boston. The city's banks, always better capitalized than banks elsewhere in the United States, remained the only ones in the nation to sustain the capacity to make specie payments on banknotes. This led speculators to buy up New England banknotes for specie redemption. The cost of defending the region had mounted rapidly in 1814, and Madison's government refused to promise any national reimbursements for state war expenses. With the state war debt mounting, state taxation already high from war expenses, and New England's banks pressed for cash, the region's traditional ability to finance its own defense looked increasingly precarious as 1814 progressed.

The British Army sacked and burned Washington, DC, in August, making it appear as though the nation was defenseless, and that the union's fiscal and military resources had been squandered on a useless aggressive war against Canada. With the British Army taking the town of Castine, sacking Bangor, and gaining a hold on Maine's eastern region down to the Penobscot River, New England looked to bear the brunt of British retribution for Madison's folly. The military situation was exactly the reverse of the Revolutionary

War. Now Boston and its hinterland were the least committed members of the union, and Britain's military assault on the region was designed to split them off from the rest.

In this heated atmosphere, state legislators in the General Court spoke out in favor of an autonomous Massachusetts customs house, open defiance of the embargo, and raising an army of thirty thousand men "to protect the citizens of this commonwealth in the enjoyment of their constitutional rights." Massachusetts governor Caleb Strong secretly wrote to the military governor of Nova Scotia, assessing the possibility of a separate peace for Massachusetts in order to recover the Maine territory that the British Army had captured. At the same time, Governor Strong called the General Court into special session on October 5, 1814, to deal with the commonwealth's military and fiscal crisis.[134]

In so many ways, this critical moment called to mind the crisis of 1774. The British military blockaded Boston's trade and threatened its harbor, while the towns in the Massachusetts interior supported Boston's most radical leaders in pressing for drastic measures. In September 1814, with the British Army sweeping down the Maine coast, and refugees from Castine, Belfast, and Portland pouring into Boston, the city undertook a frenzy of defensive measures to fortify Boston Neck and strengthen strategic points throughout the harbor, while militia units from the countryside were on the march to defend the city.[135] But in other ways, the situation was completely different from 1774. The British military threat was not the main enemy of the moment. The separation that the radical leadership wanted was not from Britain but from the Virginia-dominated United States. Although the actions of the Jefferson and Madison administrations could easily be portrayed as a "long train of abuses" against the political economy of Boston and New England, there was no equivalent to the horrifying shocks of Lexington and Concord or Bunker Hill to galvanize political will; Captain Bainbridge's threat to "fire on the city" remained empty.

A deeper reason for the difference between 1774 and 1814 lay in the nature of the political divisions present at each moment within the commonwealth. Loyalism had certainly been a significant factor in Boston and Massachusetts in the 1770s, as demonstrated by the many exiles who left Boston when the British Army evacuated. But as a political force, loyalism had been limited by the thin reach of Crown patronage into the republican structure and practices of the commonwealth. Yes, the royal governor had appointed a small number of judges and civil servants, Whitehall had supplied customs agents, and during wartime, opportunities for military service expanded. But Crown service had not been a widely accessible avenue to political careers or local power for many citizens of the city-state of Boston in the colonial period. When the indigenous political structure of town governments and the General Court, for a century and a half the main path to political power, turned decisively against Crown rule in the wake of the Coercive Acts, the veneer of Crown patronage crumbled in the face of the popular onslaught.

Circumstances in 1814 were radically different. Federalists like Quincy, Governor Strong, Pickering, and Lowell did have strong popular support in both the city and hinterland, much as the radicals of 1774 like Hancock and the "brace of Adamses" had enjoyed. Nevertheless, over the course of the preceding twenty-five years, the growth of the Democratic-Republican Party across the United States, including New England, had created an alternative avenue to political power at both the local and national level. The United States as a whole had developed a participatory allegiance structure that the British Empire lacked for its colonies. Party organization provided a coherent framework for people throughout the commonwealth to seek access to office, replacing the loose and shifting factionalism of the colonial era. Although Federalists generally dominated Boston and Massachusetts politics, the Democratic-Republicans made strong inroads in many locations and won several statewide elections, exploiting the cracks in the unity of Massachusetts' political economy that the Regulator movement of 1786–87 had exposed.[136]

Quincy and the other leaders of the separatist movement had to consider this population and its allegiances in making a plan of resistance. Without a strong sense of consensus, if not unanimity, akin to that of 1774, an attempt at separation from the union would risk the prospect of violence or civil war within New England. When Governor Strong called the General Court into special session to address the crisis, some leading politicians like Otis proceeded cautiously. Despite popular calls for nullification of federal laws and secession from the union, the General Court proposed a more moderate path: a convention of delegates from all the New England states to deliberate on remedies for their current predicament. Part of the reason for their caution lay in the fluidity of the situation. Napoléon's abdication suggested that the French threat was over, and the war against Britain had gone so disastrously for the Madison administration that perhaps the Virginia dynasty in America was reaching its end as well. If there remained a prospect, however dim, for the restoration of balance within the union that would end New England's subordination, then secession at this moment might be a grave mistake.

The Massachusetts General Court overwhelmingly supported the "Otis Report" calling for a convention, as did the Connecticut and Rhode Island legislatures.[137] New Hampshire's legislature was not in session at the time of the call, but two of its counties sent delegates voluntarily. One Vermont county sent a delegate as well, though the state legislature was controlled by Democratic-Republicans. Hartford was chosen to host the meetings in order to convey that the protest against Mr. Madison's war was not confined to Boston and Massachusetts. But when Federalist leaders from both houses of the General Court met to choose the Massachusetts delegates, they excluded the most radical supporters of separation and nullification, such as Quincy, Lowell, and Pickering. The only truly radical member of the twelve delegates from Massachusetts was Timothy Bigelow Jr., a lawyer whose father, a Worcester blacksmith, had led the rural uprisings of 1774–75 that had overthrown Crown government in advance of Lexington and Concord.[138]

The Massachusetts Federalist leadership looked to the Hartford Convention as a means to restrain the radicalism of the local population, much as the Stamp Act Congress of 1765 and the First Continental Congress of 1774 had assessed the degree to which resistance to Parliament in places like Boston was supported by more distant colonies. The delegates themselves saw their task in exactly these terms. As Boston merchant George Cabot said to James Jackson, “We are going to keep you young hotheads from getting into mischief.”[139]

“A GREAT PAMPHLET” AND THE DEMISE OF FEDERATIVE POLITICS

The moderate delegates at the Hartford Convention, which assembled on December 15, 1814, were led by Otis and Cabot. They arrived in Hartford with a plan for the convention’s proceedings, much as the Virginia delegates had done in Philadelphia in 1787. The convention chose Cabot as its presiding officer, and he immediately called on Otis, who had prepared a series of proposals to shape the agenda for the convention’s debates. The sessions themselves were held in secret (also mimicking the Philadelphia convention), and no detailed record of the proceedings exists. Several delegates recounted its events in subsequent memoirs, and the convention’s published report describes its main concerns.[140] Within the convention, Otis and Cabot excluded the more radical members, such as Bigelow of Worcester and Connecticut’s James Hillhouse, from positions on important committees.[141] In the end, what the Hartford Convention produced was what Quincy, once he had been excluded from its deliberations, had expected: not secession, nullification, or insurrection, but “A GREAT PAMPHLET!”[142]

In the convention’s twice-daily sessions, the many grievances of New England’s citizens and their desire for action, even separation from the union, were acknowledged. But the final outcome of three weeks of discussions was, as Quincy had feared, a pamphlet—a twenty-five-page document, unanimously approved by the twenty-six delegates, describing the collective grievances of the New England states, followed by a series of carefully worded amendments to the Constitution designed to remedy those grievances and restore balance to the union. It was, in spirit and purpose, one last attempt at conducting federative politics, designed to both defend the region's interests and heal the nation's woes. Its final provision allowed for the possibility that any two of the three state delegations present could call for "another meeting of this convention, to be holden at Boston, . . . if in their judgment the situation of the country shall urgently require it." But the provision was never used.[143] The Hartford Convention would be the last attempt at federative politics undertaken by the city-state of Boston.

The convention report offered a thorough summation of the issues that Ames, Quincy, and their many New England Federalist colleagues had addressed for twenty-five years, along with a last-ditch attempt to restore the balance among the states and their interests that the Constitution had originally framed.[144] The report's opening section acknowledges the extreme danger and suffering that the Jefferson and Madison administrations had brought on New England, and even uses language echoing the Declaration of Independence to suggest a radical response. The report's lament, "but when abuses, reduced to a system, and accumulated through a course of years, have pervaded every department of government and spread corruption through every region of the state," draws its meaning and language from the Declaration, and aims toward a similar conclusion: "No summary means of relief can be applied without recourse to direct and open resistance."[145] Otis's prose lacks Jefferson's pellucid vigor, but the intent is the same.

Where the Declaration proceeded directly to an indictment of the king and his government for establishing an "absolute tyranny" over the colonies, the Hartford Convention pulls back. It acknowledges the many reasons why doubt remains whether the United States has reached the stage of absolute tyranny, or whether the long years of Jefferson and Madison have simply been a "miserable and afflicting reverse" that might still be corrected. But even should worse come to worst, the convention affirmed its commitment to the politics of federation: that if the current union collapsed, "some new form of confederacy should be substituted among those states which shall intend to maintain a federal relation to each other." With these provisions, the report stepped back from the possibility that the convention was calling for violent resistance or secession in the midst of a war.[146]

Nevertheless, the Hartford delegates were not shy in enumerating their grievances. These included the federal government's unconstitutional mistreatment of the states' militias and its neglect of the defense of New England. One of the most striking, if seldom noticed, indictments of Madison's administration was the report's charge that the federal takeover of state militias actually violated the three-fifths clause of the Constitution. Most historical attention to the notorious Federal Ratio focuses on the advantage in representation it gave to the slave states. But in the compromise that created this clause, every five slaves were to be counted as the equivalent of three free persons for the sake of direct taxation as well as representation. Until the War of 1812, no direct taxation had ever been imposed by the federal government. But the Hartford Convention argued that the federal takeover of state militias to support a foreign invasion was precisely a direct tax by the national government conducted on a state-by-state basis. When each state's proportion of militia contribution to the national cause was determined, however, only the free white population, not three-fifths of the slave population, had been counted in determining state allotments. This directly echoes Boston's objections to the British military's imperial policies of the 1750s to 1770s, when the people of New England, known for their martial spirit in self-defense, complained bitterly over the misuse of their soldiers by tyrants: "An iron despotism can impose no harder servitude upon the citizen, than to force him from his home and his occupation, to wage offensive wars, undertaken to gratify the pride or passions of his master." King George II, the Emperor Napoléon, or Madison—it mattered not. The principle was the same, whether the object of conquest was Cuba, Corsica, or Canada. Fierce opposition to aggressive foreign wars and government by soldiers remained at the forefront of Boston's grievances.[147]

The Hartford Convention's second major grievance paralleled the first, but in fiscal terms, describing the damage and peril imposed on New England by the Jefferson and Madison administrations' neglect of the region's defense and their mismanagement of finances. The national government was financially incapable of assisting the very region it had milked for revenues at the moment the British were threatening invasion. In consequence, "these [New England] states have no capacity of defraying the expense requisite for their own protection, and, at the same time, of discharging the demands of the national treasury." From these immediate concerns, the report then turned to deeper causes and enumerated something similar to the Declaration of Independence's long train of abuses: the Virginia dynasty's plan to engross national power under its leadership, eject Federalists from appointive offices, dismantle the Hamiltonian fiscal system, admit new states to undermine the original balance of power, bring "naturalized foreigners" into position of high power, create "hostility to Great Britain, and partiality to the late government of France," and "lastly and principally,—A visionary and superficial theory in regard to commerce, accompanied by a real hatred but a feigned regard to its interests, and a ruinous perseverance in efforts to render it an instrument of coercion and war." Ames and Quincy had advanced these concerns in Congress since 1789. Now the Hartford Convention proposed to address them with a series of recommended amendments to the Constitution, in precisely the way that the Massachusetts Ratification Convention of 1788 had approached the Constitution.[148]

The substance of these seven amendments should come as no surprise. The First Amendment proposed an end to the three-fifths clause. The second was equally simple: "No new state shall be admitted into the Union by Congress . . . without the concurrence of two-thirds of both houses." The third denied Congress the power "to lay any embargo . . . for more than sixty days." The fourth denied Congress the power "to interdict the commercial intercourse between the United States and any foreign nation" without a two-thirds majority in both houses. The Fifth Amendment would prohibit Congress from declaring war against foreign nations, except in defense "of the territories of the United States when actually invaded," without a two-thirds majority in both houses. The Sixth Amendment would prevent naturalized citizens of foreign birth from serving in the House or Senate, or "holding any civil office under the authority of the United States." And the seventh recommended that "the same person shall not be elected president of the United States a second time; nor shall the president be elected from the same state two terms in succession."[149]

The deep roots of all these amendments in Boston's suffering under the federal government should be clear, with the possible exception of the sixth. The Sixth Amendment was an unfair attack on Albert Gallatin, Madison's secretary of the treasury, as well as an expression of xenophobia in the wake of fraught relations with France during the Napoleonic Wars. But it was also an equivalent with respect to individual persons of the theory that the constitution was a compact among sovereign states, as Quincy had argued in opposing the admission of Louisiana. As Otis's report asserted, "Why admit to a participation in the government aliens who were no parties to the compact—who are ignorant of the nature of our institutions, and have no stake in the welfare of the country but what is recent and transitory?"[150] While this position echoed Quincy's opposition to the admission of Louisiana, it also reached back to Boston's founding years, when Winthrop issued an order on behalf of the General Court excluding uninvited migrants as a way to fend off the Antinomian crisis, or when the towns of Massachusetts developed laws for "warning out" strangers to preserve the integrity of their internal political economies. A fundamental aspect of the republican city-state mentality and the federative politics it pursued had always required control over who was admitted to the compact or commonwealth. In every element, the Hartford Convention's report contended for an understanding of the nature of republican polity and its relationships to other commonwealths that was deeply consistent with the traditions of Boston and New England.

The convention issued its report on January 5, 1815. When the Massachusetts General Court met soon thereafter, it passed a resolution in support of the convention's report and called on Governor Strong "to appoint three commissioners to proceed immediately to the seat of the National Government."[151] The governor chose three leading though moderate Boston Federalists, Harrison

Gray Otis, William Sullivan, and Thomas Handasyd Perkins, as "ambassadors"—none of the three was a member of Congress—to send to Washington. This point bears repeating. Boston, Massachusetts, and New England as a whole were already represented in Congress. This delegation was something extraordinary—essentially diplomats for New England's ad hoc confederation, gone to Washington to plead the case for adjustments to the union's foundation. There they were to argue the case for allowing Massachusetts and its neighbors to conduct their own defense, to keep the money they raised for that defense in their own treasuries, and to present the convention's recommended amendments to Congress.

The Commonwealth of Massachusetts paid for a private coach to carry the three ambassadors to the Potomac. But on their journey, they encountered one stunning piece of news: Andrew Jackson's forces had defeated the British military invasion of New Orleans on January 8, 1815. They were met on arrival in Washington with another shock: the Treaty of Ghent had ended the war between Britain and the United States on December 24, 1814, restoring all territorial claims to their prewar status.[152] The end of the Napoleonic Wars also eliminated the only real grievances that had caused Madison to seek war in the first place: Britain's Orders in Council and impressment of American sailors. The war had been a costly and bloody standoff, with no particular gains made through American arms. Yet the sudden announcement of peace at a moment that had looked extremely perilous, followed by the news of military victory at New Orleans, despite its irrelevance to the war's outcome, created a surge of support for Madison in Washington and profound embarrassment for the ambassadors from Boston.

Personally, Otis and Perkins rejoiced at the news of the peace treaty. Their fears for the military destruction of Boston and New England had been real. But politically, they were in an awkward spot. They had come to Washington prepared to argue for changes in military defense and finance policy that were now irrelevant, and with instructions to press for constitutional amendments that the party in power reviled. President Madison refused to meet with them ("a mean and contemptible little blackguard," Otis called him).

Figure 8.1. *The Hartford Convention, or Leap No Leap*, by William Charles (Philadelphia, 1814). This satirical print depicts King George III on the lower right, encouraging convention leaders Harrison Gray Otis (as Brother Mass) and James Hillhouse (as Brother Conn) and their diminutive Rhode Island colleague (possibly Samuel Ward Jr.) to leap into his waiting arms, while Timothy Pickering prays that he might become "Lord of Essex."

The pro-administration press ridiculed the Boston ambassadors with satirical doggerel and cartoons, referring to Otis as "Titus Oates," the seventeenth-century English clergyman who concocted the hoax of a "Popish Plot" to assassinate Charles II that led fifteen men to be wrongly executed.[153] In addition to the ridicule, the coincidence of the Treaty of Ghent and the Battle of New Orleans gave Madison's party the opportunity to paint the Hartford Convention and its Boston leadership as traitors in wartime, a secessionist "conspiracy" against the government. John Quincy Adams took it on himself to make this case in a published pamphlet, and the epithet has stuck to the Hartford Convention ever since.[154]

The irony is that those who most wanted the Hartford Convention to consider separation from the union, men like Quincy, Lowell, Bigelow, and Pickering, saw the convention as a failure precisely because it was so moderate. They had been attempting to practice federative politics in Congress for a quarter century and were now convinced it was hopeless, that the South's dominance was permanent. Had these men led the convention and pushed it toward the separation that popular opinion supported, there is no telling what the Treaty of Ghent and peace with Britain would have meant for the prospects of an independent New England Confederation led by Boston. But the actual outcome of the Hartford Convention's attempt to temper New England's radicalism and try once more to reshape the balance of the national confederation, when met with an unexpected peace treaty, an unlikely military victory, and ridicule from the victorious party in America's winner-take-all politics, meant the end of Boston's long and futile effort to conduct federative politics within the United States. Federalism was over. On Sunday, February 26, 1815, Otis, Sullivan, and Perkins, the ambassadors from Boston, climbed back in their coach and rode home into permanent exile from the main course of the political future of the United States.

Chapter 9

From Merchant Princes to Lords of the Loom

Remaking Boston's Political Economy

> The only circumstance which made him distrust his own calculations was, that he could bring them to no other result but one which was too favorable to be creditable.
>
> —Nathan Appleton, remembering Francis Cabot Lowell's reaction to the profits of the Lowell Mill, 1858

Boston's political economy, stable since the mid-seventeenth century, was the deep cause of its alienation from national politics in the early United States. The city's heavy reliance on overseas commerce steered its region's economic leadership toward Atlantic trade and away from continental expansion, making it an outlier in the Jeffersonian republic. But at the time of the debacle of the Hartford Convention, these economic patterns were beginning to change in ways that even the prominent Boston merchants who delivered the Hartford results to Washington only dimly perceived. Congress's power to regulate overseas trade posed a perpetual threat; Boston's livelihood was in the hands of political agents it lacked the power to control. The solution, if one was to be found, seemed to lie in redirecting the city's wealth toward productive enterprises less vulnerable to the shifting winds of the national government's international policies.

This transformation was slow in coming. In the aftermath of the destruction caused by British Army occupation and the exile of Loyalists in the Revolutionary War, Boston's initial impulse was to rebuild the old seafaring economy under new leadership and exploit new opportunities that independence from Britain had generated. Despite many past decades of hostility toward French Catholics during the colonial period, Boston's leading merchants demonstrated a surprising willingness to embrace French commercial opportunities once the United States had allied with France. For the first three decades after the city's liberation from its British occupiers, Boston's merchants would rebuild the old model of overseas commerce, but expand it to a far wider range of legitimate trading partners than Parliament's Navigation Acts had allowed.

Yet toward the end of the first decade of the nineteenth century, when the embargo made it plain that Jefferson and Congress could be more punitive than king and Parliament, merchants who had thrived under Boston's expanded postwar commerce began to shift their investments to less vulnerable enterprises. They established modern textile factories along the Charles and Merrimack Rivers, developing the limited-liability business corporation to consolidate and protect their capital. The textile mills spun off hundreds of auxiliary industries, trades, and businesses, generating enormous growth in the city's wealth and population over the subsequent three decades.

This dramatic transformation, the most radical change in the city's economic pattern since its initial coalescence in 1643, would have at least two unintended consequences. First, although the shift to textile manufacturing aimed to preserve Boston's autonomy in the face of national threats, it would also accelerate the economic separation of Boston and eastern Massachusetts from the rest of New England. Overseas trade had generally integrated the hinterland with Boston; merchants relied on the products of the New England countryside for export goods, and rural farmers relied on the merchants to supply them with manufactured imports. The rise of textile production meant a newfound reliance on a commodity, cotton, that New England farmers could not produce and on consumer markets with little interest in buying the region's traditional farm products. Second, the demand for cotton as the central factor in production meant that the quest for autonomy from national political control would turn out to be a fool's errand, as the Cotton

Kingdom, still unimaginable at the time of Jefferson's embargo, would become the dominant force in American national politics in a few short decades. This chapter follows the course of these dramatic changes, which began when France momentarily replaced Britain as Boston's chief commercial partner.

France Comes to Boston, and Boston Goes to France

When the king's soldiers departed and General Washington's army marched across the Neck, Boston lay in ruins. From April 19, 1775, to March 17, 1776, the Continental Army, formed from the New England militia that turned out to defend Lexington and Concord, lay siege to the city. During those eleven months, the occupying army penned inside Boston ravaged the city's buildings in search of firewood, imported from the mainland in ordinary times. The meetinghouse of the North Church, where generations of the Mather family had preached, was leveled. So were more than a hundred older wooden houses. The Old South meetinghouse, known for its large seating capacity and used for many public meetings during the resistance movement, was torn apart inside and turned into riding stables for British Army officers. A collection of precious historical documents amassed by the church's former minister, Thomas Prince, and stored in the meetinghouse bell tower disappeared during the occupation. Over the unusually cold winter, hardship, hunger, and a smallpox epidemic took their toll on the city's remaining residents. When the British Army evacuated Boston, they destroyed Castle William, the fortress defending the harbor, leaving the town exposed to future enemy assaults. Thousands of loyalists, including many leading merchants, left with the evacuating troops, ripping apart the town's social fabric.[1]

But severe as the destruction was, it did not fundamentally restructure Boston's economy. Merchants from the New England hinterland as well as local Bostonians committed to the rebellion eagerly filled the vacuum left by exiled loyalists and set about to rebuild the city's economy on its prewar model. They found new overseas markets for New England's products, and tried new ports around the globe to expand the reach and profits of their commerce. If war against Britain closed many familiar channels of trade, the alliance with France opened others and spurred experiments with new routes.

This rebuilding enterprise can be traced through the careers of a small group of Bostonians who seized the opportunities created by dramatic changes in the city's relationship with the Francophone world. I begin here with the two Samuel Brecks, father and son: the elder, a merchant who realized the profits to be made in supplying the French Navy in Boston; and his son, the first native Bostonian to be educated in France, convert to Roman Catholicism, and introduce Catholic worship in the city. Then I turn to the calculating approach to French commerce and French republicanism taken by one of Boston's most successful merchants, Thomas Handasyd Perkins, and his family and business associates. The affairs of the House of Perkins in Saint-Domingue and France were based on a continuous assessment of the shifting configuration of commercial opportunity, trading liberties, and political (in)stability at play in the revolutionary French Atlantic.

The prospect of a French naval invasion had long been Boston's worst nightmare. To defend itself during many decades of imperial warfare between Britain and France, the city had maintained fortresses, one on Castle Island, directly across the harbor from Long Wharf, and another on Fort Hill in the old South End, along with batteries armed with artillery near the North End and South End wharves.[2] But a French attack never came. The only naval fleet ever to seize control of Boston Harbor was British, during the military occupation from 1768 to 1776. Not long after Bostonians and their New England allies had driven King George's Royal Navy out of Boston, the United States' new alliance with King Louis brought the French Navy to Boston on terms unthinkable before the rebellion.

As we have seen in earlier chapters, Boston and its New England hinterland had been the British colonies most deeply involved in the wars against France. Beginning in 1689, imperial warfare spilled over into North America, and the proximity of New England to New France made for brutal guerrilla war across the northern forests. For nearly a century, New Englanders had learned to believe that French Catholics were their inveterate enemies. Gravestones in the Massachusetts countryside tell of soldiers who "in six campaigns Intrepid trod ye Field / Nor to ye Gallic Foe would ever Yield."[3] During the Seven Years' War, fully one-third of Massachusetts' adult male population served against the "Gallic Foe."[4] In the city of Boston, every November 5 saw the observation of "Pope's Day," the anniversary of the foiling of Guy Fawkes's plot to blow up Parliament in 1605. Boston street gangs would fight to take possession of an effigy of the pope paraded around town on a wagon. The victorious gang won the honor of burning the effigy in a bonfire.[5] Despite the fact that France's Bourbon monarchs and the eighteenth-century papacy were in reality often at odds, in the popular mind of Boston, the pope and French king merged into a single model of absolutist tyranny, spiritual and temporal, and all Frenchmen were their slavish subjects. So strong were these prejudices that during the imperial crisis of the 1760s, many New Englanders believed that the inexplicably noxious acts and decrees of Parliament and king must have been the secret work of Jesuits and Frenchmen.[6]

The 1778 alliance between France and the United States opened the way to striking changes in Boston's relationship to all things French. Because the colonists' successful siege of Boston had forced the British to abandon the city, Boston became the North American port most accessible to the French Navy. Beginning in 1778, French naval fleets became a frequent presence in Boston, where they could be reliably refitted and safely sheltered. In April of that year, the Comte d'Estaing sailed from Toulon in command of a fleet of twenty-six ships. A violent summer storm thwarted his plan to attack the British fleet near Newport, Rhode Island, and forced him to sail to Boston to repair his damaged ships. Here, according to the reminiscences of the elder Breck, the crowd watching the fleet's arrival was shocked to discover that French sailors were not "the gaunt, half-starved" crews they had come to expect and doubted that "these hearty-looking people belong[ed] to the lantern-jawed,

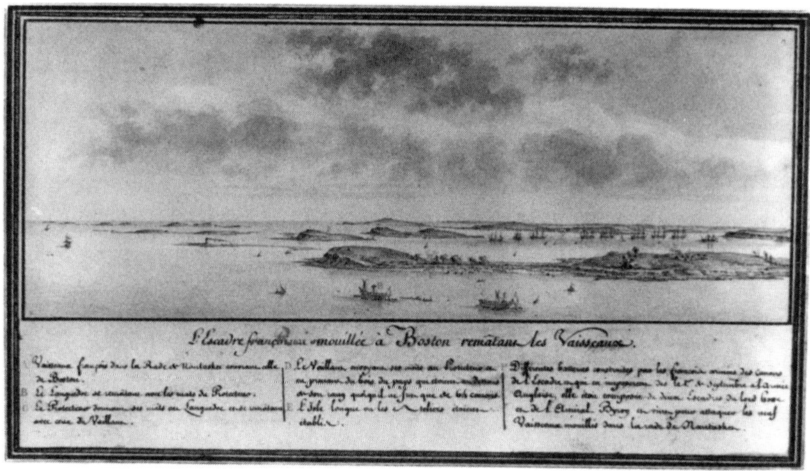

FIGURE 9.1. *L'escadre française mouillée à Boston remâtant les vaisseaux* (the French fleet anchored at Boston for repairs), by Pierre Ozanne, 1778.

spindle-shank race" they imagined their inveterate foes to be. A wealthy local merchant, Nathaniel Tracy, entertained Admiral d'Estaing and Phillip Joseph de l'Etombe, the French consul in Boston, taking great pains to acquire a large number of live frogs for the soup course. When l'Etombe, in some astonishment, fished the frog out of his soup plate, he exclaimed, "'Ah, mon Dieu! un grenouille [a frog]!' then turning to the gentleman next to him, gave him the frog. He received it, and passed it round the table. Thus the poor *crapaud* [toad] made the tour from hand to hand until it reached the admiral."[7]

Despite Tracy's misguided belief that whole-frog soup was the French national dish, Boston in fact had significant connections to France and French culture. One was the presence of Huguenot refugees in eighteenth-century Boston who had assimilated so successfully into the dominant culture that several families became mercantile, artisanal, and political leaders, including the Faneuils, Bowdoins, and Reveres, and Paul Mascarene, whose children married into the Hutchinson-Oliver clan. The French Protestant church that they founded on School Street, sustained for several decades through the mid-eighteenth century, eventually melded into the puritan establishment.[8] Another French connection was the long and profitable relationship between Boston's trading community and Acadia, the so-called French Neutrals who remained in the region after Britain formally took possession of Nova Scotia in 1710. Despite their Roman Catholicism, the Acadians had been excellent customers for Boston's coastal merchants—until the British Army brutally expelled them in the 1750s. Despite the powerful prejudices shaped by decades of war, it was possible for Bostonians to imagine that the French people were not their enemies by nature but instead simply victims of spiritual and temporal tyrants, the popes and kings who ruled over them.

During the American War of Independence, the avenue for change, especially in Boston's cultural attitudes toward all things French, was provided by commerce. The French presence in Boston offered rich opportunities for local merchants to supply the navy with food, clothing, naval stores, and financial services, much as they had done for the British Army during the Seven Years' War. In 1779, Breck Sr. was offered a contract by Louis XVI's government to be the permanent agent for French forces in Boston: "He sold their prize-goods, negotiated their bills of exchange and furnished the ships of war with all they wanted."[9] Arrangements like these had a long history in Boston; some of city's great fortunes, including the Belchers' and Hancocks', had been made by supplying the British military.[10] These commercial relationships lent themselves to social and cultural connections as well. As we have seen, wartime opportunities in the early eighteenth century had opened new avenues for Bostonians to explore in England, the Netherlands, and Germany.[11] Now France became part of Boston's Atlantic world, a new partner in a familiar process.[12]

Although the Breck family, like many rebel sympathizers, had fled Boston during the British occupation in 1775–76, after the British evacuation the elder Breck purchased a fine estate across from the Boston Common. Here in 1781, he hosted a lavish fete for the entire town to celebrate the birth of the dauphin, Louis Joseph—surely a first for Boston.[13] The party for the dauphin was but one element in a general craze for all things French that swept Boston during the war. Few Bostonians had studied French before 1778, but now the demand for French tutors soared. The elder Breck found his business with the French Navy hindered by his limited language skills; his dependency on the French consul, l'Etombe, for translation eventually forced him to share his profits with l'Etombe. Together with John Hancock, the elder Breck hired a tutor to learn French, without much success. Instead he determined that his children would learn French, even if he could not.[14]

Breck made plans in 1782, while the war was still going on, to send his eleven-year-old child to France for his education—another first in Boston's history. Breck turned for advice to Louis-Phillippe de Rigaud, Marquis de Vaudreuil, commander in chief of French naval forces in America.[15] The marquis recommended the College of Sorèze, near his own village of Vaudreuil in the Lower Languedoc (not far from Paul Mascarene's birthplace), a school run by Benedictine monks that combined liberal arts with military training. On his journey there, the younger Breck directly experienced the craze for Boston in France equal to the craze for France in Boston. Because the war for independence had begun in Boston, and because of the limited European knowledge of American geography, "Boston" was taken to be a synonym for all of revolutionary America. In the city of Nantes, his first stop after landing at the mouth of the Loire, the young Breck attended a stage play for the first time in his life; theatrical entertainments had always been prohibited in Boston. Afterward, the actresses adopted him as "le petit Bostonian," as "it was indeed by the name of Bostonian that all Americans were known in France then." He learned to sing a French song then in fashion, "the chorus of which was: 'Bon, Bon, Bon, / C'est à Boston / Qu'on entend souflé les canons'" (Boston is where one hears the cannons). He also learned a new card game called "Boston," which remained popular throughout Europe (except in Britain) for decades afterward.[16] On the long overland journey to the school, which took him through La Rochelle, Rochefort, Bordeaux, and Toulouse, Breck discovered a café in the town of Montauban that had taken to calling itself the "Café de Boston."[17]

Breck Jr. spent more than four years at the College of Sorèze, and under the care of the Benedictine monks he gradually converted to

Roman Catholicism, despite his puritan upbringing and ancestry. Earlier in the eighteenth century, young Boston travelers in Europe had encountered Roman Catholic clerics frequently enough that a typical response developed—at least in the written evidence that these encounters left behind. The characteristic pattern involved the young traveler engaging his Catholic (often Jesuit) interlocutor in heated conversation about religious doctrine, eventually besting his opponent with devastating logic and tenacious Protestant faith.[18] For young Breck, the experience was rather different. To his surprise, the monks "ever treated me with parental tenderness and the most watchful solicitude for my happiness here and hereafter," but they did not make "the smallest effort to turn me from the religion of my fathers"—a restriction that Breck Sr. had insisted on. Rather, the conversion was inspired by another student at the school, "a young man of the greatest piety and application," whose behavior, "studious, orderly, every way exemplary," offered a model to young Breck that induced the change. The superior of the order even insisted that Breck wait a week and reconsider before offering him a confessor.[19]

Breck was converted by education and culture, not only by that of the College of Sorèze, but by the changes in Boston that made it possible for descendants of Puritans to recognize the essential humanity of their former enemies.[20] We might call Breck's embrace of Roman Catholicism a "social conversion." It should come as no surprise that after his return to Boston, he gradually slipped back to a middle position between his Calvinist upbringing and his French Catholic education, joining the Episcopal Church in post-revolutionary Boston. Never a zealot, the younger Breck sought to conform to the culture and society in which he found himself, and after 1778, Boston's culture had made a small tolerant space for France and its religion, built on the commercial opportunities that the French alliance afforded.[21]

French Commerce and the House of Perkins

Boston's new French alliance also expanded the potential for Boston merchants to conduct legitimate trade with France. During the colonial era, this trade had been extensive but illegal, centered mainly on smuggling sugar from the French West Indies into Boston to avoid Parliament's customs duties.[22] After the war for independence, this situation was reversed: the formerly illegal trade was now thrown open to American ships, while Britain's Orders in Council closed off the British West Indian ports that had once been Boston's mainstay. In Boston, these shifting opportunities were seized by the new merchant families that came to prominence after the departure of many of the older loyalist families. Among these new families, the Perkins brothers, James, Thomas, and Samuel, became especially prominent.

Technically, the Perkins brothers were not newcomers. They were born to a Boston family engaged in trade since the seventeenth century. But although their father and grandfather had been reasonably prosperous traders, they had never attained the top rank of Boston's Atlantic merchants, or been prominent in the city's social or political affairs. What was worse, James Perkins Sr., father of the three boys, died young in 1773, when his eldest son was only eleven. Their mother earned a small income as a shopkeeper, but the family fortunes suffered. The three sons entered apprenticeships in Boston commercial houses rather than Harvard College, to which their talents and pedigree would have earned them a place had their father lived. As the boys came of age in the mid-1780s, they sought to make their own fortunes in trade and were drawn to the most prosperous location opened by the French alliance: the colony of Saint-Domingue.[23] In 1782, as the war in North America drew to a close, the French fleet, with thousands of troops on board, sailed from Boston to Saint-Domingue in expectation of further fighting against Britain. In its wake came some of Boston's most enterprising merchants.

The following year, James Perkins, the oldest brother, joined a Boston merchant firm already established in Cap-Français, Saint-Domingue's capital and commercial center on the island's northern coast. He learned the business quickly and soon struck out on his own. His younger brother, Thomas Handasyd Perkins, joined him in Saint-Domingue in 1785, and together with a third partner, they established a trading house in Cap-Français. Within a few more years, the youngest brother, Samuel, would join them as well.

The brothers purchased goods brought to the cape by other merchants and sold them to local planters.[24] A tremendous amount of this business involved the trade in slaves or provisions to maintain the slave system. In the mid-1780s, the population of Saint-Domingue comprised roughly half a million African or African-descended slaves, ruled by a free white population of about thirty thousand. During the decade that the Perkins brothers conducted business there, the island's slave trade was at its height, importing thirty to forty thousand slaves every year, absorbing one-third of the entire African slave trade to the Americas between 1783 and 1791. This huge importation of labor was matched by the island's enormous output. Saint-Domingue produced 40 percent of the sugar and 60 percent of the coffee consumed in Europe.[25] Cap-Français served as the commercial entrepôt for much of this trade. The profits they made from their business here formed the original foundation of the tremendous riches that the House of Perkins would acquire.

Although the Perkins family had owned slaves in Boston in every generation going back to the seventeenth century, the active trade in African slaves had never played a large part in their business or that of Boston in general. Boston merchants had traditionally made large profits by provisioning the West Indian plantation economies. Yet Boston itself had a limited market for labor, and its merchants were not heavy investors in the slave trade, even compared to their Rhode Island competitors. This did not seem to impede the Perkins brothers' trade in Cap-Français, however, nor did the fact that the Commonwealth of Massachusetts had abolished slavery and the slave trade by the early 1780s. As commission merchants, the buying and reselling of imported slaves constituted a steady part of their business in Cap-Français, along with supplying imported flour, dried fish, and horses that kept the plantations running. The coffee and sugar they acquired in return helped the Perkins brothers expand their operations throughout the Atlantic and before long around the globe.[26]

Smuggling played an essential part in their business. In the historiography of the American Revolution, the smuggling habits of colonial American merchants are often viewed as patriotic acts, defenses of liberty and free trade in defiance of Parliament's restrictive regulations.[27] The activities of the Perkins brothers and many others like them, however, show that smuggling was simply the way that business was done, an act of pure commercial self-interest, regardless of whose regulations were violated. As leaders of a small city-state operating in a world controlled by large empires, Boston merchants saw smuggling as a means to retain a competitive edge and continued to practice it vigorously even after American independence.[28]

The correspondence of the Perkins brothers contains detailed instructions to their clients explaining how to avoid the customs duties imposed by France, Spain, Britain, China, the United States, and even the Commonwealth of Massachusetts. A 1786 letter from Saint-Domingue to a client reads, "Our J. P. [James Perkins] will be in Boston last of September and will communicate to you the means of Introducing Flour to this Port and taking away Contraband Goods."[29] Samuel Breck Jr., who returned to Boston from his schooling in France and joined his father's business in 1787, had a similar experience. He observed that even Massachusetts' own custom duties (in effect before the ratification of the US Constitution in 1789) received little respect from Boston merchants: "So soon as a vessel arrived, one-half the cargo was hoisted into the upper part of the store, and the other half only entered at the custom-house; and thus we were initiated into the secret of smuggling. . . . The only apology was the universality of the custom."[30]

The profits and commodities that the Perkins brothers acquired from their business in Saint-Domingue became the basis for their next and most lucrative enterprise. In 1788, the middle brother, Thomas Handasyd, left Le Cap and returned to Boston to prepare for the next venture: the beginnings of trade with China. He arranged a cargo of goods by assembling local New England products (butter, rum, codfish, and spermaceti candles) together with items acquired through trade in Saint-Domingue, including a hundred tons of Russian bar iron, which the House of

Perkins had acquired by shipping Caribbean sugar to Saint Petersburg.[31] The *Astrea* sailed for China in February 1789, and opened a new phase in Boston's global commerce. In Whampoa, the foreign trading station on the Pearl River below Canton, Perkins noticed a spike in demand in China for sealskin and sea otter furs that another Yankee ship had brought from the Oregon coast of North America (this too required smuggling to get the furs past Chinese customs agents). From this point forward, he rearranged the trade priorities of the Perkins family business. Because of the Perkins's tremendous success, the rest of the overseas merchant community of Boston followed suit, and came to dominate the American trade to the Pacific Northwest and China for several decades.[32]

Profits from the trade in Saint-Domingue made this global expansion possible. James and Samuel Perkins continued to pursue them, even after the French National Assembly's decree of May 15, 1791, offering political rights to free people of color in the colonies. Violence quickly followed the decree's arrival in Le Cap. In fall 1791, slave uprisings broke out on the plantations in the hills above Cap-Français. James Perkins and family were visiting one such plantation when the alarm began, and after a harrowing coach journey through the countryside, made it safely back to the city.[33] Despite the burning of Port-au-Prince and the cane fields in flames above the city, business went on as usual in Cap-Français. James Perkins took command of the white Americans pledged to defend the city, yet all the while continued to purchase newly arrived African slaves, expecting to sell them to the plantations once order was restored—or to Havana or South Carolina, if necessary. Like many Americans, the Perkins brothers saw the outbreak of revolution in France as a joyous event, a sign that yet another country was turning to a republican model of self-government. But they were unwilling to view the slave rebellions in Saint-Domingue as part of the same process or imagine independent self-government by the island's African majority. They continued to operate in Le Cap until 1793, when the city was at last overrun by rebel forces and the last brother, Samuel, abandoned the business and returned to

Boston, leaving behind the (unpaid) debts owed to the firm by the planters of Saint-Domingue.[34]

The violence of the Haitian Revolution, when Saint-Domingue's enslaved population rose against its masters, and the loss of their business on the island did not dissuade the House of Perkins from supporting France and the French Revolution. In January 1793, Russell Sturgis, the Perkins's business partner and husband of their sister Elizabeth, organized a "CIVIC FEAST in commemoration of the glorious struggles and brilliant successes of the Citizen Soldiers of Liberty in France."[35] The news had just reached Boston of the French victory at Valmy over the Duke of Brunswick (whose Hessian and Brunswick troops had threatened New England during the American Revolution), and the subsequent abolition of the monarchy and declaration of the French Republic. These events, combined with the September Massacres that targeted the clergy and the beginnings of the legal de-Christianization of the French state, made it appear to Bostonians as though the twin pillars of tyranny of their former "Gallic Foe," the "Canon and Feudal Law" that John Adams so abhorred, were at long last crumbling.[36] The feast organized by Sturgis, the largest of many across the United States, was held at Faneuil Hall, the famous public market given to Boston by the Huguenot merchant Peter Faneuil, with a whole roast ox to feed the crowds and bonfires and fireworks at night, reminiscent of the old "Pope's Day" revels but now in celebration of the French Republic.[37]

With the outbreak of war between Britain and France in 1793, and President Washington's declaration of American neutrality, direct commerce with France appeared to the Perkins brothers as yet another opportunity, an extension of Boston's Atlantic commerce. War meant contracts for military provisions, and the destructive civil wars in revolutionary France created food shortages. Bread was in high demand, and food riots had broken out in Paris in February 1793, shortly after the declaration of war against Britain. In June, James Perkins sailed from Boston for the West Indies (now stopping on Martinique, as Saint-Domingue was in flames) and then on to France, where profits of 200 percent could be made on American grain.[38] James returned to Boston in January 1794.

Unfortunately, no record survives of his experiences during the Reign of Terror, but they must not have discouraged his commercial aspirations, for the following fall, Thomas Handasyd Perkins made a similar voyage and spent most of 1795 touring France, pursuing business in Paris, and keeping a journal of what he saw.

Perkins's journal is not filled with anti-Gallic prejudices that the dominant American historiography on Boston Federalism has taught us to expect. He approached France with an open and acquisitive mind. Perkins's ship arrived in Bordeaux early in February 1795, whence he traveled overland to Paris: "We passed so near the theatre of war in La Vendée as to hear the reports of the cannon of the belligerent parties." On Perkins's arrival in Paris, the food shortages were immediately obvious: "There was a great scarcity of breadstuffs during the winter and spring. It was produced partly by the farmers having their ploughshares turned into swords, partly by the waste attendant on war, and in part by an unwillingness to sell for *assignats*," the depreciating paper money of the republic, a problem familiar to Americans from their own revolutionary war.[39]

Perkins arrived during the last spasms of violence after the fall of Maximilien Robespierre and the radical Jacobins. He witnessed at close hand the execution by guillotine of Antoine Quentin Fouquier-Tinville, the public prosecutor under Robespierre, along with fifteen judges and jurymen of the court. Perkins measured with his pocket watch the astonishing speed of this process: "From the time the prisoners descended from the carts, until their heads were all in long baskets, placed in the same carts with the lifeless trunks, was fourteen minutes."[40] He was disturbed by the violence, and by the fear that regular exposure to such bloodshed had coarsened the French people and hardened them to human suffering.[41] He assisted in surreptitious efforts to smuggle the son of the imprisoned Marquis de Lafayette, French hero of the American Revolution, out of the country and across to America.[42] In late March 1795, he attended the trials of Bertrand Barère, Jean-Marie Collot d'Herbois, and Jacques-Nicolas Billaud-Varenne, and dined with current members of the convention who wanted to punish these leaders of the Terror without reduplicating their excesses: "They do not hesitate to say that the present trial is a decision between Jacobinism with its excesses and the reign of reason and moderation. God send the latter may triumph! . . . Were the *modérés* to pursue all concerned in the system for which the accused are now on trial, it would be destroying one system of terror by another." When the convention condemned Barère and the others to prison in French Guiana rather than execution, Perkins expressed his approval: "It would have been dangerous to have got the guillotine again in operation."[43]

The bloodshed and injustice of the Terror and its aftermath did not shake Perkins's belief in the essential virtue of France and the French Revolution. He loved French art, architecture, and culture: "The Opera House is the most beautiful I have yet seen; and the dancing is so far beyond what I had seen before, that it appeared to me like magic." He visited the country estate of Jean-Jacques Rousseau in Ermenonville and the palace of Versailles. A great observer of urban life and industry, he toured manufacturing centers, and studied methods of making pottery, porcelain, iron, and cloth. His Boston friend and traveling companion Joseph Russell even used the profits from his own successful trading in France to purchase a château outside Paris. In Paris itself, Perkins was impressed by the public spirit of the citizen guard, as tens of thousands of volunteers turned out daily to preserve the peace and prevent a Jacobin resurgence during spring 1795. He watched the parade of national troops before the Tuileries and remarked on the "fine-looking" cannoneers: "To them the Republic is indebted for some of the best victories she has to boast. May every man be a cannoneer when opposed to tyrants, and every cannoneer an army in himself!" (Napoléon Bonaparte may have been among the cannoneers Perkins saw, as he spent much of his time in Paris that summer). Perkins also visited the Hôtel des Invalides, and "when one contemplates the causes which have produced the misfortunes of those people, . . . and traces them to the ambitions of kings, or tyrants under other names, he is led to wish that all the world would have the resolution to throw off the yoke, and enlist under a republican government."[44]

Similar thoughts occupied Perkins when he visited "the place where the Bastille stood. . . . When one contemplates the misery which that place once contained, the blood runs cold in the veins, and the soul is quickened with hatred against tyrants, wherever they are found,—whether they rule in a *body*, or severally. *There have been, unfortunately, a great many Bastilles in France since that one was destroyed.*" His general opinion, however, was that the excesses of the revolution had ended. Perkins commented approvingly on the report of the committee of the National Convention to frame a new constitution for the republic: "It promises to put the country, which has been torn up by the roots by dissensions of every kind, under a lasting and good government. The principles are much the same as those upon which our government is founded." Like John Adams before him, Perkins would have preferred a singular executive with veto power over the legislature after the American fashion rather than a directory of five, but he imagined the new constitution would bring peace and order to the republic.[45]

Most important, Perkins confirmed this belief in making his commercial plans. After yet another dinner with members of the convention, he reported, "Pelet was very inquisitive about our commerce, and seemed anxious to know if it was our opinion that we should be largely connected with France after the war. This, I have no doubt, will be the fact, and that it will be advantageous to us in a great degree. He tells me that the quantity of wheat raised in France was never equal to its wants . . . and that wheat, in the best of times, was always worth twelve livres tournois in specie per quintal. This would give a good peace freight from America." Despite his intimate observations of the aftermath of the Reign of Terror and the turbulence of French politics, Perkins remained confident enough in the republic's success to imagine a large role for France in Boston's commercial future. He left Paris on July 26, 1795, "with a light heart at the idea of once more bending my course towards my native country."[46] Ten weeks later, on the 13th Vendémiaire, Napoléon Bonaparte would defend the directory's government in the Tuileries against insurgent royalist forces, using artillery—"a whiff of grapeshot"—to cut down the republic's enemies in the streets of Paris.

The political, cultural, and commercial overtures that Boston made to revolutionary France were quite extraordinary, given its historic antipathy to France before 1776. For those like the Perkins brothers, who were less interested in the distractions of national politics than in the immediate success of their own business, and who viewed the infant American republic as one among many commercial powers within their larger trading orbit, the republic of France and city-state of Boston could be partners—until the United States' response to the wars between Britain and France made that impossible.

Property and Theft: Industrial Espionage and the Rise of the Mills

In 1804, exactly one hundred years after Jonathan Belcher made a similar voyage, a young man named Joseph Warren Revere, son of the famous patriot-craftsman Paul Revere, journeyed to England, the Netherlands, and parts of France, across Germany to Denmark, and then across the Baltic to Sweden. His aim was "to visit the major copperworks in Britain and northern Europe to learn their methods and study their equipment."[47] His father, a renowned silversmith, wanted to move into metallurgy on a larger scale, building rolling mills to produce copper sheeting for the bottoms of naval vessels, and casting iron into cannons and church bells. At a similar moment of economic transition in the 1640s, John Winthrop the younger had traveled to the Low Countries and Germany to gain information for the development of an ironworks in Saugus, just north of Boston, and to recruit alchemical adepts to return with him to Massachusetts.[48] A century and a half later, Europeans' strict prohibitions on the emigration of skilled artisans and the export of advanced technology forced Paul Revere's son to sail for Europe as an industrial spy.

The young Revere traveled in Europe on a Massachusetts passport signed by the commonwealth's governor—an indicator of the state's sovereign authority in the early years of the confederated American republic. During the Napoleonic Wars, possession of

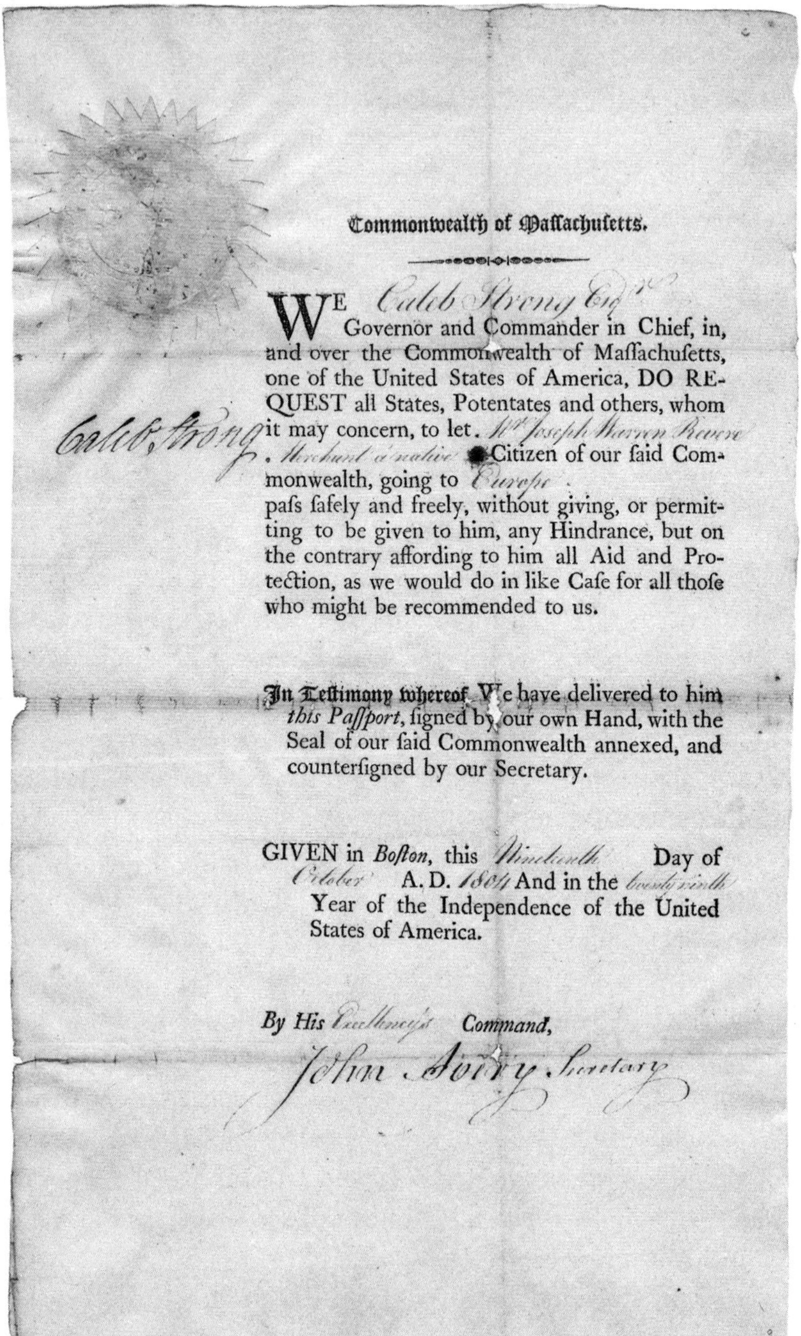

Commonwealth of Maſſachuſetts.

WE *Caleb Strong Esq.*
Governor and Commander in Chief, in, and over the Commonwealth of Maſſachuſetts, one of the United States of America, DO REQUEST all States, Potentates and others, whom it may concern, to let *Mr. Joseph Warren Revere, Merchant a native* Citizen of our ſaid Commonwealth, going to *Europe* paſs ſafely and freely, without giving, or permitting to be given to him, any Hindrance, but on the contrary affording to him all Aid and Protection, as we would do in like Caſe for all thoſe who might be recommended to us.

Caleb Strong

In Teſtimony whereof We have delivered to him *this Paſſport*, ſigned by our own Hand, with the Seal of our ſaid Commonwealth annexed, and counterſigned by our Secretary.

GIVEN in *Boſton*, this *Nineteenth* Day of *October* A. D. *1804* And in the *twenty ninth* Year of the Independence of the United States of America.

By His Excellency's Command,

John Avery Secretary

FIGURE 9.2. Passport of Joseph Warren Revere from the Commonwealth of Massachusetts, 1804.

strong credentials was important for travelers, and a Boston identity carried considerable cachet, as the young Samuel Breck had experienced on his journey through France.[49] Joseph Warren Revere unknowingly visited many of the same places that had inspired Belcher a century earlier, like the mines of the Harz Mountains, but with a more practical set of aims. Belcher, the rich merchant's son, had hoped to ascend in aristocratic circles and therefore relished the attention of royalty. Revere, the craftsman's son, hoped to ascend from his father's leather-apron status to become a new kind of gentleman, the manager of a large industrial enterprise with a permanent staff of skilled employees. British and continental authorities seemed less concerned about protecting the technology of metallurgy than textile machinery, so Revere was able to draw makeshift sketches of rolling mills without having them confiscated. On his return to Boston, his drawings, together with his observations about the organization of these large enterprises, enabled his father to build New England's largest copperworks and bell and cannon foundry, ten miles southwest of Boston along the Neponset River in Canton, using the river's falls to power the mills. By the time Paul Revere retired in 1811 and handed the growing business over to his son, they had acquired the contract to supply copper sheeting for the boilers on Samuel Fulton's new steamboats, getting in on the ground floor of one of the major growth industries of nineteenth-century America.[50]

Successful as it was, Joseph Warren Revere's industrial spying paled in comparison to the boldness of Francis Cabot Lowell. Lowell was the scion of one of the lesser merchant families that prospered in Boston in the wake of the Loyalist exile. The Lowells moved into the city from Essex County and made fortunes for themselves in overseas trade. Then Francis Cabot Lowell launched New England's shift to industrial production through a remarkable act of intellectual theft—industrial espionage, information piracy, call it what you will.[51] On an extended family sojourn in Britain during the interval between the end of Jefferson's embargo and the start of the War of 1812, Lowell toured the mechanized textile mills in Lancashire. He evaded Britain's strict laws against technology transfer by committing to memory the operations of the machinery. By 1815, Lowell's Boston Manufacturing Company had replicated Manchester's power looms, driven by the falls of the Charles River in Waltham, ten miles upstream from Boston.

Revere's European fact-finding tour predated Jefferson's embargo, while Lowell's espionage came in the wake of the embargo's devastating blow to Boston's commerce. Whether from the artisan perspective represented by the Revere family or from the viewpoint of the Lowells and their wealthy merchant kin, the problem of the new century was the same. Boston's economy of earlier days had waxed and waned on the shifting tides of Atlantic commerce. Fortunes were made on the skill and daring with which merchants braved the risks of overseas trade. Now Boston faced a persistent threat that no amount of individual or community enterprise could overcome: the consolidated power of the national government in the hands of its rivals to foreclose trade altogether. This threat drove Lowell's strategy to remake Boston's economy.

Born in the year of Paul Revere's "midnight ride," Francis Cabot Lowell had transformed the modest fortune that his father had accumulated as a lawyer and judge into a large one. In his late teens, Lowell shipped out on several voyages to Europe and the Mediterranean as supercargo on a ship owned by his uncle, Thomas Russell, an established Boston merchant. Lowell traded American products, especially grain, in Bilbao and Bordeaux, then spent 1795–96 living in France, including extended stays in Paris and Tours, where he was enchanted by the quiet beauty of the Loire Valley. Like Thomas Handasyd Perkins before him, Lowell found American fears of the French Revolution's violence to be much exaggerated: "The ideas you have of France in America are quite erroneous. There is full as much safety here as in America." Other Boston merchant families, including Lowell's cousins the Higginsons and the Bromfields, shared similar views. While in Paris, Lowell stayed with his Higginson cousins, George and John, who had purchased "a very handsome place" and settled there permanently as agents for other Boston merchants. Like James and Thomas Handasyd Perkins, Lowell saw France's wartime condition as an opportunity for Boston merchants to sell flour and other foodstuffs, and would continue to pursue this trade well into the nineteenth century, braving the risks of war for the sake of profit.[52]

After returning to Boston in 1796, Lowell set himself up as an overseas merchant, and over the next several years greatly expanded his business, in part by developing India Wharf on Boston Harbor as the centerpiece of Boston's burgeoning trade to the Far East. By the time the pall of embargo fell across the region in 1807, the Lowells had joined the ranks of Boston's richest families.[53] But it was exactly this pall—the potential of the national government, despite Josiah Quincy's impassioned representation of Boston's interests, to destroy in a legislative stroke what Lowell had devoted his life to building—that turned Lowell's attention to manufacturing on a scale that might rescue his and his city's fortunes.

Lowell was understandably reticent about these plans in his own writings. But in later years his business partner, Nathan Appleton, who visited Lowell in Scotland in 1811, remembered that Lowell "had determined before his return to America, to visit Manchester, for the purpose of obtaining all possible information on the subject, with a view to the introduction of the improved manufacture in the United States."[54] As Lowell knew well, a small and widely dispersed cotton textile industry already existed in New England. Samuel Slater, an English craftsman experienced in working with Richard Arkwright's spinning technology, had disguised himself as a common farmer to evade English customs agents and emigrated to America. Moses Brown of Rhode Island hired Slater to build a water-powered spinning mill in Pawtucket.[55] Similarly, Lowell's Cabot family relatives in Beverly, Massachusetts, north of Boston, had established a small cotton mill in the late 1780s. In both cases, though, and in dozens of similar enterprises that emerged in the embargo's wake, the limited machine technology required considerable amounts of hand labor to produce yarn or cloth that could not compete with British manufactures or imports from India for quality or price.[56] Lowell's determination to copy the great Lancashire factories reflected his belief that scale and mechanization would transform Boston's political economy, and make it immune from the vagaries of overseas trade and the national politics that undermined it.

The Boston Manufacturing Company was a wild success. Lowell recruited a skillful self-taught mechanic named Paul Moody, who transformed his vision into a reality, mechanizing and integrating more aspects of cotton cloth production under a single roof than ever before. Equally important, Lowell turned to his Boston relatives and business associates, and the joint-stock form of corporate organization, to raise the massive capital investment his plan required. In addition, the corporate form's usefulness as a tool for the governance of capital and the management of business made it attractive to Boston's merchant elites. The interlocking boards of directors of these new corporations became the eighteenth-century successors of the "town fathers" who had developed New England's corporate towns two centuries earlier, though with far greater economic power than their predecessors.[57] The resumption of war with Britain in 1812, and its repetition of the embargo's stifling effect on Boston's overseas trade, made Boston's wealthiest merchants eager to find a safe and productive haven for their idle resources, especially one that might in future insure them against the risks of merchant life.[58] Lowell's Boston Manufacturing Company began producing cotton in 1815, and within only a few years it developed new plans for a far larger complex at the more powerful falls of the Merrimack River north of Boston, near the original boundary of the Massachusetts Bay Colony's charter.

Even in its early years, the Boston Manufacturing Company yielded such large returns on its owners' investments that Lowell himself could scarcely believe the figures. As he told Appleton, "The only circumstance which made him distrust his own calculations was, that he could bring them to no other result but one which was too favorable to be creditable." By 1817, the company was paying its stockholders dividends of 17 percent, and that figure increased to 27.5 percent by 1822.[59] Over the next several decades, the city's political economy and the resources necessary for its civic development shifted from the old formula of using the region's humble products as a stake for creative trade throughout the world to a new model of large-scale industrial production for a domestic market. For that economic transformation to take place, a political adjustment was necessary as well.

During the War of 1812, with British-American trade suspended, dozens more cotton mills had sprung up across the United States, especially in New England and the mid-Atlantic region. These were small-scale enterprises, with machinery for spinning thread but no power looms for weaving cloth.[60] When the war ended and trade with Britain resumed, British merchants dumped enormous quantities of cotton textiles on the American market, both cheap imports from India and high-quality British machine-made goods, selling at discounted prices in a deliberate effort "to glut, to stifle in the cradle those rising manufactures in the United States, which the War has forced into existence, contrary to the natural order of things."[61] Britain's plan worked, driving many American cotton mills out of business. But with its massive capitalization (Lowell raised $400,000 for the firm's initial operations, tenfold greater than most American mills) and its mechanized efficiency producing cotton cloth cheaply, the Boston Manufacturing Company survived the onslaught.[62] Nonetheless, Lowell took it on himself to travel to Washington, DC, to lobby for a tariff to protect American manufacturing in the face of British and East Indian competition.

In 1816, lobbying was not yet an established practice in Congress. In effect, Lowell was continuing the tradition that George Cabot, Harrison Gray Otis, and Thomas Handasyd Perkins had pursued in their disastrous trip a year earlier to present the results of the Hartford Convention, acting not as formally elected representatives *of* the national government, but as informal agents *to* the national government, in much the same way that in the colonial period, agents for the colonies or spokesmen for interest groups (religious dissenters, merchants, land speculators, etc.) would lobby in Whitehall, given that they had no direct representation in Parliament.[63] Lowell's move was both shrewd and necessary, because New England's elected congressmen did not support a protective tariff. Historically, the region's economy relied on overseas trade, and any form of import tax had usually been anathema to the merchants who dominated Boston's politics. Lowell and his small circle of supporting investors had now come to see the advantages of a modest tariff, yet the bulk of the merchant community, not only in Boston, but other nearby towns like Salem, Portsmouth, and Providence, were wary of further national measures that might restrict their trade. At the same time, the small-scale producers of cotton throughout the region hoped for *very* high tariffs that would double the price of imported cotton, especially cheaper cotton from India, and allow their businesses to survive.

Lowell found the means to thread his way through these conflicting interests by locating the right allies in national politics. He focused his lobbying on the leading figures in South Carolina's congressional delegation, John C. Calhoun and William Lowndes, the latter chairman of the powerful House Ways and Means Committee. Though a native southerner and large plantation owner, Calhoun had attended Yale College, trained as a lawyer in Litchfield, Connecticut, and at this point in his career favored a strongly nationalist vision, fostered by his sense of the country's embarrassment in the War of 1812. The Washington in which Lowell approached these Carolina planters still smoldered from the British Army's sacking of the city and burning of the Capitol. Congress was holding sessions in Blodgett's Hotel, "which it were unfair to criticize, as a place for Congress to sit in, as it was originally intended only for a tavern, or boarding house."[64] Calhoun, Lowndes, and some other southern and western members of Congress favored a tariff as a means to pay down the debt from the recent war, and supported the idea that the promotion of manufacturing in the United States would lessen the country's dependency on foreign powers, particularly Britain.[65] Another factor that encouraged Calhoun's and Lowndes' support for the tariff was the prospect that Lowell's new mills offered a potential market for the raw cotton that Carolina planters produced.

Lowell knew that the 100 percent tariff favored by New England's small cotton mills would never gain southern support. At those prohibitive rates, high enough to keep out all English-made cloth, demand for Carolina's raw cotton would plummet, as British mill owners would retaliate by purchasing their cotton elsewhere. Instead, Lowell suggested a much lower tariff of only 20 percent on all imported cotton textiles, with an additional provision that a minimum selling price of twenty-five cents per yard be established for all imports. Twenty-five cents per yard happened to be just about the price at which the Boston Manufacturing Company produced its sturdy low-end cloth. The effect of this tariff would be exclusionary for the cheap textiles made in India, which ordinarily sold for much less than twenty-five cents per yard, but not for high-quality British-made textiles already priced well above twenty-five cents per yard. Consequently, British manufacturers would continue to purchase Carolina cotton, especially the fine long-staple variety grown on the Sea Islands, and Lowell's mechanized mills would produce cheaper cotton for the domestic market without the threat of Indian competition.[66] Lowndes, as chair of the Ways and Means Committee, introduced Lowell's tariff plan, Calhoun supported it with speeches on the House floor, and the measure passed on the basis of strong votes from the South and West, overcoming nearly unanimous opposition from New Englanders in Congress.

With this calculated (and decidedly unrepresentative or perhaps even antirepresentative) diplomacy, Lowell achieved a remarkable victory for his vision of the future of New England's political economy, while circumventing the chronic disadvantage that New England customarily faced in national politics as determined by electoral majorities. The tariff system, which would endure into the 1850s (though at decreasing rates after 1846 when the minimum valuation of imported cloth was eliminated), secured the establishment of New England's textile industry on the model that Lowell had pioneered: a highly mechanized, heavily capitalized factory system with a corporate management structure. By keeping out low-cost textiles that his own factories were ideally suited to produce, Lowell forced New England's small-scale, low-tech cotton producers out of business unless they chose to follow the Boston Manufacturing Company model, purchase the advanced machinery that the company produced, and capitalize their enterprises on a scale that could compete with the Lowell juggernaut. By creating the conditions that allowed his own factories to yield huge dividends to investors, he also offered convincing reasons for Boston merchants to shift their investments from trade to manufacturing—a carrot to offset the painful stick that the tariff laid on importers of East Indian cloth. As a result, Boston's merchants became the voluntary source of the capital necessary for many more textile companies to follow in Lowell's footsteps.[67]

An unintended consequence of Lowell's innovations in technology, investment, management, and legislative protection for the cotton textile industry was to deepen the divide, already visible since the time of the Regulation of 1786–87 (the so-called Shays's Rebellion), between Boston's political economy and the interests of its New England hinterland. One of the remarkable features of the political economy of the city-state of Boston had been the convergence of interests among its rural producers of food and timber products, its fleets of fishermen, and its overseas merchants. They were equally dependent on one another and on the autonomy of the region's overseas trade for their mutual prosperity. In the old system, the success of the largest merchants or producers enhanced the strength of the system as a whole. The great fortunes made by the largest overseas merchant houses did not prevent small-scale coastal traders from prospering as well. Likewise, government regulation and the moral economy of the crowd had always prevented large merchants from depressing prices or forestalling markets, so that farmers and fishermen could get fair prices whether they sold to the big fish or the small fry.[68] Independence, and with it Boston's newfound (and short-lived) authority over a state-governed monetary system, had been at the heart of the Shaysite upheaval. But here too, internal political negotiation ultimately healed the conflict over the proper balance between hard money and plentiful currency, as demonstrated by the region's remarkable unity during the embargo and War of 1812.

Lowell and his mills introduced something new. Economies of scale, both with respect to the technology of production and the capital necessary to achieve this productive level, created for the first time a sharp distinction between the source of Boston's great fortunes and the economy of New England's rural hinterland. The success of Lowell's system made it impossible for small cotton-cloth producers to flourish in New England. The only way to compete with the Lowell system was to imitate it, and only those with access to large capital resources and corporate charters could do that. And the raw materials driving this productive industrial system, unlike those of the old mercantile system, were not and could not be produced by New England's farmers. (Molasses used in Boston's preindependence rum industry was not produced by New England farmers either, but it was acquired through direct trade in goods New England did produce, especially fish; this was precisely Fisher Ames's argument against James Madison's proposed molasses duty in 1789.) This structural divide, a fundamental difference between the city's economy, defined now by the concentration of capital in Boston and the industries that it had planted at nearby strategic water-power centers, and that of the rest of New England, became a permanent feature of the region's political economy.

Francis Cabot Lowell's industrial and managerial innovations, together with the protective legislation for which he lobbied, were not the ruthless maneuvers of a cutthroat capitalist bent on "creative destruction" or "disruptive innovation." Or if they were, then the destructive blows fell directly on his own interests. His cousins and in-laws, the Cabot family, were among the small cotton producers eliminated by the new system, and the India Wharf project that he developed himself would suffer from his tariff's prohibitive rates on Indian cotton. But the strongest evidence that the new divide across New England's political economy was not Lowell's intention comes from his plan for the mill's workforce. He was deeply aware of the dismal conditions of the laboring poor in Lancashire's mills and the poverty that blighted Britain's new industrial cities. He had no interest in creating a wage-laboring dependent underclass that would, in Jefferson's famous formulation, produce a "canker" on the republican body politic.[69]

Lowell therefore aimed to produce an entirely different labor system, first in Waltham and then at the far-larger Lowell Mills. Much speculation has been devoted to the source of Lowell's benevolently paternalistic ideals, including a strained effort to suggest the influence of Robert Dale Owen's utopian New Lanark project outside Glasgow.[70] But to find the source of Lowell's willingness to forego maximized profits from proletarian labor, and instead offer high wages, comfortable housing, and educational opportunities to entice the daughters of respectable New England farm families to work in the mills, one need look no further than the traditional political economy of the New England town. The creation of a disciplined and educated labor force paid at sustainable wages had always been central to the community ethos of New England towns.[71] In its intent, if not in its ultimate outcome, the Lowell system was motivated by a deeply conservative impulse to replicate New England's traditional communal culture on a scale demanded by its newest mode of production. Yet at best, the Lowell Mills could never be more than a Potemkin Village reproduction of the traditional New England town. The young women who came to work there gained skills, education, time discipline, and cash to enter the consumer economy. They could not, however, replicate their ancestors' ownership of the means of production of the goods that linked New England to the Atlantic economy.[72]

The other element that Lowell introduced to the city's political economy, perhaps unintentionally as well, was a new connection for Boston with slavery and the American South. As earlier chapters have shown, slavery had always been essential to Boston's economy from the days in the 1640s when William Peirce and George Downing discovered the profits to be made selling New England products to West Indian planters. Neither Peirce nor Downing could have envisioned the next two centuries of expansion in the slave-based plantation complex, the Atlantic trade it generated, or the political evolution of the British Empire around it. But in all that time, the economic ties between Boston and the islands never placed the city under the direct political influence of the sugar plantation owners in Barbados and Jamaica. The deal that Lowell made with Lowndes and Calhoun changed that as well. Lowell forged an economic link between Boston's future principal industry and an expanding Cotton Kingdom, whose political power would shape Boston's fate within the United States.

In retrospect, the links between Lowell's Boston Manufacturing Company and the cotton boom that transformed the American South seem obvious, even inevitable. We can envision the boilerplate made in Paul Revere's Canton copperworks powering the steamboats that brought slaves down the Ohio and Mississippi from the Old South to the New. But in 1816, neither Lowell nor Calhoun understood the long-term impact that their bargain on tariffs would have on their respective regions and their relationship within the union. For the moment, Lowell could only see, before his untimely death the next year at the age of forty-two, that he had laid the economic foundation for a transformation of his city's social and cultural institutions.

Lords of the Loom and Lords of the Lash

In the two decades after the establishment of the Boston Manufacturing Company, the complex of textile mills spawned by the Boston Associates on the falls of the Merrimack River generated enormous growth for the city and its immediate neighbors. In 1837, the state of Massachusetts conducted its first industrial survey of the commonwealth's productive power. The results were striking. In 1821, the district known as East Chelmsford had been the site of about a dozen houses near the thirty-foot falls of the Merrimack. In 1837, transformed into the new industrial city of Lowell, it was now home to twenty thousand people, the second-largest town in the state.[73] About seven thousand of those residents, mostly young women, worked in Lowell's twenty-two cotton mills, which annually processed over sixteen million pounds of raw cotton into more than forty-eight million yards of finished cloth of ever-increasing variety, worth more than $5 million.[74] The mills themselves were capitalized at more than $6 million. The investors, still a tight circle of family and friends in Boston, received handsome annual dividends, averaging around 10 percent in the decade between 1825–35 for the Merrimack Company's mills at Lowell.[75]

The growth, productivity, and profits of the mills also spun off an enormous number of other commercial and industrial enterprises, which transformed the economic life of the city of Boston and its relationship to the larger region. These enterprises included sales corporations for the marketing and distribution of the mills' products, and the growth of dozens of ancillary industries for processing the products of the mills and serving the needs of the mill workers. The mills drove a boom in the transportation industry, too—most significantly, the railroads. Thomas Handasyd Perkins had the distinction of financing the first railroad in the United States, a horse-powered line designed to haul granite from a Quincy quarry to the coast, so that the stone for building the Bunker Hill Monument could be shipped to Charlestown. Based on this example, the state chartered the construction of a rail line from Lowell to Boston, encouraged by Patrick Tracy Jackson, a leading member of the Boston Associates. The introduction of steam-powered locomotives expanded the potential for the rapid and efficient marketing of textiles. By 1835, the Boston and Lowell was in operation, soon to be followed by another line to Worcester, described by one of its investors as "a forty-four mile extension of Boston Long-Wharf." This revolution in transportation financed by textile mill profits provided a new opportunity for Boston to reclaim some of the economic hegemony over its New England hinterland that had been draining away since the ratification of the US Constitution. Additional railroad lines to the Connecticut River and as far west as Albany further implemented that purpose.[76] Maps from this era illustrate this rapid transformation. An 1824 map of Massachusetts prominently depicts the Middlesex Canal, built in the 1790s and opened in 1803, which connected the Merrimack River directly to Massachusetts Bay and helped to make Lowell's textile mills on the Merrimack possible. An 1846 map of railroads linked to Boston demonstrates the rapid spread of the new transport technology. And by depicting Boston as a large oval space firmly on the mainland, with no trace of the peninsula jutting into Boston Harbor, it suggests how dramatically the railroads worked to reorient the popular conception of the city away from the sea and toward the continent.

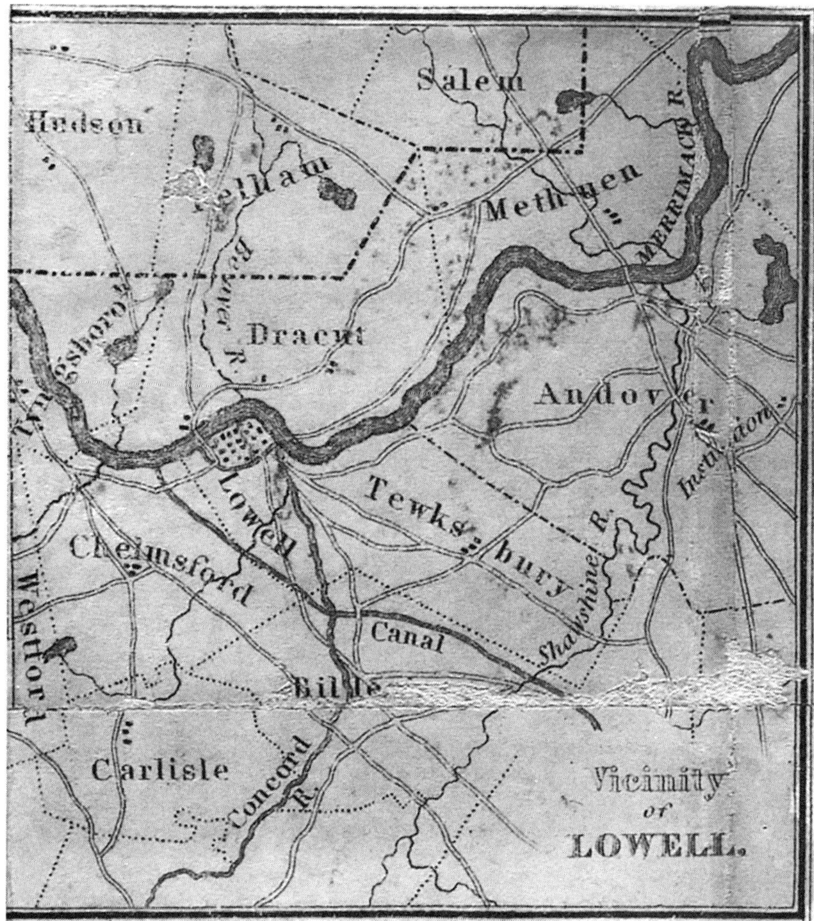

MAP 9.1. *Massachusetts*, by J. H. Goldthwaite, 1824. Detail. Although the cotton mills at Lowell did not begin operations until 1823, this 1824 map already depicts Lowell, along with Boston and Springfield, with a special detailed map inset, showing the site of the new mills adjacent to the Middlesex Canal.

In the city proper (still confined to the Shawmut Peninsula though its population grew from 43,000 in 1820 to 61,000 in 1830 to 93,000 in 1840), the booming textile industry reshaped economic life at every level. The 1837 industrial survey listed some 8,375 people now employed in manufacturing industries in the city of Boston, not counting some of the older, pre-Lowell businesses such as the rum distilleries. Many of these jobs, such as those filled by nearly 3,000 workers (mostly women) in "Manufactories of Clothing,"

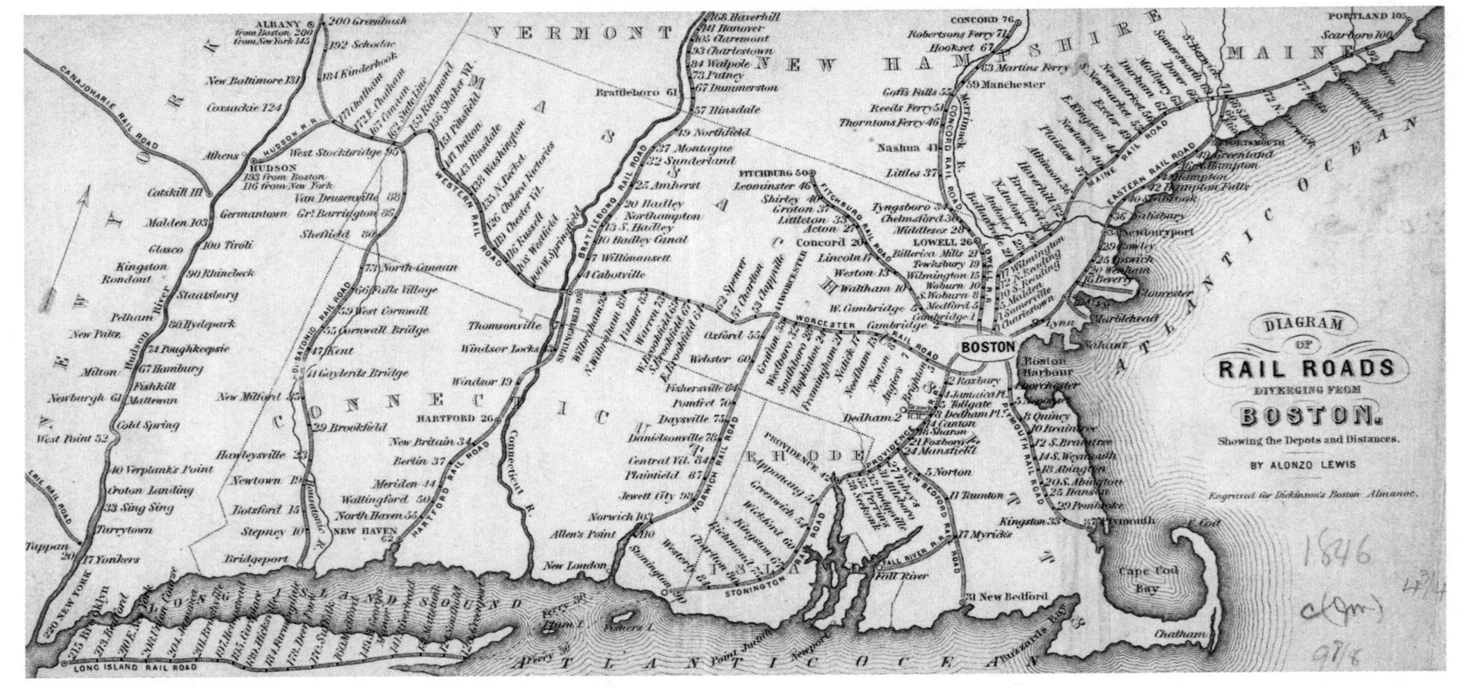

Map 9.2. *Diagram of Rail Roads Diverging from Boston*, by Alonzo Lewis, 1846.

and 456 more in "Manufactories of Neck Stocks and Suspenders," were clearly affiliated with the textile boom.[77] But the shift to textiles also created thousands of new positions for clerks, accountants, and managers of the sales corporations, banks, and insurance companies fostered by the growth of the mills, as Boston became a major financial center in these decades.[78] In addition, the growth in the coastal shipping routes dedicated to trading with the American South complemented the continuing vigorous pursuit of international trade, making this era the most lucrative in Boston's maritime history.[79]

These rapid changes meant that Boston and its regional hinterland now staked an enormous amount of their prosperity on the ability to purchase, process, and sell a single commodity that they did not produce: cotton. As a result, the city's interests were increasingly entangled with those of the Cotton Kingdom, the enormous economic system that over the same few decades, stretched rapidly west from its birthplace in Georgia and South Carolina. Its plantation developers, abetted by the US government, displaced the region's indigenous landowners in order to fill the rich river valleys of new states like Louisiana (admitted in 1812), Mississippi (1817), Alabama (1819), and Arkansas (1836) with cotton plantations powered by enslaved African workers.[80] Between 1800 and 1840, the enslaved population of Mississippi grew from 3,500 to 195,000, and its cotton production correspondingly increased from 0 to 193 million pounds per year.[81] No coincidence, then, that in the year 1831, for the first time in Boston's history, the total volume of its coasting trade—that is, its trade with other parts of the United States—exceeded that of its foreign trade. In the words of Boston's maritime historian Samuel Eliot Morison, "Year by year the wealthy Cotton Belt wore out more boots and shoes, purchased more cottons for her slaves, used more Quincy granite in her public buildings, and consumed more Fresh Pond ice in her mint juleps. The New England mills, on their part, were calling for more cotton; and every pound of it that they received, before the Civil War, came by sailing vessel from Charleston, Savannah, Mobile, and New Orleans."[82]

It might be argued that this was more a change in commodity than in condition. In the colonial period, Boston's political economy had likewise been dependent on slave-produced sugar from the West Indies. Morison went on to describe the cotton trade as "the last sailing-ship phase of a Massachusetts interest two centuries old—the carrying of Southern staples to a market."[83] But there was a fundamental difference from earlier times created by this new staple: the Caribbean sugar islands never had any direct *political* authority over Boston. Massachusetts and Jamaica had merely been mutually interdependent parts of the same loose network of British colonial possessions. The West India lobby may have had greater influence over the general shape of Whitehall's colonial policy than its Massachusetts counterparts did, but the planters of Barbados could not legislate for the merchants of Boston, and vice versa.

The assent of Massachusetts to the US Constitution in 1788, however, and subsequent developments in the practice of national politics and the rapid growth of the slaveholding South, meant that national laws made by majorities garnered elsewhere in the union, often with the help of the three-fifths clause and its boost to planter representation, bore directly on the Bay State's political economy and autonomy.[84] Consequently, the transformations that linked Boston's economy to the Cotton Kingdom demanded political adaptations as well. The troubling entanglements caused by these new connections between Boston's lords of the loom and the slaveholding lords of the lash are nowhere more evident than in the tortuous career of Daniel Webster.

Black Dan's Dilemma

Had he been born ten or fifteen years later, and in closer proximity to Boston, Webster might have been among those talented young New England men who would travel to Germany for their education in the years after 1815. Prodigiously gifted he was, with a mind both enormously acquisitive and sharply analytic, and a talent for oratory arguably unmatched in American history. In an era known for its rhetorical excellence, Webster was unexcelled. His "godlike" reputation was largely a product of his way with words, yet it was matched by an imposing physical presence—a powerful physique, jet-black hair, lowering brow, and eyes with a look that arrested. But Webster was born in 1782 in the remote village of Salisbury, New Hampshire, near the headwaters of the Merrimack River. Webster's father, Ebenezer, was a man much like John Adams's father had been: an exemplar of local civic virtue in this frontier New England town. Salisbury's distance from Boston and the family's relative poverty, though, meant that young Daniel developed his talents closer to home at Dartmouth College rather than Harvard, read law with a New Hampshire neighbor, and became a successful lawyer and promising young politician in Portsmouth instead of Boston.

Yet Webster's aspirations always turned him toward New England's metropolis. He was chronically short of money, and highly conscious of that shortcoming as a limitation on his ambitions. At the age of twenty-two, he managed to gain a brief stint in the Boston law office of Christopher Gore before family responsibilities dragged him back to New Hampshire. By age twenty-four, he was submitting articles and reviews to Boston's *Monthly Anthology*. He married a local Salisbury woman, Grace Fletcher, set up practice in Portsmouth, and in 1812, at the age of thirty, won a seat in Congress as a Federalist from New Hampshire. Unlike Adams fifty years earlier, Webster was already a mature and powerful figure in his own right, prominent in Boston's hinterland, before moving into Boston's elite circles.[85] (See plate 20.)

Though Webster lived in the hinterland, he espoused the politics of Boston. He embraced the Federalist views championed by Boston's representatives Fisher Ames and Josiah Quincy in Congress. He detested Napoléon's imperial aspirations. As a free trade advocate, he denounced Napoléon's Continental System. Once Jefferson's embargo was enacted, Webster attacked it in print as an unconstitutional assault on New England's interests by an "administration-party . . . continually singing the praises of the French Emperour."[86] In one of many famous Fourth of July orations he would give in his career, Webster addressed the Washington Benevolent Association of Portsmouth in 1812, denouncing

Madison's war and defending the concept that the US Constitution was a pact among states, adopted to promote the commerce that Virginia's dynasts were now destroying.[87] Later that summer, as a delegate to a Federalist convention in Rockingham County, New Hampshire, Webster drafted a memorial to President Madison expressing the convention's objections to the war. Claiming to "shrink from a separation of the states," Webster's memorial nonetheless lamented that disunion might be the result "when one portion of the country undertakes to control, to regulate, and to sacrifice the interest of another."[88]

Although not a member of the Hartford Convention of 1814 (he was serving in Congress at the time), Webster's political views aligned with the report that Otis, Sullivan, and Perkins delivered to Washington in 1815, including support of a state's right to "interpose" its authority against national government conscription of state militias for military service. Webster also shared the cultural prejudices of Boston's Federalists. On his own first journey to Washington when elected to Congress, he expressed the same shock and dismay over "the general appearance of this Country" that many of his Boston predecessors had felt: "It has not the wealth nor the People which I expected. From Baltimore to this place, the whole distance, almost, you travel thro woods, & in a worse road than you ever saw." Other than a few plantations that were "tolerable well,—all the rest is a desert."[89] When he finally moved to Beacon Hill in Boston in summer 1816, set up a law practice on Court Street, joined the Athenaeum and the Brattle Square Church, Webster felt he had come home.[90]

The previous winter in Washington, Webster had met Francis Cabot Lowell and assisted him in preparing the tariff bill that would protect Lowell's textiles from cheap foreign competition. When the actual floor vote came, Webster managed to absent himself from the roll call so as not to have to vote against the free trade interests of his Portsmouth constituency and the rest of New England's congressmen, who still saw tariffs as akin to the hated British Navigation Acts.[91] By the time he arrived in New England's metropolis, Webster was positioned to be the legal and political spokesman for the Boston Associates and their manufacturing interests. But because Webster had already married a clergyman's daughter from rural New Hampshire nearly a decade earlier, he could not marry into the city's riches. Many nineteenth-century Boston men made their reputations from their learning and wits, but married into merchant or industrial fortunes, including Edward Everett, Andrews Norton, George Ticknor, Henry Wadsworth Longfellow, George Bancroft, Jared Sparks, and Charles Francis Adams.[92] Webster longed to live the life of wealth and grace that his Beacon Hill neighbors displayed, and to do so required that he become the hired hand, in Congress and the courts, of the merchants, manufacturers, and bankers of the new Boston.[93]

For his first few years in the city, Webster continued to espouse positions consistent with his earlier convictions. As controversy emerged in 1819 over the possible admission of Missouri to the union as a slave state, Webster spoke out at a public meeting in Boston, denouncing slavery as a "great evil" and arguing for Congress's right to restrict its expansion into new territories.[94] The following year, as a delegate in the Massachusetts convention to revise its state constitution, Webster argued in favor of retaining the Senate as a body representing property rather than persons, citing the republican writings of Aristotle, Hugo Grotius, and above all, James Harrington, much as Adams had done in drafting the 1780 Constitution.[95]

Later that year, Webster delivered the oration in Plymouth celebrating the bicentennial of the landing of the Pilgrims. This address, among Webster's greatest, showed the influence of Boston's newfound fascination with ancient Greece. Webster cast the tiny Plymouth Colony as a metaphor for New England as a whole and seized the occasion to trace the region's history from its founding to the present. For Webster, ancient Greece offered the best model for understanding New England's origins: "Roman settlement resembled, far less than that of the Greeks, the original settlement of this country." The Romans sought "dominion," while for the Greeks, "colonization and commerce, indeed, would naturally become objects of interest to an ingenious and enterprising people." Webster compared the influence of the decisive Battle of Marathon on the future of Athens in producing a "Socrates and Plato, Demosthenes, Sophocles and Phidias," to the influence of Plymouth's founding on the future glories of New England. He surveyed New England's achievements from the Glorious Revolution to the American Revolution, attributing them to the region's republican values, including the protection of private property and its equitable distribution among the population: "A great subdivision of the soil, and a great equality of condition; the true basis most certainly of a popular government," again citing Harrington to support his case. Then, in a surprising and stirring conclusion, Webster returned to the question of slavery, reminding his audience that despite these accomplishments, "the land is not yet wholly free from the contamination of a traffic, at which every feeling of humanity must forever revolt—I mean the African slave trade." From his rhetorical arsenal, he summoned the claim that "it is not fit that the land of the pilgrims should bear the shame longer. I hear the sound of the hammer, I see the smoke of the furnaces where manacles and fetters are still forged for human limbs. I see the visages of those, who by stealth, and at midnight, labour in this work of hell, foul and dark, as may become the artificers of such instruments of misery and torture. Let that spot be purified, or let it cease to be of New England."[96]

Webster stopped short of calling for the end of American slavery. And while he clearly meant that all America was now "the land of the pilgrims," he remained ambiguous about whether he included the internal, interstate slave trade, then in the midst of selling a million human souls from the Chesapeake to the Mississippi, as part of this "work of hell, foul and dark." He tried, as always, to balance the rights of property against the claims of liberty and equality. But as of 1820, he was clearly willing to stand for the superiority of moral claims over social convenience or political compromise. Four years later, when he had become Boston's member of Congress, Webster spoke out in support of the righteous cause of Greek independence in the face of the Monroe administration's caution and politics of prudence: "Does it not become us, then, is it not a duty imposed on us, to give our weight to the side of liberty and justice, to let mankind know that we are not tired of our own institutions . . . ?"[97]

Nevertheless, from the time that Webster took his seat as Boston's representative in 1823, to his elevation to the US Senate in 1827 and the serious aspirations to the presidency that quickly followed, Webster's politics shifted steadily toward upholding the interests of his wealthy Boston backers and staking out positions that would make him a viable national leader. Insofar as the Boston Associates now sought cooperation with their suppliers and customers in the Cotton Kingdom, these goals went hand in hand. Yet his ambitions led Webster to back away from the moral and principled positions of his Federalist youth. In 1828, Theodore Lyman Jr. published an article that named Webster (in passing) among other Federalists who conspired to plan New England's secession from the union during the embargo crisis of 1807–8. Although Webster, unlike other Federalists such as Timothy Pickering, had never taken part in any secession plans, Lyman's article was not far from the mark in describing Webster's position at the time. It was Webster's good fortune that his 1814 speech in Congress against conscription and in favor of state interposition had not been entered into the Congressional Record. This made it possible in later years to downplay his earlier sectional sentiments.[98] With a national reputation to defend, however, Webster felt compelled to bring a criminal charge of libel against Lyman, a Boston neighbor and friend. The case ended with a deadlocked jury, but Webster's determination to reposition himself as a committed nationalist was apparent.[99]

Within two more years, the transformation was complete. As Webster became an open supporter of the protective tariffs that in 1816 he had dodged by avoiding roll call, he became embroiled in Senate debates over the tariff in which slavery was the omnipresent subtext. By the time of his famous "Second Reply to Hayne" in 1830 regarding the so-called Tariff of Abominations, he had performed a full about-face. Webster now denounced South Carolina's Robert Hayne, who called for the "independence of the States" against pernicious national legislation like the tariff, whereas in

1814, Webster had defended state "interposition" against the national conscription of state militias. At the same time, while Webster continued to insist that slavery was "one of the greatest evils," he now argued that it was up to the individual states where it existed to deal with the problem: "It is their affair, not mine." Thus, on national tariff policy (which favored the Boston Associates), Webster championed Congress's unquestioned supremacy, while on the question of southern slavery (which also favored the Boston Associates), Webster championed state sovereignty. No longer supporting the Hartford Convention's proposal to amend the Constitution's three-fifths clause, he now argued for "the Constitution as it is, and for the Union as it is." For the rest of his life, Webster would continue to uphold this convoluted position, summarized in the conclusion to his second reply to Hayne, "Liberty and Union, now and forever, one and inseparable!"[100] Only a few days before, Webster had presented a petition to the Senate on behalf of a South Carolina railroad asking for federal support—a request that aligned perfectly with the nationalism that he asserted in his reply to Hayne. But it also demonstrated that cheap cotton from Carolina was now an integral aspect of the national welfare that benefited the Boston Associates and their textile mills. Textile magnate Abbott Lawrence endorsed this sentiment when he presented Webster with a silver tea service inscribed to the "Defender of the Constitution" and remarked that "Mr. Webster never stood so high in this country as at this moment, and I doubt if there be any man, either in Europe or America, his superior."[101]

The success of the cotton textile enterprise in remaking Boston's economy had, over the space of only fifteen years, pushed its leading (or at least its wealthiest) citizens away from the Federalist and federative politics of Ames, Quincy, and the Hartford Convention, and into the arms of South Carolina and Mississippi. Boston's leaders were now not merely republicans in the traditional New England sense of Harrington's *Oceana* and John Adams, but also National Republicans of the sort defined by "Black Dan" Webster, a Faustian character who sold his soul to the money devil in search of fame, power, and glory on a national stage.

Under the governing umbrella of the British Empire, Boston's economy had always been deeply intertwined with the slave-labor-based plantation economies of the West Indies. In effect, New England had been a slave society where the bulk of its slaves happened to live an ocean passage away, out of sight and too often out of mind. No matter how deep the economic connections with Jamaica, Antigua, and Barbados had been under British rule, these sugar islands never had any direct governing authority over Boston, no power to subordinate New England's interests to their own—a fact that the revolution itself had demonstrated when these colonial regions went their separate ways. Immediately after independence, Boston's economic connections to the southern slave states were quite limited. Under the Articles of Confederation, the equality among the states and the restricted powers of the national government made it difficult to imagine that the slave states could ever influence the domestic governance of New England.

But the enhanced powers of Congress under the 1787 Constitution and the rise of a winner-take-all form of national politics that defeated Boston's federative aspirations, combined with the strong economic link between New England's textile mills and the Cotton Kingdom's plantations, meant that Boston's economic growth now came with choking limitations on its political autonomy. In economic terms, the relationship between the Cotton Kingdom and the northern seaports that shipped and processed its cotton was a colonial one, with the underdeveloped South dependent on the technologically sophisticated and commercially developed North. In America's colonial past, British courts had decided in the Somerset Case that the slaveholding colonies could not legislate for the metropolitan homeland. Yet under the US Constitution, the slave South's economic dependency was offset by its enhanced political power in the national government. The slaveholding states could, and did, legislate for the United States as a whole. Even if Boston's new economy imposed new limits on its political autonomy, however, it offered another avenue for sustaining the region's traditional independence, found in the realm of culture.

CHAPTER 10

On the German Road to Athens

Boston at a Crossroads

> Many years ago, when [Edward Everett] was a very young man, he was addressing an assembly of Boston merchants whom he had invited to meet him at Faneuil Hall, and whom he was endeavoring to persuade to purchase for the use of Harvard College, a work of art, the Panorama of Athens, . . . which had just arrived from Greece. He was showing the value of art in a young community like our own, and in the course of his argument put the question into the mouth of his hearers, "What is it good for?" I shall never forget the force of manner and expression which he threw into his reply, put also into the form of a question, "What is anything good for except as it refines and ennobles and brings out the divine in man?"
>
> —*A Memorial of Edward Everett, from the City of Boston*, 1865

Boston had never experienced anything like the political debacle brought on when William Sullivan, Harrison Gray Otis, and Thomas Handasyd Perkins delivered the results of the Hartford Convention to Washington, DC, in January 1815.

In 1689, when Boston's political, religious, and economic autonomy were endangered by the dictates of a British monarch, Bostonians vented their ire against the noxious king's local representative, Sir Edmund Andros, the military governor of the newly created Dominion of New England. Fortunately, their rebellion took place in the year when the revolt against James II was ratified in the crowning of William and Mary as constitutional monarchs.

In 1775, Britain's monarch again threatened the city's political, religious, economic, and military authority. Once more, Bostonians' hostility focused on a military governor of the province, General Thomas Gage, his handpicked councillors, and his regiments of regulars. In this instance, the willingness of a dozen other British colonies to declare that the cause of Boston was the cause of all America sustained Boston's defiance and proved ultimately victorious.

By contrast, in the first two decades of the nineteenth century, when the elective executives of the United States, the "Virginia Dynasty" residing in the new federal city on the Potomac, pursued measures that undermined Boston's economy, defied its political will, and ignored its military capacities, there was no local scapegoat to blame, no arm of an overweening distant authority to attack, arrest, or expel. Under the federal system that the US Constitution created, Boston's traditional leadership class still dominated the politics of the city and its New England hinterland (although the hinterland's allegiance, now divided between Boston's long-standing influence and new national sources of power, was waning). But the enduring strength of traditional local authority seemed to matter not at all within the larger confederation of American states, in which congressional majorities corralled elsewhere in the expanding nation could impose their will on each of the union's component parts.

The Hartford Convention, unlike the similarly extralegal political conventions of 1689 or 1775, had been gathered among New England's leaders not to confront the local spokesman of a distant authority, but to strategize against an authority in which they were formally represented, yet whose actions seemed increasingly alien and hostile. The purpose had been to strike boldly at a moment when the national government seemed weakest, even on the verge of toppling, in order to renegotiate the federal compact to which Boston had (perhaps mistakenly) assented a quarter century earlier. When that moment of weakness turned, almost miraculously, into a triumph for the Madison administration, the plan that at Hartford had seemed so moderate, so plausible, as a way to concentrate New England's political force within the larger national compact, now was made to appear subversive, radical, even treasonous, when it had been nothing of the kind, certainly not by the standards of 1689 or 1775.

In both 1689 and 1775, the success of Boston's rebellions and the resulting changes in their larger imperial contexts had opened new avenues for enterprising citizens to explore, and new sources of inspiration for their efforts to develop and refine their own city—the Dutch and German opportunities seized on by Jonathan Belcher and Cotton Mather in the aftermath of the Glorious Revolution, and the French moment of Samuel Breck (father and son) and the Perkins brothers in the wake of the American Revolution. In 1815, something more complex happened. The closing of US national politics to Boston's Federalists forced an inward turn. After 1815, many of the city's bright and ambitious young people rejected the national arena in which the federative politics of their fathers had been spurned. Instead, they worked to develop the economic strength, social stability, and cultural prospects of Boston and its hinterland.

Yet this inward turn paradoxically involved another outward reach as well. Europe in the aftermath of Napoléon became the center, once again, of young Bostonians' aspirations. The French Revolution's disruption of the tight association between Roman Catholicism and French political and military power, together with Boston's own halting steps toward a more ecumenical religious culture, made a wider range of European destinations available to Boston's nineteenth-century travelers than their predecessors. Nonetheless, much as it had been a century earlier, Germany was a source of inspiration for Bostonians in this era, and with the end of the Napoleonic Wars, many of Boston's leading young men went to Germany for their education. But this was a Germany quite different from the one that Belcher had explored, a Germany no longer plagued by wars of religion, but scarred by the French revolutionary wars and Napoléon's ambition to re-create a neo-Roman imperium across all of Europe, a Germany whose intellectual world was now obsessed with Greek antiquity as a source of identity and a resource for German recovery and unification.

The young Bostonians who went to Germany imagined, on their return, that they were building the Athens of America, reviving on the Atlantic's western shore a tradition rooted in ancient Greece.

The remaking of the city's fortunes through the dramatic shift from merchant to industrial enterprise, as described in the preceding chapter, underwrote the cost of rebuilding its distinctive culture. Shut out as Boston was by the Hartford Convention debacle from any leading role in national political affairs, the city's newfound wealth and economic stability made it possible for a generation of the city's leadership to focus its energies instead on the cultivation of literature and the arts, education, science, and social reform. It also allowed Bostonians to act as agents of political liberation overseas, promoting republican self-government for downtrodden and anti-imperial states and principalities in Europe and elsewhere. The following pages will travel alongside a series of these adventurers to Europe, including Edward Everett and George Ticknor, Samuel Gridley Howe and Horace Mann, and encounter with them an astonishing array of European intellectuals, reformers, and politicians whose ideas and programs they would bring back to Boston in an effort to transform the city's social and cultural life.

But over the course of this generation's careers, no amount of success in cultural or civic improvement could ultimately spare the city of Boston from the conflict generated by its deepening entanglement with the Cotton Kingdom. Indeed, the social and culture movements that these adventurers' European travels brought back to Boston would unintentionally exacerbate the tensions generated by the turn to a cotton textile economy, both within the city and between Boston and the national government. In the end, the terms of the city's entanglements in the constitutional compact and the growing internal rift over slavery that it generated made Boston's inward turn away from national politics impossible to sustain, and undermined this last-ditch attempt to remake the city-state of Boston as the Athens of America.

The Lure of Germany

With culture, as with industry, scale mattered. Individual Bostonians had traveled to Germany before, and some had developed an awareness of its intellectual riches. Yet the cultural chasm created by the revolutionary break and the Loyalist exile, including the descendants of Jonathan Belcher, seems to have eradicated the memory of Belcher's German sojourns. Later Boston travelers to Germany, like Joseph Warren Revere, unknowingly followed in his footsteps. Benjamin Thomson, a Loyalist exile from the siege of Boston who gained fame for his experiments in thermal physics and practical inventions, moved in 1785 to Bavaria, where he oversaw the defortification of Munich and established its English Gardens on the remnants of the city's ramparts; he was awarded the title of Count Rumford by the Holy Roman Empire in 1791.[1] John Quincy Adams served as minister to Prussia from 1797 to 1801, acquired a substantial library of German books, and composed his *Letters on Silesia*.[2] But over the next two decades, Boston's fascination with Germany grew rapidly in ways that would profoundly reshape the city and its region's culture.

In 1806–7, Joseph Stevens Buckminster, the young pastor of Boston's Brattle Street Church, toured the Rhineland and German Switzerland, spending his inheritance on a collection of three thousand books. Buckminster was among the liberally minded theologians, centered in Boston and at Harvard, who were transforming the Congregational Church from within, challenging the orthodoxies of the puritan past, including the doctrine of the trinity. The new forms of biblical criticism that German universities were developing through the intense philological study of ancient texts offered an important resource for the emergent Unitarian movement. On Buckminster's return to Boston, he used his library to compose brilliant essays for the *Monthly Anthology*, the city's first literary magazine, and to make forays into biblical criticism that led to his appointment in 1811 as Harvard's first lecturer in scriptural studies.[3] After the Napoleonic Wars ended in 1815, these few individual visitors grew into a wider stream of young Bostonians traveling to Germany, particularly to the University of Göttingen, creating a widening current of travel, study, and return.

Before his untimely death in 1812 at the age of twenty-eight, Buckminster had convinced Edward Everett, a younger friend and parishioner, to follow him into the ministry. Everett, the son of Oliver Everett, minister of Boston's New South Church, graduated from

Harvard in 1811 at the precocious age of seventeen. When Buckminster died, Everett was appointed to the Brattle Street pulpit, and two years later was named to a newly endowed chair in Greek literature at Harvard. This appointment came with the extraordinary opportunity of two years of travel and study in Europe to prepare for the new position.[4] Everett recruited another young Bostonian, George Ticknor, a few years older and the son of a wealthy Boston grocer, to accompany him to Europe and study at the University of Göttingen.

Why Göttingen? Part of the university's attraction lay in its connection to the Anglo-American Protestant world. Britain's King George II (Georg August) had founded the Georg-August-Universität there in 1734, when Göttingen lay within his Hanoverian realm. Benjamin Franklin, seeking inspiration for the college that would become the University of Pennsylvania, had visited Göttingen in 1766. In the 1780s, George III sent three of his sons there, and later English authors such as Samuel Taylor Coleridge studied in Göttingen as well.[5] But for Ticknor and Everett, the attraction of Göttingen was more direct. By way of Buckminster's library and Adams's books, Ticknor and Everett knew that Europe's finest scholars of classical civilizations and its most advanced biblical critics, historians, and natural philosophers had done pioneering work at Göttingen. Christian Gottlob Heyne and his pupil Friedrich August Wolf conducted critical investigations into the authorship of Homer's works, which launched the field of modern philology.[6] Buckminster learned, through English translations, of the Göttingen scholars Johann David Michaelis and Johann Gottfried Eichhorn, professors of oriental languages and biblical exegesis, who pioneered the field of Old Testament criticism. Göttingen was also the home of Johann Friedrich Blumenbach, Germany's great naturalist and comparative anatomist, and a roster of other scholars, Dissen on the Greek and Roman classics, Planck and Heeren on church history and modern history, Bouterwek on modern philology and literature—in all some forty professors. (At the time, Harvard had eight professorships—three in medicine, two in natural science, and one each in rhetoric, divinity, and Hebrew.)[7] Of all the German universities, Göttingen had been the least damaged by the recent wars. Napoléon had "considered Göttingen as an University belonging neither to Hanover nor Germany but to Europe and the world." Its magnificent library of two hundred thousand volumes made Harvard's seem like "a closetful of books" by comparison.[8] If Everett meant to introduce the study of Greek Literature to Harvard, then Göttingen was the place to go, and Ticknor eagerly accompanied him.[9] (See plates 21 and 22.)

A Southern Interlude

Before their voyage to Germany, Ticknor and Everett each independently visited the American South, an important prelude to their European travels, because the jarring differences between New England and the southern states prepared them to appreciate the affinities between Boston and Germany. Before his southern journey, Ticknor wrote, "The next winter I shall pass at the South, to see the men the cities contain, and get some notion of the state of my own country; and, in the spring, I shall go to the land of strangers."[10] But like Josiah Quincy and John Adams forty years earlier, Ticknor and Everett would both find that Virginia was actually "the land of strangers," at least with respect to their cultural expectations. The sense of alienation these two young Bostonians experienced in the capital of their own national confederation would frame their very different encounter with German culture.

Ticknor and Everett kept remarkably similar diaries of their southern travels. Everett observed, "There are no towns in Virginia, few cities, and those not large, . . . the mass of the population must dwell upon their lands in the country." Ticknor commented disparagingly on the absence of bridges across Virginia's many streams, its lack of decent roads, and the "miserable hovel, though called a tavern," where he and his five traveling companions were forced to stay, where men and pigs both slept indoors, and there was no hay for their horses.[11] Compared with New England's carefully tended landscape of prosperous towns and well-made roads and bridges, where even livestock were well housed and fed, life in Virginia struck Ticknor and Everett as squalid. In addition, when Ticknor and Everett contemplated the problem of slavery, they feared that Virginia would one day experience an uprising like the recent Haitian Revolution. On the journey south from Boston, Ticknor reported that Samuel Perkins (the younger brother of James and Thomas Handasyd Perkins) had spent an entire day providing "an account of the Revolution in St Domingo," from which the brothers had barely escaped.[12] Everett, in his journal, speculated at length what would happen in Virginia "should the slaves ever rise." He imagined violent and bloody scenarios: "The blacks would be subdued, exterminated, or resubjugated." Or else the slaves would succeed, "which would drench the state in its best blood, strew it with the ruins of its noblest fortunes, and drive out those that escape the sword, into a heady exile in the middle and Eastern states." The exiled masters would likely gain their revenge, however, and the "soil would thus be restored to the whites, who would as likely as not, cover it in ten years, with another population of slaves." Especially striking in this grim vision of the future is that Everett saw slavery as Virginia's problem, or at most a southern one: "I confess the situation of the slave holding states . . . is the greatest political problem I have met." In 1814, when the mills outside Boston were just beginning to produce cotton cloth and Francis Cabot Lowell's tariff bargain with South Carolina had yet to be struck, young Everett could not yet imagine that the "greatest political problem" would entangle Boston too.[13]

As Everett rode from Washington to Mount Vernon hoping to see the home of the late president, he puzzled over "the absence of all small tenements in which the yeomanry might dwell. You everywhere perceive nothing but handsome seats, and the cabins of slaves." Everett knew that Virginia must have a considerable population of free whites who worked their own land, but their invisibility suggested that "this class of yeomanry instead of being as with us [in Massachusetts], the strength and pride of the state, are probably a depressed, despised, and consequently embittered class; the genuine materials for demagogues to work upon."[14] If Thomas Jefferson feared the "mobs of great cities" as a threat to republican government, Everett and Ticknor found the materials for demagogues among the very people that Jefferson considered the "chosen people of God," the vaunted yeomanry of Virginia.[15]

In Washington, Everett clambered through the ruined Capitol building, gutted and burned by the British invasion. He visited the desolate Navy Yard, observing the wreck of the ship *Boston*, built and furnished by Thomas Handasyd Perkins and burned by the British in the late pointless war. His musings on the "vanity of life" were prompted by the devastation that Virginia's leaders had brought on his home city.[16] In their travels through Virginia, Everett and Ticknor were each imbued with a sense of Boston's distance from the dominant social and political strain of the United States.

Göttingen

The Germany that Everett and Ticknor encountered in 1815 felt more familiar than the American South and its rural plantations. The cities and towns of the independent regions of Germany, once part of the now-defunct Holy Roman Empire, bore striking similarities to the political conditions and cultural aspirations of Boston.[17] Like Boston, many of these cities had been ravaged by the imperial wars of the previous half century. Some, like Bremen and Hamburg, independent port cities (or "Free Imperial Cities" in the language of the Holy Roman Empire), had suffered economic distress under Napoléon's Continental System of trade restriction, much like Boston under Jefferson's embargo.[18] Göttingen had been spared the war's worst destruction, but even so it had changed hands numerous times. French forces occupied Göttingen during the Seven Years' War, and in the Napoleonic Wars it fell under Prussian domination in 1806. Taken over by Napoléon's Kingdom of Westphalia the following year, it was ruled by the emperor's brother, the unstable Jerome Bonaparte ("a weak and uncertain little blockhead," Ticknor called him), before returning to the Elector of Hanover following Napoléon's first great defeat in 1813.[19] Among the many still-independent principalities squeezed between France to the west, Prussia to the northeast, and Austria to the south, city after city in central Germany had experienced terrible suffering at the hands of Napoléon's armies, and consequently cultivated a strong hatred of all things French.[20]

During the wars, the German intellectual who best articulated a vision of the independent German city was Johann Gottlieb Fichte. In response to the Prussian Army's humiliating defeat at the Battle of Jena in 1806, Fichte published his *Reden an die deutsche Nation* (addresses to the German nation) in 1808, aiming to rally the German people against French domination. In his sixth address, Fichte resurrected the medieval German city as a model for resistance to Napoléon's empire. Fichte saw medieval German cities as the creations not of princes and kings but of the German people, and centers of resistance to the power of the Roman Empire and its successors: "In these cities every branch of culture quickly developed into the fairest bloom. In them arose civic constitutions and organizations which, though but on a small scale, were none the less of high excellence."[21] In comparison with European countries dominated by princes and nobles, "I say that the German burghers were the civilized people, and the others the barbarians." For Fichte, the spirit, the "Geist," in which the German burghers cultivated their civic virtue was "the spirit of piety, of honour, of modesty, and of the sense of community. . . . Seldom does the name of an individual stand out or distinguish itself, for they were all of like mind and alike in sacrifice for the common weal."[22] The spiritual qualities embodied in this urban tradition convinced Fichte that the German nation, uniquely among Europeans, was "capable of enduring a republican constitution."[23] The qualities that Fichte described in these independent German cities had been embodied in the solid walls that formed their defensive perimeters and symbolized the "honor" of the city. In premodern Europe, what distinguished a city from the countryside was not population size or density but rather the fact of the walls surrounding it, separating those with the privileges and rights of citizens from those outside the walls.[24] A great surge of urban defortification brought on by decades of war had devastated many of these cities. In some cases, as in the great Rhineland fortresses along the French border, Napoléon's armies had demolished the fortifications.[25] In others, independent towns chose to dismantle their own walls to avoid becoming targets of siege or occupation.[26] En route from Göttingen to Hanover, Everett observed that "almost every little town (and all the population is gathered in towns) had its ruined castle, and frequently its ruined wall."[27] Göttingen had begun to remove its fortifications in the wake of French occupation in the Seven Years' War, and as Ticknor wrote, "The whole town was originally surrounded with pretty strong walls; but they are now in ruins, and serve only as the foundation of a public walk, shaded with fine trees, that extends around the city."[28]

Everett and Ticknor made themselves at home as students in Göttingen, and soon began to visit some of the nearby cities. They were impressed by the learned culture of the German universities and intellectual character of the society in which they thrived. On vacation in September 1815, Ticknor and Everett journeyed to Hanover, where Belcher had preceded them a century earlier. Belcher's main purpose had been to access the power of the Hanoverian court. The world of learning and culture, including his accidental meeting with Leibniz, was a pleasant diversion. Ticknor and Everett's goal was just the opposite. As their carriage passed by Herrenhausen's formal gardens, where Belcher had spent many a happy hour strolling with Princess Sophia, Everett and Ticknor didn't bother to get out, preferring to meet an antiquarian bookseller instead. They were eager to meet Professor Georg Friedrich von Martens, a famous jurist recently returned from the Congress of Vienna, and J. G. H. Feder, professor of ethics at Göttingen and now the librarian of the Electoral Library. They spent the day in the great library of eighty thousand volumes that Leibniz had created, marveling at rare and ancient manuscripts, and "above all the rest, the entire collection of Leibnitz MSS on subjects of politics, mathematics, philosophy, history, divinity, and indeed nearly every branch of human knowledge, in Latin, Greek, English, French, Italian, and German."[29]

Like Boston in Massachusetts, these German cities had long traditions of autonomy, albeit within a loose imperial confederation, including a proud faith in the local militia, "the city in arms," as a force for self-defense. On October 18, 1815, Everett observed the ceremonies in Göttingen commemorating the second anniversary of the Battle of Leipzig, "the occasion for administering the oath of allegiance and fidelity to the Landsturm (militia) of the city."[30] Under the Holy Roman Empire, these city-states owed allegiance to the emperor (in whose election some of them participated), but had retained myriad independent rights and privileges, including the power to form independent commercial associations outside imperial control such as the Hanseatic League, of which Göttingen had been a member. The consolidation of imperial power, embodied most recently in Napoleonic France, fostered a powerful anti-French and anti-imperial culture that melded easily with the universities' dedication to the investigation of all things Greek. Eighteenth-century German philhellenism originated in the belief that Greek art and language were the purest source of beauty and aesthetics. But it was strengthened by the war experience, when "German identification with the Athenian Empire—politically fragmented, conquered by force of arms, but united by a single language and spirit—became much more palpable."[31] Autonomy, a martial spirit, and a tradition of commercial association against imperial domination—all these features of Göttingen and its neighbors were tremendously appealing to the young Bostonians of 1815.

Everett and Ticknor were soon joined by two other Bostonians, Joseph Cogswell (in 1816) and George Bancroft (in 1818), forming the beginnings of an American "colony" at Göttingen that would continue through the nineteenth century.[32] Cogswell (b. 1786) was older than Everett, Ticknor, and Bancroft, having been married and pursued a law career in Maine, only to lose his young wife to tuberculosis in 1813. In his grief, he began shipping out on voyages to Europe, but was drawn to study at Göttingen through correspondence with Ticknor and Everett. Bancroft (b. 1800), like Everett before him, had received an appointment from Harvard to travel to Göttingen for further education in languages and biblical criticism. Bancroft was accompanied by twelve-year-old Frederic Henry Hedge, son of a wealthy Boston merchant, who would go on to become a distinguished professor of German at Harvard. If France was the educational destination of choice for merchants' children in the 1770s and 1780s, Germany, and particularly Göttingen, was now the prime location. In 1815, Everett and Ticknor had similarly been tasked with finding a school in Göttingen for the young son of Samuel Perkins, and in 1816, Cogswell had the charge of finding schooling for Augustus Thorndike from another Boston merchant family.[33]

Together, this cohort threw themselves into Göttingen's ascetic culture of learning. Its heroic figures, the professors at Göttingen, were no dilettantes or amateurs, but dedicated professionals, craftsmen of learning.[34] As Ticknor commented of his Greek instructor, Dr. Gottlob Schultze, "It never entered into my imagination to conceive that any expense of time or talent could make a man so accomplished in this forgotten language as he is." Bancroft likewise wrote that his Göttingen professors were all "men of talent, arduous and miraculous industry, . . . superior in this respect to anything we have in America."[35] Although dismayed by the theological skepticism of professors such as Eichhorn, whose philological lectures on the origins of the Gospels they attended, they were in awe of their professors' *scholarly* piety.[36] In the intensity of their devotion to ancient texts, in their belief that philology would recover the original meaning of the works of antiquity, the Göttingen scholars resembled Boston's puritan founders—but Homer was as much their scripture as Moses.[37]

If not to the content of their professors' theology, then at least to the model of their scholarly regime, the Boston visitors applied themselves. Ticknor's daily schedule went as follows: rise at five o'clock, for several hours studying Greek. Then German lessons at eight, three days a week with Professor Georg Friedrich Benecke. At nine o'clock every day, Eichhorn's "lectures on the first three Evangelists." From ten o'clock to noon, more Greek, then after midday dinner and a brief nap, an hour and a half's reading in preparation for Blumenbach's lecture on natural history. At five o'clock, he meets Dr. Schultze, "the best Greek instructor in Göttingen," and recites to him in Greek. "The evenings I pass in reading German, principally such books as will profit me in Italy and Greece."[38]

As latecomers to this learned world, the Boston scholars were bound to fall short of its standards, no matter how many hours they studied each day.[39] Having been educated at the admittedly backward Harvard College, the initial group of Everett, Ticknor, Cogswell, and Bancroft would never gain sufficient command of philological methods or ancient languages to replicate Göttingen in New England. Because it would require many decades for American universities to approach the standards of their German counterparts, these initial expeditions have often been deemed a failure or at best a naive experiment.[40] But such criticisms overlook two important factors.

First, the absence in Boston and New England of the social and educational infrastructure that supported the German universities, like the state-run gymnasia that prepared students for careers in the Prussian bureaucracy, made the immediate replication of German-style universities unthinkable. The city-state of Boston had neither students prepared to pursue German higher education nor more than a handful of positions for such graduates to fill. More significant, to call these first experiments in Göttingen a failure is to overlook the accomplishments of Ticknor, Everett, Bancroft, Cogswell, and their successors. Without discounting the impact of Everett as professor of Greek, Ticknor in romance languages, or the Round Hill School founded by Cogswell and Bancroft to reform Massachusetts' secondary education, more important was their channeling of a continuous stream of educational travel, study, and engagement. After Everett, Ticknor, and company, many other Bostonians followed their footsteps to Göttingen and then other German universities (especially Berlin) as well as to Paris, Rome, and above all Greece, seeking membership in the transatlantic Republic of Letters. Their experiences would influence Boston's culture, learning, arts, and civil society, and they would engage in the promotion of republicanism, even to the point of revolution, in parts of Europe where autonomous self-governing states still seemed possible.

In an extraordinary letter to his father, written after a year in Göttingen, Ticknor described the allure of this vision. "We have always been accustomed to hear and talk of the republic of letters as a state of things in which talent and learning make the only distinction." But in actuality, "the thing itself remained as unreal as [Philip] Sidney's 'Arcadia,' or Sir Thomas More's 'Utopia.' " By Ticknor's lights, the "system of universal patronage" in England was "essentially bad." The "splendor of the Court of France" could only create "literary men as cold and polished as itself." The "little tyrants of Italy and the great ones of Spain and Portugal" stood in the way of any "liberal union of the men of letters" in those countries. But Germany was different: "From the force of circumstances and character, a literary democracy has found full room to thrive and rule." The people and governments in Germany were too poor and small for English-style patronage to dominate. Without a single great metropolis, a London or Paris, the "splendor of a court can have no influence." And except for the recent French invasions, tyranny had never "pressed very hard on Germany." As a result, "the men of letters here . . . have always been dependent for their bread and reputation on their own unassisted and unembarrassed talents and exertions. . . . In this way, a genuine republic of letters arose in the north of Germany."[41]

By a *Republic* of Letters, Ticknor meant not just a jovial association among scholarly sorts but a form of real power. In Germany, "a republic has been formed, extending though all the great and small governments, and independent of the influence of them all, which by its activity unites all the interests of learning, and . . . by its aggregate power resting, as it must, on general opinion, it is able to exert a force which nothing that naturally comes under its influence can resist." To exemplify this power, Ticknor offered two "proofs." First was the distinction between civil life and the Republic of Letters throughout Germany. The civil attachment of most Germans, especially politicians, lay strongly with the principality of their birth. Yet for a man of letters, "when he speaks of his country he is really thinking of all that portion of Germany, and the neighboring territories, through which Protestant learning and philosophical modes of thinking are diffused," and will happily move from one principality to another in pursuit of learning. Ticknor's second "proof" was that the various governments of Germany recognized the independent status of scholars: "The king of Prussia would not appoint to any military or civil service, even to any clerical office in his dominions, any but a Prussian; the king of Hanover, any but a Hanoverian, etc.; but if a man of letters is wanted, all such distinctions are not even thought of; . . . Thus Eichhorn was brought from Weimar; Boeckh, now so famous in Berlin, was a Hanoverian; Heyne was a Saxon." Ticknor lacked the time to include "details too numerous for a letter" about the influence the Republic of Letters had "upon the individuals, institutions, and territories which fall within its sphere." But Ticknor, Everett, Bancroft, Cogswell, and the many who followed in their wake would bring the influence of Germany's Republic of Letters back to Boston over the next several decades.[42]

Ticknor, a twenty-four-year-old with only a year's residence in Göttingen, may not have had a fully accurate reading of intellectual life in Germany.[43] Still, what he was projecting onto Germany, what he clearly longed for, was a Republic of Letters of his own that would create powerful ties among intellectuals, scholars, and the public spirited and civic minded, and transcend the narrow allegiances all too familiar among the weakly united American states. At the same time, he seemed to understand intuitively what Fichte had articulated in his *Address to the German People*. Such a republic could not be an abstraction, a free-floating ideal. It gained power by emanating from specific social and political conditions, not the centralized empires of France, Britain, or Spain, not the splendid courts and metropolises reflecting one another in their mutual brilliance, but from small states of middling wealth and active intellects, the city-states of modern Boston, medieval Germany, or ancient Greece. In its first quarter century, the United States had not coalesced into a unified entity, and its widely varying economies and populations made such a prospect seem unlikely. Nonetheless, perhaps it could foster an internal Republic of Letters like that of Germany, with Boston, the Athens of America, leading the way. This was a significant reduction in Boston's aspirations in the forty years since Adams wrote *Thoughts on Government* as an apostle for the Massachusetts model for all the American republics. Yet it was an optimistic vision for the influence of Boston's cultural power and reflected the vision of Europe's leading men of letters.

Byron, Goethe, and Greece

The Boston travelers' turn toward Greece was encouraged not only by their Göttingen professors but also by their repeated encounters with two of the great literary lights of the Romantic age, Lord Byron and Johann Wolfgang von Goethe—the former in his mid-twenties, the enfant terrible of British letters, the latter in his late sixties, a living monument in the German-speaking world. By reputation, these authors were understood by proper Bostonians to be amoral and irreligious, but the air of scandal only enhanced the attraction for the young travelers, whose European journeys came in the interval between 1812, when Byron published the first two cantos of his narrative poem *Childe Harold's Pilgrimage*, based on his travels in Greece, and 1818, when the last two cantos appeared. In June 1815, stopping over in England on their way to Germany, Everett and Ticknor met Byron in London. Ticknor was enthralled by Byron's account of Greece: "He gave me a long, minute, and interesting account of his journeys and adventures, not only in Greece, but in Turkey; . . . and told me what I ought to be most anxious to see and investigate in that glorious country."[44] Byron also gave Ticknor a "splendid pistol" to present to Ali Pasha, the renowned warrior and Albanian-born ruler of the Ottoman Empire's Macedonian provinces whom Byron had visited in 1809, "to insure me a kind reception with the perverse Turk." During this initial encounter, Ticknor claimed that he "received more kindness from Lord Byron than from any person in England," including a night at the theater in Drury Lane with Lord and Lady Byron in their private box, and parted from the poet with a "lively impression of the goodness and vivacity of his disposition."[45]

Everett's experience paralleled Ticknor's. Ancient Greece was at the forefront of cultural conversation in Britain at the time. Parliament was debating whether to purchase the marbles that Lord Elgin had removed from the Parthenon. Everett "went to see Lord Elgin's marbles, but was . . . disappointed in finding them fewer, less perfect, and less interesting than I expected."[46] Lord Byron did not disappoint. Over several visits, Byron autographed Everett's copy of *Childe Harold*, bantered with him about Britain's system of literary patronage, admired a poem that Everett had written, and provided letters of introduction for Everett and Ticknor on their planned trip to Greece.[47] George Bancroft, who came to Göttingen later than the others, also encountered Byron during a tour through Italy in 1822, when they both happened to visit the *U.S.S. Constitution*, then in the harbor at Leghorn (Livorno). Byron invited the young Bostonian to his villa, and like Everett and Ticknor before him, Bancroft's prejudices about the poet's scandalous reputation were swept away: "I . . . was treated by him with more civility than I have ever been by any man in Europe."[48] And like Everett and Ticknor, Bancroft's conversations with Byron frequently turned to Germany and Goethe.[49]

Everett, Ticknor, Bancroft, and Cogswell, who joined the group in Göttingen in 1816, had strikingly similar encounters with the German poet and polymath. The first part of Goethe's *Faust* had appeared in 1808, but the second part, more strongly influenced by Greek art and mythology, would not be published until after Goethe's death in 1832. In these later years, Goethe dwelled in Weimar, a hundred miles southeast of Göttingen, and the Boston voyagers made special pilgrimages to see him there. As with Byron, Goethe's "immoral" reputation led the Bostonians to expect the poet to be slovenly or repulsive. Yet when Ticknor first encountered Goethe, he found him to be "in his person not only respectable, but imposing. . . . In his manners, he is simple. He received us without ceremony, but with care and elegance."[50] Everett's experience was similar, but among the Bostonians, Joseph Cogswell was the most enamored, visiting the poet many times and forming an enduring bond, initiated by their mutual interest in mineralogy,

FIGURE 10.1. Portrait of Johann Wolfgang von Goethe, by Ferdinand Jagemann, 1818.

but cemented by affection and mutual respect. On first meeting Goethe in March 1817, Cogswell wrote, “From all that I had heard of him, I was prepared to meet with the most repulsive reception, but, I . . . actually experienced the directly opposite. . . . A grand and graceful form, worthy of a knight in the days of chivalry, with a dignity of manners that marked the court rather than the closet."[51] Through the course of several more visits, their friendship was sealed when Cogswell ordered a copy of Goethe's portrait—made by the original artist, Ferdinand Jagemann—which he sent home to Boston.[52]

Goethe had been fascinated by ancient Greece since his youth, when the appearance in 1764 of Johann Joachim Winckelmann's *Geschichte der Kunst des Alterthums* (The history of ancient art) had launched the German obsession with Greek culture. Winckelmann argued that Greek art was a general expression of Greek culture rather than simply the talent of individual geniuses.[53] Winckelmann (b. 1717) had been raised in the Pietist educational system that Jonathan Belcher had witnessed on his visits to Germany, and although Winckelmann converted to Catholicism and moved to Italy, he retained a Pietist's intensity in his worshipful attitude toward Greek art, much as the Göttingen philologists applied the rigor of puritan biblical scholarship to the interpretation of Greek texts.[54] To Goethe, Winckelmann was the "Columbus to the undiscovered continent of the Greeks," the explorer of Greek artistic spirit, not to be slavishly imitated, but to infuse the works of modern artists.[55] In his 1818 essay "Antik und Modern," Goethe made this idea an artistic motto: "Jeder sei auf seine Art ein Grieche! Aber sei's!" (Everyone should be Greek in his own fashion! But be Greek!). (See plate 23.)

Byron's fashion was to be Greek in a literal sense. In 1816, Byron told Ticknor of "the extravagant intention he had formed of settling in Greece."[56] A year after his encounter with Cogswell in 1822, Byron sailed to Missolonghi to join the Greek Revolution against the Ottoman Empire, spending much of his fortune on a plan to support the Greek rebels' assault on the Turkish fortress in Lepanto, only to die of a fever before the attack. Goethe chose to be Greek in a figurative sense. His works such as *Iphigenie auf Tauris* (1779) and *Faust* drew inspiration from Greek art and mythology. Goethe began composing the second part of *Faust* in 1825, after Byron's death in Missolonghi, and based the character of Euphorion, the son of Faust and Helen of Troy, on Byron.[57] Given the two poets' mutual admiration and their common interest in Greece, it is not surprising that whenever the Bostonians met Byron, the conversation turned to Goethe, and whenever they met Goethe, the German poet asked them about Byron. When Ticknor and Everett visited Goethe in 1816, "of Lord Byron, he spoke with interest and discrimination,—said that his poetry showed great knowledge of human nature and great talent in description."[58] On one of Cogswell's visits to Goethe, the two sat up until midnight dining and drinking: "I made him talk of the literature of the day. . . . He was enthusiastic in his praises of Byron, pronounced him the greatest and the only living poet, which was no small gratification to me, from its coincidence with my own opinion."[59]

The fate of these Boston travelers, by virtue of their newfound education and their associations with Europe's finest poets and scholars, was overdetermined. Raised in Boston and educated at Harvard where their teachers were challenging traditional doctrines, they were prepared to leave behind the Trinitarian orthodoxy of their puritan forebears. Yet they barely realized how deeply imbued they were with their city and region's culture, its habits, expectations, and assumptions, until they traveled elsewhere and found it missing, as in their journeys to the American South. But in the universities and cities of Protestant Germany, in romantic figures like Byron and Goethe, and in the idealized image of ancient Greece dangled before them, the Boston travelers found practices and beliefs both strange and new, yet still recognizable, familiar enough to embrace as an appealing path to their own future.

The Germans' love of Greek antiquity and their intense scrutiny of its texts grew out of a Pietistic culture that mirrored Boston's puritan past—the very thing that Cotton Mather had recognized in August Hermann Francke's Halle Institute a century earlier. The idealized version of Greek culture that Winckelmann and his successors promoted already infused the biblicism of New England's puritan heritage. The road from Jerusalem to Boston had from the beginning gone through Philippi. And the Germans' promotion of the "Graechophile's conception of art as [the] historical and national-cultural product" of an educated society that possessed "security, order, and leisure in order to develop noble perceptions and knowledge," flattered the Bostonians' deep-seated belief in New England's carefully cultivated social institutions.[60] Finally, the strong political identification of the German city-states in the Napoleonic age with the ancient Greek city-states' resistance to conquering empires as well as the modern Greek rebellion against the Ottoman Empire resonated with the political sensibilities of Bostonians.[61] Once baptized by high priests like Eichhorn, Dissen, and Schultze in the German cult of Greek antiquity, they too would have to "sei auf seine Art ein Grieche"—be Greek in their own fashion. Like their mentors, Byron and Goethe, their fashions ranged from the literal to the figurative. But the Athens of America of nineteenth-century Boston was the product of young men who went to Germany to learn to be Greek.

Literal Greeks: Edward Everett, Samuel Gridley Howe, and the Greek Revolution

Among the literal Greeks, Edward Everett took the lead. Even before his voyage to Germany, he was badly smitten by philhellenism, having read *Childe Harold's Pilgrimage* in 1812. Over the next few months, Everett prepared an article titled "On the Literature and Language of Modern Greece," in which he argued that the modern Greek language was closer in its "purity" to ancient Greek than was modern Hebrew to the language of ancient Israel, or modern Italian to classical Latin. All that was required for the restoration of the language (and with it, the glory of ancient Greek poetry and philosophy) was the liberation of the Greek homelands from Turkish despotism. "If then, in the page of revolutions, which is opening on the world, there is written an hour of political revival for Greece, we may prophesy, without enthusiasm, that their language may be restored."[62] The following year, a merchant ship from Smyrna called the *Jerusalem* arrived in Boston Harbor, allowing Everett to speak with some actual modern Greeks, perhaps the first ever to come to Boston.[63] For his master's oration at Harvard that summer, Everett declaimed on the topic "The Restoration of Greece," and by year's end, before he turned twenty-one, he was appointed the Eliot Professor of Greek Literature, which occasioned the venture to Göttingen and beyond.[64]

From the time he left Boston for Göttingen, "beyond" always included Greece. Everett clung to this agenda throughout his time in Europe and even planned to write an extended poem modeled on Byron's *Childe Harold*, to be called "An American Pilgrimage." At Göttingen, he befriended a Greek student, Georgios Glarakis, from the Aegean island of Chios (the island of Homer); Glarakis was also learning ancient Greek from Schultze, Dissen, and Eichhorn. Everett traveled with Glarakis ("Glary" in his journals) and continued to meet other Greeks, collecting an impressive array of letters of introduction for his eventual journey to the East. Ticknor had planned to join the Greek pilgrimage, but Harvard appointed him professor of Spanish and romance languages, and he instead went off to the Iberian Peninsula to learn Spanish and collect books for Harvard's library.[65] Everett found another Bostonian, Theodore Lyman Jr., to accompany him to Greece in spring and summer 1819. From Corfu in the Ionian Sea, they went inland to Ioannina to meet the fearsome Ali Pasha (and deliver Byron's pistols), who quizzed them about American interests in the Mediterranean. From there they journeyed overland to ancient Byzantine monasteries (where Everett used his newfound learning to hunt for ancient manuscripts), on to Delphi, through the pass at Thermopylae, and down to Athens. Then on to Sparta, Corinth, and more monasteries (the monks had never encountered Americans before, let alone Americans who could read ancient Greek manuscripts illegible to them). And finally, by boat to the Aegean islands and Constantinople, where Everett purchased six medieval Greek manuscripts for Harvard's collections.[66]

Everett's companion, Lyman, acquired something more substantial, not in Greece, but in London, where the two sailed after a tour through the Levant. As a gift to Harvard College, Lyman spent more than $1,000 on an enormous panorama of Athens, painted by London artists Henry Barker and John Burford, a "perfect representation of the city and plain of Athens . . . from the most

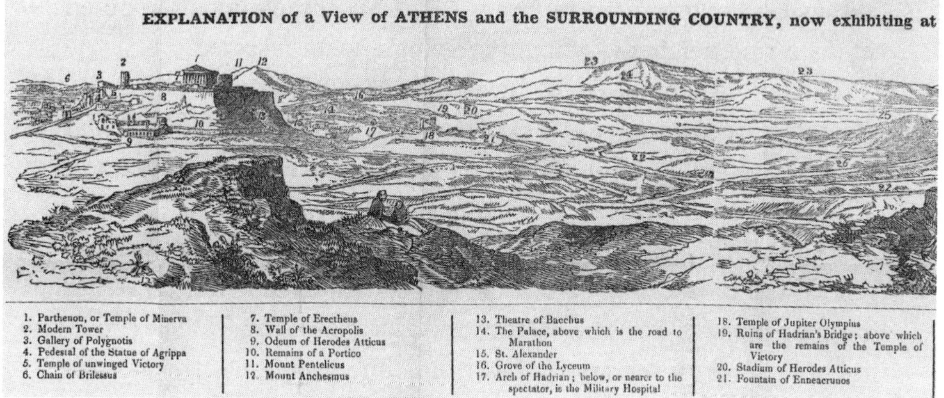

FIGURE 10.2. Description of the *View of Athens, and Surrounding Country, Now Exhibiting in Henry Aston Barker and John Burford's Panorama, Strand* (London, 1818). Detail. This publication, with a foldout image tucked inside, gave readers a miniature version of the enormous panorama on public display.

elevated part of Museum Hill."[67] By August 1821, this enormous artwork was on display at Roulstone's Circus on Mason Street in Boston, near the edge of the Common.

Back home that fall, Everett delivered a series of popular public lectures on ancient Athens, and combined his earnings with donations by John Lowell, son of the mill founder Francis Cabot Lowell, and James Perkins, to construct a building in Cambridge for the panorama to be "exhibited for the gratification and instruction of the students of the University and the liberal public."[68] The panorama inspired Henry Pickering (whose brother John wrote a guide to modern Greek pronunciation) to publish an extended poem, "Athens," in which the author imagined:

> Lo! Here upon the sacred hill where sleeps
> The great Musaeus, bard of old renown'd—
> Lo! Here, amid *The City's* bounds I stand.
> How swells the varied landscape on the eye!
> How glows the extended verdant plain beneath!
> How rural all, and pastoral, the scene![69]

The quality of Pickering's verse ran rapidly downhill from this ecstatically punctuated starting point, but the enthusiasm for all things Greek generated by Everett and his companions remained at the fervid heights to which Pickering's poetry aspired.

The outbreak of the Greek Revolution in 1821 lent political force to Boston's Greco-mania. At a Fourth of July celebration in Paris that summer attended by the Marquis de Lafayette, George Bancroft raised a toast to "The Land of Minerva . . . may her sons rebuild in her climes the home of liberty." In his private journal he added, "Since the days of the American war for independence, there has been no scene of exertion so pure and glorious as this."[70] The promise of pure glory served to recruit Boston's greatest enthusiast for the literal way of being Greek, Samuel Gridley Howe.

Howe was born in 1801, the son of a prosperous Bostonian in the rope-making business and a member of Boston's liberal Brattle Street Church. He was raised under the preaching of Joseph Stevens Buckminster, Edward Everett, and John Gorham Palfrey, the future dean of the Unitarian Harvard Divinity School.[71] After graduating from Brown University, Howe returned in 1821 to attend Harvard Medical School, located at that time on Mason Street in Boston, only a few steps from Roulstone's Circus where the panorama of Athens was on display.[72]

In spring 1821, news arrived in Boston that the secretive Filiki Eteria (Friendly Society) had launched an insurrection in the Ottoman Empire's Danube Principalities. At the same time, Ali Pasha and his forces defied Ottoman authority in Roumelia (the part of Greece north of the Gulf of Corinth), while Greek forces under Theodoros Kolokotronis rose against the Turks in the Morea, south of the Gulf.[73] That fall, Everett, Howe's former minister, delivered his lecture series on ancient Athens. Over the next two years, Boston leaders including Everett, William Ingalls (the medical school professor with whom Howe apprenticed), and Howe's father, Joseph Howe, formed the Boston Committee for the Aid of Greece. In December 1823, Everett delivered a stirring address on the "atrocities" that "surpass almost the bounds of Turkish barbarity" and called on Bostonians to support the Greeks, "who are struggling against a tyranny infinitely more galling than that, which our fathers thought it beyond the power of man to support."[74] That same month, Boston's congressman, Daniel Webster, introduced a motion supporting Greek independence and proposing to send an American agent to Greece, with Everett as the likely choice.[75] The following spring brought the news of Byron's death in Missolonghi in Greece.[76]

In summer 1824, Howe formed a secret design to join the growing group of European and American philhellenes fighting alongside the Greek rebels (he had already begun to take fencing lessons). That August at his Harvard Medical School commencement, Howe listened as the Marquis de Lafayette, returned to America for the fiftieth anniversary of the revolution, spoke passionately in favor of Greek independence, embodying the revolutionary reciprocity that Everett had called on Boston to support. For Howe, the die was cast. In November, he sailed on the *Triton* with Everett's letters of introduction and Byron's *Childe Harold* in his trunk.[77]

With such a buildup, Howe was bound for disillusion. His romantic vision of Byronic heroism in the service of a noble but oppressed people, inflated by America's recent celebrations of its own romanticized rebellion, grew cloudy through contact with actual Greeks. The Greek rebels fought among themselves, sought personal gain over national liberation, and were as capable as their Turkish foes of wartime atrocities: "The folly, ignorance, and instability of the present race of Greeks is most lamentable."[78] Howe saw extensive service in the brutal 1825 campaigns throughout the Morea against the Egyptian forces of Ibrahim Pasha. He was officially employed as surgeon to the troops, but often engaged in combat. He abandoned Western dress for the local costume and learned to live the life of a soldier on the march, while his estimate of modern Greek soldiers plummeted.[79] His opinions of his fellow European and American philhellenes were likewise dashed; most of them had come to Greece "for personal distinction; and for honour," but "were generally discontented and disappointed because there was hard fare, hard marches, and no glory."[80] (See plate 24.)

Next Howe joined on as surgeon to the Greek fleet in its futile attempt to relieve the island of Crete. The following year he took up a post in a hospital in the seaport of Nauplion, then the capital of the provisional government of the rebellion (the First Hellenic Republic) and the largest city on the Greek peninsula (though its population was considerably smaller than Boston's). Late in 1826, he rejoined the fleet in its efforts to secure the Greek islands in the Aegean Sea.[81] On the island of Amorgos in December 1826, Howe wrote, "Landed at nine this morn on the beach, on which are a few miserable huts inhabited by still more miserable beings, refugees from the most miserable part of miserable Greece."[82] And yet, despite having "got rid of those foolish romantic ideas with which my head was once stuffed," Howe somehow retained his enthusiasm for the Greek cause and developed a fondness, even a love, for the Greek people in their "state of misery almost beyond conception or endurance."[83]

At this point in the war, in spring 1827, Howe turned from fighting to relief efforts. As early as his 1823 address to the Boston Committee for Greek Relief, Everett had used extreme language to describe the plight of the Greeks under Turkish brutality; a "decree of extermination against five millions of Christians was pronounced," and "the infuriated Janisaries constituted themselves its executioners."[84] Many aspects of the Ottoman attempt to put down the rebellion, such as the "massacre of Scio" (Chios) in 1822, where perhaps twenty-five thousand Greek civilians were put to the sword, drew widespread attention and originated one of the first international discussions of humanitarian intervention.[85] But for every major European power, reason of state trumped humanitarian and romantic sentiments. The only head of state to offer direct support was the king of the small Rhineland principality of Wurttemberg; he gave sixty thousand florins for "an armament of volunteers fitted out in Germany for the aid of the Greeks."[86] The Monroe administration refused to lend anything more than vague moral support, and in December 1823, issued the Monroe Doctrine, asserting American neutrality in European affairs while warning Europe's powers against meddling in the Americas.[87]

The United States' refusal to recognize the Greek cause marked the beginning of Howe's disillusionment with government. By 1827, it was clear that no European power would come to Greece's aid for fear of upsetting the network of alliances assembled by Austria's

Count Metternich in the aftermath of the Napoleonic Wars. Private organizations for the relief of the Greeks, both in Europe and America, raised money for aid and even military support, but Howe had learned to expect corruption in the provisional Greek government's administration of this aid. As ships from the American relief committees began to arrive in spring 1827, Howe took charge of aid distribution, bypassing the government to bring food, clothing, and equipment to the naked and starving Greeks.[88] Riding mule trains over mountain passes, Howe witnessed the conditions of near slavery that centuries of Ottoman rule had forced on the Greek peasantry. He even purchased and then freed a "negro" slave woman who begged him to rescue her from her owner, a local priest.[89] Disabused of the notion that political independence would magically restore the modern Greeks to the glories of their ancient past, Howe now believed that "it is not for this generation that we fight; they are sunk in trespasses and sins, but their children may and will be better."[90]

Howe's journey to Greece had begun as a romantic adventure, but in the relief work for the poor, the injured, and the sick, he found his life's calling. Late in 1827, at the urging of the Greek government and the Boston Relief Committee, Howe returned home to pursue American fund-raising. Before he left Greece, he purchased the military helmet that had once belonged to Lord Byron to use as a prop in his fund-raising tour.[91] Howe also rapidly wrote a history of the Greek revolution, published in August 1828. Although he insisted that "the Author has never, for an instant, let his enthusiasm blind him to the faults of the Greeks," he was willing to sustain the romantic illusion with the book's epigraph, from Byron's *Childe Harold's Pilgrimage*, canto II, stanza LXXV:

> ——————————————and who
> That marks the fire still sparkling in each eye,
> Who but would deem their bosoms burn'd anew
> With thy unquenched beam, lost Liberty!
> And many dream withal the hour is nigh
> That gives them back their fathers' heritage.[92]

With the money from his lectures, his writings, and the various American relief committees, Howe returned to Greece in November 1828. The political outcome of the war had been determined the previous year when the combined naval forces of Britain, France, and Russia had destroyed the Turkish fleet at the battle of Navarino.[93] But eight years of brutal warfare left a dire need for humanitarian aid. On the island of Aegina, near Athens, in addition to feeding and clothing refugees, Howe paid hundreds of local workers to repair the once-prosperous harbor, using stones reclaimed from a ruined ancient temple to build a mole (a stone pier) that ships would use for decades to come.[94]

From Aegina, Howe turned to building a farming colony for refugees on the Greek mainland, selecting a site at Hexamilia on the Gulf of Corinth, where the prospects for a new canal or even a railroad encouraged hopes for the region's economic future: "I decided at once in my own mind to ask five thousand *stremmata*, about two thousand acres, of land (all about here being national) from the Government, and plant a colony of poor families upon it."[95] With the government's permission, Howe established his colony, alternately called Columbia and Washingtonia, bringing almost to full circle the inspiration that had brought Boston into being two centuries earlier, when the Massachusetts founders imagined themselves as latter-day apostles at Philippi.[96] Howe's colony bore an uncanny resemblance to the early plantations of Massachusetts. Land was distributed widely to refugee families, many of them persecuted by a government hostile to their religion. The settlers raised livestock and crops (including Indian corn and cotton, Boston's oldest and newest staples), using seed, tools, and animals supplied by the relief committees. The colonists kept part of what they produced for themselves, while part went to the colony to pay its expenses, including a hospital to care for the poor as well as a school and church.[97]

As administrator of this benevolent enterprise, Howe was at last in his element. In later years, he would remember this as "perhaps the happiest part of my life," even though he was stricken with malaria during the spring of 1829.[98] The local population treated Howe as their new "Effendi" (lord), and he willingly took on the role of minor potentate: "I laboured here day and night, in season and out, and was governor, legislator, clerk, constable, and everything but *patriarch*." Howe's experience was oddly reminiscent of John Winthrop's first year in Boston, when despite the fact that other colonists were dying around him, Winthrop "never fared better in his life, never slept better, never had more content of mind."[99] By fall 1829, Howe had managed to get fifty refugee families established in the colony (a number comparable to many early Massachusetts towns) and believed that he was laying the groundwork for the Greek future. As he looked ahead, the profits generated by the colony's agriculture would be used to settle still more families and expand the hospital's services: "In ten years these poor will probably be augmented to two hundred families, or one thousand souls; a large hospital will be supported, and a useful example given to the rest of Greece of improved agriculture."[100]

But the newly independent Greek republic lacked the integrity of the Massachusetts Bay Company. Its government failed to honor the commitments on which Howe had based the colony. Promised supplies never materialized, and the settlers were denied title to the land they had cultivated, without which Howe despaired of the colony's future. By June 1830, Howe had left Greece behind.[101] Within another year, the republic's head of state had been assassinated by members of a rival Greek family. The Great Powers—Britain, France, and Russia—ended Greece's experiment in republicanism by placing Prince Otto, the teenage son of Bavaria's Ludwig I, on the throne as King Otto of Greece.[102] Howe's attempt to resuscitate the glories of Greece had left him disillusioned about the powers of government, but he had found his calling in humanitarian reform, which he would pursue on his return to Boston.

Figurative Greeks: German Reform in the Athens of America

During the 1820s, the other members of Everett's cohort in Göttingen were bringing the spirit of Greek antiquity to bear on Boston through the application of their German experience to local problems, and through the recruitment of German intellectuals and reformers to Boston. These figurative Greeks, Ticknor, Cogswell, and Bancroft, began by addressing the need for educational reform at home that their travels in Germany had revealed, and from there moved on to many other social issues.

George Ticknor, on his return in 1819, took up his position as Harvard's professor of French and Spanish languages and literatures and professor of belles lettres. Thankfully he was allowed to live in Boston rather than Cambridge, and avoid the parietal duties that plagued the lives of the residential tutors and professors. The college was in a low condition. With respect to student discipline and scholarly standards, Harvard in the 1820s lagged far behind not only Germany's universities but even its gymnasia. As the rare Harvard instructor who was not an alumnus (and therefore unsentimental about its traditions), Ticknor had a clear-eyed view of its shortcomings, and his experience in Germany provided models for reform. For the next decade, he tried to develop a scholarly division of labor at Harvard by creating academic departments, starting with his own modern languages. Ticknor also hoped to expand the college library, end rote recitations as the chief method of instruction, raise admissions standards, and reform the curriculum to give students greater choice in their studies. But these efforts foundered amid the institution's complex politics, torn between the inertia of the instructors on the internal governing corporation and reforming interests of the Boston elites on the external Board of Overseers. President John Thornton Kirkland waffled between the two. A decade of bitter infighting and student rebellions led to a reorganization of the college's governance and the loss of its public subsidies from Massachusetts, ending in Kirkland's resignation in 1828. Ticknor's reforms never reached beyond his department of modern languages.[103]

When Cogswell and Bancroft returned from their time in Europe, they also spent time teaching at Harvard—Cogswell as professor of mineralogy, and Bancroft as instructor in ancient Greek—and Cogswell recatalogued Harvard's library according to methods that he had observed in Göttingen.[104] Yet both men realized that even the modest reforms Ticknor proposed, let alone the creation of a German-style university, were hopeless without improvements in secondary education. If they, as some of Harvard's brightest graduates, had been overwhelmed by the demands of study at Göttingen, how could graduates of American high schools be expected to thrive in a true university? While in Europe, Cogswell and Bancroft visited well-known centers of secondary education; Cogswell made several visits to Phillip Emmanuel von Fellenberg's famous school in Hofwyl near Bern where "the children of beggars and of sovereigns were to be taught in what their duty and their happiness consists," and to Johann Heinrich Pestalozzi's famous school in Yverdon.[105]

Bancroft's inquiries into German secondary education were driven by his task of finding a suitable school for Frederic Henry Hedge, the twelve-year-old son of the Boston merchant Levi Hedge who accompanied him to Göttingen. After several failures, they found the Schulpforta near Leipzig, an ancient Cistercian monastery converted into a boarding school and run by the Prussian government. Fichte had studied there, and its beautiful rural setting gave the school a "mixture of grandeur and mildness" that Bancroft found "delightful." In a letter to Levi Hedge, Bancroft described how students of varied social backgrounds were brought together "by the strongest ties of proximity, and to form one large and well organized family."[106] This emphasis at Schulpforta and Hofwyl on integrating what John Winthrop had called "the high and eminent in dignity" with the "mean and in subjection" accorded well with Boston's social and educational traditions.

During a semester spent at the University of Berlin, Bancroft attended lectures by Friedrich Schleiermacher on the philosophy of education and studied their influence on Berlin's schools, where they "unite gymnastic exercises, music, and the sciences; and this is the mode of educating, which Plato has extolled as the perfect art."[107] Well before his return to Boston in 1822, Bancroft was planning how to improve New England's education. The region's secondary schools, whether the older public grammar schools such as Boston Latin or newer private academies that sprang up after the revolution, still subjected students to a curriculum little changed for a century or more, focused on Latin and (to a lesser extent) Greek, and heavy on memorization of grammatical rules and recitation of standard texts.[108] Encouraged by Everett and backed by Boston businessmen, Bancroft joined forces with Cogswell and in October 1823 opened the experimental Round Hill School, not in Boston, but in rural Northampton along the Connecticut River, in a location that reminded Bancroft of the Schulpforta.

The plan for Round Hill closely followed the one outlined by Bancroft after his visit to the Prussian boarding school ("1: Greek should be the first language taught"), supplemented by ideas that Cogswell learned at Hofwyl and Yverdon.[109] Bancroft himself taught German, Greek, and Latin. History courses were modeled on those taught at Göttingen. In addition to scholarly subjects, the school stressed ethics and morality, fine arts, "gymnastics, bathing, and dancing," and "all the labors of husbandry and gardening."[110] Although it lay a hundred miles from Boston, Round Hill was dominated by students from New England's metropolis, in particular the sons of mercantile and industrial families. The roster included Amorys, Appletons, Lawrences, Lowells, Lymans, Otises, Peabodys, Perkinses, Shaws, Storrows, and Thorndikes—families that would come to be known as Boston Brahmins. But Bancroft and Cogswell also aimed at a wider clientele. The roster included substantial numbers of students from New York and Rhode Island, from Maryland and South Carolina, where the booming cities of Baltimore and Charleston lacked suitable educational institutions, and from as far afield as Mississippi, Louisiana, Mexico, and Brazil. Strangely, the Round Hill School attracted almost no students from Connecticut, its near neighbor only a few miles down the well-traveled Connecticut River. Twice as many Mexicans (four) as Connecticut students (two) attended Round Hill in the school's first decade—a mark of the degree to which Connecticut was now alienated from the liberal transformation of religious culture and radical reforms in education that Boston's sons brought back from Europe.[111]

The deepening connection with Germany stood out among Round Hill's achievements. The school followed the advice of

Arnold Heeren, Bancroft's history professor at Göttingen, to hire a native speaker to teach the German language. A German drawing teacher, Dr. Graeter, conveyed the Greek ideal in art, and the school imported German-made gymnastics equipment for the boys to use under the direction of Karl Beck of Heidelberg. Beck had studied with Friedrich Ludwig Jahn, the founder of the gymnastics movement, and translated Jahn's *Deutsche Turnkunst* for English publication.[112] Among the beneficiaries of this training was John Lothrop Motley, son of Boston merchant Thomas Motley and Anna Lothrop of a distinguished clerical family. The young Motley was gifted at languages, excelled at Round Hill, and entered Harvard as the youngest in his class. After delivering an address on "The Genius and Character of Goethe" at his senior class exhibition, Motley went off for three years of further study at Göttingen, where he formed a lifelong friendship with Otto von Bismarck.[113]

As the connections forged by Boston's initial wave of students in Germany proliferated, Motley's experience became a norm for ambitious young men wanting to make their name in Boston. Henry Wadsworth Longfellow, Horace Mann, James Russell Lowell, and Theodore Parker were among those who followed Everett, Ticknor, Bancroft, and Cogswell to Germany, and returned to become transformative figures in Boston's cultural life. Eventually the University of Berlin came to eclipse Göttingen as the prime destination for American students, but even so, the memory of Göttingen's prominence lingered.[114] Long into the nineteenth century, Harvard students continued to sing this bit of doggerel:

Where 'er with haggard eyes I view
This dungeon that I'm rotting in,
I think of those companions true
Who studied with me at the U-
  niversity of Göttingen
  niversity of Göttingen.[115]

Göttingen also influenced Bostonians who stayed at home. In the Emerson family, Ralph Waldo's older brother William studied at Göttingen for two terms in 1824. But the younger brother learned much from William's experience, having already been exposed to German learning from Professor Everett's Harvard course on Greek literature. According to Ralph Waldo, Everett's influence on his contemporary Harvard undergraduates "was almost comparable to that of Pericles in Athens."[116]

When the Transcendental Club began in Boston in 1836, it was centered around the same Frederic Hedge (in fact it was initially called the "Hedge Club") whose schooling at the Schulpforta had been arranged by Everett and Ticknor.[117] Most of the other members of the Transcendental Club had not been educated *in* Germany, but their intellectual outlook was shaped *by* Germany. George Ripley, Unitarian minister of the Purchase Street Church in Boston and future founder of the Brook Farm utopian colony, "had a library full of philosophy and biblical criticism, including Kant, Fichte, Schleiermacher, Herder, Cousin, Hegel, Schopenhauer, Eichhorn, Paulus, Bauer, and Tholuck." Born in Greenfield in western Massachusetts, Cambridge and Boston were as near to Germany as Ripley would ever go. But his education at Harvard College and Divinity School in the 1820s under the tutelage of Everett, Ticknor, and company prepared him to write articles on subjects like "Schleiermacher as a Theologian" that would place him at the forefront of the emerging transcendentalist movement.[118] If we recall that Everett and Ticknor, before their departure in 1815, had been hard put to find any German books or anyone in Boston who could teach them the language, the rapidity with which their cohort transformed Boston's intellectual world appears all the more remarkable.

Equally profound was the influence of German-inspired attempts to "be Greek" on Boston's social and cultural institutions. Educational reforms were only one strand of a wider project, which included Everett and Ticknor's effort to establish the Boston Public Library. The city had been served by the more or less private Boston Athenaeum since 1807 (itself the product of the desires of Buckminster and the other founders of the Anthology Society to bring a Greek sensibility to Boston). But the Athenaeum restricted its books and art collections to Boston's elites. Ticknor came to believe, in part through his exposure to Göttingen's enormous library, that since mass education was necessary for wise self-government, then "a very free use of books, furnished by an institution supported at the expense of the community, would be one of the effective means for obtaining this result."[119] A similar sensibility informed Horace Mann, who became secretary of the Massachusetts Board of Education. In company with Howe, Mann toured Germany's schools and became convinced that the Prussian state educational system should be the model for Massachusetts.[120] Likewise, the bequest of John Lowell Jr. (son of the mill founder Francis Cabot Lowell), who died in India after extensive travels in Europe and the Middle East, created the Lowell Institute to provide free public lectures on education, science, religion, and morality to the population of Boston. The younger Lowell was also a major supporter of the Lyceum movement, another forum for public education named for the school of Aristotle in ancient Athens. Even before the Lowell Institute was launched in 1839, the Boston Society for the Diffusion of Useful Knowledge organized dozens of public lecture courses "attended in the aggregate by about thirteen thousand five hundred persons, at an expense of less than twelve thousand dollars."[121]

In addition to schools, libraries, and general public education, Bostonians supported an array of institutions to address the health and well-being of its population, beginning with the Massachusetts General Hospital and its sister institution, the McLean Asylum. The Massachusetts General Hospital, as its name implied, was intended to promote the health of the community at large. Although Boston's rich donors and state funding played significant roles in its creation, the doctors who founded the hospital raised money in small amounts from the public, extending the tradition of Boston's commitment to taking care of its own people, but on a scale that the growing city demanded. In 1810, when James Jackson and John Collins Warren first proposed the idea for a "well-regulated hospital," the city's population of thirty-three thousand was twice what it had been before the revolution, and by 1830 it had doubled yet again. But as former congressman and soon-to-be mayor Josiah Quincy declared at its foundation ceremonies in 1818, the Massachusetts General Hospital was the product of "all classes of . . . citizens combining and concentrating their efforts," with half of the thousand or more donations made in the amount of ten dollars or less.[122]

Over the next three decades, as reformers created new institutions to meet specific community needs, Samuel Howe came to play the most prominent role. After his return home from the Greek Revolution, a restless Howe volunteered to go back to Europe on behalf of the American Polish Committee, a voluntary organization supporting Polish revolutionaries' attempts to free their country from Russian domination, like the Greeks a decade earlier. By the time Howe reached Paris, the forces of Czar Nicholas I had suppressed the Polish rebellion, causing many of the rebels to flee to neighboring Prussia. The American Polish Committee had been sending its funds to the elderly Lafayette in Paris, but Howe's experience in Greece made him the natural person to take over the distribution of relief to the Polish refugees. In January 1832, Howe left for Prussia, his first trip to Germany. Although no friend to the czar, the Prussian government viewed the Boston republican with suspicion, and Howe was arrested by the Prussian police in Berlin and held in solitary confinement for more than a month.[123] Howe was shocked by his treatment. Had he been in an autocratic country like Russia or Austria, or in the hands of the "Turk or Tartar," he might not have been surprised. But the Prussians, "though a bit suspicious, are nevertheless Christian and civilized. . . . There are laws and judges in this land."[124]

After nearly a decade of frustration with state power and political revolution, Howe turned his humanitarian passion toward work that, in Everett's phrase, "refines and ennobles and brings out the divine in man." Howe henceforth aimed to refine and ennoble suffering humanity one person at a time.[125] In 1831, before he left for Paris and Prussia, Howe had been offered a position as director of the New England Institution for the Education of the Blind, incorporated by the Massachusetts legislature in 1829 at Horace Mann's instigation.[126] The new Boston school was the first of its kind in North America, an extension of the impulse that created the Massachusetts General Hospital and McLean Asylum. In Paris in the winter of 1831–32, before his ill-fated Prussian adventure, Howe toured the Royal Institute for Blind Youth, founded in 1784 by the

French philhellene Valentin Haüy, where Louis Braille was a young teaching assistant. Before his arrest, Howe also visited Berlin's school for the blind, and after his return to Paris continued his studies there, acquired books and materials, and hired a teacher of the blind, Emile Trencheri, to return with him to Boston. There he opened the new school at his father's old house at 140 Pleasant Street, in the south end of town between the Neck and Boston Common.[127]

Like the Massachusetts General Hospital, the New England Institute for the Blind was chartered by the state, but required to raise funds from a combination of public and private donations. Howe hoped that rich and poor alike would contribute to the welfare of this neglected group. As he began admitting the first pupils, chosen for their potential to benefit from his teaching methods (raised alphabet printing to teach reading as well as vocational education, music, and gymnastics), Howe realized that the students were their own best advocates. Despite unease at the potential for exploitation of the children, Howe organized a series of demonstrations of the students' abilities—musical and reading performances along with displays of craft production—at venues ranging from Boston's Masonic Temple to lyceum programs, Ladies' Fairs, and the state legislatures of Massachusetts, Connecticut, New Hampshire, and Vermont. The results were rewarding. In 1833, the Massachusetts legislature voted an annual appropriation of $6,000 for the school to underwrite the education of twenty students. The governments of Connecticut, New Hampshire, and Vermont together contributed another $2,700, and "the whole town of Boston, from the stevedore on the wharf to John P. Cushing, the great Canton merchant . . . was interested . . . in this new Institution for the Blind."[128] Boston's tradition of turning public resources to the benefit of the poor and unfortunate would now be shaped by the European learning of its young elites.

Philanthropy and Its Limits in the Age of Cotton

Despite this broad support for Howe's school for the blind, in the two decades since Lowell's founding of the Boston Manufacturing Company at Waltham and the nearly simultaneous creation of the

Massachusetts General Hospital, the nature of wealth and philanthropy in Boston had changed. The immense fortunes accumulated by the investors in textile companies converged with those of families that continued to pursue overseas trade—a pattern best exemplified in the later career of Thomas Handasyd Perkins. From its early days trading slaves in Saint-Domingue and selling flour to revolutionary France, the House of Perkins had gone on to pioneer the New England trade to China. Over the first two decades of the nineteenth century, Perkins was enticed by the potential of China's opium market. Since British merchants had a lock on opium produced in India, he looked to corner the market on Turkish opium, which accounted for about 8 percent of the overall Chinese market. By 1823, Perkins was purchasing half of Turkey's annual opium production and aiming for more. At the same time, he was investing in textile production. Although not initially part of the Lowell investment group, Perkins quickly appreciated the mills' wealth-generating potential. By the early 1820s, he had formed his own corporation with some of his Cabot relatives, purchased machinery from the Lowell firm, and developed a factory at the falls in Newton. Over the next decade, he became a major investor in the Lowell and Lawrence mills, and a director of their efforts to build canals and railroads.[129]

With the profits from these ventures, Perkins became one of Boston's great benefactors, supporting the effort to "be Greek," to make Boston the Athens of America. Yet there were limits to Perkins's support, defined by his mercantile interests. At the outbreak of the Greek Revolution, Edward Everett, Perkins's trusted friend and former minister, had taken the lead in organizing the Boston Committee for the Relief of the Greeks, arguing for US recognition of an independent Greek state. Perkins had nothing against the cause of Greek independence per se, but he feared that American recognition of Greece, or Boston's support for the Greek rebels, would anger the Ottoman government and undermine his opium business. Consequently, Perkins wrote two anonymous letters to the *Boston Daily Advertiser* (signed "A Merchant") arguing against hazarding "a valuable trade to show our goodwill."[130]

FIGURE 10.3. *Plan of Boston, with Parts of the Adjacent Towns*, by George W. Boynton, 1835. Detail. The margins of Boynton's *Plan of Boston* depict important buildings in the city, including the "Asylum for the Blind," formerly the home of Thomas Handasyd Perkins on Pearl Street.

Nevertheless, Perkins gave lavishly to uncontroversial local institutions: Harvard College, the Athenaeum (where an enormous portrait of Perkins hangs to this day), Massachusetts General Hospital, McLean Asylum (where his son received frequent treatment), and many other Boston charities.[131] In the year that the state legislature granted $6,000 per annum to Howe's school for the blind, Perkins donated his mansion on Pearl Street, worth $25,000, to be the new home for the growing school, renamed the Perkins Institute in his honor. Pearl Street, in the old South End, was becoming too plebian for Perkins's tastes, and he moved his clan to a newly fashionable neighborhood on the edge of Boston Common.[132] But as a condition for his gift, Perkins insisted that the school raise an additional $50,000 for an endowment. Here the large bequests of other wealthy merchants and industrialists, including John P. Cushing, who built his fortune as agent for Perkins and Russell in China, along with members of the Appleton, Eliot, Lowell, and Lawrence families, raised the money rapidly.[133] (See plate 25.)

The symbolism of the school's renaming and move into Perkins's discarded mansion is unmistakable. It marked another step in the growing divide between rich and poor, and the emergence of a new Boston in which the institutions of charity and philanthropy were dominated by a wealthy elite, and understood as an ornament of their power.[134] When Cushing built a country retreat in Watertown to complement his town house in Boston, the Watertown selectmen visited to determine its value for tax assessment purposes. Cushing told the selectmen to charge the town's entire tax assessment amount to him.[135] While obviously an act of considerable generosity, the notion that a single wealthy man would assume complete fiscal responsibility for one of the commonwealth's oldest towns contradicted the deepest tradition of Massachusetts' egalitarian self-rule. The great fortunes that had sponsored the European education of Boston's new reformers were now taking greater control over its social institutions, concentrating its charitable traditions in the hands of an elite. This transformation was by no means complete in 1833, but it was nonetheless exemplified in the career of Samuel Howe's star pupil, Laura Bridgman.

As the school's financial well-being depended on Howe's success in improving the lives of its blind students, Howe was always seeking promising students, and in 1837 he learned of a seven-year-old girl, blind and deaf, yet "sprightly and joyous of spirit," who lived on a farm in Hanover, New Hampshire. That summer Howe traveled north, accompanied by a distinguished group of fellow Boston luminaries—Mayor Samuel Eliot, the lawyers Rufus Choate and George Hillard, and Howe's friend Longfellow—to meet Bridgman and convince her reluctant parents to let Howe bring their daughter to his school in Boston. By using raised-letter printing and the hand spelling of sign language that he had observed in Europe, Howe taught Bridgman to read and write—the first deaf and blind person ever to manage this feat.

Bridgman, Howe, and the Perkins Institute all became internationally famous. Howe's annual reports for the Perkins Institute were translated into French and German, and read widely throughout Europe.[136] The school became a tourist attraction for Boston's visitors, including Charles Dickens, whose chapter on Boston in *American Notes* (1842) was devoted mostly to his meeting with Laura Bridgman.[137] So great was Bridgman's renown that the press suggested she be sent as America's representative to London's Crystal Palace Exhibition in 1851. As a product of "American art," she would surpass "the looms of England, the delicate fabrics of France, and all the products of Germany."[138]

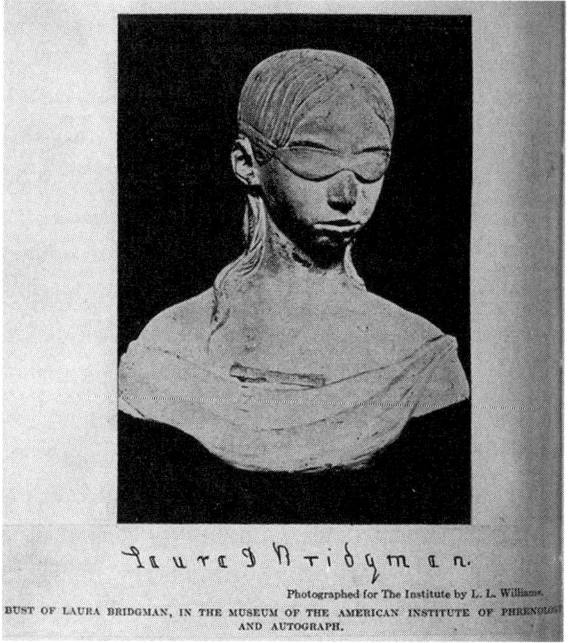

Photographed for The Institute by L. L. Williams.
BUST OF LAURA BRIDGMAN, IN THE MUSEUM OF THE AMERICAN INSTITUTE OF
AND AUTOGRAPH.

FIGURE 10.4. Clipping with photograph of Laura Bridgman Bust, made by Sophia Peabody, and sample of Laura Bridgman's handwritten autograph. Detail.

In all of Howe's efforts and those of his contemporary Boston reformers, there is a powerful sense that the *person* being "ennobled and refined" (to paraphrase Everett again) was really the reformer, benefactor, or philanthropist, while the *object* of charity was so much clay, waiting to be formed by the hand of "American art."[139] Although his devotion to Bridgman was real, Howe also viewed her in instrumental terms from the beginning; he referred to her as his "prize" on the first journey to meet her. Howe treated Bridgman's education as an experiment to refute New England's Calvinist doctrines of original sin and human depravity, and promote the Unitarian belief in humankind's innate goodness and perfectibility through proper training, education, and social institutions.[140] In many respects, Bridgman's life is yet another variant of the common pattern of the New Englanders from the hinterland, drawn to Boston by their ambitions or special talents, favored by local elites, and risen to the heights of fame. Perhaps the best comparison is with Phillis Wheatley. Like Wheatley's loss of freedom, home and family, it was what Bridgman had been robbed of, her lost hearing and sight, along with her obvious talents and accomplishments, that made her the object of widespread interest and adoration.

And object she was. Like Phillis Wheatley, Bridgman was used as evidence in philosophical and religious controversies over whether physical disability, like the perceived "defects" of racial difference, could be overcome through education or faith. Like Wheatley, she became a distributed commodity. Howe commissioned Sophia Peabody, the artist and future wife of Nathaniel Hawthorne, to make a bust of Bridgman, copies of which, like Byron's helmet, were eminently suitable for fund-raising. Samples of Bridgman's handwriting and the products of her manual labor became highly prized as well.[141] But while Wheatley's fame declined because the revolutionary crisis tore apart her network of supporters, Bridgman's significance dissipated when her actual life took a course that contradicted Howe's educational theories and personal aspirations. Despite Howe's efforts to keep her from the tenets of orthodox religion, with its emphasis on original sin and human depravity, Bridgman was drawn toward it and eventually joined the Baptist church of her parents. When his star pupil's choices in life no longer supported his cherished theories of human perfectibility, Howe lost interest and moved on to other causes—insanity, mental disability, and prison reform. As her youthful fame passed, Bridgman lived out her adult life in obscurity as a permanent ward of the Perkins Institute.

Howe, who liked to be called "Chev" (he had been awarded the title of "Chevalier of the Greek Legion of Honor"), was not the only Boston humanitarian whose reforming efforts served to elevate and separate them from the objects of their philanthropy.[142] Witness the immodest testimony of the gravestone in Mount Auburn Cemetery of Doctor Charles T. Jackson of Harvard Medical School, a pioneer in the use of sulphuric ether for painless surgery:

Thy Godlike crime was to be kind,
To render with thy precepts less
The sum of human wretchedness,
And strengthen man with his own mind.

Witness the language showered on Boston's rising political star, Daniel Webster, known to admirers and detractors alike as "the god-like Daniel," for "he trod the earth like a god" and "spoke like a Divinity"; "it seemed to me as if he was like the mount that might not be touched, and that burned with fire."[143] Note that in 1828, William Ellery Channing, the guiding light of Boston Unitarianism and bellwether of the transcendentalist movement, preached a sermon called "Likeness to God," in which he maintained "that true religion consists in proposing, as our great end, a growing likeness to the Supreme Being."[144] And consider the dream that Longfellow recorded in his journal one midsummer morning: "I dreamed last night that Goethe was alive and in Cambridge. I gave him a supper at Willard's Tavern. . . . I told him I thought Clärchen's song in Egmont was one of his best lyrics. The god smiled."[145]

Longfellow had never met Goethe. Germany's national poet, whom Emerson would include four years later in his study of humanity's six Representative Men (the others were Plato, Swedenborg, Montaigne, Shakespeare, and Napoléon), was near death at the time of Longfellow's first European tour. The Bostonians who had first gone to Germany—Everett, Ticknor, Bancroft, and Cogswell—had expected the immoral Goethe that they half knew from the reputation of his writings to be deformed and depraved. Instead, they found a surprisingly ordinary and amiable man, and for Cogswell, a lasting friend. But a generation later, the Goethe conjured in Longfellow's dreamscape had become an *übermensch*, a god. Longfellow's dream calls to mind Samuel Sewall's similar dream a century and a half earlier, when Christ came to Boston and stayed with John Hull. For the dreaming Sewall, the divine presence honored Boston, but humbled the dreamer and made him worry in his waking hours about the dangers of idolatry. For Longfellow and his fellow elite Bostonians approaching the mid-nineteenth century, a growing gulf separated godlike men of the sort they aspired to be from the mortal and suffering masses.

Die Unbedingten: The Unconditionals in Boston

In this widening distance between Boston's wealthy philanthropists and the objects of their charity, the limitations that the pursuit of wealth placed on the political commitments of a man like T. H. Perkins, and the abandonment by the likes of Webster and Everett of the principles they had held as young Federalists in the face of King Cotton, we begin to glimpse emerging rifts in the Athens of America—divisions within the exemplary culture that Boston's new industrial wealth had aspired to create. Had they been more mature or politically astute at the time, perhaps the Boston sojourners to Göttingen might have perceived yet another source of division in the uncompromising youth culture of post-Napoleonic Germany.

A form of radicalism was stirring in the intellectual and political world that Ticknor, Everett, Cogswell, and Bancroft encountered in Germany. Many of the students and faculty at Germany's universities cultivated intellectual, moral, and ethical convictions that would shake the foundations of German politics through the first half of the nineteenth century, with reverberations that would undermine the complacency of the Boston Associates' worldview as well. Throughout their time in Germany, the young Bostonians were vaguely aware of but tried to resist the radical elements of German universities. Even before they went to Göttingen, Ticknor, Everett, Cogswell, and Bancroft had been warned of the dangers of the higher biblical criticism and religious skepticism of their future instructors. While in Germany, they endeavored to keep the infection of infidelity at arm's length. With respect to political matters, however, the Bostonians remained unaware of just how radical some of the Germans they encountered were. This was partly due to the difficulty of parsing Germany's complex political scene, but also because the specific beliefs that constituted radicalism in post-Napoleonic Germany were long-established norms in republican Boston.

Ticknor's 1816 letter depicting the Republic of Letters in Germany had accurately described how Germany's intellectuals were emancipated from the chauvinism and particularism of the small states that comprised much of the German-speaking world. Scholars moved freely across political boundaries from university to university in ways that were unimaginable for political, military, or bureaucratic personnel.[146] Yet Ticknor failed to recognize how this asymmetry generated intense conflict between scholars and their governments over the future of the German lands—conflict that emerged in the cultural life of the German universities.

For generations, German universities had fostered fraternal organizations known as *Landsmannschaften*—provincial student associations that perpetuated German particularism and cultivated the ignoble aspects of student life, such as dueling, drinking, and brawling. But in the early nineteenth century, in response to the humiliating defeat by Napoléon's armies, radical students created a new organization called the *Burschenschaft* (youth association). Friedrich Ludwig Jahn, or "*Turnvater* Jahn," who had trained in theology and philology at Halle and Göttingen, founded the gymnastics or "Turner" movement. Jahn believed that vigorous physical education would promote the recovery of German national pride and help to expel Napoléon's occupying forces. Jahn and other young veterans developed the Burschenschaft as a national movement to improve the morals and behavior of students, and turn their energies toward the creation of a liberal, unified German republic.[147]

The Burschenschaften aimed to promote social harmony across a united Germany built around a common language, culture, and Christian religion, believing that religion united with German nationalism could overcome the confessional divisions that had plagued Germany since the Reformation. They called for a single unified German federal state, the end of intra-German tolls between states, a unified religion, popular sovereignty, elected representatives, the abolition of the police system in favor of local administration, and a common German militia in which all men would serve. The students also demanded freedom of speech, the end to privileges of birth, the abolition of serfdom, and equality before the law.[148] With the exception of a unified religion and language, their ideal closely resembled the founding principles of the United States. What distinguished the more radical elements from the moderates, however, was the means that the radicals contemplated for achieving these goals in the face of opposition from conservative and reactionary forces.

Among the members of the radical wing of the Burschenschaften was a student at the University of Giessen named Karl Follen, who shared the fervor and intensity of Fichte, Jahn, and the leaders of the new movement. After supporting peasant resistance to oppressive tax measures in his home province, and fearing recriminations from the government, Follen left Giessen for Jena in 1818, where he reshaped the radical members of its Burschenschaft into a secret organization. They called themselves *die Unbedingten*—the Unconditionals. Follen's group had the same goals as the moderate Burschenschaften, but the Unconditionals differed in their belief, articulated by Follen, that the freedom to act on one's individual convictions was the most basic human right: "No man can demand of another that he recognize any higher law than his own free conviction."[149] For Follen, the pursuit of the good and true could justify violence: "Where the ethical necessity exists, all means are permitted for those who are convinced of this necessity," and "if necessary, those who have an opinion which varies must be sacrificed."[150] Before he left Giessen, Follen had composed a lyric verse, which he called "Das Grosse Lied" (the great song), to express his movement's vision:

> Only the equality of man, the will of the *Volk*,
> Is Sovereign by God's grace.
> Up, up my people! God created you free.
> Call yourselves up out of slavery's wasteland
> To the haven of freedom. . . .
> Germany's need calls to all,
> To each calls the Lord's commandment:
> Destroy your tormentors,
> Rescue the nation![151]

While Follen envisioned a bloody revolution led by the masses someday (much as his contemporary Everett had imagined slave revolts in Virginia), in the near term Follen and his fellow Unconditionals were willing to contemplate acts of violent resistance to "take out the knife of freedom . . . [and] Pierce the dagger through the throat!" Follen was implicated when in March 1819, Carl Sand, another of the Unconditionals, stabbed to death August von Kotzebue, the monarchist German playwright, "seducer of virtue," and satirical critic of the Turnverein and Burschenschaft movements. Follen knew of the plan, took charge of Sand's personal papers, and even paid for the assassin's fatal journey to Kotzebue's Mannheim home.[152]

In the wake of Kotzebue's assassination, Count Metternich, the guiding hand of the Congress of Vienna and bastion of conservativism, outlawed the Burschenschaften, censored the press, and prosecuted radical students and faculty throughout the German states. After being arrested and interrogated, Follen fled to Switzerland, where other German radicals including Karl Beck gathered in refuge. By 1824, as Metternich and the Prussian government pressured the Swiss for the extradition of radicals, Follen decided to leave Europe for America. Assisted by letters of introduction from Lafayette to Ticknor, Follen made his way to Boston.[153]

Boston was the obvious place, the perfect place, for Follen to go. The principles for which the Burschenschaft movement stood, radical as they seemed to Metternich and the autocratic governments of many German principalities, were the established values and reigning political conditions of the city-state of Boston. Popular sovereignty, equality before the law, representative government, free speech, property rights, local authority, and compulsory civilian militia training (as opposed to standing or mercenary armies)—all had been standard practice in Boston and its hinterland for generations. Even Follen's intense religiosity, his political piety, harked back to Boston's puritan origins, as did his belief in the integrity of personal convictions, which was a key element for Unitarian Boston's rethinking of its puritan tradition in the face of changing theological beliefs brought home by the higher criticism.[154] This odd synchronicity explains how an ultraradical German fugitive from justice, a defender of political assassination and violent revolution, was rapidly embraced by the highest ranks of Boston's establishment.

With Ticknor's support, Harvard appointed Follen as its first instructor of the German language in 1825. The most radical

FIGURE 10.5. *Gymnastics*, by David Claypoole Johnston, ca. 1826.

member of a movement whose aims Everett had a decade earlier thought were "ruinous" for Germany was now Everett's colleague on the Harvard faculty. Follen would soon be appointed as lecturer on ethics and church history at Harvard Divinity School, teaching "the foundations of moral obligations."[155] Karl Beck, fellow Unconditional and Follen's traveling companion in exile, had already accepted a position as German and gymnastics instructor at Bancroft and Cogswell's Round Hill School, where he was now teaching the sons of Boston's elite. Harvard tried to recruit Turnvater Jahn, who had been imprisoned and then exiled from Berlin, to introduce gymnastics instruction in the college, but Jahn declined. Instead, with the support of Dr. John Collins Warren of Harvard Medical School and the Massachusetts General Hospital, Follen opened a public open-air gymnasium, a "Turnplatz," in the city of Boston, located in Washington Gardens at Tremont and West Streets, adjacent to the Medical School and on the site of the panorama of Athens.[156] Within a year, Warren, at Follen's suggestion, had recruited Franz Lieber, another Burschenschaft radical who was imprisoned as a suspect after Kotzebue's murder, to succeed Follen as the Turnplatz's superintendent.[157]

In 1827, Follen married Eliza Lee Cabot, daughter of Samuel Cabot of the illustrious merchant and industrial family, and founder of the Sunday school in William Ellery Channing's Federal Street Church.[158] Soon thereafter, the Cabot family, with financial support from Thomas Handasyd Perkins, transformed Follen's appointment at Harvard from instructor to professor of German language and literature. Follen became an occasional member of the Transcendental Club that formed around Frederic Hedge, Follen's eventual successor as Harvard's German professor. And with encouragement from Channing, Follen pursued training as a Unitarian minister and was ordained in 1836.[159]

But no matter how well integrated he became within Boston's establishment, Charles Follen (for he had Anglicized his name) remained an Unconditional at heart, and this spirit would find a home in Boston's emerging abolitionist movement. With his belief that individual conviction was the highest law and that violent measures were justified to bring about an ethical necessity, Follen turned his attention to the central moral dilemma facing Boston and its relationship to the United States. He became aware of a radical pamphlet written by the African American clothing dealer, David Walker, *An Appeal to the Colored Citizens of the World*, and was taken by Walker's insurrectionary rhetoric, especially its similarity to his own "Great Song" of 1818.[160] Soon thereafter, Follen sought out William Lloyd Garrison, who in 1831 began publishing the *Liberator*, which from its first issue renounced the gradualist opposition to slavery and called for immediate, unconditional abolition.[161]

By the winter of 1832–33, Follen's correspondence concerning slavery reveals that his Unconditional commitments had pushed him to question the value of the American union: "A republic secures blessings to mankind only so far as it actually exists; I mean, so far as it really acknowledges the equal rights of every individual. There are many in this country, who value the union of the States above every thing, higher even than the individual rights, the protection of which is the only lawful ground of its existence. This overrating of the union proceeds . . . from an honest superstition, (something like a *ci-devant* European feeling of awe at the mysterious nature of kings,) which makes them shrink from calculating the value of the union."[162]

From their former positions in 1815, Everett and Follen had now traded places. Everett, who had visited the American South and seen how different its political economy, morals, and social conditions were from New England, and who with his elders and mentors had endured the embargo and War of 1812's destruction of Boston's economy at the hands of Virginia, had in 1815 believed that the unification of small states into a great republic without a common principle was a ruinous idea. Follen, who with his elders and mentors had endured Napoléon's occupation of Germany, had taken part in the War of Liberation, and were still oppressed by the dead hand of ancient autocracies in the German principalities, in 1815 saw the unification of Germany into a great republic as the only hope for liberal reform. Now, a common principle that transformed Everett's, Webster's, and the Boston Associates' views of the question had emerged in the form of King Cotton. And now, Follen and his fellow Boston abolitionists saw that superstition about the union's sacred value, perhaps masking allegiance to King Cotton, obscured a clear vision of the one thing that prevented a true republic from actually existing in the United States: slavery.

By 1833, Charles and Eliza Cabot Follen had joined Garrison's New England Anti-Slavery Society. Although he knew that it would cost him his position at Harvard—his professorship was terminated in 1835—Follen assumed a leading role.[163] In 1833, Samuel Howe began to speak out against slavery for the first time. Other radicals such as Samuel May and Wendell Phillips started to emerge as leaders in the group as well. Their strident call for immediate abolition began to generate hostility within the city of Boston, mainly from the thousands of men and women whose livelihoods were now bound up in the cotton economy. It quickly turned violent.

In 1835, George Thompson, a leading British abolitionist, toured the United States, facing death threats and hostile mobs everywhere he went. In that year, ninety thousand bales of southern cotton were imported in Boston—twice the amount of only five years before.[164] When Thompson came to Boston, Garrison arranged for him to address the anniversary meeting of the Boston Female Anti-Slavery Society (Eliza Cabot was one of many members). Shortly before, a virulent antiabolitionist meeting, "filled with the best elements of Boston society," had been staged at Faneuil Hall, with speeches by Boston politicians and businessmen. At the meeting, Harrison Gray Otis, once a supporter of the Hartford Convention and its amendment to end the three-fifths clause, now spoke of the Constitution as a compact that "binds every man's conscience by all that is sacred in good faith."[165] In the days before Thompson's lecture, Garrison's front door was adorned in the night with a gallows, rope, and a note from "Judge Lynch." Meanwhile, all the available venues in the city refused to host Thompson's lecture, forcing Garrison to hold the meeting in his own cramped New England Anti-Slavery Society headquarters at 46 Washington Street, a block away from the Old State House in the center of town. The *Boston Commercial Gazette* warned that if Thompson persisted in addressing the Female Society, he would be "roughly treated by the emissaries of Judge Lynch," and "this resistance will not come from a *rabble*, but from men of property and standing who have a large interest at stake in this community."[166] With public spirit so fervently opposed to Thompson, on October 21, Garrison canceled Thompson's appearance and volunteered to address the Female Anti-Slavery Society himself.

By the early afternoon, the streets around the center of town were so thronged with opponents that the society's members could barely climb the stairs to the meeting, surrounded as they were "with horrible execrations, howling, stamping, and finally shrieking with rage."[167] Garrison offered to address the ladies' assembly, but fearing for his safety, the society's president, Mary S. Parker, declined. Nevertheless, in attempting to leave the building by a second-story rear window after the women had been safely escorted out the front entrance, Garrison fell into the hands of the mob. They wrapped a rope around his chest, tore his clothes, broke his spectacles, and threatened to "hang him on the Common." Rescued by a pair of supporters, Garrison was dragged across the square just east of the Old State House where the Boston Massacre had occurred sixty-five years before, thrust into the old building, now used as the city hall, and brought to the office of Boston's mayor.

The mayor was Theodore Lyman, Everett's friend and traveling companion in Greece, the man who purchased the panorama of Athens for display in Boston. Lyman realized that the only way to save Garrison was to arrest him and bring him to the city jail. This feat was accomplished with the help of two carriages, one a decoy, and an unnamed black coachman who was unafraid to wield the whip in driving off Garrison's attackers.[168] The mob around the society's headquarters became so enraged that in a fit of iconoclasm, they seized the Anti-Slavery Society's sign on 46 Washington Street and tore it "into a thousand pieces," "dash[ing] it into splinters." In addition, "a number of persons, who resembled in their personal appearance, Thompson and Garrison, were severely beaten by the gentlemen assembled."[169]

In Garrison and his abolitionist circle, Follen had found and helped to build a new group of Unconditionals. In its "acknowledgment of the justice and necessity of *immediate emancipation*," the

FIGURE 10.6. *The Abolition Garrison in Danger, & the Narrow Escape of the Scotch Ambassador*, ca. 1835. Garrison, hatless at the center, is being dragged by a rope held by various "respectable" gentlemen, who say "Lynch the rascal" and "Give him a coat of Tar and feathers," while the figure of George Thompson, dressed as a Scottish woman, escapes at the right.

constitution of the Boston Female Anti-Slavery Society echoed the spirit of the "Draft Constitution for a Future German Empire" that August and Karl Follen had written in 1818.[170] The Society's hymns, including "Where Is Thy Brother" by Eliza Cabot, extended to the antislavery cause the same ferocious Christian martyrology that Follen had called on in his "Great Song" of the Burschenschaften.[171] Had it not been Follen's misfortune to die in a steamboat accident in 1840, he was on course to join Garrison, Theodore Parker, Wendell Phillips, Maria Weston Chapman, and Lydia Maria Child among Boston's leading radical abolitionists. Shortly after Follen's untimely death, Garrison named his next child Charles Follen Garrison, and rightly so. The abolitionist movement that would tear Boston apart over the next two decades was an Americanized version of a radical German impulse, an "unconditional" approach that had taken root in Boston, brought home from an excursion begun by Everett and Ticknor on the German road to Athens.

Chapter 11

Dismembering the Body

Boston's Spatial Fragmentation

> We had been a great family. If we choose by wards, there is danger of us splitting into twelve little towns.
>
> —William Tudor, *Debates . . . on Changing the Form of Government . . . of Boston*, 1822

Things fell apart slowly.

Two centuries earlier, they had come together all in a rush. In a confluence of disparate events happening around the year 1643, Boston swiftly consolidated its economic future in Atlantic commerce, defended its commitment to self-governing autonomy, and extended its hegemony over the New England region's many polities. These developments transformed Massachusetts Bay from a puritan hiding place into the hub of a new kind of Atlantic colony, an intermediary between the slave-based commodity monocultures of the Caribbean colonies and the mature trading economy of the imperial metropole. Boston proper, the town on the Shawmut Peninsula, became New England's link to the Atlantic world, the center of its seafaring trade as well as the capital of its varied hinterland, the metropolis of a region of confederated settlements. From this advantageous position, at once marginal and central, the city-state of Boston pursued its own interests and framed its own ideals, as a middling homogeneous godly society sustained by a wide array of Atlantic global connections.

For two centuries, Boston had retained these defining characteristics while weathering a series of challenges to its integrity.

From Britain came attempts to force Boston to conform to models of colonial subordination better suited to dependent plantation colonies or alien populations under military rule than to its own tradition of English republican autonomy. After American independence came the subtler challenge of coexistence within the United States, where the dominant powers in the nation's political economy differed radically from Boston's own practices, and the line between internal and external authority became harder to define. But beginning around the year 1822, when the city of Boston received a municipal corporate charter from the Commonwealth of Massachusetts, the city-state of Boston slowly pulled itself apart.

The remaining two chapters bear witness to this slow destruction, the dismemberment of the city-state of Boston. Here I focus on changes in the physical body of the city, its land area and surrounding waters, its boundaries and defenses, its shifting residential, industrial, and commercial zones, in response to demographic growth and an evolving economic relationship with the New England interior. These spatial alterations were accompanied by a political restructuring mandated by the new city charter, but this new professional form of civic government also meant a more fragmented political body, one distinctly different from the rest of Massachusetts and New England. Along with these spatial and structural changes, this era experienced rapid population growth within the constricted space of the Shawmut Peninsula.

The four decades following municipal incorporation was a period of profound disruption, when the large-scale immigration of new ethnic and religious groups, along with changes in the economy of the city and region, generated growing segregation and violence on the streets and wharves of the city—a rage within the body politic that turned citizen against citizen. The decade of the 1830s, particularly its middle years from 1834 to 1837, marked a breaking point, a moment when latent strains burst forth into open hostility. A decade later, the arrival of hundreds of thousands of Irish immigrants, most of them destitute victims of a catastrophic famine, forced a further physical transformation of the city, reorienting it toward and attaching it to the mainland through land-making and transportation-building projects, and obscuring its former identity as a seaward-facing island.

Separating City from State and Citizen from City

Before 1822, Boston's status as a legal entity was murky. No record remains of its creation as a separate town, and its earliest surviving town records from 1634 begin practically in mid-sentence, with its selectmen already conducting ordinary business. The General Court directive that gave Massachusetts towns the power to grant land to their inhabitants did not occur until 1636, after Boston had already done this work. Until 1822, it's hard to say when and how Boston became a distinct corporate entity. And although it may seem counterintuitive, the granting of a corporate charter creating the city of Boston in 1822, after nearly two centuries of existence as a town, marked an important step in the *dis*memberment of the corporate body that somehow took shape in the 1630s.

When the 1780 Massachusetts Constitution remade the commonwealth's frame of government, it barely mentioned the towns, and Boston not at all, presumably because it envisaged little change in the town-commonwealth relationship from the colonial period.[1] Neither did it grant the General Court any specific power to create incorporated cities. But in the early nineteenth century, growing demand for a municipal charter to create a government for the city adequate to its complex needs caused a legal and constitutional problem for the state. At earlier times in its history, various groups in Boston, often merchants and political leaders, had raised the possibility of incorporating Boston after the fashion of other colonial cities or common European norms. New Amsterdam had been incorporated by the Dutch in 1654 and rechartered as New York in 1665. In 1708, Boston's selectmen appointed a committee to "draft a charter of incorporation for the better government of the town," but at the next town meeting the "town's men" rejected the draft and the issue was dropped.[2]

Similar schemes were raised in the 1780s and 1790s, but no concerted efforts for a corporate charter were made until 1815. These were prompted by a sense that the town's growing population and "the want of an efficient police" required a more elaborate government than the quarterly town meetings and a small board of selectmen could provide. Over the course of the eighteenth century, Boston's selectmen had created a series of standing committees to manage ongoing tasks—a school committee, fire wardens, overseers of the poor, and a board of health—but there was no structure for coordination among them. Annual elections of board members by the entire town meeting made it difficult to sustain long-term plans. And by 1820, with nearly eight thousand eligible voters (out of a total population of forty-three thousand), mass town meetings on contentious issues became chaotic and unmanageable, while ordinary business went neglected by all but a handful of interested parties.[3]

Delegates to the Massachusetts Constitutional Convention of 1820 addressed the absence of formal state powers to incorporate cities. Boston's Daniel Webster and Lemuel Shaw argued that a town consisting of "a numerous people" required a more sophisticated form of government than smaller towns. Since 1780, when Boston's population, shrunken by wartime occupation, had numbered around ten thousand, the city had grown rapidly, mostly through natural increase and the influx of migrants from the New England hinterland, reaching fifty-eight thousand by 1825. The convention approved an amendment allowing large towns to exempt themselves from the requirement that all voters meet in a single place to choose selectmen and instead divide into districts, with each district electing representatives to a municipal governing body. Under this provision, Boston's town meeting called for the creation of the City of Boston. The powers of government would be vested in a mayor, a board of eight aldermen, and a "Common Council" of forty-eight citizens, four from each of the city's twelve wards, with elections taking place in the wards themselves. The plan was approved by Boston's voters and the General Court in 1822.[4] This corporate charter distinguished Boston from all the other towns in the commonwealth, giving it a unique governmental structure and, for the first time, a sharply distinct identity from Massachusetts as a whole. After the construction of Charles Bulfinch's new Massachusetts State House on the slope of Beacon Hill in 1798, the commonwealth had ceded the Old State House to the town, marking a symbolic separation of state from town government. The city's corporate charter confirmed that separation.[5] (See plate 26.)

Unlike the town meeting, where all the voters met in Faneuil Hall to determine major issues and choose a small group of selectmen to handle the day-to-day business, now, in the words of "An Old Bostonian," the city's government had switched "from a simple *democracy* to a Representative Republic."[6] The four town councilmen who represented each of the city's twelve wards would now have to vie with their counterparts from the other eleven wards for the benefit of their own district rather than act collectively for the general welfare of the city as a single body. As Federalist William Tudor put it, "We had been a great family. If we choose by wards, there is danger of us splitting into twelve little towns."[7] The new city government did not create competing interest groups—they had been present in the city for centuries—but it now gave concentrated institutional power over the whole to the victors of these contests. Boston's political restructuring resembled the United States' transformation from the Articles of Confederation to the Constitution, with similarly destructive consequences for the ideal that government should seek consensus around a common good.

The new and powerful office of the mayor became a prize for which interest groups in the city now competed. John Phillips served a single brief term, cut short by illness, as the city's first mayor. In 1823, Josiah Quincy, Boston's former congressman, was elected to the first of five consecutive terms. Mayor Quincy concentrated executive authority under his own control. He revamped all the former town committees and appointed professional administrators to oversee their functions. He applied the city's growing financial power to street widening, sanitation, and the development of a new marketplace on the site of the old town dock. Quincy also proposed an elaborate new water system for the city, gradually implemented over the next two decades, building aqueducts and pipelines to bring fresh water into Boston from distant reservoirs.

The shift in political structure quickly yielded evidence of an altered social reality, of sharp distinctions between personal or local interests and the welfare of the community as a whole. Under Quincy, the city's traditional volunteer fire companies, which had long cajoled Boston's citizens to join bucket brigades to fight fires, were reorganized in the wake of a devastating 1825 conflagration. In the new system, chief engineers oversaw a professional firefighting department. Quincy justified this change by claiming that citizens could no longer be counted on to assist in firefighting, imagining what he took to be the public's new attitude: "I am insured; why should I keep fire buckets? . . . I go to the expense of protecting myself. I ask no protection from others, and I mean not to incur the risk of health and life in protecting them."[8] Now that the structure of Boston's government no longer encouraged an ethic of citywide communal responsibility, a more costly professional system using water reservoirs, the latest fire engines, and hoses rather than bucket brigades became an urban necessity.[9]

The new expenses of professional administration also included street sanitation and widening, the building of a new "House of Industry" for the able-bodied poor, and the redevelopment of Faneuil Hall marketplace. With these new costs, the city's debt soared, from $100,000 in 1822 to nearly $900,000 when Quincy left office in 1829. With rising debt came higher taxes on the city's property owners.[10] Some of Boston's well-to-do abandoned the ethic of mutual obligation in favor of new strategies to evade taxes. Since the mid-eighteenth century, it had been common for Boston's wealthiest merchants and civic leaders to build estates in the countryside, and the practice became increasingly popular in the early nineteenth century.[11] But the rural retreats now became means for the wealthy to dodge their tax burdens in the city, as "[many] of the 'rich inhabitants' of Boston took up a 'temporary residence in the Country' during the spring collection of taxes."[12]

After Boston's incorporation, these evasive practices became more elaborate. Some rich Bostonians, especially merchants retiring from the hectic life of trade, chose to move out of the city altogether. Others took advantage of new transportation services into Boston's neighboring towns. By 1826, a regular stagecoach connected Boston to Roxbury, its neighbor across the Neck. The rapid building of bridges connecting the city to Charlestown and then Cambridge, soon to be followed by rail service, made these once-rustic towns accessible to commuters who could afford the fare. The Perkins brothers built rural retreats in Roxbury and Brookline, their former commercial agent in China John Cushing constructed his estate, "Belmont," on a hill in Watertown, and other prominent men such as Dr. John Collins Warren, chief surgeon at the Massachusetts General Hospital, joined the rural exodus. By midcentury, only half of Boston's bankers still lived in Boston.[13]

This rural movement to avoid the taxes of a rapidly urbanizing world soon replicated itself in Boston's surrounding towns. By the early 1840s, the area of "Lower Roxbury" nearest Boston, just across the Neck, had effectively become part of Boston's urban environment, with its expanding population employed by tanneries, leather factories, and other light industry. In 1846, Roxbury applied to become the fourth incorporated city in the commonwealth, imitating Boston, Salem, and Lowell in framing a representative government with a professional administration.[14] Within five years, though, the upper or western part of Roxbury, where wealthy Bostonians had their retreats, petitioned to break away and return their rustic enclave to the status of a town, not a city.

In arguing for West Roxbury's return to town status, Boston lawyer Rufus Choate asserted a fundamental distinction between rural and urban life—a distinction that would have been unthinkable among Bostonians in earlier generations: "God the first garden made, . . . And the first city Cain." Choate envisaged upper Roxbury as a pastoral garden, "dotted here and there with a beautiful locality." Lower Roxbury had "the artificial sidewalks, the gas-lighted stores, the artificial supply of water, the crowded and noisome population" characteristic of modern urban life. To govern both under a single system violated the natural order of things: "Only a town government would provide the conditions under which 'the agricultural mind breathes freely and trains itself perfectly to the duties of citizenship.' "[15] In Boston's past, Choate's claim would have been profoundly counterintuitive (and etymologically preposterous): that the best citizens are those people who do not live in cities. But Choate's rhetoric was merely a self-flattering justification for why some Boston elites were now manipulating the boundaries of civic institutions to serve personal interests and avoid contributing to the collective good. By implication, urbanized and "artificial" Boston, since 1822 formally cordoned off *from* the commonwealth, could no longer be seen as a microcosm *of* the commonwealth. Synecdoche had been the prevalent trope for understanding Boston's relationship to Massachusetts and New England—a part that stood for the whole. Choate and the elites he represented were dismantling this image.

Yet it was not only men of wealth and power who were making this argument. In 1841, members of Boston's Transcendental Club led by George Ripley formed a utopian colony in West Roxbury called Brook Farm as a rustic counterpoise to Boston's urban problems. A Unitarian minister, Ripley was deeply influenced by Friedrich Schleiermacher during his studies at Harvard Divinity School in the 1820s—another of the many effects of the connections forged in Göttingen. The neighborhood around Ripley's Unitarian church on Purchase Street in Boston, near the wharves and Fort Hill in the old South End, changed from middle class to working class. The sorry condition of its working poor prompted Ripley to seek a solution to the ills of social inequality increasingly prevalent in the city.

Ripley and his Brook Farm cofounders formed a joint-stock company to attract investor-participants, who would own the property in common and receive annual returns on their collective agricultural and aesthetic endeavors. They purchased a 170-acre dairy farm in West Roxbury near the home of Theodore Parker, a leading clergyman in the transcendental movement. There they opened a school, and set to work at collective farming and handmade textile production, believing that shared manual labor would leave the participants plentiful free time for artistic, intellectual, and scientific work. The experiment drew thirty full participants and as many as two hundred residents at its height. Brook Farm lasted only a few years and never made ends meet. But its idealistic founders' notion that the city of Boston, itself founded two centuries earlier as a quasi-utopian colony on a joint-stock model, now required a new colony, a rural retreat removed from the baneful influence of urban life, mirrored Choate's cynical argument for West Roxbury's separation from the "crowded and noisome population" of the city.[16] (See plate 27.)

Defortification: Dismantling the City's "Honor"

The city-state's dismemberment was accelerated by the topographical transformation of Boston in the nineteenth century. In the colonial era, Boston was essentially an island fortress. In the 1770s, when Boston's rebellion against the British Crown stirred intense curiosity across Europe, a German artist named François Xavier Habermann produced an engraving of Boston for widespread distribution. Habermann, who had never been to America or seen how Boston actually looked, depicted it as a European-style walled city with turrets and parapets. His image has subsequently been derided as so much fanciful nonsense, "figments of the engraver's imagination."[17] (See plate 28.)

But Habermann unwittingly captured something essential about Boston that its later physical transformation has made difficult to recall. Colonial Boston *was* a European-style walled city, only its walls were made of water as well as stone. Unlike many European cities, Boston was never completely encircled by stone walls because its protection and regulation did not require them. Nearly an island, Boston was naturally defensible. Its watery barriers were enhanced by a hilly topography and by fortifications built during the colonial period. Maps of Boston made by its enemies carefully noted these features. During the Anglo-French War of 1689–97, Jean-Baptiste-Louis Franquelin, New France's most prominent cartographer, charted the New England coast for a possible French invasion, including a map of "Baston" that highlighted its defenses.[18] Franquelin's map emphasizes the fortified batteries at the north

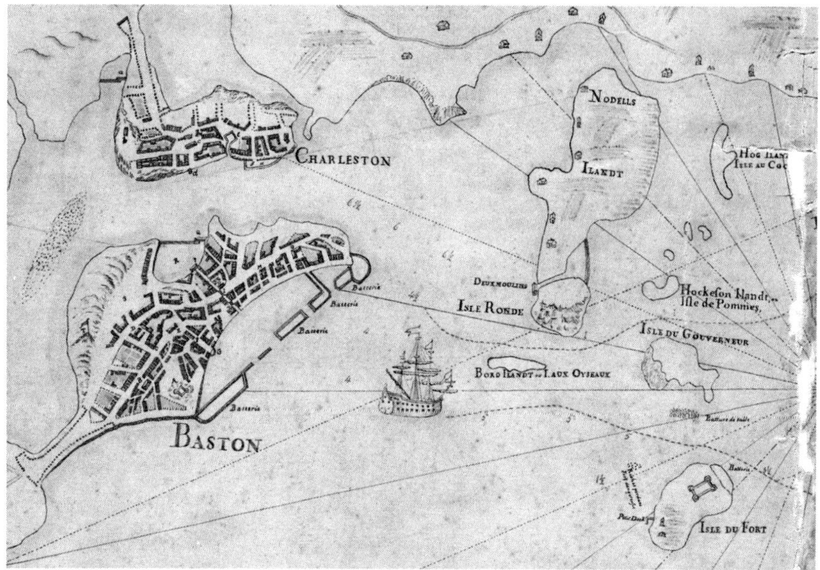

MAP 11.1. *Carte de la ville, baye et environs de Baston*, by Jean-Baptiste-Louis Franquelin, 1693. Detail.

and south ends of town facing the harbor, built in 1646 and 1666, respectively. It depicts the "Barricado," a series of rough stone fortifications across the shallow flats at the entrance to the inner harbor as yet another "Batterie."[19] Franquelin's map also carefully delineates the fortifications atop Fort Hill in the South End, just behind the South Battery, as well as the stone walls built around the Neck, protecting the area adjoining the South Cove and Back Bay where the water turned to mudflats at low tide. In addition, Franquelin shows the fort and battery on Castle Island (the "Isle du Fort") guarding the shipping lane by which oceangoing vessels approached the inner harbor.

These fortifications were no fantasies. Their presence, depicted in engravings on enlistment documents for artillerymen ("montrosses") during the Seven Years' War, helped to assure that during the many years of Anglo-French warfare from 1689 to 1815, Boston was never directly assaulted by military forces (including those of General George Washington during the siege of 1775–76). A 1757 successor to Franquelin's map carefully noted the strength of the

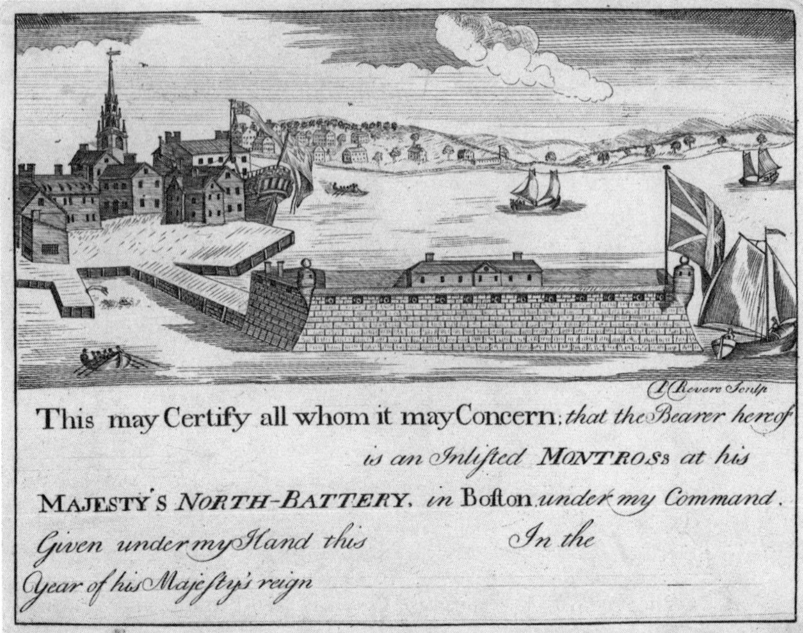

P. Revere Sculp

This may Certify all whom it may Concern; that the Bearer hereof is an Inlisted MONTROSS at his MAJESTY'S NORTH-BATTERY, in Boston under my Command. Given under my Hand this In the Year of his Majesty's reign

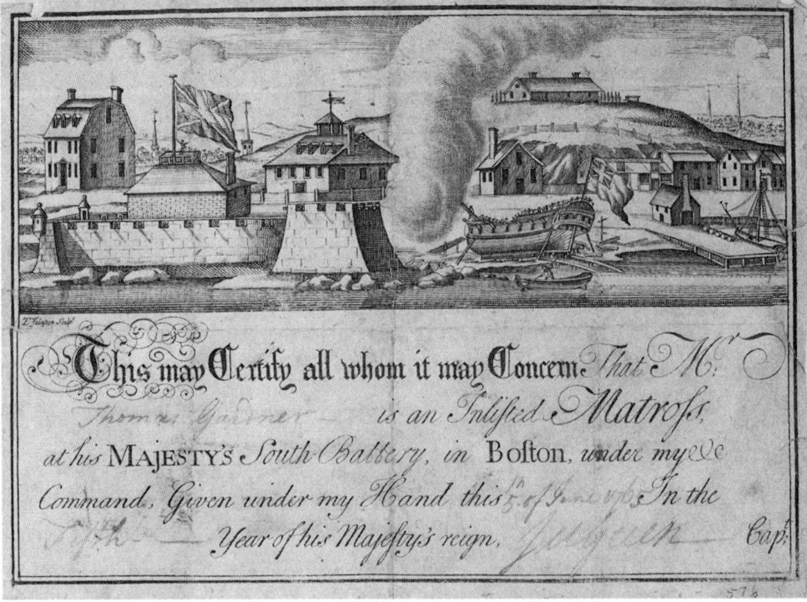

This may Certify all whom it may Concern. That Mr. Thomas Gardner is an Inlisted Matross, at his MAJESTY'S South Battery, in Boston, under my Command, Given under my Hand this 5 of June 1765 In the Fifth Year of his Majesty's reign, Capt.

FIGURE 11.1. (a and b) Enlistment documents depicting the fortifications at Boston's North Battery and South Battery, ca. 1765.

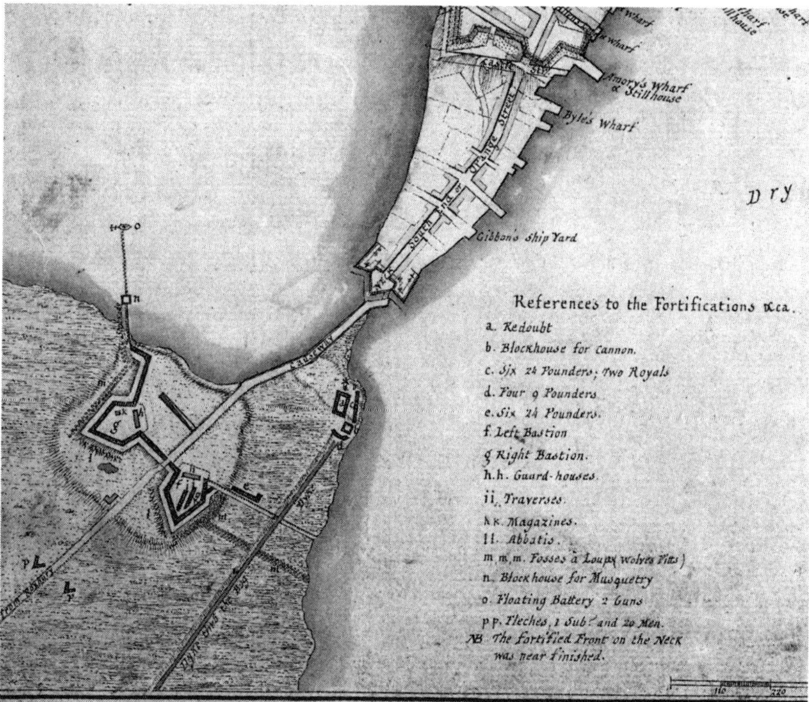

Map 11.2. *A Plan of the Town of Boston with the Intrenchments &ca. of His Majesty's Forces in 1775*, by Sir Thomas Hyde Page, 1777. Detail.

defenses at the North and South Batteries and on the Long Wharf, with twenty-five, twenty-five, and sixteen "pièces de Canon," respectively. It likewise showed that the Neck was defended by a ditch ("un fossé"), which served as a moat when filled by the tide, and "2 Batteries." These were the stone- and brickworks that the town built in 1710, armed with a "suitable number of great guns."[20] At night and on Sabbath, town officials closed the gates at the Neck to shut off travel in and out of Boston, much like a European walled city. And while the Neck may have been the least heavily fortified entrance to the city in the 1750s, when no one would have expected a French attack by land, by the 1770s this too had changed. A map drawn by Sir Thomas Hyde Page depicts the enhanced fortifications at the Neck ordered by General Thomas Gage in the wake of Lexington and Concord; vestiges of the fortifications remained as late as 1822. Although Habermann may not have known it, his image of Boston as a walled city in the 1770s was remarkably accurate in spirit. But the subsequent history of the city's land development, the wholesale remaking of Boston's built environment, has obscured these forgotten features.

The last time foreign invasion threatened Boston came during the closing months of the War of 1812. British forces occupied Castine, a town midway down the Maine coast (then still part of Massachusetts), and prepared to advance toward Boston. Terrified residents of Portland and even Salem fled toward the capital. A Boston town meeting in October 1814 called for defensive preparations in the face of the federal military's abandonment of New England.[21] Thomas Handasyd Perkins oversaw the strengthening of the Neck's fortifications—an attack by land forces was now plausible—along with plans to build new forts on Noddles Island and Bunker Hill and repair the existing batteries.[22] But when the peace treaty was signed in Ghent in December, the threat subsided. And like many of the walled cities of post-Napoleonic Europe, though perhaps less self-consciously, Boston began the slow process of defortification.

In the colonial period, the long road that leads from Roxbury across the Neck and meanders into central Boston was segmented into differently named sections: Orange Street, Newbury Street, Marlborough Street, and Cornhill. The names changed as the road moved through town, with Cornhill finally passing the west side of the Old State House at the head of King Street as it entered the heart of the city. Yet the entire avenue gradually adopted the single name of Washington Street in the decades after 1789, when the quasi-monarchical hero of the Revolutionary War made his *second* triumphal entry into the city along its path. The first entry had come at the lifting of the siege on March 17, 1776, when the generalissimo (as Phillis Wheatley called him) led his victorious army through Gage's abandoned fortifications and into the ruins of the evacuated city. The second entry followed the same path. As the newly inaugurated president, Washington toured the United States, arriving in Boston on October 24, 1789. The president passed throngs of admirers lining the mile's length of road from the Neck to the Old

FIGURE 11.2. *View of the Triumphal Arch and Colonnade Erected in Boston, in Honor of the President of the United States, October 24, 1789*, engraving by Samuel Hill, *Massachusetts Magazine* 2, no. 1 (Boston, 1790).

State House. There he rode under a triumphal arch built by Charles Bulfinch for the occasion, on which stood a chorus singing an ode in praise of "Columbia's Favorite Son."

Bulfinch designed this arch after the style (though not on the scale) of triumphal arches from ancient Rome, specifically the third-century Porte de Mars in Reims. In imperial Rome and in subsequent European history, arches like these, along with the gates to fortified cities, marked the ritual entry of the emperor or monarch into the independent city—sometimes by force, as in the aftermath of a siege, and sometimes by invitation, as a city's gesture of tribute to the sovereign's authority. With his 1789 entry, Washington had now come to Boston in both guises, and the reception he received in 1789 demonstrated the lingering power of these traditions. Once the president had arrived, John Hancock insisted that protocol required Washington, whom he "undertook to regard . . . as a sort of foreign potentate," to present himself as a visitor to Hancock, the governor of the sovereign Commonwealth of Massachusetts, in Hancock's Beacon Hill mansion. Washington believed otherwise. He waited for Hancock at his guest residence below the hill. A day later, Hancock finally submitted, claiming gout had kept him away. Wrapped in flannel and carried down Beacon Hill on a litter by servants, Hancock paid a call to Washington, who then reciprocated the following day.[23]

President Washington asserted his superior rank over Boston and Massachusetts in a manner far gentler than the monarchs who defortified Europe's independent cities. Beginning in the seventeenth century with Louis XIII's siege of La Rochelle (where John Winthrop Jr. had joined the English attempt to relieve the Huguenots), the Bourbon monarchs' desire for a centralized, unitary, and sovereign state made the fortified city anathema. When Louis's army finally defeated La Rochelle in 1629, the year of the Massachusetts Bay Company's original charter, Cardinal Richelieu ordered a general defortification of cities in the French interior as well, because urban walls "do not allow the state to control important, mutinous cities."[24] Henceforth, the king's army and navy would protect the realm as a whole; interior cities would not need to build walls whose only purpose would be to resist the sovereign. The project begun by the Bourbon monarchs was eventually completed by Napoléon, who extended its scope beyond France to defortify most of the walled cities of continental Europe, as we saw in the previous chapter.

In the seventeenth century, the Stuart monarchs' attacks on the corporate charters of England's cities and colonies was the legal equivalent of defortification, a way of breaking down vestiges of organized local opposition to the sovereign. So too were Parliament's punitive measures against colonial resistance in the 1770s, such as the Massachusetts Government Act. These assaults on local power were key aspects of European centralized state making on the eve of modernity. But it was uncertain whether the newly formed United States, in rejecting the dominion of the British Crown, would follow the European model of state consolidation. As late as the War of 1812, it remained unclear whether the US government would use national military forces to obviate the need for Boston (or any other city or state) to provide its own defense against invasion. This uncertainty explains the frenzy of Boston's defensive preparations as

British forces attacked Maine in 1814. After Napoléon's final defeat at Waterloo the following summer, and the Congress of Vienna's construction of a new balance of power in Europe, Boston performed its own slow and halting absorption into the sovereign uniformity of the United States, marked by the gradual dismantling of its fortifications against attacks from land and sea.

A city with stone walls can tear them down. Many European cities did so (as Ticknor, Everett, and Cogswell noted in their German travels), often replacing them with parks or green space for public promenading. The English gardens that the exiled Boston loyalist, Benjamin Thompson, designed for Munich followed this pattern. Walls of water are harder to destroy, but over the course of the nineteenth century, Boston managed this feat by accelerating its traditional practice of making land where water had been. Since Boston's earliest days, the practice of "wharfing out" had been used to make land along Shawmut's shallow shorelines, where low tides exposed mudflats. By building wharves atop stones embedded in the mud, then using more stones and earth to fill the gap between adjacent wharves, the shoreline could be extended outward, making new land. Historians tend to focus on what was gained in the making of new ground, but land making was an unmaking as well, an abandonment of Boston's traditional character as a martial city, an island fortress defending its magnificent harbor and keeping its hinterland safe from foreign invasion.[25]

This aspect of Boston's transformation was more evident to outsiders, such as visiting Scotsman Robert Fleming Gourlay. In 1844, Gourlay dreamed up a scheme for Boston's future development inspired by his own experiences in Edinburgh: "Seventy years ago, the capital of Scotland was noted for discomfort. The necessities of a warlike age had driven the people within narrow bounds, to have protection from rocks and ravines. . . . [B]ut at last, a stupendous bridge gave access to a plain, whereon a new town grew up, on a regular plan, unrivalled for beauty and convenience. So it may be here [in Boston], more easily, and on a grander scale."[26] In the years after 1814, with the necessities of a warlike age giving way to a new era of Boston's integration into the economic sphere of the

Cotton Kingdom, Bostonians would build a variety of stupendous bridges and artificial land designed to enhance the city's access to the surrounding plains.

In 1786, the Charles River Bridge Company built a wooden span connecting Charlestown, site of the Battle of Bunker Hill, to Boston's North End. A second bridge soon crossed the Charles and connected the city's sparsely populated West End to the eastern edge of Cambridge, where Gage's redcoats had landed on their march to Lexington and Concord. In 1805, a third bridge was added from the Neck to South Boston (formerly known as Dorchester Heights), where Henry Knox's cannons had forced the British Army to evacuate Boston. That this third bridge marked a defortification, the creation of yet another avenue into the city skirting the old stone walls at the Neck, was recognized in the celebrations on its opening. Boston's Legionary Brigade, the city militia formed during the quasi-war with France in the 1790s, including cavalry, light infantry, and artillery, performed martial maneuvers on Boston Common. From there, "a detachment advanced and took possession of South Boston Bridge and the neighboring [Dorchester] heights; after which the remainder of the Brigade marched thither to dispossess them—displaying a representation of real battle."[27] Despite the fanfare of this mock combat, the new bridge proved a disappointment to its investors. There was little traffic to sparsely populated South Boston, and the bridge did not significantly shorten the journey from Boston. But it did "furnish a fashionable promenade for Boston residents because of its agreeable view of the town," much like the walkways built on dismantled fortifications around European cities.[28]

Along with the bridges that provided new routes into Boston for pedestrians, carriages, and farmers' wagons, the city's population growth stimulated a new wave of land making on an unprecedented scale. The North End's terrain had been slightly altered in the seventeenth century, when a dam was built across the mouth of a marshy cove, turning the area into the Mill Pond. Its proprietors dug a narrow channel across the North End's own "neck" to connect the Mill Pond to the bay. Through this channel at high tide, water spilled into the Mill Pond, turning the wheels of flour mills and sawmills.[29]

FIGURE 11.3. *View of Boston from the South Boston Bridge*, by Jacques Gérard Milbert, ca. 1820–29. Note how the clothing of the promenading gentlemen resembles that of the "mob" that nearly lynched Garrison.

By the early nineteenth century, these mills had ceased to be profitable, and the sanitary conditions of the shallow Mill Creek and Mill Pond, together with the growing demand for space in the city, prompted a movement to fill in the Mill Pond.

Over the next twenty years, construction crews filled the Mill Pond with gravel and dirt from the tops of Copp's Hill in the North End and Beacon Hill in the city's center. Bulfinch designed a plan to develop more than forty acres of land where the Mill Pond had been.[30] Similar methods were used to fill in the South Cove, building up new streets where in 1773, the East India Company tea had been dumped into the harbor. A second and more direct bridge was built to narrow the distance between Boston and South Boston, and the Neck was gradually widened to the point where it ceased to be recognizable as a neck. With all this new land, Boston's old fortifications were transformed. When Uriah Cotting and Francis Cabot Lowell built India Wharf and Broad Street in the 1810s, their project absorbed the old South Battery. The North Battery became Battery Wharf, retaining only in name its former defensive function.

Map 11.3. *Map of Boston in the State of Massachusetts*, by John Groves Hale, 1814. The former Mill Pond, having now been filled in, is the light-colored, vaguely triangular region at the top end of the map.

The fort atop Fort Hill was dismantled at the turn of the nineteenth century, replaced with new housing for the rich, and renamed Washington Place.[31]

Land making and defortification opened new areas of the city for residential and commercial development, but foreclosed other prospects for the city's future. One such possibility arose concurrently with Lowell's experiments in developing water-powered textile mills. The filling of Boston's Mill Pond deprived the city of a power source that had driven small-scale industries in the North End. In its stead, Uriah Cotting, Lowell's India Wharf partner, developed a grand (if ultimately unrealistic) plan to turn the entire city and its surrounding waters into a tide-powered perpetual motion machine. By building an interconnected set of dams on the (western) Charles River side of the city, and another dam on the (eastern) South Cove side, the Boston and Roxbury Mill Corporation planned to create a giant reservoir of water at high tide west of the Neck. This water would flow through man-made cuts or sluices across the Neck, and into a receiving basin on the east side, which could then be drained at low tide. The waterpower produced by the tides would drive dozens of mills of all sorts—flour mills, sawmills, textile mills, and iron- and copper-rolling mills—enhancing the growing city's industrial capacity.[32] (See plate 29.)

Had Cotting's company succeeded in turning the Neck into an industrial powerhouse, Boston would have remained essentially an island far into its future, with little room for further land making or population growth without severe overcrowding. But Cotting's death in 1819, together with Roxbury's objection that the proposed dam would cut off its access to the harbor, scaled back the project. The Boston and Roxbury Mill Corporation did build a new mill dam across the Back Bay, but not the South Cove receiving basin. Instead, the Back Bay was divided into two parts by a smaller internal dam. This created a small high water basin to the west and a larger receiving basin to the east, with a few mills built at Gravelly Point across the smaller dam that divided the two basins. Sadly, the waterpower generated by this diminished version failed to meet expectations. The few mills built at Gravelly Point never generated enough profits to offset the costs of the dam. And the concerns voiced by one opponent in the *Daily Advertiser* proved to be prophetic: "Citizens of Boston! . . . What think you of converting the beautiful sheet of water which skirts the Common into an empty mud-basin, reeking with filth, abhorrent to the smell, and disgusting to the eye? By every god of sea, lake, or fountain, it is incredible."[33] The gods of sea, lake, and fountain had it right. From 1821, when the Mill Dam was completed, the Back Bay became a stinking reminder of the growing city's "filth," dumped by sewers into the mudflats but no longer washed away by the tides. In an era of frequent cholera epidemics, the damming of the Back Bay raised fears that the city now harbored a source of deadly disease.

Instead of dozens of factories driven by tidal power, Boston built still more land, often to promote new railroads that reoriented the port city toward the American interior. The area's first railway began in 1826 as a horse-drawn conveyance to move granite for the Bunker Hill Monument from a quarry in Quincy down to the harbor. Its success led rapidly to plans for steam train lines from Boston to Lowell, Worcester, and Providence. Within less than a decade, all three lines had opened with Boston terminals built on newly made land. The Boston and Lowell Railroad built its terminal on the site of the former Mill Pond. The South Cove, the marshy tidal area south of the main harbor and nearest to South Boston, became the next target. The Boston and Worcester Railroad's extensive terminal complex was built on fifty-five acres of landfill created by the South Cove Corporation east of the Neck. By the time that this railroad-driven landfill project was completed in the 1850s, the wide expanse of water that had once separated the Shawmut Peninsula from Dorchester Heights, which in 1776 prevented General Gage from dislodging the cannons there, had been reduced to a narrow channel easily spanned by railroad and pedestrian bridges. With the Boston and Worcester line soon extended to Albany, the new-made streets near the its terminal ("that vomitory of the travel and the trade of the Great West and South") were given appropriate corresponding names: Albany, Hudson, Erie, Oneida, Oswego, Genesee, Rochester, and Troy. This was the first time that a set of streets in Boston had been named for neither a Massachusetts nor an overseas location—another sign of Boston's slow reorientation from the sea to the national landscape.[34]

By midcentury, a dozen bridges connected Shawmut to the surrounding mainland. Landfill in the South Cove and Back Bay had

Map 11.4. *New Map of Boston, Comprising the Whole City, with the New Boundaries of the Wards*, by George W. Boynton, 1852. Detail. The streets named for Erie Canal cities are shown just below the number 10.

FIGURE 11.4. *Boston from Willis Creek*, by J.F.W. Des Barres, 1775. This image, taken from the west side of the Charles River near the Cambridge-Charlestown boundary, depicts Boston's North End on the left, the Trimountain in the center, and to the right, barely visible, the narrow strip of the Neck connecting the city to the mainland. Like most early images of Boston, it emphasizes its island-like topography.

unmade the narrow Neck with its once-fortified gate. Boston no longer seemed like an island at all, and it had long since ceased to be a defensible fortress. Although it remained an active maritime trading city, Boston had now become part of the American mainland as well. The balcony and front steps of the Old State House had faced eastward down State Street toward Long Wharf, the harbor, and the sea. The new Bulfinch State House with its grand staircase faced the Boston Common, oriented toward the mainland. Once-popular images depicting the city as an island floating offshore in the harbor were superseded by new images showing it as the place where the New England mainland came down to meet the sea.

The era of railroad building coincided with the moment when land pressure in Boston proper, concern for filth and disease, and the rise of the romantic English garden inspired Boston's Unitarian leadership to develop Mount Auburn Cemetery in Cambridge. Mount Auburn was formed as a joint-stock corporation in which investors in cemetery plots collectively owned the land—a kind of colony for the departed. Henceforth, the city's honored dead would

FIGURE 11.5. *Bird's Eye View of Boston,* by John Bachmann, 1850. Bachmann's image, taken from the southwest edge of the city, lacks any sense that Boston was once a mountainous near-island.

be buried beyond the fortified walls of the peninsula, where historically everyone from John Winthrop and John Cotton to the martyrs of the Boston Massacre had been laid to rest. The new burial ground for the city's politicians, preachers, scholars, artists, and industrialists would be in the countryside of western Cambridge. New railroads could easily deposit city visitors at Mount Auburn's Egyptian gates for the contemplation of eternity or a frolic in a rustic setting. As in ancient Rome, Boston's fallen heroes would be found outside the city walls—except now the walls were gone.[35]

In the medieval and early modern European city-in-arms, the city's walls were synonymous with the city's "honor," a tangible manifestation of what separated the city, with its distinctive privileges, functions, and culture, from the undifferentiated mass of the surrounding countryside. They protected the city's sovereign authority from the encroachments of external powers. In the dismantling of its fortifications, both literally and through the less obvious process of land making, Boston not only dispersed its sovereignty and honor but also disguised the fact that it had ever had them, undoing its island-like past and reorienting itself toward the mainland of which it had now become a part.

Immigration and Ethnic Segregation in the Corporate City

The movement of people and the rapid growth in human numbers played as powerful a part in the spatial remaking of Boston as did concerns about land, transportation, and sanitation—the relationship was always a symbiotic one. With the exception of the devastation caused by military occupation and siege, population growth had been a steady aspect of Boston's history. This was easily visible in the many iterations and editions of John Bonner's 1722 map of the city, where decade by decade more of the Shawmut Peninsula was filled in by residential neighborhoods and burgeoning industries. But the era of Boston's municipal incorporation saw new patterns of growth, mainly in the noticeable increase in migration of an ethnically and religiously distinctive minority. Before this time, Boston's neighborhoods were relatively undifferentiated with respect to status and class; rich and poor lived cheek by jowl in every part of town. But the influx of ever-larger numbers of Irish Catholics from the 1820s onward, and the wary-to-hostile response of Boston's Yankees to the newcomers accentuated the segregation and fragmentation that the city's division into wards had initiated.

Irish immigrants were early Boston's oldest and most notable ethnic minority in a city known for its Anglo-Saxon homogeneity. Yet for the city's first two centuries, the majority of its Irish citizens were Protestants from Ulster. Like their fellow Protestants, the Huguenots, the small numbers of Irish immigrants had mostly assimilated with the English majority. If Peter Faneuil and Paul Mascarene were emblematic of Boston's successful Huguenots, then James Sullivan was their Irish equivalent. The son of an Irish Catholic migrant to Berwick, Maine, Sullivan drifted away from his father's religion, studied law, and eventually moved to Boston, where he became a member of the Brattle Street Church and an important figure in revolutionary politics. It was Sullivan who suggested ratifying the US Constitution with recommended amendments, helping to end the impasse at the Massachusetts convention. In 1807, Sullivan was elected governor of the commonwealth—the first man of Irish descent to hold the office.[36]

Through the first decades of the nineteenth century, the character of Irish immigration to Boston adhered to the colonial pattern, while its numbers grew. After the end of the Napoleonic Wars, wartime trade restrictions that intensified Britain's reliance on Irish agriculture ended too. The Irish economy slumped. Irish farmers facing high rents and skilled workers seeking better wages flocked to North America. As many as a million people left Ireland in the three decades after Waterloo, even before Ireland's famine of 1846. But until around 1830, most Irish migrants to Boston were still Protestant farmers and artisans from Ulster. In the next decade, migration patterns shifted, and poor tenant farmers and laborers from Ireland's southern counties predominated.[37] The 1830s witnessed a growing Irish presence in Boston, and noticeably more Roman Catholics among them. In 1830, there were already seven thousand people of Irish birth or descent living among Boston's population of sixty-one thousand, or more than triple the number of African Americans in the city.[38] The poverty of newer Irish immigrants channeled them into cheap housing near the wharves of the North and South End. The influx of poor Irish Catholics rapidly changed the neighborhood around George Ripley's Purchase Street Church and precipitated his creation of the utopian colony at Brook Farm.

As Irish immigrants crowded Boston's waterfront neighborhoods, the character of Roman Catholicism in the city began to shift. In its earliest days, Boston's Catholic Church served a rarefied group, including French military officers stationed in Boston during the Revolutionary War. Some of Boston's earliest Catholic priests such as Father Francis Matignon, and the city's first bishop, Jean-Louis Lefebvre de Cheverus, were exiles from the French Revolution. In this aspect, the early Catholic Church in Boston resembled Boston's nascent Anglican Church a century earlier, when it had catered to the first royally appointed governor, Edmund

Andros, and the small contingent of military officers and civil servants surrounding him.

The new Irish immigrant population made increasing demands on the Catholic Church's local leadership. When Bishop Benedict Fenwick was appointed as Cheverus's successor in 1825, he found only three priests in the diocese to serve some five thousand Catholics. Instead of serving new parishioners, the resources of the church were devoted to projects reaching back to its eighteenth-century foundations. Father John Thayer, the first local Boston Protestant to convert to Roman Catholicism, had left the city after a stormy career of conflict with both Protestant adversaries and the French Catholic leadership, and had been resettled in Limerick, Ireland. Before leaving Boston, Thayer had dreamed of opening an Ursuline convent, inspired by the Ursulines in Quebec and their mission to educate the daughters of Quebec's creole elites. Thayer continued to pursue this idea in Limerick, where he befriended a cloth merchant named James Ryan, taught French to Ryan's daughters, and convinced them to take up his project.

Mary, Catherine, and Margaret Ryan moved to the Ursuline convent at Trois Rivières in Quebec, supported by Thayer's estate of some $10,000, left to the sisters when the priest died suddenly in 1815. By 1820, under the guidance of Bishop Cheverus, Thayer's money was used to open Boston's Ursuline convent and school on Franklin Street in the South End, adjacent to the Cathedral of the Holy Cross. Mary, now Sister Mary Joseph, was its first mother superior. Within a few years, tuberculosis cut short the lives of Sister Mary Joseph and the other Ryan sisters. The convent, seeking a more salubrious location outside the city, purchased land on a hillside in neighboring Charlestown. With the remainder of Thayer's estate and a gift from Bishop Cheverus, the convent built a handsome new building for the nuns and a boarding school for the daughters of Boston's elite, many of them Unitarians, whose parents were dismayed at the limited educational opportunities for young women and disdained the conservative Trinitarian emphasis in the public schools.[39]

In the early 1830s, the Ursuline convent became the focal point for animosity between working- and middle-class Yankee Bostonians and Irish newcomers. Around Ann Street in the North End and Broad Street in the South End where the Irish immigrants congregated, frequent riots erupted. Gangs of Protestant workingmen attacked Irish residences, breaking windows and even pulling down small houses, forcing the new professional police force to expand its patrols.[40] At the same time, a growing antipopery movement in the religious press, represented by the appearance of magazines such as the *Protestant* and the *Boston Recorder*, encouraged readers to believe that Roman Catholicism posed a dire threat to traditional orthodox Protestant values. Lyman Beecher, the Calvinist patriarch of the famous family of preachers and writers, and former minister of Boston's Hanover Street Church, preached a series of fiercely anti-Catholic sermons in Boston in 1834.[41] Beecher's staunch Calvinism could be as hostile to the Unitarian elites of Boston as toward Roman Catholicism. His animosities were shared by many of the men from rural New England who had emigrated to Boston and neighboring Charlestown and Roxbury to work in the brickyards and factories.

These smoldering prejudices burst forth in a wave of arson and destruction in August 1834, after one of the Ursuline nuns, in a state of nervous exhaustion, fled from the convent. A committee of Charlestown's selectmen visited the troubled young woman and were assured that she had returned to the convent voluntarily. But many of the locals, including workers in a nearby brick factory along with several volunteer fire companies in Charlestown and Boston, were convinced that the nun's distress was caused by foul and mysterious rites among the cloistered Catholics. They vented their anger on the night of August 10, attacking the convent and burning it to the ground, while firefighters either stood by or, more likely, aided the destruction.[42] The convent's combative mother superior, Mary Ann Moffatt, exacerbated the trouble by threatening the gathering mob that "if you meddle with us, the Bishop has 30,000 men, who will burn your houses over your heads," confirming the fears of secret Catholic power that Beecher's sermon had warned about the previous day.[43]

The razing of the convent revealed not only the resurgence of vitriolic anti-Catholicism in Boston, instigated by the presence of a growing immigrant population, but also a widening divide within the once-united community. This was a class-based but also ideological split between the Unitarian mercantile and intellectual leaders and the more traditional orthodox Protestant working and middle classes. The previous year, this internal division had caused the final dissolution of the state religious establishment in Massachusetts. With churches and towns across Massachusetts no longer capable of internal agreement on doctrinal fundamentals and a minister who could preach them, it became impossible to sustain the state-mandated system where towns raised taxes to support a local church.[44] The violence aimed at the Ursuline convent and school was directed not only at Irish Catholics but also at the liberal elites who tolerated and cooperated with them. It was no surprise that in the aftermath of the Charlestown convent riot, the city's Unitarian leaders, including former and current mayors Harrison Gray Otis and Theodore Lyman, joined Bishop Benedict Fenwick in pleading for peace, and calling out the city's militia to discourage retaliation by Irish Catholics and avert the threatened destruction of the Catholic cathedral on Franklin Street.[45]

Three years later, in June 1837, the militia would be called out again, and this time forced into action. A Boston volunteer fire company returning to the city from an alarm in Roxbury crossed paths with an Irish funeral procession. Fighting broke out, and more fire companies were called in. By evening, a crowd of fifteen thousand was sweeping through the Broad Street district near the waterfront, flushing Irish residents out of their tenements and beating them. It took a cavalry regiment of eight hundred horsemen from the city's militia under the direction of Mayor Samuel Eliot to quell the riot.[46] In its aftermath, Mayor Eliot accelerated Mayor Quincy's earlier project of converting the city's fire department into a paid professional organization. The middle- and working-class Yankee volunteer fire companies could no longer be trusted to maintain the peace among the city's bitter ethnic and religious divisions. Even as the land-making and transportation enterprises were reshaping the city and extending its effective boundaries into neighboring towns, the segregation emerging within Boston was undermining the capacity of its civic institutions.

At the time of the Charlestown and Broad Street riots, the tidal wave of immigration that the Irish famine of 1846 would propel toward the Atlantic's western shore was still a decade in the future. Although Boston's Irish population grew significantly in the 1820s and 1830s, there were still no more than five hundred Irish voters on the rolls in 1839 out of a total population of eligible voters nearing fifteen thousand.[47] Yet the alarming violence of the 1830s indicated that from the perspective of Boston's Anglo-Saxon majority, the Irish Catholic minority was "extravasat blood" in Boston's political body, as Samuel Sewall had once described Boston's African population.[48] In the historian Oscar Handlin's blunt summation of Yankee prejudices, the Irish were "a massive lump in the community, undigested, undigestible."[49]

The Great Hunger and the Collapse of Christian Charity

Even with the best of intentions, even had there been no festering prejudice against them, even had they been English Protestants and not Irish Catholics, the sheer numbers and desperate condition of the migrants fleeing Ireland's famine would have overwhelmed Boston's capacity to sustain its commitment to Christian charity. The story is, first of all, one of numbers. The potato blight (*Phylophthora infestans*) caused the failure in 1845–46 of two consecutive potato crops, which triggered the Great Hunger. British economic policy turned the blight into a famine that killed a million Irish people by starvation and hunger-related diseases, and drove more than two million others to flee their homeland in the next decade.[50] Boston received a tremendous number of these migrants, especially in relation to its population size and the constricted physical space in the city.

As it happens, Boston had conducted a municipal census in 1845, enumerating 114,366 residents.[51] The author of the census report, in addressing future needs for water and sanitation services, judged that Boston's population could grow no further: "The flats have been filled up nearly to the channel prescribed by the commissioners of the State; and no new land can be made; and the vacant lots are nearly all occupied. Where is there room for more?"[52] Despite this warning from Lemuel Shattuck, over the next decade a quarter of a million Irish immigrants landed in Boston by ship. Countless thousands more made their way overland to the city from ports in Canada. In 1846 alone, 112,664 ship passengers arrived in a city of 114,000 residents. That number would be surpassed annually over the next several years as the devastation in Ireland spread.[53]

Not all of the Boston-bound passengers were Irish. Not all of them aimed to stay in Boston. But the horrific conditions from which they fled and the cost of their ocean passage meant that few Irish migrants had the wherewithal to travel far beyond the docks where they landed. The most destitute decamped in the crowded waterfront districts in the North and South Ends that had already become Irish neighborhoods. The luckier ones spilled over into the burgeoning towns ringing Boston, or found work in the mills along the Merrimack, where immigrant Irish labor supplanted the rural farm girls.[54] By 1855, Boston's resident population, which its census reporter in 1845 had estimated could grow no further, had in fact grown by 50 percent, to 159,171. And from 1840 to 1855, the aggregate population of Boston's immediate neighbors—Brighton, Brookline, Cambridge, Charlestown, Chelsea, Dorchester, and Roxbury—more than doubled from 40,400 to 88,435.[55]

The infrastructure that Boston had constructed over two centuries, including its housing stock, water supply, and sanitation systems, its schools, churches, and businesses, and its network of hospitals, poorhouses, workhouses, orphanages, asylums, and prisons, simply could not contain, let alone alleviate, the misery that landed on its wharves.[56] This is not to say that the city's charitable habits failed entirely. As the early news of the severity of Ireland's famine spread, relief efforts similar to those that had supported the

Greek rebellion in the 1820s or the Polish refugees of the 1830s, and led by many of the same people, were organized to support the hungry in Ireland. Boston raised more money for Ireland than any other American city save the far-larger New York.[57]

Early in 1847, a mass meeting was held at Faneuil Hall. Samuel Howe and Edward Everett spoke, and the New England Relief Committee for the Famine in Ireland and Scotland was formed, with Josiah Quincy as its chairman.[58] Robert C. Winthrop, congressman from Boston and speaker of the House, formally requested Congress to allow the warship *U.S.S. Jamestown*, then stationed in Boston Harbor, to bring food and relief materials to Ireland. Under the command of Robert Forbes, the *Jamestown* was loaded with eight hundred tons of food and supplies, and sailed to Cork in record time. Forbes and crew joined the work of food distribution before sailing the *Jamestown* back to Boston—carrying no Irish emigrants. The purpose of the relief effort, from the perspective of Boston's establishment figures, had been much like the campaigns for Greece and Poland: to support the suffering people of Ireland and their campaign for liberation from imperial misrule, not to bring more Irish migrants to Boston.[59]

The Irish came, regardless. And they came in such numbers, and in such desperate poverty, sickness, social and mental dislocation, as to overwhelm Boston's resources. Genteel neighborhoods near the North and South End wharves that had been popular with merchants like the Perkins brothers, who once built their mansions on tree-lined Pearl Street to be close to their business, now packed in Irish refugees by the thousands. Unscrupulous landlords divided old houses into warrens of apartments, renting out attics, crawl spaces, basements, cellars, or shanties thrown up in former courtyards, any space at all, often devoid of fresh water or sanitation. Within four years of the start of the Irish famine, there were six hundred basements in Boston being used as separate dwellings, each one averaging between five and fifteen residents. One basement housed thirty-nine people.[60]

Half-Moon Place, the epicenter of the worst slums, wedged between Broad Street and Fort Hill in the South End, was investigated by the Cholera Commission of 1849 after Boston suffered a "mysterious epidemic" of the disease. Henry Clark, the doctor heading the Cholera Commission, found twelve to fourteen ill-constructed and overflowing privies in this densely occupied alley, which also received human waste tumbling down from the Fort Hill slums up above.[61] In addition to the cholera scare, the Irish influx brought renewed smallpox outbreaks not seen since the 1790s and Edward Jenner's development of vaccination. Tuberculosis swept through Boston as well. In 1847, the city established two new hospitals for "Foreign Diseased Paupers" on Deer Island in the harbor to attend to those immigrants, nearly all of them Irish, needing immediate medical care.[62] Although the Irish famine migrants were younger on average than Boston's overall population, the city's death rates climbed to new heights after 1845. Infant mortality reached unprecedented levels by 1850, when over half the city's new births were the children of Irish newcomers.[63]

From the time in 1630 when its founders relocated their settlement from Charlestown to the Shawmut Peninsula, Boston had prided itself on being one of the healthiest cities in the Atlantic world. According to one modern historian, at the end of Josiah Quincy's term as mayor in 1828, "Boston was very likely the cleanest, most orderly, and best governed city in the United States."[64] On his 1842 visit, Charles Dickens had remarked that "the public institutions and charities of this capital of Massachusetts are as nearly perfect, as the most considerate wisdom, benevolence, and humanity, can make them."[65] As late as 1845, the British geologist Charles Lyell commented on Boston's "almost entire absence of pauperism" and the beneficent work of the "committee in Boston to see that the poor who are too old to work have all the necessary comforts."[66] But over the following decade, the city's expenditures on poor relief quadrupled, from $15,000 to $60,000 per year. The tiny peninsula had become one of the most crowded, slum-ridden, filthy, and disease-prone urban spaces in the world. The public institutions and charities that had captivated Dickens and Lyell only a few years before now struggled desperately to keep up with the overwhelming demand for their services.

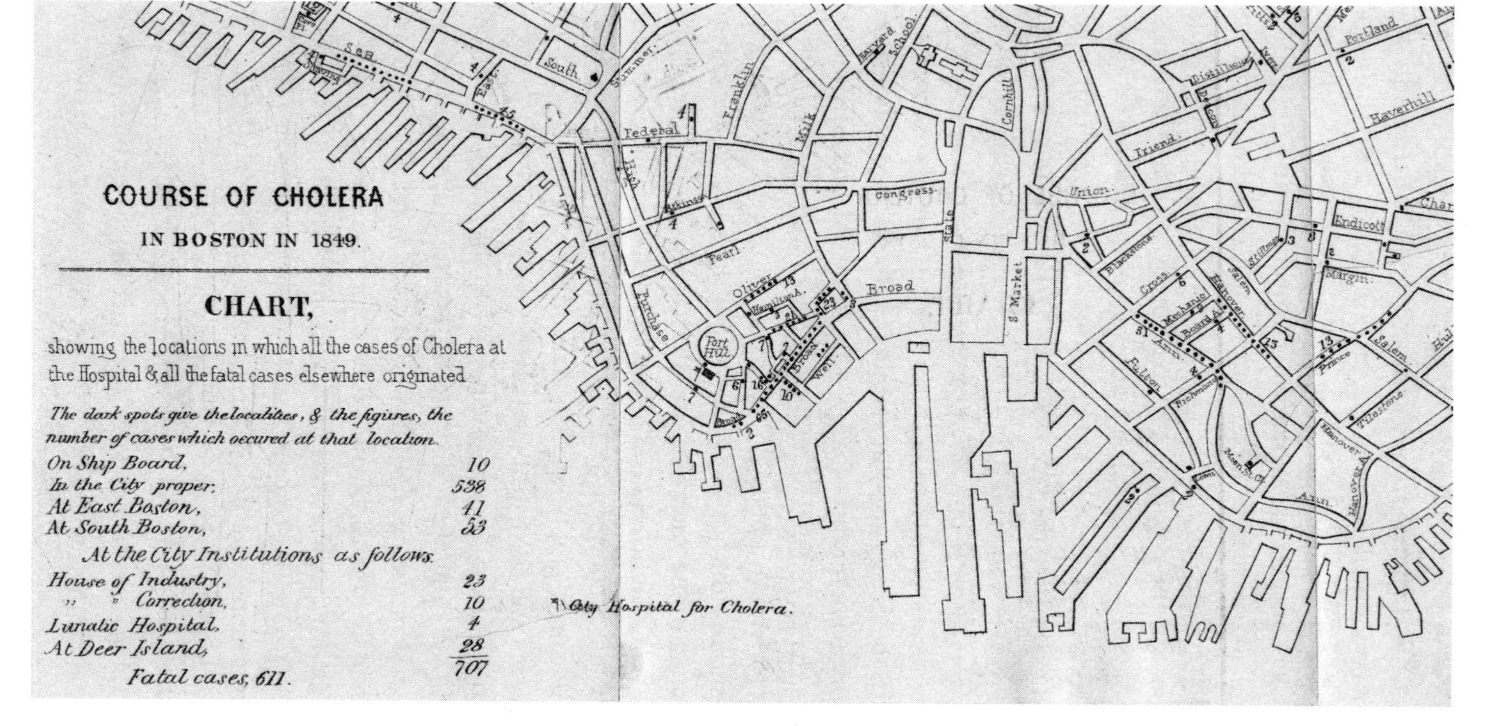

Map 11.5. *Course of Cholera in Boston in 1849*, by the Boston Committee on Internal Health. Detail. The concentration of cholera cases closely tracks the residence of Boston's impoverished Irish famine immigrants near Broad Street and Fort Hill in the South End, and Ann, Prince, and Hanover Streets in the North End.

This surge in poverty spurred an increase in alcohol abuse and crime, but the justice system was unequipped to handle it. The number of liquor dealers in the city, after declining from the 1830s to the mid-1840s, grew by 50 percent between 1846 and 1849, strongly concentrated in neighborhoods around Ann Street in the North End and Fort Hill in the South End that were rapidly becoming Irish slums. By 1851, there were fifteen hundred shops selling liquor in the city, nine hundred run by Irishmen, and most of these sold only liquor, making no pretense of being a tavern or inn.[67] Arrests by the police and detentions in Boston's limited jail cells skyrocketed. By the late 1850s, those being arrested and detained were overwhelmingly Irish born, outnumbering all others combined.[68] The city's police force grew rapidly, from twelve regular patrol officers in 1846 to sixty-six by 1851. Not one of them was Irish. With the force's growing numbers came its first police chief, the authoritarian Francis Tukey, who amassed near-dictatorial powers as the city's head of public health as well as its chief constable. Tukey stoutly opposed the movement in 1851 to add even a single Irishman, Barney McGinniskin, to the force. Police expenditures quadrupled between Marshal Tukey's appointment in 1846 and 1851. Night raids on suspected dens of vice in the Irish slums became a common tactic of the police. The Boston police force increasingly emphasized its paramilitary aspects, with formal uniforms and the use of firearms issued to the constables.[69]

Theodore Parker, the transcendentalist minister of Boston's Twenty-Eighth Congregational Society, assessed the rapidly changing character of the city in a powerful sermon titled "The Moral Condition of Boston," preached on February 11, 1849. As a biblical text, Parker drew on the same passage from 1 Samuel 7:12 that Cotton Mather had used a century and a half earlier when he preached a similar sermon, "The Bostonian Ebenezer: Some Historical Remarks on the State of Boston." But where Mather's celebratory history of Boston cited the prophet Samuel—"Hitherto the Lord hath helped us"—in order to describe "some agreeable methods for preserving and promoting the good state" of the city, Parker offered a dire warning about Boston's low moral condition and fear for a calamitous future.[70]

At the heart of Parker's jeremiad lay his claim that "trade is to Boston what the Church is to Rome and the Imperial Court is to St. Petersburg:—it is the pendulum which regulates all the common and authorized machinery of the place."[71] As in these other cities, Boston's regulating pendulum had become an idol. Now "love of money is out of proportion to love of better things"—a sin apparent in the way that landlords and shopkeepers preyed on the immigrants, charging exorbitant rents and prices for squalid hovels and shoddy goods. The result was an epidemic of poverty in the city, and with poverty came barbarism, intemperance, and crime.[72] Boston's jeremiad tradition was more than two centuries old by the time of Parker's sermon. Blaming moral decay on the love of money is as old as morality and money. Yet Parker's analysis differed from earlier jeremiads in asserting that the cause for Boston's poverty, intemperance, and crime "is of foreign origin; we are to deal with it, to be blamed if we allow it to continue; not at all to be blamed for its origin." Parker's point was not to fault the Irish for their misery. Parker blamed the British government and the Catholic Church for their failure to educate the people of Ireland and prepare them for self-government.[73] Rather, the novel element in Parker's rendition of Boston's oldest rhetorical genre was his stark separation of the city into the civilized and the barbarous, the native proprietors of a cultural tradition and the alien barbarians: "*they* will violate *our* laws." Parker remained optimistic that through the redirection of the city's resources, both material and moral, the reformers' goals could be attained. But now, even for Boston's most progressive, open-minded, and tolerant intellectual leaders, the city was no longer imaginable as a unified space tending to the cultivation of its own. Boston had become a place of *us* versus *them*, and would continue to be so as far as Parker saw it: "This increase of foreigners is prodigious: more than half the children in your public schools are children of foreigners; there are more Catholic than Protestant children born in Boston."[74]

Theodore Parker's wary optimism of 1849, like that of many of his fellow self-styled reformers, would dissipate over the next decade. For even if native Bostonians could harness the resources and the will to ameliorate the "foreign" problems that Parker identified, the resurgence of national conflict over slavery and its expansion would drive the city's old order to tear itself apart from within. Parker was the grandson of the militia captain who defended Lexington against the onslaught of the redcoats on April 19, 1775. He soon joined radicals like William Lloyd Garrison and Charles Follen in the abolitionist movement, accompanied by other scions of old Boston families: Wendell Phillips, son of the city's first mayor; Thomas Wentworth Higginson, son of a Boston merchant and grandson of a member of the Continental Congress; Edmund Quincy, the congressman and mayor's son; and Samuel E. Sewall, namesake and direct descendant of the puritan merchant and judge. New leaders of talent and dynamism joined the cause as well: Samuel Howe, Charles Sumner, Horace Mann, Samuel May, Ellis Gray Loring, and Amasa Walker. But this group was arrayed against an equally formidable set of talented, wealthy, and powerful figures, the lords of the loom, represented by Amos and Abbott Lawrence, Nathan Appleton, Robert Winthrop, Edward Everett, George Ticknor, the Lowells, the Cabots, and their political champion, Daniel Webster. It was already clear in 1835, at the near lynching of Garrison, that these divisions ran deep among the working people of Boston whose livelihoods depended on cotton. The huge influx of Irish immigrants only deepened them.

Ironically, Garrison and the abolitionists had once hoped that the Irish would be natural supporters of the antislavery cause as a result of their own oppression at the hands of their British overlords. Indeed, Garrison named his newspaper the *Liberator* in honor of Ireland's Daniel O'Connell, who earned that nickname fighting for Irish Catholic emancipation and against West Indian slavery. As late as 1842, Charles Remond, a black abolitionist from Salem, returned from a lecture tour in Ireland with a petition signed by O'Connell and sixty thousand other Irishmen, urging their Irish American countrymen to "unite with the abolitionists" to liberate enslaved

African Americans.[75] Yet the increase in Irish immigrants after 1845, whose employment options were limited to the most menial jobs, exacerbated Irish fears that liberated slaves would shove them off even the lowest rung on the social ladder.[76]

The great wave of Irish immigrants and their segregation in the city's poorest neighborhoods was the last stage in the spatial dismemberment of Boston in the years following its incorporation. With the dismantling of its military defenses, large-scale land making, and consequent reorientation toward the mainland, and with the division of Boston into competing wards and increasingly stratified neighborhoods, the development of ethnic and religious conflict completed the slow process of breaking down the spatial integrity of the old colonial capital. But in the unprecedented internal violence that erupted over the city's relationship to slavery, the very idea of what Boston had always stood for would be tested beyond endurance.

Chapter 12

"There Was a Boston Once"

> I would wish, candidly, however, before the Lord, to be understood, that I would not give a pinch of snuff to be married to any white person I ever saw in all the days of my life.
>
> —David Walker, *An Appeal to the Colored Citizens of the World*, 1829

Throughout its existence, Boston, after the fashion of most city-states through the ages, had been willing to form alliances with larger entities, even to fight for them, so long as its internal autonomy was preserved and it was not governed by hostile forces. Twice in its history, in 1689 and 1775, Bostonians committed themselves to open rebellion in the name of these ideals, each time at great risk but with remarkable success. They approached this prospect again early in the nineteenth century. In 1814, they failed to withdraw from or rebel against the United States as they had against British monarchs, but not because the United States were so strong. Rather, the American republic seemed so weak, even on the verge of collapse, that it was difficult to envision that Boston would long be under Virginia's thumb. In the aftermath of the surprising events that rescued the Madison administration and preserved US authority over New England, Boston's leaders restructured its economy and launched a new set of cultural projects. They set out to re-create Boston as the Athens of America, yet in the process imported cultural and political imperatives that would make it impossible to hold the city-state together.

One of those imperatives, most fully embodied in the character of Karl Follen, the "unconditional" German radical who married into Boston's Cabot family, was a commitment to equality among men that was blind to racial distinctions. This commitment was reinforced by a belief that moral convictions stood higher than the laws of states, and by a willingness to consider violent means to bring about ethical ends. But as Follen's position found allies among Bostonians, black and white, male and female, it brought increased attention to the growing conflict among Boston's population with respect to race and ethnicity, and to the intimate level of family life and relations between the sexes, where further fissures emerged. Despite often sharing a common vision of a more equitable and charitable world, in many ways consistent with the founders' aspirations two centuries before, Boston's reformers nonetheless split themselves into warring camps over matters of race and sex. If the previous chapter traced the spatial dismemberment of Boston, its division into clashing neighborhoods, ethnic groups, and social classes, here I turn to the destruction of the ideals that had held the city-state of Boston together for so long.

These internal chasms dividing Boston mirrored similar divisions across the nation as a whole. As Boston's economy became increasingly integrated with the Cotton Kingdom, and as the reach of Boston's magnetic power over the issue of slavery began to take in the whole country as its hinterland, the city staged an internal version of the war that would tear the nation asunder. As a last-ditch effort to rescue the Athens of America, Bostonians reached for new theories of mind and spirit, desperate to find reform measures that could salvage a corporate cohesion that was fast slipping away. But the cure failed to take. The city's internal turmoil intensified as the nation's bonds of unity crumbled, and Boston witnessed a cascade of violence. A microcosm of the nation in which it was ever more tightly embedded, Boston tore itself apart.

"Extravasat Blood": Racial Segregation in the Corporate City

To external observers, one of colonial New England's most striking features was the homogeneity of its population's ethnic origins, religious commitments, and cultural values. The migration of twenty thousand English Puritans to Massachusetts in the 1630s, and their good health, long lives, and large families, quickly filled up New England's limited arable lands. By the eighteenth century, when large numbers of more ethnically diverse migrants started to arrive in British America, these German and Scots Irish migrants saw little to attract them to New England. Colonization had destroyed or displaced most of the Indians of southern New England by the late seventeenth century, and there had been little cross-cultural amalgamation between English and Indians; puritan missionaries attempted to create separate "praying Indian" communities rather than intermingle the English population with Christianized Indians.

The homogeneity of the English population was enhanced by the political economies of early New England towns, including Boston. Strict efforts to control labor markets resulted in town "warning out" laws that prohibited the permanent settlement of unwanted laborers.[1] Boston also used its political power to shelter the city from religious or cultural threats, from the famous Order in Court of 1637 to discourage the immigration of further "antinomian" supporters of Anne Hutchinson, to the violent measures taken against Quakers in the 1650s and the resistance to Anglicanism in the 1680s. Boston's homogeneity, its cultural exclusivity, had always been both a strength and a weakness, a source of pride and shame. A sense of common identity made it easier for Boston, more than most colonial cities, to sustain the goals that John Winthrop articulated: "That they might be all knitt more nearly together in the Bond of brotherly affeccion," and "that every man afford his help to another in every want or distresse." Yet religious and ethnic homogeneity tended to promote a restrictive interpretation of the golden rule, limited to those who were "a brother in Christ allsoe, and in the communion of the same Spirit."[2] Although some ethnically divergent immigrants like the Huguenots were comfortably able to share "communion of the same Spirit" with Boston's dominant culture, most would find it difficult.

During the city's first two centuries, enslaved Africans were the most visible minority population, working everywhere from the waterfront docks to merchants' mansions. In the mid-eighteenth century, Africans comprised as much as 8 to 10 percent of the city's population of roughly fifteen thousand. Most Africans were enslaved and lived under the roofs of their masters, so they were dispersed widely throughout the city.[3] Even though they were not geographically segregated, widespread racial prejudice kept them a people apart from the white majority. Samuel Sewall, among the more sympathetic Englishmen toward Africans in colonial Boston and the first outspoken voice against the slave trade, declared in *The Selling of Joseph* that blacks would always remain outsiders: "There is such a disparity in their Conditions, Color & Hair, that they can never embody with us, and grow up into orderly Families, to the Peopling of the Land; but still remain in our Body Politick as a kind of extravasat Blood."[4] Extravasat blood literally meant blood extruded from its natural place within the arteries and veins, and instead spread harmfully among bodily tissues, like a bruise. Figuratively, Sewall meant that African slaves in Massachusetts might live within the corporate body's perimeter, but would never function as an integral part of the body politic.

Slave emancipation in the 1780s transformed earlier demographic patterns and rendered Sewall's metaphor visible on a map of the city. No longer housed by their masters, Boston's free blacks began to congregate in neighborhoods with cheap housing and proximity to employment opportunities, at first in the North End near the wharves and increasingly in the West End on the northern side of Beacon Hill—the cold, dark side that came to be known as "Negro Hill." In these newly concentrated residential districts, members of the black community organized new institutions to promote their own welfare.[5] Among these were the African Mutual Aid Society (1796); the African Masonic Lodge founded by Prince Hall after the revolution and later renamed in his honor; a privately funded African School (the Smith School, founded in 1798); and a growing number of literary societies, dramatic clubs, musical groups, and benevolent organizations.[6]

Equally important were the new African churches, starting with Thomas Paul and Scipio Dalton's 1805 founding of the African Baptist Church in Smith Court on Beacon Hill. This was followed by the African Methodist Episcopal (AME) Church in 1818, then a

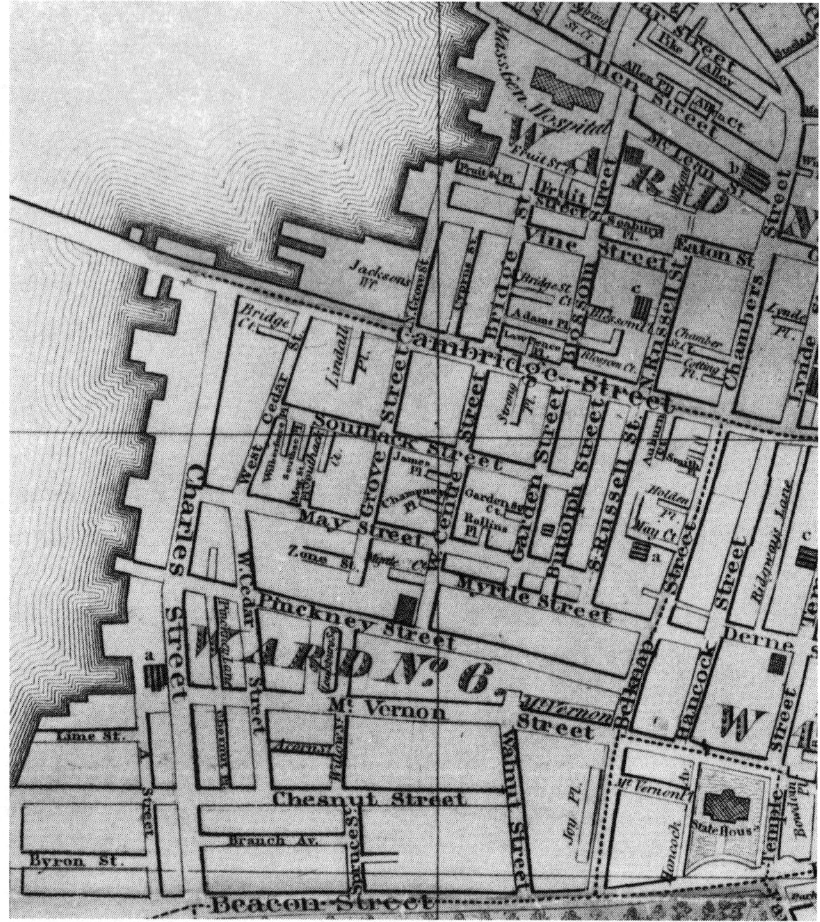

Map 12.1. *Plan of Boston, Comprising a Part of Charlestown and Cambridge*, by George G. Smith, 1846. Detail. Antebellum Boston's black neighborhood formed in the northern half of Ward 6, between Myrtle and Cambridge Streets, and from Belknap Street down to Charles Street.

second AME church that broke away from the first in the 1830s, an African Methodist Episcopal Zion Church in 1838, and the Twelfth Baptist Church from a division within the African Baptist Church. All five churches built their meetinghouses within the five- to six-block confines of the West End where Boston's black population was now concentrated.[7]

Each of these institutions produced new community leaders. Some were clergymen like Thomas Paul, Leonard Grimes, Samuel

Snowden, John T. Raymond, Jehial Beman, and John Sella Martin. Others were business and social leaders like the craftsman Prince Hall, dry goods dealers David Walker and Lewis Hayden, barbers Peter Howard and James Barbadoes, education activist William Cooper Nell, temperance organizers Jane Putnam and Susan Paul, political activist Maria Stewart, and medical practitioner and lawyer John Swett Rock.[8] But their organizations were also the product of segregationist impulses in white Boston society, an "extravasation" (to borrow Sewall's archaic term) of blacks from churches and other societies where they had once been part of the communal body. Early in the nineteenth century, James Easton, a successful blacksmith, was ejected from his church for refusing to sit in the "negro gallery." When he bought a pew for his family in another church, the white members first tried to cancel the purchase and then spread tar on the pew to prevent the Eastons from using it. Similar racial segregation began to appear in Boston's schools, theaters, and other public places as well as on streetcars, horse-drawn omnibuses, and later "negro cars" on passenger railroads.[9]

At the same time, public attacks and insults from whites against blacks seemed to be increasing, much as Yankee violence against the Irish would soon increase too. David Walker, in an 1828 speech, commented on "the very derision, violence, and oppression, with which we as a part of the community are treated by a benevolent and Christian people." Hosea Easton noted how "universally common" it was for blacks in the streets of Boston to be taunted by whites about their "physical features, intellectual capacities, and poverty."[10] Popular white print culture derided the cultural activities of the black community, such as the annual July 14 parade commemorating the abolition of the Atlantic slave trade, which the Boston press grotesquely lampooned as "Bobalition Day."[11] This intensifying racial hostility, unlike the parallel Yankee hostility toward the Irish, played out against the backdrop of a relative *decline* in Boston's black population, increasingly concentrated in one or two narrow corners of the city.[12] By 1860, Boston had become the most racially segregated major city in the United States.[13]

FIGURE 12.1. *Grand Bobalition of Slavery!!*, broadside, 1819. Detail.

Boston's black leaders responded with a new form of black radicalism, beginning in the mid-1820s by founding the Massachusetts General Colored Association, designed not only to promote the interests and equality of blacks in Boston but also to address the plight of Africans in the larger Atlantic world. Several of its leaders, including Walker, took part in the publication of *Freedom's Journal*, the first national black newspaper, which staunchly opposed the American Colonization Society's plans to repatriate free blacks to Africa.[14]

David Walker was a remarkable figure. Born in North Carolina to at least one free black parent, he learned to read and write through the auspices of the Methodist Church. Walker made his way as a young man to Charleston, South Carolina, where he was exposed to the city's separate free black churches and the wider world of communications that the South's leading seaport offered.[15] Walker focused his attention on the brutality of American slavery, especially in the wake of Charleston's ferocious suppression of the alleged Denmark Vesey insurrection conspiracy of 1822.[16] Shortly thereafter, Walker made his way north to Boston. He arrived sometime late in 1824, joined Samuel Snowden's AME church and Prince Hall's

Masonic Lodge, married a Boston woman named Eliza Butler, opened a second-hand clothing shop on Brattle Street near other black-owned businesses, and moved to Belknap Street on the north slope of Beacon Hill.[17]

Walker's trajectory is a pattern that we have seen many times before. Boston was a magnet for talented young people from the hinterland. Daniel Webster had likewise settled in Boston—on the fashionable south slope of Beacon Hill—just eight years before. But for Walker and black Bostonians, the pattern had two striking differences. First, Boston's hinterland in the 1820s now included the entire Cotton Kingdom, at least with respect to free blacks and fugitive slaves, who looked to Boston as a place of safety and opportunity, despite its prejudices. A remarkable number of Boston's black leaders shared Walker's background as a free black or former slave from the American South or the West Indies. Among them were Hall, Snowden, Grimes, Nell, Barbadoes, Martin, and Hayden. Their life patterns reflect a larger trend. In the decades before the Civil War, the city's population included an increasing number of southern-born and a declining number of Boston-born blacks.[18] The second difference is that white Boston's prejudices prevented talented blacks like Walker from rising any further than the top of Boston's highly segregated African community. They were excluded from the heights of power, fame, or authority in the body of the city as a whole. Thus it was from a privileged and yet circumscribed position that David Walker published his coruscating pamphlet *An Appeal to the Colored Citizens of the World* (1829).

The radical quality of Walker's pamphlet and the hardening of racial divisions in Boston can be seen by comparison to similar publications from earlier eras in the city's history, such as Samuel Sewall's *The Selling of Joseph* or Phillis Wheatley's poetry. Like these predecessors, Walker's *Appeal* sets the problem of American slavery in the context of biblical history as well as the history of the Atlantic world. While Sewall had denounced the selling of Joseph, and Wheatley had assumed the position and power of Joseph in her poetry, Walker's *Appeal* indicts white Christian America's treatment of Africans by comparison with the Egyptians' treatment of the children of Israel and Pharaoh's empowerment of Joseph: "I make this extract [from Genesis] to show how much lower we are held, and how much more cruel we are treated by the Americans, than were the children of Jacob, by the Egyptians."[19] Wheatley's hopes that Africans in Britain's colonies would eventually receive the benefits of Joseph under a benevolent empire of liberty had clearly not been realized in the first four decades of US independence. There arose a king in Egypt—King Cotton—who knew not Joseph.

Wheatley had been confident that the Christian liberty promoted by New England orthodoxy would reform the British Empire. Walker, equally committed to evangelical Protestantism, argues that it has been perverted by the Pharisees of white American Christianity. His *Appeal* proclaims that the "Coloured Citizens of the World" are the possessors of true Christianity. They are the actual body of Christ in the world, they alone can bring the kingdom of God to all nations, and as a free black Christian, Walker is a full citizen only in this community.[20] Free blacks in American cities like Boston, where slavery has been abolished, are still only partially free so long as they remain under the dominion of the United States.[21] Walker admonished the white majority not to think that their "charitable deeds to the Greeks, Irish, &c" would compensate for their crimes against Africans.[22] In addition to castigating white America, Walker's *Appeal* aims to rouse Africans from their subservience, to dispel the illusion that they are not self-possessed and that their claim to a birthright in America is any less than their white overlords.[23] Walker reserves his most virulent attacks for the colonization movement and its attempts to "return" freed slaves to Africa. In Walker's view, the Colonization Society's motive was not Christian duty to free blacks but rather the desire to transform free Americans into commodities for overseas export. By deporting free blacks and silencing their voices, America would keep the nation's slaves in wretched ignorance.[24]

Samuel Sewall—wealthy merchant, council member, and superior court judge—spoke from a position of privilege and authority when he declared in 1700 that Africans could never "embody with *us*," that black men could never . . . make husbands for "*our* daughters." The teenage slave girl Phillis Wheatley displayed a preternatural confidence in her ability to speak for New England as a whole, as when she thanked the Earl of Dartmouth for restoring the colony's liberty. In 1829, David Walker rejected Wheatley's optimism in the potential for Africans to become fully incorporated in Boston's society and turned the tables on Sewall's rhetoric of exclusion: "I would wish, candidly, however, before the Lord, to be understood, that I would not give a *pinch of snuff* to be married to any white person I ever saw in all the days of my life."[25] As a newcomer to this homogeneous and exclusive city, Walker rejected the notion that he or his fellow colored citizens had any interest in embodying with white people in a single corporate whole. Two centuries of mistreatment at the hands of American pharaohs had squelched any such desire.

To spread his insurrectionary pamphlet beyond Boston, Walker, like Sewall before him, relied on commercial contacts in Atlantic seafaring and religious communities. As a used clothing merchant, Walker enclosed copies of his *Appeal* in packages of cheap garments made in New England textile mills from cotton produced by slaves. Through the efforts of dockworkers, ship stewards, sailors, black clergymen, and missionaries, Walker's message was distributed in southern seaports, where it generated hostile reactions from white authorities. Savannah, Richmond, and other southern cities passed new restrictive laws against free blacks. In Virginia and the Carolinas, free blacks and whites were arrested for possessing or distributing Walker's pamphlet.[26] When William Lloyd Garrison began publishing the *Liberator* in 1831, Boston's radicalized black community, already opposed to gradualist measures and colonization, came to his support. Black Bostonians lent their strength to the movement that would soon attract white Bostonians such as Wendell Phillips, Charles Follen, and Lydia Maria Child, who were willing to alienate themselves from the city's social and political elites.[27] Although the heavily segregated black community gained a tiny number of allies among white radical reformers, they also suffered tremendous enmity from the white majority. This hatred would plague the city for a generation in the form of escalating violence, especially as the slave states came to resent what a magnet for fugitives Boston had become.

"The Body Comprehends Men and Women of Every Shade and Color"

From the city's earliest days, women of intellect, ambition, and talent had occasionally made a mark on Boston's public culture, from Anne Hutchinson and Anne Bradstreet in the founding generation, to Phillis Wheatley, Mercy Otis Warren, and Hannah Adams in the revolutionary era. Women were never a minority in the city. As in many a seaport that sent its men off to dangerous maritime work, females usually outnumbered males in Boston's population. But until the early nineteenth century, Boston remained a traditional society in its patriarchal domestic arrangements. The family, the little commonwealth, was the basic unit of society, and the household head was usually male. The voices speaking and writing within the greater commonwealth of state and church were expected to be husbands and fathers, who represented their dependents: wives, children, servants, or slaves. No clearer example could be offered than the life of Abigail Adams, whose remarkable gifts for politics and language are better known today than they were to her contemporaries.[28] *We* know that in spring 1776, she asked her husband John to "Remember the Ladies" in any "new Code of Laws which I suppose it will be necessary" for the Continental Congress to make. At the time, though, her advice was buried in personal correspondence, not broadcast in public.[29]

In the years after American independence, this traditional pattern began to change. The impetus of revolutionary rhetoric about equality and liberty, together with the wartime experiences of thousands of women, inspired new confidence in women's capacities, including their suitability for higher education. The shifting structure of family life and women's responsibilities brought on by changes in the workplace, especially in urban America, also brought women greater public visibility, as did the influence of new modes of religious belief and expression.[30] Hannah Adams

(1755–1831), who gained fame as a historian, the first woman to be admitted to the library of the Boston Athenaeum, was a transitional figure. Her talents were obvious to those who knew her, and her unusual social circumstances allowed exceptions to be made for her. Bereft of family support from an early age, Adams never married, and made her living from her reading and writing skills. Her first publication, a dispassionate survey of world religions, appeared in 1784 and went through four editions. She subsequently published a history of New England, several defenses of Christianity, and in 1812, *A History of the Jews*.[31]

Beyond exceptions like these, the first sign of significant change in the gender dynamics of Boston's public culture burst forth in the 1830s. A new generation of women born in Boston or its hinterland after 1800 stepped forward as public speakers, writers, and organizers, exerting a powerful influence on civic affairs. Among the notable figures in this cohort (not unlike the cohort of young men who went to Göttingen after 1815) were Lydia Maria Child (1802–80), Dorothea Dix (1802–87), Maria Stewart (1803–80), Sophia Willard Dana Ripley (1803–61), Prudence Crandall (1803–90), Maria Weston Chapman (1806–85), Margaret Fuller (1810–50), and Abby Kelley Foster (1811–87). Several older or younger outliers also joined the activism of this cohort, including Eliza Cabot Follen (1787–1860), Lucy Stone (1818–93), and Julia Ward Howe (1819–1910). The young men who journeyed to Göttingen were supported by Boston's economic and political elites. By contrast, the generation of women who forged a public presence in the 1830s risked being treated as pariahs by polite society because of their commitments to antislavery and radical social reform. Among the first to take this risk were Maria Stewart and Lydia Maria Child.

A free black woman, Stewart was born Maria Miller in Hartford, Connecticut, orphaned at age five, and bound out as a servant in a clergyman's family, where she learned to read and write. Somehow she made her way to Boston and married James W. Stewart, but was widowed in 1829. In that year, Walker published his *Appeal to the Colored Citizens of the World*, which powerfully influenced Stewart. She wrote, "Many will suffer for pleading the cause of oppressed

Africa . . . and I shall glory in being one of her martyrs. . . . God is able to take me to himself, as he did the most noble, fearless and undaunted David Walker." When Garrison launched the *Liberator* in 1831, Stewart approached him with the manuscript of this essay, which Garrison published as *Religion and the Pure Principles of Morality, the Sure Foundation on Which We Must Build*. The following year Garrison encouraged her to accept public speaking engagements, and Stewart began in Boston's Franklin Hall on September 21, 1832, where she followed Walker's lead by attacking the colonization movement.

Over the next two years, Stewart moved from arguing for the rights of African Americans to insisting on the rights of black *women* "to develop their highest intellectual capacities, to enter, without apology, into all spheres of the life of the mind, . . . from religion and education to politics and business."[32] Stewart encouraged black women to pool their resources to fund higher education for themselves. With education they might escape from domestic service jobs little better than the slavery of the South. In 1831, Stewart joined in forming the African American Female Intelligence Society of Boston (AAFIS), even before Garrison and his colleagues organized the New England Anti-Slavery Society. In one of Stewart's addresses to the AAFIS, she referred to the recent Greek revolution to call on free black women similarly to unite their efforts in the cause of African liberation.[33] After a "Farewell Address" in 1833, however, Stewart abruptly ended her speaking career (though she lived another forty years). Little evidence remains to explain her decision, but her farewell address alludes to the "ridicule" and the "profound current of prejudice that flows against us at present."[34]

As a white woman, Child criticized the prejudice that Stewart suffered, and was herself ostracized for her efforts. She was born Lydia Francis, a baker's daughter from Medford, the town north of Boston through which Paul Revere galloped on his midnight ride. Her older brother Convers Francis went to Harvard Divinity School and became a Unitarian minister. When their mother died in 1814, Child, the youngest of five children, moved in with a married sister on the Maine frontier until her brother invited her to join him in the parsonage of his new church in Watertown, just west of Boston.[35] Over the next decade, inspired by her brother's literary connections, Child wrote novels, children's literature, and guides for housewives and young mothers. Beginning with *Hobomok: A Tale of Early Times* (1824), and then with the founding in 1826 of the *Juvenile Miscellany*, America's first children's magazine, she became a popular author, producing several more novels including *The Rebels: or, Boston Before the Revolution* (1825) and publishing *The American Frugal Housewife* (1829), which went through more than thirty editions. In 1828, she married David Lee Child, a Boston lawyer and editor of the *Massachusetts Journal*, and seemed well on the way to a promising literary career.

Their political convictions brought the Childs closer to the radical antislavery circle forming around Garrison. As early as 1830, Garrison had identified Child as "the first woman of the republic"—both a tribute to her literary talent and an expression of hope that she would join the cause. Inspired by Garrison's *Liberator* and Walker's *Appeal*, Child now directly addressed issues of racial justice that she had foreshadowed in *Hobomok* and in stories she had written for *Juvenile Miscellany*, including a sympathetic account of the Haitian Revolution and opposition to President Andrew Jackson's Indian removal. The Childs joined Garrison's New England Anti-Slavery Society at its founding in 1832. Even while she was composing guidebooks to domestic life, Child conducted research in the Boston Athenaeum, where her literary success had won her membership privileges, on the history of slavery, the slave trade, and the condition of Africans in the United States. In 1833, Child published *An Appeal in Favor of That Class of Americans Called Africans*. Its title paid tribute to Walker's *Appeal*, but its force was directed more to white Americans and their prejudices than to the "Colored Citizens of the World."

Like Walker's, Child's *Appeal* is an extraordinary work of polemical scholarship. She traces the history of Atlantic slavery from the Portuguese in fifteenth-century West Africa to the modern United States. She demonstrates slavery's "inevitable effect upon all concerned in it," including her fellow New Englanders, to be a brutal coarsening of human character and society.[36] Child's pioneering work offered a comparative study of slavery throughout human history, using fourteen "distinct propositions" to show how modern US slave codes are more brutal and dehumanizing than those of the ancient Hebrews, Greece and Rome, Slavic Europe, and modern French and Iberian systems. She reviews arguments from contemporary political economy to prove that free labor is more productive than slave labor and that emancipation can be accomplished safely without economic damage. Child explains how slavery has warped American politics, giving the slave states "an undue advantage, which they have maintained with anxious jealousy."[37] She echoes the many arguments of Fisher Ames and Josiah Quincy regarding the national taxing power, the embargo, and the War of 1812 to demonstrate how slavery distorts representative government.

Like Walker, Child denounces the American Colonization Society for its tendency "to put public opinion asleep, on a subject where it needs to be wide awake," and champions the immediate abolitionist position of the New England Anti-Slavery Society.[38] She asserts that Africans and Europeans are intellectual and moral equals, and cites dozens of examples, from Queen Zhinga of Angola to Phillis Wheatley and Toussaint l'Ouverture, to make her case. Finally, Child attacks the prejudice of white Americans against people of color, insisting that northern bigotry "is even more inveterate than it is at the South," denouncing Massachusetts laws against interracial marriage, and reminding her readers that Boston shares in the guilt of slavery: "Several fortunes in this city have been made by the sale of Negro blood."[39]

By ending her attack with a denunciation of Boston's prejudices, Child knew that like Stewart before her, she would be subject to "gross ridicule."[40] Her fears were more than fulfilled. After her *Appeal* appeared in print, subscriptions to *Juvenile Miscellany* withered away, sales of her novels dried up, and her books went out of print. Family and friends snubbed the Childs, Lydia was ostracized from literary salons, and the Athenaeum revoked her library privileges.[41] George Ticknor, who had patronized her literary efforts in the 1820s, "cut her dead in the street."[42]

Only the tiny group of Boston abolitionists received Child's *Appeal* with enthusiasm. Child quickly became a force in the circle of Garrison and Follen, and her work drew new converts to the cause. John Gorham Palfrey, Wendell Phillips, Thomas Wentworth Higginson, and Charles Sumner all attested to the power of Child's book in swaying their opinions.[43] In addition, her *Appeal* inspired William Ellery Channing, Boston's leading Unitarian minister, held in the highest esteem by the city's merchant and industrial elites, to publish his own antislavery (though not overtly abolitionist) tract in 1835.[44] Channing, by throwing the great weight of his reputation behind a moderate antislavery position, made it impossible for any literate, thinking Bostonian *not* to have an opinion on slavery. Like Thomas Paine's *Common Sense* on the independence question in 1776, Child's radical *Appeal* forced the slavery question to the center of public discourse in Boston. But it had the further effect of entwining the controversy over women's public role with the issue of slavery.

In fall 1833, a dozen women formed the Boston Female Anti-Slavery Society (BFASS), which played a central role in the city's antislavery agitation and became a proving ground for politically active women in Boston. Child's friend and supporter, Maria Weston Chapman, took the organizational lead but was soon joined by dozens of other women, both white and black. By 1835, there were more than a hundred members.[45] The BFASS organized an annual Christmas fair, the Boston Anti-Slavery Bazaar, to raise money for Garrison's *Liberator* and the American Anti-Slavery Society. Chapman, Child, Follen, and other society members produced *The Liberty Bell* to be sold at the Bazaar, an annual gift book with contributions from female and male authors, both white and black, promoting the abolitionist cause.[46]

The BFASS could offer women a platform for political activism precisely because it was on the fringes of social approval. Even so, the propriety of women seeking such an active public role caused

FIGURE 12.2. Portrait of Lydia Maria Child, photographer unknown, no date.

violent controversy. Just as the 1834 destruction of the Ursuline convent in Charlestown carried an undercurrent of animosity toward the education of the daughters of Unitarian elites, so the violence against Garrison in October 1835 was intensified by the fact that English abolitionist George Thompson's lecture was supposed to take place at a meeting of the BFASS. The mostly male crowd's rage

FIGURE 12.3. Portrait of Maria Weston Chapman, daguerreotype, ca. 1846.

was directed at politicized women as well as at abolitionists. In addition to nearly lynching Garrison and threatening the hundred women in attendance, the mob of several thousand "respectable" Bostonians attacked the organization's sign on the building's exterior; it was taken down "and torn into a thousand pieces by the enraged multitude."[47] In her annual report for 1836, Chapman recounted the attack in order to prove that abolition was an appropriate cause for women. The mob's attack was so ferocious precisely because their male critics knew the power of women as consumers: slavery would end if all women agreed to purchase only "the product[s] of free labor, in preference to those produced by the labor of the slave."[48]

Challenges to women's activism were not limited to violent opponents of abolition; they also appeared within the movement itself. Abolitionists anticipated social ostracism, as when Karl Follen lost his Harvard professorship, but there were many men in the movement, along with conservative women, who disapproved of female activism, fearing that agitation for women's rights would divert attention from immediatist abolition.[49] In 1836, Child published a novel, *Philothea, A Romance*, set in ancient Athens, exploring the title character's struggle over the role of women in society, especially a slave society in which "Grecian women" were treated little better "than mere domestic slaves."[50] But over the next three years, these debates split the abolitionist movement. Massachusetts' orthodox clergymen issued a pastoral letter, read from every Congregational pulpit in the commonwealth, denouncing women who dared to be "public reformers." The evangelicals withdrew from the New England Anti-Slavery Society when Garrison insisted that women could take part in its proceedings, and formed a new antislavery society that excluded women. In 1840, the BFASS likewise dissolved when a conservative faction denounced Garrisonian "Non-Resistance, Women's Rights, &c."[51]

A decade after David Walker and Maria Stewart created an opening for women's activism through radical abolitionism, the movement had splintered, torn apart by "a new order of things" in gender and race relations.[52] In 1839, Harriet Martineau, the English sociological writer and radical sympathizer, a Bostonian by heart if not by birth, reviewed these tumultuous years in *The Martyr Age of the United States*.[53] She painted a striking picture of "the abolitionists of the United States" as a remarkable set of people

> with a consonance of will and understanding which has perhaps never been witnessed among so large a number of indi-

> viduals of such diversified powers, habits, opinions, tastes, and circumstances. *The body* comprehends men and women of every shade of color, of every degree of education, of every variety of religious opinion, of every gradation of rank, bound together by no vow, no pledge, no stipulation but of each preserving his individual liberty; and yet they act as if they were of one heart and of one soul.[54]

Martineau exaggerated the unity of a movement that was actually on the verge of schism. Her description of abolitionism's internal qualities was exactly the opposite of what was happening in Boston, where divisions over race, education, rank, religion, and gender were more contentious than ever before. But most startling is her choice of an organic metaphor to identify the movement's nature. Martineau was describing a quite abstract "body," a kind of invisible church, dispersed and made of disparate parts, not concentrated in a single space—in that way unlike the organic polity, the harmonious physical community, that Bostonians had been pursuing since the days of Winthrop and Cotton. Martineau's image of the abolitionist movement is reminiscent of Walker's invocation of the "Colored Citizens of the World" as the true body of Christ—an idealistic vision, but like Walker, abandoning hope that blacks and whites might embody in one place as a single people.

A Phrenological Solution?

Amid Boston's wrenching divisions—spatial, racial, religious, ethnic, gender, class, and political divisions all twisted one around the next—one hopeful remedy, one promise for a new way to cure the ailments of the social body, was embraced by Boston's liberal elites. Its origins, like many other intellectual currents of the time, lay in German universities, in a new science called phrenology. Its doctrines offered a program for individual and communal improvement that was tremendously appealing to Boston's Unitarian leaders. And in 1832, it arrived in Boston in the person of Johann Gaspar Spurzheim.

Spurzheim was born in 1776 in the Rhineland and studied at the University of Vienna under Franz Joseph Gall, a German anatomist.

Gall pioneered efforts to connect the physiology of the human brain to specific mental faculties and personal characteristics.[55] Spurzheim learned dissection from Gall, and adopted Gall's system of correspondences between organs of the brain and personality characteristics. But Spurzheim broke from his mentor by extending phrenology from a science of mind and brain into a philosophical system. Spurzheim wanted to transform the commonplace notion that external appearances were signs of inner qualities into an exact science, useful for living people. Postmortem dissections were not much good if they could only show that virtuous people had virtuous brains, or that criminals' brains had criminal features. Spurzheim's goal was to make anatomical findings into methods for promoting health, virtue, and social order.

Central to Spurzheim's system was his belief in the organic connection between the individual body and the social realm. Disease, disorder, and sin, whether personal or social, were caused by imbalances, excesses in the function of one or more organic elements, and deficiencies in others. This was not a Manichean system; for Spurzheim there were no bad or evil organs of the brain, any more than there were inherently bad people in society or evil races among the nations. Gall had believed that there were organs of the brain associated with "murder" and "theft," but Spurzheim argued instead that these sinful behaviors were caused by excesses or imbalances in otherwise-useful portions of the brain such as "destructiveness" and "acquisitiveness." The mutual health and balanced functioning of all the varied parts in nature were necessary for the well-being of the individual body and for social harmony.[56]

Spurzheim and his followers believed that they were reconciling science with religion, making room for free will and moral action within a world otherwise explained by materialistic determinism. In the post-Calvinist world of liberal Christianity, the belief that the mind was the product of the brain's material form and its relationship to the body, and that these physical and mental characteristics could be inherited from one generation to the next, was a satisfactory substitute for the abandoned doctrine of original sin. It salvaged the belief that the sins of the fathers (now redefined as bodily defects) were visited on the children to the third and fourth generations. But phrenology offered a complementary doctrine: the defects of brain and body could be remedied through the proper exercise of mental and moral virtues. And these virtues happened to correspond remarkably well with the doctrines of liberal Christianity, to the point that Spurzheim published a tract called *A Philosophical Catechism of the Natural Laws of Man*, which used biblical passages to illustrate phrenology's "natural laws" of human behavior and social relations.[57] Spurzheim's traveling lecture tours were thus a kind of Unitarian variation on George Whitefield's itinerant evangelical preaching a century earlier, replete with attacks from skeptics, triumphal conversions of doubters into believers, and waves of converts fanning out to preach their leader's doctrine.

Like Whitefield, Spurzheim's fame preceded him. He arrived in Boston in August 1832, following a triumphal tour through Britain. He offered lectures for the general public at the Boston Athenaeum, but audiences were so large that he was forced to move to Tremont Temple. He spent his days visiting Boston's "prisons and institutions of beneficence," displaying his "great interest for the welfare of man."[58] Then, at the height of his fame, Spurzheim died. He fell ill in late October with typhus and shuffled off his mortal coil on November 10, 1832.[59] Boston's leading citizens—Harrison Gray Otis, Josiah Quincy, Nathaniel Bowditch (renowned astronomer and authority on celestial navigation), Joseph Story (US Supreme Court justice), and Spurzheim's countryman Karl Follen—organized the funeral, held at the Old South Meeting House and attended by three thousand people, where Follen delivered the eulogy. Spurzheim's body was embalmed, the brain removed and measured (it weighed fifty-seven ounces, or 20 percent more than an average human brain), and the remains buried near the entrance of the newly dedicated Mount Auburn Cemetery. Spurzheim was its first star attraction.[60]

After the funeral, Spurzheim's converts organized the Boston Phrenological Society and named Samuel Howe its recording secretary. For the next decade, the society promoted phrenology in Boston, organized lecture series, and developed an affiliated publishing

FIGURE 12.4. *Tomb of Spurzheim, Mount Auburn Cemetery*, by R. Martin, 1847.

house.[61] Spurzheim had many followers, but none more devoted than Howe, who made phrenology central to all the institutions for social reform that he directed, including the Perkins School for the Blind.[62] In 1837, Howe delivered "A Discourse on the Social Relations of Man" in which he laid out his philosophy as a social reformer, specifically his belief that human intellect, spirit, and morality are all dependent on the body's "corporeal organization." Human moral freedom depended on whether the functioning of the body's "organs is according to the general laws of nature," or whether the "original organization is unnatural" or "becomes diseased." It was imperative for scientific research to study the "certain known laws" of "the human race in general," because the overall condition of society depends "upon the use or abuse, exercise or neglect of his organization, by each individual."[63]

Howe's *Discourse*, written in the same year that he "discovered" Laura Bridgman, illuminates his excitement over the progress of Bridgman's education. Howe believed she provided the opportunity to refute both the Lockean position that the mind was purely a product of sensory experience, and the Calvinist doctrines of original

1848.] SENATE—No. 51. 3

Numbers for reference to names in the MSS.	Actual size, by Measurement, in inches and tenths.								Development of various parts of the cranium, and activity of various mental faculties as compared with that of 1000 ordinary persons of the same age and sex; 10 being the standard among ordinary persons.												
	Depth of Chest.	Width of Chest.	Greatest Circumfer'e of Cranium.	Greatest Diameter of Cranium.	Diameter from the root of the Nose to the Occipital Spine.	Transverse Diameter over the Ears.	Arc of Cranium from root of Nose to Occipital Spine.	Arc from Ear to Ear.	Size of the Lower Frontal Region.	Skill in the use of the Perceptive Faculties	Size of the Upper Frontal Region.	Skill in the use of the Reflective Faculties.	Size of the Lateral Region.	Activity of the Faculties of Self-Preservation.	Size of the Posterior Region.	Activity of the Social Attachments.	Size of the Coronal Region.	Activity of the Moral Sentiments	Size of the Cerebellum.	Activity of the Animal Nature.	Degree of ability to support themselves.

FIGURE 12.5. Table recording physical measurements of Massachusetts "idiots" with respect to phrenological attributes, in S. G. Howe, *Report Made to the Legislature of Massachusetts, upon Idiocy* (Boston, 1848). Detail.

sin and human depravity. By teaching Bridgman to function far beyond expectations for a blind and deaf child, Howe could demonstrate the superiority of phrenological science, linked with Unitarian religion, as a means to bring about individual and social improvement—a method for healing the body and restoring harmony to society. The busts of Bridgman that Howe commissioned Sophia Peabody to make were phrenological models as well as souvenirs, intended to show that even a blind and deaf child could, through proper education and exercise, improve her corporeal organization, and become a "free moral agent" and a "fit temple for the transient dwelling" of the divine spirit.[64]

From his early successes at the Perkins Institute, Howe turned to other social ills that by phrenological lights, were caused by deficiencies or imbalances in bodily function or social organization. When the Broad Street riots erupted in summer 1837, Howe blamed working-class Yankees as much as immigrant Irishmen, and saw the riot as an indication of the growing "vice, corruption, and irrational passion" that threatened Boston's social and moral stability.[65] To combat these threats, Howe applied phrenology to prison reform, insanity, and idiocy, and encouraged Horace Mann to reform the Massachusetts public schools along phrenological principles. In

1846, the Massachusetts General Court appointed Howe to head a commission to investigate "the condition of Idiots of the Commonwealth, . . . and whether any thing can be done in their behalf."[66]

Howe's report discovered some 574 "idiots"—mentally deficient or handicapped individuals—among the state's children. From this sample, he projected a total of some 1,200 to 1,500 school-age idiots in the commonwealth—"a fearful number"—a third to half of them children of paupers.[67] To Howe's phrenological eye, the causes were clear: "THE CONDITION OF THE BODILY ORGANIZATION."[68] Howe's report used statistical tables to portray the physical measurements of hundreds of idiots as they indicated "self-preservation," "social attachments," "moral sentiments," and other faculties in phrenology's lexicon. Since phrenological theory insisted that physical defects could be "visited upon the race to the third and fourth generation," Howe also paid attention to the parents and relatives of idiots, noting whether the parents were "drunkards, or not" (frequently "yes") along with other categories of vice that might be passed onto their children through their bodily organization.[69]

In response to Howe's report, the commonwealth granted funding and a charter to open the Massachusetts School for Idiotic and Feeble Minded Youth. The new school followed Howe's organizational model from the Perkins Institute and was housed in South Boston immediately adjacent to the school for the blind. The purpose was twofold: to improve the lives of a small number of students carefully selected for their "teachability," and to demonstrate that the organic and scientific approach taught by phrenology would solve wider social ills.[70]

In 1848, the year of Europe's revolutions and the publication of *The Communist Manifesto*, Howe wrote a review article on the problem of idiocy. He refused to blame the victims of idiocy for their own fate, but suggested that their plight was a symptom of deeper social ills. The bodily organization of the mass of humanity was being deranged by the oppressive conditions of modern labor, and by the social ills and depravity it produced. Howe assails the tyranny of slave owners in the American South as well as Boston's elites with their factories and mills, where the conditions of labor "cause a great degeneracy of the race, and great frequency of moral and mental idiocy." As hope against this despairing vision, Howe held out the phrenological remedy: with proper education and training, "the frightful number of those unfortunates whose numbers encumber the march of humanity;—the insane, the idiots, the blind, the deaf, the drunkards, the criminals, the paupers, will dwindle away."[71]

Phrenology's doctrines were attuned to the liberal religion that dominated Boston's cultural and charitable institutions. And there was no shortage of men and women like Howe, Dorothea Dix, or Horace Mann, ready to devote their lives to these measures. The goal resonated with Boston's history: to restore a sense of mutual interdependency in social relations, "let none of them be uncared for . . . no matter how deformed, how vicious, how loathsome, even, he may be; let it be regarded as a call to help a brother."[72] Phrenology seemed the perfect reform vehicle, retaining aspects of the Mosaic law, a version of original sin, but tempered by Unitarian hopefulness for human perfectibility. The trouble was that phrenology, now implemented in Boston's prisons, schools, temperance societies, and asylums for the deaf, blind, and mentally deficient, did not work.

Many of these reform projects may have been none the worse for phrenology's influence. Its emphasis on educating the whole person, body and mind, its interest in promoting general health, and indeed, its basic optimism that individuals and society were capable of improvement, were not intrinsically destructive. Some of the worst conditions in asylums and prisons were improved; care for the physically and mentally impaired was no doubt better for the students lucky enough to be chosen for Howe's schools, and their education sometimes gave them useful opportunities. But phrenology's failure went deeper than that. The belief that its principles, when applied to profound medical and social ills, would actually heal individuals and create social harmony, was bound to exceed any attainable improvements and instead leave a profound sense of disappointment, as it did for Laura Bridgman and the students in Howe's "Idiot School."

From the beginning, Howe only accepted children whom he believed to be educable. Even among his handpicked students, however, the degree of improvement was limited. Phrenological education did not reshape the children's brains or restructure their cranial capacities. The most teachable student at Idiot School was George Rowell, whom the other students (including Bridgman) called "Littlehead." Other students with greater cranial capacities inexplicably did less well than Rowell. As the years went by and Howe's interests shifted, the school became more of a glorified almshouse than a force for social change.[73] Other institutions shaped by phrenological thought suffered similar trajectories, much as Brook Farm failed to create a transcendentalist utopia in these years. After the initial surge of enthusiasm, government funding, private donations, the construction of buildings, and the implementation of new curricula or health regimens, some people experienced modest improvements, but intractable ailments and social ills remained uncured. The phrenological millennium failed to arrive.[74]

What was worse, in the wake of phrenology's failures at social reform, other features of its scientific approach exacerbated the social splintering that its supporters had aimed to heal. Embedded in phrenological thought was its commitment to the *hereditary* basis of the physical condition of the brain and body, and therefore of mental, moral, and behavioral traits too. Accompanying this belief was a strong impulse to categorize human beings in racial, ethnic, class, and sociological groups in order to explain differences in appearance, behavior, and status between black and white, rich and poor, English and Irish, virtuous and vicious. Spurzheim's *Phrenology* asserted that inherited differences made some races superior to others, and illustrated this claim with images of four representative skulls depicting "a cannibal of Brazil, . . . a woman of the savage tribe Wabash, in North America[,] . . . the Hindoo skull, . . . and from Blumenbach's work, . . . a specimen of the ancient Greek." The last skull came from the collection of Johann Friedrich Blumenbach, the Göttingen naturalist who taught Edward Everett, Ticknor, Joseph Green Cogswell, and George Bancroft, and who was among the first scientists to divide humankind into five distinct races.[75]

With this impulse to categorize races by physiological qualities came an emphasis on the hereditary transmission of infirmities and deficiencies, for which the phrenological remedy lay in eugenics. Howe's survey of idiots in Massachusetts was a case in point. By seeking to prove the hereditary nature of mental deficiency, Howe aimed to prevent its transmission to future generations.[76]

Phrenology's bright hope for individual and social transformation ended in failure. After the gradual realization that its principles would not eliminate alcoholism, crime, poverty, and disease, what remained were popular conceptions of the racial, ethnic, class, and character categories that phrenology promoted. These traits were no longer seen as malleable characteristics, but as fixed and immutable conditions, separating person from person and group from group, best kept separate lest the purer races be sullied. Phrenology's failure left in its wake a virulent source for the emergence of "scientific racism" in the 1840s and 1850s. A new science and philosophy that had been embraced for its promise to heal the suffering members of an organic social body and restore harmony among its parts, now declared those parts to be irreconcilable by their very nature. What had begun as diagnosis ended as destiny.[77]

Violent Renditions

From the mid-1830s onward, from the time of the burning of the Ursuline convent, the mobbing of Garrison, and the Broad Street riots, the lines of fracture in Boston's social and political order—rich versus poor, black versus white, foreign versus native, Irish versus Yankee, male versus female, Cotton versus Conscience Whigs—generated an escalating sequence of violent incidents—violence that was increasingly linked to national affairs. Again and again, conflict emerged over bodies—who defined their identity, where they could legally go, who controlled them, where and what they were allowed to speak. The cacophony of angry voices provoked bloody responses, an eruption of hatred that pulled the city apart just as the United States as a whole was pulled apart. Boston's events became national events, and national politics overwhelmed Boston's tradition of local autonomy, merging the dissolution of the city and union into a single story of fratricide.

In November 1837, an abolitionist clergyman, printer, and newspaper editor, Elijah Lovejoy, was murdered by a mob in Alton, Illinois, just across the Mississippi from Saint Louis. Unlike the pacifist Garrison, Lovejoy had been deputized by Alton's mayor to defend himself from heavily armed mobs. Lovejoy was gunned down while trying to protect his printing press from the mob's firebombs. The violence shocked many of the nation's moderate antislavery voices. In Boston, William Ellery Channing, the city's most revered Unitarian minister, a slow convert to antislavery and reluctant supporter of organized movements, now demanded that a public meeting be held in Faneuil Hall to discuss this outrage.[78]

The meeting was chaotic. Channing began by condemning violence and affirming the freedom of speech and the press. But almost immediately one of his own parishioners, the Massachusetts attorney general James T. Austin, rose to defend the Alton mob's right to kill Lovejoy to protect the peace of their city and nearby slaveholding regions. Austin compared the Alton mob to John Hancock, Sam Adams, and the patriots of Boston who had destroyed the East India Company tea. Loud shouts of approval from Austin's supporters threatened to overwhelm the meeting.

In response, Wendell Phillips made a dramatic appeal, his first public speech, defeating the crowd's attempt to shout him down. Phillips excoriated Austin's vile denigration of Hancock, Adams, and Phillips's own ancestors, and reframed the abolitionist movement as an extension of the city-state of Boston's revolutionary tradition. Gesturing to the portraits of Adams, Hancock, Quincy, and Otis on the walls of Faneuil Hall, he argued that Lovejoy's legally authorized defense of the rights of conscience and freedom of the press were consistent with the actions of revolutionary patriots. Phillips likewise cited John Cotton and Hugh Peter, puritan founders of the commonwealth, for their approbation of the use of force in defense of higher law.[79] In one impassioned stroke, Phillips localized the abolitionist cause as an extension of Boston's revolutionary tradition, and turned the force of this tradition against a usurping slavocracy that threatened to overwhelm it, much as Charles I, James II, and George III had threatened the commonwealth in past eras. Yet the violent division within Faneuil Hall that December afternoon was radically different from the unity that Bostonians had mustered against these earlier threats. It presaged the brutal struggle that would divide the city and nation over the next two decades.

A principal source of this conflict lay in the US Constitution. Article 4, Section 2 guaranteed that a slave escaping from a master in one state would not be set free by the laws of another state, "but shall be delivered up on claim of the party to whom such service or labour may be due." A 1793 act of Congress gave force to this clause, allowing slave owners and their agents—bounty hunters—to seize fugitive slaves in free states without a legal warrant. So long as they satisfied a local judge that the fugitive was indeed the claimant's slave, bounty hunters were free to take fugitives back to slavery without a trial.[80]

Boston's black community grew adept at defending fugitives from slave catchers. In 1836, two women, Eliza Small and Polly Ann Bates, who had escaped from slavery in Baltimore and stowed away on a brig bound for Boston, were rescued from the courthouse in Boston where their fate was about to be decided. A large group of black Bostonians rushed in, seized the fugitives, and spirited them away to a ship bound for Nova Scotia and freedom. Escape to Canada would become a common pattern for blacks endangered by the slave catchers and a bitterly ironic comment on Boston's lost autonomy. The place where, in the 1780s, Loyalist exiles from Boston's defense of its liberties had taken refuge now became a refuge for those whose liberties Boston could no longer defend.[81]

In 1842, a similar attempt to free George Latimer, an escaped slave from Norfolk, Virginia, failed. Boston's black activists led by Henry Tracy tried without success to rescue Latimer by attacking city constables hired by slave catchers, who then detained Latimer in the Suffolk County Jail for safekeeping. Samuel E. Sewall, descendant of the Boston judge who first denounced the slave trade in 1700, attempted to gain Latimer's release through a writ of personal replevin, to no avail. Ultimately Latimer's defenders succeeded only by purchasing Latimer from his owner for $400. Even this outcome divided the city's antislavery community. Garrison and other radical abolitionists denounced the purchase as financial compensation for the sin of slavery, and tacit acceptance of the principle that human beings can be bought and sold.[82] The outrage caused by the use of city police and the county jail to assist the slave hunters led to a campaign to outlaw these practices. The following March, after receiving a petition with over sixty thousand signatures, the General Court passed the Massachusetts Personal Liberty Law forbidding state or local officials and public facilities in the commonwealth from being used to enforce the Federal Fugitive Slave Law.[83]

Theodore Parker, inching his way closer to abolitionism, commented on the Latimer crisis in an essay that unwittingly and uncannily echoed the argument that Sewall had made in *The Selling of Joseph*. Sewall had contended that slavery was nothing more than "manstealing," and that it was no better to condone manstealing in unknown Africa than to allow a fishing party in Massachusetts to enslave its weaker neighbors. Parker's similar analogy compared Latimer's case to an "Algerian pirate" or "merchant of Tripoli" coming to Faneuil Hall, and under Tripoli's laws claiming possession of a Boston man. Against these claims, Parker conjured up the ghost of John Robinson, minister of the Pilgrim fathers, to insist on the superiority of "GOD'S LAW" to "MAN'S COMMAND."[84] John Greenleaf Whittier, the Quaker poet and protégé of Garrison, responded to the Latimer crisis with a literary denunciation of the national government, making a similar identification of divine law with the laws of Massachusetts:

> Look to it well, Virginians! In calmness we have borne,
> In answer to our faith and trust, your insult and your scorn;
> You've spurned our kindest counsels; you've hunted for our lives;
> And shaken round our hearths and homes your manacles and
> gyves!
> But for us and for our children, the vow which we have given
> For freedom and humanity is registered in heaven;
> No slave-hunt in our borders,—no pirate on our strand!
> No fetters in the Bay State,—no slave upon our land![85]

Like Everett in 1815, Whittier in 1842 saw the potential for slave revolt as Virginia's problem to deal with. But the slave hunters within Massachusetts' borders presented a different problem: as fetters in and on the Bay State.

The following year, another attempt was made to protect Boston bodies from alien state laws, only to precipitate further violence. South Carolina law forbade the entry of free blacks into the state, levied fines on ship captains who brought free black sailors into port, held free black sailors in jail during the ship's time in port, and threatened enslavement for failure to pay the fines. Because numerous free blacks from Boston and the ship captains who employed them had suffered under these laws, the governor of Massachusetts sent a distinguished Boston lawyer, Samuel Hoar, to collect information to test the constitutionality of Carolina's statutes. An opponent of slavery but no abolitionist, Hoar was met on arrival in Charleston with a resolution by the South Carolina legislature directing that Hoar be expelled forthwith from the state. A mob was prepared to take direct action. They surrounded and threatened to destroy the hotel where Hoar was staying until a "deputation" of seventy prominent local citizens arrived to escort Hoar to a waiting carriage and onto a ship returning to Boston. In his report on his aborted commission, Hoar questioned whether the US Constitution had any force in South Carolina, if the state could expel another American citizen for his opinions: "Are the other states of the Union to be regarded as the conquered provinces of South Carolina?"[86] Judge Hoar's son, a state senator from Concord, declared in the Massachusetts State House that "the Legislature should represent the conscience as [well as] the cotton of the Commonwealth," coining the terms by which the state's dominant Whig party would henceforth be divided.[87]

The movement by the national government under Presidents John Tyler and James Knox Polk to annex Texas and attack Mexico pushed these divisions among Boston's Whigs to the forefront of local politics. Younger Conscience Whigs such as Charles Sumner, John Andrew, Charles Francis Adams, and Samuel Howe now aligned themselves with ostracized abolitionists such as Phillips,

Edmund Quincy, and Sewall. In September 1846, a fugitive slave from New Orleans known as "Joe" had stowed away on a ship owned by Boston merchant John H. Pearson. Joe survived the voyage from New Orleans, only to be discovered by the ship's captain on arrival in Boston Harbor. Pearson wanted to keep Joe's presence a secret and hold him on one of the harbor islands until he could be returned to Louisiana and slavery. But Joe stole a rowboat and escaped to South Boston, until Pearson's crew hunted him down and brought him back to another ship, also owned by Pearson and bound back to New Orleans.[88]

This incident differed from the Latimer crisis not only in Joe's return to slavery but also in the absence of a slaveholder claimant—a Boston merchant and not a southern planter was the slave catcher. The "irreparable shame to Boston of this abduction" caused a "wave of revulsion" to run through the city. Howe organized a protest meeting in Faneuil Hall, where he made his own first abolitionist speech, calling for a campaign of permanent watchfulness against slave hunters, to use the public gaze of indignation to shame them out of the state.[89] Phillips took a more radical step, insisting that this kidnapping of a free man from Boston had led him to "calculate the value of the Union." Just as when British regulars had occupied the city seventy years earlier, the time for a revolutionary break had come. The laws of the union were no longer worthy of respect: "It is idle to say, now, that this thing and that thing is unconstitutional. Constitution,—Mr. President, I abjure the word—there is no constitution in the country, and everybody knows it,—it is a farce." Yet even in this avowedly antislavery meeting, few in Faneuil Hall were prepared to go as far as Phillips. As the report of the meeting next states, "The speaker was here obliged to pause for some time, in consequence of the shouts and hisses in all parts of the hall."[90] Hisses and shouts marked a growing fissure between those still wanting to use the political process to repair the union, and those like Phillips ready for revolutionary action. The meeting voted to establish the Boston Vigilance Committee and unanimously elected forty men, both black and white, to serve on it. A standing reward of $100 was offered for information about captured fugitive slaves.[91]

The Boston Vigilance Committee succeeded in rescuing a number of fugitives and attempted to extend its power beyond Boston. In April 1848, abolitionist ship captain Daniel Drayton and pilot Edward Sayres organized the escape of seventy-six slaves from Washington, DC. But their ship *Pearl*, slowed by adverse winds, was captured by an armed posse traveling by steamboat, and Drayton was nearly lynched by a Washington mob. The Boston Vigilance Committee sent Horace Mann, Boston's representative in Congress, to act as attorney for their defense. Despite death threats and open displays of handguns in the courtroom, Mann managed to reduce Drayton's and Sayres's punishment from a potential death sentence to a steep fine and prison term.[92] Another dramatic case in 1848 involved William and Ellen Craft, a married couple who escaped from their Georgia owner, Dr. Robert Collins. Ellen, the half sister of her master's wife, was light skinned. She passed as a sickly white gentleman while her dark-skinned husband, William, played the role of personal valet. In this guise, they made their way by train and steamboat to Boston and freedom, where they became speakers on the antislavery circuit.

In 1850, Congress passed a new Fugitive Slave Act as part of the compromise to dispose of the vast tracts of land gained by the United States from the Mexican War. In a famous speech of March 7, 1850, Massachusetts senator Daniel Webster defended the act as necessary to preserve the union. In the opinion of Boston's antislavery community, Webster's speech marked his final debasement as the tool of Boston's Cotton Whigs and servant of slavocracy. Ralph Waldo Emerson marked the change: "I have lived all my life without suffering any known inconvenience from American Slavery. I never saw it; I never heard the whip; I never felt the check on my free speech and action, until the other day, when Mr. Webster, by his personal influence, brought the Fugitive Slave Law on the country."[93] The new act preempted the personal liberty law that Massachusetts had passed in 1843 following the Latimer case. State and local authorities were now mandated to assist federal marshals in executing orders to return escaped slaves to their masters. Anyone aiding fugitives or obstructing their return faced stiff fines and prison sentences.

Ordinary citizens of free states had now been made unwilling deputies of the slave catchers. While moderate and reluctant sympathizers like Emerson were radicalized by the new law, the brute force of it fell on the bodies of the fugitives and their defenders. Hundreds of fugitives living in Boston, many of them members of the city's black churches, fled to Canada.[94] Dr. Collins of Georgia became one of the first slave owners to test its power by sending two agents to Boston in October 1850 to arrest the Crafts. The Boston Vigilance Committee hid the Crafts from the bounty hunters, Willis Hughes and John Knight. Black businessman and Vigilance Committee leader Lewis Hayden, himself a fugitive from slavery, was concealing William in his home when he confronted Hughes and Knight from his barricaded front door, and threatened to ignite the two barrels of gunpowder stored in the basement if they advanced any farther. White abolitionists, including Theodore Parker, harassed the bounty hunters with lawsuits and threats of arrest for kidnapping, and warned that they could not protect them from antislavery mobs. Knight and Hughes abandoned the hunt, but Dr. Collins appealed to US president Millard Fillmore to enforce the law. Fillmore authorized the use of military force to arrest the Crafts, but not before the couple had escaped to Nova Scotia.[95]

The Fugitive Slave Act ratcheted up the violence in Boston, both in the rhetoric of personal attacks between the Cotton and Conscience factions of Boston's Whig politicians, and for the fugitives threatened by the slave hunters. Just weeks after the Crafts' flight to Canada, another fugitive named Shadrach Minkins, recently escaped from Virginia and working as a waiter in Taft's Cornhill Coffee House, was seized by two US marshals posing as customers. The marshals dragged Minkins to the nearby courthouse to initiate the legal rendition. Under the Fugitive Slave Law, this was an alarmingly simple proceeding. The federal commissioner, Judge George Ticknor Curtis, a staunch supporter of Webster, affirmed that the fugitive was indeed the property of the slaveholding claimant and issued a certificate for his return to slavery.

The Boston Vigilance Committee, alerted immediately to Minkins's arrest, sent lawyers—Samuel E. Sewall, Ellis Gray Loring, Richard Henry Dana, and Robert Morris, a black lawyer and protégé of Loring who had recently been admitted to the bar. Their petition for a writ of habeas corpus was denied by Massachusetts chief justice Lemuel Shaw. But the legal proceedings gave the Vigilance Committee, led by Hayden, time to assemble a determined rescue party. They fought their way past courtroom guards, seized Minkins bodily and carried him away to the West End, where he was hidden until he could be brought to Canada by the Underground Railroad.[96] The rescue of Minkins from the hands of federal marshals profoundly embarrassed Webster, now serving as Fillmore's secretary of state. Webster insisted that the rescue was an act of treason that must be prosecuted. Although nine men were arrested and seven charged, including Hayden and Morris, all were acquitted by sympathetic Boston juries, resurrecting the practice of jury nullification common in the days of the resistance movement to Britain.[97]

The Minkins rescue heightened the vigilance of the federal marshals and pro-union forces in the city. Slave owners seeking to recapture their lost property never lacked for paid assistance among Boston's proslavery and pro-union citizens. Two months later, on April 3, 1851, marshals arrested Thomas Sims, a fugitive slave from Georgia. Sims resisted, wounding deputy marshal Asa Butman's leg with a knife before the marshals subdued him and brought him to the courthouse. This time, city authorities were prepared to enforce President Fillmore's proclamation. Marshal Francis Tukey's police surrounded the courthouse. A dozen personal guards were assigned to watch over Sims and prevent another rescue. Overnight, Tukey ordered that the entire courthouse be encircled by a great iron chain, suspended three feet above the ground, to keep away the crowd that swarmed the surrounding streets.

The Boston Vigilance Committee's legal team stepped forward to defend Sims. Mann, Phillips, Parker, and Howe organized mass meetings on the Common and at Tremont Temple. Higginson plotted an escape whereby Sims would leap from a third-story window onto mattresses and into a waiting carriage, only to be foiled when Tukey installed iron bars on the courthouse windows. The legal maneuvers of the Vigilance Committee failed to dissuade Judge Curtis from issuing the certificate to return Sims to slavery. The mayor of Boston, John Bigelow, ordered three companies of city militia to assist the federal marshals in carrying Sims out of the city and permitted Tukey to arm his policemen with US military weapons. At four o'clock on the morning of April 12, a guard of three hundred volunteer soldiers and policemen brandishing military swords formed a hollow square around Sims. They marched down State Street past lines of militia to Long Wharf and a waiting ship that returned Sims to Savannah; Sims was nearly killed by the public whipping that he received in Georgia as punishment for his escape. As soldiers paraded Sims from Boston's courthouse to the wharf, another parade of a hundred abolitionists followed behind, bearing a black coffin marked with the name "liberty." Sims's Georgia owner wrote an open letter to the merchants of Boston, thanking them for returning his property according to federal law.[98]

The Fugitive Slave Law had at last been enforced in Boston, but at enormous expense to the city and at the symbolic cost of putting its courthouse in chains. For the next few years, southern slaveholders shied away from repeating the Sims experience and more commonly sought to recover escaped slaves from cities less hostile than Boston. But in May 1854, in the wake of the passage of the Kansas-Nebraska Act, which allowed for the possibility that slavery might be introduced in territories where it had been banned by the Missouri Compromise of 1820, Charles Suttle, an emboldened slave owner from Alexandria, Virginia, came to Boston to demand that federal marshals arrest his escaped slave, Anthony Burns. When Burns was arrested, Boston erupted.

Over the preceding three years, public opinion in the city had moved slowly toward an antislavery position. The state legislature elected Charles Sumner as US senator to succeed Webster. Harriet Beecher Stowe's novel, *Uncle Tom's Cabin*, converted many thousands of northern readers to at least a moderately antislavery position. Nevertheless, abolitionists were still widely reviled. Their meetings, including a return of British abolitionist George Thompson to Boston in 1851, were attacked by violent mobs. With the Whig Party collapsing over the conflict between its pro- and antislavery factions, its former members converged temporarily on the anti-immigrant American Party (the "Know-Nothings") that swept into power in local and statewide elections in 1854. The still largely disenfranchised Irish were made the scapegoats for Boston's and New England's ills.

Anthony Burns was seized by Asa Butman, the same deputy marshal wounded in the arrest of Sims, on the evening of May 24, 1854.[99] The ensuing conflict resembled the Sims case, with a similarly dismal outcome. But it burned with greater intensity and threw off still more explosive sparks that spread far beyond Boston. On the night of May 26, five thousand people gathered at Faneuil Hall, the largest crowd that the venerable building had ever held. Wendell Phillips and Theodore Parker gave keynote addresses. As a clergyman, Parker called himself a "man of peace," but he also argued that "liberty is the end, and sometimes peace is not the means towards it." Many in the crowd shouted for immediate action. Men thronged out of Faneuil Hall and ran the few blocks to the courthouse, where Thomas Wentworth Higginson was waiting with newly purchased axes and a heavy beam to ram open the courthouse's oaken double doors. With US marshals lined up against them inside, Higginson's group finally crashed through the door and a battle ensued. The rescuers fired pistols and thrust swords into the opening. The US marshals swung their clubs to drive them back. The marshals prevailed; Higginson and company were forced back out into the street, but not before a hired deputy marshal, a young Irish immigrant named James Batchelder, had been stabbed in the groin and bled to death. By sunrise the next morning, two companies of US Marines and two more of state militia were guarding the courthouse.[100]

Despite attempts by the Vigilance Committee to delay the proceedings and purchase Burns from his owner, the judicial wheels

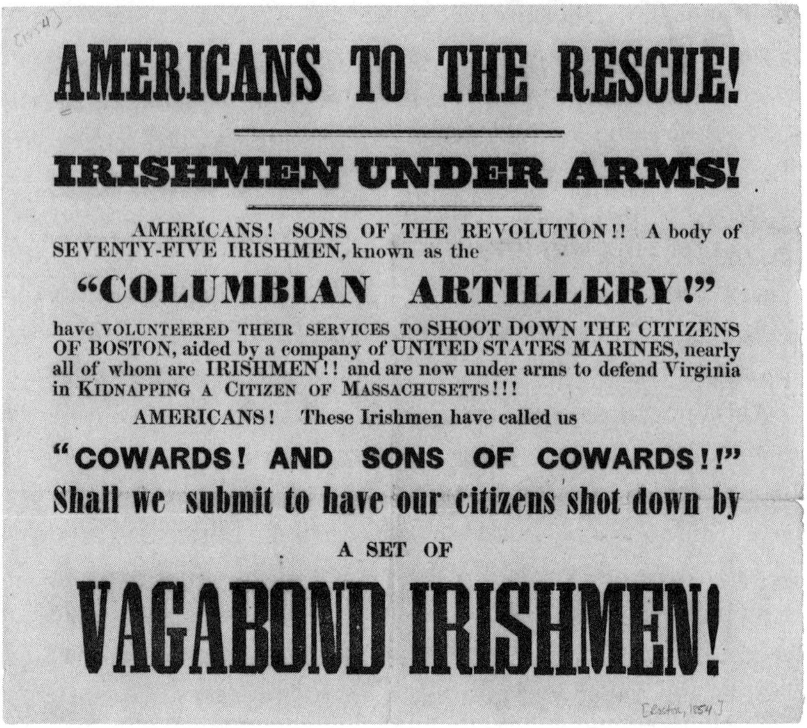

AMERICANS TO THE RESCUE!

IRISHMEN UNDER ARMS!

AMERICANS! SONS OF THE REVOLUTION!! A body of SEVENTY-FIVE IRISHMEN, known as the

"COLUMBIAN ARTILLERY!"

have VOLUNTEERED THEIR SERVICES TO SHOOT DOWN THE CITIZENS OF BOSTON, aided by a company of UNITED STATES MARINES, nearly all of whom are IRISHMEN!! and are now under arms to defend Virginia in KIDNAPPING A CITIZEN OF MASSACHUSETTS!!!

AMERICANS! These Irishmen have called us

"COWARDS! AND SONS OF COWARDS!!"

Shall we submit to have our citizens shot down by

A SET OF

VAGABOND IRISHMEN!

[Boston, 1854]

FIGURE 12.6. *Americans to the Rescue! Irishmen under Arms!*, broadside, 1854.

ground on. Burns was deemed to be Suttle's property and ordered to be returned to Virginia on a US Revenue Cutter. On the morning of June 2, the mayor put Boston under martial law. Major General B. F. Edmands of the state militia took command of two thousand soldiers carrying muskets and bayonets, including US Marines armed with horse-drawn artillery loaded with grapeshot, along with several companies of cavalry, to escort Burns from the courthouse down to the harbor.

The military presence was meant to thwart any rescue attempts and prevent rioting between pro- and antislavery factions, but the ethnic composition of the troops aggravated the situation. A company of Irish militia volunteered their services. In response, the streets were plastered with broadsides announcing that the Irish had volunteered to "SHOOT DOWN THE CITIZENS OF BOSTON." Thousands of spectators—estimates ran as high as fifty thousand—lined the streets to watch the cortege make its way from the courthouse down State Street to the harbor, past the site of the Boston Massacre in 1770, past the spot where militia from Boston and the surrounding towns had arrested Edmund Andros in 1689. Antislavery merchants and residents draped State Street's windows with black bunting and American flags bordered in black or hung upside down. Down the street moved the hollow square of soldiers and cavalry, with Burns at the center, surrounded by hired ruffians, or in the words of a spectator, "The worst pimps and blacklegs of the city."[101] (See plate 30.)

Martial law and the massing of troops did the job they were meant to do. The US marshals moved Burns out of Boston and back to Virginia. The blow to the city's identity and civic pride, the shame felt by many citizens that Boston lay under Virginia's thumb, was intensely painful. Many moderate antislavery or formerly pro-union figures switched sides because of the Burns rendition. More than nineteen hundred merchants signed a petition calling for the repeal of the Fugitive Slave Act. At the head of the list was John Pearson, the merchant responsible for the rendition of "Joe" in 1846. Samuel A. Eliot, Boston's congressman, the only member of the Massachusetts congressional delegation to vote for the Fugitive Slave Act, now called for its repeal. Charles Devens, the US marshal who returned Sims to slavery, now volunteered money to purchase Sims's freedom.[102] And Amos A. Lawrence, son of the founder of the Lawrence mills, owner of the Ipswich mills, described the dramatic change: "We went to bed one night old fashioned, conservative, Compromise Union Whigs, and waked up stark mad Abolitionists."[103] But it was an outsider who best perceived the shame of Boston.

Prompted by Burns's rendition, New York's Walt Whitman composed "A Boston Ballad—1854." In it he imagined the parade of "government cannon," of "Federal foot and dragoons," drawing apparitions of Boston's heroes out of their graves, "phantoms" with "cock'd hats of mothy mould, crutches made of mist, arms in slings." Whitman's narrator instructs the martial ghosts to retreat to their graves; valiant figures from the past do not belong at Boston's scene of surrender. Instead, he suggests that the mayor of Boston "send a committee to England," and ask Parliament to "dig out King George's coffin" and ship him on a swift Yankee clipper to Boston, where the rendition of Burns can be restaged for his enjoyment: "Open the box, set up the regal ribs, glue those that will not stay, clap the skull on top of the ribs, and clap a crown on top of the skull. You have got your revenge, old buster."[104] It was fitting that Whitman should banish the moldy and broken ghosts of past heroes, and conjure up the decaying mortal remains of a king that the city had once defied. What better witness to the failure of a fractured Boston to defend its independence in the face of King Cotton? Theodore Parker put it more simply: "There is no Boston to-day. There was a Boston once. Now, there is a north suburb to the city of Alexandria; that is what Boston is. And you and I, fellow-subjects of the State of Virginia."[105]

The most radical Bostonians clung to the possibility of disunion, of the Bay State's secession from a union dominated by Virginia and South Carolina, from a constitution that remained a covenant with hell. But after the rendition of Anthony Burns, the possibility of any future autonomy for the city-state of Boston under the umbrella of the United States, a prospect ever diminishing from the Constitution's ratification, was now finished. In this sense, Parker was right: there once was a Boston, but no longer. The violence spurred by ethnic division and conflict over slavery continued. Bodies would break and bleed and pile up in greater numbers, but now the fight became increasingly a contest within and about the future ownership of the United States. Amos Lawrence may have become a "stark mad abolitionist" (by his own standards, anyway), but he remained a union man. After the Burns affair, Lawrence threw his support behind the New England Emigrant Aid Company, a corporate colonizing venture echoing the origins of the Massachusetts Bay Company. It moved thousands of antislavery New England settlers to the Kansas frontier, aiming to outnumber and outvote the proslavery migrants under the "Popular Sovereignty" terms of the Kansas-Nebraska Act. If guns were needed to arm the New England colonists, then Amos Lawrence would supply the guns. "Bleeding Kansas" was the result.

Charles Sumner of Boston delivered his famous speech in the US Senate on "The Crime against Kansas" on May 19 and 20, 1856, decrying the organized violence of Missouri "Border Ruffians" and denouncing efforts to engineer the admission of Kansas to the union as a slave state. Sumner insisted that the bloodshed in Kansas was not confined to this single US territory: "Already the muster has begun. The strife is no longer local, but national . . . foreshadowing a strife, which, unless happily averted by the triumph of Freedom, will become war."[106] The fury of the propagandists of slavery came quickly. The next day, Missouri Border Ruffians ransacked Lawrence, Kansas, named for the Boston benefactor of the New England Emigrant Aid Company. The following day, Preston Brooks, South Carolina congressman and cousin of South Carolina senator Andrew Butler, whom Sumner had verbally attacked for promoting slavery in Kansas, walked up behind the seated Sumner and bludgeoned his head with a gold-handled cane. Sumner was left unconscious on the Senate floor, blinded by his own blood. Two days later, one of the antislavery Kansas emigrants, John Brown, led an assault that seized five proslavery settlers in Pottawatomie, Kansas, and hacked them to death with broadswords.

John Brown agreed with Sumner. The strife was "no longer local, but national." He left Kansas after the Pottawatomie massacre and returned to his native New England, where he began to plan a general slave insurrection. In Boston, he found financial backing and moral support among its abolitionist leaders, including Parker, Higginson, Howe, George Luther Stearns and Franklin Sanborn. These men, along with Gerrit Smith of New York, formed the "Secret Six" to raise money and weapons for Brown—two hundred Sharps rifles and a thousand pikes. In October 1859, Brown carried out his assault on the federal armory at Harpers Ferry, Virginia. The armory held ten thousand muskets that Brown planned to distribute among local slaves. They would launch a general insurrection sweeping southward down the Blue Ridge Mountains and into the heart of slave territory. Local militia and the US Marines captured Brown and snuffed out the slave insurrection. Brown was hanged for his crimes.

Recall that Harpers Ferry threatened exactly what the young Edward Everett had envisioned as the "slave states' problem" back in 1815: a general slave insurrection that would "drench [Virginia] in its best blood." Only now, Everett's fellow Bostonians, including his protégé, Samuel Howe, whom he had inspired to fight in the Greek Revolution in order to "refine and ennoble and bring out the divine in man," had supplied the rifles and pikes, hoping to begin the bloodletting. In the wake of Brown's raid, Howe joined the exodus of free blacks from the Fugitive Slave Law and temporarily fled to Canada, fearing arrest for his part in abetting Brown.[107] No longer could Everett believe that "greatest political problem I have met" belonged to the slave states only. Boston owned it too, symbolized by Everett's willingness to stand alongside John Bell of Tennessee as the Constitutional Union Party's nominee for vice president, a newly formed party with the sole purpose of keeping the disintegrating union together.

Abraham Lincoln won a stunning election victory in 1860 on a platform promising to honor slavery in its current locations but limit its further expansion. Lincoln received no electoral votes and virtually no individual votes from the slaveholding states. As a result, it was the slavocracy of the South rather than the disunionists of Massachusetts who attempted to withdraw from the United States. Lincoln's election, with less than 40 percent of the nation's popular vote, was a shocking departure from the long tradition of southern control of the national government—an aberration brought about by divisions among the multiple candidates who opposed the fledgling Republican Party's platform. But even though Lincoln won every county in Massachusetts (indeed, every county in New England—an outcome replicated in no other part of the union), Boston remained deeply divided over the slavery question and chose a unionist Democrat as its mayor in 1860.

A month after Lincoln's election, as the South Carolina secession convention was assembling, a meeting at Boston's Tremont Temple to commemorate the first anniversary of John Brown's execution was invaded by a mob. The fifty policemen present did nothing to stop the rioting, except to hustle Frederick Douglass from the stage as he strove to be heard over the jeering crowd. Another meeting that night was held at the African Baptist Church on Joy Street, but here too a mob of two thousand rioters tried to seize the main speaker, Wendell Phillips. One opponent shouted, "Damn him! He has depreciated stocks three million dollars by his slang!"[108] In January 1861, by which time South Carolina and six other states had declared their secession, Phillips spoke at Boston's Music Hall in favor of disunion, arguing that the departure of the South would free Boston from the rule of slave owners. Afterward, "His path was beset & his way obstructed by a mob of well dressed, but evidently coarse & uncultivated men, who howled & yelled & pressed in upon the body guard which surrounded him."[109] In the months after Lincoln's election, Boston's antislavery leaders went in fear of their lives, protected by armed German radicals—members of the Turners union, holdovers from the Unbedingten in the days of Follen.[110]

With the union unraveling and the city violently divided, a rising literary celebrity, one of the many young men educated at Göttingen in the wake of Ticknor, Everett, and Bancroft, returned to Boston after an extended stay in Europe. For much of the preceding decade, John Lothrop Motley had been toiling in European archives, preparing his multivolume work, *The Rise of the Dutch Republic* (1856), and its sequel, *The History of the United Netherlands*. Though removed from the scene of the previous decade's growing sectional conflict, Motley had kept himself informed of events in Boston and the nation. From his European vantage point, he captured the sense of looming crisis and the uncertainty of its outcome that, given our hindsight, is difficult to recover. Already in 1858, he feared that it might be untenable for Boston and New England to remain in the union: "A man in . . . Massachusetts must either be a rebel and bend his energies to the dissolution of the Union, or he must go heart in hand with Alabama and Carolina in acquiring Cuba and Central America, and carving out an endless succession of slave States for the future."[111]

Motley returned to Boston shortly after Lincoln's election and immediately sensed the air of panic in the city. He described Boston's fears to his wife, who remained in London: "The Confederate flag was to wave over Washington before May 1, and over Faneuil Hall before the end of this year; there was to be a secession party in every Northern State, and blood was to flow from internecine combats in every Northern town," just as it had been flowing in Kansas for years.[112]

Of course we know that's not what happened. Instead, Union troops turned out in the hundreds of thousands in response to Lincoln's call. By 1863, sons of Boston Brahmins were leading regiments of black Yankee soldiers against the citadels of South Carolina. The long-feared slave insurrection had become a reality, sponsored by a national government that the plantation aristocracy had once dominated and had now abandoned. But given the long history of slave owners' dominance of national government and Boston's futile resistance, from the embargo of 1807 to the War of 1812, from the Louisiana Purchase to the Mexican War, from the Fugitive Slave Act to the humiliating renditions of Thomas Sims and Anthony Burns, it was not foolish for Motley and his anxious contemporaries to imagine a Confederate flag waving over Faneuil Hall. In their eyes, it had actually been there for decades. Southern secession merely revealed a long-hidden truth: the city-state of Boston had been absorbed by a nation-state that the South had built. There was a Boston once, but the city-state of Boston was no more.

Conclusion

The Making of US History and the Disappearance of the City-State of Boston

The preceding chapters have offered a distinctive description of Boston in New England through three centuries, as a city-state making its own way in the larger Atlantic world. Its individual elements may be familiar to those schooled in this history, but in its overall narrative and interpretation, the story told here may seem deeply unfamiliar. It contradicts many of the home truths that Boston's remembrancers (to borrow a term from Cotton Mather) have been telling themselves for generations. It is not the story endorsed by the Freedom Trail and Boston's heritage industry. It may well lead readers to ask, "If this story is true, why is it so strange? Why don't we know it already?"

My answer is this: the demise of the city-state of Boston came as a whimper, drowned out by an enormous bang. Boston was neither occupied nor destroyed during the American Civil War, as it had been during the American Revolutionary War. Instead, the Civil War made Boston bigger, richer, and more powerful (though at the same time, more unequal and more internally divided). Boston's influence in and commitment to the United States expanded as a result of the Civil War. And that is precisely why the history of the city-state of Boston has been overshadowed.

The disappearance of the city-state ideal and Boston's full embrace of the US national project did not occur without effort. Cultural work was required to reconfigure Boston's relationship to the United States, to reshape mythical contours to make it seem as though the city's place in US history had been assured all along.

Here, let me remind the reader of an important distinction, too seldom made by historians, between the origins of the colonial rebellion against British rule, and the development of the early United States. Boston's part in the former has always been easy to comprehend. The rebellion had deep roots in the city's long-contentious relationship with royal government; on this issue, loyalist Peter Oliver and rebel Mercy Otis Warren agreed in their otherwise-conflicting accounts. But from the earliest sessions of Congress under the Constitution in 1789, even from John Adams's attempt to influence the crafting of other state constitutions in 1776, Boston found it nearly impossible to shape the development of the United States after its own image, or to make the union function according to New England ideals of federal governance. Consequently, when the surprising outcome of the Civil War created a new opportunity for Boston to put its impress on the future of the United States, Boston's historians constructed new narratives, making it possible to imagine that Boston and New England had always been central to the rise of this continental empire. Boston's historians performed the cultural heavy lifting necessary to recast the city's relationship to the United States and to develop a new mythical narrative of American history.

Traces of these efforts can be detected in gradual shifts in the historical scholarship conducted by Bostonians across the nineteenth century—before, during, and after the cataclysm of the Civil War. Boston's historians, among them William Hickling Prescott, John Lothrop Motley, and most prominently, Francis Parkman, played key roles in transforming historical scholarship in America while at the same time refiguring the historical relationship between Boston and the United States. By the time Parkman completed his life's work, a historical profession had emerged from America's universities, taking the practices that these earlier authors had pioneered as the basis for training doctoral students in history. The cumulative effect of their labors was to paper over the contentious relationship that Boston had endured with the dominant powers of the United States in the decades between the Constitution and Civil

War. In addition, the professional scholarship foreshadowed by these Boston historians encouraged the apotheosis of the consolidated nation-state as the natural and inevitable subject, framework, and destination for historical inquiry, advancing a historical teleology that made the small, autonomous city-state seem like a thing of the antique past, historical debris swept away by modernity.

Prescott, Motley, and Parkman were not Boston's only significant historians of the nineteenth century. Obviously missing from the list are George Bancroft and Henry Adams, who each in his way provides a bookend and a contrasting approach to the writings of these three. Bancroft hewed closer to the romantic and mythic styles of earlier historians; he worked largely from secondary sources and, as he pursued a career in Democratic politics, drifted away from Boston as the center of his identity, moving to New York and finally settling in the national capital. Adams was of a later generation, and his most important historical work, the nine-volume *History of the United States of America, 1801–1817* (1889–91), belongs to the era of professional scholarship that he helped to inaugurate as a Harvard history professor and early president of the American Historical Association. Adams, like Bancroft and some of his forebears (including John Quincy Adams), was alienated from Boston; he, too, preferred the culture of Washington. In their historical outlooks and personal politics, Bancroft and Adams were nationalists much sooner and more wholeheartedly than Prescott, Motley, and Parkman. The latter were lifelong Bostonians whose writings expressed the struggle between their native city's identity and its shifting relationship to the power and consolidating force of the United States.[1]

Many other worthy authors might be included in this discussion: Mercy Otis Warren, whose three-volume *History of the Rise, Progress, and Termination of the American Revolution* appeared in 1805; Hannah Adams, who published a survey of world religions, a history of New England, and a history of the Jews; Jared Sparks, the biographer of George Washington; John Gorham Palfrey, author of a multivolume history of colonial New England; and Richard Hildreth, Bancroft's ideological opponent who wrote his own multivolume US history. But these three—Prescott, Motley, and Parkman—found that they could best understand Boston's place in history by looking away from it, by explaining the rise of the powerful republics, kingdoms, and empires of Europe and their American colonies in order to make sense of the world in which Boston, New England, and the United States came to be.

Theirs was an audacious act of world making. Before the nineteenth century and the rise of professional academic scholarship, most histories were written by people recounting their own past for their own people. The boldness of Prescott, Motley, and Parkman lay in believing that from their provincial situation in Boston, at the outer margins of European literary society—Sidney Smith asked in the *Edinburgh Review* in 1820, "In the four quarters of the globe, who reads an American book?"—they could nonetheless produce primary-source-based, scrupulously factual, and definitive accounts of people and nations whose languages, experiences, customs, and countries were not their own.

Prescott, Motley, and Parkman shared a quality that set them off from their predecessors and contemporaries among Boston's historians: a commitment "to distinguish fact from fiction, and to establish the narrative on as broad a basis as possible of contemporary evidence," as Prescott wrote in his preface to *The Conquest of Mexico*.[2] Like many other historical writers of their era, these three were impressed by the power of historical fiction in the hands of authors like Walter Scott and James Fenimore Cooper to bring the past to life.[3] (Both Motley and Parkman tried their hand as novelists early in their careers.)[4] Yet they were equally influenced by the new historical methods that Leopold von Ranke was establishing in Germany. Ranke taught at Berlin University at the time Motley studied there, and Ranke's archivally grounded histories of the Roman and Latin peoples, the Papacy, Prussia, France, England, and many more began to appear in the 1820s.[5] Prescott, Motley, and Parkman synthesized Scott and Ranke by writing history with the emotional power and narrative coherence of romantic fiction while adhering closely to evidence from primary sources. When Prescott portrayed the *Noche Triste*, the climactic scene of Hernán Cortés's conquest of Tenochtitlán, he relied on evidence from Spanish and Nahua sources to prove that the event had indeed taken place on a dark and stormy night, allowing him to enhance its dramatic quality.[6] Prescott pioneered the technique among American historians of using footnotes to identify his sources and assess their strengths and weaknesses in plain view of the reader.

In pursuit of this scholarly rigor, Prescott, Motley, and Parkman went to extraordinary lengths to acquire their sources. Ill health and partial blindness plagued both Prescott and Parkman, so both men spent their fortunes paying agents to acquire trunkfuls of documents in the archives of Madrid, Paris, and London and ship them to Boston. They hired college students to read aloud from these treasure troves, and used specially constructed machines to aid their visually impaired writing.[7] Motley's health was not at issue; he moved his family to live for years near archives in Dresden, Brussels, and The Hague.[8] The results were prodigious. The works of all three historians were well received, not only by American readers, but in the countries whose histories they depicted. Their books were published in many editions, translated into multiple European languages, and became definitive accounts of their subjects well into the era of academic scholarship. The three authors became transatlantic literary celebrities, convincing many Europeans to read American books.

In the United States, their works sharpened the distinctions between scholarly history, popular history, and romantic historical fiction. They marked the start of a transition from history as the avocation of leisured gentry to the discipline's professionalization. In the year that Parkman published *Montcalm and Wolfe* (1884), the culminating volume in his series on the conflict between France and England over North America, the American Historical Association was formed. At the same time, the earliest American students to earn doctoral degrees in history began to develop formal training programs at Johns Hopkins, Columbia, Harvard, and soon many other universities. With the American Historical Association and the universities, the expectation emerged that future college teachers of history would receive professional training in the language study and critical approach to sources, if not the romantic modes of storytelling, that Prescott, Motley, and Parkman had championed.[9]

These three Boston historians produced their works in an overlapping chronology: first Prescott (1796–1859), who published his studies of Spain and its New World conquests from 1837 to 1858, then Motley (1814–77), whose histories of the Dutch Republic appeared between 1856 and 1874, and finally Parkman (1823–93), who published his seven-volume history of "France and England in America" starting in 1865. As they painstakingly assembled their accounts, Prescott, Motley, and Parkman also projected an implicit narrative of how the United States could be seen as a rightful successor to these predecessor empires and republics, and they found ingenious ways to place Boston and New England at the center of this mythic national story.

Of the three, Francis Parkman is the most significant, for although his historical sensibilities were framed in the antebellum era, his seven-volume history of France and Britain in North America was profoundly shaped by the Civil War, and it in turn framed a new way of understanding Boston in New England as central to the making of imperial America. When Parkman embarked on the first volume, his working title for the series was "France in the New World," and he continued to refer to the series as "a connected history of France in the New World" for years to come—and rightly so. In the first five volumes, *Pioneers of France in the New World* (1865), *The Jesuits in North America* (1867), *LaSalle and the Discovery of the Great West* (1869), *The Old Regime in Canada* (1874), and *Count Frontenac and New France under Louis XIV* (1877), the English colonies play an extremely limited role. To the extent that he acknowledges an English presence in North America, Parkman attends almost exclusively to New England. *The Jesuits in North America* devotes a single chapter to "Priest and Puritan," and *The Old Regime in Canada* briefly describes the quarrel between Acadian claimants Charles de La Tour and Charles d'Aulnay that spilled over into Boston in the 1640s. For these five volumes, Parkman's series might more accurately be called "France and Boston in North America."

The narrowed focus allowed Parkman to use New England as his sole reference point when comparing the French and the English, imbuing all the English colonies with the characteristics of New England. For Parkman, Anglo-American history was Boston's history writ large. By the time the series concluded with *Montcalm and Wolfe*, Parkman could depict Wolfe's victory in 1759 at the Plains of Abraham as the ultimate triumph of New England virtues over Gallic vices, after which nothing remained but for the "advancing waves of Anglo-American power" to sweep aside the futile conspiracies of proud but doomed opponents, be they Indians and their French supporters in the 1760s, or the slaveholding oligarchs of the American South in the 1860s.[10] In his introduction to *Pioneers of France in the New World*, written in January 1865 and dedicated to the memory of Theodore Parkman, Robert Gould Shaw, and Henry Ware Hall, his kinsmen recently "slain in battle," Parkman explicitly linked Britain's vanquishing of "Feudalism, Monarchy, and Rome" in New France to the moment "at this hour, [when] half a million of bayonets are vindicating the ascendancy of a regulated freedom"—a freedom for which New England was Parkman's model and source.[11]

By collapsing the century between 1763 and 1865 into this single sentence, Parkman performed the neat trick of projecting an implicit history of the United States without ever addressing the American Revolution and the first eight decades of the republic under the Constitution. Remarkable, though seldom noted, is the fact that Parkman devoted his life to recounting the conflict between France and England over North America, yet neglected to address the final act, when France returned to play a crucial role in winning America's independence. This was no accident. By avoiding the revolution, Parkman also avoided having to explain the messy reality of a bloody conflict between Boston and Britain in the 1770s, and the fateful role of France on the patriots' behalf, scrambling the moral binaries that organized his seven volumes. The actual events of the revolution muddied the projection of Anglo-Saxon virtues onto a victorious New England at the head of an American Republic, and that was the story, vindicated by his kinsmen's Civil War sacrifice, that Parkman wished to tell.

When the Civil War reached its end, Parkman took decisive action to secure New England's cultural victory. In April 1865, after four years of the most gruesome warfare the world had yet known, the Confederate capital in Richmond, Virginia, surrendered to Union forces. Into that scene of chaos moved a party from the Boston Athenaeum, the stately temple of literature at the foot of the State House on Beacon Street. Organized and led by Francis Parkman, the party was charged with acquiring state papers, military records, financial documents, newspapers, books, sheet music, photographs—virtually any record or publication produced in the Confederacy—for the Athenaeum's collections. In the words of the Athenaeum Library Committee's annual report in January 1866,

> The sudden collapse of the Rebellion in the early part of the year seemed to the Committee to furnish an opportunity, which should be instantly used, of obtaining the newspapers and other publications issued at the South during the war; . . . These fugitive publications had a peculiar historical interest; and, unless secured promptly, before they were destroyed, or had fallen into the hands of collectors, they would be forever beyond our reach. A *Poor Richard's Almanac* of the year 1752 is priced on an English sale catalogue at five times its weight in gold; and one hundred years hence, a rebel almanac, or a dingy file of Southern newspapers, may; perhaps, reach a corresponding value.

There was wealth and power to be had in confiscating the means of historical production from the defeated enemy. By seizing the records of the vanquished foe, the Boston Athenaeum became one of the finest repositories anywhere for studying the history of the

American South during its rebellion, and it continued to pursue these acquisitions aggressively for the next century.[12]

There could be no better symbol than the Athenaeum's roundup of Confederate records for the dramatic transformation that the Civil War brought to Boston's relationship to the United States. For the first eighty years under the Constitution, Boston's interests had been subordinated, again and again, to those of a southern slavocracy. Boston's Congressmen Fisher Ames and Josiah Quincy had fought to no avail to redirect the winner-take-all politics of Virginia's dynasts in the national government. When Boston's industrial and political leaders hitched the city's interests to the economic power of southern planters, they created a terrible and widening rift within Boston's political culture. But now, at enormous cost, the slavocracy had been decisively beaten. African American troops, many of them former slaves, led by Boston Brahmins like Parkman's cousin Robert Gould Shaw, had assaulted the citadels of the South, put down the rebellion, and brought an end to slavery. As the Reconstruction project began, Bostonians were at the forefront of seizing the spoils of victory and embracing the imperial aims of the United States without reservation. In that transformation, the centuries-old idea of Boston as an autonomous city-state, a polity in its own right, slipped away largely unnoticed.

In its place emerged a Whiggish, Anglo-Saxon narrative placing New England at the center of a great *translatio imperium* from Britain to the United States. This narrative, hesitantly projected by Prescott and Motley before the Civil War, perfected by Parkman afterward, constituted their collective legacy to the nascent American historical profession. The scholarship produced by the new scientific historians who were now being trained in PhD programs differed more in style and presentation than in substance from their gentleman-scholar predecessors. The first professional scholars holding PhDs such as Herbert Baxter Adams, founder of the American Historical Association, explored topics such as *The Germanic Origins of New England Towns*.[13] Adams's early student and later Yale professor Charles McLean Andrews wrote his dissertation on *The River Towns of Connecticut* (1889), which began with the claim that "the spirit of trade inherent in the Teutonic life, and given broader and newer fields by contact with an unopened country, led to the first . . . settlements in the Connecticut valley."[14] Henry Cabot Lodge, the first student to earn a history PhD at Harvard, wrote his dissertation on the German origins of Anglo-Saxon land law.[15] Adams, Andrews, and Lodge shared what were now common assumptions: New England's roots lay in the primordial past of the Anglo-Saxon tribes, these roots shaped social customs and governance in the villages of East Anglia, Puritan migrants imported these practices to New England, and the United States was New England writ large.

At the founding of the American historical profession, the idea that Boston and New England might *not* have been destined to lead the development of the United States was simply unthinkable. This condition lasted well into the twentieth century. In the 1920s, the young Perry Miller (according to his own mythic narrative) found himself unloading American oil drums on the banks of the Congo. Comparing his own experience to Edward Gibbon's inspiration among the ruins of Rome for writing his *Decline and Fall of the Roman Empire,* Miller imagined that "it was given to me, equally disconsolate on the edge of a jungle of central Africa, to have thrust upon me the mission of expounding what I took to be the innermost propulsion of the United States."[16] Oddly, Miller did not take this mission to mean investigating what the United States had to do with central Africa but instead to discover America's origins in "The New England Mind." Miller never questioned whether there was any discord between the founding vision of Boston's Puritans and the "innermost propulsion of the United States." The reworking of American historical narratives in the wake of the Civil War had obliterated that discord and made the autonomous aspirations of the city-state of Boston fade from historical view.

Coda

Looking Forward to *Looking Backward*

> That blue ribbon winding away to the sunset—was it not the sinuous Charles?
>
> —Julian West, on waking up in Boston in the year 2000, in Edward Bellamy, *Looking Backward, 2000–1887*

In 1888, a curious book about Boston became a runaway success, the third most popular American title of the nineteenth-century, outselling all but *Uncle Tom's Cabin* and *Ben-Hur*. *Looking Backward* was a utopian novel with a preposterous plot: a young man named Julian West falls asleep in Boston in 1887 and wakes up in the year 2000 to a world utterly transformed. Its author, Edward Bellamy, was an earnest young man with socialist inclinations, deeply troubled by post–Civil War industrial society, its economic inequalities and chronic labor unrest. Bellamy likened modern society to a giant carriage, "a prodigious coach" in which the fortunate few rode in comfort on top, while the great mass of humankind struggled to pull the behemoth along a rough and hilly road strewn with pitfalls and hazards.[1] *Looking Backward* envisioned a solution to inequality and misery based on the creation of a vast national industrial army that would solve economic problems much as the Union Army had won the Civil War. Although Bellamy's work was a tract for its times, there are many striking similarities between *Looking Backward* and the utopian literature that influenced Boston's founding three centuries earlier.

Dr. Leete, the character from the Boston of 2000 who explains this new world to Julian West, resembles Raphael Hythlodae in Thomas More's *Utopia*, guiding the reader topic by topic through a society that has solved all the old world's problems—not least of them the labor problem. Just as sixteenth-century English authors had worried about the rising tide of "masterless men" displaced from agricultural labor and turning cities into sites of misery, Bellamy's concern was the plight of the urban industrial poor, exploited by factory owners and ever threatening to rise against them. In describing the twentieth century's solution to this problem, Dr. Leete takes us through a host of other issues that also troubled the utopian writers of early modernity: money (in the Boston of 2000, currency no longer exists); inequality (in *Looking Backward*, every man, woman, and child receives the same annual resource stipend); relations among the classes (Bellamy's utopia demands equal service from each individual for the good of the whole); and vocation (an elaborate scheme allows each person to find their calling); not to mention production and consumption, education and religion, sickness and health, crime and punishment. These problems had troubled the world in which Boston was founded, and the city lavished its resources on them through the centuries. All were resolved in the Boston of 2000.

But there were two issues, critical to the rise and fall of the city-state of Boston, that Bellamy's novel overlooked and thereby obscured how much had changed from the city's early modern origins. The first is the more obvious of the two. *Looking Backward* ignores race, slavery, and ethnicity. Whether we mean the indigenous people who were brutally excluded from Boston's New England hinterland, or the enslaved Africans whom Emmanuel Downing imagined might "do all our business," and who actually did much of Boston's business from afar in the West Indies and the Cotton Kingdom, or the Irish immigrants whose numbers and desperate condition overwhelmed Boston's capacity for Christian charity—in each of these cases, the failure to integrate or accommodate outsiders marked the point at which the ideals of Boston's founders most obviously faltered. Especially with respect to slavery, the essential bargain of the colonial period, that Boston would be a slave society in which the slaves mainly lived elsewhere, and that it could prosper as a commercial economy so long as its West Indian trading partners remained a plantation society of enslaved Africans, constituted the fatal flaw in the city-state's tragic demise. Once Boston committed itself to a constitutional compact with other slave societies like South Carolina and Virginia, and eventually Louisiana, Mississippi, and Texas as well, then the autonomy it had struggled to sustain while an English colony came to an end. Instead, the dominance of slave-holding interests in the United States gradually forced its way into the city's politics. This change was embraced by some for economic reasons, rejected by others for moral reasons, but ultimately destroyed the capacity for consensus on which the city-state of Boston had rested.

To read *Looking Backward*, one might think that Bellamy had never heard of these problems. The Julian West of 1887 does employ a black servant, "a faithful colored man by the name of Sawyer," but otherwise there is no mention at all of African Americans, Irish immigrants, or any other ethnic group, either in 1887 or 2000. Bellamy refers to "minorities" only in the sense of consumer minorities with idiosyncratic tastes, whom West worries might be unsatisfied by the Industrial Army's production system.[2] (Fear not: Dr. Leete explains how niche markets work in this consumer paradise.) All social ills in the novel are attributed to economic causes; race as a social problem does not exist. Although it had been abolished only twenty years before, the history of slavery in America plays no part in Bellamy's story.

This, too, is part of the legacy of the Civil War and the creation of a mythic national narrative placing Boston and New England at its center. As victors in the Civil War, Francis Parkman and the professional historians who came after him made sure to wipe clean from their story of the Anglo-Saxon origins of American democracy any possibility that slavery shaped the innermost propulsions of the United States. Slavery was made to be the "peculiar institution" of the American South, and an exogenous import at that, as foreign to American soil as the "Feudalism, Monarchy, and Rome" that Parkman's Anglo-Saxon heroes banished in their fight against the French, and that his cousins defeated in their conquest of the slavocracy. Postwar Bostonians cultivated a collective amnesia about their own past as a slave-based economy and society with a legacy of slaveholding. Boston celebrated its antislavery accomplishments, as in August Saint-Gaudens's gorgeous sculpture on Boston Common commemorating Robert Gould Shaw and the Massachusetts 54th, but preferred to forget that angry mobs of respectable Boston gentlemen had threatened to lynch the city's abolitionists.

Race and slavery in Boston are obviously missing from *Looking Backward*. A more subtle absence can be seen by comparing *Looking Backward* to the utopian writings of Boston's founding era. What Bellamy's Boston of 2000 lacks is any sense of the city itself—the polis, city-republic, or small commonwealth—as an ideal unit of collective self-government. From More's *Utopia* to Campanella's *City of the Sun*, from Bacon's *New Atlantis* to Andreae's *Christianopolis*, to the Massachusetts Bay Company's fixation on Philippi for the colony's seal, city thinking had been a dominant force in framing ideals of government in the early modern world.[3] By the mid-nineteenth century, these beliefs were rapidly slipping away. Rufus Choate offered a preview of this change in his argument for West Roxbury's separation from the "crowded and noisome" incorporated city of Roxbury, which he claimed was inimical "to the duties of good citizenship." By the 1880s, the shift was complete. The explosive growth of urban America, the concentration of industrial labor in cities, and the political unrest generated there made the city itself seem ever more the problem. The opening chapters of *Looking Backward* dwell at length on these urban miseries.

For Bellamy, the vast scale of the continental nation consolidated by the Union victory in the Civil War enabled solutions to the problems of industrial society. The Boston that Julian West wakes up to in 2000 is unrecognizable from the perspective of 1887: "At my feet lay a great city. Miles of broad streets, shaded by trees and lined with fine buildings, for the most part not in continuous blocks but set in larger or smaller enclosures, stretched in every direction. Every quarter contained large open squares filled with trees, along which statues glistened and fountains flashed in the late-afternoon sun. Public buildings of a colossal size and architectural grandeur unparalleled in my day raised their stately piles on every side." Only by looking westward and recognizing the shape of the river, "that blue ribbon winding away to the sunset—was it not the sinuous Charles?"—does Julian West realize that he is still in Boston.[4]

All the problems of 1887 have now been solved by the enormous scale of America's national organization: millions of workers perfectly coordinated to produce all the goods and services that a country could want, an enormous national distribution system for all of life's desires, a national school system, national health care, even national distribution of what had formerly been women's household chores. "The broad shoulders of the nation," explains Dr. Leete, "bear now like a feather the burden that broke the backs of the women of your day."[5] The consolidated nation created these solutions; state governments have been abolished as impediments to large-scale organization. And among nations, first came the United States (of course), for *it* (no longer *they*) had pioneered the industrial organization of corporate and labor interests, which superseded the older polity of the federal Constitution and its independent states. Then "the great nations of Europe, as well as Australia, Mexico, and parts of South America," followed the United States' lead. Bellamy left aside Asia and Africa so that the world of 2000 could still have some historical achievements to anticipate. As Dr. Leete explains, "We all look forward to an eventual unification of the world, as one nation. That, no doubt, will be the ultimate form of society."[6] As *Looking Backward*'s popularity grew, thousands of enthusiastic Bellamy readers created a new socialist political movement in the United States. Its supporters, known as "Nationalists," published a magazine, the *Nationalist*, and founded Nationalist Clubs (the first was in Boston) seeking to achieve the nationalization of industry that *Looking Backward* projected.

By the time *Looking Backward* was published, the city-state of Boston had come and gone. Although many of the ideals of its founders remained relevant to late nineteenth-century problems, the notion that these ideals were best embodied in a compact, integrated, and unified polity had been swept away.

But now the year 2000 has come and gone as well, and we are no closer to Bellamy's ideal of an egalitarian society balanced with personal liberty, let alone a unified world government, than we are to discovering utopia on the remote island of Bensalem in a distant ocean. The large consolidated nation-states with imperial ambitions that have played major roles in world history since Bellamy's day—Great Britain, France, Germany, Russia, China, Japan, and the United States—all have left legacies of misery across the twentieth century that would surely have saddened Bellamy. The League of Nations and the United Nations, constructed in the wake of unspeakable disasters to promote the collective power of nation-states as a force for peace, have not brought about world unification. In the twenty-first century, it has become less certain than it was in Bellamy's day whether the nation-state should be the normative form of governance, and whether the ideals of responsible self-government can be achieved in units reaching the hundreds of millions or even billions of citizens. This book will have served its purpose if it encourages readers to calculate the value of a common form of polity that national consolidation brushed aside, once embodied in the city-state of Boston.

Notes

Introduction

1. "Speech of Theodore Parker at the Faneuil Hall Meeting," in Charles Emery Stevens, *Anthony Burns: A History* (Boston: John P. Jewett, 1856), appendix M, 291.
2. "Establishment of the Freedom Trail," Freedom Trail Foundation, accessed January 1, 2018, http://www.thefreedomtrail.org/about-foundation/establishment.shtml; "The Revolution Was in the Minds and Hearts of the People . . . ," National Park Service, Boston National Historical Park, accessed January 1, 2018, https://www.nps.gov/bost/index.htm.
3. Nathaniel Hawthorne, "The Gray Champion" (1835), in *Twice-Told Tales* (Boston: American Stationers Co., 1837), 22.
4. Walt Whitman, "A Boston Ballad—1854," in *The Complete Writings of Walt Whitman* (New York: G. P. Putnam's Sons, 1902), 2:25–27.
5. *Estado de los negros introducidos en La Habana, 1789–1820*, Archivo General de Indias, Santo Domingo 2207. Thanks to Elena Schneider for this reference.
6. Edward Randolph, *Edward Randolph: . . . Letters and Official Papers . . . , 1676–1703*, ed. Robert N. Toppan and Alfred T. S. Goodrick (Boston: Prince Society, 1909), 4:187, 6:72, 6:74.
7. King Charles to . . . , March 10, 1676, in W. Noel Sainsbury, ed., *Calendar of State Papers, Colonial Series, America and West Indies* (Vaduz, Liechtenstein: Kraus Reprint, 1964), 9:358, item 838.
8. Louis Jolliet, *Nouvelle decouverte de plusiers nations dans la Nouvelle France, en l'année 1673 et 1674* (New France, ca. 1674), John Carter Brown Library, Providence, RI.
9. Amblard-Marie-Raymond-Amédée, Vicomte Noailles, *Marins et Soldats Français en Amérique pendant la Guerre de l'Independence des États-Unis (1778–1783)* (Paris: Perrin et Cie, 1903), 317.
10. W. Warde Fowler, *The City-State of the Greeks and Romans* (London: Macmillan, 1893).
11. Mogens Herman Hansen, "The Concepts of City-State and City-State Culture," in *A Comparative Study of Thirty City-State Cultures: An Investigation*, ed. Mogens Herman Hansen (Copenhagen: Kongelige Danske Videnskabernes Selskab, 2000), 18.
12. At present, such concerns appear frequently in popular and scholarly media. See, for example, Jamie Bartlett, "Return of the City-State," *Aeon*, September 5, 2017, accessed January 27, 2018, https://aeon.co/essays/the-end-of-a-world-of-nation-states-may-be-upon-us; Bill McKibben, *Radio Free Vermont: A Fable of Resistance* (New York: Blue Rider Press, 2017).
13. John Winthrop, "A Modell of Christian Charity," in *The Winthrop Papers*, ed. Samuel Eliot Morison, Allyn Bailey Forbes, and Malcolm Freiberg (Boston: Massachusetts Historical Society, 1929–), 2:295. For the continuing ubiquity and conventionality of this interpretation, see the first paragraph of the Wikipedia entry for John Winthrop, accessed January 27, 2018, https://en.wikipedia.org/wiki/John_Winthrop.
14. Reagan used this phrase in his presidential nomination acceptance speech at the 1984 Republican National Convention as well as in his 1989 "Farewell Address."

15. Perry Miller, *Errand into the Wilderness* (Cambridge, MA: Harvard University Press, 1956), 15, 5.
16. Winthrop, "Modell of Christian Charity," 2:295; Hugh Dawson, "'Christian Charitie' as Colonial Discourse: Reading Winthrop's Sermon in Its English Context," *Early American Literature* 33 (1998): 117–48.
17. The *Arbella* crossed the Atlantic from March 29 to June 14, 1630. Winthrop wrote an entry in his journal for every day of the voyage, but made no mention of writing or presenting a lengthy discourse to his fellow passengers. See Richard S. Dunn, James Savage, and Laetitia Yeandle, eds., *The Journal of John Winthrop, 1630–1649* (Cambridge, MA: Belknap, 1999), 1–34.
18. Hugh Dawson, "John Winthrop's Rite of Passage: The Origins of the 'Christian Charity' Discourse," *Early American Literature* 26 (1991): 221–22; Abram C. van Engen, "Origins and Last Farewells: Bible Wars, Textual Form, and the Making of American History," *New England Quarterly* 86 (December 2013): 543–92.
19. George Bancroft later paraphrased the city upon a hill passage in revised editions of his *History of the United States*, but other nineteenth-century writers such as John Gorham Palfrey, John Fiske, Brooks Adams, and Charles Francis Adams Jr. never referred to it in their histories of early New England.
20. Several eyewitnesses reported hearing Cotton preach his sermon in Southampton. Francis J. Bremer, *John Winthrop: America's Forgotten Founding Father* (New York: Oxford University Press, 2003), 173–74.
21. John Cotton, *Gods Promise to His Plantation* (London, 1630), 8–9.
22. Sargent Bush Jr., introduction to *The Correspondence of John Cotton* (Chapel Hill: University of North Carolina Press, 2001), 1–11.
23. Theodore Dwight Bozeman, *To Live Ancient Lives: The Primitivist Dimension in Puritanism* (Chapel Hill: University of North Carolina Press, 1988).
24. See also John Winthrop, "The Humble Request, April 7, 1630," in *The Winthrop Papers*, 2:231–33.
25. On Philippi under Macedonian and Roman authority, see Joseph H. Hellerman, *Reconstructing Honor in Roman Philippi* (Cambridge: Cambridge University Press, 2005), 64–72. In early modern England, knowledge of ancient Philippi would have been found in the works of Strabo, the Greek geographer and historian, and Plutarch's *Lives of the Noble Grecians and Romans*, translated into English by Sir Thomas North, including a 1612 edition that featured biographies of Philip of Macedon and Octavius.
26. Acts 16:14–21 (King James Version). Hellerman notes that scholars "consistently highlight the Romanness of Philippi . . . because the Roman colonists, mainly military veterans, had dispossessed and disenfranchised the earlier Macedonian landowners. The tenacious manner in which Philippi retained its Roman orientation thus distinguished the settlement from colonies in Asia Minor, where assimilation of Hellenistic culture and values was much more pronounced. Only in Italy could one find a Roman settlement even comparable to Philippi." Hellerman, *Reconstructing Honor*, 66–67.
27. Ibid., 67–72.
28. Likewise, the "Humble Request" of the governor and Company of Massachusetts written in 1630 "to the rest of their Brethren in and of the Church of England" also cited the example of Philippi to justify their cause: "You are not ignorant, that the Spirit of God stirred up the Apostle *Paul* to make continuall mention of the Church of *Philippi* (which was a Colonie from *Rome*) let the same Spirit, we beseech you, put you in mind, that are the Lords remembrancers, to pray for us without ceasing." Winthrop, "Humble Request," 2:231–33.

29. See David D. Hall, *A Reforming People: Puritanism and the Transformation of Public Life in New England* (New York: Alfred A. Knopf, 2011), 22–53, 159–91; Michael P. Winship, *Godly Republicanism: Puritans, Pilgrims, and a City on a Hill* (Cambridge, MA: Harvard University Press, 2012), 183–232.
30. Quotation is from the title of Ralph Robinson's English translation of *Utopia* published in 1551. See Phil Withington, *Society in Early Modern England: The Vernacular Origins of Some Powerful Ideas* (Cambridge, UK: Polity, 2010), 157.
31. Christiaan van Adrichem, *A Briefe Description of Hierusalem and the Suburbs Therof, as It Florished in the Time of Christ*, trans. Thomas Tymme (London, 1595), "Epistle Dedicatory" and "Preface."
32. David Underdown, *Fire from Heaven: Life in an English Town in the Seventeenth Century* (New Haven, CT: Yale University Press, 1992), 105; Charles Herbert Mayo, ed., *The Municipal Records of the Borough of Dorchester, Dorset* (Exeter: W. Pollard, 1908), 667.
33. [Robert Burton], *The Anatomy of Melancholy* (Oxford, 1621), 56.
34. Donald R. Dickson, *The Tessera of Antilia: Utopian Brotherhoods and Secret Societies in the Early Seventeenth Century* (Leiden: Brill, 1998), 50–53; Walter W. Woodward, *Prospero's America: John Winthrop, Jr., Alchemy, and the Creation of New England Culture, 1606–1676* (Chapel Hill: University of North Carolina Press, 2010), 31–33.
35. Robert Appelbaum, *Literature and Utopian Politics in Seventeenth-Century England* (Cambridge: Cambridge University Press, 2002), 64–101; Amy Boesky, *Founding Fictions: Utopias in Early Modern England* (Athens: University of Georgia Press, 1996), 23–83; Jeffrey Knapp, *An Empire Nowhere: England, America, and Literature from Utopia to the Tempest* (Berkeley: University of California Press, 1992); Woodward, *Prospero's America*, 43–74. For a compelling account of the development of puritan colonization schemes in the context of English and European politics of the early seventeenth century, see Karen Ordahl Kupperman, "Errand to the Indies: Puritan Colonization from Providence Island to the Western Design," *William and Mary Quarterly* 45, no. 1 (January 1988): 70–99.
36. Underdown, *Fire from Heaven*, ix, 91.
37. Keith L. Sprunger, *Dutch Puritanism: A History of the English and Scottish Churches of the Netherlands in the Sixteenth and Seventeenth Centuries* (Leiden: E. J. Brill, 1983), 63–64, 334–35; Edmund S. Morgan, *Visible Saints: The History of a Puritan Idea* (Ithaca, NY: Cornell University Press, 1963), 48–50; Winship, *Godly Republicanism*, 89–110.
38. See David Beers Quinn, "The First Pilgrims," in *England and the Discovery of America, 1481–1620* (New York: Alfred A. Knopf, 1974), 337–63; Richard Hakluyt, *The Principal Navigations, Voyages, Traffiques, and Discoveries of the English Nation* (Glasgow, 1904), 8:166–81.
39. Karen Ordahl Kupperman, "A Welter of Colonial Projects," in *The Jamestown Project* (Cambridge, MA: Harvard University Press, 2007), 183–209. On Calvert's Avalon colony, see Luca Codignola, *The Coldest Harbour of the Land: Simon Stock and Lord Baltimore's Colony in Newfoundland, 1621–1649*, trans. Anita Weston (Kingston, ON: McGill-Queen's University Press, 1988).
40. Edmund S. Morgan, *American Slavery, American Freedom* (New York: Alfred A. Knopf, 1975), 73, 100.
41. William Bradford, *Of Plymouth Plantation, 1620–1647*, ed. Samuel Eliot Morison (New York: Alfred A. Knopf, 1952), 77–79.
42. John Winthrop, "General Observations: Autograph Draft," in *The Winthrop Papers*, 2:116–17.

43. Kupperman, "Errand to the Indies"; Karen Ordahl Kupperman, *Providence Island, 1630–1641: The Other Puritan Colony* (Cambridge: Cambridge University Press, 1993).
44. Charles E. Clark, *The Eastern Frontier: The Settlement of Northern New England, 1610–1763* (New York: Alfred A. Knopf, 1970), 16–20; James Phinney Baxter, *Sir Ferdinando Gorges and His Province of Maine* (Boston, 1890); Henry S. Burrage, *The Beginnings of Colonial Maine* (Portland, 1914).
45. James Phinney Baxter, *Agamenticus, Bristol, Gorgeana, York* (York, ME, 1904), 16–18.
46. Cotton, *Gods Promise*, 14, 16.
47. For a gigantic example, which ran to four volumes and nearly three thousand pages, see Justin Winsor, ed., *The Memorial History of Boston, 1630–1880* (Boston: James R. Osgood, 1882–86).

Chapter 1: Boston Emerges

1. Thomas Hutchinson, *History of the Colony of Massachusetts Bay*, 2nd ed. (London, 1765), 20–21.
2. Thomas Dudley "Letter to the Countess of Lincoln," March 1631, in *New Hampshire Historical Collections* (1834): 4:224–249, especially 229–32.
3. "A Court of Assistants Holden att Charlton the 7th of September 1630," in *Records of the Court of Assistants of the Colony of Massachusetts Bay, 1630–1692* (Boston: County of Suffolk, 1902), 2:4; Charles C. Smith, "Boston and the Colony," in *The Memorial History of Boston, 1630–1880*, ed. Justin Winsor (Boston: James R. Osgood, 1882–86), 1:217–40.
4. Nathaniel B. Shurtleff, ed., *Records of the Governor and Company of the Massachusetts Bay in New England* (Boston: William White, 1853), 1:172.
5. "Boston Town Records," in *Second Report of the Record Commissioners of the City of Boston*, 2nd ed. (Boston: Rockwell and Churchill, 1881), 1–3.
6. Shurtleff, *Records of Massachusetts Bay*, 1:101.
7. Ibid., 4:327, part 1.
8. For references to New England as a kingdom, see Richard S. Dunn, James Savage, and Laetitia Yeandle, eds., *The Journal of John Winthrop, 1630–1649* (Cambridge, MA: Belknap, 1999), 365, 429.
9. B. H. McPherson, "Revisiting the Manor of East Greenwich," *American Journal of Legal History* 42, no. 1 (January 1998): 35–56. This language was used in many colonial charters as well as for land grants in England to free the recipients of the land from the future possibility that the Crown could demand quitrents or other services or fees from tenants. These alternative forms of land tenure were abolished in England in 1660, but James II would attempt to resuscitate their use in the colonies in the 1680s, after most of the original charters of the colonies had been revoked.
10. Shurtleff, *Records of Massachusetts Bay*, 1:3–19.
11. Some documentary collections, when reprinting the Massachusetts 1629 charter, omit the references to mines of gold and silver altogether. See "No. 6, The First Charter of Massachusetts," in *Documentary Source Book of American History, 1606–1898*, ed. William MacDonald (New York: Macmillan, 1914), 22–26.
12. For complete versions, see *The Federal and State Constitutions, Colonial Charters, and Other Organic Laws of the States, Territories, and Colonies Now or Heretofore Forming the United States of America*, comp. Francis Newton Thorpe (Washington, DC: Government Printing Office, 1909). For New Sweden, see Berthold Fernow, ed.,

Documents Relating to the Colonial History of the State of New York, vol. 11 (Albany, NY: Weed, Parsons, and Company, 1853–87).

13. John J. McCusker and Russell R. Menard, *The Economy of British America, 1607–1789*, 2nd ed. (Chapel Hill: University of North Carolina Press, 1991).
14. Walter W. Woodward, *Prospero's America: John Winthrop, Jr., Alchemy, and the Creation of New England Culture, 1606–1676* (Chapel Hill: University of North Carolina Press, 2010), 75–105.
15. "Roger Williams to John Winthrop, Jr., 15 December 1648," in *The Correspondence of Roger Williams*, ed. Glenn W. LaFantasie (Providence: John Carter Brown Library, 1988), 1:263.
16. For a telling comparison, see Karen Ordahl Kupperman, *Providence Island, 1630–1641: The Other Puritan Colony* (Cambridge, UK: Cambridge University Press, 1993), 142–46.
17. This book will not attempt to sort out a precise definition of Puritanism or the puritan movement, as this is not its central focus. Instead, following the overwhelming predominance of the scholarship on this subject, it assumes that the bulk of the settlers who came to the "orthodox" colonies—Massachusetts, Plymouth, Connecticut, and New Haven—were committed to pursuing a godly way of life, were dissatisfied with the Church of England as a means to this end, and saw New England's experimental churches as a promising alternative. At the same time, it acknowledges the diverse views among the godly over questions of church polity and practice as well as a substantial population of religious outliers, from intense religious radicals for whom even New England's congregational system was too tame and conformist, to the religiously indifferent fishermen and traders who populated the periphery. See Michael P. Winship, "Were There Any Puritans in New England?" *New England Quarterly* 74, no. 1 (March, 2001): 118–38.
18. Virginia DeJohn Anderson, *New England's Generation: The Great Migration and the Formation of Society and Culture in the Seventeenth Century* (New York: Cambridge University Press, 1992).
19. Karen Ordahl Kupperman, "A Welter of Colonial Projects," in *The Jamestown Project* (Cambridge, MA: Harvard University Press, 2007), 183–210.
20. Darrett B. Rutman, "Governor Winthrop's Garden Crop: The Significance of Agriculture in the Early Commerce of Massachusetts Bay," *William and Mary Quarterly* 20, no. 3 (July 1963): 397–401.
21. Charles Francis Adams Jr., "The Earliest Exploration and Settlement of Boston Harbor," in Winsor, *Memorial History of Boston*, 1:63–86; Walter Muir Whitehill and Lawrence Kennedy, *Boston: A Topographical History*, 3rd ed. (Cambridge, MA: Harvard University Press, 2000), 1–4.
22. William Wood, *New England's Prospect* (London: John Bellamie, 1634), 40.
23. Dudley, "Letter to the Countess of Lincoln," 4:232, 236, 247. A "strike" was an archaic English unit of measure, usually used for grain and often the equivalent of a bushel.
24. Peter E. Pope, *Fish into Wine: The Newfoundland Plantation in the Seventeenth Century* (Chapel Hill: University of North Carolina Press, 2004), 11–44.
25. G. D. Ramsay, *The English Woollen Industry, 1600–1700* (London, 1982); Carla Rahn Phillips and William D. Phillips Jr., *Spain's Golden Fleece. Wool Production and the Wool Trade from the Middle Ages to the Nineteenth Century* (Baltimore: Johns Hopkins University Press, 1997).
26. James F. Shepherd and Gary M. Walton, *Shipping, Maritime Trade, and the Economic Development of Colonial North America* (New York: Cambridge University Press, 1972).

27. See Regina Grafe, "The Globalisation of Codfish and Wool: Spanish-English-North American Triangular Trade in the Early Modern Period" (working paper 71/03, Department of Economic History, London School of Economics, February 2003), 14–15.
28. Bernard Bailyn, *The New England Merchants in the Seventeenth Century* (Cambridge, MA: Harvard University Press, 1955), 80–83; Regina Grafe, *Entre el mundo ibérico y el Atlántico: Comercio y especialización regional en el norte de España, 1550–1650* (Bilbao: Diputación Foral de Bizkaia, Departamento de Cultura, 2005).
29. Bailyn, *New England Merchants*; Grafe, "Globalisation of Codfish and Wool"; McCusker and Menard, *Economy of British America*; Daniel Vickers, *Farmers and Fisherman: Two Centuries of Work in Essex County, Massachusetts, 1630–1850* (Chapel Hill: University of North Carolina Press, 1994).
30. "John White to John Winthrop, 16 Nov. 1636," in *The Winthrop Papers*, ed. Samuel Eliot Morison, Allyn Bailey Forbes, and Malcolm Freiberg (Boston: Massachusetts Historical Society, 1929–), 3:322; Vickers, *Farmers and Fisherman*, 92.
31. Francis X. Moloney, *The Fur Trade in New England, 1620–1676* (Cambridge, MA: Harvard University Press, 1931), 67–78; Bailyn, *New England Merchants*, 23–32, 49–60; William Cronon, *Changes in the Land: Indians, Colonists, and the Ecology of New England* (New York: Hill and Wang, 1983), 82–107.
32. Shurtleff, *Records of the Governor*, 1:214, 304.
33. Lynn Ceci, "Native Wampum as a Peripheral Resource in the Seventeenth-Century World System," in *The Pequots in Southern New England*, ed. Laurence M. Hauptmann and James D. Wherry (Norman: University of Oklahoma Press, 1990), 48–68; Jonathan L. Fairbanks, ed., *New England Begins: The Seventeenth Century* (Boston: Museum of Fine Arts, 1982), 1:74–75.
34. Numerous early European observers, such as Peter Lindeström, Roger Williams, William Wood, and Daniel Gookin, recount similar practices among a variety of Indian peoples—Delaware, Susquehannock, Iroquois, and Algonquians of southern New England. See Peter Lindeström, *Geographia Americae, with an Account of the Delaware Indians* (1654–56) (New York: Arno Press, 1979).
35. Daniel K. Richter, *The Ordeal of the Longhouse: The Peoples of the Iroquois League in the Era of European Colonization* (Chapel Hill: University of North Carolina Press, 1992), 47; Christopher L. Miller and George R. Hamell, "A New Perspective on Indian-White Contact: Cultural Symbols and Colonial Trade," *Journal of American History* 73 (1986–87): 311–28.
36. Daniel Gookin, *Historical Collections of the Indians in New England* (1674), repr. ed. with notes by Jeffrey H. Fiske (Towtaid, MA, 1970), 18.
37. Roger Williams, *A Key into the Language of America* (1643), ed. Howard M. Chapin (Providence, RI, 1936), 152, 161.
38. On the volume of Dutch trade, see Ceci, "Native Wampum," 58–59. By comparison, the value of the Spanish wool imported into England in the early 1640s was roughly two hundred thousand pounds. See Grafe, "Globalisation of Codfish and Wool," 12.
39. Cronon, *Changes in the Land*, 95–103; Alfred A. Cave, *The Pequot War* (Amherst: University of Massachusetts Press, 1996), 49–68.
40. On Pynchon and the fur trade, see Stephen Innes, *Labor in a New Land: Economy and Society in Seventeenth-Century Springfield* (Princeton, NJ: Princeton University Press, 1983); Bailyn, *New England Merchants*, 49–57. On the relationship between the fur trade and the town founders of New England, see John Frederick Martin, *Profits in the Wilderness. Entrepreneurship and the Founding of New England Towns in the Seventeenth Century* (Chapel Hill: University of North Carolina Press, 1991).

41. Darrett B. Rutman, *Winthrop's Boston: A Portrait of a Puritan Town, 1630–1649* (Chapel Hill: University of North Carolina Press, 1965), 183–85; Margaret Newell, *From Dependency to Independence: Economic Revolution in Colonial New England* (Ithaca, NY: Cornell University Press, 1998), 53–55.
42. Sylvester Sage Crosby, *Early Coins of America and the Laws Governing Their Issue* (Boston, 1875), 26–28; William B. Weeden, *Indian Money as a Factor in New England Civilization*, ed. Herbert Baxter Adams (Baltimore: Johns Hopkins University Press, 1884), 6–30; Shurtleff, *Records of Massachusetts Bay*, 1:138.
43. Wood, *New England's Prospect*, 81.
44. Cave, *Pequot War*, 40–44.
45. Ibid., 63–68; Faren Siminoff, *Crossing the Sound: The Rise of Atlantic American Communities in Seventeenth-Century Eastern Long Island* (New York: NYU Press, 2004), 34–56.
46. Cave, *Pequot War*, 58–61.
47. Dunn, Savage, and Yeandle, *Journal of John Winthrop*, 134.
48. Ibid., 133–34.
49. Cave, *Pequot War*, 69–98; Francis Jennings, *The Invasion of America: Indians, Colonialism, and the Cant of Conquest* (New York: W. W. Norton, 1976), 189–99.
50. Cave, *Pequot War*, 104–8; Jennings, *Invasion of America*, 206–9.
51. Michael Leroy Oberg, *Uncas: First of the Mohegans* (Ithaca, NY: Cornell University Press, 2003), 63–70.
52. See Dunn, Savage, and Yeandle, *Journal of John Winthrop*, 213–21; Lieutenant Lion Gardener, *Relation of the Pequot Wars* (1660), *Collections of the Massachusetts Historical Society* 3rd ser., 3:140–50; John Underhill, *Newes from America* (London, 1638). See Cave, *Pequot War*. See also Jennings, *Invasion of America*, 209–27.
53. Cave, *Pequot War*, 163.
54. Oberg, *Uncas*, 87–109. See also Michael Leroy Oberg, *Dominion and Civility: English Imperialism and Native America, 1585–1685* (Ithaca, NY: Cornell University Press, 1999), 81–112.
55. Ceci, "Native Wampum," 61; Shurtleff, *Records of Massachusetts Bay*, 1:208, 302, 329, 2:261, 279.
56. Patrick Manning, *Slavery and African Life: Occidental, Oriental, and African Slave Trades* (New York: Cambridge University Press, 1990), 8–23; David Eltis, *The Rise of African Slavery in the Americas* (New York: Cambridge University Press, 2000), 164–92.
57. Shurtleff, *Records of Massachusetts Bay*, 4:3–4, part 2; Weeden, *Indian Money*, 28–29.
58. Jan Hagendorn and Marion Johnson, *The Shell Money of the Slave Trade* (Cambridge: Cambridge University Press, 1986), 101–24.
59. Ibid., 37–63.
60. Cronon, *Changes in the Land*, 97–103; Bailyn, *New England Merchants*, 24; Weeden, *Indian Money*, 25–33. See Shurtleff, *Records of Massachusetts Bay*, 2:167, 4:3–4, part 2.
61. George Parker Winship, ed., *The Journal of Madam Knight* (1704) (Boston: Small Maynard and Co., 1920), 41.
62. David Murray, *Indian Giving: Economies of Power in Indian-White Exchanges* (Amherst: University of Massachusetts Press, 2000), 116–40.
63. "Lucy Downing to John Winthrop, c. Jan. 1640/41," in *The Winthrop Papers*, 4:303–4.
64. Dunn, Savage, and Yeandle, *Journal of John Winthrop*, 34, 44–45, 59, 95.

65. Ibid., 227, 246, 352. Peirce is listed in Rutman's compilation of "Boston Gentry, 1634–36," based on Peirce's contributions to the building of a school and fort in the town. Rutman, *Winthrop's Boston*, 73–75. For an imaginative reconstruction of the social meaning of Peirce's wealth, see Wendy Warren, *New England Bound: Slavery and Colonization in Early America* (New York: W. W. Norton, 2016), 197–98.
66. Dunn, Savage, and Yeandle, *Journal of John Winthrop*, 246, 323. The movement toward the Caribbean occurred in the context of an additional Puritan return migration to England, prompted by the outbreak of civil war. See Susan Hardman Moore, *Pilgrims: New World Settlers and the Call of Home* (New Haven, CT: Yale University Press, 2007).
67. Frances Rose-Troup, "John Humphrey," in *Essex Institute Historical Collections* (1929): 65:293–308; Bailyn, *New England Merchants*, 17; Louise A. Breen, *Transgressing the Bounds: Subversive Enterprises among the Puritan Elite in Massachusetts, 1630–1692* (New York: Oxford University Press, 2001), 100–110; Kupperman, *Providence Island*, 146–47, 322–25.
68. Dunn, Savage, and Yeandle, *Journal of John Winthrop*, 356.
69. Ibid., 356–57; Kupperman, *Providence Island*, 325, 335, 341.
70. Dunn, Savage, and Yeandle, *Journal of John Winthrop*, 409; Kevin Butterfield, "Puritans and Religious Strife in the Early Chesapeake," *Virginia Magazine of History and Biography* 109, no. 1 (2001): 11–17.
71. Dunn, Savage, and Yeandle, *Journal of John Winthrop*, 328, 489. On the price decline and economic crisis in early Boston, see Bailyn, *New England Merchants*, 47; Rutman, *Winthrop's Boston*, 183–84.
72. Dunn, Savage, and Yeandle, *Journal of John Winthrop*, 345; Stephen Innes, *Creating the Commonwealth: The Economic Culture of Puritan New England* (New York: W. W. Norton, 1995), 276; Rutman, *Winthrop's Boston*, 189.
73. Dunn, Savage, and Yeandle, *Journal of John Winthrop*, 301–2.
74. Ibid., 386.
75. Ibid., 424.
76. Bailyn, *New England Merchants*, 82–86; Grafe, "Globalisation of Codfish and Wool," 1–40.
77. Saint Augustine, *Of the Citie of God* (London, 1610); Thomas More, *Utopia* (1516), trans. Ralph Robynson, ed. David Harris Sacks (Boston: Bedford Books, 1999).
78. Dunn, Savage, and Yeandle, *Journal of John Winthrop*, 286–87.
79. Ibid., 602–4; Robert E. Moody, ed., *The Saltonstall Papers, 1607–1815* (Boston, 1972), 1:138–39; Shurtleff, *Records of Massachusetts Bay*, 2:129, 136, 168, 3:46. See also Warren, *New England Bound*, 37–42.
80. *New Englands First Fruits* (London: Henry Overton, 1643), 10–11.
81. Dunn, Savage, and Yeandle, *Journal of John Winthrop*, 573–74, 761. On the labor crisis in the Anglo-Atlantic world of the 1640s, see Peter Linebaugh and Marcus Rediker, *The Many-Headed Hydra: Sailors, Slaves, Commoners, and the Hidden History of the Revolutionary Atlantic* (Boston: Beacon Press, 2000), 104–42; Carla Gardina Pestana, *The English Atlantic in an Age of Revolution, 1640–1661* (Cambridge, MA: Harvard University Press, 2004), 183–212. On the development of a labor regime in colonial Massachusetts, see Barry Levy, *Town Born: The Political Economy of New England from Its Founding to the Revolution* (Philadelphia: University of Pennsylvania Press, 2010), 34–50.
82. Dunn, Savage, and Yeandle, *Journal of John Winthrop*, 601; John Langdon Sibley, "George Downing," in *Biographical Sketches of the Graduates of Harvard University* (Cambridge, MA: Charles William Sever, University Bookstore, 1873), 1:28–51.
83. "George Downing to John Winthrop, Jr.," in *The Winthrop Papers*, 5:42–45.

84. Richard S. Dunn, *Sugar and Slaves: The Rise of the Planter Class in the English West Indies* (New York: W. W. Norton, 1972), 59–62.
85. "Emmanuel Downing to John Winthrop," in *The Winthrop Papers*, 5:38–39.
86. Innes, *Creating the Commonwealth*, 237–70; Woodward, *Prospero's America*, 93–137.
87. Richard Cogley, *John Eliot's Mission to the Indians before King Philip's War* (Cambridge, MA: Harvard University Press, 1999).
88. Neal Salisbury, *Manitou and Providence: Indians, Europeans, and the Making of New England, 1500–1643* (New York: Oxford University Press, 1984), 79–82, 188–90.
89. Dunn, Savage, and Yeandle, *Journal of John Winthrop*, 51–52.
90. Jennings, *Invasion of America*, 177–201; Salisbury, *Manitou and Providence*, 166–202.
91. For the essential introduction to the tangled history of charters and land claims in colonial British America, see Charles McLean Andrews, *The Colonial Period of American History*, vols. 1–2, *The Settlements* (New Haven, CT: Yale University Press, 1934).
92. Mark A. Peterson, "Boston Pays Tribute: Autonomy and Empire in the Atlantic World, 1630–1714," in *Shaping the Stuart World: The Atlantic Connection*, ed. Allan I. Macinnes and Arthur H. Williamson (Leiden: Brill, 2006), 311–35.
93. Jenny Hale Pulsipher, *Subjects unto the Same King: Indians, English, and the Contest for Authority in Colonial New England* (Philadelphia: University of Pennsylvania Press, 2005), 16–30.
94. Harry M. Ward, "The Articles of Confederation of the United Colonies of New England, May 19, 1643," in *The United Colonies of New England, 1643–1690* (New York: Vantage Press, 1961), 384–90.
95. Hannah Farber, "The Rise and Fall of the Province of Lygonia, 1643–1658," *New England Quarterly* 82, no. 3 (September, 2009): 490–513.
96. Robert Emmett Wall, *Massachusetts Bay: The Crucial Decade, 1640–1650* (New Haven, CT: Yale University Press, 1972), 121–56.
97. Oberg, *Uncas*, 87–109; Woodward, *Prospero's America*, 97–100.
98. Oberg, *Uncas*, 87–109; Pulsipher, *Subjects unto the Same King*, 25–28.
99. Dunn, Savage, and Yeandle, *Journal of John Winthrop*, 481. Note that wampum here was used as a diplomatic gift, not as money or payment.
100. Alden Vaughan, *New England Frontier: Puritans and Indians, 1620–1675* (Boston: Little, Brown, 1965), 169–73; Jennings, *Invasion of America*, 272–276; Salisbury, *Manitou and Providence*, 225–35. See also Oberg, *Uncas*, 87–109; Pulsipher, *Subjects unto the Same King*, 25–32.
101. Jaap Jacobs, *The Colony of New Netherland: A Dutch Settlement in Seventeenth-Century America* (Ithaca, NY: Cornell University Press, 2009), 19–61; Susanah Shaw Romney, *New Netherland Connections: Intimate Networks and Atlantic Ties in Seventeenth-Century America* (Chapel Hill: University of North Carolina Press, 2013), 26–65.
102. Isabel MacBeath Calder, *The New Haven Colony* (New Haven, CT: Yale University Press, 1934).
103. Amandus Johnson, *The Swedish Settlements on the Delaware: Their History and Relation to the Indians, Dutch, and English* (New York: University of Pennsylvania Press, 1911), 380–97.
104. Washington Irving, *A History of New York* (1809; New York: Penguin, 2008), 137; Ward, *United Colonies of New England*, 161.
105. Wall, *Massachusetts Bay*, 161; Shurtleff, *Records of Massachusetts Bay*, 2:60; Dunn, Savage, and Yeandle, *Journal of John Winthrop*, 521–22.

106. Ward, *United Colonies of New England*, 188–92.
107. Dunn, Savage, and Yeandle, *Journal of John Winthrop*, 440–51. For a general account, see M. A. MacDonald, *Fortune and La Tour: The Civil War in Acadia* (Toronto: Methuen, 1983).
108. Dunn, Savage, and Yeandle, *Journal of John Winthrop*, 358, 393.
109. William Bradford, *Of Plymouth Plantation, 1620–1647*, ed. Samuel Eliot Morison (New York: Alfred A. Knopf, 1952), 275–79; Dunn, Savage, and Yeandle, *Journal of John Winthrop*, 153–55.
110. Dunn, Savage, and Yeandle, *Journal of John Winthrop*, 153, 366.
111. Ibid., 442n.
112. Thomas Hutchinson, *The History of the Colony and Province of Massachusetts-Bay*, ed. Lawrence Shaw Mayo (Cambridge, MA: Harvard University Press, 1936), 1:110–16.
113. Dunn, Savage, and Yeandle, *Journal of John Winthrop*, 642–43.
114. Hutchinson, *History of the Colony*, 1:114.
115. John G. Reid, *Acadia, Maine, and New Scotland: Marginal Colonies in the Seventeenth Century* (Toronto: University of Toronto Press, 1981), 96–101.
116. Dunn, Savage, and Yeandle, *Journal of John Winthrop*, 365, 429.
117. Edmund S. Morgan, *The Puritan Dilemma: The Story of John Winthrop* (New York: Pearson Longman, 2007), 196.
118. Dunn, Savage, and Yeandle, *Journal of John Winthrop*, 524–27.
119. Ibid.
120. Ibid., 606; Shurtleff, *Records of Massachusetts Bay*, 2:116.
121. Dunn, Savage, and Yeandle, *Journal of John Winthrop*, 326–28.

Chapter 2: The World in a Shilling

1. The Crown's revocation effort was sidetracked by the growing contention within English politics. See Herbert Levi Osgood, *The American Colonies in the Seventeenth Century*, vol. 3, *Imperial Control: Beginnings of the System of Royal Provinces* (New York: Macmillan, 1907), 69–71.
2. From the fifteenth century on, the word "sovereign," meaning "one of the greatest power or potency," referred both to the monarch and to an especially valuable gold coin, worth twenty-two shillings, six pence—thirty pence more than the pound sterling. See "sovereign," *Oxford English Dictionary*, online ed., A.4.a.
3. A JSTOR search for the words "political economy" appearing in articles in the *William and Mary Quarterly* yields hundreds of results, but nearly every one of these articles is primarily concerned with the revolutionary period.
4. For such metropolitan analyses, see John J. McCusker and Russell R. Menard, *The Economy of British America, 1607–1789*, 2nd ed. (Chapel Hill: University of North Carolina Press, 1991); Nuala Zahedieh, *The Capital and the Colonies: London and the Atlantic Economy, 1660–1700* (Cambridge: Cambridge University Press, 2010).
5. Adam Smith, *An Inquiry into the Nature and Causes of the Wealth of Nations* (London: W. Strahan and T. Cadell, 1776), 2:1.
6. By imputing political economy "goals" to Boston, I do not suggest that its colonists spelled out such goals explicitly. Instead, I follow the method used by scholars such as Edward Luttwak, discovering their goals in actions taken persistently over time by persons and institutions committed to the success of the state. See Edward Luttwak, *The Grand Strategy of the Byzantine Empire* (Cambridge, MA: Harvard University Press, 2009).

7. Margaret E. Newell, *From Dependency to Independence: Economic Revolution in Colonial New England* (Ithaca, NY: Cornell University Press, 1998), 70, 75, 88, 91.
8. The only comparable example involves the limited success of Barbadian planters in creating South Carolina. See Peter Wood, *Black Majority: Negros in Colonial South Carolina from 1670 through the Stono Rebellion* (New York: W. W. Norton, 1996), 13–34; Richard S. Dunn, *Sugar and Slaves: The Rise of the Planter Class in the English West Indies* (New York: W. W. Norton, 1972), 111–16.
9. For an alternative to the declension model, see Mark A. Peterson, *The Price of Redemption: The Spiritual Economy of Puritan New England* (Stanford, CA: Stanford University Press, 1997).
10. Lewis Hanke, *The Imperial City of Potosí: An Unwritten Chapter in the History of Spanish America* (The Hague: Nijhoff, 1956). For the Manila galleon and flota, see Henry Kamen, *Empire: How Spain Became a World Power, 1492–1763* (New York: Perennial, 2004), 197–239, 262–63, 285–93.
11. Regina Grafe, "The Globalisation of Codfish and Wool: Spanish-English-North American Triangular Trade in the Early Modern Period" (working paper 71/03, Department of Economic History, London School of Economics, February 2003), 14–15.
12. To put this amount in context, 100,000 pesos in 1676 would have been worth roughly £40,000 sterling, a huge sum of money for a single individual to provide as a gift. Recall that in the 1640s, the entire value of the wool trade from Spain to England was roughly £200,000.
13. Peter Bakewell, *Silver and Entrepreneurship in Seventeenth-Century Potosí: The Life and Times of Antonio López de Quiroga* (Albuquerque: University of New Mexico Press, 1988), 121–23. On silver mining and Indian labor at Potosí, see Peter Bakewell, *Miners of the Red Mountain: Indian Labor in Potosí, 1545–1640* (Albuquerque: University of New Mexico Press, 1984).
14. Carlos Newland and Maria Jesus san Segundo, "Human Capital and Other Determinants of the Price Life Cycle of a Slave: Peru and La Plata in the Eighteenth Century," *Journal of Economic History* 56, no. 3 (September 1996): 698.
15. In the familiar ratio known and used across Europe and the Americas, there were 12 pence to the shilling, and 20 shillings to the pound.
16. For estimates, see Louis Jordan, *John Hull, the Mint, and the Economics of Massachusetts Coinage* (Lebanon, NH: University Press of New England, 2002), 102–17.
17. Nathaniel Hawthorne, *Grandfather's Chair and Biographical Stories* (Boston: Houghton Mifflin, 1896), 32–33.
18. Thomas Hutchinson, *The History of the Colony of Massachusetts Bay*, 2nd ed. (London, 1765), 178n.
19. John Hull, "Account Books" (manuscript, New England Historic and Genealogical Society, Boston), 1:72.
20. Jordan, *John Hull*, 110–11.
21. There were many experiments by English colonies involving the production of fiduciary or token coins, beginning with the brass "Hog Money" of Bermuda. But these were always made from inexpensive materials, and never pretended to compete with English sterling or Spanish money. See Robert Chalmers, *A History of Currency in the British Colonies* (London, 1893), 150–51.
22. Thomas J. Sargent and François R. Velde, *The Big Problem of Small Change* (Princeton, NJ: Princeton University Press, 2002), 65.
23. Ibid., 48.
24. Ibid., 134; Rogers Ruding, *Annals of the Coinage of Great Britain and Its Dependencies* (London: J. Hearne, 1840), 1:275.

25. Deborah Valenze, *The Social Life of Money in the English Past* (New York: Cambridge University Press, 2006), 35.
26. According to Sargent and Velde, "Over 12,700 different types of tokens have been catalogued for the period from 1644 to 1672, issued in 1,700 different English towns. An estimated 3,000 were issued in London alone . . . ; [t]he circulation of each token was limited geographically to a few streets, but there existed in London at least one 'changer of farthings' in Drury Lane, who issued his own farthings." Sargent and Velde, *Big Problem of Small Change*, 267. See also George Berry, *Seventeenth-Century England: Traders and Their Tokens* (London: Seaby, 1988).
27. Daniel Vickers, *Farmers and Fisherman: Two Centuries of Work in Essex County, Massachusetts, 1630–1850* (Chapel Hill: University of North Carolina Press, 1994), 47–48, 99–100.
28. Richard S. Dunn, James Savage, and Laetitia Yeandle, eds., *The Journal of John Winthrop, 1630–1649* (Cambridge, MA: Belknap, 1999), 642–43. See also Mark G. Hanna, *Pirate Nests and the Rise of the British Empire, 1570–1740* (Chapel Hill: University of North Carolina Press, 2015), 92–94.
29. Eric Helleiner, *The Making of National Money: Territorial Currencies in Historical Perspective* (Ithaca, NY: Cornell University Press, 2003).
30. Curtis Putnam Nettels, *The Money Supply of the American Colonies before 1720* (Madison: University of Wisconsin, 1934); 236–37; Sylvester Sage Crosby, *Early Coins of America and the Laws Governing Their Issue* (Boston, 1875), 80; Nathaniel B. Shurtleff, ed., *Records of the Governor and Company of the Massachusetts Bay in New England* (Boston: William White, 1853), 4:533, part 2.
31. Marc Shell, *Art and Money* (Chicago: University of Chicago Press, 1995), 10. On the commonplace nature of clipped and cut coins in seventeenth-century England, see Valenze, *Social Life of Money*, 36.
32. Recall that "departing" or dividing coins was seen in fourteenth-century England as a desperate measure to take in the face of coin shortages.
33. Thomas Babington Macaulay, *The History of England, from the Accession of James the Second* (London, 1855), 4:187. By the 1690s, the state of England's coinage was so poor, and coins were so routinely found to be clipped or underweight, that the Crown conducted a "Great Recoinage" at considerable expense. See Peter Laslett, "John Locke, the Great Recoinage, and the Origins of the Board of Trade, 1695–1698," *William and Mary Quarterly* 14, no. 3 (July 1957): 370–402.
34. Jordan, *John Hull*, 150.
35. Bakewell, *Silver and Entrepreneurship*, 36–44.
36. Quoted in ibid., 38.
37. Ibid., 40–44.
38. The various colonial governments in Spanish America responded with measures to compensate for the scandal, although distance and information-control problems allowed merchants in some places, such as Buenos Aires, to hide the facts of the scandal well into the 1650s. The French government also responded with measures regulating the acceptance of Spanish coins as legal tender starting in the late 1640s. See Philip L. Mossman, "The Potosí Scandal and the Massachusetts Mint," *Colonial Newsletter: A Research Journal in Early American Numismatics* 48, no. 2 (August 2008): 3289–309; Sewall Menzel, *Cobs, Pieces of Eight, and Treasure Coins: The Early Spanish-American Mints and Their Coinages, 1536–1773* (New York: American Numismatic Society, 2005).
39. John Hull, "The Diaries of John Hull, Mint-Master and Treasurer of the Colony of Massachusetts Bay," in *Transactions of the American Antiquarian Society* (Boston: John Wilson and Son, 1857), 145. Furthermore, an address to King Charles II written

by the Massachusetts General Court in October 1684 to justify the Massachusetts coinage and gain leave to continue the mint's operations suggests a strong awareness of the problem created by the Potosí mint scandal: "And as for the minting and stamping pieces of silver to pass among ourselves for XIId, VId, IIId, we were necessitated thereunto, having no staple commodity in our country to pay debts or buy necessaries but fish and corn. . . . Then comes in a considerable quantity of light, base Spanish money, whereby many people were cousened, and the Colony in danger of being undone thereby; which put us upon the project of melting it down, and stamping such pieces as aforesaid to pass in payment of debts amongst ourselves." "Report of a Committee Appointed October 30, 1684," political volume of manuscripts, vol. 1, Massachusetts State Archives, reprinted in Hull, "Diaries of John Hull," 282.

40. The original order for stamping foreign coins has disappeared from the Massachusetts General Court records. Our knowledge of its contents comes from the language of the surviving directive calling for its repeal. See Crosby, *Early Coins of America*, 30–31.
41. Ibid., 43.
42. *Holinshed's Chronicles* claimed that "King Edward I [r. 1272–1307] did first coine the penie and smallest peeces of siluer roundwise, which before were square." See "coin," *Oxford English Dictionary*, online ed., 1.a. Similarly, the 1497 Spanish law that determined that value of the real declared that the smallest coin, the eighth real, be square: "e que los ochavos sean quadrados." See "*Pragmatica* of Medina del Campo, June 13, 1497," in *Compendio de las piezas de ocho reales*, ed. Gabriel Calbeto de Grau (San Juan: Ediciones Juan Ponce de Leon, 1970), 2:536, reprinted in Jordan, *John Hull*, 151–52.
43. Sargent and Velde, *Big Problem of Small Change*, 266–67. Later, in the 1690s, the English diarist John Evelyn's tract on the history of medals and money described square coins in use as farthings and halfpennies in the era of the Norman Conquest. John Evelyn, *Numismata, A Discourse on Medals, Antient and Modern* (London, 1697), 10.
44. The technical literature on the exact weight of the Massachusetts shilling and its relationship to English and Spanish silver coinage suggests that when precisely measured, the Massachusetts shilling weighed 22.5 percent less than an English shilling. But for practical purposes, the Massachusetts shilling was valued at three-quarters of an English shilling. See Jordan, *John Hull*, 64–73.
45. Shurtleff, *Records of Massachusetts Bay*, 3:353–54.
46. The legislation allowed customers bringing silver to the mint to stay to watch the coining process and get exact receipts from Hull for the amount of silver received, assayed, and coined and for the fees charged. See Shurtleff, *Records of Massachusetts Bay*, 3:261–62.
47. Louis Jordan, "On the Founding of the Hull Mint," *Colonial Newsletter: A Research Journal in Early American Numismatics* 49, no. 3 (2009): 3477–88.
48. On the location of the mint, see Jordan, *John Hull*, 1–17.
49. Ibid., 115.
50. Mass General Court Records, May 2, 1662, reprinted in Hull, "Diaries of John Hull," 294.
51. Starting in the 1660s, Barbados, Jamaica, Montserrat, Antigua, Nevis, and Bermuda all cried up the value of their silver to keep it from being sent to Massachusetts in return for staples. See Chalmers, *History of Currency*, 48, 64, 98, 153.
52. Jordan, *John Hull*, 172–74.
53. For a book that speaks eloquently to these questions, see John McCusker, *How Much Is That in Real Money? A Historical Commodity Price Index for Use as a Deflator of Money* (Worcester, MA: American Antiquarian Society, 2001).

54. Sargent and Velde, *Big Problem of Small Change*, 116 (emphasis added).
55. The account books simply list the value of the consignment of mackerel and pork at seventy-eight pounds, ten shillings. John Hull, "Account Books," 1:53.
56. Account book of Philip English, Essex Institute, cited in James McWilliams, *Building the Bay Colony: Local Economy and Culture in Early Massachusetts* (Charlottesville: University of Virginia Press, 2007), 82. McWilliams traces the relationship between New England's commercial farmers and the producers they supplied, but pays no attention to the importance of currency in lubricating the exchange.
57. Shurtleff, *Records of Massachusetts Bay*, 1:327.
58. Hermann Frederick Clarke, *John Hull: A Builder of the Bay Colony* (Portland, ME: Southworth-Anthoesen Press, 1940), 87–89.
59. "Deed of Webucksham and Nonmonshot to John Winthrop, Jr., Oct 8, 1644," and "Deed of Nodawahunt to John Winthrop Jr., Nov 11 1644," in *The Winthrop Papers*, ed. Samuel Eliot Morison, Allyn Bailey Forbes, and Malcolm Freiberg (Boston: Massachusetts Historical Society, 1929–),4:496; Shurtleff, *Records of Massachusetts Bay*, 1:82.
60. On the relationship between black lead and silver in alchemical thought, see Walter W. Woodward, *Prospero's America: John Winthrop, Jr., Alchemy, and the Creation of New England Culture, 1606–1676* (Chapel Hill: University of North Carolina Press, 2010), 78–89.
61. Cited in Clarke, *John Hull*, 88.
62. A dozen years later, Hull was still contemplating the possibility of "sending home the blacke lead either to England or to Hollon upon Joynt Account." See John Hull to Benedict Arnold, December 2, 1674, in "Letter Book of John Hull," John Hull Papers, American Antiquarian Society, 221.
63. John Hull to Benedict Arnold, April 16, 1677, in "Letter Book of John Hull," 335–36.
64. "Records of a Meeting of the Pettequamscutt Partners, June 4, 1668," in Clarke, *John Hull*, 90.
65. Hull was not alone among Boston's leading merchants in pursuing a vertical integration strategy. Newell, *From Dependency to Independence*, 85.
66. John Hull to Thomas Broughton, October 17, 1673, in "Letter Book of John Hull," 138–39.
67. John Hull to Roger Plaisted, November 4, 1673, in "Letter Book of John Hull," 139–40.
68. The *Oxford English Dictionary* defines "entreprenour" as "one who undertakes; a manager, controller; champion," with the following usage example: "1475 *Bk. Noblesse* (1860) 64 That most noble centoure Publius Decius, so hardie an entreprenoure in the bataile." Decius was a republican Roman general who sacrificed himself in battle to save his army.
69. Hull, "Diaries of John Hull," 144.
70. Ibid., 145.
71. In addition to the "Diaries of John Hull," the best accounts of Hull's career remain Clarke, *John Hull*; Samuel Eliot Morison, *Builders of the Bay Colony* (Boston: Houghton Mifflin, 1930).
72. William Cronon, *Changes in the Land: Indians, Colonists, and the Ecology of New England* (New York: Hill and Wang, 1983), 91–101.
73. William Wood, *New England's Prospect* (London: John Bellamie, 1634), 94.
74. Bernard Bailyn, *The New England Merchants in the Seventeenth Century* (Cambridge, MA: Harvard University Press, 1955), 56. For another work focusing on the decline of the fur trade, see Francis X. Moloney, *The Fur Trade in New England,*

1620–1676 (Cambridge, MA: Harvard University Press, 1931), 109–19. See also Cronon, *Changes in the Land*, 99.

75. John Hull to Edward Hull, September 12, 1681, in "Letter Book of John Hull," 492. See also ibid., 522.
76. Samuel Maverick to Earl of Clarendon, n.d. (ca. 1662), "Clarendon Papers," in *Collections of New-York Historical Society for the Year 1869* (New York, 1869), 42–43.
77. Daniel Gookin, *Historical Collections of the Indians of New England* (1792), *Collections of the Massachusetts Historical Society*, 1:158.
78. Francis Jennings, *The Invasion of America: Indians, Colonialism, and the Cant of Conquest* (Chapel Hill: University of North Carolina Press, 1975).
79. Hull's account books for King Philip's War remain largely unused by historians of the war. Kyle Zelner investigates the process of conscription in Essex County, but does not use Hull's account books to see how the soldiers were paid. Kyle Zelner, *A Rabble in Arms: Massachusetts Towns and Militiamen during King Philip's War* (New York: NYU Press, 2009). Douglas Leach mentions Hull's account books, but does not explore their relevance. Douglas Leach, *Flintlock and Tomahawk: New England in King Philip's War* (New York: Macmillan, 1958).
80. George Bodge, *Soldiers in King Philip's War* (Leominster, MA, 1896), 479.
81. John Hull to Edward Hull, February 2, 1674, in "Letter Book of John Hull," 158.
82. The council of the United Colonies had used funds collected by the New England Company, the charitable organization that raised money for Indian missions in New England, to purchase arms and ammunitions, ostensibly for the praying Indians' defense. See Jennings, *Invasion of America*, 286–87. Once King Philip's War began, Hull's orders for muskets and "carbins with swivels" continued apace. See John Hull to Edward Hull, September 22, 1675, in "Letter Book of John Hull," 281; John Hull to Edward Hull, November 4, 1675, in "Letter Book of John Hull"; John Hull to John Ive, November 4, 1675, in "Letter Book of John Hull," 285. Hull ordered more than two hundred additional firelock muskets and fifty carbines from two separate correspondents here.
83. Bodge, *Soldiers in King Philip's War*, 479. An attack on Hadley, Massachusetts, in June 1676 was repulsed when "the inhabitants discharged a great gun upon them, whereupon about fifty Indians were seen running out of the house in great haste, being terribly frighted with the report and slaughter made amongst them by the great gun." Increase Mather, *A Brief History of the War with the Indians of New England* (Boston, 1676), 33. Similarly, in Medfield, Massachusetts, in February 1676, "the enemy were frightened away by the firing of a cannon." Bodge, *Soldiers in King Philip's War*, 34. These inland towns were defended by artillery that clearly had been stationed for the purpose of Indian warfare, not coastal defense.
84. John Hull to Mr. John Harris, March 4, 1674, in "Letter Book of John Hull," 164.
85. John Hull to Thomas Papillon, August 20, 1674, in "Letter Book of John Hull," 202.
86. Saltpeter had other uses among seventeenth-century alchemical and metallurgical experimenters, but Hull's correspondence clearly emphasizes its use in making gunpowder. See Woodward, *Prospero's America*, 147–48.
87. John Hull to Thomas Papillon, January 4, 1675, in "Letter Book of John Hull," 233–34. Hull also purchased saltpeter from other London merchants, including his cousin Daniel Allen. In 1675, Hull complained that "yor salt peter was verry bade small blacke stuff I would have had East India petr this was Barbarie petr." John Hull to Daniel Allen, January 5, 1675, in "Letter Book of John Hull," 229.
88. John Hull to Thomas Papillon, September 4, 1675, in "Letter Book of John Hull," 274.

89. John Hull to John Ives, January 4, 1675, in "Letter Book of John Hull," 233–34; John Hull to Edward Hull, January 4–7, 1675, in "Letter Book of John Hull," 236.
90. Gookin, *Historical Collections*, 4:166–71.
91. Virginia DeJohn Anderson, "King Philip's Herds: Indians, Colonists, and the Problem of Livestock in Early New England," *William and Mary Quarterly* 51, no. 4 (October 1994): 601–24; Richard W. Cogley, *John Eliot's Mission to the Indians before King Philip's War* (Cambridge, MA: Harvard University Press, 1998).
92. For other major accounts of the origins of the war, see Leach, *Flintlock and Tomahawk*; Jennings, *Invasion of America*; James D. Drake, *King Philip's War: Civil War in New England, 1675–1676* (Amherst: University of Massachusetts Press, 1999); Jenny Hale Pulsipher, *Subjects unto the Same King: Indians, English, and the Contest for Authority in Colonial New England* (Philadelphia: University of Pennsylvania Press, 2005).
93. George D. Langdon, *Pilgrim Colony: A History of New Plymouth, 1620–1691* (New Haven, CT: Yale University Press, 1966), 156–87.
94. For a discussion of the war's expansion from a conflict between Plymouth and the Wampanoags in June 1675, to the major confrontation between the United Colonies and Narragansetts in fall 1675, see Pulsipher, *Subjects unto the Same King*, 101–27. On the Boston-based Atherton Company's land interests in Rhode Island as a basis for war against the Narragansetts, see Jennings, *Invasion of America*, 305–7.
95. For contemporary accounts, see William Hubbard, *The Present State of New-England, Being a Narrative of the Troubles with the Indians in New-England* (London, 1677); Increase Mather, *Brief History of the War.*
96. Hull, "Diaries of John Hull," 162.
97. Zelner describes the impressment of soldiers during King Philip's War, but focuses exclusively on Essex County towns, and does not coordinate town impressment records with Hull's account books of soldiers' payment, missing the link between colony and confederation coordination and town contributions. Zelner, *Rabble in Arms.*
98. John Hull to Edward Hull, May 6, 1676, in "Letter Book of John Hull," 308.
99. John Hull to John Flint, April 27, 1676, in "Letter Book of John Hull," 303.
100. John Hull to John Pynchon, September 23, 1675, in "Letter Book of John Hull," 282–83.
101. See, for example, Hull's record of payments to "Wounded Men" in John Hull, "Account Books," 3:5.
102. "John Hull to the Honorable General Court Now Sitting in Boston, October 25, 1681," reprinted in Hull, "Diaries of John Hull," 263–64.
103. See T. H. Breen, "War, Taxes, and Political Brokers: The Ordeal of Massachusetts Bay," in *Puritans and Adventurers: Change and Persistence in Early America* (New York: Oxford University Press, 1980), 82–89; Robin L. Einhorn, *American Taxation, American Slavery* (Chicago: University of Chicago Press, 2006), 59–71.
104. John Hull to Robert Webster, February 1, 1675, in "Letter Book of John Hull," 243–44.
105. John Hull to Philip French, September 2, 1675, in "Letter Book of John Hull," 271. The same refrain was repeated in another letter to his cousins, Thomas Buckham and Daniel Allen: "Gentlemen, I have so much business forced upon me by the country since our warrs began, yt I have no time to do as I would." John Hull to Thomas Buckham and Daniel Allen, June 19, 1676, in "Letter Book of John Hull," 308.
106. John Hull to Edward Hull, June 22, 1676, in "Letter Book of John Hull," 311.
107. John Hull to Daniel Quincy, January 15, 1677, in "Letter Book of John Hull," 327.
108. Margaret Newell, *Brethren by Nature: New England Indians, Colonists, and the Origins of American Slavery* (Ithaca, NY: Cornell University Press, 2015), 131–58.

109. Carla Gardina Pestana, *The English Atlantic in an Age of Revolution, 1640–1661* (Cambridge, MA: Harvard University Press, 2004), 183–212.
110. Margaret Ellen Newell, "The Changing Nature of Indian Slavery in New England, 1670–1720," in *Reinterpreting New England Indians and the Colonial Experience*, ed. Colin G. Calloway and Neal Salisbury (Boston: Colonial Society of Massachusetts, 2003), 112–15.
111. Ibid.
112. John Hull to Philip French, September 2, 1675, in "Letter Book of John Hull," 272. See also John Hull to John Ive, September 22, 1675, in "Letter Book of John Hull," 280.
113. Hull, "Account Books," 2:398, 446.
114. The names of these "Lads," Pomham and Matoonas, are curious, as these were the names of two experienced sachems, one Narragansett, and the other Nipmuck, who led Indian forces in attacks against the English during the war. It is possible that these children were descendants of the sachems, but more likely that they were given these names derisively by English captors. It is doubtful that the Sachem Pomham, who had been involved in Anglo-Indian politics since the 1640s, would have been described as a lad. See Jennings, *Invasion of America*, 264–65, 309; Pulsipher, *Subjects unto the Same King*, 26–30, 202.
115. For a general discussion of New England's trade in captive Indians, see Wendy Warren, *New England Bound: Slavery and Colonization in Early America* (New York: W. W. Norton, 2016), 83–115.
116. M. Halsey Thomas, ed., *The Diary of Samuel Sewall, 1674–1729* (New York: Farrar, Straus and Giroux, 1973), 1:18.
117. Max Cavitch, "Interiority and Artifact: Death and Self-Inscription in Thomas Smith's 'Self-Portrait,'" *Early American Literature* 37, no. 1 (2002): 107–8; Roger B. Stein, "Thomas Smith's Self-Portrait: Image/Text as Artifact," *Art Journal* 44, no. 4 (Winter 1984): 320.
118. For a thorough discussion of the sale of captives from King Philip's War into Atlantic slave markets, the "second native diaspora," see Newell, *Brethren by Nature*, 159–88. On the relationship between refined metalwork in silver and gold, and the crude, brutal, but effective metalwork of chains and handcuffs, see Fred Wilson, *Mining the Museum: An Installation* (New York: New Press, 1994).
119. John Hull to John Ive, September 2, 1678, in "Letter Book of John Hull," 388.
120. John Hull to William Loveridge, January 30, 1679, in "Letter Book of John Hull," 409.
121. Mary Rowlandson, "The Sovereignty and Goodness of God" (1682), in *Puritans among the Indians: Accounts of Captivity and Redemption, 1676–1724*, ed. Alden T. Vaughan and Edward Clark (Cambridge, MA: Harvard University Press, 1981), 71.
122. Mark A. Peterson, "Puritanism and Refinement in Early New England: Reflections on Communion Silver," *William and Mary Quarterly* 58, no. 2 (April, 2001): 322, figure 6.
123. Wilcomb Washburn, *The Governor and the Rebel: A History of Bacon's Rebellion in Virginia* (Chapel Hill: University of North Carolina Press, 1957); Edmund S. Morgan, *American Slavery, American Freedom* (New York: Alfred A. Knopf, 1975); Bernard Bailyn, "Politics and Social Structure in Virginia," in *Seventeenth-Century America: Essays in Colonial History*, ed. James Morton Smith (Chapel Hill: University of North Carolina Press, 1959), 90–115.
124. John Hull to Samuel Allin, October 23, 1676, in "Letter Book of John Hull," 322.
125. For the classic account of this division, see Morgan, *American Slavery*.
126. One recent historian has described King Philip's War as a civil war in New England. See Drake, *King Philip's War*.
127. Ibid., 146–47.

128. Ibid., 147–62.
129. Pulsipher, *Subjects unto the Same King*, 154–55.
130. After her return from captivity, Rowlandson was shocked to see one of her former captors, a man who as a soldier had bragged of killing many Englishmen, walking unnoticed on the streets of Boston. Rowlandson, "Sovereignty and Goodness of God," 51.

Chapter 3: Boston Pays Tribute

1. For an exploration of English-Indian relations within this framework, see Jenny Hale Pulsipher, *Subjects unto the Same King: Indians, English, and the Contest for Authority in Colonial New England* (Philadelphia: University of Pennsylvania Press, 2005).
2. For the creation and structure of the United Colonies, see Harry M. Ward, *The United Colonies of New England, 1643–1690* (New York: Vantage Press, 1961), 49–89.
3. See Richard S. Dunn, "John Winthrop, Jr., and the Narragansett Country," *William and Mary Quarterly* 13, no. 1, (January 1956): 68–86.
4. The enduring use of this name explains why salt cod that Boston merchants sold in Bilbao was described in Spanish records as "Birginia" bacalao. See Regina Grafe, "The Globalisation of Codfish and Wool: Spanish-English-North American Triangular Trade in the Early Modern Period" (working paper 71/03, Department of Economic History, London School of Economics, February 2003), 15.
5. Sir Ferdinando Gorges, "A Briefe Relation of the Discovery and Plantation of New England," reprinted in J. P. Baxter, ed., *Sir Ferdinando Gorges and His Province of Maine* (Boston: Prince Society, 1890), 1:203–40.
6. Baxter, *Sir Ferdinando Gorges*, 1:174–96; Charles E. Clark, *The Eastern Frontier: The Settlement of Northern New England, 1610–1763* (New York: Alfred A. Knopf, 1970), 16–20.
7. Neither Gorges nor Mason ever set foot in Maine or New Hampshire. See Clark, *Eastern Frontier*, 19–20; John G. Reid, *Maine, Charles II, and Massachusetts: Governmental Relationships in Early Northern New England* (Portland: Maine Historical Society, 1977), 6–11.
8. Jeremy Belknap, *The History of New Hampshire*, ed. John Farmer (Dover, NH: George Wadleigh, 1862), 17–34; Clark, *Eastern Frontier*, 36–47.
9. See Herbert Levi Osgood, *The American Colonies in the Seventeenth Century*, vol. 3, *Imperial Control: Beginnings of the System of Royal Provinces* (New York: Macmillan, 1907), 69–71.
10. Hannah Farber, "The Rise and Fall of the Province of Lygonia, 1643–1658," *New England Quarterly* 82, no. 3 (September 2009): 490–513. See also Reid, *Maine, Charles II, and Massachusetts* , 1–35.
11. "An Account of the Colony and Fishery of New Foundland" (manuscript, John Carter Brown Library, Providence, RI, 1678), cited in Margaret Newell, *From Dependency to Independence: Economic Revolution in Colonial New England* (Ithaca, NY: Cornell University Press, 1998), 75. See also Peter E. Pope, *Fish into Wine: The Newfoundland Plantation in the Seventeenth Century* (Chapel Hill: University of North Carolina Press, 2004).
12. Pulsipher, *Subjects unto the Same King*, 46; Nathaniel B. Shurtleff, ed., *Records of the Governor and Company of the Massachusetts Bay in New England* (Boston: William White, 1853), 4:79–80, part 1.
13. October 2, 1678, Shurtleff, *Records of Massachusetts Bay*, 5:200.
14. October 10, 1683, Shurtleff, *Records of Massachusetts Bay*, 5:414–15; Newell, *From Dependency to Independence*, 80.

15. Reid, *Maine, Charles II, and Massachusetts*, specifically 127–211.
16. Shurtleff, *Records of Massachusetts Bay*, 4:355–56, part 1; George A. Rawlyk, *Nova Scotia's Massachusetts: A Study of Massachusetts-Nova Scotia Relations, 1630 to 1784* (Montreal: McGill-Queen's University Press, 1973), 27–33.
17. John R. Reid, *Acadia, Maine, and New Scotland: Marginal Colonies in the Seventeenth Century* (Toronto: University of Toronto Press, 1981), 136–41; Arthur Howland Buffington, "Sir Thomas Temple in Boston: A Case of Benevolent Assimilation," *Colonial Society of Massachusetts Publications* 27 (1932): 308–19; Richard R. Johnson, *John Nelson, Merchant Adventurer: A Life between Empires* (New York: Oxford University Press, 1991), 11–15.
18. Andrew Eliot to Thomas Hollis, May 25, 1768, in *Memoirs of Thomas Hollis, Esq.* (London, 1780), 397. After the defeat of his army at the Battle of Worcester in September 1651, Charles hid in an oak tree at Boscobel House to escape capture by Oliver Cromwell's forces. After the Restoration, images of the king hiding in a tree became a popular element in English material culture. Antonia Fraser, *King Charles II* (London: Weidenfeld and Nicolson, 1979), 143–56.
19. In justifying its actions, the General Court claimed, "Nor did we know it [coining money] to be against any Law of England, or against His Majesties Will or pleasure, till of late; but rather that there was a tacit allowance & approbation of it. For in 1662, when our first Agents were in England, some of our Money was showed by Sir Thomas Temple at the Council-Table, and no dislike thereof manifested by any of those right honourable Persons: much less a forbidding of it." Massachusetts Archives, 106:336, cited in Sylvester Sage Crosby, *Early Coins of America and the Laws Governing Their Issue* (Boston, 1875), 76.
20. Colonel Nichols was a key figure in the household of James, Duke of York, the future James II, during the English Civil Wars. Maverick was a longtime Bostonian and opponent of the puritan leadership. Carr and Cartwright, the other two commissioners, were well-connected Englishmen who saw the appointment as an opportunity to enrich themselves. See Reid, *Maine, Charles II, and Massachusetts*, 61–62; Michael G. Hall, *Edward Randolph and the American Colonies, 1676–1703* (Chapel Hill: University of North Carolina Press, 1960), 13–15.
21. Shurtleff, *Records of Massachusetts Bay*, 4:211–13, part 2.
22. Ibid.; Pulsipher, *Subjects unto the Same King*, 61–62.
23. Shurtleff, *Records of Massachusetts Bay*, 4:150, part 2; Pulsipher, *Subjects unto the Same King*, 60–69.
24. Shurtleff, *Records of Massachusetts Bay*, 4:317–18, part 2.
25. John Hull, "The Diaries of John Hull, Mint-Master and Treasurer of the Colony of Massachusetts Bay," in *Transactions of the American Antiquarian Society* (Boston: John Wilson and Son, 1857), 223, 227.
26. Reid, *Maine, Charles II, and Massachusetts*, 114; Pulsipher, *Subjects unto the Same King*, 83. Breedon refers to a passage from I Samuel 15 in which King Saul refused to obey God's command to kill every living thing in the land of the Amalekites, and instead offered a sacrifice of only a few choice animals. Breedon's analogy could be nothing but alarming to the biblically hyperliterate Bostonians.
27. Shurtleff, *Records of Massachusetts Bay*, 4:347, part 2; Louis Jordan, *John Hull, the Mint, and the Economics of Massachusetts Coinage* (Lebanon, NH: University Press of New England, 2002), 15; Crosby, *Early Coins of America*, 78.
28. The return of the bubonic plague in 1665–66, followed by the Great Fire of London in September 1666, along with the second Anglo-Dutch War (1665–67) and subsequent war with France (1667–68), left colonial North America as a low priority for the Crown.
29. Reid, *Maine, Charles II, and Massachusetts*, 61, 95, 254.

30. For administrative purposes, Massachusetts had previously named the nearer part of Maine "York County."
31. Reid, *Maine, Charles II, and Massachusetts*, 132–39.
32. Esmond Samuel de Beer, ed., *The Diary of John Evelyn* (Oxford: Oxford University Press, 1955), 3:579–81. The Crown created the Council for Trade and Foreign Plantations in 1672 to bring greater oversight to the American settlements, restore the maritime northeast to royal patentees, and bring Massachusetts in line with the norms of English government. See Osgood, *American Colonies*, 3:281.
33. Pulsipher, *Subjects unto the Same King*, 237; Reid, *Maine, Charles II, and Massachusetts*, 162. Warfare with the Abenaki resumed in 1688 "because the English refused to pay that yearly tribute of corn, agreed upon in the 'articles of peace' formerly concluded with them by the English commissioners." Cotton Mather, *Magnalia Christi Americana* (Hartford, CT: Silas Andrus, 1853), 2:584.
34. For a detailed account of Randolph's career, see Hall, *Edward Randolph*. See also Richard R. Johnson, *Adjustment to Empire: The New England Colonies, 1676–1715* (New Brunswick, NJ: Rutgers University Press, 1981).
35. Edward Randolph to the Lord Commissioners of Trade and Plantations, September 20–October 12, 1676, in Thomas Hutchinson, *Original Papers* (Boston, 1769), 480.
36. Ibid., 495–96. See also Newell, *From Dependency to Independence*, 79.
37. Randolph to Lord Commissioners, in Hutchinson, *Original Papers*, 495.
38. Hull, "Diaries of John Hull," 130–31; John Hull to John Phillips, master of the ship *Blessing*, December 24, 1677, in "Letter Book of John Hull," John Hull Papers, American Antiquarian Society, 368.
39. Crosby, *Early Coins of America*, 90–95; Jordan, *John Hull*, 41–45.
40. King Charles to . . . , March 10, 1676, in W. Noel Sainsbury, ed., *Calendar of State Papers, Colonial Series, America and West Indies* (Vaduz, Liechtenstein: Kraus Reprint, 1964), 9:358, item 838.
41. Hall, *Edward Randolph*, 20–52; Reid, *Maine, Charles 11, and Massachusetts*, 162–77; Pulsipher, *Subjects unto the Same King*, 195–99.
42. Pulsipher, *Subjects unto the Same King*, 207–37.
43. Instruction for William Stoughton, Esq., & Mr Peter Bulkeley, September 16, 1676, Shurtleff, *Records of Massachusetts Bay*, 5:115–16.
44. Reid, *Maine, Charles II, and Massachusetts*, 170.
45. Michael G. Hall, *The Last American Puritan: The Life of Increase Mather* (Middletown, CT: Wesleyan University Press, 1988), 198.
46. John Hull to John Ive, November 26, 1678, in "Letter Book of John Hull," 399.
47. Hull had previously extended large sums of money to Bulkeley and Stoughton. When the two were first appointed as the colony's agents in 1676, Hull gave them a letter of credit for £300 to present to Thomas Papillon when they arrived in London, "for their use, as they shall need it." John Hull to Thomas Papillon, October 20, 1676, in "Letter Book of John Hull," 317–18.
48. John Hull to William Stoughton and Peter Bulkeley, November 26, 1678, in "Letter Book of John Hull," 400.
49. John Hull to John Ive, June 20–21, 1679, in "Letter Book of John Hull," 416–17. Not only did Hull put aside his own business to pay off the debt for Maine, but he asked Ive to advance, on his credit, £50 to pay the ransom for "Poore Mr Elson," a Boston mariner taken captive by Algerian pirates.
50. Belknap, *History of New Hampshire*, 85–90; Clarke, *Eastern Frontier*, 56–60.
51. On challenges to town corporations and the writ of quo warranto (literally, "under what warrant") as a legal method for challenging corporate charters, see Paul D. Halliday, *Dismembering the Body Politic: Partisan Politics in England's Towns,*

1650–1730 (Cambridge: Cambridge University Press, 1998), 149–235, especially 175 (on oysterers and the Stationers Company) and 204–9 (on London).

52. Philip S. Haffenden, "The Crown and the Colonial Charters, 1675–1688: Part I," *William and Mary Quarterly* 15, no. 3 (July 1958): 298–311; Philip S. Haffenden, "The Crown and the Colonial Charters, 1675–1688: Part II," *William and Mary Quarterly* 15, no. 4 (October 1958): 452–86; Johnson, *Adjustment to Empire*, 53–63.
53. John Hull to Thomas Glover, June 20, 1683, in "Letter Book of John Hull," 550.
54. Edward Randolph, "Articles against the Government of Boston" (June 4, 1683), in *Edward Randolph: Including His Letters and Official Papers from the New England, Middle, and Southern Colonies in America, with Other Documents Relating Chiefly to the Vacating of the Royal Charter of the Colony of Massachusetts Bay, 1676–1703*, ed. R. N. Toppan and A. T. S. Goodrick (Boston: Prince Society, 1909), 3:229.
55. Because of a technicality in its preparation, the writ of quo warranto in the end failed to nullify the charter, but the following year, an alternative legal strategy, a writ of *scire facias et alias*, was used to the same effect. Hall, *Edward Randolph*, 79–83; David S. Lovejoy, *The Glorious Revolution in America*, 2nd ed. (Middletown, CT: Wesleyan University Press, 1987), 148–57.
56. John Hull to William Stoughton and Peter Bulkeley, February 1, 1679, in "Letter Book of John Hull," 410.
57. John Hull to William Stoughton and Peter Bulkeley, November 26, 1678, in "Letter Book of John Hull," 401.
58. Hull, "Diaries of John Hull," 245.
59. John Hull to the selectmen of Salisbury, June 25, 1681, in "Letter Book of John Hull," 485–86. Hull's letters to only these three towns survive in his "Letter Book," but the towns of Salem, Newbury, Medfield, Topsfield, and perhaps others were in Hull's debt for back taxes as well. See Hull, "Diaries of John Hull," 264.
60. Hull, "Diaries of John Hull," 264–65.
61. John Hull to William Stoughton and Peter Bulkeley, February 1, 1679, in "Letter Book of John Hull," 410–11.
62. John Hull to Peleg Sanford and Josiah Arnold, August 21, 1679, in "Letter Book of John Hull," 427–36.
63. John Hull to William March, June 20–21, 1679, in "Letter Book of John Hull," 417; John Hull to James Elson, December 27, 1680, in "Letter Book of John Hull," 470–73; Hull, "Diaries of John Hull," 245–46.
64. John Hull to Sir Henry Ashurst, December 17, 1679, in "Letter Book of John Hull," 438–39.
65. "William Berkeley to John Winthrop Jr., June 25, 1648," in *The Winthrop Papers*, ed. Samuel Eliot Morison, Allyn Bailey Forbes, and Malcolm Freiberg (Boston: Massachusetts Historical Society, 1929–), 5:232.
66. Richard S. Dunn, James Savage, and Laetitia Yeandle, eds., *The Journal of John Winthrop, 1630–1649* (Cambridge, MA: Belknap, 1999), 399–400.
67. Peter Earle, *The Treasure of the Concepcion: The Wreck of the Almiranta* (New York: Viking Press, 1980), 46–47, 112–16.
68. John Hull and Eliakim Hutchinson to Richard Rook, Peres Savage, and Francis Lester, May 16, 1683, in "Letter Book of John Hull," 549.
69. John Hull and Eliakim Hutchinson to Richard Rook, May 16–24, 1683, in "Letter Book of John Hull," 547–48.
70. At exactly this time, two West Indian informants approached Sir John Narborough, a Royal Navy officer with a long history of interest in shipwrecks, to outfit an expedition with the support of the Crown and Royal Navy. See Earle, *Treasure of the Concepcion*, 118–20.

71. Hull, "Diaries of John Hull," 122; Hermann Frederick Clarke, *John Hull: A Builder of the Bay Colony* (Portland, ME: Southworth-Anthoesen Press, 1940), 182–94.
72. Viola F. Barnes, *The Dominion of New England* (New Haven, CT: Yale University Press, 1923).
73. For accounts of this era from a New England perspective, see Johnson, *Adjustment to Empire*; Barnes, *Dominion of New England*; Lovejoy, *Glorious Revolution in America*; Hall, *Edward Randolph*; Hall, *Last American Puritan*. For important documentary editions, see W. H. Whitmore, ed., *The Andros Tracts*, 3 vols. (Boston: Prince Society, 1974); R. N. Toppan and A. T. S. Goodrick, eds., *Edward Randolph: Including His Letters and Official Papers from the New England, Middle, and Southern Colonies in America, with Other Documents Relating Chiefly to the Vacating of the Royal Charter of the Colony of Massachusetts Bay, 1676–1703* (Boston: Prince Society, 1909); Robert Earle Moody and Richard Clive Simmons, eds., *The Glorious Revolution in Massachusetts: Selected Documents, 1689–1692* (Boston: Colonial Society of Massachusetts, 1988).
74. See Richard S. Dunn, "The Glorious Revolution and America," in *The Origins of Empire*, vol. 1, *The Oxford History of the British Empire*, ed. Nicholas Canny (Oxford: Oxford University Press, 1998), 445–66.
75. Hall, *Edward Randolph*, 122. By contrast, for works that highlight the discord within the New York and Maryland uprisings, see Dunn, "Glorious Revolution and America," 458–60; Lovejoy, *Glorious Revolution in America*, 251–70. On the bitter internal conflict in New York that drove Leisler's Rebellion to a tragic end, see David William Voorhees, "The 'Fervent Zeal' of Jacob Leisler," *William and Mary Quarterly* 51, no. 3 (July 1994): 447–72.
76. Cotton Mather, *Pietas in Patriam: The Life of Sir William Phips*, in *Magnalia*, books I–II, ed. Kenneth Murdock (Cambridge, MA: Harvard University Press, 1977), 294.
77. Richard S. Dunn, *Puritans and Yankees: The Winthrop Dynasty of New England* (New York: W. W. Norton, 1971), 254–56.
78. Edmund S. Morgan, *American Slavery, American Freedom* (New York: Alfred A. Knopf, 1975), 98–107.
79. Robert C. Ritchie, *The Duke's Province: A Study of New York Politics and Society, 1664–1691*, 2nd ed. (Chapel Hill: University of North Carolina Press, 2009), 9–24; J. M. Sosin, *English America and the Restoration Monarchy of Charles II: Transatlantic Politics, Commerce, and Kinship* (Lincoln: University of Nebraska Press, 1980), 138–49.
80. "I arrived at N. Hampshire and after great Opposition made by ye Bostoners, settled his [Majesty's] Government in that Province." Toppan and Goodrick, *Edward Randolph*, 4:187. See also ibid., 6:72, 74.
81. In his history of New England, Massachusetts writer Edward Johnson enumerated "the charges expended by this poor people, to injoy Christ in his purity of Ordinances." Johnson came up with the figure of £192,000, breaking the cost down according to categories—transportation, livestock, food, tools, arms, and so on—and asked, "Where had this poore people this great sum of money? The mighty Princes of the Earth never opened their Coffers for them, and the generality of these men were meane and poore in the things of this life." Edward Johnson, *Wonder Working Providence of Sion's Savior in New England* (1654), ed. J. Franklin Jameson, (New York: Charles Scribner's, 1910), 54–55.
82. Among Andros's supporters were several Roman Catholics, including Anthony Brockholls, Gervais Baxter, George Lockhart, and David Condon, who served on the Royal Navy frigate *Rose* stationed in Boston Harbor. On fears of Roman Catholic conspiracy as a cause of the rebellion, see Lovejoy, *Glorious Revolution in America*,

281–88; Owen Stanwood, "The Protestant Moment: Anti-Popery, the Revolution of 1688–89, and the Making of an Anglo-American Empire," *Journal of British Studies* 46, no. 3 (July 2007); Johnson, *Adjustment to Empire*, 43. On the justification for the uprising, see [Cotton Mather], *The Declaration of the Gentlemen, Merchants, and Inhabitants of Boston, and the Countrey Adjacent* (Boston, 1689).

83. "A Narrative of the Proceedings of Sir Edmund Androsse and his Complices . . . ," in *The Andros Tracts*, cited in Michael G. Hall, Lawrence H. Leder, and Michael G. Kammen, eds., *The Glorious Revolution in America: Documents on the Colonial Crisis of 1689* (Chapel Hill: University of North Carolina Press, 1964), 31. The narrative asserted that the fees to be charged for surveying and regranting land titles were so extensive that "it hath by some been computed that all the money in the Country would not suffice to patent the Lands therein contained." Ibid., 34. See also Toppan and Goodrick, *Edward Randolph*, 4:168.

84. "Randolph to Sir Nicholas Butler Proposing a Romanist Mission," in Toppan and Goodrick, *Edward Randolph*, 6:240–42. See also "The Humble Petition of Edward Randolph (to Be Secretary of All New England)," in Toppan and Goodrick, *Edward Randolph*, 4:165–66. Randolph knew exactly how lucrative this office could be, as he was the author of "A Table of Ffees Humbly Presented to His Excellencie the Governour and Councell for Their Allowance to the Secretaries Office in New England," in Toppan and Goodrick, *Edward Randolph*, 4:147–48. Randolph also wrote the list of fees due to the customs collector in Boston—an office he held as well. See Toppan and Goodrick, *Edward Randolph*, 4:149.

85. "Petition of Edward Randolph for Nahant Neck," October 1, 1687, in Toppan and Goodrick, *Edward Randolph*, 4:171; "Warrant for Cambridge Proprietors of Land to Appear and Put in Claims Adverse to Petition of Edward Randolph," in Toppan and Goodrick, *Edward Randolph*, 4:207.

86. "Objections of Lynn to the Petition of Edward Randolph," in Toppan and Goodrick, *Edward Randolph*, 4:202–4. See also "Reply of Proprietors of Lands between Sanders Brook and Spy Pond," in Toppan and Goodrick, *Edward Randolph*, 4:213–16. These complaints became item 5 of "A Narrative of the Proceedings of Sir Edmond Androsse and His Complices": "The Enjoyment and Improvement of Lands not inclosed, and especially if lying in common amongst many was denied to be possession." Hall, Leder, and Kammen, *Glorious Revolution in America*, 34.

87. Later seventeenth-century economists such as Josiah Childs, William Davenant, Thomas Mun, and Thomas Manley began to appreciate the value of the carrying trade as a productive enterprise in its own right, but they followed Randolph in seeing New England's growing trade as a loss to English revenue, "so that New England is become the great mart and staple, by which means the navigation of the kingdom is greatly prejudiced." See Newell, *From Dependency to Independence*, 70, 81–83.

88. "Randolph to Sir Nicholas Butler, March 29, 1688," in Toppan and Goodrick, *Edward Randolph*, 6:245.

89. Johnson, *Adjustment to Empire*, 52. Several governors in the charter period impoverished themselves in their devotion to colony service; Winthrop was the prime example. According to Johnson, the early magistrates of Massachusetts "have hitherto been Volunteers, governing without pay from the People, onely the Governor of Mattacusets hath some years 100 l. allowed to him, some years less." Johnson, *Wonder Working Providence*, 141. See also Francis J. Bremer, *John Winthrop, America's Forgotten Founder* (New York: Oxford University Press), 105–24.

90. "The Boston Declaration of Grievances, April 18, 1689," in *Narratives of the Insurrections*, ed. Charles M. Andrews (New York: Barnes and Noble, 1967), 175–82; Hall, Leder, and Kammen, *Glorious Revolution in America*, 43.

91. Johnson, *Adjustment to Empire*, 55.
92. Ibid., 40.
93. "The Boston Declaration of Grievances, April 18, 1689," in Hall, Leder, and Kammen, *Glorious Revolution in America*, 42–46.
94. Hall, *Last American Puritan*, 212–54.
95. Daniel Defoe, *An Essay upon Projects* (London, 1697), 16.
96. Mather, *Pietas in Patriam*, 278. Mather's biography of Phips, written shortly after his death, is the most important contemporary source of information on Phips's life. For the best modern biography, see Emerson W. Baker and John G. Reid, *The New England Knight: Sir William Phips, 1651-1695* (Toronto: University of Toronto Press, 1998).
97. Mather, *Pietas in Patriam*, 280.
98. Baker and Reid, *New England Knight*, 5. On the connections of early Maine colonists to the claims of English aristocrats, see Johnson, *John Nelson*, 49–86.
99. Baker and Reid, *New England Knight*, 25–29; Mather, *Pietas in Patriam*, 280–82; Earle, *Treasure of the Concepcion*, 124–28.
100. Mather, *Pietas in Patriam*, 283.
101. Ibid., 284.
102. Ibid., 285.
103. Earle, *Treasure of the Concepcion*, 201. The king's tenth amounted to roughly £21,000, and the largest investor, the Duke of Albemarle, received £43,000.
104. John Maynard Keynes, *A Treatise on Money* (London: Macmillan, 1930), 2:151, 156–57; John Clapham, *The Bank of England, A History* (Cambridge: Cambridge University Press, 1944), 1:13–14.
105. Defoe, *Essay upon Projects*, 11–12, 16.
106. Andrew O'Shaughnessy, *An Empire Divided: The American Revolution and the British Caribbean* (Philadelphia: University of Pennsylvania Press, 2000), 4–18.
107. Mather, *Pietas in Patriam*, 288.
108. Baker and Reid, *New England Knight*, 66–67; Barnes, *Dominion of New England*, 282–83, Mather, *Pietas in Patriam*, 286–88; Toppan and Goodrick, *Edward Randolph*, 4:200–201.
109. Mather, *Pietas in Patriam*, 285.
110. M. Halsey Thomas, ed., *The Diary of Samuel Sewall, 1674–1729* (New York: Farrar, Straus and Giroux, 1973), 1:167, 172.
111. Mather, *Pietas in Patriam*, 295–98; Baker and Reid, *New England Knight*, 78–79; Hall, *Last American Puritan*, 210–11. That Phips had never been baptized reflects how weak the establishment of churches on the Maine frontier had been.
112. Hall, *Last American Puritan*, 220–24. On Mather's abrupt shift to William, see "Increase Mather to William of Orange [January 9, 1689]," in Moody and Simmons, *Glorious Revolution in Massachusetts*, 423.
113. "The Declaration of the Gentlemen, Merchants, and Inhabitants of Boston, and the Country Adjacent. April 18, 1869," in Moody and Simmons, *Glorious Revolution in Massachusetts*, 49–50.
114. See "Bill for Volunteers against the French," "Committee to Consult Referring to an Expedition against Port Royal," and "Proposals for the Reducing of Nova Scotia," in Moody and Simmons, *Glorious Revolution in Massachusetts*, 191–95. See also Baker and Reid, *New England Knight*, 87–95.
115. See Tony Claydon, *William III and the Godly Revolution* (Cambridge: Cambridge University Press, 1996), 122–47.
116. Baker and Reid, *New England Knight*, 83.

117. Richard Harding, *Amphibious Warfare in the Eighteenth Century: The British Expedition to the West Indies, 1740–1742* (Rochester, NY: Boydell and Brewer, Inc., 1991).
118. Moody and Simmons, *Glorious Revolution in Massachusetts*, 192–93; Emerson and Reid, *New England Knight*, 84–85.
119. Mather, *Pietas in Patriam*, 307. For an important contemporary source for the 1690 expeditions, see *A Journal of the Proceedings in the Late Expedition to Port-Royal* (Boston: Benjamin Harris, 1690). See also Baker and Reid, *New England Knight*, 86–109; Johnson, *Adjustment to Empire*, 190–99.
120. Mather, *Pietas in Patriam*, 308.
121. Anonymous, *A Model for Erecting a Bank of Credit with a Discourse in Explanation Thereof, Adapted to the Use of Any Trading Countrey, Where There Is a Scarcity of Moneys: More Especially for His Majesties Plantations in America* (1688; repr., Boston, 1714), 23–24.
122. Mather, *Pietas in Patriam*, 309.
123. Ibid.
124. Newell, *From Dependency to Independence*, 121–31. See also Jeffrey Sklansky, *Sovereign of the Market: The Money Question in Early America* (Chicago: University of Chicago Press, 2017).
125. Mather, *Pietas in Patriam*, 308–9.
126. Carl Wennerlind, "Credit Money as the Philosopher's Stone: Alchemy and the Coinage Problem in Seventeenth-Century England," annual supplement, *History of Political Economy* 35 (2003): 234–61.

Chapter 4: *Theopolis Americana*

1. Sewall's edition was probably David Pareus, A *Commentary upon the Divine Revelation of the Apostle and Evangelist John*, trans. Elias Arnold (Amsterdam, 1644).
2. M. Halsey Thomas, ed., *The Diary of Samuel Sewall, 1674–1729* (New York: Farrar, Straus and Giroux, 1973), 1:91.
3. A few men with Boston connections, such as John Humfry and Robert Sedgwick, took an interest in these Caribbean ventures, but Cromwell's call for Puritans to abandon New England for the West Indies mostly met with indifference. See Louise A. Breen, *Transgressing the Bounds: Subversive Enterprises among the Puritan Elite in Massachusetts, 1630–1692* (New York: Oxford University Press, 2001).
4. Mark Peterson, "Boston Pays Tribute: Autonomy and Empire in the Atlantic World, 1630–1714," in *Shaping the Stuart World, 1603–1714: The Atlantic Connection*, ed. Allan I. Macinnes and Arthur H. Williamson (Leiden: Brill, 2006), 311–36.
5. Owen Stanwood, "The Protestant Moment: Anti-Popery, the Revolution of 1688–89, and the Making of an Anglo-American Empire," *Journal of British Studies* 46, no. 3 (July 2007): 481–508.
6. Michael C. Batinski, *Jonathan Belcher, Colonial Governor* (Lexington: University Press of Kentucky, 1996); Clifford K. Shipton, "Jonathan Belcher," in *Sibley's Harvard Graduates* (Cambridge, MA: Harvard University Press, 1933), 4:439–48.
7. The scholarship on Cotton Mather is too voluminous to be cited here. For general biographies, see David Levin, *Cotton Mather: The Young Life of the Lord's Remembrancer, 1663–1703* (Cambridge, MA: Harvard University Press, 1978); Kenneth Silverman, *The Life and Times of Cotton Mather* (New York: Harper and Row, 1984). For some of the better specialized studies of Mather's career, see

Richard F. Lovelace, *The American Pietism of Cotton Mather: Origins of American Evangelicalism* (Grand Rapids, MI: Wm. B. Eerdmans, 1979); Michael P. Winship, *Seers of God: Puritan Providentialism in the Restoration and Early Enlightenment* (Baltimore: Johns Hopkins University Press, 1996). For the best exploration of Mather's engagement with continental Pietism, see Jan Stievermann, *Prophecy, Piety, and the Problem of Historicity: Interpreting the Hebrew Scriptures in Cotton Mather's Biblia Americana* (Heidelberg: Mohr Siebeck, 2016).

8. Samuel Sewall, *The Selling of Joseph: A Memorial* (Boston, 1700), reprinted in *Diary of Samuel Sewall*, 2:1117–21.
9. *Diary of Samuel Sewall*, 1:432–33.
10. Lawrence Towner, "The Sewall-Saffin Dialogue on Slavery," *William and Mary Quarterly* 21 (1964): 40–52.
11. A history of slavery in Massachusetts published in 1866 reprinted Sewall's pamphlet in full, "probably for the first time in the [nineteenth] century," claiming that it had been "unknown to our historians" and that there had been "no quotation from it later than 1738, when it was reprinted in Pennsylvania." George H. Moore, *Notes on the History of Slavery in Massachusetts* (New York: D. Appleton and Co., 1866), 82–87. For further discussions, see Towner, "Sewall-Saffin Dialogue," 40–52; David Brion Davis, *The Problem of Slavery in Western Culture* (New York: Oxford University Press, 1966), 341–48.
12. Sewall, *Selling of Joseph*, 1117.
13. Moore, *Notes on the History of Slavery*, 48–50; Lorenzo Johnston Greene, *The Negro in Colonial New England* (New York: Atheneum, 1968), 79–95. Both Moore and Greene cite the same estimates made by colonial officials of Boston's and Massachusetts' slave populations.
14. A French Huguenot refugee in Boston in 1687 claimed that "there is not a house in Boston, however small may be its means, that has not one or two [negroes]." This cannot be accurate. Boston's tax record from 1687 lists 1,226 households, which would make for a slave population closer to 2,000, roughly one-fourth of the city. It nonetheless reflects the perception shared by Sewall of the growing "numerousness" of slaves in the city. See Wendy Warren, *New England Bound: Slavery and Colonization in Early America* (New York: W. W. Norton, 2016), 9, 265n20.
15. Greene, *Negro in Colonial New England*, 20–26. On the Royal African Company, see Robin Blackburn, *The Making of New World Slavery: From the Baroque to the Modern, 1492–1800* (London: Verso, 1997), 254–55, 266–67; Kenneth Davies, *The Royal African Company* (New York: Holiday House, 1970), 129–52; William A. Pettigrew, *Freedom's Debt: The Royal African Company and the Politics of the Atlantic Slave Trade, 1672–1752* (Chapel Hill: University of North Carolina Press, 2013), 11–44.
16. Mather provides a thoroughly biased account of the war. See Cotton Mather, *Decennium Luctuosum* (1699; repr., New York: Garland Publishing, 1978). For a modern account, see Philip S. Haffenden, *New England in the English Nation, 1689–1713* (Oxford: Clarendon Press, 1974).
17. *Diary of Samuel Sewall*, 1:176.
18. John Demos, *The Unredeemed Captive: A Family Story from Early America* (New York: Alfred A. Knopf, 1994).
19. Sewall, *Selling of Joseph*, 1118.
20. "Cotton Mather's Letter Justifying His Part in Nelson's Capture and Release," in Richard R. Johnson, *John Nelson, Merchant Adventurer: A Life between Empires* (New York: Oxford University Press, 1991), 142–45.
21. Emerson W. Baker and John G. Reid, *The New England Knight: Sir William Phips, 1651–1695* (Toronto: University of Toronto Press, 1998), 86–109, 156–60.

22. Sewall, *Selling of Joseph*, 1120.
23. *Diary of Samuel Sewall*, 1:156; Samuel Sewall, *Letter Book of Samuel Sewall* (1886–88), *Collections of the Massachusetts Historical Society* 6th ser., 1:28, 34, 38, 45, 49, 76–77, 112, 234–35. See also Cotton Mather, *A Pastoral Letter to the English Captives in Africa* (Boston: B. Green and J. Allen, 1698).
24. See John Barnard, *Ashton's Memorial: An History of the Strange Adventures and Signal Deliverances of Mr. Philip Ashton* (Boston: Samuel Gerrish, 1725). See also George Francis Dow and John Henry Edmonds, *The Pirates of the New England Coast, 1630–1730* (New York: Dover Publications, 1996); Mark G. Hanna, *Pirate Nests and the Rise of the British Empire, 1570–1740* (Chapel Hill: University of North Carolina Press, 2015).
25. Dow and Edmonds, *Pirates*, 99–115. For the best recent account of Atlantic piracy, see Hanna, *Pirate Nests*. On Captain Quelch, see ibid., 330–64.
26. *Diary of Samuel Sewall*, 1:406n2; C. C. Smith, "The French Protestants in Boston," in *The Memorial History of Boston, 1630–1880*, ed. Justin Winsor (Boston: James R. Osgood, 1882–86), 2:249–68; Jon Butler, *The Huguenots in America: A Refugee People in New World Society* (Cambridge, MA: Harvard University Press, 1983). On Maine refugees' involvement in the witchcraft crisis, see Mather, *Decennium Luctuosum*; John McWilliams, "Indian John and the Northern Tawnies," *New England Quarterly* 69 (1996): 580–604; Mary Beth Norton, *In the Devil's Snare: The Salem Witchcraft Crisis of 1692* (New York: Alfred A. Knopf, 2002), 82–111. On Sewall's anguish, see *Diary of Samuel Sewall*, 1:366–67.
27. Gary Nash notes the social problems that Boston faced during the wars of the 1690s, but not the traffic in human beings as a key element. Gary Nash, *The Urban Crucible: The Northern Seaports and the Origins of American Revolution* (Cambridge, MA: Harvard University Press, 1986), 33–39.
28. Jonathan I. Israel and Geoffrey Parker, "Of Providence and Protestant Winds: The Spanish Armada of 1588 and the Dutch Armada of 1688," in *The Anglo-Dutch Moment: Essays on the Glorious Revolution and Its World Impact*, ed. Jonathan I. Israel (Cambridge: Cambridge University Press, 1991), 335–64; Tony Claydon, *William III and the Godly Revolution* (Cambridge: Cambridge University Press, 1996), 24–63, 122–47.
29. Stewart P. Oakley, *William III and the Northern Crowns during the Nine Years War, 1689–1697* (New York: Garland Publishing, 1987).
30. Blackburn, *Making of New World Slavery*, 266; John J. McCusker and Russell R. Menard, *The Economy of British America, 1607–1789*, 2nd ed. (Chapel Hill: University of North Carolina Press, 1991), 162–63; Richard Pares, *Yankees and Creoles: The Trade between North America and the West Indies before the American Revolution* (Cambridge, UK: Longmans, Green, and Co., 1956), 9–13.
31. Sewall handed out copies of Louis XIV's revocation of the Edict of Nantes and recorded rumors of Louis's death in his diary. *Diary of Samuel Sewall*, 1:92, 176, 330–31, 365, 393, 492, 530, 801. See also Cotton Mather, *A Letter concerning the Terrible Suffering of Our Protestant Brethren, On Board the French King's Galleys* (Boston, 1701).
32. For the strange case of Thomas Pound, see Dow and Edmonds, *Pirates*, 54–72.
33. Philip Otterness, *Becoming German: The 1709 Palatine Migration to New York* (Ithaca, NY: Cornell University Press, 2004); Mack Walker, *The Salzburg Transaction: Expulsion and Redemption in Eighteenth-Century Germany* (Ithaca, NY: Cornell University Press, 1992).
34. Sewall's reasoning echoes that of Augustine, who explained why the expansion of a commonwealth by a just war was at best a thing "of necessitie," not a morally justifiable good: "For it was the badnesse of those against whome iust warres were whilome

under-taken, that hath aduanced earthly soueraignties to that part they now hold: which would haue been little still, if no enemy had giuen cause nor prouocation war by offring his neighbour wrong. If men had always beene thus conditioned, the Kingdomes of the earth would haue continued little in quantity, and peacefull in neighbourly agreement." Saint Augustine, *Of the Citie of God* (London, 1610), book 4, chapter 15, 174–75.

35. Sewall, *Selling of Joseph*, 1119–20.
36. Ibid., 1117–18.
37. Moore, *Notes on the History of Slavery*, 52.
38. Greene described this legislation as "The Machinery of Control." Greene, *Negro in Colonial New England*, 124–43. See also Moore, *Notes on the History of Slavery*, 52–58; Robert C. Twombly and Robert H. Moore, "Black Puritan: The Negro in Seventeenth-Century Massachusetts," *William and Mary Quarterly* 24 (1967): 224–42. For a comparative view of slavery and taxation practices regarding property versus polls, see Robin L. Einhorn, *American Taxation, American Slavery* (Chicago: University of Chicago Press, 2006), 24–78.
39. *Diary of Samuel Sewall*, 1:532.
40. See James J. Allegro, "'Increasing and Strengthening the Country': Law, Politics, and the Antislavery Movement in Early Eighteenth-Century Massachusetts Bay," *New England Quarterly* 75 (March 2002): 5–23.
41. Cotton Mather, *Rules for the Society of Negroes* (Boston: B. Harris, 1693); Cotton Mather, *The Negro Christianized* (Boston: B. Green, 1706). See also Silverman, *Life and Times of Cotton Mather*, 263–65. On baptism and slavery, see Travis Glasson, "'Baptism Doth Not Bestow Freedom': Missionary Anglicanism, Slavery, and the Yorke-Talbot Opinion, 1701–30," *William and Mary Quarterly* 67, no. 2 (April 2010): 279–318; Rebecca Anne Goetz, *The Baptism of Early Virginia: How Christianity Created Race* (Baltimore: Johns Hopkins University Press, 2012).
42. Mather's organization of religious education for slaves continued the work that John Eliot had begun as an extension of his missionary work with Indians. See Greene, *Negro in Colonial New England*, 237–38, 263–67.
43. See G. B. Warden, *Boston, 1689–1776* (Boston: Little, Brown, 1970), 101–26; Mark A. Peterson, *The Price of Redemption: The Spiritual Economy of Puritan New England* (Stanford, CA: Stanford University Press, 1997), 163–90. Mather compiled two decades of effort along these lines. Cotton Mather, *Bonifacius: An Essay upon the Good* (Boston: B. Green, 1710). See also George Selement, "Publication and the Puritan Minister," *William and Mary Quarterly* 37 (1980): 219–41.
44. See Batinski, *Jonathan Belcher*, 3–9; Shipton, "Jonathan Belcher," 4:439–42. Bernard Bailyn describes Andrew Belcher and his descendants as "prototypes of the ascending merchant families in the late seventeenth and early eighteenth centuries." Bernard Bailyn, *The New England Merchants in the Seventeenth Century* (Cambridge, MA: Harvard University Press, 1955), 195–97.
45. Batinski, *Jonathan Belcher*, 4–11.
46. Jonathan Belcher, "A Journal of My Intended Voyage and Journey to Holland, Hanover, &c, July 8, 1704 to October 5, 1704" (manuscript, Massachusetts Historical Society, Boston).
47. C. D. van Strien, *British Travelers in Holland during the Stuart Period: Edward Browne and John Locke as Tourists in the United Provinces* (Leiden: E. J. Brill, 1993).
48. For the effect of tumultuous Anglo-Dutch relations on British travelers to the Netherlands during Queen Anne's reign, see ibid., 8–13.
49. See Robert Earle Moody and Richard Clive Simmons, eds., *The Glorious Revolution in Massachusetts: Selected Documents, 1689–1692* (Boston: Colonial Society of Massachusetts, 1988), 4–5, 54, 60–64.

50. Belcher, "Journal of My Intended Voyage," 14–16. On the House of Nassau and construction of Dutch patriotism, see Simon Schama, *The Embarrassment of Riches: An Interpretation of Dutch Culture in the Golden Age* (New York: Vintage, 1997), 51–125.
51. Belcher declined the college trustees' suggestion that the building be named "Belcher Hall," preferring to honor "the immortal Memory of the glorious King William the 3d. who was a Branch of the illustrious House of Nassau." Batinski, *Jonathan Belcher*, 170. See also Annie Haven Thwing, *The Crooked and Narrow Streets of the Town of Boston* (Boston: Marshall Jones Co., 1920), 228, 237–41.
52. In 1716, Andrew Belcher dissuaded the newly arrived royal governor, Samuel Shute, from attending a dance hosted by the organist of the Anglican King's Chapel. See *Diary of Samuel Sewall*, 2:838; Peterson, *Price of Redemption*, 173–84.
53. Ebenezer Pemberton, *Advice to a Son: A Discourse at the Request of a Gentleman in New-England, upon His Son's Going to Europe* (London: Ralph Smith, 1705). Belcher took time while in London to arrange for this publication.
54. Belcher, "Journal of My Intended Voyage," 26.
55. Belcher writes, "The English gentlemen there . . . spend most of their time in reading, . . . a Court life, being very Idle; . . . and they live in an entire oblivion of Religion and will (I fear) insensibly fall into atheism, they never go to any Chh nor mind Sunday any more than any other day." Belcher, "Journal of My Intended Voyage," 53, 118–25.
56. On shipping, see Bernard Bailyn and Lotte Bailyn, *Massachusetts Shipping, 1697–1714* (Cambridge, MA: Harvard University Press, 1959), 20–21. For population estimates, see Carl Bridenbaugh, *Cities in the Wilderness: The First Century of Urban Life in America, 1625–1742* (New York: Oxford University Press, 1971), 143–44; Nash, *Urban Crucible*, 33–34.
57. Nash, *Urban Crucible*, 34–39; Warden, *Boston*, 60–79; Elizabeth E. Dunn, "'Grasping at the Shadow': The Massachusetts Currency Debate, 1690–1751," *New England Quarterly* 71 (March 1998): 54–76.
58. Belcher, "Journal of My Intended Voyage," 23–24. On stock exchanges and cosmopolitan culture, see Margaret C. Jacob, *Strangers Nowhere in the World: The Rise of Cosmopolitanism in Early Modern Europe* (Philadelphia: University of Pennsylvania Press, 2006), 66–94.
59. On market reform in Boston, see Warden, *Boston*, 53–54, 76–77, 106–7, 117–21.
60. During the paper money and banking schemes of 1740–41, Belcher denounced the so-called Land Bank, which might "defraud Men of their Substance," and praised the rival Silver Bank, saying that its notes were "of service to the people as a medium in commerce, for they are truly & really equal to gold and silver to the possessors." Batinski, *Jonathan Belcher*, 142; Dunn, "Grasping at the Shadow," 61–66; Rosalind Remer, "Old Lights and New Money: A Note on Religion, Economics, and the Social Order in 1740 Boston," *William and Mary Quarterly* 47 (October 1990): 566–73.
61. Belcher, "Journal of My Intended Voyage," 19, 28–30. On Dutch philanthropy in the seventeenth century, see van Strien, *British Travelers in Holland*, 134–36, 191–98; Schama, *Embarrassment of Riches*, 570–79; Sheila D. Muller, *Charity in the Dutch Republic: Pictures of Rich and Poor for Charitable Institutions* (Ann Arbor, MI: UMI Research Press, 1985).
62. See Eric G. Nellis, "Misreading the Signs: Industrial Imitation, Poverty, and the Social Order in Boston," *New England Quarterly* 59 (1986): 486–507. During Belcher's decade as Massachusetts governor in the 1730s, Boston's poor relief, education, and charity received a major overhaul. See Nash, *Urban Crucible*, 78–79; Warden, *Boston*, 101–26; Bridenbaugh, *Cities in the Wilderness*, 392–94; Horace E. Scudder, "Life in Boston in the Provincial Period," in Winsor, *Memorial History of Boston*, 3:458–61.

63. Belcher, "Journal of My Intended Voyage," 16. Von Bothmar would play an important role as the Hanoverian elector's representative in Britain, ensuring George I's peaceful accession when the death of Queen Anne stirred speculation about a challenge from the Stuart pretender. See Ragnhild Hatton, *George I, Elector and King* (Cambridge, MA: Harvard University Press, 1978), 97, 107–9, 147–51.
64. On court life at Herrenhausen during this era, see Maria Kroll, *Sophie, Electress of Hanover: A Personal Portrait* (London: Victor Gollancz, 1973), 183–247.
65. Belcher, "Journal of My Intended Voyage," 41–47.
66. Ibid., 45.
67. Belcher described the scene thus: "Ye Electress gave over play and went into her closet, being a little frighted, because of her son in the Army, at length the Elector came in again and told us the good news, of the French and Bavarians being intirely defeated by our Army." Belcher, "Journal of My Intended Voyage," Ibid., 42, 46.
68. Ibid., 55. For portraits of George's Turkish servants, Mahomet and Mustapha, see Joyce Marlow, *The Life and Times of George I* (London: Weidenfeld and Nicolson, 1973), 71.
69. Jonathan Belcher to John White, December 27, 1704 (manuscript, Belknap Papers, Massachusetts Historical Society, Boston); Julius H. Tuttle, "Note on the Portrait of the Electress Sophia of Hanover," in *Publications of the Colonial Society of Massachusetts* (Boston, 1920), 20:96–103.
70. Other travelers who encountered Catholics and Jesuits included Benjamin Colman, Jeremiah Dummer, John Williams, and John Nelson. See Ebenezer Turell, *Life and Character of the Reverend Benjamin Colman* (Boston: Rogers and Fowle, 1749), 5–14; Clifford K. Shipton, "Jeremiah Dummer," in *Sibley's Harvard Graduates* (Cambridge, MA: Harvard University Press, 1933), 4:464; John Williams, *The Redeemed Captive Returning to Zion* (1853; repr., Bedford, MA: Applewood Books, 1987), 183–96; Johnson, *John Nelson*, 91.
71. Belcher, "Journal of My Intended Voyage," 57–61. On the monastery at Lambspring along with its connections to English Benedictines and the later Stuarts, see Dom Bennet Weldon, *Chronological Notes Containing the Rise, Growth, and Present State of the English Congregation of the Order of St. Benedict* (London: J. Hodges, 1881), 184–86, 189–93, 232–33, appendix 8, 23–27.
72. Belcher, "Journal of My Intended Voyage," 63–68. For a contemporary description of the Harz silver mines, see Georg Henning Behrens, *The Natural History of the Hartz Forest* (London, 1730).
73. Richard Harvey Phelps, *A History of Newgate of Connecticut, at Simsbury, Now East Granby* (Albany, NY: J. Munsell, 1860), 10–14. Parliamentary legislation prohibited the making of copper coins in the colonies. Even copper smelting defied the Navigation Acts, though this did not stop Belcher's from pursuing it.
74. The King of Prussia's palace was so lavish that "it put me in mind of the Queen of Sheba, who when she had seen Solomon's glory, it is said there was no more spirit in her." Belcher, "Journal of My Intended Voyage," 73. The Queen of Prussia was Sophia's only daughter and favorite child, Sophia Charlotte, known as "Figuelotte." See Kroll, *Sophie*, 206–12.
75. Belcher, "Journal of My Intended Voyage," 76–78.
76. On Leibniz and alchemy, see Roger Ariew, "G. W. Leibniz, Life and Works," in *The Cambridge Companion to Leibniz*, ed. Nicholas Jolley (Cambridge: Cambridge University Press, 1995), 20–21, 41n11. Harvard students in Belcher's era would have been exposed to alchemical theories of matter in the college's natural philosophy curriculum, especially in Charles Morton's *Compendium of Physics*, introduced in 1687. Throughout Belcher's lifetime, alchemical theses were defended at the college's

commencement exercises. See William R. Newman, *Gehennical Fire: The Lives of George Starkey, an American Alchemist in the Scientific Revolution* (Cambridge, MA: Harvard University Press, 1994), 32–39.

77. Batinski, *Jonathan Belcher*, 16–18.
78. Jonathan Belcher to "Dear Brother," November 16, 1708, Belcher Miscellany, Princeton University Library. Thanks to Professor Michael Batinski for this reference. Little else is known of the fate of this Indian servant, whose name may have been derived from classical mythology. According to Ovid, Io was a servant girl taken by Zeus as a lover, transformed into a heifer because of Hera's jealousy, and then restored to human form and elevated to the status of the gods. Perhaps Belcher bestowed this name on the Indian servant expecting him to be similarly transformed through contact with royalty.
79. Belcher would prove to be mistaken; Frederick died while still Prince of Wales, leaving his son to succeed to the throne as George III.
80. Jonathan Belcher to "Dear Brother," November 16, 1708, Belcher Miscellany, Princeton University Library. The medal was a copy of one that Sophia had made for Lord Macclesfield, the English ambassador who presented her with official news of the Act of Settlement. See Kroll, *Sophie*, 202–3, 220, 237.
81. In this sense, the Mather library bears comparison to the "private" fortune of John Hull, often used in service of the public good.
82. Hugh Amory, "Printing and Bookselling in New England, 1638–1713," in *A History of the Book in America*, vol. 1, *The Colonial Book in the Atlantic World*, ed. Hugh Amory and David D. Hall (Cambridge: Cambridge University Press, 2000), 83–116.
83. Anne Goldgar, *Impolite Learning: Conduct and Community in the Republic of Letters, 1680–1750* (New Haven, CT: Yale University Press, 1995).
84. On the concept of material objects as "distributed personhood," see Alfred Gell, *Art and Agency: An Anthropological Theory* (Oxford: Clarendon Press, 1998).
85. On the puritan movement's continuity with Roman Catholic piety and discipline, see Theodore Dwight Bozeman, *The Precisianist Strain: Disciplinary Religion and Antinomian Backlash in Puritanism to 1638* (Chapel Hill: University of North Carolina Press, 2004), 63–144.
86. Luther had used a similar image in his treatise criticizing the Roman Catholic Church's doctrine of the sacraments. Martin Luther, *Prelude on the Babylonian Captivity of the Church* (1520).
87. Michael G. Hall, *The Last American Puritan: The Life of Increase Mather* (Middletown, CT: Wesleyan University Press, 1988), 44–46; Robert Kingdon and Michel Reulos, "'Disciplines' réformées du XVIe siècle français: une découverte faite aux Etats-Unis," *Bulletin de la Société de l'Histoire du Protestantisme Français* 130, no. 1 (1984): 69–86.
88. Isaac de La Peyrère, *Men before Adam, A System of Divinity* (London, 1656), 18.
89. See Anthony Grafton, "Isaac La Peyrère and the Old Testament," in *Defenders of the Text: The Traditions of Scholarship in the Age of Science, 1450–1800* (Cambridge, MA: Harvard University Press, 1991), 204–13; Richard Popkin, *Isaac La Peyrère (1596–1676): His Life, Work, and Influence* (Leiden: E. J. Brill, 1987).
90. For seminal works in framing this argument, see Steven Shapin and Simon Shaffer, *Leviathan and the Air Pump: Hobbes, Boyle, and the Experimental Life* (Princeton, NJ: Princeton University Press, 1985); Steven Shapin, *The Social History of Truth: Civility and Science in Seventeenth-Century England* (Chicago: University of Chicago Press, 1994). See also Bruno Latour, *We Have Never Been Modern* (Cambridge, MA: Harvard University Press, 1993); Mario Biagioli, *Galileo, Courtier: The Practice of Science in the Culture of Absolutism* (Chicago: University of Chicago

Press, 1993); Lorraine Daston and Katharine Park, *Wonders and the Order of Nature, 1150–1750* (New York: Zone Books, 1998).

91. Newman, *Gehennical Fire*, especially 54–91.
92. Shapin, *Social History of Truth*, 126–92.
93. Margaret Jacob offers a comparable argument that alchemical forms of scientific investigation were driven underground in England after 1660, because the religious and political radicalism of many alchemical practitioners of the 1640s and 1650s were no longer acceptable in Restoration England. Jacob provides a comparison with France, where alchemy continued to thrive well after 1660, to demonstrate the significance of politics in the construction of communities of knowledge in England. Margaret Jacob, *Strangers Nowhere in the World: The Rise of Cosmopolitanism in Early Modern Europe* (Philadelphia: University of Pennsylvania Press, 2006), 41–65. But an equally strong case could be made through comparison with New England, where alchemical thought and practice continued to thrive beyond the reach of Restoration politics and royal authority.
94. David D. Hall, *World of Wonders, Days of Judgment: Popular Religious Belief in Early New England* (New York: Alfred A. Knopf, 1989), 67–68.
95. Ola Elizabeth Winslow, *A Destroying Angel: The Conquest of Smallpox in Colonial Boston* (Boston: Houghton Mifflin, 1974); John B. Blake, *Public Health in the Town of Boston, 1630–1822* (Cambridge, MA: Harvard University Press, 1959), 52–98; Perry Miller, *The New England Mind: From Colony to Province* (Cambridge, MA: Harvard University Press, 1953), 345–66; Silverman, *Life and Times of Cotton Mather*, 336–63; Margot Minardi, "The Boston Inoculation Controversy of 1721–1722: An Incident in the History of Race," *William and Mary Quarterly* 61, no. 1 (January 2004): 47–76.
96. Emmanuel Timoni, "An Account, or History, of the Procuring the Small Pox by Incision, or Inoculation: As It Has for Some Time Been Practised at Constantinople," *Philosophical Transactions* 29, no. 339 (1714): 72; Jacobus Pylarini, "Nova & Tuta Variolus Excitandi per Transplantationem Methodus, Nuper Inventa & in Usum Tracta," *Philosophical Transactions* 29, no. 347 (1716): 393–99.
97. Thomas Bartholini, "Historia Medica de Variolis, Anno 1656, Hafniae Epidemiis," in *Cista medica Hafniensis . . . Accedit ejusdem Domus anatomica brevissime discripta* (Hafniae [Copenhagen]: Petri Hauboldi, 1662, 590–608).
98. *New England Courant*, August 7 and August 14, 1721; *Boston Newsletter*, July 24, 1721.
99. For a recent overview, see Douglas H. Shantz, *An Introduction to German Pietism: Protestant Renewal at the Dawn of Modern Europe* (Baltimore: Johns Hopkins University Press, 2013).
100. *Diary of Cotton Mather*, 2 vols. (1911–12), *Collections of the Massachusetts Historical Society* 7th ser., 2:23. For the earliest English version of Francke's reports, see August Hermann Francke, *Pietas Hallensis: or, an Abstract of the Marvellous Footsteps of the Divine Providence*, trans. Anton Wilhelm Böhme (London, 1707).
101. Gary R. Sattler, *God's Glory, Neighbor's Good: A Brief Introduction to the Life and Writings of August Hermann Francke* (Chicago: Covenant Press, 1982); F. Ernest Stoeffler, *German Pietism during the Eighteenth Century* (Leiden: E. J. Brill, 1973), 1–88. On Mather's correspondence with Francke, see Kuno Francke, "Cotton Mather and August Hermann Francke," in *Studies and Notes in Philology and Literature*, vol. 5, *Child Memorial* (Boston, 1896), 57–67; Kuno Francke, "The Beginning of Cotton Mather's Correspondence with August Hermann Francke," *Philological Quarterly* 5 (July 1926): 193–95.
102. Published the following year as Crescentio Mathero, *De Successu Evangelij apud Indos in Nova-Anglia epistola ad cl. virum D. Johannem Leusdenum, . . .* (London, 1688).

103. Cotton Mather, *Triumphs of the Reformed Religion in America: The Life of the Renowned John Eliot* (London: John Dunton, 1691); Thomas J. Holmes, *Cotton Mather: A Bibliography of His Works* (Cambridge, MA: Harvard University Press, 1940), 3:1124–30.
104. See Patrick Gordon, "To the Reader," in *Geography Anatomiz'd: or, a Compleat Geographical Grammar* (London, 1693), n.p. Compare to Patrick Gordon, preface to *Geography Anatomiz'd: or the Compleat Geographical Grammar* (London, 1699), n.p., 346, 391–402.
105. Gordon, a chaplain in the Royal Navy and fellow of the Royal Society, joined the SPCK and went to America as one of its first missionaries. W. K. Lowther Clarke, *Eighteenth Century Piety* (London: Society for Promoting Christian Knowledge, 1944), 91–95. Gordon's *Geography* also influenced Cotton Mather's "Desiderata," a list of proposals for "general services for the Kingdom of God among mankind." See Cotton Mather, *Bonifacius: An Essay upon the Good*, ed. David Levin (Cambridge, MA: Belknap, 1966), 139.
106. W. O. B. Allen and Edmund McClure, *Two Hundred Years: The History of the Society for Promoting Christian Knowledge, 1698–1898* (New York: Burt Franklin, 1970), 7.
107. W. R. Ward, *The Protestant Evangelical Awakening* (Cambridge: Cambridge University Press, 1992), 302–7; Arno Sames, *Anton Wilhelm Böhme: Studien zum ökumenischen Denken und Handeln eines halleschen Pietisten* (Göttingen, 1990).
108. On Böhme's death in 1722, Newman wrote to Mather, "In him I have lost one of my dearest and intimate companions, and every place where I used to enjoy him seems desolate as if one half of me was gone to the grave." Henry Newman to Cotton Mather, August 31, 1722, in Allen and McClure, *Two Hundred Years*, 231–33; Leonard W. Cowie, *Henry Newman: An American in London, 1708–1743* (London: Society for Promotion of Christian Knowledge, 1956), 47.
109. Samuel Newman wrote the most comprehensive biblical concordance in any modern European language prior to the nineteenth century. See Cotton Mather, "Bibliander Nov-Anglicus, the Life of Samuel Newman," in *Magnalia Christi Americana* (1702; repr. New York: Arno Press, 1972), 3:113–16.
110. Cowie, *Henry Newman*, 195–222.
111. See Francke, "Beginnings of Cotton Mather's Correspondence," 193–94; Cotton Mather, *Nuncia Bona e Terra Longinqua: A Brief Account of Some Good and Great Things a Doing for the Kingdom of God in the Midst of Europe* (Boston, 1715). For Mather's text published together with an edited version of Francke's Latin original, see Kuno Francke, "Further Documents concerning Cotton Mather and August Hermann Francke," *Americana Germanica* 1, no. 4 (1897): 32–66.
112. Francke, "Further Documents," 51–52. Anton Wilhelm Böhme published a loose English translation of Francke's letter to Mather. See Francke, *Pietas Hallensis, Part III* (London: J. Downing, 1716). Increase Mather's letter to Johannes Leusden was published in Utrecht in 1693, with a discussion of missions to the East Indies appended to Mather's text. The enlarged work was translated into German and published at Halle in 1696. See Increase Mather, *Ein Brieff von dem glucklichen Fortgang des Evangelii bey den West-Indianern in Neu-Engeland an den beruhmten Herrn Johann Leusden* (Halle, 1696), copy in Houghton Library, Harvard University, Cambridge, MA.
113. *Diary of Cotton Mather*, 2:332–33, 2:563.
114. Cotton Mather, *India Christiana: A Discourse Delivered unto the Commissioners for the Propagation of the Gospel among the American Indians* (Boston: B. Green, 1721). The pamphlet reprints Mather's correspondence with Ziegenbalgh and Gıundler, including Latin originals and English translations on facing pages. See ibid., 62–87.
115. *Diary of Cotton Mather*, 2:193, 335–36, 348, 364, 400, 490, 497–99.

116. Mather, *Bonifacius*, 138–42.

117. See Ernst Benz, "The Pietist and Puritan Sources of Early Protestant World Missions (Cotton Mather and A. H. Francke)," *Church History* 20 (1951): 28–55; Ernst Benz, "Ecumenical Relations between Boston Puritanism and German Pietism: Cotton Mather and August Hermann Francke," *Harvard Theological Review* 54 (1961): 159–93; Richard F. Lovelace, *The American Pietism of Cotton Mather: Origins of American Evangelicalism* (Grand Rapids, MI: Wm. B. Eerdmans, 1979).

118. Lovelace, *American Pietism of Cotton Mather*, 73–109.

119. See Cotton Mather, *Theopolis Americana: An Essay on the Golden Street of the Holy City* (Boston: B. Green, 1710), 21–23. Mather dedicated this essay to Sewall. In addition to *The Selling of Joseph*, Sewall published a Boston edition of an antislavery exchange from the London's Athenian Society. See *The Athenian Oracle*, 2nd ed. (London, 1704), 1:545–48; *Whether Trading for Negroes i.e. Carrying Them out of Their Own Country into Perpetual Slavery, Be in It Self Unlawful, and Especially Contrary to the Great Law of Christianity* (Boston, 1705).

120. See Mather, *Letter concerning the Terrible Suffering of our Protestant Brethren*; Butler, *Huguenots in America*; J. F. Bosher, "Huguenot Merchants and the Protestant International in the Seventeenth Century," *William and Mary Quarterly* 52 (January 1995): 77–102; Charles C. Smith, "The French Protestants in Boston," in Winsor, *Memorial History of Boston*, 2:249–68. On German refugee migrants to North America, see A. G. Roeber, *Palatines, Liberty, and Property: German Lutherans in Colonial British America* (Baltimore: Johns Hopkins University Press, 1996); Philip Otterness, *Becoming German: The 1709 Palatine Migration to New York* (Ithaca, NY: Cornell University Press, 2004).

121. This obsession with international Catholicism turned up in the frequent rumors of the death of Louis XIV, along with reports of Louis's persecution of Protestants. See *Diary of Samuel Sewall*, 1:92, 102, 176, 267, 330–31, 365, 492.

122. [Paul Dudley], *An Essay on the Merchandize of Slaves and Souls of Men, with an Application Thereof to the Church of Rome* (Boston, 1731). Dudley endowed Harvard with the Dudleian Lecture, and every four years its theme was to be devoted to "detecting and convicting and exposing the Idolatry of the Romish Church, Their Tyranny, Usurpations, damnable Heresies, fatal Errors, abominable Superstitions, and other crying Wickednesses in their high Places." See Clifford K. Shipton, "Paul Dudley," in *Sibley's Harvard Graduates* (Cambridge, MA: Harvard University Press, 1933), 4:52–53.

123. Mather, *India Christiana*, 64; Mather, *Bonifacius*, 138.

124. Inspired by the German Pietists, Mather attempted to reduce the fundamentals of Christianity to fourteen *axiomata evangelii aeterni*. He later reduced these fourteen to an even more simplified three points: belief in the divine trinity as the world's creator to whom mankind owes obedience; belief in Jesus Christ's sacrificial atonement as the sole basis for human salvation; and upholding the golden rule as a guide to human relations. See Mather, *India Christiana*, 64–74; Benz, "Pietist and Puritan Sources," 43–46.

125. James Knowlton, *Universal Language Schemes in England and France, 1600–1800* (Toronto: University of Toronto Press, 1975).

126. Mather, *Nuncia Bona e Terra Longinqua*.

127. For his medical opinions, see Cotton Mather, *The Angel of Bethesda*, ed. Gordon W. Jones (Barre, MA: American Antiquarian Society, 1972). On alchemy and medicine in New England, see Mather's biographical sketch of the younger Winthrop. Cotton Mather, "Hermes Christianus," in *Magnalia Christi Americana* (Hartford, CT: Silas Andrus, 1853), 2:30–33; Newman, *Gehennical Fire*, 28, 32–40. See also

Patricia A. Watson, *The Angelical Conjunction: The Preacher-Physicians of Colonial New England* (Knoxville: University of Tennessee Press, 1991); Walter W. Woodward, *Prospero's America: John Winthrop, Jr., Alchemy, and the Creation of New England Culture, 1606–1676* (Chapel Hill: University of North Carolina Press, 2010).

128. Cotton Mather, *Lex Mercatoria: or, the Just Rules of Commerce Declared* (Boston: Timothy Green, 1705); Benjamin Colman, *Some Reasons and Arguments Offered to the Good People of Boston . . . for the Setting up Markets in Boston* (Boston: S. Gerrish and J. Edwards, 1719); Thomas Prince, *Vade Mecum for America: or, a Companion for Traders and Travelers* (Boston: S. Kneeland and T. Green, 1731).
129. Mather, *Theopolis Americana*, 42–43.
130. Samuel Sewall, *Phaenomena Quaedam Apocalyptica ad Aspectum Novi Orbis configurata; Or, Some Few Lines towards a Description of the New Heaven as It Makes to Those Who Stand upon the New Earth* (Boston: Green and Allen, 1697), epistle dedicatory "To the Honorable William Stoughton Esq."
131. Sewall worked for the Company for the Propagation of the Gospel to the Indians in New England and dedicated this tract to Sir William Ashurst, its governor.
132. Sewall, *Phaenomena*, 49, 64–65.
133. Samuel Sewall, *Proposals Touching the Accomplishment of Prophesies Humbly Offered* (Boston: Bartholomew Green, 1713), 4–5.
134. *Diary of Cotton Mather*, 2:333. See also Mather, *Bonifacius*, 15; Cotton Mather, *Shaking Dispensations: An Essay upon the Mighty Shakes, Which the Hand of Heaven, Hath Given . . . with Some Useful Remarks on the Death of the French King* (Boston: B. Green, 1715); Silverman, *Life and Times of Cotton Mather*, 303.
135. Batinski, *Jonathan Belcher*, 45–53.
136. Ward, *Protestant Evangelical Awakening*, 93–115.
137. George Fenwick Jones, ed., *Henry Newman's Salzburger Letterbooks* (Athens: University of Georgia Press, 1966).
138. George Fenwick Jones, ed., *Detailed Reports on the Salzburger Emigrants Who Settled in America . . . Edited by Samuel Urlsperger* (1733–36; repr., Athens: University of Georgia Press, 1968–72), 1:188–89, 2:vii, 2:xxi, 2:14, 3:xix, 3:1. Colman's letter to Urlsperger is omitted from volume 3 of Jones's edition of the Salzburger reports, but can be found in the original text. Samuel Urlsperger, *Der Ausfuhrlichen Nachrichten von der Koniglich-Gross-Britannischen Colonie Saltzburgischer Emigranten in America* (Halle, 1741), held at the Houghton Library, Harvard University, Cambridge, MA.
139. "Travel Diary of Commissioner Von Reck," in Jones, *Detailed Reports*, 1:128.
140. Ibid., 1:116–34. On Philadelphia, see ibid., 119–20. On New York, see ibid., 122–23. On Belcher and Boston, see ibid., 127–30. On slavery and the slave trade, see ibid., 122–23, 126–27.
141. Sewall continued to cite Pareus in his millennial writings. See, for instance, Sewall, *Proposals*, 7.
142. Frances Yates, *The Rosicrucian Enlightenment* (London: Routledge and Kegan Paul, 1972), 1–29.
143. Ibid., 171–205.
144. James Holstun, *A Rational Millennium: Puritan Utopias of Seventeenth-Century England and America* (New York: Oxford University Press, 1987), 102–9.
145. On Sophia's ancestry, see Kroll, *Sophie*, 21–51.
146. Mather, *Theopolis Americana*, 50.

Chapter 5: "God Deliver Me and Mine from the Government of Soldiers"

1. Jonathan Belcher to Thomas Coram, October 6, 1733, in *Jonathan Belcher Letterbooks*, part I, 6th series (Boston: Massachusetts Historical Society, 1893), 6:392.
2. Ibid.
3. See Daniel K. Richter, *Facing East from Indian Country: A Native History of Early America* (Cambridge, MA: Harvard University Press, 2001), 152–88.
4. For general accounts, see Geoffrey Plank, *An Unsettled Conquest: The British Campaign against the Peoples of Acadia* (Philadelphia: University of Pennsylvania Press, 2001); John Mack Faragher, *A Great and Noble Scheme: The Tragic Story of the Expulsion of the French Acadians from Their American Homeland* (New York: W. W. Norton, 2005). My account retells this bitter story from a vantage point that distinguishes Boston's interests from those of British military authorities. For a similar interpretation, see George A. Rawlyk, *Nova Scotia's Massachusetts: A Study of Massachusetts–Nova Scotia Relations, 1630 to 1784* (Montreal: McGill-Queens University Press, 1973).
5. Faragher, *Great and Noble Scheme*, 180–81; Richard R. Johnson, *John Nelson, Merchant Adventurer: A Life between Empires* (New York: Oxford University Press, 1991), 16–29. See also Jean Daigle, "Nos Amis les Ennemis: relations commerciales de l'Acadie avec le Massachusetts, 1670–1711" (PhD diss., University of Maine, 1975).
6. William Bradford, *Of Plymouth Plantation, 1620–1647*, ed. Samuel Eliot Morison (New York: Alfred A. Knopf, 1952), 201–2, 244–46, 275–79.
7. Hannah Farber, "The Rise and Fall of the Province of Lygonia, 1643–1658," *New England Quarterly* 82, no. 3 (September, 2009): 490–513.
8. Among the advantages that Boston gained was the remarkable population growth among the founding migrants of New England. The twenty thousand colonists of the 1630s had grown to a hundred thousand by 1700. As the principal commercial center for the region, Boston had a far larger array of goods to sell and far larger internal demand to be met by way of its overseas trading. See Bernard Bailyn, *The New England Merchants in the Seventeenth Century* (Cambridge, MA: Harvard University Press, 1955), 98–100.
9. Evan Haefeli and Kevin Sweeney, *Captors and Captives: The 1704 French and Indian Raid on Deerfield* (Amherst: University of Massachusetts Press, 2003); John Demos, *The Unredeemed Captive: A Family Story from Early America* (New York: Alfred A. Knopf, 1994).
10. For a description of the opposition of New England soldiers to these plans, in a slashing attack on Joseph Dudley, the much-despised Massachusetts royal governor, see Cotton Mather, *The Deplorable State of New England, by Reason of a Covetous and Treacherous Governor, and Pusillanimous Counsellors* (London, 1708).
11. The name "Nova Scotia" had been associated with this region since the late 1620s, when Scottish Presbyterians supported by Sir William Alexander, a courtier of James I, wrested Acadia away from the French, only to return it in 1632. See John G. Reid, *Acadia, Maine, and New Scotland: Marginal Colonies in the Seventeenth Century* (Toronto: University of Toronto Press, 1981), 37–39.
12. Vetch was reinventing a plan that Bostonians led by Sir William Phips had developed twenty years earlier. Military patterns of invasion and conquest tend to repeat themselves, none more so than New England plans for attacking French Canada.
13. G. M. Waller, *Samuel Vetch, Colonial Enterpriser* (Chapel Hill: University of North Carolina Press, 1960).
14. See Plank, *Unsettled Conquest*, 40–63. For a description of the alienation of New Englanders by Vetch and Nicholson, and their plans for conquest, see Geoffrey Plank,

"New England and the Conquest," in *The Conquest of Acadia, 1710: Imperial, Colonial, and Aboriginal Constructions*, ed. John G. Reid, Maurice Basque, Elizabeth Mancke, Barry Moody, Geoffrey Plank, and William C. Wicken (Toronto: University of Toronto Press, 2004), 67–86.

15. On Mascarene's personal history, see Faragher, *Great and Noble Scheme*, 126–27. See also Maxwell Sutherland, "MASCARENE, PAUL," in *Dictionary of Canadian Biography, Volume III (1741–1770)*, University of Toronto and Université Laval, accessed February 24, 2018, http://www.biographi.ca/en/bio/mascarene_paul_3E.html. Contrary to Faragher, Sutherland has Mascarene's post-1706 education taking place in Geneva. In either case, his family's commitment to Protestantism would have been sustained by his education.
16. Waller, *Samuel Vetch*, 189, 240–41; Faragher, *Great and Noble Scheme*, 131.
17. Faragher, *Great and Noble Scheme*, 132; Paul Mascarene, "A Narrative of Events at Annapolis from the Capture in October 1710 till September 1711," in "Hon. Samuel Vetch, First English Governor of Nova Scotia," in *Nova Scotia Historical Society Collections*, ed. George Patterson (Halifax, 1885), 4:11–12, 78–79.
18. Waller, *Samuel Vetch*, 195–96.
19. Plank, *Unsettled Conquest*, 90–98.
20. Samuel Drake, *Old Landmarks and Historic Personages of Boston* (Boston: James Osgood, 1873), 60.
21. This plan was precisely how Thomas More imagined the Utopians would colonize neighboring lands.
22. Plank, *Unsettled Conquest*, 102–5; Faragher, *Great and Noble Scheme*, 200–201.
23. St. Poncy had once been deported from Acadia to Louisbourg for saying masses in private homes on the fringes of Annapolis Royal rather than in the Catholic Church under the watch of British government.
24. In the same year, Smibert painted Sewall, and would also do portraits of Thomas Hancock, the Oliver family, the Dudleys, the Tyngs, the Quincys, and many other leading families. Richard H. Saunders, *John Smibert, Colonial America's First Portrait Painter* (New Haven, CT: Yale University Press, 1995), 69–71, 155–56.
25. *Boston Gazette*, January 22, 1728; February 26, 1729; January 5, 1731; January 8, 1729; November 27, 1732.
26. Faragher, *Great and Noble Scheme*, 210.
27. Ibid., 212.
28. John A. Schutz, *William Shirley, King's Governor of Massachusetts* (Chapel Hill: University of North Carolina Press, 1961), especially 3–5.
29. Ibid., 16–22.
30. Ibid., 22.
31. Ibid., 37.
32. David Syrett, "The Raising of American Troops for Service in the West Indies during the War of Austrian Succession, 1740–41," *Historical Research* 73, no. 180 (February 2000): 20–32; Richard Harding, *Amphibious Warfare in the Eighteenth Century: The British Expedition to the West Indies, 1740–1742* (Rochester, NY: Boydell and Brewer, Inc., 1991).
33. Schutz, *William Shirley*, 39–41. On the banking controversy, see Margaret Newell, *From Dependency to Independence: Economic Revolution in Colonial New England* (Ithaca, NY: Cornell University Press, 1998), 214–36; Rosalind Remer, "Old Lights and New Money: A Note on Religion, Economics, and the Social Order in 1740 Boston," *William and Mary Quarterly* 47 (October 1990): 566–73.
34. One advertisement described "the Island of Cuba, a Land well known in History to be a Place of Health and Plenty, and is bless'd with a fertile Soil, which abounds with Cattle, Greens, Fish, &c. having in it Springs, Brooks and Rivers, and produces all kind

of Commodities which grow in the other West India Islands." John Winslow, broadside advertisement, October 19, 1741, American Antiquarian Society, Worcester, MA.

35. For a description of the slow learning process of the British Army and Navy and their colonial recruits, see Harding, *Amphibious Warfare*.
36. See Rawlyk, *Nova Scotia's Massachusetts*, 141–43.
37. A. J. B. Johnston, "From Port De Pêche to Ville Fortifiée: The Evolution of Urban Louisbourg, 1713–1758," *Proceedings of the Meeting of the French Colonial Historical Society* 17 (1993): 24–43.
38. "Journal of Colonel John Bradstreet," in *Louisbourg Journals, 1745*, ed. Louis Effingham de Forest (New York: Society of Colonial Wars, 1932), 170–78; William G. Godfrey, *Pursuit of Profit and Preferment in Colonial North America: John Bradstreet's Quest* (Waterloo, ON: Wilfrid Laurier University Press, 1982).
39. *Boston Evening Post*, July 15, 1745, cited in John A. Schutz, "Imperialism in Massachusetts during the Governorship of William Shirley, 1741–1756," *Huntington Library Quarterly* 23, no. 3 (May, 1960): 219.
40. See John Brewer, *The Sinews of Power: War, Money, and the English State, 1688–1783* (Cambridge, MA: Harvard University Press, 1990).
41. Schutz, *William Shirley*, 88–101; Robert Emmet Wall, "Louisbourg, 1745," *New England Quarterly* 37, no. 1 (1964): 64–83.
42. *Boston Evening Post*, July 29, 1745.
43. Charles Chauncy, *Marvellous Things Done by the Right Hand and Holy Arm of God in Getting Him the Victory. A Sermon Preached the 18th of July, 1745* (Boston: T. Fleet, 1745).
44. Denver Brunsman, "The Knowles Atlantic Impressment Riots of the 1740s," *Early American Studies* 5, no. 2 (2007): 324–66.
45. Douglas Edward Leach, "Brothers in Arms? Anglo-American Friction at Louisbourg, 1745–1746," *Proceedings of the Massachusetts Historical Society* 89 (1977): 36–54; Jack M. Sosin, "Louisbourg and the Peace of Aix-la-Chapelle, 1748," *William and Mary Quarterly* 14, no. 4 (October 1957), 516–35; Daniel Robinson, "Giving Peace to Europe: European Geopolitics, Colonial Political Culture, and the Hanoverian Monarchy in British North America, ca. 1740–63," *William and Mary Quarterly* 73, no. 2 (2016): 291–332.
46. Schutz, *William Shirley*, 101–8.
47. For population figures and rates of growth, see Rawlyk, *Nova Scotia's Massachusetts*, xiii–xiv; Naomi Griffiths, *The Contexts of Acadian History, 1686–1784* (Montreal: McGill-Queen's University Press, 1992), 64–68.
48. Report of the Council, cited in Faragher, *Great and Noble Scheme*, 229.
49. See Geoffrey Plank, *Rebellion and Savagery: The Jacobite Rising of 1745 and the British Empire* (Philadelphia: University of Pennsylvania Press, 2006), 155–80.
50. [William Shirley], *Memoirs of the Principal Transactions of the Last War between the English and French in North America Containing in Particular an Account of the Importance of Nova Scotia or Acadie and the Island of Cape Breton to Both Nations*, 3rd ed. (London, 1757), 11.
51. William Shirley to Duke of Newcastle, July 8, 1747, cited in Faragher, *Great and Noble Scheme*, 241. Faragher and Plank show that although the specific methods Shirley envisioned wavered over the years, the removal of Acadians who would not adopt Protestant ways was essential for Shirley's plan. In the years after 1746, Shirley increasingly despaired of converting Acadians or settling Protestants peaceably among them.
52. Schutz, *William Shirley*, 168–81.
53. Fred Anderson, *Crucible of War: The Seven Years' War and the Fate of Empire in British North America, 1754–1766* (New York: Alfred A. Knopf, 2000), 3–8, 108–23.

54. Faragher, *Great and Noble Scheme*, 245–78, 296–301; Schutz, *William Shirley*, 187–204.
55. Faragher, *Great and Noble Scheme*, 299–301.
56. See John Frederick Martin, *Profits in the Wilderness: Entrepreneurship and the Founding of New England Towns in the Seventeenth Century* (Chapel Hill: University of North Carolina Press, 1991), 18–20.
57. Mary Rowlandson, "The Sovereignty and Goodness of God" (1682), in *Puritans among the Indians: Accounts of Captivity and Redemption, 1676–1724*, ed. Alden T. Vaughan and Edward Clark (Cambridge, MA: Harvard University Press, 1981), 71.
58. Seymour Van Dyken, *Samuel Willard, 1640–1707: Preacher of Orthodoxy in an Era of Change* (Grand Rapids, MI: Wm. B. Eerdmans, 1972).
59. Henry Stedman Nourse, *The Military Annals of Lancaster, Massachusetts, 1740–1865* (Lancaster, MA, 1889), 16–22.
60. The names, occupations, and hometowns of the New England recruits are recorded in the *Journal of John Winslow*, 3 vols. (manuscript, photostat copy, Massachusetts Historical Society, Boston). Volume 1 contains material from the Acadian removal, and volumes 2 and 3 pertain to Winslow's later experiences as an officer in expeditions to Crown Point and the Saint Lawrence Valley under General Jeffrey Amherst.
61. Rawlyk, *Nova Scotia's Massachusetts*, 209–11; Schutz, *William Shirley*, 175–79, 189, 228–29.
62. Abijah Willard, *A Journal on the Intended Expedition to Novicotia* (original manuscript, Henry E. Huntington Library, San Marino, CA). For a printed version, see *Collections of the New Brunswick Historical Society* (Saint John, 1930), 13:1–75.
63. Willard, *Journal*, 2–4.
64. Ibid., 20–23.
65. Faragher, *Great and Noble Scheme*, 335–50.
66. Godfrey, *Pursuit of Profit*, 51, 58.
67. Willard, *Journal*, 30.
68. Ibid., 31, 33–35.
69. Ibid., 41–42.
70. Ibid., 36–37.
71. *Journal of John Winslow*, vol. 1 (manuscript, Massachusetts Historical Society, Boston).
72. Pierre Belliveau, *The French Neutrals of Massachusetts: The Story of Acadians Rounded Up by Soldiers from Massachusetts and Their Captivity in the Bay Province, 1755–1766* (Boston: K. S. Griffin, 1972), 180–96.
73. A number of leading Massachusetts citizens, especially those with family ties to Huguenots or Acadians, treated the refugees with kindness and respect. Thomas Hutchinson, the future governor of Massachusetts, took ailing Acadian families into his own home in Boston's North End. Huguenot families such as James Bowdoin's were also generous to the exiles, and used their power in the General Court to provide for far more refugees than Massachusetts had initially been allotted. James K. Hosmer, *The Life of Thomas Hutchinson* (Boston: Houghton Mifflin 1896), 40–41.
74. Petition of February 22, 1757, in *The Acts and Resolves, Public and Private, of the Province of Massachusetts Bay* (Boston, 1878), 3:1060.
75. Belliveau, *French Neutrals of Massachusetts*, 26.
76. Plank, *Unsettled Conquest*, 149.
77. Belliveau, *French Neutrals of Massachusetts*, 30.
78. Ibid., 34.

79. Abijah P. Marvin, *History of the Town of Lancaster, Massachusetts* (Lancaster, 1879), 299–300.
80. T. H. Breen, *American Insurgents, American Patriots: The Revolution of the People* (New York: Hill and Wang, 2010), 94; Ray Raphael and Marie Raphael, *The Spirit of '74: How the American Revolution Began* (New York: New Press, 2015), 80–81.
81. Marvin, *History of the Town of Lancaster*, 299–300; Ann Gorman Condon, "WILLARD, ABIJAH," in *Dictionary of Canadian Biography, Volume IV (1771–1800)*, University of Toronto and Université Laval, accessed February 24, 2018, http://www.biographi.ca/en/bio/willard_abijah_4E.html.
82. Samuel Sewall, *The Selling of Joseph: A Memorial* (Boston: Green and Allen, 1700), 3.

Chapter 6: Cutting Off the Circulation

1. Fred Anderson, *A People's Army: Massachusetts Soldiers and Society in the Seven Years' War* (Chapel Hill: University of North Carolina Press, 1984), 59–60. On the war generally, see Fred Anderson, *Crucible of War: The Seven Years' War and the Fate of Empire in British North America, 1754–1766* (New York: Alfred A. Knopf, 2000).
2. Vincent Carretta, *Phillis Wheatley: Biography of a Genius in Bondage* (Athens: University of Georgia Press, 2011), especially 1–66.
3. Ibid., ix–xi.
4. Among these was the first religious magazine published in America. Thomas Prince, *The Christian History* (Boston, 1744).
5. On the Great Awakening in Boston, see Mark A. Peterson, *The Price of Redemption: The Spiritual Economy of Puritan New England* (Stanford, CA: Stanford University Press, 1997), 224–39; Thomas Prince, "Some Account of the Late Revival of Religion in Boston," in *The Christian History* (Boston, 1744).
6. For a powerful account of the impact of Britain's conquest of Havana during the Seven Years' War, see Elena A. Schneider, *The Occupation of Havana: War, Trade, and Slavery in the Atlantic World* (Chapel Hill: University of North Carolina Press, 2018).
7. Edmund S. Morgan and Helen M. Morgan, *The Stamp Act Crisis: Prologue to Revolution* (1953; repr., Chapel Hill: University of North Carolina Press, 1995), 130–31.
8. Eric Hinderaker, *Boston's Massacre* (Cambridge, MA: Harvard University Press, 2017), 110–20. Hinderaker draws attention to the significance of military rule in bringing about Boston's rebellion against the Crown. See also Richard Archer, *As If an Enemy's Country: The British Occupation of Boston and the Origins of Revolution* (New York: Oxford University Press, 2010).
9. For a thorough account of the tea crisis, see Benjamin Woods Labaree, *The Boston Tea Party* (New York: Oxford University Press, 1964).
10. For a detailed account of the Lexington and Concord battles as well as the beginning of the siege, see David Hackett Fischer, *Paul Revere's Ride* (New York: Oxford University Press, 1994).
11. For a vivid account of the siege and its destruction of the city, see Jacqueline Barbara Carr, *After the Siege: A Social History of Boston, 1775–1800* (Boston: Northeastern University Press, 2005), 13–42. See also Richard Frothingham, *History of the Siege of Boston* (Boston: Little, Brown, 1849).
12. Bernard Bailyn, *The Ordeal of Thomas Hutchinson* (Cambridge, MA: Harvard University Press, 1974).
13. For important titles on Wheatley's life and work, see Carretta, *Phillis Wheatley: Biography*; Henry Louis Gates Jr., *The Trials of Phillis Wheatley: America's First Black Poet and Her Encounters with the Founding Fathers* (New York: Basic Books, 2003); William H. Robinson, ed., *Critical Essays on Phillis Wheatley* (Boston: G.

K. Hall, 1982); Merle A. Richmond, *Bid the Vassal Soar: Interpretive Essays on the Life and Poetry of Phillis Wheatley and George Moses Horton* (Washington, DC: Howard University Press, 1974); David Grimsted, "Anglo-American Racism and Phillis Wheatley's 'Sable Veil,' 'Length'ned Chain,' and 'Knitted Heart,'" in *Women in the American Revolution*, ed. Ronald Hoffman and Peter Albert (Charlottesville: University of Virginia Press, 1989), 338–444; Vincent Carretta and Philip Gould, eds., *Genius in Bondage: Literature of the Early Black Atlantic* (Lexington: University of Kentucky Press, 2001). Major editions of Wheatley's writings contain biographical and critical commentaries. See Vincent Carretta, ed., *Phillis Wheatley: Complete Writings* (New York: Penguin Books, 2001); Julian D. Mason Jr., ed., *The Poems of Phillis Wheatley*, rev. (Chapel Hill: University of North Carolina Press, 1989); William H. Robinson, *Phillis Wheatley and Her Writings* (New York: Garland Press, 1984); John C. Shields, ed., *The Collected Works of Phillis Wheatley* (New York: Oxford University Press, 1988). For Pope's influence on Wheatley, see Albertha Sistrunk, "The Influence of Alexander Pope on the Writing Style of Phillis Wheatley," in *Critical Essays on Phillis Wheatley*, ed. William H. Robinson (Boston: G. K. Hall, 1982), 175–88.

14. Henry F. Stecher, *Elizabeth Singer Rowe, the Poetess of Frome: A Study in Eighteenth-Century English Pietism* (Bern, Switzerland: Herbert Lang, 1973); Arthur W. H. Eaton, *The Famous Mather Byles* (Boston: W. A. Butterfield, 1914).
15. Linda Colley, *Britons: Forging the Nation, 1707–1837* (New Haven, CT: Yale University Press, 1992), 11–54; David Armitage, *The Ideological Origins of the British Empire* (Cambridge: Cambridge University Press, 2000), 170–98. Both Colley and Armitage cite the famous lines from Thompson's "Rule Britannia" as an epigraph. See also Kathleen Wilson, *The Island Race: Englishness, Empire, and Gender in the Eighteenth Century* (London: Routledge, 2003), 1–53; David S. Shields, *Oracles of Empire: Poetry, Politics, and Commerce in British America, 1690–1750* (Chicago: University of Chicago Press, 1990).
16. Carretta, *Phillis Wheatley: Biography*, 4–11.
17. For a speculative but plausible account of Wheatley's early life in Africa and arrival in Boston, see Robinson, *Phillis Wheatley and Her Writings*, 3–10.
18. Joseph Fisk, *A Few Lines on the Happy Reduction of Canada, . . .* (Boston, 1761), 3.
19. James A. Rawley, "The World of Phillis Wheatley," *New England Quarterly* 50 (1977): 266–77; Grimsted, "Anglo-American Racism," 370–94.
20. For newspaper advertisements announcing the arrival of the *Phillis* and sale of its "parcel of likely Negroes, imported from Africa," which John Avery, the Boston agent, referred to as "the meanest Cargo I Ever had Come," see Robinson, *Phillis Wheatley and Her Writings*, 3–5.
21. The Wheatleys' large house stood at the northeast corner of King Street and Mackerel Lane (later Kilby Street), three blocks east of the town house, the center of government. See ibid., 12–15; Caretta, *Phillis Wheatley*, 15–16.
22. Linda K. Kerber, *Women of the Republic: Intellect and Ideology in Revolutionary America* (Chapel Hill: University of North Carolina Press, 1980); Linda K. Kerber, "'History Can Do It No Justice': Women and the Reinterpretation of the American Revolution," in *Women in the Age of the American Revolution*, ed. Ronald Hoffman and Peter Albert (Charlottesville: University Press of Virginia, 1989), 3–42; Linda Colley, *Captives: Britain, Empire, and the World, 1600–1850* (London: Jonathan Cape, 2002), 137–240; Wilson, *Island Race*, 92–128. On the role of evangelical women in creating Wheatley's circle, see Grimsted, "Anglo-American Racism," 370–94.
23. On Lathrop, see Clifford K. Shipton, *Sibley's Harvard Graduates* (Cambridge, MA: Harvard University Press, 1933), 15:428–36.

24. On Cooper, see Charles Akers, "'Our Modern Egyptians': Phillis Wheatley and the Whig Campaign against Slavery in Revolutionary Boston," *Journal of Negro History* 60, no. 3 (July 1975): 397–410. For Wheatley's correspondence with Occom, see Carretta, *Phillis Wheatley: Complete Writings*, 152–53. On the Sewall connection, see Mark A. Peterson, "*The Selling of Joseph*: Bostonians, Antislavery, and the Protestant International, 1689–1733," *Massachusetts Historical Review* 4 (2002): 1–22.
25. Robinson, *Phillis Wheatley and Her Writings*, 19.
26. Ibid., 23–24.
27. See Phillis Wheatley, "A REBUS, by I. B." and "An ANSWER to the *Rebus*, by the Author of These POEMS," in Carretta, *Phillis Wheatley: Complete Writings*, 64–65.
28. Catherine A. Brekus, *Sarah Osborn's World: The Rise of Evangelical Christianity in Early America* (New Haven, CT: Yale University Press, 2013), especially 170–91, 248–89.
29. Sarah Osborn, diary, March 18, 1767, cited in Grimsted, "Anglo-American Racism," 380.
30. Samuel Eliot Morison, *Harrison Gray Otis: The Urbane Federalist* (Boston: Houghton Mifflin, 1969), 464–77. On Eliot, see Bernard Bailyn, "Religion and Revolution: Three Biographical Sketches," in *Faces of Revolution* (New York: Vintage Books, 1990), 106–24.
31. On eighteenth-century Anglo-American humanitarianism and the problem of slavery, see Christopher Leslie Brown, *Moral Capital: Foundations of British Abolitionism* (Chapel Hill: University of North Carolina Press, 2006), 33–101.
32. Joanna Brooks, *American Lazarus: Religion and the Rise of African American and Native American Literatures* (New York: Oxford University Press, 2003); William DeLoss Love, *Samson Occom and the Christian Indians of New England* (Syracuse, NY: Syracuse University Press, 2000). On the global mission of New England Christianity, see Ezra Stiles, *A Discourse on the Christian Union* (Boston: Edes and Gill, 1761).
33. On Whitefield's connection with the Wheatley family, see Carretta, *Phillis Wheatley: Biography*, 33–34; Grimsted, "Anglo-American Racism," 384.
34. Phillis Wheatley, "On the Death of the Rev. Mr. GEORGE WHITEFIELD. 1770," in Carretta, *Phillis Wheatley: Complete Writings*, 15–16.
35. Grimsted, "Anglo-American Racism," 384; Sara Dunlap Jackson, "Letters of Phillis Wheatley and Susanna Wheatley," *Journal of Negro History* 57 (1972): 212–15.
36. Boyd Stanley Schlenther, *Queen of the Methodists: The Countess of Huntingdon and the Eighteenth-Century Crisis of Faith and Society* (Durham, UK: Durham Academic Press, 1997); Edwin Welch, *Spiritual Pilgrim: A Reassessment of the Life of the Countess of Huntingdon* (Cardiff: University of Wales Press, 1995); Alan Harding, *The Countess of Huntingdon's Connexion: A Sect in Action in Eighteenth-Century England* (Oxford: Oxford University Press, 2003), 1–172.
37. Welch, *Spiritual Pilgrim*, 131–47; Schlenther, *Queen of the Methodists*, 83–92; Harding, *Countess of Huntingdon's Connexion*, 371.
38. See Phillis Wheatley to David Worcester, October 18, 1773, in Carretta, *Phillis Wheatley: Complete Writings*, 146–47. On Sharp's role in British abolitionism, see Brown, *Moral Capital*, 155–204.
39. B. D. Barger, *Lord Dartmouth and the American Revolution* (Columbia: University of South Carolina Press, 1965), 1–23. Dartmouth became the patron of John Newton, the former slave trader who adopted abolitionist beliefs. See Adam Hochschild, *Bury the Chains: Prophets and Rebels in the Fight to Free an Empire's Slaves* (Boston: Houghton Mifflin, 2005), 130–31.
40. Letter from Thomas Woolridge, November 24, 1772, Dartmouth Manuscripts, cited in Barger, *Lord Dartmouth*, 58.

41. Carretta, *Phillis Wheatley: Complete Writings*, 39–40.
42. See "translation, n.," *Oxford English Dictionary*, online ed., accessed February 25, 2018, http://www.oed.com/view/Entry/204844?redirectedFrom=translation; Michael Wintroub, "Translations: Words, Things, Going Native, and Staying True," *American Historical Review* 120 (2015): 1185–1217.
43. Jerome M. Segal, *Joseph's Bones: Understanding the Struggle between God and Man in the Bible* (New York: Penguin Books, 2007), 1–34.
44. Carretta, *Phillis Wheatley: Complete Writings*, 13–15, 50–51.
45. Ibid., 40, lines 40–43.
46. Ibid., 41, lines 7–10 and 13–16.
47. Ibid., 41–42, lines 3, 10, 7, 11.
48. Ibid., 47–48, stanza 3, lines 17–24.
49. Ibid., 62–64, stanzas 2, 7, 8; Timothy Gantz, *Early Greek Myth: A Guide to Literary and Artistic Sources* (Baltimore: Johns Hopkins University Press, 1993), 1:81–82.
50. Carretta, *Phillis Wheatley: Complete Writings*, 13, lines 1–4.
51. For an essay on the evolution of Wheatley criticism and her place in the modern canon of African American literature, see Gates, *Trials of Phillis Wheatley*.
52. See John Demos, *The Unredeemed Captive: A Family Story from Early America* (New York: Alfred A. Knopf, 1994), 140–66.
53. Phillis Wheatley to John Thornton, October 30, 1770 [1774], in Carretta, *Phillis Wheatley: Complete Writings*, 158–60.
54. Carretta, *Phillis Wheatley: Complete Writings*, 8.
55. Ibid., 39–40, lines 2, 5–6, 9–10, 12.
56. Ibid., 39–40, lines 21, 24–25, 26–29.
57. Ibid., 152–53. See also Akers, "Our Modern Egyptians," 405–7.
58. Ibid., 39–40, lines 29, 19, 17.
59. For a facsimile of Wheatley's 1773 publication, see Shields, *Collected Works of Phillis Wheatley*, 1–127.
60. Scipio, Wheatley's fellow slave in Boston, may have been the artist who created Wheatley's portrait for the frontispiece, but there is no solid evidence to support this otherwise-attractive idea.
61. Shields, *Collected Works of Phillis Wheatley*, frontispiece.
62. Phillis Wheatley, "To the Publick," in Shields, *Collected Works of Phillis Wheatley*, 7.
63. Shields, *Collected Works of Phillis Wheatley*, 13–14, 15–16, 19–21, 22–24.
64. Ibid., 3, 9–12, 17, 24, 73–75. Maecenas's patronage extended to Virgil, Horace, and "Terence, an African by birth" as well as Maecanas's own freed slave. Shields, *Collected Works of Phillis Wheatley*, 11; N. G. L. Hammond and H. H. Scullard, eds., *Oxford Classical Dictionary*, 2nd ed. (Oxford: Clarendon Press, 1970), 636.
65. Phillis Wheatley, "On Being Brought from Africa to America," in Shields, *Collected Works of Phillis Wheatley*, 18.
66. Wheatley speaks of all New England as a single "race," and includes herself among New England's grateful souls offering "our thanks" to past favors of Dartmouth, including the repeal of the Stamp Act. Shields, *Collected Works of Phillis Wheatley*, 73–75.
67. In a further irony, this claim is today quite literally true. In 2005, a single autographed letter of Wheatley's sold at auction for $253,000. Carretta, *Phillis Wheatley: Biography*, ix. For further discussion of Wheatley's poetic achievement and its relationship to her enslaved status, see John C. Shields, "Phillis Wheatley's Struggle for Freedom in Her Poetry and Prose," in Shields, *Collected Works of Phillis Wheatley*, 229–70; Grimsted, "Anglo-American Racism."
68. Benjamin Woods Labaree, *The Boston Tea Party* (New York: Oxford University Press, 1964), 126–32.

69. Shields, *Collected Works of Phillis Wheatley*, 7. On British emancipation during the American Revolution, see Brown, *Moral Capital*, 209–58.
70. Steven M. Wise, *Though the Heavens May Fall: The Landmark Trial That Led to the End of Human Slavery* (Cambridge, MA: De Capo Press, 2005), 182.
71. See David Waldstreicher, "The Wheatleyan Moment," *Early American Studies* 9, no. 3 (Fall 2011): 522–51. On how Wheatley's career shapes and is shaped by Mansfield's decision, see also David Waldstreicher, *Slavery's Constitution: From Revolution to Ratification* (New York: Hill and Wang, 2009), 21–56.
72. Carretta, *Phillis Wheatley: Complete Writings*, 12–13, lines 14–15.
73. Frank Shuffleton, "On Her Own Footing: Phillis Wheatley in Freedom," in *Genius in Bondage: Literature of the Early Black Atlantic*, ed. Vincent Carretta and Philip Gould (Lexington: University of Kentucky Press, 2001), 175–89.
74. See Henry Wiencek, *An Imperfect God: George Washington, His Slaves, and the Creation of America* (New York: Farrar, Straus and Giroux, 2003), 205–14. For her ode to Washington, see Carretta, *Phillis Wheatley: Complete Writings*, 88–90. Carretta doubts that Wheatley ever met Washington and suggests that she may have been in Providence, Rhode Island, with the family of Nathaniel Wheatley during this time. Carretta, *Phillis Wheatley: Biography*, 154–58.
75. Carretta, *Phillis Wheatley: Complete Writings*, 90–94; Shuffleton, "On Her Own Footing," 187–88.
76. Carretta, *Phillis Wheatley: Complete Writings*, 101–2, lines 11–12.
77. Ibid., 101–2, lines 47–48, 15, 17–20, 35.
78. Carretta, *Phillis Wheatley: Biography*, 190–93.
79. Thomas Jefferson, *Notes on the State of Virginia* (1781), ed. David Waldstreicher (Boston: Bedford Books, 2002), 178. Barbé-Marbois would become the intendant of Saint-Domingue in 1785, and later negotiated the sale of Louisiana to the Jefferson administration in 1803; he was also one of the greatest promoters of the expansion of slavery in all of French history.
80. Caroline Winterer, *American Enlightenments: Pursuing Happiness in the Age of Reason* (New Haven, CT: Yale University Press, 2016), 88–89.
81. Gates, *Trials of Phillis Wheatley*, 40–56.

Chapter 7: John Adams, Boston's Diplomat

1. "Tully" was the name that eighteenth-century New Englanders used for Marcus Tullius Cicero, the famed Roman orator frequently read in schoolbooks. The Tory historian Peter Oliver disparaged the young Adams by suggesting that he stooped to teaching schoolgirls. Peter Oliver, *Peter Oliver's Origin and Progress of the American Rebellion: A Tory View* (1707), ed. Douglass Adair and John A. Schutz (Stanford, CA: Stanford University Press, 1961), 83–84.
2. In his diary for February 9, 1772, Adams recorded the following remarks made by Shirley: "'Who are the Boston Seat?' says the Governor.—'Mr. Cushing, Mr. Hancock, Mr. Adams, and Mr. Adams' says the Gentleman.—'Mr. Cushing I know,' quoth Mr. Shirley, 'and Mr. Hancock, I know, but where the Devil this Brace of Adams's came from, I cant conceive.'" John Adams Diary 16, January 10, 1771–November 28 [i.e., 27], 1772, p. 69, in Adams Family Papers: An Electronic Archive, Massachusetts Historical Society, accessed July 5, 2018, https://www.masshist.org/digitaladams/archive/doc?id=D16.
3. The important exception is Elbridge Gerry, who attended the Constitutional Convention (but refused to sign the finished product) and later became James Madison's vice president. The contrast with Virginia is striking: George Washington, Thomas

Jefferson, James Madison, James Monroe, George Mason, Richard Henry Lee, Edmund Randolph, George Wythe, and John Marshall all played important parts in national as well as Virginia politics. Among the major leaders of Virginia's revolutionary movement, only Patrick Henry followed the Massachusetts pattern and shunned national politics.

4. David McCullough's biography of Adams, later made into the HBO seven-part television series, devotes only 40 of its 650 pages to the first forty years of Adams's life, before he joined the Continental Congress. David McCullough, *John Adams* (New York: Simon and Schuster, 2002), 29–71. John Ferling's biography of Adams dedicates a larger percentage of his text to these years, but narrates events in Boston's resistance movement as if they were necessary parts of Adams's biography, even when Adams was not involved—another way of suggesting that the essence of Adams's identity was aligned with a teleology of US nationalism. John Ferling, *John Adams: A Life* (Knoxville: University of Tennesse Press, 1992), especially 39–114. For other works in this vein, see Joseph Ellis, *Founding Brothers: The Revolutionary Generation* (New York: Alfred A. Knopf, 2000); Gordon S. Wood, *Friends Divided: John Adams and Thomas Jefferson* (New York: Penguin, 2017).
5. Gordon S. Wood, *The Creation of the American Republic, 1776–1787* (Chapel Hill: University of North Carolina Press, 1969), 567–92.
6. This was the trajectory of his younger brother, Peter. McCullough, *John Adams*, 46, 58, 64; Ferling, *John Adams*, 12.
7. Some of Adams's expenses were deferred by a scholarship. McCullough, *John Adams*, 34.
8. Adams complained that Ned and Samuel Quincy, the sons of Colonel Josiah, called him a "Numbskull and a Blunder Buss." Ferling, *John Adams*, 12.
9. John Adams, "Monday. December 18th. 1758," in *Diary and Autobiography of John Adams, Vol. 1, Diary 1755–1770*, ed. L. H. Butterfield (Cambridge, MA: Harvard University Press, 1961), 63. See also Bernard Bailyn, "Butterfield's Adams: Notes for a Sketch," *William and Mary Quarterly* 19, no. 2 (1962): 238–56.
10. L. H. Butterfield, ed., *Diary and Autobiography of John Adams, Vol. 1, Diary 1755–1770* (Cambridge, MA: Harvard University Press, 1961), 63.
11. By contrast, Wheatley's personal writings reveal little anxiety in her encounters with far-grander people. Perhaps the fact that she was such an anomaly, that there was no place on any social scale for "female slave literary prodigy," made the comparisons of rank and quality that generated so much anxiety for Adams simply unthinkable for Wheatley.
12. Butterfield, *Diary*, 83. On Adams's and Boston's legal community, see William Pencak, "John Adams and the Massachusetts Provincial Elite," in *John Adams and the Founding of the Republic*, ed. Richard Alan Ryerson (Boston: Massachusetts Historical Society, 2001), 43–71. For biographies of other legal figures, see the following sketches in Clifford K. Shipton, *Sibley's Harvard Graduates* (Cambridge, MA: Harvard University Press, 1933): "Timothy Ruggles," 9:199–223; "Benjamin Prat," 10:226–39; "Oxenbridge Thacher," 10:322–28; "Jeremiah Gridley," 8:518–30; "Benjamin Kent," 8:220–30.
13. Peter and Andrew Oliver were nephews of Jonathan Belcher; their mother was Belcher's sister Elizabeth. On the Hutchinson-Oliver clan, see Bernard Bailyn, *The Ordeal of Thomas Hutchinson* (Cambridge, MA: Harvard University Press, 1974), 30–32.
14. "Peter Oliver," in Shipton, *Sibley's Harvard Graduates*, 8:743.
15. John Adams, *Novanglus 2*, January 30, 1775, in *The Papers of John Adams*, ed. Robert J. Taylor et al. (Cambridge, MA: Belknap, 1977–), 2:233–36.

16. On Adams's hatred for Hutchinson and his circle, see Bailyn, *Ordeal of Thomas Hutchinson*, 2–3, 51–53, 66–67, 163, 375–77.
17. Thomas Hutchinson, *The History of the Colony of Massachusetts Bay* (Boston: Thomas and John Fleet, 1764); Thomas Hutchinson, *The History of the Province of Massachusetts Bay, from 1691 to 1750* (Boston: Thomas and John Fleet, 1767); Thomas Hutchinson, *The History of the Province of Massachusetts Bay, from 1749 to 1774* (London: John Murray, 1828).
18. Oliver, *Peter Oliver's Origin and Progress*, 21–22. For Hutchinson, this was exacerbated by his family's personal connection to Anne Hutchinson, the arch enthusiast of the first generation.
19. John Adams, *Thoughts on Government: Applicable to the Present State of the American Colonies* (Philadelphia: John Dunlap, 1776). A decade earlier in his *Dissertation on the Canon and Feudal Law* (Boston, 1765), Adams made a virtually identical statement about the puritan founders. Adams, *Papers*, 1:115. For the connections between New England's political economy tradition and the English commonwealth writers, see David D. Hall, *A Reforming People: Puritanism and the Transformation of Public Life in New England* (New York: Alfred A. Knopf, 2011); Mark Peterson, "Why They Mattered: The Return of Politics to Puritan New England," *Modern Intellectual History* 10, no. 3 (2013): 683–96.
20. For a look at the young Adams's constitutional thinking rooted in the New England tradition, see Timothy H. Breen, "John Adams' Fight against Innovation in the New England Constitution: 1776," *New England Quarterly* 40, no. 4 (December 1967): 501–20. Adams's deepest encounter with the commonwealth writers (such as Marchamont Nedham) took place later, in the 1780s. See ibid., 509–10. See also Richard Alan Ryerson, "'Like a Hare before the Hunters': John Adams and the Idea of Republican Monarchy," *Proceedings of the Massachusetts Historical Society* 107 (1995): 16–29.
21. See R. B. Bernstein, "John Adams's Use of Reading as Political and Constitutional Armory," in *The Libraries, Leadership, and Legacy of John Adams and Thomas Jefferson*, ed. Robert C. Baron and Conrad Edick Wright (Golden, CO: Massachusetts Historical Society, 2010), 81–93.
22. John Adams to Joseph Warren, September 26, 1775, in Adams, *Papers*, 3:95. On Adams's book collecting, see Beth Prindle, "Thought, Care, and Money: John Adams Assembles His Library," in *The Libraries, Leadership, and Legacy of John Adams and Thomas Jefferson*, ed. Robert C. Baron and Conrad Edick Wright (Golden, CO: Massachusetts Historical Society, 2010), 3–19.
23. This timing was coincidental. His diaries show that Adams was drafting these thoughts as early as February 1765. See Charles Francis Adams, ed. *The Works of John Adams: Second President of the United States* (Boston: Little, Brown, 1856), 3:448.
24. Adams, *Dissertation on the Canon and Feudal Law, No. 1*, 1:111–14.
25. Breen concurs: "When Adams spoke about the founding of the New World, he referred only to Massachusetts. The possible significance of St. Augustine or Jamestown did not occur to him." Breen, "John Adams' Fight," 501–2.
26. Adams, *Dissertation on the Canon and Feudal Law, No. 1*, 1:114. Adams was probably thinking of the Mather family library, among the principal artifacts still surviving in Boston from the founders' world of learning.
27. Adams, *Dissertation on the Canon and Feudal Law, No. 2*, 1:117.
28. John Cotton, *Gods Promise to His Plantation* (London, 1630), 12.
29. The loyalist Peter Oliver agreed. He offered a similar narrative of the founding of Massachusetts among the "procatarctick Causes" of the American rebellion, even transcribing in full the 1630 "Humble Request" in which the Philippi analogy was

reiterated. But Oliver saw the puritan religious impulse as so much hypocrisy, a danger to good government, and a source of perpetual rebellion. The rebellion of 1775 simply continued this spirit: "You will see Religion dressed up into a Stalkinghorse, to be skulked behind, that Vice might perpetrate its most atrocious Crimes, whilst it bore so fair a Front to mislead & decieve the World around." Oliver, *Peter Oliver's Origin and Progress*, 10–26.

30. Adams, *Disseration on the Canon and Feudal Law, No. 4*, 1:128.
31. C. F. Adams, *Works of John Adams*, 2:466–67.
32. Ibid., 2:484–85.
33. John Adams Diary 15, January 30, 1768, August 10, 1769–August 22, 1770, p. 1, in Adams Family Papers: An Electronic Archive, Massachusetts Historical Society, accessed May 31, 2018, https://www.masshist.org/digitaladams/archive/popup?id=D15&page=D15_1.
34. "Sui Juris," *Boston Gazette*, May 23, 1768, in John Adams, *Revolutionary Writings*, ed. Gordon S. Wood (New York: Library of America, 2001), 1:174–75.
35. Hiller Zobel, *The Boston Massacre* (New York: W. W. Norton, 1970), 241–94; Eric Hinderaker, *Boston's Massacre* (Cambridge, MA: Harvard University Press, 2017), 187–220.
36. Richard L. Bushman, *King and People in Provincial Massachusetts* (Chapel Hill: University of North Carolina Press, 1985), 201–6.
37. John Adams, "On the Independence of the Judges, No. 1," in *Revolutionary Writings*, 1:223–27; John Adams, "Reply of the Massachusetts House of Representatives to Governor Hutchinson's First Message, January 26, 1773," in *Revolutionary Writings*, 1:234–50.
38. Benjamin Woods Labaree, *The Boston Tea Party* (New York: Oxford University Press, 1964), 142–52; Benjamin L. Carp, *Rebels Rising: Cities and the American Revolution* (New York: Oxford University Press, 2007), 55–58.
39. Adams, *Revolutionary Writings*, 1:286–87.
40. John Adams to Abigail Adams, May 12, 1774, in Frank Shuffelton, ed., *The Letters of John and Abigail Adams* (New York: Penguin, 2004), 3.
41. John Adams to James Burgh, Braintree, December 28, 1774, in *Revolutionary Writings*, 1:350–51. "Alva" refers to the Duke of Alba, famous for his brutal suppression of the Dutch Revolt of the 1560s.
42. John Adams, *Novanglus 4*, February 13, 1775, in *Papers*, 2:256–58.
43. For a comparable reading of Wheatley's "Ode to Dartmouth" in October 1772, see David Waldstreicher, "Phillis Wheatley: The Poet Who Challenged the American Revolutionaries," in *Revolutionary Founders: Rebels, Radicals, and Reformers in the Making of a Nation*, ed. Alfred F. Young, Gary B. Nash, and Ray Raphael (New York: Alfred A. Knopf, 2011), 97–100.
44. John Adams, *Novanglus 7*, March 6, 1775, in *Papers*, 2:314.
45. Ibid.
46. John Adams, "First Reply to Hutchinson," January 26, 1773, in *Revolutionary Writings*, 1:245–47.
47. Adams, *Novanglus 7*, 2:311–12.
48. Ibid., 2:313.
49. John Adams, *Novanglus 6*, February 27, 1775, in *Papers*, 2:299–300.
50. Ibid., 2:300.
51. Ferling, *John Adams*, 133.
52. John Adams to Horatio Gates, March 23, 1776, *Revolutionary Writings*, 2:47.
53. John Adams to Richard Henry Lee, November 15, 1775, in C. F. Adams, *Works of John Adams*, 4:186–87.

54. John Adams, "Diary of John Adams," in *Revolutionary Writings*, 1:163; Butterfield, *Diary*, December 24, 1766, 1:327.
55. Breen, "John Adams' Fight," 512.
56. These included George Wythe of Virginia, William Hooper and John Penn of North Carolina, and Jonathan Sergeant of New Jersey. John Adams to James Warren, April 20, 1776, *Warren-Adams Letters* (Boston: Massachusetts Historical Society, 1917), 230.
57. Adams, *Revolutionary Writings*, 2:69. Adams drafted the resolution, along with the preamble that accompanied its formal issuance, on May 15, 1776.
58. John Adams, *Thoughts on Government*, in *Revolutionary Writings*, 2:50.
59. Ibid., 2:55.
60. Ibid., 2:56.
61. Nathaniel Hawthorne, "The Gray Champion," in *Tales and Sketches: Including Twice-Told Tales, Mosess from an Old Manse, and the Snow-Image* (New York: Library of America, 1982), 236–44.
62. Adams, *Thoughts on Government*, in *Revolutionary Writings*, 2:56.
63. In October 1775, the acting provincial legislature of Massachusetts appointed Adams as chief justice of the commonwealth—a remarkable transformation, given that his predecessors on the bench had been his arch nemeses Hutchinson and Oliver. Adams's congressional duties prevented him from serving, and he resigned the position in February 1777.
64. See Oscar Handlin and Mary Flug Handlin, eds., *The Popular Sources of Political Authority: Documents on the Massachusetts Constitution of 1780* (Cambridge, MA: Harvard University Press, 1966).
65. Ray Raphael, *The First American Revolution: Before Lexington and Concord* (New York: New Press, 2002), 57–168.
66. Cited in Handlin and Handlin, *Popular Sources of Political Authority*, 40.
67. Breen, "John Adams' Fight," 513–18.
68. Cited in John Patrick Diggins, ed., *The Portable John Adams* (New York: Penguin Books, 2004), 219.
69. John Adams to Patrick Henry, June 3, 1776, in *Revolutionary Writings*, 2:78.
70. John Adams to James Sullivan, May 26, 1776, in *Revolutionary Writings*, 2:73. Adams's position is consonant with recent research on social equity in early New England. See Hall, *Reforming People*, especially 127–58.
71. John Adams to Elbridge Gerry, November 4, 1779, in *Revolutionary Writings*, 2:278; Ryerson, "Like a Hare before the Hunters," 16–29.
72. "The Report of a Constitution or Form of Government for the Commonwealth of Massachusetts," in *Revolutionary Writings*, 2:249–77; Ryerson, "Like a Hare before the Hunters," 20–21.
73. Adams, *Novanglus 7*, 2:322–23; Wood, *Creation of the American Republic*, 210–13.
74. Jefferson's draft for the Virginia Constitution in 1776 followed Adams's recommendation that senators be elected by a lower House of Delegates, but gave them nine-year terms of office. Wood, *Creation of the American Republic*, 213–15. The "Essex Result," the most extensive local response to the first Massachusetts Constitution, criticized exactly this problem. See Handlin and Handlin, *Popular Sources of Political Authority*, 324–66. On the defects of a dependent Senate, see ibid., 349–50.
75. John Adams, "The Report of a Constitution," in *Revolutionary Writings*, 2:257.
76. From 1784 to 1786, as an internal crisis over taxation and debt collection in Massachusetts mounted, the former Continental Army general from Massachusetts, Benjamin Lincoln, published articles in the *Boston Magazine* and *Independent*

Chronicle under the pseudonym "The Free Republican," defending the Senate's structure in the Massachusetts Constitution. Lincoln argued that unless the interests of wealth were segregated in a separate house of the legislature, the rich would use "cunning and corruption" to secure "the power they cannot constitutionally obtain." Cited in Wood, *Creation of the American Republic*, 220–21. Wood, however, views Adams's and Lincoln's understanding of the separate interests of people and property, the many and few, as a position that "directly confronted the Revolutionary assumptions of 1776," an "extraordinary change in American thinking," as "eighteenth-century Whiggism had made no rigid distinction between people and property." Ibid., 218–20. Adams's writings in 1776, however, along with his citations of both Harrington and Massachusetts tradition show that this manner of thinking about the relationship between the power of people and property had a long tradition in the city-state of Boston.

77. John Adams to Joseph Ward, October 24, 1809, cited in Pencak, "John Adams," 62.
78. John Adams to James Sullivan, May 26, 1776, in *Revolutionary Writings*, 2:73.
79. John Adams to James Warren, October 19, 1775, in *Revolutionary Writings*, 2:28.
80. John Adams to Mercy Otis Warren, April 16, 1776, in *Revolutionary Writings*, 2:62.
81. On the physiocrats, Jeffersonian political economy, and their connection to Adams, see Drew McCoy, *The Elusive Republic: Political Economy in Jeffersonian America* (Chapel Hill: University of North Carolina Press, 1980), 41–56, 66–69.
82. See *The Acts and Resolves of the Province of Massachusetts Bay*, vol. 18, *Resolves, 1765–1774* (Boston: Wright and Potter, 1912), 225.
83. Adams, "Report of the Committee," 2:258.
84. Bushman, *King and People*, 190–206.
85. For this important insight, see Leonard Richards, *Shays's Rebellion: The American Revolution's Final Battle* (Philadelphia: University of Pennsylvania Press, 2001), 92, 102.
86. Ibid., 63–88.
87. James Madison, "Vices of the Political System of the United States," in *The Writings of James Madison*, ed. Gaillard Hunt (New York: G. P. Putnam's Sons, 1900), 2:361–69.
88. Richards, *Shays's Rebellion*, 118–19.
89. *Journal of the Convention for Framing a Constitution of Government for the State of Massachusetts Bay* (Boston: Dutton and Wentworth, 1832), 43.
90. Adams, *Thoughts on Government*, in *Revolutionary Writings*, 2:56. Adams describes a fair and adequate representation of the *colonies*—not the people—and disputes between *colonies*, not between persons. He was not imagining a national government with sovereign power over individuals.
91. John Adams to Joseph Hawley, November 25, 1775, in *Revolutionary Writings*, 2:36–38.
92. John Adams to Horatio Gates, March 23, 1776, in *Papers*, 4:58–60.
93. [Carter Braxton], *An Address to the Convention of the Colony and Ancient Dominion of Virginia* (Philadelphia: John Dunlop, 1776), 17, 20.
94. John Adams to Patrick Henry, June 3, 1776, in *Revolutionary Writings*.
95. Woody Holton, *Forced Founders: Indians, Debtors, Slaves, and the Making of the American Revolution* (Chapel Hill: University of North Carolina Press, 1999), 35–38.
96. Jefferson employed similar logic in his *Summary View of the Rights of British America* (Williamsburg, VA, 1774), but emphasized the deep history of the Anglo-Saxon tribes and their self-government as a historical source, in contrast to Adams's reliance on New England's history.

97. Adams, *Revolutionary Writings*, 2:48. "Duck" was heavy cotton fabric used in sail making.
98. John Adams to James Warren, April 16, 1776, in *Papers*, 4:122.
99. Adams, *Revolutionary Writings*, 2:113–24; Adams, *Papers*, 4:265–76.
100. Adams, *Papers*, 4:261; Butterfield, *Diary*, 3:337–38.
101. See James H. Hutson, *John Adams and the Diplomacy of the American Revolution* (Lexington: University Press of Kentucky, 1980); John Ferling, "John Adams, Diplomat," *William and Mary Quarterly* 51 (April 1994): 227–52.
102. Adams, February 11, 1779, in Butterfield, *Diary*, 2:351.
103. John Adams to Samuel Perley, June 19, 1809, in C. F. Adams, *Works of John Adams*, 9:623.
104. Richard Price, *Observations on the Importance of the American Revolution, . . . to Which Is Added, a Letter from M. Turgot* (London: T. Cadell, 1785), 113–14. This English translation as well as the original French version of Turgot's letter were printed in the 1785 edition.
105. Ryerson, "Like a Hare before Hunters," 24; Joyce Appleby, "The New Republican Synthesis and the Changing Political Ideas of John Adams," *American Quarterly* 25, no. 5 (December 1973): 583; John Adams to Thomas Jefferson, November 30, 1786, in *The Adams-Jefferson Letters; The Complete Correspondence between Thomas Jefferson and Abigail and John Adams*, ed. Lester J. Cappon (Chapel Hill: University of North Carolina Press, 1959), 1:163; John Adams to James Warren, January 9, 1787, in *Warren-Adams Letters, Being Chiefly a Correspondence among John Adams, Samuel Adams, and James Warren, 1743–1814* (Boston: Massachusetts Historical Society, 1917–25), 2:280.
106. John Adams, *A Defence of the Constitutions of Government of the United States of America, against the Attack of M. Turgot*, in C. F. Adams, *Works of John Adams*, 5:45.
107. Pauline Maier, *Ratification: The People Debate the Constitution, 1787–1788* (New York: Simon and Schuster, 2010), 207–8.
108. Adams, *Thoughts on Government, in Revolutionary Writings*, 2:56.
109. [James Winthrop], "Agrippa, IV," December 3, 1787, *Massachusetts Gazette*, reprinted in Paul Leicester Ford, ed., *Essays on the Constitution of the United States* (Brooklyn, NY: Historical Printing Club, 1892), 67.
110. [James Winthrop], "Agrippa, X," January 1, 1788, *Massachusetts Gazette*, reprinted in Paul Leicester Ford, ed., *Essays on the Constitution of the United States* (Brooklyn, NY: Historical Printing Club, 1892), 87–88.

Chapter 8: The Failure of Federalism

1. Joyce Appleby, *Inheriting the Revolution* (Cambridge, MA: Harvard University Press 2000); Stanley Elkins and Eric McKitrick, *The Age of Federalism* (New York: Oxford University Press, 1993); Gordon S. Wood, *Empire of Liberty: A History of the Early Republic, 1789–1815* (New York: Oxford University Press, 2009).
2. John Locke, *Two Treatises of Government, Second Treatise concerning the Origin, Extent, and End of Civil Government*, 6th ed. (London: A. Millar, 1764), chap. 12, sec. 146.
3. Ibid., chap. 12, sec. 145.
4. Alison LaCroix, *The Ideological Origins of American Federalism* (Cambridge, MA: Harvard University Press, 2010), 11–30. See also Lee Ward, "Early Dutch and German Federal Theory," 91–106, Ann Ward and David S. Fott, "Montesquieu on Federalism and the Problem of Liberty in the International System," 107–20, both in *The Ashgate Research Companion to Federalism*, ed. Ann Ward and Lee Ward (Farnham, UK: Ashgate, 2009).

5. David Hendrickson, *Peace Pact: The Lost World of the American Founding* (Lawrence: University Press of Kansas, 2003), especially 115–60, 211–56.
6. Pauline Maier, *Ratification: The People Debate the Constitution, 1787–1788* (New York: Simon and Schuster, 2010), 92–95.
7. Merrill Jensen advocates this position most fervently among modern historians. Merrill Jensen, *The New Nation: A History of the United States during the Confederation, 1781–89* (New York: Alfred A. Knopf, 1950). See also Hendrickson, *Peace Pact*, 281–98.
8. "It is to be the assent and ratification of the several States, derived from the supreme authority in each State, the authority of the people themselves. The act therefore establishing the Constitution, will not be a *national* but a *federal* act." [James Madison], *The Federalist*, no. 39 (January 16, 1788), ed. Jacob E. Cooke (Middletown, CT: Wesleyan University Press, 1961), 254; Hendrickson, *Peace Pact*, 283.
9. James Madison, "Virginia Resolutions, 21 December 1798," in *Writings of James Madison*, ed. Gaillard Hunt (New York: G. P. Putnam's Sons, 1900), 6:326.
10. Kenneth M. Stampp, "The Concept of a Perpetual Union," *Journal of American History* 65, no. 1 (June, 1978): 5–33.
11. Ames and then Quincy represented Massachusetts' First District, essentially Suffolk County, which included the city of Boston and neighboring towns to the south and west. The proportion of population to representatives in the new Congress was 30,000:1—a ratio so large that only Philadelphia and possibly New York were cities big enough to merit their own representative, an antiurban bias to the national government that rankled Bostonians.
12. John P. Kaminski et al., eds., *The Documentary History of the Ratification of the Constitution* (Madison: State Historical Society of Wisconsin, 1976–), 6:1263; Maier, *Ratification*, 177. Ames made this remark during the Massachusetts convention that ratified the Constitution in defending the "federal" versus "consolidated" nature of the new Constitution.
13. Robert A. McCaughey, *Josiah Quincy, 1772–1864: The Last Federalist* (Cambridge, MA: Harvard University Press, 1974), 76.
14. Elisha P. Douglass, "Fisher Ames, Spokesman for New England Federalism," *American Philosophical Society Proceedings* 103 (October 1959): 713; Richard Buel, *America on the Brink: How the Political Struggle over the War of 1812 Almost Destroyed the Young Republic* (New York: Palgrave Macmillan, 2005), 49–50.
15. See Clifford K. Shipton, "Nathaniel Ames," in *Sibley's Harvard Graduates* (Cambridge, MA: Harvard University Press, 1933), 15:3–15; Clifford K. Shipton, "Fisher Ames," in *Sibley's Harvard Graduates* (Cambridge, MA: Harvard University Press, 1933), 18:367–80.
16. Winfred E. A. Bernhard, *Fisher Ames: Federalist and Statesman, 1758–1808* (Chapel Hill: University of North Carolina Press, 1964), 3–43; J. T. Kirkland, *The Works of Fisher Ames, with a Selection from His Speeches and Corresponence*, ed. Seth Ames (Boston: Little, Brown, 1854), 1:3–8.
17. Fisher Ames to George Richards Minot, September 3, 1789, in Kirkland, *Works of Fisher Ames*, 1:69.
18. Bernhard, *Fisher Ames*, 39.
19. Fisher Ames, "Lucius Junius Brutus" October 12, 1786, *Independent Chronicle*, in Kirkland, *Works of Fisher Ames*, 2:91–97.
20. Bernhard, *Fisher Ames*, 64–75; Kirkland, *Works of Fisher Ames*, 1:8–10; Ames, "Lucius Junius Brutus."
21. Joseph Gales, ed., *The Debates and Proceedings in the Congress of the United States Contains the Records for Sessions of the U.S. Congress Including Summaries of*

Proceedings, Letters, and Speeches for the Senate and House of Representatives (Washington, DC: Gales and Seaton, 1834), 1:100.

22. Fisher Ames to George Richards Minot, April 4, 1789, in Kirkland, *Works of Fisher Ames*, 1:32–33.
23. Quoted in Bernhard, *Fisher Ames*, 90.
24. Fisher Ames to George Richards Minot, May 16, 1789, in Kirkland, *Works of Fisher Ames*, 1:39; Bernhard, *Fisher Ames*, 93.
25. Fisher Ames, "Speech on the Impost of Molasses," in *Speeches of Fisher Ames in Congress, 1789–1796*, ed. Pelham W. Ames (Boston: Little, Brown, 1871), 9–18.
26. Gales, *Debates and Proceedings in the Congress*, 1:311.
27. Ibid., 1:139.
28. Bernhard, *Fisher Ames*, 88.
29. Gales, *Debates and Proceedings in the Congress*, 1:236.
30. Fisher Ames to George Richards Minot, May 14, 1789, in Kirkland, *Works of Fisher Ames*, 1:37.
31. Gales, *Debates and Proceedings in the Congress*, 1:224. Fifty dollars was actually a smaller percentage of the mean value of imported slaves than eight cents was of the price of a gallon of molasses.
32. Ibid., 1:227.
33. Fisher Ames to George Richards Minot, May 3, 1789, in Kirkland, *Works of Fisher Ames*, 1:35.
34. Ibid.
35. See Elkins and McKitrick, *Age of Federalism*, 68–74, 381–88.
36. Fisher Ames to George Richards Minot, September 3, 1789, in Kirkland, *Works of Fisher Ames*, 1:69.
37. Fisher Ames, "Speech on the Assumption of State Debts," in Ames, *Speeches of Fisher Ames*, 33–42.
38. James Ferguson, *Power of the Purse: A History of American Public Finance (1776–1790)* (Chapel Hill: University of North Carolina Press, 1961), 205–6.
39. Thomas McCraw, *Founders and Finance: How Hamilton, Gallatin, and Other Immigrants Forged a New Economy* (Cambridge, MA: Harvard University Press, 2010), 87–109; Ferguson, *Power of the Purse*, 203–20; Elkins and McKitrick, *Age of Federalism*, 133–62.
40. Fisher Ames, "Speech on the Public Credit," in Ames, *Speeches of Fisher Ames*, 19–32; Ames, "Speech on the Assumption of State Debts," 32–56.
41. This dinner has now been immortalized in Lin-Manuel Miranda's popular Broadway musical *Hamilton!* in the song "The Room Where It Happens."
42. Elkins and McKitrick, *Age of Federalism*, 146–61.
43. Fisher Ames to Thomas Dwight, June 27, 1790, in Kirkland, *Works of Fisher Ames*, 1:84.
44. Bernhard, *Fisher Ames*, 154n48.
45. Thomas Jefferson, *Notes on the State of Virginia* (1781), ed. David Waldstreicher (Boston: Bedford Books, 2002), 8.
46. On spatial expansion in Jefferson's political ideology, see Drew R. McCoy, *The Elusive Republic: Political Economy in Jeffersonian America* (Chapel Hill: University of North Carolina Press, 1980). On Jefferson's presidency, see ibid., 185–209.
47. "Mémoire pour servir d'instruction au Citoyen Genet Adjudant-General-Colonel, allant en Amérique en qualité de Ministre Plénipotentiaire de la République Française près le Congrès des Etats Unis," December 2, 1792, in Frederick Jackson Turner, ed., *Correspondence of the French Ministers to the United States, 1791–1797* (Washington, DC: Government Printing Office, 1904), 2:204.

48. Turner, *Correspondence of the French Ministers*, 2:204, translation cited in Elkins and McKitrick, *Age of Federalism*, 333.
49. Ferguson, *Power of the Purse*, 251–89; Elkins and McKittrick, *Age of Federalism*, 375–451.
50. Fisher Ames to Thomas Dwight, August 1793, in Kirkland, *Works of Fisher Ames*, 1:129.
51. Elkins and McKitrick, *Age of Federalism*, 350–54; Turner, *Correspondence of the French Ministers*, 2:221; Frederick Jackson Turner, "The Origins of Genet's Projected Attack on Louisiana and the Floridas," *American Historical Review* 3 (July 1898): 650–71.
52. Fisher Ames, "Speech on the British Treaty," in Ames, *Speeches of Fisher Ames*, 115.
53. Bernhard, *Fisher Ames*, 332–34.
54. Fisher Ames, "Falkland, Nos. 1–4," in Kirkland, *Works of Fisher Ames*, 2:128–44.
55. Fisher Ames, "Phocion, No. 4," in Kirkland, *Works of Fisher Ames*, 2:163. In another of the "Falkland" essays, Ames wrote, "New England now contains a million and a half of inhabitants, . . . In spirit and enterprise no nation exceeds them." Fisher Ames, "Falkland, No. 2," in Kirkland, *Works of Fisher Ames*, 2:134.
56. Fisher Ames, "The New Romans, No. 1," *New England Palladium*, September 1801, in Kirkland, *Works of Fisher Ames*, 2:174–76.
57. Fisher Ames, "Political Review, No. I," *New England Palladium*, October 1802, in Kirkland, *Works of Fisher Ames*, 2:240.
58. Fisher Ames, "The New Romans, No. III," in Kirkland, *Works of Fisher Ames*, 2:181. In a subsequent essay, Ames juxtaposes France as Rome to Britain as Carthage, while allowing modern Britain a number of strengths that ancient Carthage lacked. See Fisher Ames, "Foreign Politics, No. II," in Kirkland, *Works of Fisher Ames*, 2:195–99. On Carthage as metaphor and analytic tool, see Caroline Winterer, "Ancient Carthage and the Science of Politics in Revolutionary America," *William and Mary Quarterly* 67, no. 1 (January 2010): 3–30.
59. For Ames's references to universal monarchy, see Fisher Ames to Timothy Pickering, February 14, 1806, in Kirkland, *Works of Fisher Ames*, 2:363; Fisher Ames, "The Duration of French Despotism (1807)," in Kirkland, *Works of Fisher Ames*, 2:336; Fisher Ames, "The Observer," *New England Palladium*, February 1801, in Kirkland, *Works of Fisher Ames*, 2:146.
60. Ames, "Political Review, No. I," 2:240.
61. Jon Kukla, *A Wilderness So Immense* (New York: Alfred A. Knopf, 2003), 214–15.
62. William Stinchcombe, "Talleyrand and the American Negotiations of 1797–1798," *Journal of American History* 62, no. 3 (December 1975): 577–78.
63. Fisher Ames, "Political Review, No. II," in Kirkland, *Works of Fisher Ames*, 2:242–43.
64. George William Van Cleve, *A Slaveholders' Union: Slavery, Politics, and the Constitution in the Early American Republic* (Chicago: University of Chicago Press, 2010), 220; "Jefferson to DeWitt Clinton," in Paul Leicester Ford, ed., *Writings of Thomas Jefferson* (New York: G. P. Putnam's Sons, 1892–99), 8:283.
65. Fisher Ames, "Dangers of American Liberty," in Kirkland, *Works of Fisher Ames*, 2:352–54.
66. Edmund Quincy, *Life of Josiah Quincy of Massachusetts* (Boston: Ticknor and Fields, 1868), 88.
67. Ibid., 42.
68. Fisher Ames, "The New Romans, No. V," in Kirkland, *Works of Fisher Ames*, 2:191.
69. Bernard Bailyn, *The Ideological Origins of the American Revolution* (Cambridge, MA: Harvard University Press, 1967), 22.

70. Ames and Quincy both lost their fathers in childhood, and were raised primarily by their mothers, who instilled in them a profound sense of New England's republican heritage. See Linda K. Kerber, *Women of the Republic: Intellect and Ideology in Revolutionary America* (Chapel Hill: University of North Carolina Press, 1980).
71. McCaughey, *Josiah Quincy*, 1–18; Quincy, *Life of Josiah Quincy*, 1–33.
72. M. A. De Wolfe Howe, ed., "Journal of Josiah Quincy, Jr., 1773," *Massachusetts Historical Society Proceedings* 49 (1916): 456–57, 455.
73. Ibid., 454; Josiah Quincy III, *Memoir of Josiah Quincy, Jr.* (Boston, 1825), 114–15.
74. McCaughey, *Josiah Quincy*, 19–23; Quincy, *Life of Josiah Quincy*, 58–68.
75. Josiah Quincy to Charles Lowell, March 30, 1857, in Charles Lowell, "Letters of Hon. John Lowell and Others," *Historical Magazine* 1 (1857): 257.
76. Quincy, *Life of Josiah Quincy*, 67–68.
77. Ibid., 66. The Constitution provides that two-thirds of the state legislatures can call for a national convention to consider constitutional amendments. Although the proposal failed to get sufficient support from other state legislatures, Massachusetts senator Timothy Pickering nonetheless introduced it for debate in Congress, but it was immediately tabled and never discussed. Linda K. Kerber, *Federalists in Dissent: Imagery and Ideology in Jeffersonian America* (Ithaca, NY: Cornell University Press, 1970), 36, 64–66.
78. See "A Plain Fact," *New England Palladium*, January 20, 1801. Jefferson's opponents referred to him derisively as "The Negro President" for this reason. See Garry Wills, *"Negro President": Jefferson and the Slave Power* (Boston: Houghton Mifflin, 2003). For Quincy's view, see Quincy, *Life of Josiah Quincy*, 65–66; Kerber, *Federalists in Dissent*, 36–37; James Banner, *To the Hartford Convention: The Federalists and the Origins of Party Politics in Massachusetts, 1789–1815* (New York: Alfred A. Knopf, 1970), 102.
79. Quincy, *Life of Josiah Quincy*, 312–13.
80. For differing interpretations of Pickering's plan, see Gerard H. Clarfield, *Timothy Pickering and the American Republic* (Pittsburgh, PA: University of Pittsburgh Press, 1980), 219–28; Wills, *"Negro President,"* 106–46.
81. Kevin M. Gannon, "Escaping 'Mr. Jefferson's Plan of Destruction': New England Federalists and the Idea of a Northern Confederacy, 1803–1804," *Journal of the Early Republic* 21, no. 3 (Autumn 2001): 413–43; Wills, *"Negro President,"* 114–39.
82. Quincy, *Life of Josiah Quincy*, 96. The act specifically prohibited the import of all leather, silk, hemp, flax, tin or brass goods, most woolen cloths, window glass and all other types of glass, silver, paper, nails, spikes, hats, ready-made clothing, millinery, playing cards, beer, ale, porter, and pictures and prints. Ninth Congress, 1st Sess., chap. 29, April 18, 1806, in Richard Peters, ed., *The Public Statutes at Large of the United States of America* (Boston: Little, Brown, 1845), 2:379–81.
83. Josiah Quincy Jr., *Observations on the Act of Parliament Commonly Called the Boston Port-Bill; with Thoughts on Civil Society and Standing Armies* (Boston: Edes and Gill, 1774), reprinted in Quincy, *Memoir of Josiah Quincy, Jr.*, 468.
84. Quincy, *Life of Josiah Quincy*, 97.
85. In this era, the "eastern states" meant New England and sometimes New York.
86. Quincy, *Life of Josiah Quincy*, 100–101.
87. Ibid., 101.
88. Carl Seaburg and Stanley Patterson, *Merchant Prince of Boston: Colonel T. H. Perkins, 1764–1854* (Cambridge, MA: Harvard University Press), 188–90.
89. McCraw, *Founders and Finance*, 276; Bradford Perkins, *Prologue to War: England and the United States, 1805–1812* (Berkeley: University of California Press, 1970), 162–68.

90. Quincy, *Life of Josiah Quincy*, 152.
91. Ibid., 147.
92. Traditionally, governments had used embargoes as temporary measures in preparation for war, not prohibitions on all commerce intended to last months or years. McCraw, *Founders and Finance*, 275–77.
93. Quincy, *Life of Josiah Quincy*, 147.
94. Ibid., 151–52.
95. Ibid., 154 (emphasis in original).
96. Ibid. (emphasis in original).
97. By the 1850s, Troup would be known as the "Hercules of States' Rights," but not in 1808, when Massachusetts was the state whose rights were in question. See K. R. Constantine Guzman, "Troup, George Michael," in *American National Biography*, accessed May 20, 2018, http://www.anb.org/articles/03/03-00501.html?a=1&n=george%20troup&d=10&ss=0&q=1.
98. Quincy, *Life of Josiah Quincy*, 158.
99. Robin L. Einhorn, *American Taxation, American Slavery* (Chicago: University of Chicago Press, 2006), 157–200, 220–30.
100. Quincy, *Life of Josiah Quincy*, 275–76.
101. Ibid., 155 (emphasis added). George Campbell had already wounded one fellow congressman in a duel that year. The following year, John G. Jackson would be severely wounded in a duel with another congressman. See Joanne Freeman, *Affairs of Honor: National Politics in the New Republic* (New Haven, CT: Yale University Press, 2001); Kenneth Greenberg, *Honor and Slavery* (Princeton, NJ: Princeton University Press, 1996).
102. Harrison Gray Otis to Josiah Quincy, December 15, 1808, in Quincy, *Life of Josiah Quincy*, 164–65.
103. Quincy, *Life of Josiah Quincy*, 165.
104. Seaburg and Patterson, *Merchant Prince of Boston*, 196.
105. Quincy, *Life of Josiah Quincy*, 89.
106. Article 4, Section 3, provides that "New States may be admitted by the Congress into this Union" from territory not "within the jurisdiction" of any current state, and grants Congress the "Power to dispose of and make all needful Rules and Regulations respecting the Territory or other Property *belonging* to the United States" (emphasis added). It says nothing about how Congress (or the president) can acquire new territories, or make new states out of acquired territories.
107. Wills, *"Negro President,"* 115; Josiah Quincy, *Political Sermon Addressed to the Electors of Middlesex* (Boston, 1803).
108. Quoted in Wills, *"Negro President,"* 119–20.
109. Quincy, *Life of Josiah Quincy*, 91; Wills, *"Negro President,"* 124. Critics of Quincy and other Federalist opponents of the Louisiana Purchase have emphasized the racism and xenophobia of their opposition to the incorporation of Louisiana, and there is certainly truth in these charges. On another occasion, Quincy referred to the "race of Anglo-Hispano-Gallo-Americans who bask on the sands in the mouth of the Mississippi." Quincy, *Life of Josiah Quincy*, 209. But Quincy's Democratic-Republican opponents, from Eustis to Jefferson, shared these sentiments. More significant is the similarity of Quincy's objections to the ethnic hostility and xenophobia that Bostonians expressed in opposing the Quebec Act of 1774. The authoritarian provincial governments erected by Parliament for Quebec was, in the eyes of Bostonians like Quincy, similar to that which Jefferson and Congress proposed for Louisiana.
110. The original US territory still not admitted to statehood in 1811 when Louisiana joined the union included the present states of Indiana, Illinois, Michigan, Wisconsin,

Alabama, and Mississippi. Their collective land area of 357,400 square miles was 40 percent of the original land area of the United States under the Treaty of Paris.

111. Quincy expressed what historian Wills has called the "Ideology of 'the Thirteen,'" a variation on what I describe as Boston's approach to its federative powers under the US Constitution. Wills, *"Negro President,"* 122–26.
112. "Municipal" in this sentence has an archaic meaning closely aligned with Quincy's usage: "Pertaining to the internal affairs of a state or nation, rather than to international affairs." Quincy's critique aimed at the notion that adding a new state from originally alien territory is "merely municipal," within the ordinary powers of confederation government, rather than impinging on the nature of the federal compact itself.
113. Quincy, *Life of Josiah Quincy*, 206 (emphasis in original).
114. Ibid., 207.
115. Ibid., 208.
116. Ibid., 209.
117. Wills, *"Negro President,"* 122–26.
118. Quincy, *Life of Josiah Quincy*, 209.
119. Ibid., Quincy, 210.
120. Ibid., 212.
121. Ibid.
122. Ibid., 260–61.
123. See Alan Taylor, *The Civil War of 1812: American Citizens, British Subjects, Irish Rebels, and Indian Allies* (New York: Alfred A. Knopf, 2010); Donald Hickey, *The War of 1812: A Forgotten Conflict* (Urbana: University of Illinois Press, 2012); Jon Latimer, *1812: War with America* (Cambridge, MA: Belknap, 2007); George C. Daughan, *1812: The Navy's War* (New York: Basic Books, 2011); Donald Hickey, ed., *The War of 1812: Writings from America's Second War of Independence* (New York: Library of America, 2013).
124. Quincy, *Life of Josiah Quincy*, 274, 287.
125. "Memoir of Eliza Quincy," in Quincy, *Life of Josiah Quincy*, 262.
126. Banner, *To the Hartford Convention*, 306–8.
127. Quincy, *Life of Josiah Quincy*, 314–15, 315–16. Quincy is paraphrasing Jude 1:3, "Beloved, when I gave all diligence to write unto you of the common salvation, it was needful for me to write unto you, and exhort you that ye should *earnestly contend for the faith which was once delivered unto the Saints.*"
128. Quincy, *Life of Josiah Quincy*, 292–94.
129. [John Lowell Jr.], *Mr. Madison's War: A Dispassionate Inquiry into the Reasons Alleged by Mr. Madison for Declaring an Offensive and Ruinous War against Great Britain* (Boston: Russell and Cutler, 1812).
130. Quincy, *Life of Josiah Quincy*, 323.
131. Hickey, *War of 1812*, 265.
132. Banner, *To the Hartford Convention*, 313–14. Forty Massachusetts towns submitted petitions to the General Court, describing their grievances and calling for some means to address them. See Samuel Eliot Morison, *Harrison Gray Otis: The Urbane Federalist* (Boston: Houghton Mifflin, 1969), 2:85–86.
133. Hickey, *War of 1812*, 269. Similar forms of resistance occurred in Portland, Maine, which had been burned by British forces in 1775. In New Hampshire, state officials refused to allow militia to aid federal troops defending the navy yard at Portsmouth. In Vermont, the state governor recalled state militia troops that had been taken to New York under federal command. Buel, *America on the Brink*, 213; Hickey, *War of 1812*, 269–73.

134. Hickey, *War of 1812*; Banner, *To the Hartford Convention*, 317–18, 321–22.
135. Compare Ray Raphael, *The First American Revolution: Before Lexington and Concord* (New York: New Press, 2002), especially 57–168; T. H. Breen, *American Insurgents, American Patriots: The Revolution of the People* (New York: Hill and Wang, 2010), especially 99–159; Seaburg and Patterson, *Merchant Prince of Boston*, 251–55.
136. The career of John Quincy Adams reflects this trend. Like his father, the younger Adams developed far stronger interests in national politics than he ever did in Boston's political world (he served a sum total of six months in the Massachusetts General Court). While serving as senator from Massachusetts in 1808, at the height of the embargo crisis, Adams supported Jefferson's embargo, left the Federalist Party, and joined the Democratic-Republicans, where he served as a diplomat under Madison and as Monroe's secretary of state—a position that vaulted him to the White House. See Paul C. Nagel, *John Quincy Adams: A Public Life, A Private Life* (New York: Alfred A. Knopf, 1997).
137. Suffolk County was unanimous in its support. See Morison, *Harrison Gray Otis*, 2:104. The "Otis Report" was printed in Boston's *Columbian Centinel* on October 12, 1814, adjacent to the announcement that the Congress of Vienna had been called "to decide the territorial destinies of so many powers of Europe."
138. On Bigelow, see Raphael, *First American Revolution*, 38–45.
139. Similarly, Massachusetts delegate Nathan Dane, founder of what would become Harvard Law School, wrote while on the way to Hartford that "somebody must go to prevent mischief." Banner, *To the Hartford Convention*, 332.
140. Theodore Dwight, *History of the Hartford Convention, with a Review of the Policy of the United States Government That Led to the War of 1812* (Boston: Russell, Odiorne, and Co., 1833), 352–79. Dwight served as the secretary of the convention.
141. Banner, *To the Hartford Convention*, 335–37.
142. Quincy, *Life of Josiah Quincy*, 358.
143. Morison, *Harrison Gray Otis*, 2:156.
144. Lowell signed a series of articles that he wrote during the Hartford Convention under the pen name "Refederator." Ibid., 2:122.
145. Dwight, *History of the Hartford Convention*, 352–53.
146. Ibid., 354–55.
147. Ibid., 356, 360.
148. Ibid., 365, 369–70.
149. Ibid., 377–78.
150. Ibid., 374.
151. Morison, *Harrison Gray Otis*, 2:161.
152. This earlier news had farther to travel and thus reached the Atlantic coast later.
153. Morison, *Harrison Gray Otis*, 2:164–65, 168; Seaburg and Patterson, *Merchant Prince of Boston*, 259–60.
154. John Quincy Adams, "Reply to the Appeal of the Massachusetts Federalists," in *Documents Relating to New England Federalism, 1800–1815*, ed. Henry Adams (Boston: Little, Brown, 1877), 107–329.

Chapter 9: From Merchant Princes to Lords of the Loom

1. Richard Frothingham, *History of the Siege of Boston* (Boston, 1849); William Tudor, ed., *Deacon [John] Tudor's Diary* (Boston, 1896); Anne Rowe Cunningham, ed., *Letters and Diary of John Rowe, Boston Merchant* (Boston, 1903); Winthrop Sargent,

ed., *Letters of John Andrews . . . of Boston* (Cambridge, MA, 1866); Elizabeth Ellery Dana, ed., *The British in Boston, Being the Diary of Lt. John Barker* (Cambridge, MA, 1924); Allen French, ed., *A British Fusilier in Revolutionary Boston, Being the Diary of Lt. Frederick Mackenzie* (Cambridge, MA, 1926); Jacqueline Barbara Carr, *After the Siege: A Social History of Boston, 1775–1800* (Boston: Northeastern University Press, 2005).

2. T. W. Higginson, "French and Indian Wars," 2:93–130, and E. L. Bynner, "Topography and Landmarks of the Provincial Period," 2:491–532, both in *The Memorial History of Boston, 1630–1880*, ed. Justin Winsor (Boston: James R. Osgood, 1882–86); Walter Muir Whitehill and Lawrence W. Kennedy, *Boston: A Topographical History*, 3rd ed. (Cambridge, MA: Harvard University Press, 2000).
3. Mark A. Peterson, "Stone Witnesses, Dumb Pictures, and Voices from the Grave: Monuments and Memory in Revolutionary Boston," in *Commemoration in America: Essays on Monuments, Memorialization, and Memory*, ed. David Gobel and Daves Rossell (Charlottesville: University of Virginia Press, 2013), 60–86.
4. Fred Anderson, *A People's Army: Massachusetts Soldiers and Society in the Seven Years' War* (Chapel Hill: University of North Carolina Press, 1984), 3–25.
5. See Peter Benes, "Night Processions: Celebrating the Gunpowder Plot in England and New England," in *New England Celebrates: Spectacle, Commemoration, and Festivity* (Boston: Boston University Press, 2002), 9–28; Samuel Eliot Morison, *Harrison Gray Otis: The Urbane Federalist* (Boston: Houghton Mifflin, 1969), 7–8; Alfred F. Young, *Liberty Tree: Ordinary People and the American Revolution* (New York: NYU Press, 2006), 111.
6. Bernard Bailyn, *The Ideological Origins of the American Revolution* (Cambridge, MA: Harvard University Press, 1967), 63–66, 98, 144–58.
7. Samuel Breck Jr., *The Recollections of Samuel Breck*, ed. Horace Scudder (Philadelphia, 1877), 24–27. The house that Tracy purchased, on Brattle Street in Cambridge, had been abandoned by the loyalist John Vassall. Washington used the house as headquarters during the siege of Boston. It later descended to the poet Henry Wadsworth Longfellow.
8. Charles C. Smith, "The French Protestants in Boston," in Winsor, *Memorial History of Boston*, 2:249–68.
9. Breck, *Recollections of Samuel Breck*, 43; Robert A. East, *Business Enterprise in the American Revolutionary Era* (New York: Columbia University Press, 1938), 57–58.
10. William T. Baxter, *The House of Hancock: Business in Boston, 1724–1775* (Cambridge, MA: Harvard University Press, 1945).
11. Mark A. Peterson, "*Theopolis Americana*: The City-State of Boston, the Republic of Letters, and the Protestant International, 1689–1739," in *Soundings in Atlantic History: Latent Structures and Intellectual Currents, 1500–1825*, ed. Bernard Bailyn (Cambridge, MA: Harvard University Press, 2009), 329–71.
12. The French military officers recognized Boston's city-state relationship to its New England hinterland, as evidenced in the records of their assistance in planning the invasion of Penobscot in Maine in 1782, which refer to *l'Etat de Boston*. See Amblard-Marie-Raymond-Amédée, Vicomte Noailles, *Marins et Soldats Français en Amérique pendant la Guerre de l'Independence des États-Unis (1778–1783)* (Paris: Perrin et Cie, 1903), 317.
13. Breck, *Recollections of Samuel Breck*, 38.
14. Ibid., 46–48.
15. George Washington to Louis Philippe de Rigaud, Marquis de Vaudreuil, *George Washington Papers at the Library of Congress, 1741–1799*, series 3rd, Varick

Transcripts, subseries D, Foreign Officers and Subjects of Foreign Nations, Letterbook 2, https://www.loc.gov/resource/mgw3d.002/?sp=53&st=text, accessed July 5, 2018.

16. In book I, chapter 18 of Leo Tolstoy's *War and Peace*, Count Rostov frequently plays Boston.
17. Breck, *Recollections of Samuel Breck*, 53–58.
18. Peterson, "*Theopolis Americana*," 339, 578n35.
19. Breck, *Recollections of Samuel Breck*, 77–78.
20. Ibid.
21. Ibid., 83. For a similar Catholic conversion experience by another Bostonian, John Thayer, see Mark Peterson, "Boston à l'heure française: religion, culture et commerce à l'époque des révolutions atlantiques," *Annales historiques de la Révolution française* 363 (January–March 2011): 7–31.
22. John J. McCusker, *Rum and the American Revolution: The Rum Trade and the Balance of Payments of the Thirteen Continental Colonies* (New York: Garland Publishing Inc., 1989); John W. Tyler, *Smugglers and Patriots: Boston Merchants and the Advent of the American Revolution* (Boston: Northeastern University Press, 1986); Thomas Truxes, *Defying Empire: Trading with the Enemy in Colonial New York* (New Haven, CT: Yale University Press, 2010).
23. "Memoir of James Perkins," *Massachusetts Historical Society Proceedings* 1 (1795–1835): 353–68. See also Thomas G. Cary, *Memoir of Thomas Handasyd Perkins, Containing Extracts from His Diaries and Letters* (Boston, 1856); Carl Seaburg and Stanley Paterson, *Merchant Prince of Boston: Colonel T. H. Perkins, 1764–1854* (Cambridge, MA: Harvard University Press), 3–36.
24. Seaburg and Paterson, *Merchant Prince of Boston*, 33–43; "Memoir of James Perkins," 353–57.
25. C. L. R. James, *The Black Jacobins: Toussaint L'Ouverture and the San Domingo Revolution* (New York: Random House, 1963), 6–84; Laurent DuBois, *Avengers of the New World: The Story of the Haitian Revolution* (Cambridge, MA: Harvard University Press, 2004), 20–35; David Geggus, "Saint-Domingue on the Eve of the Haitian Revolution," in *The World of the Haitian Revolution*, ed. David Geggus and Norman Fiering (Bloomington: Indiana University Press, 2009), 3–20.
26. Seaburg and Paterson, *Merchant Prince of Boston*, 144–45.
27. Tyler, *Smugglers and Patriots*; Arthur M. Schlesinger, *The Colonial Merchants and the American Revolution, 1763–1776* (New York: Columbia University, 1918); Charles McLean Andrews, "The Boston Merchants and the Non-Importation Movement," *Colonial Society of Massachusetts Transactions* 19 (1916–17): 159–259.
28. Truxes, *Defying Empire*, 43–48.
29. Seaburg and Paterson, *Merchant Prince of Boston*, 41.
30. Breck, *Recollections of Samuel Breck*, 93.
31. Kalevi Ahonen, *From Sugar Triangle to Cotton Triangle: Trade and Shipping between America and Baltic Russia, 1783–1860* (Jyväskylä, Finland: University of Jyväskylä, 2005), 362–76.
32. Cary, *Memoir of Thomas Handasyd Perkins*, 42–44; Seaburg and Paterson, *Merchant Prince of Boston*, 43–60.
33. "Memoir of James Perkins," 53–68.
34. Seaburg and Paterson, *Merchant Prince of Boston*, 72–88; Samuel Perkins, "Sketches of St. Domingo from January, 1785 to December, 1794," in *Proceedings of the Massachusetts Historical Society* (Boston, 1885–86), 2:307–90.
35. *Columbian Centinal* 18, no. 38 (January 19, 1793): 3; Chandler Robbins, *An Address, Delivered at Plymouth, on the 24th Day of January, 1793, . . . to Celebrate the Victories of the French Republic* (Boston, 1793); cf. Simon Newman, "La Révolution

française vue de loin: la célébration de Valmy à Boston, en janvier 1793," *Revue d'Histoire Moderne et Contemporaine* 58, no. 1 (2011): 80–99.

36. Thomas W. Jodziewicz, "American Catholic Apologetical Dissonance in the Early Republic: Father John Thayer and Bishop John Carroll," *Catholic Historical Review* 84, no. 3 (1998): 458–59.
37. Stanley Elkins and Eric McKitrick, *The Age of Federalism* (New York: Oxford University Press, 1993), 310; Simon P. Newman, *Parades and the Politics of the Street: Festive Culture in the Early American Republic* (Philadelphia: University of Pennsylvania Press, 1997), 1–3, 122–30.
38. Seaburg and Paterson, *Merchant Prince of Boston*, 106–8.
39. Cary, *Memoir of Thomas Handasyd Perkins*, 54, 55.
40. Ibid., 112–13.
41. Ibid., 113–14. See also Rachel Hope Cleves, *The Reign of Terror in America: Visions of Violence from Anti-Jacobinism to Antislavery* (New York: Cambridge University Press, 2009).
42. Seaburg and Paterson, *Merchant Prince of Boston*, 110–11; Cary, *Memoirs of Thomas Handasyd Perkins*, 57–59.
43. Cary, *Memoir of Thomas Handasyd Perkins*, 77, 87.
44. Ibid., 64, 69, 93.
45. Ibid., 79–80, 179–80.
46. Ibid., 96, 186.
47. Robert Martello, *Midnight Ride, Industrial Dawn: Paul Revere and the Growth of American Enterprise* (Baltimore: Johns Hopkins University Press, 2010), 290.
48. Walter W. Woodward, *Prospero's America: John Winthrop, Jr., Alchemy, and the Creation of New England Culture, 1606–1676* (Chapel Hill: University of North Carolina Press, 2010), 81–83.
49. Vincent Denis, "The Invention of Mobility and the History of State," trans. Chad Denton and Carla Hesse, *French Historical Studies* 29, no. 3 (Summer 2006): 359–77.
50. Martello, *Midnight Ride, Industrial Dawn*, 290–307. On the steamboat industry, see Robert Gudmestad, *Steamboats and the Rise of the Cotton Kingdom* (Baton Rouge: Louisiana State University Press, 2011); Walter Johnson, *River of Dark Dreams: Slavery and Empire in the Cotton Kingdom* (Cambridge, MA: Harvard University Press, 2013), 73–96.
51. Robert F. Dalzell Jr., *Enterprising Elite: The Boston Associates and the World They Made*, (Cambridge, MA: Harvard University Press, 1987), 5–25; Ferris Greenslet, *The Lowells and Their Seven Worlds* (Boston: Houghton Mifflin, 1946), 127–30; Chaim Rosenberg, *The Life and Times of Francis Cabot Lowell, 1775–1817* (Blue Ridge Summit, PA: Lexington Books, 2011), 167–257; Robert Sobel, "Francis Cabot Lowell: The Patrician as Factory Master," in *The Entrepreneurs: Explorations within the American Business Tradition* (New York: Weybright and Talley, 1974), 1–40.
52. Rosenberg, *Life and Times of Francis Cabot Lowell*, 71.
53. Ibid., 141–56.
54. Nathan Appleton, *Introduction of the Power Loom, and Origin of Lowell* (Lowell, MA, 1858), 7; Dalzell, *Enterprising Elite*, 5; Rosenberg, *Life and Times of Francis Cabot Lowell*, 178–79.
55. Sobel, "Francis Cabot Lowell," 14–15.
56. Caroline F. Ware, *The Early New England Cotton Manufacture: A Study in Industrial Beginnings* (Boston: Houghton Mifflin, 1931), 39–59.
57. See John Frederick Martin, *Profits in the Wilderness: Entrepreneurship and the Founding of New England Towns in the Seventeenth Century* (Chapel Hill: University of North Carolina Press, 1991); Edward M. Cook, *The Fathers of the Towns:*

Leadership and Community Structure in Eighteenth-Century New England (Baltimore: Johns Hopkins University Press, 1978).

58. Dalzell emphasizes this aspect of the Boston Associates' motives for the shift to manufacturing. See Dalzell, *Enterprising Elite*, especially 5–74.
59. Appleton, *Introduction of the Power Loom*, 14; Sobel, "Francis Cabot Lowell," 31; Dalzell, *Enterprising Elite*, 38.
60. Ware lists seventy-three such mills founded in New England alone between 1812 and 1815. See Ware, *Early New England Cotton Manufacture*, 37.
61. Henry Brougham, Scottish member of Parliament, founder of the *Edinburgh Review*, and future lord chancellor, in a speech before Parliament, 1815, cited in Rosenberg, *Life and Times of Francis Cabot Lowell*, 260.
62. Appleton, *Introduction of the Power Loom*, 13–14; Dalzell, *Enterprising Elite*, 26; Sobel, "Francis Cabot Lowell," 23–25, 33.
63. Alison Gilbert Olson, *Making the Empire Work: London and American Interest Groups, 1690–1790* (Cambridge, MA: Harvard University Press, 1992), 59, 158.
64. Edward Everett, *Journal of a Visit to Washington*, 1815, in Everett Papers, Massachusetts Historical Society, typescript, 1.
65. Norris W. Preyer, "Southern Support for the Tariff of 1816—a Reappraisal," *Journal of Southern History* 25, no. 3 (August 1959): 313, citing Calhoun's speech in Congress, *Annals of Congress*, 14th Cong., 1st Sess., 1329–32.
66. Douglas A. Irwin and Peter Temin, "The Antebellum Tariff on Cotton Textiles Revisited," *Journal of Economic History* 61, no. 3 (September 2001): 778–79; Edward Everett, *A Memoir of John Lowell, Junior* (Boston: Little, Brown, 1840), 23–35; Rosenberg, *Life and Times of Francis Cabot Lowell*, 259–71; Greenslet, *Lowells and Their Seven Worlds*, 158–59.
67. Dalzell, *Enterprising Elite*, 45–67.
68. M. Halsey Thomas, ed., *The Diary of Samuel Sewall, 1674–1729* (New York: Farrar, Straus and Giroux, 1973), 2:637–38; Mark A. Peterson, *Price of Redemption: The Spiritual Economy of Puritan New England* (Stanford, CA: Stanford University Press, 1997), 87; Daniel Vickers, *Farmers and Fishermen: Two Centuries of Work in Essex County, Massachusetts, 1630–1850* (Chapel Hill: University of North Carolina Press, 1994), 24–28, 47–48, 103–4.
69. Thomas Jefferson, Query 19, "Manufactures," in *Notes on the State of Virginia* (1781), ed. David Waldstreicher (Boston: Bedford Books, 2002), 196–97.
70. See Dalzell, *Enterprising Elite*, 15–25.
71. Appleton, *Introduction of the Power Loom*, 14–16; Barry Levy, *Town Born: The Political Economy of New England from Its Founding to the Revolution* (Philadelphia: University of Pennsylvania Press, 2010), especially 42–50.
72. Thomas Dublin, *Women at Work: The Transformation of Work and Community at Lowell, Massachusetts, 1826–1860* (New York: Columbia University Press, 1979).
73. Dalzell, *Enterprising Elite*, 47.
74. John P. Bigelow, *Statistical Table Exhibiting the Condition and Products of Certain Branches of Industry in Massachusetts, for the Year Ending April 1, 1837* (Boston: Dutton and Wentworth, 1838), 31.
75. Dalzell, *Enterprising Elite*, 51.
76. Charles Francis Adams, "The Canal and Railroad Enterprise of Boston," in Winsor, *Memorial History of Boston*, 4:136; Dalzell, *Enterprising Elite*, 82–92.
77. Figures compiled from Bigelow, *Statistical Table*, 1–4.
78. Dalzell, *Enterprising Elite*, 79–112; Henry F. Kidder and Francis H. Peabody, "Finance in Boston," 4:151–78, and Osborne Howes Jr., "The Rise and Progress of Insurance in Boston," 4:179–94, both in Winsor, *Memorial History of Boston*.

79. Samuel Eliot Morison, *The Maritime History of Massachusetts, 1783–1860* (Boston: Houghton Mifflin, 1941), 225–30.
80. See Gavin Wright, *The Political Economy of the Cotton South: Households, Markets, and Wealth in the Nineteenth Century* (New York: W. W. Norton, 1978); Adam Rothman, *Slave Country: American Expansion and the Origins of the Deep South* (Cambridge, MA: Harvard University Press, 2005); Johnson, *River of Dark Dreams*; David J. Libby, *Slavery and Frontier Mississippi, 1720–1835* (Oxford: University Press of Mississippi, 2004); Daniel S. Dupre, *Transforming the Cotton Frontier: Madison County, Alabama, 1800–1840* (Baton Rouge: Louisiana State University Press, 1997).
81. Stuart Bruchey, *Cotton and the Growth of the American Economy, 1790–1860* (New York: Harcourt, Brace, and World, 1967), 111–15. For the American South as a whole, cotton production rose from 178,000 bales in 1810 to 732,000 bales in 1830. See Robert Fogel and Stanley Engerman, *Time on the Cross: The Economics of American Negro Slavery* (Boston: Little, Brown, 1974), 44.
82. Morison, *Maritime History of Massachusetts*, 297–98.
83. Ibid., 298.
84. For a southern perspective, see Brian Schoen, *The Fragile Fabric of Union: Cotton, Federal Politics, and the Global Origins of the Civil War* (Baltimore: Johns Hopkins University Press, 2009).
85. I have relied here on the most definitive recent biography. Robert Remini, *Daniel Webster: The Man and His Time* (New York: W. W. Norton, 1997). See also Irving H. Bartlett, *Daniel Webster* (New York: W. W. Norton, 1978).
86. Daniel Webster, *Considerations on the Embargo Laws* (Boston, 1808), 13.
87. Daniel Webster, *An Address Delivered Before the Washington Benevolent Society at Portsmouth, July 4, 1812* (Portsmouth, NH: Oracle Press, 1812); Remini, *Daniel Webster*, 97–99.
88. Remini, *Daniel Webster*, 100.
89. "Daniel Webster to Samuel Ayer Bradley, 28 May 1813," cited in Remini, *Daniel Webster*, 104.
90. Remini, *Daniel Webster*, 144–45; Bartlett, *Daniel Webster*, 70–75.
91. Remini, *Daniel Webster*, 137–40.
92. On the social circumstances of the "New England clerisy," see James Turner, *The Liberal Education of Charles Eliot Norton* (Baltimore: Johns Hopkins University Press, 1999), 1–20.
93. Carl E. Prince and Seth Taylor, "Daniel Webster, the Boston Associates, and the U. S. Government's Role in the Industrializing Process, 1815–1830," *Journal of the Early Republic* 2 (Fall 1982): 283–99; Dalzell, *Enterprising Elite*, 191–95.
94. Daniel Webster, "Memorial to Congress on Restraining the Increase of Slavery, 15 December 1819," cited in Remini, *Daniel Webster*, 169.
95. Remini, *Daniel Webster*, 175.
96. Daniel Webster, *A Discourse Delivered at Plymouth, December 22, 1820, in Commemoration of the First Settlement of New-England*, 4th ed. (Boston: Wells and Lilly, 1826), 19, 17, 10–12, 41, 52–53.
97. "Daniel Webster, 19 January 1824 Address to Congress," cited in Bartlett, *Daniel Webster*, 102.
98. Remini, *Daniel Webster*, 129; Bartlett, *Daniel Webster*, 62–64.
99. See John W. Whitman, *Report of a Trial in the Supreme Judicial Court, . . . of Theodore Lyman, Jr., for an Alleged Libel on Daniel Webster . . .* (Boston: Putnam and Hunt, 1828); Josiah H. Benton Jr., *A Notable Libel Case: The Criminal Prosecution of Theodore Lyman Jr. by Daniel Webster . . .* (Boston: Charles E. Goodspeed, 1904).

100. Remini, *Daniel Webster*, 325–28; Bartlett, *Daniel Webster*, 114–20. For the full text, see Daniel Webster, "Speech of January 26–27, 1830," in *The Writings and Speeches of Daniel Webster* (Boston, 1903), 6:3–75.
101. Bartlett, *Daniel Webster*, 118; Richard N. Current, *Daniel Webster and the Rise of National Conservatism* (Boston: Little, Brown, 1955), 62; Remini, *Daniel Webster*, 330.

Chapter 10: On the German Road to Athens

1. George E. Ellis, *Memoir of Sir Benjamin Thompson, Count Rumford* (Boston: American Academy of Arts and Sciences, 1871); Yair Mintzker, *The Defortification of the German City, 1689-1866* (Cambridge: Cambridge University Press, 2012), 85–184.
2. John Quincy Adams, *Letters on Silesia: Written during a Tour through That Country in the Years 1800, 1801* (London, 1804).
3. Buckminster published an English translation of Johann Jakob Griesbach's critical edition of the Greek Testament. See Eliza Buckminster Lee, *Memoirs of Reverend Joseph Buckminster, D. D., and of His Son, Reverend Joseph Stevens Buckminster* (Boston: Crosby and Nichols, 1849), 318–19. On the acquisition of books for the Athenaeum, see ibid., 393–411. On his appointment at Harvard, see ibid., 440–42.
4. Edward Everett Hale, "Memoir of Edward Everett," in *A Memorial of Edward Everett, from the City of Boston* (Boston, 1865), 9–12.
5. Paul G. Buchloh and Walter T. Rix, eds., *American Colony of Göttingen: Historical and Other Data Collected between the Years 1855 and 1888* (Göttingen: Vandenhoeck and Ruprecht, 1976), 11–14.
6. Carl Diehl, *Americans and German Scholarship, 1770-1870* (New Haven, CT: Yale University Press, 1978), 7–48; Suzanne Marchand, *Down from Olympus: Archaeology and Philhellinism in Germany, 1750-1970* (Princeton, NJ: Princeton University Press, 2003), especially 3–36. Among the works that Ticknor and Everett read were Charles de Villers, *Coup d'œil sur les universités et le mode d'instruction publique de l'Allemagne protestante* (1808), and Madame de Staël, *De l'Allemagne* (1810). Ticknor borrowed a copy of Johann Wolfgang von Goethe's *Werther* and translated it into English to practice his German. David B. Tyack, *George Ticknor and the Boston Brahmins* (Cambridge, MA: Harvard University Press, 1967), 36; Orie William Long, *Literary Pioneers: Early American Explorers of European Culture* (New York: Russell and Russell, 1963), 5.
7. Josiah Quincy, *The History of Harvard University* (Cambridge, MA: John Owen, 1840), 2:555.
8. Tyack, *George Ticknor*, 53; Anna Ticknor, ed., *Life, Letters, and Journals of George Ticknor*, 2nd ed. (Boston: Houghton Mifflin, 1909), 1:72, 75.
9. See William Clark, *Academic Charisma and the Origins of the Research University* (Chicago: University of Chicago Press, 2006), 158–82.
10. Ticknor, *Life, Letters, Journals*, 1:24.
11. Ibid., 1:32.
12. Ibid., 1:13.
13. "Everett Journal," November 19, 1814, in Edward Everett Papers, Massachusetts Historical Society, Boston, 28–31.
14. Ibid., November 18, 1814, 15–16.
15. Thomas Jefferson, Query 19, "Manufactures," in *Notes on the State of Virginia* (1781), ed. David Waldstreicher (Boston: Bedford Books, 2002), 196–97. Everett was familiar with Jefferson's *Notes*, as he quoted from Query 18 at length in his journal entry of November 19, 1814.
16. "Everett Journal," November 15, 1814, 2–5.

17. The "independent regions" were the smaller kingdoms and principalities not controlled by Prussia, Austria, or France, such as the Kingdoms of Hanover, Saxony, and Württemberg, the Duchies of Baden, Brunswick, and Hesse, or free imperial cities such as Hamburg, Bremen, Frankfurt am Main, and Lübeck, along with dozens of others that made up the Confederation of Germany, a loosely reconstituted version of the Holy Roman Empire constructed at the Congress of Vienna.
18. Mintzker, *Defortification of the German City*, 167–68.
19. Jerome had threatened to remodel Göttingen as a French university, with French professors. Ticknor, *Life, Letters, Journals*, 84.
20. On the visit to Göttingen of Field Marshal Gebhard Leberecht von Blücher, the conqueror of Napoléon at Leipzig, and the "burning hatred of the French" that accounted for Blücher's idolization, see "Everett Journal," January 27, 1816, 48. See also ibid., June 13, 1815, 70.
21. Johann Gottlieb Fichte, *Addresses to the German Nation*, trans. R. F. Jones and G. H. Turnbull (Chicago: Open Court Publishing, 1922), 104.
22. In the original German, Fichte asks, "Und mit welchem Geiste brachte hervor und genoss dieser deutsche Stand diese Blüte?"—And with what Spirit did this German class bring forth and enjoy this flowering? J. G. Fichte, *Reden an die deutsche Nation* (Berlin: Deutsche Bibliothek, 1912), 107.
23. Fichte, *Addresses*, 104–6. See also Carl E. Schorske, "The Idea of the City in European Thought: Voltaire to Spengler," in *The Historian and the City*, ed. Oscar Handlin and John Burchard (Cambridge, MA: MIT Press, 1963), 95–114. Schorske's work contrasts Fichte's vision of the city as a creation of the people with Voltaire and Adam Smith, who saw monarchs as the chief figures in the creation of cities.
24. See Mintzker, *Defortification of the German City*, 5–12.
25. Joseph Green Cogswell spent October 1816 in these cities—"Cologne, Coblentz, Mentz, and Frankfort"—as he made his initial journey to Göttingen. Joseph Green Cogswell to C. S. Daveis, Portland, February 16, 1817, in Anna Eliot Ticknor, ed., *The Life of Joseph Green Cogswell, as Sketched in His Letters* (Cambridge, MA: Riverside Press, 1874), 50.
26. Mintzker, *Defortification of the German City*, 147–48.
27. "Everett Journal," September 18, 1815, 21.
28. George Ticknor to Elisha Ticknor, August 10, 1815, in Ticknor, *Life, Letters, and Journals*, 74–75. See also "Everett Journal," Amsterdam to Göttingen, August 6, 1815, 9. In 1843, when Horace Mann visited Germany, he made similar comments about Hamburg. Horace Mann, "Mann, Journal, July 1843," in *Life of Horace Mann*, ed. Mary Mann (Boston: Lee and Shepard, 1891), 198.
29. Ticknor, *Life, Letters, Journals*, September 20, 1815, 77–78; "Everett Journal," September 20, 1815, 22–26.
30. "Everett Journal," September 20, 1815, 32. On the city in arms, see Mintzker, *Defortification of the German City*, 39. For Everett's comparison of the military culture of monarchical Göttingen with republican Boston (Boston shoots more cannons), see "Everett Journal," December 12, 1815, 40–41.
31. Marchand, *Down from Olympus*, 24. On the political and cultural sources of German philhellenism, see ibid., 3–35.
32. Buchloch and Rix, *American Colony of Göttingen*.
33. Ibid., 15–17; Ticknor, *Life, Letters, Journals*, 68; "Everett Journal," Amsterdam to Göttingen, August 9, 1815, 10–11. On Cogswell, see Ticknor, *Life of Joseph Green Cogswell*, 37–59; Long, *Literary Pioneers*, 77–99. On Bancroft, see Long, *Literary Pioneers*, 108; Lilian Handlin, *George Bancroft: The Intellectual as Democrat* (New York: Harper and Row, 1984), 51–53.

34. Clark, *Academic Charisma*, 170–71.
35. November 10, 1815, in Ticknor, *Life, Letters, Journals*, 73n; "Everett Journal," September 25, 1815, 27; Handlin, *George Bancroft*, 59.
36. "Everett Journal," March 20, 1816, 48–50.
37. James Turner, *Philology: The Forgotten Origins of the Modern Humanities* (Princeton, NJ: Princeton University Press, 2014), 112–21.
38. Ticknor, *Life, Letters, Journals*, 79–80. For the similarly vigorous regimes of Ticknor's friends, see Ticknor, *Life of Joseph Green Cogswell*, 51; "Everett Journal," October 29–November 2, 1815, 33–34; Mark A. De Wolfe Howe, ed., *Life and Letters of George Bancroft* (New York: C. Scribner's Sons, 1908), 1:58.
39. Cogswell felt this problem particularly acutely. Joseph Green Cogswell to Stephen Higginson, July 1817, cited in Long, *Literary Pioneers*, 83.
40. Diehl, *Americans and German Scholarship*; Handlin, *George Bancroft*, 82–114; Tyack, *George Ticknor*, 85–128.
41. George Ticknor to Elisha Ticknor, June 20, 1816, in Ticknor, *Life, Letters and Journals*, 99–102.
42. Ibid.
43. Ticknor's understanding was shaped by his reading of Madame de Staël's famous study of Germany, which offers a similar account. See Germaine de Staël-Holstein, *Germany, by the Baroness de Staël-Holstein* (London: John Murray, 1813), 1:171–83; Tyack, *George Ticknor*, 35. Ticknor would meet the dying Madame de Staël on his visit to Paris in 1817; "11 May 1817," in Ticknor, *Life, Letters and Journals*, 132–33.
44. Ticknor, *Life, Letters, Journals*, 64.
45. Ibid., 64–68.
46. "Everett Journal," June 22, 1815, 81.
47. Ibid., June 22–25, 1815, 81, 83–85.
48. George Bancroft to Samuel A. Eliot, May 29, 1822, in Howe, *Life and Letters of George Bancroft*, 1:152.
49. "Bancroft Journal," May 22, 1822, in Howe, *Life and Letters of George Bancroft*, 1:148–50; Long, *Literary Pioneers*, 139–40.
50. October 25, 1816, in Ticknor, *Life, Letters, Journals*, 113–14; Long, *Literary Pioneers*, 128.
51. Joseph Cogswell to Mrs. C. S. Davies, April 17, 1817, in Ticknor, *Life of Joseph Green Cogswell*, 56–57; Long, *Literary Pioneers*, 79–80.
52. Joseph Cogswell to Mrs. William Prescott, July 13, 1817, in Ticknor, *Life of Joseph Green Cogswell*, 64–65.
53. Marchand, *Down from Olympus*, 10. See also Caroline Winterer, *Culture of Classicism: Ancient Greece and Rome in American Intellectual Life, 1780–1910* (Baltimore: Johns Hopkins University Press, 2002), 53–54; Nicholas Boyle, *Goethe: The Poet and the Age* (Oxford: Clarendon Press, 1991), 1:28–29.
54. Boyle, *Goethe*, 1:28.
55. Marchand, *Down from Olympus*, 7–35; Johann Wolfgang von Goethe, *Winckelmann und Seine Jahrzeit* (1805).
56. Ticknor, *Life, Letters, Journals*, 67.
57. William J. McGrath, "Freedom and Death: Goethe's Faust and the Greek War of Independence," in *Rediscovering History: Culture, Politics, and the Psyche*, ed. Michael Roth (Stanford, CA: Stanford University Press, 1994), 102–12; Marchand, *Down from Olympus*, 34.
58. October 25, 1816, in Ticknor, *Life, Letters, Journals*, 114.

59. Joseph Green Cogswell to George Ticknor, May 18, 1819, in Ticknor, *Life of Joseph Green Cogswell*, 98. See also "Bancroft Journal," October 12, 1819, in Howe, *Life and Letters of George Bancroft*, 1:67.
60. Marchand, *Down from Olympus*, 10, 21.
61. Ibid., 24–25.
62. [Edward Everett], "On the Literature and Language of Modern Greece," in *The General Repository and Review* (Boston, 1813), 84, 94.
63. One of the sailors, Nicholas Ciclitira, returned to settle in Boston and assisted in writing an essay on Greek pronunciation. See John Pickering, *An Essay on the Pronunciation of the Greek Language* (Cambridge, MA: Hilliard and Metcalf, 1818), 1–2.
64. Stephen A. Larrabee, *Hellas Observed: The American Experience of Greece, 1775–1865* (New York: NYU Press, 1957), 28–29.
65. Harvard's offer to Ticknor, who did not know Spanish and had not yet been to Spain, was a sign of the esteem in which European scholarship was now held by Boston's intellectual leaders. See Tyack, *George Ticknor*, 62–63; Ticknor, *Life, Letters, Journals*, 1:116–18.
66. Larrabee, *Hellas Observed*, 35–40; Edward Everett, *An Account of Some Greek Manuscripts, Procured at Constantinople in 1819 and Now Belonging to the Library of the University at Cambridge*, Memoirs of the American Academy of Arts and Sciences, 4 (1820), 409–15.
67. "Panorama of Athens," *Boston Daily Advertiser* 20, no. 13 (October 22, 1819): 1. See also *Description of the View of Athens and Surrounding Country, Now Exhibiting in Henry Aston Barker and John Burford's Panorama, Strand* (London: Adlard and Sons, 1818); Quincy, *History of Harvard University*, 2:401, 592; R. A. McNeal, "Athens and Nineteenth-Century Panoramic Art," *International Journal of the Classical Tradition* 1, no. 3 (Winter 1995): 80–97.
68. Edward Everett to Harvard Corporation, February 13, 1823, cited in Winterer, *Culture of Classicism*, 66–67; Larrabee, *Hellas Observed*, 40–41.
69. Henry Pickering, *Athens, and Other Poems* (Salem, MA: Cushing and Appleton, 1824), 5. John and Henry Pickering were the sons of Timothy Pickering, former Massachusetts senator, US secretary of state, opponent of the Jefferson and Madison administrations, and supporter of New England's secession in 1804. See Charles W. Upham, *The Life of Timothy Pickering* (Boston: Little, Brown, 1873), 4:398–423.
70. "Bancroft Journal," July 4, 1821, in Howe, *Life and Letters of George Bancroft*, 1:100.
71. James W. Trent Jr., *The Manliest Man: Samuel Gridley Howe and the Contours of Nineteenth-Century American Reform* (Amherst: University of Massachusetts Press, 2012), 10–11.
72. Trent, *Manliest Man*, 20–22; Thomas Francis Harrington, *The Harvard Medical School, A History, Narrative and Documentary, 1789–1905*, 2 vols. (New York: Lewis Publishing Co., 1905), 1:399–430.
73. On the causes and course of the Greek Revolution, see David Brewer, *The Greek War of Independence: The Struggle for Freedom from Ottoman Oppression and the Birth of the Modern Greek Nation* (Woodstock, NY: Overlook Press, 2001). For European and American responses to the Greek crisis, see Gary J. Bass, *Freedom's Battle: The Origins of Humanitarian Intervention* (New York: Alfred A. Knopf, 2008), 45–52; Samuel Gridley Howe, *An Historical Sketch of the Greek Revolution* (New York: White and Gallagher, 1828).
74. Edward Everett and Thomas L. Winthrop, *Address of the Committee . . . for the Relief of the Greeks* (Boston, 1823), 14, 18.
75. Larrabee, *Hellas Observed*, 70–71.

76. Brewer, *Greek War of Independence*, 194–219.
77. Trent, *Manliest Man*, 22–28.
78. "Howe Journal," July 22, 1825, in Laura E. Richards, ed., *Letters and Journals of Samuel Gridley Howe* (Boston: D. Estes, ca. 1909), 90.
79. "Howe Journal," September 5, 1825, cited in Harold Schwartz, *Samuel Gridley Howe, Social Reformer, 1801–1876* (Cambridge, MA: Harvard University Press, 1956), 18.
80. Richards, *Letters and Journals of Samuel Gridley Howe*, 219. See also Samuel Gridley Howe, "Campaigning in the Peloponnessus," *New England Magazine* 4 (October 1831): 2.
81. December 23, 1825, in Richards, *Letters and Journals of Samuel Gridley Howe*, 166; Schwartz, *Samuel Gridley Howe*, 21.
82. December 9, 1826, in Richards, *Letters and Journals of Samuel Gridley Howe*, 191; Schwartz, *Samuel Gridley Howe*, 20–22.
83. Samuel Gridley Howe to William Sampson, July 8, 1826, in Richards, *Letters and Journals of Samuel Gridley Howe*, 182; "Howe Journal," July 18, 1827, in Richards, *Letters and Journals of Samuel Gridley Howe*, 229.
84. Edward Everett and Thomas L. Winthrop, "Address of the Committee Appointed at a Public Meeting Held at Boston, December 19, 1823, for the Relief of the Greeks, to Their Fellow Citizens," ([Boston]: Press of the North American Review, 1823), 12.
85. Bass, *Freedom's Battle*, 67–75.
86. Everett and Winthrop, "Address," 7. See also Christoph Hauser, *Anfänge bürgerlicher Organisation: Philhellenismus und Frühliberalismus in Südwestdeutschland* (Göttingen: Vandenhoeck and Ruprecht, 1990). Metternich pressured the larger German states to stay out of the Greek cause for fear of reigniting revolutionary movements. Marchand, *Down from Olympus*, 32–33.
87. On the role of the Greek crisis in the Monroe Doctrine, see Schwartz, *Samuel Gridley Howe*, 88–99; Ernest May, *The Making of the Monroe Doctrine* (Cambridge, MA: Harvard University Press, 1975), 8–11, 214–18, 230–32.
88. "Howe Journal," July 5, 1827, in Richards, *Letters and Journals of Samuel Gridley Howe*, 224; Schwartz, *Samuel Gridley Howe*, 22–23; Trent, *Manliest Man*, 38–39.
89. Samuel Gridley Howe to William Sampson, July 8, 1826, in Richards, *Letters and Journals of Samuel Gridley Howe*, 182; "Howe Journal," July 23, 1827, in Richards, *Letters and Journals of Samuel Gridley Howe*, 184, 234.
90. "Howe Journal," November 7, 1826, in Richards, *Letters and Journals of Samuel Gridley Howe*, 189.
91. Schwartz, *Samuel Gridley Howe*, 24. The helmet remained a treasured item in Howe's family until the early twentieth century, when it was returned to Greece for ceremonies marking the centennial of Byron's death. See Maud Howe Elliott, *Lord Byron's Helmet* (Boston: Houghton Mifflin, 1927).
92. Samuel Gridley Howe, *Historical Sketch of the Greek Revolution*, 2nd ed. (New York: White, Gallagher, and White, 1828), title page, vi.
93. Brewer, *Greek War of Independence*, 325–36.
94. Richards, *Letters and Journals of Samuel Gridley Howe*, 305–46.
95. "Howe Journal," March 13, 1829, in Richards, *Letters and Journals of Samuel Gridley Howe*, 339.
96. Howe's writings reveal no awareness of the parallel. But he did note that the site he chose on the Gulf of Corinth had once been "the most important harbour in the Province of Corinth; it being the one . . . whence St. Paul sailed for Ephesus." Howe to the Greek Committee in America, June 16, 1829, in Richards, *Letters and Journals of Samuel Gridley Howe*, 358.

97. Richards, *Letters and Journals of Samuel Gridley Howe*, 347–69; Schwartz, *Samuel Gridley Howe*, 35–38; Trent, *Manliest Man*, 46–49.
98. Samuel Gridley Howe to Horace Mann, 1857, in Howe Papers, Houghton Library, Harvard University, Cambridge, MA, 21.
99. Richards, *Letters and Journals of Samuel Gridley Howe*, 352, 365–66; R. C. Winthrop, *Life and Letters of John Winthrop* (Boston: Ticknor and Fields, 1864–67), 1:48–49.
100. Samuel Gridley Howe to Rufus Anderson, July 14, 1829, in Richards, *Letters and Journals of Samuel Gridley Howe*, 360.
101. Schwartz, *Samuel Gridley Howe*, 37–38; Trent, *Manliest Man*, 48–50.
102. Brewer, *Greek War of Independence*, 345–51.
103. Ticknor, *Life, Letters, Journals*, 353–69; Tyack, *George Ticknor*, 90–128. Bernard Bailyn, Donald Fleming, Oscar Handlin, and Stephan Thernstrom, *Glimpses of the Harvard Past* (Cambridge, MA: Harvard University Press, 1986), 19–44.
104. George Ticknor to Samuel A. Eliot, October 9, 1822, in Ticknor, *Life of Joseph Green Cogswell*, 133–34.
105. Joseph Cogswell to Elisha Ticknor, June 6, 1818, and September 1, 1818, in Ticknor, *Life of Joseph Green Cogswell*, 80–81, 87–88; Joseph Cogswell to George Ticknor, July 10, 1819, in Ticknor, *Life of Joseph Green Cogswell*, 99; "Cogswell Journal," October 28, 1819, in Ticknor, *Life of Joseph Green Cogswell*, 114–15.
106. George Bancroft to Levi Hedge, March 6, 1821, cited in Long, *Literary Pioneers*, 136–37; Howe, *Life and Letters of George Bancroft*, 1:97.
107. George Bancroft to John T. Kirkland, November 5, 1820, in Howe, *Life and Letters of George Bancroft*, 1:89–92; Long, *Literary Pioneers*, 133.
108. Robert Middlekauff, *Ancients and Axioms: Secondary Education in Eighteenth-Century New England* (New Haven, CT: Yale University Press, 1963), 154–58.
109. "Bancroft Journal," October 27, 1821, in Howe, *Life and Letters of George Bancroft*, 1:128–29.
110. Joseph Green Cogswell, *Outline of the System of Education at the Round Hill School* (Boston, 1831), 11–13; Thomas Gold Appleton, "Some Souvenirs of Round Hill School," in *A Sheaf of Papers* (Boston: Roberts Brothers, 1875), 9–47; John Spencer Bassett, "The Round Hill School," in *Proceedings of the American Antiquarian Society* (April 1917): 18–62.
111. Cogswell, *Outline*, 19–24.
112. Appleton, "Souvenirs of Round Hill," 19–23; Bassett, "Round Hill School," 56; Charles Beck, *Treatise on Gymnasticks, Taken Chiefly from the German of F. L. Jahn* (Northampton, MA: Simeon Butler, 1828).
113. Oliver Wendell Holmes, *John Lothrop Motley, a Memoir* (London, 1878), 1–20; Long, *Literary Pioneers*, 203.
114. Carl Diehl, "Innocents Abroad: American Students at German Universities, 1810–1870," *History of Education Quarterly* 16, no. 3 (Autumn 1976): 321–41.
115. Tyack, *George Ticknor*, 60; Diehl, "Innocents Abroad," 321.
116. Long, *Literary Pioneers*, 72. See Robert Richardson, *Emerson: The Mind on Fire* (Berkeley: University of California Press, 1995), 8, 49–51.
117. Long, *Literary Pioneers*, 73–74.
118. Richardson, *Emerson*, 247.
119. Tyack, *Ticknor*, 208. On the Athenaeum, see Katherine Wolff, *Culture Club: The Curious History of the Boston Athenaeum* (Amherst: University of Massachusetts Press, 2009).
120. See Horace Mann, "Horace Mann, Journal, July–Sept, 1843," in *Life and Works of Horace Mann* (Boston: Lee and Shepard, 1981), 1:198–212.

121. Edward Everett, *A Memoir of John Lowell, Jr.* (Boston: Little, Brown, 1840), 4; Ferris Greenslet, *The Lowells and Their Seven Worlds* (Boston: Houghton Mifflin, 1946), 210.
122. Robert F. Dalzell Jr., *Enterprising Elite: The Boston Associates and the World They Made* (Cambridge, MA: Harvard University Press, 1987), 113–14, 126–28.
123. Samuel Gridley Howe to Dr. John M. Fisher, March 20, 1832, in Richards, *Letters and Journals of Samuel Gridley Howe*, 395–400; Trent, *Manliest Men*, 57–59; Schwartz, *Samuel Gridley Howe*, 45–46.
124. Samuel Gridley Howe to William Cabell Rives, March 1832, in Richards, *Letters and Journals of Samuel Gridley Howe*, 401–2.
125. In the interval following his initial return home from Greece, Howe considered taking over as editor of an anti-Jackson newspaper as well as becoming director of the American colony of free blacks in Liberia, West Africa. Schwartz, *Samuel Gridley Howe*, 40–42 Trent, *Manliest Man*, 51–55.
126. Note how the new institution's name, organization, and location continue the ancient pattern of blurring distinctions between Boston, Massachusetts, and New England as a whole.
127. Trent, *Manliest Man*, 54–59; Schwartz, *Samuel Gridley Howe*, 49–51. For Howe's description of the methods used in Paris and at the Prussian schools, see *Address of the Trustees of the New England Institution for the Education of the Blind to the Public* (Boston: Carter, Hendee, 1833), 2–6. On the Royal Institute for Blind Youth, see Zina Weygand, *The Blind in French Society from the Middle Ages to the Century of Louis Braille*, trans. Emily-Jane Cohen (Stanford, CA: Stanford University Press, 2009), especially 261–92.
128. Ernest Freeberg, *The Education of Laura Bridgman: First Deaf and Blind Person to Learn Language* (Cambridge, MA: Harvard University Press, 2001), 14–17. Quotation from Edward Everett Hale, cited in ibid., 17. See also Carl Seaburg and Stanley Paterson, *Merchant Prince of Boston: Colonel T. H. Perkins, 1764–1854* (Cambridge, MA: Harvard University Press), 377–79; *Annual Report of the Trustees of the New England Institution for the Education of the Blind*, 6–7.
129. Seaburg and Paterson, *Merchant Prince of Boston*, 296–313.
130. Cited in Seaburg and Paterson, *Merchant Prince of Boston*, 313–14.
131. Thomas G. Cary, *Memoir of Thomas Handasyd Perkins, Containing Extracts from His Diaries and Letters* (Boston, 1856), 219–22; Samuel A. Eliot, *A Sketch of the History of Harvard College, and Its Present State* (Boston: Little, Brown, 1848), 181.
132. Perkins's brother James donated his mansion on Pearl Street to provide larger quarters for the Boston Athenaeum. Seaburg and Paterson, *Merchant Prince of Boston*, 301–2; Wolff, *Culture Club*, 50.
133. *Annual Report of the Trustees of the New England Institution for the Education of the Blind*, 4–8; Seaburg and Paterson, *Merchant Prince of Boston*, 378–82; Schwartz, *Samuel Gridley Howe*, 50–54.
134. Dalzell, *Enterprising Elite*, 151–61; Ronald Story, *The Forging of an Aristocracy: Harvard and the Boston Upper Class, 1800–1870* (Middletown, CT: Wesleyan University Press, 1980).
135. "John P. Cushing," in *Other Sea Captains and Merchants of Old Boston* (Boston: State Street Trust, 1919), 18.
136. Freeberg, *Education of Laura Bridgeman*, 51–53.
137. Charles Dickens, *American Notes for General Circulation* (London: Chapman and Hall, 1842), 1:57–144. On Bridgman and the Perkins Institute, see ibid., 67–105.
138. *Boston Evening Transcript*, June 14, 1851, cited in Freeberg, *Education of Laura Bridgeman*, 1–2; Trent, *Manliest Man*, 117.

139. Honors were showered on Howe from all quarters, including, ironically, a gold medal from the king of Prussia, which Howe claimed was equal in value to the money that he had been required to pay for his prison costs when held in the Berlin jail. Schwartz, *Samuel Gridley Howe*, 89.
140. See Freeberg, *Education of Laura Bridgeman*, 66–146.
141. Ibid., 2; Trent, *Manliest Man*, 111–12. Schools for the deaf and blind throughout the United States purchased copies of the bust, as did admirers in England, France, Scotland, and other European countries. See Megan Marshall, *The Peabody Sisters: Three Women Who Ignited American Romanticism* (Boston: Houghton Mifflin, 2005), 570n.
142. Trent, *Manliest Man*, 46.
143. Comments of Benjamin Butler, Lewis G. Clark, and Cornelius Felton, cited in Daniel Walker Howe, *The Political Culture of the American Whigs* (Chicago: University of Chicago Press, 1979), 213–14; George Ticknor, cited in Robert Remini, *Daniel Webster: The Man and His Time* (New York: W. W. Norton, 1997), 184.
144. William Ellery Channing, "Likeness to God," in *The Works of William E. Channing, D. D.* (Boston: American Unitarian Association, 1877), 291.
145. "Longfellow Journal," June 21, 1846, cited in Long, *Literary Pioneers*, 194.
146. Ticknor, *Life, Letters, Journals*, 101–2.
147. See Horst Ueberhorst, *Friedrich Ludwig Jahn: 1778/1978*, with a contribution by Wolfgang Stump, trans. Timothy Nevill (Bonn-Bad Godesberg: Inter Nationes, 1978).
148. Gary D. Stark, "Ideology of the German *Burschenschaft* Generation," *European History Quarterly* 8, no. 3 (July 1978): 336.
149. Ibid., 337; Edmund Spevack, *Charles Follen's Search for Nationality and Freedom: Germany and America, 1796–1840* (Cambridge, MA: Harvard University Press, 1997), 55.
150. Stark, "Ideology of the German *Burschenschaft* Generation," 337–38.
151. Ibid., 338; Spevack, *Charles Follen*, 65–68.
152. Spevack, *Charles Follen*, 70–76; George S. Williamson, "What Killed August von Kotzebue? The Temptations of Virtue and the Political Theology of German Nationalism, 1789–1819," *Journal of Modern History* 72, no. 4 (December 2000): 890–943.
153. Spevack, *Charles Follen*, 91–125.
154. See Amy Kittelstrom, *The Religion of Democracy: Seven Liberals and the American Moral Tradition* (New York: Penguin, 2015), 57–154. Kittelstrom argues that while the orthodox Trinitarians staked their claim to the puritan heritage on theological consistency, the Unitarians based their claim on their consistent commitment to the radical pursuit of truth that had characterized the Reformation.
155. Spevack, *Charles Follen*, 181.
156. George Washington Spindler, *Karl Follen: A Biographical Study* (Chicago: German American Historical Society, 1917), 126–37.
157. Frank Freidel, *Francis Lieber, Nineteenth-Century Liberal* (Baton Rouge: Louisiana State University Press, 1947), 24–47.
158. Eliza Cabot seems never to have been fully aware of Follen's violent and radical past in Germany. See E[liza] L[ee] Follen, *The Life of Charles Follen* (Boston: Thomas Webb and Company, 1844).
159. Spevack, *Charles Follen*, 123–205.
160. Ibid., 206–10; Charles Follen, *The Works of Charles Follen, with a Memoir of His Life* (Boston: Hilliard, Gray, 1841–24), 1:304.
161. *Liberator*, January 1, 1831.

162. "Charles Follen to John Bowring, December 31, 1832, in Follen, *Works*, 1:333–34. Bowring was editor of the radical *Westminster Review* and a strong antislavery advocate.
163. Spevack, *Charles Follen*, 213–18. In addition to joining Garrison's group, Follen founded a sister organization, the Cambridge Anti-Slavery Society, proliferating organizational cells after the fashion of the Burschenschaften.
164. Henry Mayer, *All on Fire: William Lloyd Garrison and the Abolition of Slavery* (New York: W. W. Norton, 2008), 192–93.
165. Cited in Mayer, *All on Fire*, 198; cf. Samuel Eliot Morison, *Harrison Gray Otis: The Urbane Federalist* (Boston: Houghton Mifflin, 1969), 2:269–74.
166. Cited in [Maria Weston Chapman], *Right and Wrong in Boston: Report of the Boston Female Anti-Slavery Society . . .* (Boston, 1836), 13–14.
167. Ibid., 30.
168. Mayer, *All on Fire*, 200–205.
169. Chapman, *Right and Wrong in Boston*, 56.
170. Spevack, *Charles Follen*, 55–59.
171. Chapman, *Right and Wrong in Boston*, 102, 104–7.

Chapter 11: Dismembering the Body

1. The constitution's only reference to Boston is in Chapter V, Section 1, Article III, which lists Boston among six towns around Massachusetts Bay whose Congregational ministers would sit on Harvard's Board of Overseers.
2. James M. Bugbee, "Boston under the Mayors, 1822–1860," in *The Memorial History of Boston, 1630–1880*, ed. Justin Winsor (Boston: James R. Osgood, 1882–86), 4:219. Voters feared the loss of popular control over town government to wealthy merchants should incorporation occur. See G. B. Warden, *Boston, 1689–1776* (Boston: Little, Brown, 1970), 117–18.
3. Robert A. McCaughey, "From Town to City: Boston in the 1820s," *Political Science Quarterly* 8, no. 2 (June 1973): 193; Andrew R. L. Cayton, "The Fragmentation of 'A Great Family': The Panic of 1819 and the Rise of the Middling Interest in Boston, 1818–1822," *Journal of the Early Republic* 2, no. 2 (Summer 1982): 144.
4. McCaughey, "From Town to City." See also Josiah Quincy, *A Municipal History of the Town of Boston during Two Centuries, from September 17, 1630, to September 17, 1830* (Boston: Little, Brown, 1852).
5. The city government officially moved to the Old State House in 1830, on the two hundredth anniversary of Boston's founding. Bugbee, "Boston under the Mayors," 4:235–36.
6. Cayton, "Fragmentation," 155.
7. *A Full and Authentic Report of the Debates in Faneuil Hall . . . on Changing the Form of Government of the Town of Boston* (Boston, 1822), 15; Cayton, "Fragmentation," 157. Tudor was cofounder of the *North American Review* and Boston Athenaeum.
8. Josiah Quincy, "To the Citizens of Boston," in *A Complete History of the Boston Fire Department*, by Arthur Wellington Brayley (Boston: John P. Dale, 1889), 154–57; Amy S. Greenberg, *Cause for Alarm: The Volunteer Fire Department in the Nineteenth-Century City* (Princeton, NJ: Princeton University Press, 1998), 148.
9. McCaughey, "From Town to City," 205; Quincy, *Municipal History*, 153–63.
10. Bugbee, "Boston under the Mayors," 230–34. McCaughey offers an even higher figure of $1,000,000. McCaughey, "From Town to City," 208.
11. Tamara Plakins Thornton, *Cultivating Gentlemen: The Meaning of Country Life among the Boston Elite, 1785–1860* (New Haven, CT: Yale University Press, 1989).

12. Cayton, "Fragmentation," 154.
13. Michael Rawson, *Eden on the Charles: The Making of Boston* (Cambridge, MA: Harvard University Press, 2010), 154.
14. In 1836, Lowell and Salem were incorporated as cities.
15. Rawson, *Eden on the Charles*, 141–43. This paragraph is indebted to Rawson's excellent discussion in his chapter "Inventing the Suburbs," 129–78.
16. For the extensive literature on Brook Farm and transcendentalism, see Sterling F. Delano, *Brook Farm: The Dark Side of Utopia* (Cambridge, MA: Harvard University Press, 2004); Charles Crowe, *George Ripley, Transcendentalist and Utopian Socialist* (Athens: University of Georgia Press, 1967); Philip F. Gura, *American Transcendentalism: A History* (New York: Hill and Wang, 2007), 141–79; Dean Grodzins, *American Heretic: Theodore Parker and Transcendentalism* (Chapel Hill: University of North Carolina Press, 2002), 328–33.
17. Susan Danforth, ed., *A View of America* (Providence, RI: John Carter Brown Library, May 1984), 3. See also *The Changing Face of Boston over 350 Years* (Boston: Massachusetts Historical Society, 1980), 8.
18. M. W. Burke-Gaffney, "FRANQUELIN, JEAN-BAPTISTE-LOUIS," in *Dictionary of Canadian Biography, Volume II (1701–1740)*, University of Toronto and Université Laval, accessed November 2014, http://www.biographi.ca/en/bio/franquelin_jean_baptiste_louis_2E.html.
19. The General Court promoted the barricado's construction in the 1670s. Over forty private investors received the right to build wharves in the inner harbor in return for their contribution to the twenty-two-hundred-foot barricade. Walter Muir Whitehill, *Boston: A Topographical History*, 2nd ed. (Cambridge, MA: Harvard University Press, 1976), 18–20.
20. Samuel Adams Drake, *Old Landmarks and Historic Personages of Boston* (Boston: Little, Brown, 1906), 424–25.
21. Charles Willing Hare to Harrison Gray Otis, October 1814, in Donald Hickey, ed., *The War of 1812: Writings from America's Second War of Independence* (New York: Library of America, 2013), 591–93.
22. Carl Seaburg and Stanley Paterson, *Merchant Prince of Boston: Colonel T. H. Perkins, 1764–1854* (Cambridge, MA: Harvard University Press), 251–55.
23. *Massachusetts Centinel*, October 28, 1789; Henry Cabot Lodge, "The Last Forty Years of Town Government," in Winsor, *Memorial History of Boston*, 3:197–200; T. H. Breen, *George Washington's Journey* (New York: Simon and Schuster, 2016), 175–97.
24. Cited in Yair Mintzker, *The Defortification of the German City, 1689–1866* (Cambridge: Cambridge University Press, 2012), 45. In 1660, Louis XIV refused to enter Marseilles through the city's *porte reale,* insisting that a new break be made in the walls so as not to acknowledge Marseilles' history of republican autonomy. Ibid., 49.
25. Nancy S. Seasholes, *Gaining Ground: A History of Landmaking in Boston* (Cambridge, MA: MIT Press, 2003); Nancy S. Seasholes, "Gaining Ground: Boston's Topographical Development in Maps," in *Mapping Boston*, ed. Alex Krieger and David Cobb (Cambridge, MA: MIT Press, 1999), 119–45; Whitehill, *Boston*.
26. Robert Fleming Gourlay to George N. Briggs, governor of Massachusetts, et al., May 9, 1844, in Robert Fleming Gourlay, *Plans for Beautifying New York, and for Enlarging and Improving the City of Boston* (Boston: Crocker and Brewster, 1844), 17; Whitehill, *Boston*, 146–49.
27. *Boston Democrat*, October 2, 1805; Frederick Morse Cutler, *The Old First Massachusetts Coast Artillery in War and Peace* (Boston: Pilgrim Press, 1917), 21–22; Edward Stanwood, "Topography and Landmarks of the Past Hundred Years," in Winsor, *Memorial History of Boston*, 4:30.

28. Whitehill, *Boston*, 48–50, 76–77; Mintzker, *Defortification of the German City*, 152.
29. Whitehill, *Boston*, 11–12.
30. Seasholes, *Gaining Ground*, 76–96.
31. Ibid., 41–46, 59; Whitehill, *Boston*, 114–17.
32. Whitehill, *Boston*, 88–92; Seasholes, *Gaining Ground*, 155–58; William A. Newman and Wilfred E. Holton, *Boston's Back Bay: The Story of America's Greatest Nineteenth-Century Landfill Project* (Boston: Northeastern University Press, 2006), 23–29.
33. Cited in Whitehill, *Boston*, 90.
34. Quotation from Lyman Beecher, *Autobiography, Correspondence, Etc. of Lyman Beecher, D.D.*, ed. Charles Beecher (New York: Harper and Brothers, 1865), 2:50. The streets previously developed around the Boston and Lowell terminal were named Billerica, Andover, Haverhill, Lowell, and Lancaster—all towns in the vicinity of Lowell and traditionally within Boston's sphere of influence. See Whitehill, *Boston*, 95–105; Seasholes, *Gaining Ground*, 244–52.
35. Blanche Linden-Ward, *Silent City on a Hill: Landscapes of Memory and Boston's Mount Auburn Cemetery* (Columbus: Ohio State University Press, 1989); Thomas Laqueur, *The Work of the Dead: A Cultural History of Human Remains* (Princeton, NJ: Princeton University Press, 2015).
36. Thomas C. Amory, *The Life of James Sullivan, with Selections from his Writings* (Boston: Phillips, Sampson, and Co., 1859); Pauline Maier, *Ratification: The People Debate the Constitution, 1787–1788* (New York: Simon and Schuster, 2010), 193.
37. Kerby A. Miller, "From 'Emigrants' to 'Exiles': The Pre-Famine Exodus, 1815–1844," in *Emigrants and Exiles: Ireland and the Irish Exodus to North America* (New York: Oxford University Press, 1988), 193; Thomas H. O'Connor, *The Boston Irish: A Political History* (Boston: Northeastern University Press, 1995), 33–35.
38. O'Connor, *Boston Irish*, 37.
39. Nancy Lusignan Schultz, *Fire and Roses: The Burning of the Charlestown Convent, 1834* (New York: Free Press, 2000), 11–15, 37–46.
40. O'Connor, *Boston Irish*, 43; Schultz, *Fire and Roses*, 108; Roger Lane, *Policing the City: Boston, 1822–1885* (Cambridge, MA: Harvard University Press, 1967), 24–25.
41. Beecher, *Autobiography, Correspondence, Etc.*, 2:52–56, 332–36; Lyman Beecher, *A Plea for the West* (Cincinnati, 1835), 89–92.
42. Schultz, *Fire and Roses*, 147–89; Daniel Cohen, "Passing the Torch: Boston Firemen, 'Tea Party' Patriots, and the Burning of the Charlestown Convent," *Journal of the Early Republic* 24, no. 4 (Winter 2004): 527–86. The tales of another resident, Rebecca Reed, may have further inflamed the hostility. Rebecca Reed, *Six Months in a Convent* (Boston: Russell, Odiorne, and Metcalf, 1835). See also Jenny Franchot, *Roads to Rome: The Antebellum Protestant Encounter with Catholicism* (Berkeley: University of California Press, 1994), 135–54.
43. Schultz, *Fire and Roses*, 172.
44. Ray Allen Billington, "The Burning of the Charlestown Convent," *New England Quarterly* 10, no. 1 (March 1937): 4–24.
45. Schultz, *Fire and Roses*, 182–86.
46. Lane, *Policing the City*, 33–34; O'Connor, *Boston Irish*, 48–49; Samuel A. Eliot, "Being Mayor of Boston a Hundred Years Ago," *Proceedings of the Massachusetts Historical Society* 66 (October 1936–May 1941): 154–73.
47. Oscar Handlin, *Boston's Immigrants [1790–1880]: A Study in Acculturation* (Cambridge, MA: Belknap, 1959), 190, 260.
48. This was the phrase Sewall used to describe Boston's African minority in *The Selling of Joseph* (Boston, 1700).

49. Handlin, *Boston's Immigrants*, 55.
50. Cecil Woodham-Smith, *The Great Hunger: Ireland, 1845–1849* (New York: Harper and Row, 1962). For specific details and statistics, I have relied on John Crowley, William J. Smyth, and Mike Murphy, eds., *Atlas of the Great Irish Famine* (New York: NYU Press, 2012). In that anthology, see, in particular, John Feehan, "The Potato: Root of the Famine," 28–37; David Nally, "The Colonial Dimensions of the Great Irish Famine," 64–74; Cormac Ó Gráda, "Mortality and the Great Famine," 170–79; Kerby A. Miller, "Emigration to North America in the Era of the Great Famine, 1845–1855," 214–27.
51. Lemuel Shattuck, *Report to the Committee of the City Council Appointed to Obtain the Census of Boston for the Year 1845* (Boston: John H. Eastburn, 1846), 26.
52. Lemuel Shattuck, *Letter from Lemuel Shattuck . . . in Relation to the Introduction of Water into the City of Boston* (Boston: Samuel N. Dickinson, 1845), 14–15; Handlin, *Boston's Immigrants*, 89.
53. "Passengers Entering Boston by Sea, 1821–1865," table 5, in Handlin, *Boston's Immigrants*, 242.
54. Handlin, *Boston's Immigrants*, 88–100; Brian C. Mitchell, *The Paddy Camps: The Irish of Lowell, 1821–1861* (Urbana: University of Illinois Press, 1988), 101–20.
55. "Population of Boston and Its Environs," table 2, in Handlin, *Boston's Immigrants*, 239. The neighboring towns did not conduct a census in 1845 so the direct impact of the famine migration is more difficult to pinpoint. The majority of this doubling of the population probably occurred after 1845 as migrants landing in Boston made their way to surrounding towns.
56. Handlin, *Boston's Immigrants*, 88.
57. Christine Kinealy, *Charity and the Great Hunger in Ireland: The Kindness of Strangers* (London: Bloomsbury, 2013), 249. In 1850, Boston's population had reached 130,000, but New York City (not including Brooklyn) already exceeded half a million.
58. Ibid., 234–36.
59. Ibid., 242–46; Edward Laxton, *The Famine Ships: The Irish Exodus to America* (New York: Henry Holt, 1996), 49–52.
60. Handlin, *Boston's Immigrants*, 109.
61. Ibid., 110–12; *Report of the Committee of Internal Health on the Asiatic Cholera* (Boston: J. H. Eastburn, 1849), 1, 8–16.
62. Handlin, *Boston's Immigrants*, 119.
63. Ibid., 114–17, 254.
64. Robert A. McCaughey, *Josiah Quincy, 1772–1864: The Last Federalist* (Cambridge, MA: Harvard University Press, 1974), 131.
65. Charles Dickens, *American Notes for General Circulation* (London: Chapman and Hall, 1842), 1:64.
66. Charles Lyell, *A Second Visit to the United States of North America* (New York: Harper and Brothers, 1849), 1:145.
67. Lane, *Policing the City*, 63, 71; Handlin, *Boston's Immigrants*, 121.
68. The city began to keep statistics on the policing of "vice" in 1850, so comparisons with the period before 1845 can only be impressionistic. The common impression, no doubt augmented by Yankee prejudice, was that gambling, drunkenness, and prostitution all increased rapidly after 1846. Lane, *Policing the City*, 63, 111; Handlin, *Boston's Immigrants*, table 24, 257.
69. Lane, *Policing the City*, 59–84.
70. Cotton Mather, *The Bostonian Ebenezer: Some Historical Remarks on the State of Boston* (Boston: Green and Allen, 1698), title page, 3–5.

71. Theodore Parker, *A Sermon of the Moral Condition of Boston* (Boston: Crosby and Nichols, 1849), 4.
72. Ibid., 5, 6, 12–13, 15–19.
73. Ibid., 22, 26.
74. Ibid., 22, 26.
75. Angela F. Murphy, *American Slavery, Irish Freedom: Abolition, Immigrant Citizenship, and the Trans-Atlantic Movement for Irish Repeal* (Baton Rouge: Louisiana State University Press, 2010), 100–124; Richard J. M. Blackett, "'And There Shall Be No More Sea': William Lloyd Garrison and the Transatlantic Abolitionist Movement," in *William Lloyd Garrison at Two Hundred: History, Legacy, and Memory*, ed. James Brewer Stewart (New Haven, CT: Yale University Press, 2008), 25–26.
76. Handlin, *Boston's Immigrants*, 132–34; Murphy, *American Slavery, Irish Freedom*, 14–18, 104–6; David R. Roediger, *The Wages of Whiteness: Race and the Making of the American Working Class* (London: Verso, 1991), 134–50.

Chapter 12: "There Was a Boston Once"

1. Barry Levy, *Town Born: The Political Economy of New England from Its Founding to the Revolution* (Philadelphia: University of Pennsylvania Press, 2010), 39–42, 103–10; Cornelia H. Dayton and Sharon V. Salinger, *Robert Love's Warnings: Searching for Strangers in Colonial Boston* (Philadelphia: University of Pennsylvania Press, 2014).
2. John Winthrop, "A Modell of Christian Charity," in *The Winthrop Papers*, ed. Samuel Eliot Morison, Allyn Bailey Forbes, and Malcolm Freiberg (Boston: Massachusetts Historical Society, 1929–), 2:283–84.
3. William D. Piersen, *Black Yankees: The Development of an Afro-American Subculture in Eighteenth-Century New England* (Amherst: University of Massachusetts Press, 1988), 15, 25–36; Peter Benes, "Slavery in Boston Households, 1647–1770," in *Slavery/Anti-Slavery in New England*, ed. Peter Benes (Boston: Trustees of Boston University, 2005), 12–30.
4. Samuel Sewall, *The Selling of Joseph: A Memorial* (Boston: Green and Allen, 1700), 2.
5. The following discussion is indebted to James Oliver Horton and Lois E. Horton, *Black Bostonians: Family Life and Community Struggle in the Antebellum North* (New York: Holmes and Maier, 1999). See also Joanne Pope Melish, *Disowning Slavery: Gradual Emancipation and "Race" in New England, 1780–1860* (Ithaca, NY: Cornell University Press, 1998); Donald M. Jacobs, ed., *Courage and Conscience: Black and White Abolitionists in Boston* (Bloomington: Indiana University Press, 1993).
6. Horton and Horton, *Black Bostonians*, 28–39.
7. Roy E. Finkenbine, "Boston's Black Churches: Institutional Centers of the Antislavery Movement," in *Courage and Conscience: Black and White Abolitionists in Boston*, ed. Donald M. Jacobs (Bloomington: Indiana University Press, 1993), 169–89; Horton and Horton, *Black Bostonians*, 41–55; Adelaide M. Cromwell, "The Black Presence in the West End of Boston, 1800–1864: A Demographic Map," in *Courage and Conscience: Black and White Abolitionists in Boston*, ed. Donald M. Jacobs (Blooomington: Indiana University Press, 1993), 155–67.
8. Marilyn Richardson, "'What If I Am a Woman?' Maria W. Stewart's Defense of Black Women's Political Activism," in *Courage and Conscience: Black and White Abolitionists in Boston*, ed. Donald M. Jacobs (Bloomington: Indiana University Press, 1993), 191–206; Dorothy Porter Wesley, "Integration versus Separatism: William Cooper Nell's Role in the Struggle for Equality," in *Courage and Conscience: Black*

and White Abolitionists in Boston, ed. Donald M. Jacobs (Bloomington: Indiana University Press, 1993), 207–24; Horton and Horton, *Black Bostonians*, 28–69.

9. Horton and Horton, *Black Bostonians*, 73–86.
10. Peter Hinks, *To Awaken My Afflicted Brethren: David Walker and the Problem of Antebellum Slave Resistance* (University Park: Penn State University Press, 1997), 82.
11. Melish, *Disowning Slavery*, 179–84; Bernard F. Reilly Jr., "The Art of the Anti-Slavery Movement," in *Courage and Conscience: Black and White Abolitionists in Boston*, ed. Donald M. Jacobs (Bloomington: Indiana University Press, 1993), 46–73.
12. Between 1830 and 1860, Boston's black population grew slowly from 1,875 to 2,261, while the city's overall population skyrocketed from 61,000 to 178,000. The black percentage of the population shrank from 3.1 to 1.3 percent. Horton and Horton, *Black Bostonians*, 2; Peter R. Knights, *The Plain People of Boston, 1830–1860: A Study in City Growth* (New York: Oxford University Press, 1971), 29.
13. Horton and Horton, *Black Bostonians*, 5–6.
14. Hinks, *To Awaken My Afflicted Brethren*, 75–76; Horton and Horton, *Black Bostonians*, 61–62.
15. Hinks, *To Awaken My Afflicted Brethren*, 29–30; Peter Hinks, ed., *David Walker's Appeal to the Colored Citizens of the World* (1829; repr., University Park: Penn State University Press, 2000), 15.
16. Michael P. Johnson, "Denmark Vesey and His Co-Conspirators," *William and Mary Quarterly* 58, no. 4 (October 2001): 915–76.
17. Hinks, *To Awake My Afflicted Brethren*, 74–81.
18. See "Nativity of Black Bostonians," table 6, in Horton and Horton, *Black Bostonians*, 7.
19. Hinks, *David Walker's Appeal*, 9.
20. Ibid., 18.
21. In his 1828 "Address before the General Colored Association at Boston," Walker suggested that of the 2.5 million "colored people" in the United States, "more than five hundred thousand . . . are about two-thirds free." Ibid., appendix 1, 82.
22. Ibid., 42.
23. Walker's *Appeal* foreshadows the call for "self-emancipation" that Henry David Thoreau offered in *Walden*. See Carl Bode, ed., *The Portable Thoreau* (New York: Penguin Books, 1982), 259–63.
24. Hinks, *David Walker's Appeal*, 49.
25. Ibid., 11.
26. Ibid., appendix 2, 85–88; appendix 8, 104–6; Hinks, *To Awaken My Afflicted Brethren*, 116–72.
27. For Walker's influence on Garrison, see Henry Mayer, *All on Fire: William Lloyd Garrison and the Abolition of Slavery* (New York: W. W. Norton, 2008), 82–84, 107–9. When Garrison formed the New England Anti-Slavery Society, black radicals were a quarter of the subscribers to its original charter, signed in the basement of the African Meeting House. See Richard S. Newman, *The Transformation of American Abolitionism: Fighting Slavery in the Early Republic* (Chapel Hill: University of North Carolina Press, 2002), 107; Mayer, *All on Fire*, 127–31.
28. See Edith B. Gelles, *Abigail Adams: A Writing Life* (New York: Routledge, 2002); Edith B. Gelles, *Abigail and John: Portrait of a Marriage* (New York: William Morrow, 2009); Woody Holton, *Abigail Adams* (New York: Simon and Schuster, 2009).
29. Abigail Adams to John Adams, March 31–April 5, 1776, in Adams Family Papers: An Electronic Archive, Massachusetts Historical Society, accessed May 31, 2018, http://www.masshist.org/digitaladams/.

30. For works that anchor the deep scholarly literature on these themes, see Linda K. Kerber, *Women of the Republic: Intellect and Ideology in Revolutionary America* (Chapel Hill: University of North Carolina Press, 1980); Mary P. Ryan, *Cradle of the Middle Class: The Family in Oneida County, New York, 1790–1865* (Cambridge: Cambridge University Press, 1981).
31. Hannah Adams and Hannah Farnham Sawyer Lee, *A Memoir of Miss Hannah Adams* (Boston: Gray and Bowen, 1832); Gary D. Schmidt, *A Passionate Usefulness: The Life and Literary Labors of Hannah Adams* (Charlottesville: University of Virginia Press, 2004).
32. Richardson, "'What If I Am a Woman?,'" 198, 194.
33. Ibid., 200–201.
34. Maria W. Stewart, "Mrs. Stewart's Farewell Address to Her Friends in the City of Boston," in *Maria W. Stewart: America's First Black Woman Political Writer, Essays and Speeches*, ed. Marilyn Richardson (Bloomington: Indiana University Press, 1987), 69–70; Valerie C. Cooper, *Word, Like Fire: Maria Stewart, the Bible, and the Rights of African Americans* (Charlottesville: University of Virginia Press, 2011).
35. Carolyn L. Karcher, *The First Woman in the Republic: A Cultural Biography of Lydia Maria Child* (Durham, NC: Duke University Press, 1994), 1–15.
36. Lydia Maria Child, *An Appeal in Favor of That Class of Americans Called Africans*, ed. Carolyn L. Karcher (1833; repr., Amherst: University of Massachusetts Press, 1996), 35.
37. Ibid., 99.
38. Ibid., 120.
39. Ibid., 186, 187.
40. Ibid., 187, 207.
41. Deborah Weston to Anne B. Weston, May 8, 1835, in Milton Meltzer and Patricia G. Holland, eds., *Lydia Maria Child, Selected Letters, 1817–1880* (Amherst: University of Massachusetts Press, 1982), 28–29.
42. Karcher, *First Woman of the Republic*, 191–92.
43. Ibid., 192–94.
44. William E. Channing, *Slavery* (Boston: James Munroe and Co., 1835).
45. Mayer, *All on Fire*, 201; Lois A. Brown, "William Lloyd Garrison and Emancipatory Feminism in Nineteenth-Century America," in *William Lloyd Garrison at Two Hundred: History, Legacy, and Memory*, ed. James Brewer Stewart (New Haven, CT: Yale University Press, 2008), 41–76; Lee V. Chambers, *The Weston Sisters: An American Abolitionist Family* (Chapel Hill: University of North Carolina Press, 2014); Jean Fagan Yellin and John C. Van Horne, *The Abolitionist Sisterhood: Women's Political Culture in Antebellum America* (Ithaca, NY: Cornell University Press, 1994).
46. The 1845 edition included work by Henry Wadsworth Longfellow, Eliza Cabot Follen, Frederick Douglass, Abby Kelley, James Russell Lowell, William Lloyd Garrison, Charles Lenox Remond, Wendell Phillips, Edmund Quincy, Maria Weston Chapman, and many others. See [Maria Weston Chapman], ed., *The Liberty Bell, by Friends of Freedom* (Boston: Massachusetts Anti-Slavery Fair, 1845).
47. [Maria Weston Chapman], *Right and Wrong in Boston: Report of the Boston Female Anti-Slavery Society; with a Concise Statement of Events, Previous and Subsequent to the Annual Meeting of 1835* (Boston: Boston Female Anti-Slavery Society, 1836), 56, quoting the *Boston Commerical Gazette*, October 22, 1835.
48. [Chapman], *Right and Wrong in Boston*, 78–79.
49. In 1835, Child published a two-volume *History of the Condition of Women, in Various Ages and Nations* (Boston: John Allen and Co., 1835), a study of oppression across human history, but with a more muted call for women's liberation than the *Appeal*

had made on behalf of Africans. See Karcher, *First Woman of the Republic*, 220–25; Harriet Martineau, *The Martyr Age of the United States* (Boston, 1839), 54–56.

50. Lydia Maria Child, *Philothea, A Romance* (Boston: Otis, Broaders and Co, 1836), 16; Karcher, *First Woman of the Republic*, 233–37.
51. [Chapman], *Right and Wrong in Boston*, 45–48; Julie Roy Jeffrey, "The Liberty Women of Boston: Evangelicalism and Anti-Slavery Politics," *New England Quarterly* 85, no. 1 (March 2012): 38–44; Deborah Gold Hansen, *Strained Sisterhood: Gender and Class in the Boston Female Anti-Slavery Society* (Amherst: University of Massachusetts Press, 1993), 97–105; Karcher, *First Woman of the Republic*, 253–62; Mayer, *All on Fire*, 232–37, 261–69.
52. Mayer, *All on Fire*, 233.
53. See Maria Weston Chapman, ed., *Harriet Martineau's Autobiography*, 2 vols. (Boston: Houghton Mifflin, 1877); Frank Schulman, *James Martineau: This Conscience-Intoxicated Unitarian* (Chicago: Meadville Lombard Press, 2002).
54. Harriet Martineu, *The Martyr Age of the United States* (Boston: Weeks, Jordan and Co., 1839), 1 (emphasis added).
55. Andrew Carmichael, *A Memoir of the Life and Philosophy of Spurzheim* (Boston: Marsh, Capen and Lyon, 1833), 1–7. See also Nahum Capen, "Biography," in *Phrenology, in Connexion with the Study of Physiognomy*, ed. Johan Gaspar Spurzheim (Boston: Marsh, Capen and Lyon, 1833), 7–168.
56. See Johan Gaspar Spurzheim, ed., *Phrenology, in Connexion with the Study of Physiognomy* (Boston: Marsh, Capen and Lyon, 1833); Capen, "Biography," 29–30.
57. Johan Gaspar Spurzheim, *A Philosophical Catechism of the Natural Laws of Man* (1826; repr., Boston: Marsh, Capen and Lyon, 1833), 101–7.
58. Capen, "Biography," 108; Charles Follen, "Funeral Oration on Gaspar Spurzheim," in *The Works of Charles Follen, with a Memoir of His Life* (Boston: Hilliard, Gray, 1841), 5: 182.
59. Capen, "Biography," 133.
60. Ibid., 133–39; "Remains of Dr. Spurzheim," *Boston Medical and Surgical Journal* 6–7 (November 21, 1832): 226; Blanche Linden-Ward, *Silent City on a Hill: Landscapes of Memory and Boston's Mount Auburn Cemetery* (Columbus: Ohio State University Press, 1989), 233–35.
61. George Combe, *Notes on the United States of North America, during a Phrenological Visit in 1838-9-40* (Edinburgh: MacLachlan, Stewart and Co., 1841). Combe's most famous work went through dozens of editions. See George Combe, *The Constitution of Man, Considered in Relation to External Objects*, 11th American ed. (Boston: Marsh, Capen, Lyon and Webb, 1841).
62. Elisha Bartlett, *Address Delivered at the Anniversary Celebration of the Birth of Spurzheim* (Boston: Marsh, Capen and Lyon, 1838).
63. Samuel Gridley Howe, *A Discourse on the Social Relations of Man, Delivered Before the Boston Phrenological Society, at the Close of Their Course of Lectures* (Boston: Marsh, Capen and Lyon, 1837), 4–5.
64. Ernest Freeberg, *The Education of Laura Bridgman: First Deaf and Blind Person to Learn Language* (Cambridge, MA: Harvard University Press, 2001); James W. Trent Jr., *The Manliest Man: Samuel Gridley Howe and the Contours of Nineteenth-Century American Reform* (Amherst: University of Massachusetts Press, 2012), 86–118; Stephen Tomlinson, *Head Masters: Phrenology, Secular Education, and Nineteenth-Century Social Thoughts* (Tuscaloosa: University of Alabama Press, 2005), 272–79.
65. Trent, *Manliest Man*, 120.

66. Samuel Gridley Howe, *An Essay on Separate and Congregate Systems of Prison Discipline, Being a Report Made to the Boston Prison Discipline Society* (Boston: William D. Ticknor and Co., 1846).
67. Samuel Gridley Howe, *Report Made to the Legislature of Massachusetts upon Idiocy* (Boston: Coolidge and Wiley, 1848), 6; [Samuel Gridley Howe], "Causes and Prevention of Idiocy," *Massachusetts Quarterly Review* 1 (June 1848): 308–31.
68. Howe, *Report*, 8.
69. Thomas Laqueur, *Solitary Sex: A Cultural History of Masturbation* (New York: Zone Books, 2004), 185–246; April Haynes, *Riotous Flesh: Gender, Race, and the Solitary Vice* (Chicago: University of Chicago Press, 2015).
70. Tomlinson, *Head Masters*, 239–300.
71. [Howe], "Causes and Prevention of Idiocy," 320–22, 331; Trent, *Manliest Man*, 153–54.
72. [Howe], "Causes and Prevention of Idiocy," 331.
73. Samuel Gridley Howe, *Report*, 53–54, 50; Samuel Gridley Howe, *10th Report of the School for Idiotic and Feeble-Minded Youth* (Boston, 1858), 22; Trent, *Manliest Man*, 184–91; Tomlinson, *Head Masters*, 335–45.
74. David J. Rothman, *The Discovery of the Asylum: Social Order and Disorder in the New Republic*, rev. ed. (New York: Aldine de Gruyter, 2002), 237. Rebecca McLennan's analysis of the reform period focuses on the development of forced contract labor as its major outcome. See Rebecca McLennan, *The Crisis of Imprisonment: Protest, Politics, and the Making of the American Penal State, 1776–1941* (Cambridge: Cambridge University Press, 2008), 53–86. See also Gerald N. Grob, *The State and the Mentally Ill: A History of Worcester State Hospital in Massachusetts, 1830–1920* (Chapel Hill: University of North Carolina Press, 1966), 228; Thomas J. Brown, *Dorothea Dix: New England Reformer* (Cambridge, MA: Harvard University Press, 1998).
75. Spurzheim, *Phrenology, in Connexion with the Study of Physiology*, 45–46.
76. For Combe, see Samuel Morton, "Phrenological Remarks on the Relation between the Natural Talents and Dispositions of Nations, and the Development of Their Brains," in *Crania Americana* (Philadelphia, 1839); George Combe, *A System of Phrenology*, 6th American ed. (Boston: Benjamin B. Mussey, 1851); Howe, *Discourse*, 8, 17–18.
77. Thanks to Mary Woolsey for this insight. On phrenology and scientific racism, see Reginald Horsman, *Race and Manifest Destiny: The Origins of American Racial Anglo-Saxonism* (Cambridge, MA: Harvard University Press, 1981), 54–60, 116–45; Colin Kidd, "Teutonist Ethnology and Scottish Nationalist Inhibition, 1780–1880," *Scottish Historical Review* 74, no. 197, part 1 (April 1995): 45–68; Martin Staum, "Physiognomy and Phrenology at the Paris Athénée," *Journal of the History of Ideas* 56, no. 3 (July 1995): 443–62.
78. Andrew Delbanco, *William Ellery Channing: An Essay on the Liberal Spirit in America* (Cambridge, MA: Harvard University Press, 1981), 148–50.
79. Wendell Phillips, "The Murder of Lovejoy," in *Speeches, Lectures, and Letters* (Boston: Lee and Shepard, 1884), 1–10; James Brewer Stewart, *Wendell Phillips: Liberty's Hero* (Baton Rouge: Louisiana State University Press, 1986), 58–63.
80. *Annals of Congress*, 2nd Cong., 2nd Sess., (November 1792–March 2, 1793), 1414–15; Stanley W. Campbell, *Slave Catchers: Enforcement of the Fugitive Slave Law, 1850–1860* (Chapel Hill: University of North Carolina Press, 1968), 7–8.
81. Samuel E. Sewall to Comfort Winslow, July 31–August 1, 1836, in Nina Moore Tiffany, *Samuel E. Sewall, a Memoir* (Boston: Houghton Mifflin, 1898), 62–64; Horton and Horton, *Black Bostonians*, 107.

82. Bruce Laurie, *Beyond Garrison: Antislavery and Social Reform* (Cambridge: Cambridge University Press, 2005), 78–79.
83. Tiffany, *Samuel E. Sewall*, 69–70; Roger Lane, *Policing the City: Boston, 1822–1885* (Cambridge, MA: Harvard University Press, 1967), 51; Thomas D. Morris, *Free Men All: The Personal Liberty Laws of the North, 1780–1861* (Baltimore: Johns Hopkins University Press, 1974), 109–15.
84. Dean Grodzins, *American Heretic: Theodore Parker and Transcendentalism* (Chapel Hill: University of North Carolina Press, 2002), 335–38.
85. John Greenleaf Whittier, "Massachusetts to Virginia," in *The Poetical Works of John Greenleaf Whittier* (Boston: Houghton Mifflin, 1892), 3:86.
86. George Frisbie Hoar, *Autobiography of Seventy Years* (New York: Charles Scribner's Sons, 1906), 1:24–26; Lawrence Lader, *The Bold Brahmins: New England's War against Slavery, 1831–1863* (New York: E. P. Dutton, 1961), 129–30.
87. Hoar, *Autobiography of Seventy Years*, 1:134, Thomas H. O'Connor, *Lords of the Loom: The Cotton Whigs and the Coming of the Civil War* (New York: Charles Scribner's Sons, 1968), 65.
88. *Address of the Committee Appointed by a Public Meeting Held at Faneuil Hall, September 24, 1846, for the Purpose of Considering the Secret Case of Kidnapping from Our Soil* (Boston: White and Potter, 1846), 3–4; Lader, *Bold Brahmins*, 132–33.
89. Ralph Waldo Emerson, cited in Lader, *Bold Brahmins*, 132–33; *Address of the Committee*, "Appendix," 4, 6.
90. Ibid., "Appendix," 17.
91. Ibid., "Appendix," 25; Horton and Horton, *Black Bostonians*, 109.
92. Josephine F. Pacheco, *The Pearl: A Failed Slave Escape on the Potomac* (Chapel Hill: University of North Carolina Press, 2005), 140–65; Lader, *Bold Brahmins*, 136–37.
93. Ralph Waldo Emerson, *The Complete Works* (Boston: Houghton Mifflin, 1904), 11:2–3.
94. Horton and Horton, *Black Bostonians*, 111–12.
95. William Craft, *Running a Thousand Miles for Freedom; or the Escape of William and Ellen Craft from Slavery* (London: William Tweedie, 1860), 1–4, 29–80, 87–111; Horton and Horton, *Black Bostonians*, 112–13; Stephen Kantrowitz, *More Than Freedom: Fighting for Black Citizenship in a White Republic, 1829–1889* (New York: Penguin Books, 2012), 184–87.
96. Gary Collison, *Shadrach Minkins: From Fugitive Slave to Citizen* (Cambridge, MA: Harvard University Press, 1997), 1–3, 122–33.
97. Horton and Horton, *Black Bostonians*, 113–14; Lader, *Bold Brahmins*, 161–67.
98. Lader, *Bold Brahmins*, 174–80; Campbell, *Slave Catchers*, 117–21; Albert von Frank, *The Trials of Anthony Burns: Freedom and Slavery in Emerson's Boston* (Cambridge, MA: Harvard University Press, 1999), 27–30.
99. Von Frank, *Trials of Anthony Burns*, xviii. The following discussion is indebted to von Frank's work. See also *Boston Slave Riot and Trial of Anthony Burns* (Boston: Fetridge and Co., 1854); Charles Emery Stevens, *Anthony Burns: A History* (Boston: John P. Jewett, 1856).
100. Von Frank, *Trials of Anthony Burns*, 52–72.
101. *Murderers, Thieves and Blacklegs Employed by Marshal Freeman!* (Boston, 1854), Massachusetts Historical Society, accessed May 31, 2018, http://www.masshist.org/database/viewer.php?item_id=1600&mode=small&img_step=1&; Mary Blanchard to Benjamin Seaver, June 4, 1854, Seaver Family Letters, Massachusetts Historical Society.
102. Karcher, *First Woman of the Republic*, 438.

103. Von Frank, *Trials of Anthony Burns*, 207.
104. Walt Whitman, "A Boston Ballad—1854," in *The Complete Writings of Walt Whitman* (New York: G. P. Putnam's Sons, 1902), 2:25–27.
105. "Speech of Theodore Parker at the Faneuil Hall Meeting," in Charles Emery Stevens, *Anthony Burns: A History* (Boston: John P. Jewett, 1856), appendix M, 291.
106. *Speech of the Honorable Charles Sumner, in the Senate of the United States, 19th and 20th May, 1856* (Boston: John J. Jewett and Co., 1856), 6.
107. Trent, *Manliest Man*, 214–18.
108. Lader, *Bold Brahmins*, 256–57.
109. Trent, *Manliest Man*, 219; Stewart, *Wendell Phillips*, 212–15.
110. Mischa Honeck, *We Are the Abolitionists: German-Speaking Immigrants and American Abolitionists after 1848* (Athens: University of Georgia Press, 2011), 149–55; Stewart, *Wendell Phillips*, 214.
111. George William Curtis, ed., *The Correspondence of John Lothrop Motley* (London: John Murray, 1889), 1:268.
112. Ibid., 2:8–9.

Conclusion: The Making of US History and the Disappearance of the City-State of Boston

1. For the leading biographical studies of these three historians, see Wilbur R. Jacobs, *Francis Parkman, Historian as Hero* (Austin: University of Texas Press, 1991); C. Harvey Gardiner, *William Hickling Prescott: A Biography* (Austin: University of Texas Press, 1969); Joseph Guberman, *The Life of John Lothrop Motley* (The Hague: Martinus Nijhoff, 1973).For a treatment of the historical writings of these three, together with Bancroft, as a coherent literary phenomenon, see David Levin, *History as Romantic Art* (New York: AMS Press, 1967).
2. William H. Prescott, *History of the Conquest of Mexico* (New York: Harper and Brothers, 1843), I:x.
3. See Rufus Choate, "The Importance of Illustrating New-England History by a Series of Romances Like the Waverly Novels" (1833), in *The Works of Rufus Choate*, ed. Samuel Gilman Brown (Boston: Little, Brown, 1862), 1:319–46.
4. John Lothrop Motley, *Morton's Hope, or the Memoirs of a Provincial* (New York, 1839); John Lothrop Motley, *Merry Mount: A Romance of the Massachusetts Colony* (Boston, 1849); Francis Parkman, *Vassall Morton: A Novel* (Boston, 1856).
5. On the importance of German scholarship to this development, see Georg G. Iggers and James M. Powell, eds., *Leopold von Ranke and the Shaping of the Historical Discipline* (Syracuse, NY: Syracuse University Press, 1990).
6. Prescott, *History of the Conquest of Mexico*, II:361–80.
7. Gardiner, *William Hickling Prescott*, 85; Mark Peterson, "How (and Why) to Read Francis Parkman," *Common-Place* 3, no. 1 (October 2002), accessed January 1, 2018, http://www.common-place-archives.org/vol-03/no-01/peterson/index.shtml.
8. George William Curtis, ed., *The Correspondence of John Lothrop Motley*, vols. 15–17, *The Writings of John Lothrop Motley: The Netherlands Edition* (1900; repr., New York: AMS Press, 1973), I:157; Oliver Wendell Holmes, *John Lothrop Motley, A Memoir* (Boston: Houghton, Osgood, 1878), 67. For the most complete assessment of Motley's background and influences, see Levin, *History as Romantic Art*.
9. Peter Novick, *That Noble Dream: The "Objectivity Question" and the American Historical Profession* (Cambridge: Cambridge University Press, 1988), 47–60.
10. The "advancing waves" phrase first appeared in the preface to the first edition of Francis Parkman, *The Conspiracy of Pontiac* (Boston, 1851).

11. Francis Parkman, *Pioneers of France in the New World* (Boston: Little, Brown, 1865), vii–viii.
12. Walter Muir Whitehill, introduction to *Confederate Imprints: A Checklist Based Principally upon the Records of the Boston Athenaeum*, by Marjorie Crandall (Boston: Boston Athenaeum, 1955), 1:xi.
13. Herbert B. Adams, *The Germanic Origin of New England Towns* (Baltimore: Johns Hopkins Studies in Historical and Political Science, 1882).
14. Charles M. Andrews, *The River Towns of Connecticut* (Baltimore: Johns Hopkins Studies in Historical and Political Science, 1889), 5.
15. H. Cabot Lodge, "The Anglo-Saxon Land Law," in *Essays in Anglo-Saxon Law* (Boston: Little, Brown, 1876), 55–120.
16. Perry Miller, *Errand into the Wilderness* (Cambridge, MA: Harvard University Press, 1956), viii.

Coda: Looking Forward to *Looking Backward*

1. Edward Bellamy, *Looking Backward, 2000–1887* (Boston: Ticknor and Co., 1888), 11–13.
2. Ibid., 30, 253.
3. For further examples, see Paul Musselwhite, *Cities in the Air: The Urban Catalyst in the Forming of Chesapeake Society* (Chicago: University of Chicago Press, forthcoming, 2018).
4. Bellamy, *Looking Backward*, 52.
5. Ibid., 167.
6. Ibid., 193–97.

Illustration Credits

Figures

Fig. I.1. Charter of the Governor and Company of the Massachusetts Bay in New England (SC1/series 23X), Massachusetts Archives

Fig. I.2. Seal of the Governor and Company of the Massachusetts Bay in New England, Massachusetts Archives

Fig. I.3. Courtesy of the Library of Virginia

Fig. 2.1. Courtesy Lilly Library, Indiana University, Bloomington Indiana

Fig. 2.2. Order to establish a mint for coinage, with sketches of coins, 1652, v. 100, p. 36a, Massachusetts Archives Collection, 1603–1799 (SC1/series 45x), Massachusetts Archives

Fig. 2.3. (a and b) National Museum of the American Indian, Smithsonian Institution (23/9269). Photo by NMAI Photo Services

Fig. 3.1. (a) Yale University Art Gallery. (b) The Metropolitan Museum of Art, Rogers Fund, 1924

Fig. 3.2. © Trustees of the British Museum

Fig. 3.3. Courtesy, American Antiquarian Society

Fig. 3.4. Massachusetts Colony, Five Shilling Note, 1690, Currency Collection CC1, Box 1, Folder 7. Courtesy Phillips Library, Peabody Essex Museum, Salem MA

Fig. 4.1. Dutch Prints Collection (GC070); Graphic Arts Collection, Department of Rare Books and Special Collections, Princeton University Library

Fig. 4.2. Historisches Museum Hannover

Fig. 4.3. (a and b) © Trustees of the British Museum

Fig. 4.4. Collection of the Massachusetts Historical Society

Fig. 4.5. Courtesy, American Antiquarian Society

Fig. 4.6. Courtesy, American Antiquarian Society

Fig. 4.7. Courtesy, American Antiquarian Society

Fig. 4.8. Courtesy, American Antiquarian Society

Fig. 6.1. Collection of the Massachusetts Historical Society

Fig. 7.1. Collection of the Massachusetts Historical Society

Fig. 8.1. Courtesy, American Antiquarian Society

Fig. 9.1. Library of Congress, Prints and Photographs Division

Fig. 9.2. Collection of the Massachusetts Historical Society

Fig. 10.1. The State Hermitage Museum, St. Petersburg. Photograph © The State Hermitage Museum /photo by Vladimir Terebenin

Fig. 10.2. Division of Rare and Manuscript Collections, Cornell University Library

Fig. 10.3. Map image courtesy of the Norman B. Leventhal Map Center at the Boston Public Library

Fig. 10.4. Courtesy of Perkins School for the Blind Archives, Watertown, MA

Fig. 10.5. Boston Athenaeum

Fig. 10.6. National Museum of American History, Smithsonian Institute

Fig. 11.1. (a) Collection of the Massachusetts Historical Society. (b) Boston Athenaeum

Fig. 11.2. Collection of the Massachusetts Historical Society

Fig. 11.3. Print by Jacques Gérard Milbert, Boston Public Library

Fig. 11.4. Library of Congress, Geography and Maps Division

Fig. 11.5. Norman B. Leventhal Map Center, Boston Public Library

FIG. 12.1. Boston Athenaeum
FIG. 12.2. Collection of the Massachusetts Historical Society
FIG. 12.3. Boston Public Library
FIG. 12.4. Print Collection, Miriam and Ira D. Wallach Division of Art, Prints and Photographs, The New York Public Library, Astor, Lenox and Tilden Foundations
FIG. 12.5. U.S. National Library of Medicine
FIG. 12.6. Collection of the Massachusetts Historical Society

Maps

MAP I.1. Map image courtesy of the Norman B. Leventhal Map Center at the Boston Public Library
MAP I.2. Library of Congress, Geography and Maps Division
MAP 1.1. Collection of the Massachusetts Historical Society
MAP 1.2. Map image courtesy of the Norman B. Leventhal Map Center at the Boston Public Library
MAP 3.1. Map image courtesy of the Norman B. Leventhal Map Center at the Boston Public Library
MAP 5.1. Map image courtesy of the Norman B. Leventhal Map Center at the Boston Public Library
MAP 5.2. Map image courtesy of the Norman B. Leventhal Map Center at the Boston Public Library
MAP 5.3. Map image courtesy of the Norman B. Leventhal Map Center at the Boston Public Library
MAP 6.1. Map image courtesy of the Norman B. Leventhal Map Center at the Boston Public Library
MAP 9.1. Map image courtesy of the Norman B. Leventhal Map Center at the Boston Public Library
MAP 9.2. Map image courtesy of the Norman B. Leventhal Map Center at the Boston Public Library
MAP 11.1. Map image courtesy of the Norman B. Leventhal Map Center at the Boston Public Library
MAP 11.2. Map image courtesy of the Norman B. Leventhal Map Center at the Boston Public Library
MAP 11.3. Map image courtesy of the Norman B. Leventhal Map Center at the Boston Public Library
MAP 11.4. Map image courtesy of the Norman B. Leventhal Map Center at the Boston Public Library
MAP 11.5. Map image courtesy of the Norman B. Leventhal Map Center at the Boston Public Library
MAP 12.1. Map image courtesy of the Norman B. Leventhal Map Center at the Boston Public Library

Plates

PLATE 1. Collection of the Massachusetts Historical Society
PLATE 2. Print Collection, Miriam and Ira D. Wallach Division of Art, Prints and Photographs, The New York Public Library, Astor, Lenox and Tilden Foundations
PLATE 3. Courtesy, American Antiquarian Society
PLATE 4. Charter of the Governor and Company of the Massachusetts Bay in New England (SC1/series 23X), Massachusetts Archives

Plate 5. (a) Gift of the American Antiquarian Society, 1890. © President and Fellows of Harvard College, Peabody Museum of Archaeology and Ethnology, PM# 90-17-10/51063. (b) Collection of the Massachusetts Historical Society

Plate 6. Map image courtesy of the Norman B. Leventhal Map Center at the Boston Public Library

Plate 7. Yale University Art Gallery

Plate 8. Yale University Art Gallery

Plate 9. Yale University Art Gallery

Plate 10. Map image courtesy of the Norman B. Leventhal Map Center at the Boston Public Library

Plate 11. Worcester Art Museum, Massachusetts, USA/Bridgeman Images

Plate 12. Map image courtesy of the Norman B. Leventhal Map Center at the Boston Public Library

Plate 13. Collection of the Massachusetts Historical Society

Plate 14. Portrait of Major General Paul Mascarene; John Smibert (Scotland, Edinburgh, active United States, 1688–1751); United States, 1729; oil on canvas; Los Angeles County Museum of Art purchase with funds provided by Mr. and Mrs. William Preston Harrison Collection, Charles H. Quinn Bequest, Eli Harvey, and other donors (78.8)

Plate 15. William Shirley, Thomas Hudson, 1750, oil on canvas, National Portrait Gallery, Smithsonian Institute

Plate 16. Collection of the Massachusetts Historical Society

Plate 17. Harvard University Portrait Collection, Bequest of Ward Nicholas Boylston to Harvard College, 1828

Plate 18. Fisher Ames, Gilbert Stuart, c. 1807, oil on wood, National Portrait Gallery, Smithsonian Institution; gift of Geroge Cabot Lodge

Plate 19. Gilbert Charles Stuart, American, 1755–1828; Josiah Quincy, 1806; oil on panel; 30¼ × 24½ in (76.8 × 62.2 cm); The Fine Arts Museums of San Francisco, memorial gift from Dr. T. Edward and Tullah Hanley, Bradford, Pennsylvania, 69.30.195; image courtesy the Fine Arts Museums of San Francisco

Plate 20. Daniel Webster, Francis Alexander, 1835, oil on canvas, National Portrait Gallery, Smithsonian Institution; bequest of Mrs. John Hay Whitney

Plate 21. Thomas Sully, American, 1783–1872, George Ticknor (1791–1871), Class of 1807, 1831, oil on canvas. Hood Museum of Art, Dartmouth: Gift of Constance V. R. White, Nathaniel T. Dexter, Philip Dexter, and Mary Ann Streeter; P.943.130

Plate 22. Collection of the Massachusetts Historical Society

Plate 23. Image © Crown copyright: Government Art Collection, UK

Plate 24. John Elliot. Samuel Gridley Howe. Oil on Canvas. John Hay Library, Brown University Portrait Collection, Providence, Rhode Island

Plate 25. Boston Athenaeum

Plate 26. Map image courtesy of the Norman B. Leventhal Map Center at the Boston Public Library

Plate 27. Collection of the Massachusetts Historical Society

Plate 28. Collection of the Massachusetts Historical Society

Plate 29. Collection of the Massachusetts Historical Society

Index

Page numbers in **boldface** refer to illustrations.